GENERAL PRINCIPLES

GENERAL PRINCIPLES

IN THE *RISALE-I NUR* COLLECTION
FOR A TRUE UNDERSTANDING OF ISLAM

Ali Ünal

NEW JERSEY • LONDON • FRANKFURT • CAIRO • JAKARTA

TUGHRA
BOOKS

New Jersey

Published by Tughra Books

345 Clifton Ave., Clifton,

NJ, 07011, USA

www.tughrabooks.com

Library of Congress Cataloging-in-Publication Data

Ünal, Ali.
General principles in the Risale-i nur collection for a true understanding of Islam / Ali Ünal.
pages cm
Includes bibliographical references.
ISBN 978-1-59784-369-0 (alk. paper)
1. Nursi, Said, 1873-1960. Risale-i nur. 2. Nurculuk. I. Title.
BP252.U53 2015
297.8'3--dc23
2014046668

ISBN: 978-1-59784-369-0

Printed by
Imak Ofset, Istanbul - Turkey

Contents

PART 6

PART 7

PART 8

Introduction

Bediüzzaman Said Nursi, the *Risale-i Nur* and "General Principles" in Islamic Religious Sciences

*T*he end of the 19th and the beginning of the 20th centuries constitute a crucial era from the viewpoint of world history, particularly as far as the Islamic world is concerned. The thinkers of this period in the Islamic world, whose prominence in terms of material power through almost eleven centuries had long been failing, began searching for the causes of, and remedies for, this calamity. They proposed several approaches to pinpoint and treat the problem, yielding attitudes that paved the way for the birth of many currents of thought.

The years we speak of were also years that witnessed heated discussions within Islam regarding numerous issues, the influence of which is felt even today. Just as post-Renaissance developments in rational and experimental sciences sparked off discussions regarding the many truths of Christianity, and the Old and New Testaments, this era similarly opened the door to a variety of approaches and multi-faceted discussions concerning Islam, the Qur'an, Islamic history, and Islamic sciences. Certainly, the focal point of these discussions was the issue of "how to present the Qur'an or Islam for the understanding of the period." While some who spoke from within this perspective were under the spell of modern scientific and technological developments, and the economic and military superiority of the West, thus advocating the reinterpretation of the principles of Islam and the Qur'an according to this criterion, despite the obvious risk of subjecting those principles to alteration and distortion, others were overly-fervent in proposing projects of sociopolitical reform, and in the name of the Qur'an and the Sunnah, actually turned their back on the Sunnah, and on the expanse of Islamic history. This was the atmosphere in which Bediüzzaman Said Nursi (1877–1960) was born and lived.

Bediüzzaman, the author of the Collection of the *Risale-i Nur* (the Collection of the Treatises of Light), about the lofty ideal of whom and whose deep familiarity with the world and his times, as well as his simplicity, austerity, tenderness, loyalty, chastity, modesty, and contentedness, much has been said and written, is a most effective and profound representative of Islam's intellectual, moral, and spiritual strengths. In the face of the "avant-gardists," who evidently perceived Islam as a hindrance to development and associated the West's scientific and military advances with its "negative" outlook on religion, Bediüzzaman declared, "I will prove to the world that the Qur'an is a sun that cannot be extinguished." It was in such an atmosphere that Said Nursi worked towards the construction of an indestructible fortress around the Qur'an, undeterred by blasts, detonated internally or externally, and thus opted to be a tireless servant in the implementation of the Divine declaration, *"Indeed it is We, We Who send down the Reminder (i.e. the Qur'an), and it is indeed We Who are its Guardian."*[1] As a scholar who had studied almost all the positive or natural sciences of his day, he reflected, to a certain extent, the influence of modern scientific data and philosophy used to corroborate the truths of the Qur'an in his early works, where he addresses others using their own brand of logic. Later on, he asserts, "Only what has been sanctified by the Qur'an may act as corroboration for the Qur'an. Substantiating the Qur'an with whatever is not in accord with it means demoting it to a degree." However, he never despised or ignored any truth, wherever it was found, in accordance with the Prophetic Tradition: "Wisdom is like the lost property of believers. Wherever they find it, they have a greater right to take it." He was the embodiment of a distinguished spiritual master and a noble character full of respect for his history and predecessors, attached to tradition but open to new developments, endowed with love of truth, uncompromising in the face of imitation, sober and vigorous in evaluating ideas and situations, and dignified by the highest degree of faith. He carried only the purest of intentions—to earn the good pleasure of God or to serve humanity.

During the earlier period of his life, which coincided with the last years of the Ottoman State, Bediüzzaman Said Nursi was involved in the sociopolitical life of the country. He traveled much, held meetings with Kurdish leaders and religious scholars in the south-east of Turkey, visited the Balkans and the Caucasus, and saw first-hand the ignorance, poverty, and

---

[1] *Suratul-Hijr*, 15:9.

internal conflict prevalent in Turkey and the greater Muslim world. He severely criticized despotism in all fields of life and supported a constitutionalism based on the Islamic principle of consultation. He wrote many books or booklets during these years, such as *Sünuhat* (Occurrences to the Heart), *Tuluat* (Flashes of Thoughts Rising in the Heart), *Rumuz* (Subtle Allusions), *İşarat* (Indications), and *Münazarat* (Discussions). In these books or booklets, Bediüzzaman analyzed the condition of Muslims, the reasons why it was thus and discussed the ways this could be improved. He offered valuable prescriptions for a healthy social life. His two other books, *Hakikat Çekirdekleri* (Seeds of Truths) and *Leme'at* (Flashes of Truth— Flowers from Seeds of Truths), in which he offered very valuable criteria for sound thinking, can also be included in this series of works.

In 1911, Bediüzzaman delivered a sermon in the Umayyad Mosque in Damascus to approximately 10,000 people, including 100 high-ranking scholars. In this sermon, which was later published under the title of *Hutbe-i Şamiye* (The Damascus Sermon), and in the other books mentioned, Bediüzzaman analyzes why the Muslim world had remained immured in the "Middle Ages": the growth of despair, the loss of truthfulness in social and political spheres, the love of belligerency and an ignorance of the bonds that are proper among believers, despotism in all fields of life, and egocentricity. He offered his cure: hope, truthfulness and trustworthiness, mutual love, consultation, solidarity, and freedom in accordance with Islam.

In the second phase of his life, which began after the foundation of the Turkish Republic, Bediüzzaman Said Nursi devoted himself wholly to defending and explaining the truths and essentials of the Islamic faith based on religious, rational, and scientific arguments. He also elucidated Islam's main principles of thought, worship, morality, and way of life. Being one who launched an Islamic revival at the beginning of the second quarter of the twentieth-century, he emphasized the Prophetic way in serving Islam. In addition, he revised, interpreted and explained the basic principles of all Islamic religious sciences such as *Fiqh* (Jurisprudence), *Tafsir* (the Interpretation of the Qur'an), *Hadith* (the Prophetic Traditions), *Kalam* (the Islamic Theology), and *Tasawwuf* (Sufism), as well as developing new ones based on the Qur'an and Sunnah. He made extensive and profound analyses and explanations concerning the nature of humanity, things, and events. Thus, he brought up many students whose minds and hearts were re-formed in the mold of Islam or the Divine Revelation. The books he authored in this period of his life are published under the titles of *Sözler* (The Words), *Mektubat* (The Letters), *Lem'alar* (The Gleams), and *Şualar* (The Rays). *Al-Mathnawi al-Nuri* (The Seedbed of Light), which he wrote in the transitional period between the collapse of the Ottoman State and the establishment of the Turkish Republic, is like the seed of the *Risale-i Nur* Collection, as it succinctly contains almost all truths elucidated in the other books of the Collection.

The topic of "General Principles" in Islamic sciences and General Principles in the *Risale-i Nur*

The Islamic Jurisprudence or Law is the most developed one among the Laws of the world. Due to Islam being universal, and addressing all times, places, and conditions, Muslim jurists have developed it based on the Qur'an and the Sunnah to the extent that it can answer all questions concerning worldly and otherworldly life. It can solve all problems in accordance with the approval of God Almighty. One of the most significant dimensions or divisions of the Islamic Jurisprudence is the subject of *al-Qawaidu'l-Kulliyya* (General Principles). According to some scholars, such as Shihabu'd-Din al-Qarafi (1228–1285) and Ibn an-Nujaym Zaynu'd-Din ibn Ibrahim, it is through the full comprehension and knowledge of these principles that a jurist is elevated to the status of performing *ijtihad* (deduction of new laws from the Qur'an and the Sunnah).

According to the definition of the scholars, General Principles are the concise principles based on which jurists can draw conclusions concerning particular matters which allow the Shari'ah to achieve its goals (*maqasid*). These principles are based on and deduced from the Qur'an and the Sunnah. In addition to applying to many particular matters under its scope in the field of Law, a general principle has references to many other fields of knowledge and dimensions of life as well.

For example, the Qur'an declares: *No soul, as bearer of burden, bears and is made to bear the burden of another.*[2] This verse has been the basis of many legal, moral and spiritual principles. For example, it announces the privity of crime and presumption of innocence. That is, every person is responsible for his or her crime and no one can be blamed and pun-

---

[2] *Suratu'l-An'am*, 6:164; *Suratu'l-Isra'*, 17:15.

ished because of the crime of another. This principle is so important that, for example, in our time even the "most civilized" states can punish not only a family or village or city, but a whole nation, and can invade a country because of the crimes of a few persons. This is the greatest of crimes. Whereas Islam judges that even if there are nine criminals and one innocent person on a boat, that boat cannot be sunk in order to punish the nine criminals so long as the innocent one is on the boat. Secondly, everyone is innocent until he or she is legally proved to be guilty.

This principle also categorically rejects the Christian beliefs of original and inherited sin, and God's incarnation of Jesus to die on the Cross for the redemption of humanity from these sins. According to Christianity, by disobeying God's order not to eat from the forbidden fruit of knowledge, Adam sinned. The sin of Adam is inherited by all the children of Adam, and so all human beings are born sinful. Thus, Jesus Christ, the Son of God, who came from Heaven, shed his holy, sinless blood, suffered indescribable agony, and died to pay the penalty for the sins of humanity. This dogma is utterly refutable by the legal principle that every person is responsible for his or her crime or sins and cannot be called to account for others' crimes or sins.

This principle also has a significant implication in morality and human social life. For example, Bediüzzaman Said Nursi likens faith and Islamic life in a person to the Ka'ba and Mount Uhud, and certain shortcomings in him or her to pebbles. So, rancor and enmity for a Muslim, and condemning him or her because of a shortcoming or an attribute which we do not like in him or her, is enormous injustice and means preferring pebbles over the Ka'ba and Mount Uhud.

This is only a single example for the General Principles, which function like projectors illuminating people's way.

General Principles in the *Risale-i Nur* Collection

The *Risale-i Nur* Collection is full of "general principles," not only related to the Islamic Jurisprudence but also to all the fields of Islam or Islamic life and Islamic branches of knowledge. Based on or specially favored with profound wisdom having its source in the Divine Wisdom or the Divine Name of the All-Wise, the *Risale-i Nur* Collection contains numerous principles, precepts, or maxims which are standards or brilliant criteria enabling people to think, believe, and live according to Islam, and to evaluate and judge things and events in Islam's light. They also provide people with the essentials or basic principles on which the branches of Islamic knowledge and Islamic science are based. Thus, we have tried to collect many of these principles in this book under certain titles, and in certain parts or sections according to the fields of thought and branches of knowledge to which they have a greater relevance.

The first part of this book contains certain general principles related to Islamic thinking; these help us think and believe according to Islam. The second part is composed of the principles teaching us how we must believe in and support the truths concerned with the Divine Being, the Resurrection and Afterlife, the Divine Destiny with its relationship with human free will, and the metaphysical dimension of existence, to which angels, jinn, and Satan belong. The principles showing us the way to knowing and believing in the Divine Revelation and the Divine Books, including primarily the Qur'an, and instructing us in interpreting the Qur'an, comprise the third part. The fourth part consists of the brilliant standards to approach, understand, and know Prophethood and Divine Messengership and, accordingly, the Prophets and Messengers, including, first and foremost, Prophet Muhammad, upon him be peace and blessings. These standards also provide us with significant knowledge about the acts and sayings of Prophet Muhammad, peace and blessings be upon him, or the Science of *Hadith*.

The fifth part is constructed of the rules and standards related to our religious or everyday actions, and the types of worship such as Prayer, Fasting, Giving Alms and Pilgrimage, and to our relationship as His creatures and servants with God Almighty as our Creator and Lord. The sixth part is assigned to the principles and standards that instruct us in the matters concerned with Islamic Sufism and the inner dimension of Islam and Islamic life. The principles of serving Islam in accordance with the Prophetic way (Sunnah) and guidelines for a good, Islamic social life form the seventh part. The last, eighth part, contains certain important principles of eloquence, and the correct and effective use of language.

It is my hope and prayer to God Almighty that this humble study may help people understand Islam both theoretically and as a way of life.

Part I

GENERAL PRINCIPLES RELATED TO HOW TO THINK AND BELIEVE AS A MUSLIM

General Principles Related to How to Think and Believe as a Muslim

- *Bismi'llahi'r-Rahmani'r-Rahim* **(In the Name of God, the All-Merciful, the All-Compassionate) is the start of all good things or deeds.**[1]

Muslims start all their deeds with, or by uttering, *Bismi'llahi'r-Rahmani'r-Rahim.* Any deed begun without uttering this blessed word is subject to failure or the deprivation of blessing. This blessed word teaches us that it is God Almighty Who enables us to accomplish our deeds, and He who creates them. So, by uttering it at the start of our deeds, we pronounce our reliance on and trust in Him, and declare our conviction that whatever we have done or accomplished is a gift from Him out of His pure Mercy. Therefore, we must attribute to Him all of our accomplishments and any bounty reaching us, and thank Him in return.

Secondly, *Bismi'llahi'r-Rahmani'r-Rahim* is uttered at the start of not every deed, but every good, religiously lawful deed. Is is prohibited to begin an unlawful or forbidden deed with it. Therefore, Muslims, who must begin their deeds by uttering this blessed word, must refrain from evil deeds and whatever they do must be religiously lawful.

Thirdly, when we say *Bismi'llahi'r-Rahmani'r-Rahim*, we are acting in God's Name. We are like a soldier acting in the state's name, fearing no one, doing all things in the name of the law and the state, and persisting against all odds. Also, by uttering *Bismi'llahi'r-Rahmani'r-Rahim,* we declare the purity of our intention. That is, whatever good we do is for God's sake and to please Him. Thus, this blessed word teaches us that we must do, act, give and receive, and live in His Name or for His sake.

- **God Almighty has three stamps impressed upon the face of the universe, the earth, and humanity, one within the other, and each**

---

[1] *The Words*, "The First Word", p. 3.

being a pattern or sample of the others. *Bismi'llahi'r-Rahmani'r-Rahim* **(In the Name of God, the All-Merciful, the All-Compassionate) points to these stamps.**[2]

God Almighty has three stamps upon everything, showing that it is only He Who creates, sustain, maintains, and brings up everything. They are as follows:

The Supreme Stamp of Divinity: We see this in how all entities in the universe help, support and cooperate with each other, and in their general interconnectedness and reciprocity. *In the Name of God* refers to this. That is, it is God Who creates and maintains all things in the universe in cooperation and solidarity. Even for the growth or production of a single fruit, almost all parts of the universe—from the seed of the fruit tree to the sun, air, water, and soil, to the movements of the earth both around itself and around the sun—act in an extremely calculated cooperation. It is God Almighty Who has put all parts of the universe in such a cooperation, and He Who maintains it.

The Supreme Stamp of Divine Mercifulness: We see this on the face of the earth in the resemblance, proportion, order, harmony, grace, and mercy in the creation, growth, and maintenance of plants and animals. This is the work or the manifestation of God Almighty as the All-Merciful, and the All-Merciful in *In the Name of God, the All-Merciful, the All-Compassionate* refers to this.

The Supreme Stamp of Divine Compassionateness: We see this in the subtleties of kindness, fine points of affection, and rays of compassion on the face of the human's comprehensive nature. This means that God Almighty has particular compassion for humanity, due to which He has taught humanity through the Messengers the path humans must follow in their worldly life, prepared for them an eternal abode, and helps them to gain eternal happiness by finding peace and salvation in both worlds. The All-Compassionate in *In the Name of God, the All-Merciful, the All-Compassionate*, refers to this.

• **Although the absolute Unity of God Almighty is evident throughout the universe, and in the boundless multiplicity of individualized creatures, so as not to overwhelm our minds all at once, the Qur'an, being a miracle of eloquent exposition, reiterates the**

[2] *The Gleams*, "The Fourteenth Gleam', p. 132.

manifestation of Divine Absolute Oneness (*Ahadiya***) within the manifestation of Divine Unity (***Wahidiya***).**[3]

Consider this analogy: The sun encompasses innumerable things in its light. But to hold the totality of its light in our minds and be able to grasp what kind of an entity the sun is, we would need a vast conceptual and perceptual power. So lest the sun be forgotten, all shining objects from pieces of glass to drops of water and innumerable bubbles on the surface of rivers, lakes, seas, and oceans, reflect an image of the sun. That is, we can find a minute sun in every shining or transparent object, and can have certain knowledge about the nature of the sun.

Similarly—*to God applies the most sublime attribute or description*—the absolute Unity of God is evident throughout the universe, and it is possible to have knowledge of God with His Attributes and All-Beautiful Names from the totality of the universe. God's manifestation of Himself with His Attributes and Names on universal or wholes, or species of beings, is called the Manifestation of Divine Unity (*Wahidiya*). However, the boundless multiplicity of things and the vastness of the wholes or universals may overwhelm and even distract our minds. Therefore, in order to preserve our minds and hearts from being overwhelmed and distracted by the boundless of multiplicity of things and the vastness of the wholes or universals, the Qur'an draws our attention to the stamp of Divine Oneness (*Ahadiya*) within Divine Unity. That is, we can know certain knowledge of God and easily grasp that He is the One and Unique, from each and every entity in the universe. This is so because it is only God Almighty Who has created and maintains the whole universe as well as each and every entity in it, and we see the manifestations of His Attributes and Names on each and every individual entity as we see them throughout the universe or on the wholes and universals. A few examples are as follows:

> And among His signs is the creation of the heavens and the earth and the diversity of your tongues and colors.

> They have no true judgment of God, such as His being God requires, and the whole earth will be in His grasp on the Day of Resurrection, and the heavens will be rolled up in His "Right Hand." Compare with: Know that surely God comes between a person and his heart.

---

[3]   *The Gleams*, "The Fourteenth Gleam", p. 133.

God is the Creator of all things, and He is the Guardian over all things. Compare with: *God knows what they keep secret and what they disclose.*

He has created the heavens and the earth. Compare with: *He creates you and all that you do.*

This is how God wills; only whatever He wills is, and there is no power save with God. Compare with: *You cannot will unless God wills.*

The affair of the Hour is but the twinkling of an eye. Compare with: *When He wills a thing to be, He but says to it: "Be!" and it is,* and: *We are nearer to him than his jugular vein.*[4]

- **Full conviction of God's absolute Unity—His absolute dominion over the whole universe—causes the special manifestation of His Oneness for a particular occasion.**[5]

The term God's Unity (*Wahidiya*) generally implies God's overall manifestation on the whole universe, while God's Oneness indicates God's special manifestation for a particular occasion. For example, what we call the laws of nature are the results of the manifestation of God's Unity. However, His answering a call or prayer, or His coming to the aid of a single person outside the general process or course of events, is the manifestation of His Oneness (*Ahadiya*).

Prophet Jonah, upon him be peace , lived about eight centuries before Prophet Jesus, upon him be peace, and was sent to Nineveh during the early years of the second Assyrian Empire. Despite his years of preaching God's Message, his people persisted in their association of partners with God, and despairing of his people's ability to ever believe, he left them without having been ordered to do so by God, believing that God would always guard and provide for him wherever he was.[6] According to what we conclude from the Qur'an (37: 140), the ship he had boarded was about to sink in a storm because of the weight of its load, and the sailors felt constrained to lighten it. They cast lots to decide who should be thrown into the sea, and the lot fell to Jonah, upon him be peace. So, they cast him into the sea. A large fish swallowed him.

In that situation there were no apparent means or causes to which Jonah could have had recourse for salvation; he was in need of one who

---

[4]   *Suratu'r-Rum*, 30:22; *az-Zumar*, 39:67; *al-Anfal*, 8:24; *al-Baqara*, 2:77; *al-A'raf*, 7:54; *as-Saffat*, 37:96; *al-Kahf*, 18:39; *al-Insan*, 76:30; *an-Nahl*, 16:77; *Ya-Sin*, 36:82; *Qaf*, 50:16.

[5]   *The Gleams*, "The First Gleam", p. 4.

[6]   *Suratu'l-Anbiya'*, 21:87.

could command the whale and the sea, and the night and the sky if he were to be saved. The night, the sea, and the whale were united against him. Only one who could subject all three of these to his command could bring Jonah forth on the shore of salvation. Even if all of creation had become Jonah's servants and helpers, this would have been of no avail.

This means that apparent means and causes have no power of their own in the production of results. Jonah, upon him be peace, saw with the eye of certainty that there was no refuge other than the Causer of Causes, and he, through his utmost conviction of God's absolute Unity and His dominion over the entire universe, fully perceived that in addition to His overall manifestations that reign supreme over all of creation, God also has manifestations particular to each thing and being as the All-Compassionate. So he prayed to God, saying: *"There is no deity but You, All-Glorified are You (in that You are absolutely above having any partners and shortcoming). Surely I have been one of the wrongdoers (who have wronged themselves)."*[7]

Jonah's supplication served to be a means for the night, the sea, and the whale to be subjected to him. Through the light of his conviction of the Oneness of God, Who has absolute control over each and every thing and being, the belly of the whale became a submarine for him, and the awesome sea roaring with mountain-like waves became a peaceful plain, a pleasant place for an excursion. His supplication, based on and proclaiming God's Unity, also served for the sky to be cleared of all clouds and for the moon to shine over his head like a lantern. Those things that had been pressing him from all sides, threatening him, now showed to him a friendly face. So he reached the shore of salvation.

Meanwhile, when Jonah had left his people and the signs of God's impending punishment appeared, Jonah's people had implored God for forgiveness for days, and God had withdrawn His decree of punishment. Therefore, Jonah returned to his people, and more than 100,000 people, even tending to increase, believed in his message.[8]

- **Believing in God's absolute Oneness also means one's having the full conviction that He has no partners whatsoever in His absolute dominion over each and every thing.**[9]

---

[7] *Suratu'l-Anbiya', 21:87.*
[8] *Sura Yunus, 10:98; Suratu's-Saffat, 37:137–148.*
[9] *The Words,* "The Twenty-fifth Word", p. 430; "Gleams of Truth", pp. 708–710.

The general appearance of the universe and course of events, especially due to the interrelatedness among them, inevitably lead us to have conviction of God's Unity. However, the infinite multiplicity of things and complex of events, and the infinite divisibility of things down to quarks, may cause failure in understanding God's absolute dominion over each and every thing and event. This infinite multiplicity, complexity and divisibility have misled even some of the Muslim philosophers with universal fame to put certain intermediary principles between God and things in their creation. Therefore, believing in God's absolute Oneness requires having the full conviction that it is He Who creates, sustains, governs, and makes to die even the minutest things, and that He has full control over every single event.

This conviction utterly rejects the acceptance of any deity besides God Almighty, and categorically refutes idol-worship. It also negates the creative effect of causes on events, and requires believing that it is He Who creates causes. We must also believe and confess that He has no equals, peers, likes, or anything similar or analogous to Him in His Being, Attributes, or Acts. Also, He begets not, nor is He begotten. That is, one who begets or is begotten is subject to change, or production or division, and can therefore be neither Creator, nor Self-Subsistent, nor Deity. One who comes into existence within time, or is born of matter, or descends from a progenitor, can in no way be the universe's Creator, Deity, Refuge and Protector.

Something contained by time cannot be God. That is, one who came into existence within time, or was born of matter, or descended from a progenitor, cannot be the universe's Refuge and Protector.

The attribution of existence to causes (causality), the worship of stars, idolatry, and naturalism are all varieties of associating partners with God, all pitfalls of misguidance.

- **The light of reason comes from the heart.**[10]

Our eye has a white part, which resembles daytime, but it is blind and dark. But there is a pupil in it, which is dark like the night, but illuminated. Without the pupil, that piece of flesh is not an eye, and we can see nothing. Likewise, an 'eye' without insight is also worth nothing.

So, if the dark pupil of the heart is not present in the white of thought, the contents of the mind will produce no true knowledge or insight. Or as long as the ray of the mind—scientific knowledge—has not been com-

---

[10] *The Words*, "Gleams of Truth", p. 718.

bined with the light of the heart—religious knowledge and faith—the result is darkness, oppression, and ignorance. It is darkness dressed up in a false light.

- **The levels of knowledge in the mind are variable and can be confused.**[11]

There are levels of knowledge in the mind that can be confused with one another and whose results are different. One first *imagines* something, then *conceives* of it, and *clothes it in a form*.

Afterwards, one *reasons* and *reflects* on this thing, then *confirms* and *has conviction* of it. Then one *supports* or *advocates* it, and then *becomes committed* or *devoted* to it.

Your commitment is different, and so is your support, each of which results in a different state or attitude: *Steadfastness* arises from commitment or devotion, while *bigoted adherence* comes from support or advocacy. *Compliance* proceeds from conviction and *partiality* from reasoning, while *no ideas* are formed at the level of conception. If you remain at the level of imagination, the result will be *sophistry*.

- **A beautiful, scenic description of falsehood, deception, and obscenity will both injure and mislead innocent minds.**[12]

The majority of people have no certified knowledge of things. They usually act and judge according to their senses and perceptions. Therefore, a beautiful, scenic description of falsehoods , deceptions, and obscenities will both injure and mislead them.

- **Ownerless truths become worthless in worthless hands.**[13]

Rather than considering the truths themselves, the majority of people consider and judge according to the people who own and propagate them. When they see a truth in the hands of a worthless one, they refrain from accepting it. Contrarily, when they see some falsehood in the hands of those whom they like, appreciate, and trust, they tend to approve of it. Therefore, reliable people must own and preach truths. Also, those who take a positive, constructive path should be educated and follow knowl-

---

[11] *The Words*, "Gleams of Truth", p. 718–719.
[12] *The Words*, "Gleams of Truth", p. 719.
[13] *The Words*, "Gleams of Truth", p. 745.

edge. As the discredited cannot guard the Qur'an, the knowledgeable, trustworthy ones should guard it.[14]

- **Undigested knowledge should not be imparted to others. A scholarly guide should be like a sheep, not like a bird. A sheep gives its lamb its milk, whereas a bird gives its chicks regurgitated food.**[15]

Raw knowledge or information is different from confirmed and digested knowledge. The former is like the food waiting to be cooked, eaten, and digested, while the latter is like the blood nourishing the body or the milk from a mother's breasts. Therefore, teachers and educators should act like mothers or sheep, not like birds. For the former gives milk, while the latter gives regurgitated food.

- **It is unanimously agreed that a truth changing into its opposite is impossible. It is absolutely impossible that a truth becomes its very opposite while at the same time retaining its own nature.**[16]

The absolute Beauty and Mercy of God the Lord are manifest throughout the universe. Besides, His absolute Justice, which is observable in the entire parts of the universe where conscious beings have no control at all, requires the implementation of justice in the life of all creatures. However, we see that many injustices are committed and many other ugly events are observed. Also, since the end of pleasures is pain, the pleasures of loving, for example, our parents and relatives end in great pain when they die. All of these occur while God Almighty is the All-Beautiful, the All-Just, and the All-Compassionate, Who never countenances ugliness, injustices and mercilessness. So, since it is absolutely impossible that a truth changes into its opposite or becomes its very opposite while it retains its essential nature, there must be a realm where God's absolute Beauty, Justice, and Compassion will manifest themselves fully. This realm is the Hereafter.

This material world is the realm of opposites, where God Almighty allows His conscious creatures such as jinn and humanity, which He has equipped with free will, to act on their own to a certain extent. This is why God's Beauty, Justice, and Compassion can be clouded in this realm.

[14] Bediüzzaman Said Nursi, *Gleams of Truths—Prescriptions for a Healthy Social Life*, (trans.), Tughra Books, 2010; p. 54.
[15] *Gleams of Truth*, pp. 7, 35–36.
[16] *The Words*, "The Tenth Word", p. 89.

However, in the other realm or world, they will be manifested fully and in all their clarity.

The Lord of infinite compassion and mercy most compassionately fulfills the least need of His lowliest creatures in the most unexpected fashion, and answers the faintest cry of help of His most obscure creatures. However, although the greatest desire of all human beings is eternity, they are condemned to death and cannot be saved from it. More importantly, the reality of the other life is one of the greatest matters which all the Prophets, including first and foremost Prophet Muhammad, peace and blessings be upon him, the most beloved servant of God Almighty, upon him be peace and blessings, preached. Also, all of them unanimously desire the eternal happiness and pray to God to grant it. They ask for it both for themselves and for all believers from the All-Hearing, the All-Munificent, the All- Powerful, the All-Seeing, the All-Compassionate, the All-Knowing One. Therefore, since it is absolutely impossible that a truth changes into its opposite or becomes its very opposite while it retains its essential nature, the infinite, unequalled Beauty and Mercy of God will never refuse the Prophets' prayers and leave the greatest desire of humanity eternally dissatisfied by not bringing the other, eternal world, thus allowing extreme ugliness and pitilessness.

- **The truth cannot be deceptive, and one who sees it cannot be deceived. His path, which is pure truth, is free of deception. How could a fancy appear to one who sees the truth to be the truth, and deceive him?**[17]

Even an insignificant person in a small group cannot tell a small but shameful lie in an insignificant disputed matter without showing anxiety and disquiet enough for his or her enemies to remain unaware of it. Now consider God's holy Messenger, Prophet Muhammad, upon him be peace and blessings, no lies of whom were recorded by history, and who was renowned for his truthfulness; even his enemies called him *al-Amin* (the Truthful, Trustworthy One). Under a supreme mission and a tremendous task, he was addressing the whole of humanity and its history, and speaking about extremely important matters. Threatened from all sides, not only by his contemporary enemies and Arab people, but also by the followers of all other religions, particularly the Jews and Christians, he was

---

[17] *The Words,* "The Nineteenth Word", p. 250.

in dire need of security and reliability. Then, can any contradiction be found in what he speaks fearlessly, with great ease and freedom, without hesitation or anxiety, with pure sincerity, great seriousness, and in an intense, elevated manner that irritates his enemies? Can there be any deception here? What he speaks is nothing but Revelation revealed to him.[18] So, the truth cannot be deceptive, and one who sees it cannot be deceived. His path, which is pure truth, is free of deception. How could a fancy appear to one who sees the truth to be the truth, and deceive him?

- **A thing pointing to something else does not have to contain that something else, nor does it have to possess the same qualifications.**[19]

One important disease of a misguided human selfhood is that it seeks a whole or its splendor in each part of it. Not finding it, it rejects the whole. This is like the attitude of one who seeks to see the sun or all of its manifestations when it is reflected in a bubble, and when he cannot, he refuses to accept that the image belongs to the sun.

The sun's oneness does not require that its manifestations be one. A thing pointing to something else does not have to contain that something else. A thing describing something else with certain qualifications does not have to possess the same qualifications. A minute, transparent object points to the sun and displays some of its qualities. Likewise, for example, a beehive exhibits many of the All-Wise Maker's Attributes, and therefore indicates His existence and Attributes. However, in order to indicate the Maker and His Attributes, it does not have to possess all of the Maker's Attributes in their limitlessness or contain the Maker.

- **Science has many branches, each studying a particular species of beings or things. Each branch is based on or composed of certain general principles which we call laws. The existence of laws points to orderliness and a strict order, and shows the beauty of the order. We cannot speak of any law where there is no order. This order and its maintenance is a decisive proof for the existence of the Orderer.**[20]

There is a magnificent order and harmony in the universe. Every thing is interrelated or connected to everything else. We cannot see any disor-

---

[18] *Suratu'n-Najm*, 53:4.
[19] *Al-Mathnawi al-Nuri* (Seedbed of the Light), "The Fourth Treatise", p. 119.
[20] *İşaratü'l-i'caz* (Signs of the Qur'an's Miraculousness), *"Suratu'l-Baqara"*, verses 21–22.

der in any corner of the universe despite its infinite complexity and billions of years of age. This order is the source of what sciences call laws, because the laws are the results or designations of the ordered running or operation of everything and every event in the universe. This evident fact is a most clear proof for the existence of God Almighty, Who is the Orderer and Maintainer of the universe with whatever there is in it.

- **Something's result or fruit is considered first. Thus the last in existence is the first in meaning, consideration, and intention.**[21]

The existence of everything depends first on the purpose for its existence. Before doing something, first we have an intention or purpose for doing it. Then we plan it in our mind. A fruit-bearing tree is grown for its fruit, so first we consider its fruit before beginning to grow a tree. This means that something's result or fruit is the first in its existence although it comes last.

This universe, when considered with regard to the wisdom in its purposes, appears to have the meaning of a mighty tree. God Almighty has created it to be known and worshipped.[22] So there must be one who will make God known with His Attributes through the universe and call others to worship Him exclusively, as he himself knows and worships Him more than all others. Thus, this one must be both a servant and Messenger of God. Prophet Muhammad, upon him be peace and blessings, is the one most advanced in and praised for his servanthood to God, as well as being the last of God's Messengers. He was the one who came with a universal Message while the messages of all other Messengers were restricted to a certain period of time and people. So, Prophet Muhammad, peace and blessings be upon him, whose Message contains all the truths in the messages of the previous Messengers, is the most perfect among the fruits of the Tree of Creation, and is therefore the first in God's 'mind' concerning the existence of the universe, although he came as the last of the Messengers.

This reality also shows that the resemblance of structure between the species of animals in general, and between apes and human beings in particular, does never mean that they evolved from each other. For the purpose or intention for the existence of something comes first in its existence. For example, before writing an article, first we consider why we will write it. Therefore, purpose comes first in the existence of something.

---

[21] *The Words,* "The Thirty-first Word", p. 600.
[22] *Suratu'dh-Dhariyat,* 51:56.

Then we form and arrange the meanings in our mind according to our purpose, and the written words are the externalized or materialized forms of the meanings.

The material existence of something stands for the last stage of its existence and is only the externalized form of its meaning. All the alphabets in the world have almost the same letters and all the words in all the languages are based on some 30 letters. The resemblance among the structures or material of words never means that these words are issued from or made up of one another. Rather, every word has a separate existence of meaning depending on a purpose, and its material form is the manifestation of this meaning. Looking for the origin of beings in their material or physical structure and claiming evolution because of the physical resemblance among them means reversing the manifest order in existence. This is like writing innumerable words by arranging letters at random and then giving meaning to these words.

- **A clock tells the time although it is unaware of it. So, a being's lack of knowledge about the aims of its activities does not mean that it is not used for these aims.**[23]

The Lord of the worlds, the All-Majestic Lord of the heavens and the earth, the All-Gracious Builder of this world and the next, uses angels, animals, inanimate objects and plants, and humanity in this palace of the universe. He does this not out of need, but for certain instances of wisdom demanded by His Might and Honor, Grandeur and Lordship. He has charged these four classes with unique duties of worship.

The first class are angels. They are never promoted, for their ranks are fixed and determined. They receive a specific pleasure from the work itself and a radiance from worship each according to their rank. In short, their reward is found in their service. Angels are nourished by and receive pleasure from the lights of remembrance, glorification, worship, knowledge, and love of God.

The second class are animals. Since animals also have a hungry soul and a partial will, their work is not "purely for the sake of God" in the sense that, to some extent, they take a share for their selves. Therefore, since the All-Majestic and Munificent Lord of All Dominion is All-Kind and Generous, He gives them a wage as their share.

---

[23] *The Words,* "The Thirty-fourth Word", p. 374.

Animals worship and glorify God Almighty by serving in the palace of the universe or by carrying out the duties required by their existence in utmost obedience to God's laws of life, through His Power and in His Name. They thus display Divine purposes for their existence in an amazing way. These glorifications and other acts of worship they do are their gifts of praise offered to the Court of the All-Majestic Originator, the Giver of Life.

The third class of workers are plants and inanimate objects. They have no free will and whatever they do is done purely for God's sake and in His Name. However, as understood from their life cycles, they receive some sort of pleasure from carrying out the duty of, for example, pollination, producing fruits, and reproduction. While plants and trees suffer no pain, animals experience both pain and pleasure because they have some degree of choice. The fact that plants and inanimate objects have no will makes their work more perfect than that of animals.

Plants and animals are not aware of why they are being employed, but this does not mean that they are not employed for many wise purposes by God Almighty.

The fourth class are human beings. Forming a working class among the servants, they resemble both angels and animals. Also, they resemble angels in their extensive supervision and comprehensive knowledge, and in being the heralds of Divine Lordship. Indeed, we are more comprehensive in nature. Since we have a hungry soul disposed towards evil as well (angels do not), we have the potential for almost boundless advance or decline. As we seek pleasure and a share for ourselves in our work, we resemble animals. Given this, we can receive two kinds of wages: one is insignificant, animal, and immediate; the other is angelic, universal, and postponed (to the other life).

- **The All-Wise Maker has condemned nothing to inactivity, inertia, and monotony, which lead to, or even mean, non-existence. He has appointed for each thing an attainable rank of perfection and an appropriate level of existence, and accordingly, He has endowed it with a potential to work for and attain that rank. So, every thing acts towards this rank enthusiastically. This is why there is great pleasure in activity.**[24]

---

[24] *The Words,* "The Twenty-ninth Word", p. 545; "The Thirtieth Word", p. 573.

The All-Wise Maker has appointed for each and every thing a particular rank of perfection and level of existence, and urges it towards this rank and level of existence. So, every thing incessantly moves towards this end, with its potentials growing into active abilities. This is a law He has established as the Lord of all creation. Thus, plain soil can become the source of all jewelry like priceless diamonds. Each soil atom has the capacity to be the means and place of cultivation for each plant and tree seed, for any seed can find therein whatever it needs to germinate and grow.

Also, by setting everything moving for great purposes, the All-Wise Maker elevates certain atoms to the degree of minerals, as if that was their wage of perfection, and instructs them on how to glorify Him in the way of minerals. He causes inanimate minerals to move and employs them to reward them with the degree of vegetable life. He sets vegetables in motion and uses them as food for animals, thus favoring them with the rank of animal life. He employs the atoms in animal bodies as food for human beings and promotes them to the rank of human life. Lastly, by refining many of the atoms in a human body through repeated filtering, He raises them to the most delicate and subtle organs of the body: the brain and the heart. Given this, we can understand that each atom's movement is neither random nor aimless; rather, they are made to race to a sort of perfection worthy of themselves.

Humanity is endowed with unlimited potentialities that develop into unrestricted abilities. These, in turn, give rise to countless inclinations that generate limitless desires, which are the source of infinite ideas and conceptions. All of these, as confirmed by thinkers and scholars, indicate the existence of a world of eternal happiness beyond this material world. Our very nature, which is the origin of our innate inclination towards eternal happiness, makes one sure that such a world will be established.

Everything inclines towards its own perfection. An inclination grows into a need, an increased need becomes a yearning, and an increased yearning becomes an attraction. Inclination, need, yearning, and attraction work as Divine laws and operate in ways designed to lead things to realize their perfection.

- **The beginning of thought is the end of action, and the beginning of action is the end of thought.**[25]

That is, actions give rise to thoughts, which, in turn, lead to actions. Humanity has the capacity to be able to see the relationship between the cycles of causes and effects. In the light of this relationship, human beings arrive at new combinations and the forms or rules of new thoughts and behavior, as well as what we call laws which appear to be responsible for cause and effect. This is the mechanism of progress.

The way to true existence is action and thought, and this is likewise the way to renewal, both individual and collective. A Muslim society must have its own goals and act towards these goals in the way Islam has established. If Muslims are unable to initiate action in the direction of their goals and essential beliefs, they will inevitably fall under the influence of the actions of others. Right actions give rise to right or true thoughts, and true thoughts give rise to right actions. Therefore, if Muslims cannot follow their own way of action, they will inevitably be captured and carried away by the thoughts of others' actions.

- **Fancies and desires are sometimes clothed in ideas, and a greedy one mistakes his carnal desire for an idea.**[26]

People, especially greedy ones, tend to mistake their desires and fancies for ideas, and present them as ideas for the purpose of satisfying their greed.

- **Familiarity causes compounded ignorance and superficial views.**[27]

There are many things which attract our admiration in the beginning, but lose their beauty in our eyes and hearts over time due to familiarity. Especially if this is combined with purposeful opposition and the attitude maintained to silence others for the sake of obstinacy, it becomes a nest of whim and suspicion that blocks the way of reason. This attitude is the source of compounded ignorance and superficial views.

The universe is full of the clearest signs for the existence of God, allowing us to have certain knowledge of Him. However, our familiarity with them cause us to ignore them and even attribute to them to physical causes or what we call natural laws, which are themselves created. They

---

[25] *The Reasonings*, "The Third Part", p. 122.
[26] *Hutbe-i Şamiye* (The Damascus Sermon), p. 150.
[27] *The Reasonings*, "The Third Part", p. 108.

are blind, lifeless, and unconscious, and clearly have no part in creation. The Qur'an draws our attention to this compounded ignorance and superficiality, declaring: *"How many a sign there is in the heavens and earth that they pass by, being unmindful of the signs and giving no consideration to them. And most of them do not even believe in God without associating partners with Him."*[28]

- **Another important cause of compounded ignorance is giving an attractive name to something and then claiming to have full knowledge of it.**[29]

This is especially the attitude of certain scientists who are ideologically persistent regarding materialism or atheism. Although many so-called scientific facts are only theories, some scientists give them certain attractive names and think that they have full knowledge of them. Also, knowing how something happens or having even full knowledge of something's physical structure never means possessing full knowledge of it. Besides its physical structure, everything has a metaphysical nature, and every event has many other aspects in addition to the superficial way it happens. Therefore, what they call scientific knowledge or fact can cause ignorance, and block the way to true knowledge.

- **Haughtiness and self-regard rise from the weakness of character, and lead to deviation in thought and belief.**[30]

A weak character or an inferiority complex are usually the sources of haughtiness and self-regard. In order to not be in the same line as others, and to show his self-claimed superiority, such a person builds a different way for his ideas. This way never converges with the way of others, especially that of the public. Therefore, he cannot be saved from different and multi-faceted deviations in thought and belief.

- **Egotism, or love of self, and self-importance may give rise to some shameful and despicable attitudes, such as the intentional support of the opposing side merely for the sake of opposition, fanaticism, aspiring to be superior to others, unfair partisanship, exploiting a truth to justify an incorrect action, regarding weak points as being strong to justify one's desires, attempting to show**

---

[28] *Sura Yusuf*, 12:105–106.
[29] *İşarat* (Indications), in *Sünuhat, Tuluat, İşarat*, p. 152.
[30] *Hutbe-i Şamiye*, (The Damascus Sermon), p. 135; *Gleams of Truth*, pp. 16, 71.

how virtuous one is by drawing attention to the defects of others, and demonstrating one's self-claimed honesty and truthfulness by contradicting others or declaring them to be misguided.[31]

All of these are certain diseases of the heart and weak points of character, which are the sources of wrong thinking and judgment, and different falsehoods. We should turn to God Almighty for deliverance from such base attitudes and behaviors.

- **In order to be able to find the truth, we should not assume the attitude of intentional opposition, lend an ear to our whims and fancies, and look through the eyes of the customer who sees only defects and failings. In addition, we should purify the mirror of our heart from childish attitudes, and enmity, both of which tend to search for and taking shelter in pretexts. We should weigh accurately when we weigh, compare accurately when we compare, and take as evidence and guidance the shining lights of truth along our way, so that we can dispel the darkness of groundless doubts and whims that may arise. Also, we should listen with an attentive, careful ear, and not object before others' words are finished.**[32]

These are some of the basic conditions of right thinking and finding the truth.

- **There is a blind spot in the human carnal soul or self. As long as it continues to exist, even if it is only as small as the minutest particle, it remains a veil covering the truth.**[33]

The human soul or self, so long as it remains uneducated and undisciplined, concentrates on its own existence and tends to appropriate for itself whatever the Creator gives it, and seeks to deny a supreme dominant power over itself. It takes itself as the standard of every truth and is attached to its own existence. Because of this blind spot, a human being, who cannot be contained by the universe, flounders on this point.

This blind spot can be, for example, a desire clothed as an idea, or some personal interest, or an attachment to a target, or an aspiration to a social status, or partisanship, or desire for fame, or enmity, or some-

---

[31] *The Reasonings*, "The First Part", p. 44.

[32] *The Reasonings*, "The Third Part", p. 121.

[33] *Al-Mathnawi al-Nuri* (Seedbed of the Light), "The Fourth Part", pp. 123.

thing else similar. Drowned in this point, a human being looks at everything from behind it, and judges everything accordingly, committing great wrongdoing.

- **One of the reasons for human beings misjudging and committing wrong is that they weigh and judge according to their own internal scales and standards.**[34]

A person in a room illuminated with a 60 volt light bulb who has never been outside to see the sun thinks that there is no greater light than that which illuminates his room. Like this, it is well-known in Sufism that a saintly, innerly illumined one may be defeated by his spiritual light. This is because he knows only his own light, unaware of the lights of others. Similarly, a scholar can be defeated by his own information, thinking that there is no one with knowledge greater than his. This is one of the important reasons human beings fall into error. They tend to weigh everything according to the standards they find in themselves and to see everything from the windows of their particular world. They go so far as to compare God and His Acts with themselves and their acts, and even weigh Him on the scales of their defective knowledge, understanding, and reason. Whereas, as the Qur'an declares,[35] above every owner of knowledge, there is one more knowledgeable (until God, Who is the All-Knowing), and above every owner of light, there is one with greater light, and God Almighty is beyond all comparisons, having no peers or competitors.

- **Objective reasoning means impartial judgment, but the "impartial" judgment used against the basic truths of faith means siding with or following temporary unbelief.**[36]

Objective reasoning concerning the truths of faith is a trap of Satan. For what they call objective reasoning is partial judgment. However, partial judgement used against the truths of faith means temporary unbelief and siding with faith's opponents. For example, supposing the Qur'an to be a human work, and arguing as if it were, is to take the part of the opposing side; it is to side with unbelief or falsehood.

The Qur'an is a priceless item; there is an infinite distance between its owner (God) and its claimant (humanity). There cannot be a meeting point, for they are opposites, like existence and non-existence. Besides,

---

[34] *The Reasonings*, "The Third Part", pp. 105, 113.
[35] *Sura Yusuf*, 12:76.
[36] *The Letters*, "The Twenty-sixth Letter", p. 330.

since its revelation, billions of people have accepted it as God's Word. Therefore, it falls to the opposite side to prove, if it is possible, that the Qur'an is not the Word of God. If the opposing side can refute all the arguments proving the Qur'an to be God's Word and prove that it is the work of a human being, it can claim ownership of it. Who would dare to remove that brilliant Qur'an from the Greatest Throne of God, onto which it is fixed with thousands of "nails" of decisive proofs?

- **A partial or indirect view sees the impossible as possible.**[37]

A side glance usually misleads people. For example, when we are walking along a way, some things or scenes may seem to us as, say, 'giants'. This is one of the reasons human beings err. Preachers, especially, make mistakes in mentioning Qur'anic verses to support their views. Since they are not concentrated on the verses directly, and are instead trying to understand them and mention them to support their viewpoints, they may misunderstand and misinterpret them.

It is a well-known incident: a large group of people were scanning the horizon for the crescent moon to establish the beginning of the *'Iyd*, but no one could see anything. Then an old man swore that he had seen it. But what he had seen was one of his white eyelashes that curved downward before his eye. Scientist may make the same mistake. Since they are absorbed in things or occurrences, and have no direct interest in their creation and employment by God Almighty; thus, they may mistake things themselves or what they call "nature," or "natural forces," or "natural laws" is really the work of the Creator, Designer, and Director of the universe.

- **A probability or possibility based on no evidence is not worth considering. Also, a theoretical possibility does not negate certain knowledge of a present reality or contradict the demands of reason.**[38]

This is one of the established principles of the sciences of the Methodology of Islamic Law and the Foundations of Religion. Human beings are frequently misled by delusions and fancies. Satan uses these to mislead them. For example, the carnal soul or Satan whispers to them: "Why should it not be possible?" However, something being possible or probable never means that it really is or will happen.

---

[37] *Gleams of Truth*, p. 32.
[38] *The Words* "The Twenty-first Word", p. 292.

We should not confuse the theoretically possible with the reasonably likely. A theoretical possibility does not negate certain knowledge of a present reality or contradict the demands of reason. For example, it is theoretically possible that the Black Sea could sink into the ground right now. However, we know and judge with certainty that it has not done so. The theoretical possibility of its being otherwise should not cause real doubt and impair our certainty about the present reality. Theoretically, the sun might not set today or rise tomorrow. But this possibility does not, and should not, impair our certainty or engender any real doubt. Such baseless suspicions whispered by Satan, especially concerning the truths and articles of faith should and do not impair our certainty of belief.

- **The evidence put forward to prove a thesis cannot be more indistinct and unclear than the thesis itself.**[39]

Evidence is put forward to prove a thesis, and therefore should be clear, so the audience can easily understand.

Any cosmic phenomenon mentioned in the Qur'an has the following four functions: Firstly, it proclaims the grandeur of the All-Majestic Maker through the voice of its existence and functions and that of the magnificent, universal order of which it is a part, and through being in perfect harmony with all other parts or elements of creation. Secondly, since it is the subject matter of a particular science, it shows that Islam is the bedrock of all sciences. Thirdly, since it is representative of a whole species, it clearly exhibits the concord which exists between Islam and the Divine laws at work in the universe. Fourthly, since each of the cosmic phenomena is a manifestation of the truth, it serves to arouse, direct, and encourage minds towards the truth. For this reason, and because the vast majority of people do not have expert knowledge of scientific facts, the Qur'an considers the feelings and sensory perceptions of ordinary people in order to convey to them its main themes and guide them to the truth. It presents the cosmic phenomena as proofs of the basic truths and articles of faith in such a way, and such styles, that everyone, in every age, gets their share from them. If it had presented them as modern sciences teach them, it would have thrown minds into confusion for many centuries, and the evidence would be more indistinct and unclear than the thesis itself.

---

[39] *The Reasonings, "* The First Part", pp. 12–13.

- **Matters are of two kinds: those which develop after sufficient accu-mulation of information and opinions over the course of time, and those in which mutual support and assistance have no role.**[40]

The matters of the physical sciences are of the first kind, the develop-ment of which are based on mutual assistance and sufficient accumula-tion of information and opinions over the course of time. If we think about how mutual assistance is required to lift a large rock, we can understand this point easily. However, mutual support and assistance have no role in some other matters or disciplines, such as the attainment of intuitive knowledge of God or spiritual progress. An example of this would be that it is of no use for people to support or help each other while trying to jump across a gorge.

- **Something theoretical in the past may become evident and estab-lished in the present or in the future.**[41]

Human life has a tendency towards progress that arises from the uni-versal tendency towards perfection. This tendency towards progress becomes possible through opinions and theories being built upon one another over the course of centuries. Opinions and theories develop by means of the results attained—facts; then axioms or principles become established, and are used as means to implement the principles learnt. Established facts and principles impregnate the seeds of sciences that emanate from the "ribs" of creation in the womb of time, where they grow through experience and experimentation.

It is for this reason that many of the matters known to all today were only theoretical, or even incomprehensible, in the past.

- **One who is much occupied in a subject is usually more insensitive to other subjects and cannot understand these very well.**[42]

Those who are greatly occupied in physical or material matters lack sufficient knowledge or have only superficial understanding of spiritual matters. Therefore, such people's opinions and judgments concerning spiritual matters carry no weight. If a patient confounds medicine with engineering and decides to seek advice from an engineer rather than a physician, it means he has sent his relatives an early invitation to send

---

[40] *The Reasonings,* " The First Part", pp. 14–15.
[41] *The Reasonings,* " The First Part", p. 15.
[42] *The Reasonings,* " The First Part", p. 16.

condolences on his death. Similarly, applying to materialists or consulting their opinion in matters of spirituality, which are usually abstract, means that the heart, which is a faculty of faith and spirituality, will go into arrest while the intellect, which is a spiritual faculty, will atrophy.

- **Those who search for every truth in the corporeal realm have their intellects in their eyes, when eyes are blind to spiritual things.**[43]

Even though sciences themselves admit that the scope of human senses are extremely narrow and there are innumerable truths beyond human sensory perceptions, many of these sciences—especially materialist sciences— search for every truth in the material or corporeal realm. However, just as the main existences of the written words are the meanings in minds and the written words are their materialized forms, the corporeal realm is a curtain before the realms beyond. Those who search for every truth in the corporeal realm have their intellects in their eyes, whereas physical eyes are blind to spiritual or metaphysical things.

- **Time and space greatly influence human reasoning and thought. And the tidings received are not like what we personally witness or observe.**[44]

As human beings, we cannot usually save ourselves from the restrictions of time and space. For this reason, it is said that "Human beings are the children of time." In order to draw a true judgment about people and events, we should consider when and where they live and take place. Putting on the clothes of the time and place considered, we should visit the people and observe events in their own conditions, not according to our own time and place. Besides, we should not forget that tidings are not like what is personally witnessed or observed.

- **There are two viewpoints of something—say, a tree: one just and right, the other wrong. The just, right one is viewing the thing from its roots upward, while the other, wrong one, is viewing it from its fruit downward.**[45]

To acquire knowledge of an elaborate, fruit-bearing tree's life, benefits, and strength, people look at it in two ways: from its roots upward,

---

[43] *The Reasonings, "* The First Part", p. 16.

[44] *Al-Mathnawi al-Nuri* (Seedbed of the Light), "The Second Treatise", p. 21.

[45] *Al-Mathnawi al-Nuri*, "The Fourth Treatise", p. 84–85.

and from its fruits downward. The first way leads to correct conclusions, while the second is defective and leads to misconceptions. For from the first viewpoint, when we see that the roots, trunk, and branches are sound, and there are numerous sound fruits, one single fruit disappearing or being rotten never causes us to conclude that the tree is lifeless and unproductive. Rather, we conclude that the tree is full of vigor and attribute one dead fruit to external factors. However, one who does not tend to admit the liveliness of the tree views it from its fruit downward, and when he sees the single dead fruit, he concludes that the tree is dead.

Islam is like a magnificent tree, whose roots are firmly established in Divine Revelation. It is always full of vigor and has yielded, and continues to yield, innumerable lively fruits. Therefore, the shortcomings of some Muslims can never be attributed to Islam itself.

- **With all its fundamentals, divisions and truths, the Islamic faith is a palace with thousands of doors, which are its proofs. If all of the doors of a palace are open with the exception of only a few, no one can claim that the palace cannot be entered.**[46]

There is a palace with thousands of doors. If even one of its doors is opened, people can enter the palace and open the closed doors from inside.

With all of its fundamentals, divisions, and truths, the Islamic faith is that palace with thousands of doors, which are its proofs. There are numerous proofs for every truth of Islamic faith, and almost all the doors of it are opened. However, if, for some wisdom, one of the doors is kept closed, this never means that that palace cannot be entered. But Satan presents to the viewer that closed door, and tries to deceive many that the palace cannot be entered. Because of heedlessness or ignorance or wrong-doing or biased viewpoints, or for other reasons, many are unfortunately deceived by Satan.

- **Like intention, a true viewpoint may transform habitual acts into worship.**[47]

Through the intention to lead a life that is pleasing to God, permissible habitual actions may become worship. Sunnah, or the Prophetic way of life, has a division or dimension, which is described as mannerliness or

---

[46] *The Gleams*, "The Thirteenth Gleam", pp. 120–121.
[47] *Gleams of Truth*, pp. 64–65.

good manners. It comprises the everyday acts of the Holy Prophet, upon him be peace and blessings. If a believer follows or imitates the Prophet in these acts because they are the acts of the Prophet, his or her habitual acts also become worship.

A correct viewpoint, when combined with true knowledge, leads to truth, while a wrong viewpoint, even if combined with true knowledge, causes wrong conclusions and misuses true knowledge.

Physical sciences become sources of Divine knowledge with a correct viewpoint. If we study and reflect on things as signifying not themselves but their Maker, and in respect of the art they contain, we will remark on, say, a flower: "How beautifully the Maker has made this, how well He has done it!" instead of "How beautiful it is." Thus, even a single flower will become a book making the Almighty Maker known to us. But if we look at things as signifying themselves from the point of view of "nature" or "natural causes and laws," which have no creative part in things, then we will remark: "How beautiful it is!" although it has no part at all in its beauty. So, it is an unfortunate fact that *many truths become thus worthless in worthless hands.*

- **Human beings themselves are not their owners. Nor are their bodies their personal properties.**[48]

In order for somebody to claim ownership, he or she should have created or produced or bought an object. It is a most clear fact that as human beings, it is not we who have created ourselves, nor have we bought ourselves and our bodies in a market, nor have we found ourselves and our bodies on the street. Our bodies work according to the system the Creator has established for us, and we have no part in its operation. Also, we do not have the least part in the appointment of our basic or vital needs, or in the way to satisfy them. We only obey the demands of our bodies. Thus, our owner is the One Who has created us, and our bodies are His trusts to us. Therefore, we should act in accordance with the commandments of our Creator, our Owner, and use our bodies in the way He has established and wants us to follow. Otherwise we will be recorded in the notebook of usurpers and betrayers.

- **Fame is an oppressive usurper. It appropriates for a famous person that which does not belong to him.**[49]

---

[48] *Al-Mathnawi al-Nuri*, "The Fourth Treatise", p. 88.

[49] *The Reasonings*, "The First Part", 21; *Gleams of Truth*, p. 50.

It is a characteristic of human beings that in order for any words, actions, or attitudes to be justified, or at least not discredited, or to show something more important and valuable, they attribute it to one who is famous in that given field. They even attribute to that single person some good thing belonging to a whole nation.

- **When passing from the hands of knowledge to the hands of ignorance, a metaphorical expression may change into a literal description, and open a door to superstition.**[50]

Whenever the dark hand of ignorance usurps a metaphor or simile from the luminous hand of knowledge, it may be taken for a reality, and open a door to superstition. Once, during my childhood, there was an eclipse of the moon. I asked my mother about it. She answered that a snake had swallowed the moon. I asked why I could still see it then. She explained, "The snakes of the sky are semi-transparent." See how a simile taken for a reality conceals the truth? For ancient astronomers the word "snake" referred to an indistinct shape that somewhat resembles a snake during the lunar eclipse. Over time the common people took this term of science, a simile, to describe a reality, and thought that there really was in the sky a snake that sometimes swallowed the moon!

- **One who searches for truth should be like a diver, freed of the effects of time, able to dive into the depths of the past, weighing ideas on the scales of reason, and discovering the source of everything.**[51]

- **The eye of obstinacy perceives an angel as a devil.**[52]

Obstinacy causes one to behave in this way: if a devil helps or supports them or their side, they hail him as "an angel" and call down blessings upon him. But if they see an angel on the opposing side, they view him as a devil in the guise of an angel, and they call down curses on him out of enmity.

- **Demagogy is deceptive. It is demagogy to see only faults and defects, especially in multi-dimensional matters. Demagogy exaggerates faults and evils against truth and good.**[53]

---

[50] *The Reasonings*, "The First Part", 23–24.
[51] *The Reasonings*, "The First Part", 24.
[52] *Gleams of Truth*, p. 50.
[53] *Gleams of Truth*, p. 163.

Demagogy is a corruptive characteristic. Rather than seeing the good and perfections, it tends to see evils and faults, and exaggerates them against good and truth, thus condemning something or someone that is mostly good and useful. A person, movement, or group is, and should, be viewed and judged according to their own basic characteristics. Judging them from the viewpoint of opposition is also deceptive demagogy. For example, especially in our day, some Muslims who are not engaged in good, constructive deeds and activities in the service of Islam are occupied with criticizing certain other Muslims or Islamic movements because they do not show active opposition against, for example, the United States, or Israel, or Russia. This is sheer demagogy, being both a deception and deceptive.

- **Propaganda and destructive criticism are illicit children of oppressive demagogy. A single grain of truth burns away a great heap of lies.**[54]

What is necessary to a human being, especially a Muslim, is always being truthful and trustworthy. Rather than busying themselves with criticizing others, Muslims should be engaged in doing their positive and constructive duties for God's sake. The Qur'an declares: *"You are always the superior side if you are (true) believers."*[55] *"O you who believe! (Do not busy yourselves with those who follow different ways!) Your responsibility is your own selves (so consider how you are faring along your own way). Those who go astray can do you no harm if you yourselves are rightly guided (following your right way without deviation)."*[56]

Muslims cannot respond to lies and propaganda with counter lies and anti-propaganda. They must follow their own way and respond to lies and propaganda with truthfulness.

- **It is an abasing, dangerous demagogy to use the criticism of the Muslim scholars of the early centuries of Islam against each other in order to degrade them, and thus to shake the sacredness of Islam in minds and hearts.**[57]

Scholars can criticize each other for their views, provided that it be positive and constructive criticism. This does not allow others to criticize

---

[54] *Gleams of Truth*, p. 150.

[55] *Sura Al 'Imran*, 3:139.

[56] *Suratu'l-Ma'eda*, 5:105.

[57] *Tulu'at* (Flashes of Thoughts Rising in the Heart), p. 79.

them in order to degrade them. God Almighty may reprimand His Messengers, but this can never be an excuse for people to criticize them. Likewise, a father's harsh, reproachful words to his son cannot allow others to use the same words against that son. Positions have great importance in mutual behaviors and words to be uttered.

- **Materialism is a plague; it has infected humanity with a terrible fever and subjected it to Divine wrath and punishment. In proportion to the increase in humankind's tendency to criticize, inculcate, and imitate, this plague becomes more severe and spreads ever-wider.**[58]

Our most grievous illness, which is indeed a disaster, is criticism that arises from haughtiness, loquacity, and demagogy. If even a just, truth-loving one engages in such criticism, he injures the truth; if it is exercised in vanity, it destroys the truth.

What is most grievous is when such criticism is directed against the tenets of the faith and the foundations of the Religion—for faith is both an affirmation and conviction; it is also preference, submission, compliance, and observance. The criticism in question damages submission and observance, preference and compliance. Even though it may not cause doubt, this causes indifference and neutrality instead of confirmation.

At this time of doubt, suspicion, and ungrounded misgivings, it is necessary for everyone to study and follow sincerely the uncontaminated works that nurture and strengthen compliance and observance, as well as the moving ideas and words, free of doubt, that come from illuminated, warm hearts.

- **A person who desires, in debate on a subject, his own thesis to be true and is happy with its turning out to be right and the opposing side to be wrong and mistaken, is an unfair one.**[59]

Such a person is also in loss, for when they win the debate, they have learned nothing new; rather, their probable pride may cause them further loss. But if the truth turns out to be on the opposing side, they will have learned something previously unknown to them, and thereby acquired something beneficial, as well as having been saved from probable pride. Therefore, a fair, truth-loving one wounds the pride of their

---

[58] *The Letters*, "Seeds of Truth", p. 457; *Gleams of Truth*, pp. 75, 109.
[59] *The Gleams*, "The Twentieth Gleam", p. 222.

carnal soul for the sake of the truth. When they see the truth in the hand of their opponent, they willingly accept it and support it.

- **Matters of belief cannot be disputed.**[60]

Belief or faith is not theoretical knowledge but it is both digested knowledge and confirmed by reason or intellect. It is further proved through conviction and experience by the heart, feelings, spirit, and other inward human faculties. Belief or faith address all human faculties; each and every human faculty has a share in them. Also, truths of faith are not matters depending on human choice or preference but they exist independently of humanity, and what falls to human beings is to discover them. Therefore, they should be sought for, studied, and understood.

- **The falsifier of the truth adopts the false as true.**[61]

Human beings, created with an inherently noble disposition, pursue the truth. But sometimes they happen to find and embrace a falsehood. While searching for the truth, misguidance or falsehood comes upon them involuntarily; supposing it to be the truth, they wear it on their head.

- **People are directed either by their thoughts or emotions, or by right or force, or by wisdom or power, or by guidance or lusts and caprices.**[62]

What generally prevailed in the past and gave rise to spite, enmity, and superiority complexes were emotions, inclinations, and force. A powerful, convincing speech was enough to guide people. At that time, the ability to embellish a thesis in such a way that it would affect the feelings and inclinations, or make it attractive with the power of rhetoric, served as evidence. But comparing ourselves to them means returning to the corners of that time. Every age has a character peculiar to itself. We demand evidence, and are not deceived through the mere statement or embellishment of a thesis. This gives the glad tidings that Islam, which is the true and greatest humanity, and has all its truths confirmed by science and sound reason, will shine like an unclouded sun in the heavens of the future.

- **If a religion, ideology, or political system is not based on truth, evidence, and voluntary acceptance and practice, it tends to maintain power through force and despotism. Force and despo-**

---

[60] *The Letters,* "The Twelfth Letter", p. 69.
[61] *Gleams of Truth,* pp. 7, 33.
[62] *The Reasonings,* "The First Part", pp. 32.

tism give rise to fanaticism, bigotry, and denouncing others as deviant or fallacious, and therefore to enmity and conflict.[63]

Where force, desires, natural untrained dispositions, and emotions are dominant, despotism and authoritarianism prevail. Enmity towards the way of others is more popular than love of one's own way. Enmity towards a person is manifested as friendship to that person's enemies. In addition, partisanship and fanaticism prevent the appearance of the truth. Since differences of opinion supported by partisanship can cause fierce conflicts, the truth retreats and conceals itself. Bigotry and denouncing others as deviant or fallacious are the tools of despotism. These are all condemned in the sight of Shari'ah, and are also contrary to religious brother/sisterhood, to the bonds of humanity, and the mutual assistance that is required by collective life. Islam demands that truth must prevail over force, evidence over fallacies, reason over disposition, guidance over lust and caprice, steadfastness in the truth over bigotry or fanaticism, public spirit over spite, intellectual tendencies over the inclinations of the carnal soul, and thought over emotions.

- **A judgment that is given or valid for a whole may not be valid for each of its parts.**[64]

Every human being is fallible by nature, so some un-Islamic acts or attributes cannot be reason for a Muslim to be denounced as if he or she is a non-Muslim, just as some good, Islamic acts or attributes are not enough for a non-Muslim to be a Muslim.

- **The reason why humankind was set on the earth as vicegerent is that we must improve the earth and rule on it according to the commandments of God, thus establishing justice. This depends on both religious and scientific knowledge.**[65]

Humankind was created and set on the earth as vicegerent (*khalifah*) of the earth. As a term, *khilafah,* or vicegerency, denotes improving the earth on the basis of knowledge of things and the laws of creation (which we wrongly call the "laws of nature"), and ruling on the earth according to the commandments of God, thus establishing justice. Carrying out this duty requires scientific knowledge and the Divine Religion. Humankind can acquire scientific knowledge by studying nature, and we are given the

---

[63] *The Reasonings,* "The First Part", pp. 33–34.

[64] *The Reasonings,* "The Third Part", p. 130.

[65] *İşaratü'l-İ'caz,* "*Suratu'l-Baqara*", verses 30–33.

Religion through God's Messengers. The Books given or revealed to the Messengers, in addition to containing the religious principles, are, in one respect, like discourses describing nature and its meaning. That is why, in Islam, the universe, or nature, is seen as the "Created Book," and its laws as the laws of creation and the operation of the universe issuing from the Divine Attributes of Will and Power. The Qur'an is the "Revealed Book," the set of Divine laws and principles issuing from God's Attribute of Speech. For this reason, there can and should be no dichotomy or conflict between science and the Religion.

Prophet Adam, upon him be peace, the first human being, was taught the names of things, or given knowledge of things, succinctly or briefly, and this knowledge has been elaborated over time. Prophets or Messengers also acted as scientific guides to people, and God Almighty pointed to the farthest limits of scientific knowledge through the miracles He created at the hands of the Prophets, urging people to reach them.[66]

- **The Divine reason why Prophet Adam was sent out of Heaven lies in the mission of humanity on the earth.**[67]

Humanity has a unique duty in the universe. Prophet Adam, upon him be peace, was sent to the earth with so sublime a duty that humanity was honored with the ability to achieve an infinite spiritual evolution, and to be a comprehensive mirror in which all Divine Names are reflected. This duty leads humanity to develop its full potential. If Adam had stayed in Heaven, his rank would have been fixed and humanity's full potential would not have developed. Humanity was not created to worship God in the manner of angels, whose worship does not cause them to evolve spiritually. Divine Wisdom must have required a different world in which humanity could attain the highest rank, and fully develop its potential. This is why Adam was sent to earth.

There are two kinds of Shari'ah (Divine Laws): one issuing from the Divine Attribute of Speech and regulating or ordering the actions and states of humanity, the microcosm, which are voluntary; and the other issuing from the Divine Attributes of Will and Power and regulating the universe's (a macro-human) creation and opera-

---

[66] See *The Words*, "The Twentieth Word".
[67] *The Letters*, "The Twelfth Letter", p. 70.

tion. **This second one is the eternally determined system of the Lord, and it is what is wrongly termed "nature".**[68]

People are free to obey or disobey both of the Shari'as. Results for the former are usually deferred to the Hereafter, while returns for the latter usually come in this life. For example, the reward for patience is success, while the punishment for indolence is privation. Industry brings wealth, and steadfastness brings victory. Any claim to justice that is not based on giving everyone his or her due is a false claim.

Angels are a mighty community, a host of the All-Glorified One. They are God's obedient servants and workers, who are responsible for the fulfillment of the second Shari'ah; they are representatives (representing the worship of the inanimate, plant, and animal kingdoms in the Court of God). Some of them are worshipping servants of God, others are absorbed in knowledge and love of God, stationed near to Him around His Supreme Throne.

- **Misfortunes experienced by innocent children and animals contain instances of Wisdom that people usually fail to notice.**[69]

For example, Divine laws of nature and life are principles of Divine Will applied not only to intellectual beings; creatures without reason are also 'obliged' to obey them by virtue of their disposition. Those laws also appeal to the heart, feelings, and senses. A child may be considered mature in some senses or feelings. A child's feelings may even be more perfect and alert than an adult's reason. While an adult's reason might not prevent him or her from oppressing an orphan, the compassion of his or her child who watches this oppression may drive that child to tears.

That being so, if children do not heed their feelings of compassion or pity and kill a honeybee to indulge an impulse, they may be punished. For example, a female leopard feels great affection for its young and is protective of its mate. However, when these feelings do not prevent it from killing a young gazelle, it may become the target of a hunter's bullet. Is this not what it deserves, for its lawful food is the carcasses of other animals?

- **The "lawful" food of many wild carnivores is another animal's carcass. By eating them, these carnivores feed themselves and cleanse the earth's surface.**[70]

---

[68] *The Words*, "Gleams of Truth', pp. 754–755; *The Letters*, "Seeds of Truth", 455–456, 457.
[69] *Al-Mathnawi al-Nuri*, "The Fourth Treatise", pp. 116–117.
[70] *The Letters*, "Seeds of Truth", p. 454; *Al-Mathnawi al-Nuri*, "The Fourth Treatise", 116.

The Qur'an defines Islam as *fitra* (the unchangeable Divine system of the creation and operation of the whole universe with whatever is in it),[71] therefore Islam is the translation of the universal order. Things and beings with no consciousness and will-power absolutely obey this Divine system or universal order, and this is why there is no corruption and disorderliness in the parts of the universe where conscious, responsible beings like humanity and jinn are active. In this Divine system no living being is allowed to feed on or eat another living being. God Almighty has appointed animal carcasses as the food of wild carnivores. They are forbidden to eat of other living beings, whether animals or human beings.

However, we witness that wild carnivores generally feed on many species of living animals. This is because some degree of corruption has taken place on the earth and in the sea due to humanity's disobedience to the Divine Religion and the Divine system of the universe. This is clear in the Qur'an: "*Corruption and disorder have appeared on land and in the sea because of what the hands of people have (done and) earned (of evil deeds)...*"[72] This corruption and disorder has also spoiled the character of some wild carnivores. This is why they eat some innocent animals.

This is like war in human life and diseases appearing in human bodies. What is essential for human life is peace, and for human bodies it is health. What is most abhorrent in God's sight, concerning the human mission on earth is causing corruption and disorder, and shedding blood.[73] Therefore, God has allowed, even ordered, war, in order to re-establish peace and order, as He has allowed, and even ordered the performance an operation on a diseased human body. Essentially, both fighting and a surgical operation on a healthy body are evil deeds in themselves, but they become necessary for health and a healthy social life. Like this, in order to prevent wild carnivores from feeding on some innocent animals, we must re-establish order fully on earth. This requires the discovery of all the laws of the Divine universal system and obeying them, as well as living in strict accordance with the commandments of the Divine Religion.

---

[71] *Suratu'r-Rum*, 30:30.

[72] *Suratu'r-Rum*, 30:41.

[73] *Suratu'l-Baqara*, 2:30.

- **The limits of religiously permissible enjoyment are broad and adequate for our desires, and there is no need to indulge in what is forbidden.**[74]

God the All-Merciful has created numerous kinds of wholesome and licit food and drink in order to satisfy our needs and desires. They are enough for both a healthy nourishment and pleasure. Therefore, there is no need to indulge in what is forbidden.

- **Just as going to one extreme is harmful, going to the opposite extreme is also harmful; in fact, it is even more harmful. However, going to one extreme is the greater fault, as this causes others to go to the opposite extreme.**[75]

Balance is essential in everything and the destruction of balance brings with itself many other vices, even the destruction of the entire system. The Qur'an emphasizes balance: ".. *And the heaven—He has made it high (above the earth), and He has set up the balance; so you must not go beyond (the limits with respect to) the balance; and observe the balance with full equity, and do not fall short in it.*"[76]

The wonderful accord observed in the universe and its maintenance is due to this most sensitively computed balance. It is also indispensable to human life, both individually and socially. Its social manifestation is justice. With respect to human education and perfection, this balance requires that everything is given its due importance in life and that the basic faculties or impulses of anger, desire, and reason be trained, disciplined, and employed in order to develop them into the virtues of chivalrous courage, moderation and chastity, and wisdom. If the balance is just the middle point on a line, every distance from this point causes the destruction of the balance, to certain extents.

During history people have not been able to avoid going to extreme points both right and left, and going to one extreme has caused others going to the opposite extreme. For example, in the history of Islam, some went to the extreme where they denied the role of human free will in human acts; and just opposite of this, others went so far that they defended that human beings create their own deeds. As another example, the Shi'a appeared with the claim of love of the Prophet's Household but

---

[74] *The Words*, "The Sixth Word", 39.
[75] *The Reasonings*, "The First Part", p. 20.
[76] *Suratu'r-Rahman*, 55:7–9.

went so far as to claim that the Caliphate of 'Ali and some of his descendants were appointed by God and therefore those who did not accept his Caliphate just after the Prophet, upon him be peace and blessings, both usurped his right and destroyed one of the pillars of the Religion. Just opposite to this, some from among the Umayyads went to the other extreme point, and adopted an attitude of enmity towards 'Ali, may God be pleased with him, and cursed him. Many deviant sects and movements have thus appeared because of such extreme attitudes.

- **Do not overdo those things you like.**[77]

We should refrain from going to every kind of extreme in our deeds, thoughts, actions, and judgments. For example, as ill-suspicion is forbidden in the Qur'an,[78] over-estimation of people is also forbidden. The Holy Prophet, upon him be peace and blessings, declares: "While God exists and sees and hears everything, we cannot over-estimate anybody and declare them to be sinless and faultless."[79] He also warns that we should not go to extremes in either hating or loving anybody, because one whom we hate may one day be a friend, while another whom we love may appear to be an enemy.

- **The cure for one ailment may be harmful to another; what is an antidote for one becomes poison for another. If the cure is taken to excess, it causes illness and becomes fatal.**[80]

Every illness, bodily, psychological, spiritually, or socially, demands therapy and medication with different doses according to its nature, type, and intensity of severeness.

- **Religion is for examination, a test and trial to distinguish elevated and base ones from each other and so that people can develop their potential into active abilities and be witnesses as to their essence, and what sort and quality of people they are.**[81]

Just as raw materials are fired to separate diamonds from coal and gold from soil, Divine obligations test conscious beings so that the precious "ore" in the "mine" of human potential may be separated from the dross. It is also because of this that God does not compel people to

---

[77] *Gleams of Truth*, p. 54..

[78] *Suratu'l-Hujurat*, 49:12.

[79] *al-Bukhari*, "Shahada" 16: *Muslim*, "Zuhd" 65; *Abu Dawud*, "Adab" 10.

[80] *Gleams of Truth*, p. 54.

[81] *The Words*, "The Twentieth Word", pp. 278–279; "The Twenty-ninth Word", p. 549.

believe, rather, He opens the door to reason to believe without negating people's free willpower. Therefore, belief or unbelief is something people will and do choose freely. For example, the Qur'an only alludes especially to future events and scientific developments, which people will witness over time. It opens the door to reason as much as needed to prove its argument. If it had mentioned such things explicitly, testing would be meaningless. They would be so clear, as if writing *There is no deity but God* on the face of the sky with stars, that everyone would be forced to believe, and the testing and trial would mean nothing.

Testing through Religion also enables people to develop their potential into active abilities, and causes them to know themselves as to what kind and quality of people they are. They even cannot help confessing this in their own conscience and will confess it in the other world.[82]

- **God tries His servants, but they cannot try Him.**[83]

One cannot interfere in God's concerns. He takes His servant to the arena of trial and says: "If you do that, I'll do this." But the servant can never try God. If he says, "Should God give me success, I'll do this," he is transgressing his limits.

Satan said to Jesus: "Since it is He Who does everything, and His Destiny does not change, then throw yourself down off the mountain, and see what He will do with you." Jesus replied: "O accursed one! God puts His servant to the test, but His servants cannot put Him to the test!"[84]

What always falls to the servants is to obey God's commands and refrain from His prohibitions.

- **It is mistaken to feel mercy or wrath greater than God's.**[85]

As God Himself, His Attributes are also infinite. Therefore, no one can be either more merciful than Him, nor know what kind of punishment one exactly deserves. Nor can we know what amount of mercy or wrath we should show to people. We should leave matters to the All-Just, the All-Merciful One, and be resigned to both His mercy and forgiveness, and the punishment He inflicts or legislates. We should also

---

[82] *Suratu'l-Anbiya'*, 21:63; *Sura Ya–Sin*, 36:65; *Suratu'l-Muddassir*, 74:42–47.

[83] *Gleams of Truth*, pp. 52–53.

[84] 'Abdur-Rahman ibn 'Ali ibnu'l-Jawzi, *Talbisu Iblis*, p. 344; also see, *The Gospel of Matthew*, 4:5–7..

[85] *Gleams of Truth*, p. 60.

know that excessive compassion causes pain and excessive wrath is wrongful and blameworthy.

- **There are two types of Muslims and believers or faithful. Also, from another perspective,** islam **(Muslimness) is choosing the side of truth and submission to truth, while** iman **(faith) means conviction and confirmation.**[86]

There are two types of Muslims and believers (*mu'min*). One type is a true Muslim. A true believer and Muslim is the person who confirms and confesses all the truths of Islam, including those of faith primarily, and, at least, tries to practice the commandments of Islam in his or her daily life. The other type is that the one whom we see performing some of Islam's basic commandments such as the Prescribed Prayers (*Salah*) and Giving the Prescribed Alms (*Zakah*) and in whom no word or act of unbelief certain to issue from his unbelief is witnessed is accepted as a believing Muslim and treated as a Muslim citizen by a Muslim state. However, such a one may be a hypocrite, who conceals his unbelief. Therefore, there are two kinds of Muslims and believers: those who are truly Muslims and believers, and the hypocrites who are believers and Muslims in appearance but unbelievers in truth.

From another perspective, *islam*, or being a Muslim, means siding with, submitting to, and obeying the truth. *Iman*, or being a believer (*mu'min*), means confirming and confessing the truths of Islam. There are some people who strongly advocate the Qur'an's commandments even though they are not believers. Such people may be considered *Muslim* in the literal sense (of those who surrender) because they observe some of Islam's elements without believing in all of them. On the other hand, there are some believers who cannot be considered *Muslim*, for they do not pay much attention to the Qur'an's commandments or try to obey them.

- **Belief** (iman) **is a bond connecting us to our All-Majestic Maker, by virtue of which we gain the great value of being the most precious work of the All-Majestic Maker's Art. Whereas unbelief breaks this connection, thereby veiling the Divine art and reducing our value to that of a mere physical entity.**[87]

---

[86] *The Letters*, "The Ninth Letter", p. 53.
[87] *The Words*, "The Twenty-third Word", pp. 327–328.

Consider what follows: The value of the iron (or any other material) from which a work of art is made differs from the value of the art expressed in it. The art's worth is usually far more than its material according to the greatness of the artist. For example, a painting made by an artist like Picasso can be sold for a million dollars due to the artist himself, while its material may be worth of a few dollars only. It is like this with each person: they are a unique, priceless work of God Almighty's Art. We are His Power's most delicate and graceful miracles, beings created to manifest all His Names and inscriptions in the form of a miniature specimen of the universe. It is belief or faith which makes these extremely meaningful and valuable inscriptions visible, and believers read them consciously. That is, the Divine art contained in each person is revealed through such affirmations as: "I am the work of the All-Majestic Maker, the creature and object of His Mercy and Munificence." As a result, and because we gain value in proportion to how well we reflect this art, we move from insignificance (in material terms) to beings ranked above all creatures. We communicate with God, are His guests on the earth, and are qualified for Paradise.

However, should unbelief, which means the severance of this connection, manifest in us, all of the Divine Names' gifts are veiled by darkness and thus non-expressive. For if the Artist is unknown, how can the aspects expressing the worth of His Art be identified? Thus, the most meaningful instances of that sublime Art are concealed. Regarding the material aspects of our being, unbelievers attribute them to physical causes, nature and chance, thereby reducing them to plain glass instead of sparkling diamonds. They are no more significant than any other material entity, self-condemned to a transient and suffocating life, and no better than the most impotent, needy, and afflicted animal that eventually will become dust. Unbelief thus spoils our nature by changing our diamond into coal.

- **Belief establishes brotherhood, sisterhood and affinity among all things. Due to believing in the One God as the Creator and Lord of the entire universe with whatever and whoever is in it, a believer sees the universe a cradle of brotherhood or sisterhood. However, unbelief causes separation and alienation, which manifest in unbelievers as strong feelings of enmity towards others, and self-preference.**[88]

---

[88] *Al-Mathnawi al-Nuri*, "The Fourth Treatise", p. 112.

One does not find strong feelings of greed, enmity, hatred, or desolation in believers' hearts. Believers see even the strongest enemies as brothers or sisters in humanity. Whereas unbelief engenders separation, alienation, and loneliness, and causes an unbeliever to see the universe as a desolate place, life as a meaningless plaything of chance or coincidences, and all other beings as either enemies prepared to remove him from the world or take away whatever he has.

- **The seat of belief is the heart and conscience; the mind is where the light of belief is reflected.**[89]

Belief has its seat in the heart and conscience. It is conviction and experience by the heart. As for the mind, it is sometimes a warrior fighting falsehoods with rational and scientific arguments, sometimes it is a broom removing doubts. If the doubts of the mind do not enter the heart, neither belief or faith nor conscience will be shaken.

- **The degree of belief attained through certainty of knowledge based on the Qur'an and Sunnah is greater and surer than that achieved through spiritual vision or discovery.**[90]

All spiritual states, visions, and conclusions reached via contemplation, intellectual intuition, or spiritual discovery should be judged according to the principles of the Qur'an and the Sunnah, and the standards derived from them by pure people or scholars of truth.

A true spiritual vision has a reality, but like dreams, it usually requires interpretation. People of vision cannot interpret their visions while in a trance-like state, just as people cannot interpret their dreams while dreaming. Their visions can be interpreted only by pure people of truth and verification who are true heirs of the Prophetic mission (*Asfiya*). When such people of vision attain the rank of people of pure truth and become aware of their mistakes they make in their descriptions of their vision according to the standards of this world, in the light of the Qur'an and Sunnah, they correct them.

- **Grasping one matter of faith fully and making it understood in plain terms is preferred to attaining thousands of spiritual pleasures and ecstasies and working wonders. The final station of all**

---

[89] *Gleams of Truth*, p. 78.
[90] *The Letters*, "The Eighteenth Letter", pp. 108–109.

spiritual journeying is to attain the full perception of the truths of faith.[91]

Imam Rabbani Ahmad Faruq al-Sirhindi (1564–1624) writes that there are three kinds of sainthood: that known to everybody (minor), that of a medium degree, and that of major sainthood (the greatest one), which can be attained through direct succession to the Prophetic Message. This greatest one paves the way to the truth without entering the intermediate realm of spiritual orders. One can progress on a spiritual way by having a firm belief in the pillars of faith and performing the religious duties. Neglect of or deficiency in either makes this way impossible to follow.[92]

- **Faith is defined as a light God Almighty kindled in the heart of a person as a result of the person using his or her free will to choose faith; it is a conviction and confirmation of the truth of each and every fundamental of Islam, and a general affirmation of its secondary principles and commandments. Faith has as many and different degrees as the image or reflection of the sun in a drop of water to itself.**[93]

Faith is acceptance by the mind, and conviction and experience by the heart and conscience, which requires the performance of Islamic obligations. It does not consist of only a verbal declaration or a simple affirmation. It has a relation with all the dimensions of a human being's existence and all of his or her inner and outer senses. It is love and attachment by feelings, experience in the heart, compliance by the body or performance by the will-power, and affirmation by the mind. It has degrees to the number of human beings, and even to the number of the states of all human beings. It has degrees that are similar to the number and intensity of the sun's reflections in drops of water to those in a lake, a river, a sea, an ocean, and in the atmosphere, as far as the sun itself.

- **Faith or belief requires affirming Divine Unity; affirmation of Divine Unity requires submitting to God; submission to God requires relying on God; and reliance on God yields happiness in both worlds.**[94]

---

[91] *The Letters*, "The Fifth Letter", p. 30; "The Twenty-eighth Letter", p. 364.

[92] *The Letters*, "The Fifth Letter", p. 30.

[93] *İşaratü'l-İ'caz*, "Suratu'l-Baqara", verse 3; *Emirdağ Lahikası* (Addendum of Emirdağ),p. 102.

[94] *The Words*, "The Twenty-third Word!", p. 330.

Belief is both light and power. Those who attain true belief can challenge the universe and, in proportion to their belief's strength, be relieved of the pressures of events. Relying on God, they travel safely through the mountainous waves of events on the ship of life. Having entrusted their burdens to the Absolutely Powerful One's Hand of Power, they voyage through the world comfortably until their last day. The grave will be a resting place, after which they will fly to Paradise to attain eternal bliss.

We should not misunderstand reliance on God; it does not mean ignoring cause and effect, and complete negligence of the means to attain a goal. Rather, it means that we should do whatever we should in the lawful way in order to attain a lawful goal, and then expect the result only from God, the All-Mighty. As He is the sole producer of effects, we always should be grateful to Him.

- **The human carnal soul bent on unbelief is like an ostrich, that when told to fly replies: "I'm a camel, not a bird." But when told to carry a burden, it answers: "I'm a bird, not a camel."**[95]

Islam is a universal mercy. It enables even unbelievers to find some happiness in their worldly lives and ensures that their pleasure does not change into endless pain. For Islam changes absolute unbelief and denial, which cause endless despair and pain, into doubt and hesitation. Influenced by its clear announcements, unbelievers may come to regard eternal life as probable. This relieves them from suffocating pain arising from the thought of eternal extinction through death. However, when they are told to live according to God's commandments in order to gain the eternal happiness, they tend to deny the Hereafter and eternal punishment since their carnal soul does not desire to discipline itself according to the Divine Religion.

- **Faith or belief bears the seed of what is, in effect, a *Touba* tree of Paradise, whereas unbelief contains the seed of a *Zaqqum* tree of Hell. Safety and happiness are found only in *islam* (submission to God) and belief. However, the ostrich-like attitude of the human carnal soul, and the sedative and hypnotizing effects of modern life, may cause unbelievers to find some happiness in the worldly life.**[96]

---

[95] *Al-Mathnawi al-Nuri*, "The Fourth Treatise", p. 122.

[96] *The Words*, "The Second Word", p. 16; *The Gleams*, "The Thirteenth Gleam", p. 108.

Belief and the performance of the commandments of Islam give the human heart and spirit unclouded happiness and exhilaration. Also, a believer sees the world as a cradle of brotherhood and sisterhood, a place where numerous creatures glorify, praise, and exalt God Almighty, a practice arena for people and animals, and an examination hall for people and jinn where they develop their inborn abilities. Animals and humanity are demobilized so that after death believers can travel in spiritual enjoyment to the other world—for this world needs a new generation to populate and work in it. Whereas unbelievers or heedless sinners see this world as a place of general mourning, all living things as weeping orphans due to the pain of separation and decay, people and animals as lonely and uncivilized creatures cut down by death, and great masses like mountains and oceans as terrible corpses without souls. Their unbelief and misguidance breed great anxieties that torture them.

- **Belief enables us to attain true humanity, to acquire a position above all other creatures. Thus, belief and prayer are our most fundamental and important duties. Unbelief, by contrast, reduces us to the state of a brutal but very impotent beast.**[97]

A decisive proof for this truth is the difference between how human beings and animals come into existence. Almost from the very moment of birth, an animal seems to have been trained and perfected its faculties somewhere else. Within a few hours or days or months, it can lead its life according to its particular rules and conditions. This means that an animal's basic obligation and essential role does not include seeking perfection through learning, progress through knowledge, prayer and petitioning for help by displaying their impotence. Rather, their sole purpose is to act within the bounds of their innate faculties, which is the mode of worship specified for them.

Human beings, however, are born knowing nothing of life and their environment and so must learn everything. We continue to learn until we die. We are sent here with so much weakness and inability that we might need more than one year to learn how to walk. Only after fifteen years can we dimly distinguish good and evil, and our preference of good requires education until death. Thus the essential and intrinsic duty of our existence is to seek perfection through learning and to proclaim our worship

---

[97] *The Words*, "The Twenty-third Word", p. 331–332.

of and servanthood to God through prayer and supplication. Everything is, by its nature, essentially dependent on knowledge. And the basis, source, light, and spirit of all true knowledge is knowledge of God, of which belief is the very foundation.

- **All believers, according to the degree of their belief and through the Qur'an's light, can be happy with creatures' happiness and permanence, their being saved from nothingness and favored with the light of existence, and their being the valuable missives of the Lord. They may acquire thereby a light so comprehensive that it fills the world and benefits everyone according to his or her capacity.**[98]

Being the fruit of the Tree of Creation, human beings feel themselves connected to all other creatures, and derive pleasure from their happiness and grieve over their misfortune. They especially rejoice over animate beings' happiness, particularly over that of other people, and especially over that of the approved and loved people of perfection, and share their grief. Like affectionate mothers, they may sacrifice their own rest and happiness for such people's welfare.

However, this is possible through belief, which enables believers to see the universe as the cradle of brotherhood and sisterhood. Misguidance and unbelief sever the bonds of brotherhood and sisterhood among all creatures, regard death as absolute annihilation, and cause people to fall into despair and depression and become pessimists due to all creatures' misfortune and death. Unbelief causes people to become obsessed with the fear of going to absolute non-existence, and as a result they suffer hellish torment even before reaching Hell.

- **Since God exists, everything exists. Since everything is connected to God Almighty, His Unity causes each thing to be connected to everything. Thus each thing is an object of the infinite light of existence.**[99]

Since everything exists because God exists as the Creator and Lord, every and each thing is connected to God and to everything else. Due to this connection, each thing has an infinite light of existence even though it lives even for a moment. This is why people of truth conclude that a

---

[98] *The Letters*, "The Twenty-fourth Letter", p. 309.
[99] *The Letters*, "The Twenty-fourth Letter", p. 310.

moment of life enlightened through this connection is preferable to a million years of life devoid of such light.

Unbelief severs this connection and condemns everything to eternal non-existence and causes one to suffer infinite separation and non-existence due to the resulting endless despair and depression felt when a creature to which one feels a connection decays and dies. For those who do not recognize God, the universe is a vast, dark, and desolate place in which beings wait for death and separation. Consider that each fruit on a tree is connected to all fruits on that tree, and so has as many kinds of secondary existence as the number of fruits. Picking it separates it from the other fruits and envelopes it in the darkness of non-existence. The connection to the One Eternally Besought's Power gives each being or thing an actual existence. Without this connection, there are as many types of non-existence as the number of things.

- **While it is obligatory that all attributes of a Muslim are Muslim, in reality this may not always be so. Similarly, not all the attributes of an unbeliever have to be connected to unbelieving or arise from his unbelief. In the same way, all the attributes of a sinful transgressor may not be sinful, nor do they need always arise from sinfulness.**[100]

A Muslim is supposed to be Muslim in all his or her attributes and acts, but in reality every Muslim is fallible and a Muslim may have non-Muslim attributes and commit a sin. Similarly, an unbeliever may have Muslim attributes and all his or her acts do not have to issue from his or her unbelief. Having a non-Muslim attribute or committing a sin does not make a Muslim non-Muslim, nor does having a Muslim attribute or doing good, Islamic acts make a non-Muslim Muslim.

- **God raised a Messenger within every community; but either their messages were distorted and corrupted in time and therefore they came not to be known as Messengers, or since they had a small following, they did not become famous or were not recognized.**[101]

God declares in the Qur'an: *"And assuredly, We raised within every community a Messenger (to convey the primordial message): Worship God*

---

[100] *Gleams of Truth*, p. 108.
[101] *The Letters*, "The Twenty-eighth Letter", p. 377–378.

alone, and keep away from false deities and powers of evil (who institute patterns of faith and rule in defiance of God)."[102] Imam Rabbani, based on evidence, said: "Many Prophets appeared in India, but, since no one or only a few followed most of them, they either did not become famous or were not recognized as Prophets." So, there has been no community within which a Prophet was not raised.

- **The people who are not addressed by Divine Revelation or to whom the Divine Message is not conveyed are forgivable and will be excused in the Hereafter.**[103]

As stated in: "*We do not punish unless We send a Messenger,*"[104] those to whom the Divine Message is not conveyed will be exempt from Hell-fire. Imam ash-Shafi'i and Imam Abu'l-Hasan al-Ash'ari maintain that they will be saved from Hell's torment even if they did not believe and were unaware of the pillars of belief, for God holds His servants responsible for His commands only after sending a Messenger.

- **One of the reasons why some attribute everything to apparent means or agents or causes is two things—the cause and the effect—coming together, which is called "accompaniment," and the absence of the effect in the absence of the cause.**[105]

The Divine Wisdom has made in this world the existence or occurrence of something dependent on the existence of a cause or means. This has led many into the deception that the cause or means is the creator of the effect.

This incorrect supposition causes people to attribute any bounty that comes to them to apparent material causes, or to its apparent agent, and thus they offer thanks to them instead of God, the Giver of bounties. However, the existence of a bounty or something else depends on the existence of many other things, while its non-existence is possible through the non-existence of one of those things. For example, one who does not open the irrigation channels to water a garden becomes the cause of the garden drying up and the non-existence of the bounties that come through the garden. But the existence of those bounties depends on the

---

[102] *Suratu'n-Nahl*, 16:34.
[103] *The Letters*, "The Twenty-eighth Letter", p. 377; *Kastamonu Lahikası* (Addendum of Kastamonu), p. 79.
[104] *Suratu'l-Isra'*, 17:15.
[105] *The Gleams*, "The Seventeenth Gleam", p. 184.

existence of many other requirements, and the main cause for and creator of them, as well as everything else that exists or occurs, is the Divine Will and Power. Also, everything and every occurrence in the universe is extremely meaningful and has many instances of wisdom, while all of the "natural" causes are lifeless and absolutely devoid of consciousness and will-power. Therefore, we should not receive the bounties that come to us at the hands of some worldly means or agents as if these means or agents were providing these bounties for us. If any means or agent is something without consciousness and free will, like an animal or a tree for example, it gives the bounty directly on behalf of God Almighty, Who is its Creator and Lord, and Who employs it in His bounties reaching us. Since it gives in the Name of God, we should receive it, saying *In the Name of God*. If the agent has consciousness and free will, they should say while giving, *In the Name of God*; then we should receive it.

- **Belief is affirmation based on evidence, while unbelief is negation and denial. Affirmation is possible through a single evidence or the testimony of two witnesses, whereas it is not possible to prove the non-existence of something, and therefore negation or denial has no weight in the name of truth.**[106]

Two people who testify to the existence of something are able to defeat a million who deny its existence, simply by producing an example of that thing. For instance, if two trustworthy people claim that they have seen the crescent moon which heralds, say, the lunar month of Ramadan, their claim is accepted as veracious even if everyone else denies it. Similarly, if two persons testify to the occurrence of something, it is acceptable by law, although all other people deny it. Also, if two people claim that there is a garden on the earth where coconuts resembling cans of milk are grown, their claim will be verified if they bring forth a single coconut or, alternatively, indicate the place where they can be found. Those who deny this claim, however, can prove their point only by searching all four corners of the earth in order to demonstrate that no such coconuts exist anywhere.

So, it is almost impossible to prove the non-existence of something, and this is why claiming the non-existence of God is only a personal claim having no weight in the name of truth. Whereas denial or unbelief is a

---

[106] *The Rays*, "The Eleventh Ray", pp. 242–243; *The Words*, "The Twenty-ninth Word", p. 533.

judgment or conclusion which must be based on evidence. However, there can be shown no evidence to prove the claim of God's non-existence, while there are innumerable rational, even scientific, proofs for His existence and other cardinals of belief.

- **It is an established principle that once a matter is confirmed by two specialists, its denial by thousands carries no weight. Two specialists in a matter are preferable to thousands of non-specialists.**[107]

A hundred and twenty-four thousand Prophets, the most renowned of all humankind, none of whom was ever witnessed to tell a single lie, attested unanimously to the truth of all of the cardinals of belief, including first and foremost the existence of God Almighty. Hundreds of millions of people who lived together with the Prophets and believed in them sincerely based on many proofs of Prophethood that they observed, confirmed them in all their claims. Therefore, the denial of others whose denial is only a personal choice, arising from personal biases and excuses, and impossible to be proved based on any evidence, should not cast even the slightest doubt or suspicion on pillars of belief.

- **The affirmations of those who affirm support and strengthen each other, while the negations and denials of those who deny are no more than personal choices which give no support to each other.**[108]

Affirmation relates to the reality or fact itself, whereas negation depends on the one who negates. So those who believe and affirm are agreed on a reality or fact, and their affirmations support and strengthen one another. But since denial issues from many different excuses and depends on those who deny, the agreement of deniers has no power or validity. If a thick cloud makes it impossible for all people, except a few, to see the sun, can we say that the sun is not there? Of course not, for those who cannot see it will say, "I cannot see the sun," not, "The sun does not exist."

- **Value and importance are not judged by quantity. So, the agreement of the unbelievers and the misguided on denying and negating a truth of belief has no weight, for denial, even if in the form**

---

[107] *The Rays*, "The Eleventh Ray", pp. 242–243; *The Words*, "The Twenty-ninth Word", p. 533.

[108] *The Rays*, "The Eleventh Ray", pp. 242–243; *The Gleams*, "The Seventeenth Gleam", p. 169.

of affirmation, is negation or repudiation; therefore, their agreement on denial has no power.[109]

We see that although this world contains far more animals than human beings, human beings have been given supremacy over all animal species as God's vicegerents on earth. Therefore, the unbelievers being more in number than the believers has no value in the face of the truth of belief. A thousand deniers are equal to one believer. For example, if all but two people in Istanbul rejected the sighting of the crescent moon (at the beginning of Ramadan), and those two state that they have seen it, the testimony of these two would invalidate the negation and agreement of that great multitude. So, since in reality, unbelief and misguidance are negation, denial, ignorance, and acceptance of non-existence, even the agreement of unbelievers in great numbers would have no significance. In matters of belief, which have been proven and established to be true, the affirmation of two believers based on observation and experience is preferable and prevails over the agreement of multitudes of people of misguidance.

- **Non-acceptance of something's existence is usually confused with the acceptance of its non-existence, though one is doubt and the other, denial, which requires proof.**[110]

One of the important points which should be considered in the matter of belief and unbelief is that people confuse non-acceptance of the existence of something with the acceptance of its non-existence. Whereas the former is doubt and indifference, the latter is judgment, which requires proof. As explained above, it is almost impossible to prove the non-existence of something. If you claim the existence of something, it is enough to merely point it out. But if you claim its non-existence, the whole world has to be sifted through so that you will be able to prove its non-existence.

- **Minds that are absorbed in negligence, sin, and materiality become restricted and narrowed with regard to the profound issues of belief such as Divine Supremacy, Grandeur, and Infinity, and the afterlife. Because of this, they deviate towards denial and negation, puffed up by arrogance on account of the knowledge they believe they possess.**[111]

---

[109] *The Gleams,* "The Seventeenth Gleam", p. 168–169.
[110] *Gleams of Truth,* p. 179; *The Words,* "The Fifteenth Word", p. 203.
[111] *The Rays,* "The Seventh Ray", p. 118–119.

Since such people cannot encompass the extremely vast, profound, and comprehensive matters of belief within their spiritually desiccated and narrowed minds, or their corrupt and spiritually dead hearts, they throw themselves into unbelief and misguidance and they drown.

If they were able to look at the essence of their unbelief and the true nature of their misguidance, they would see how manifestly absurd and impossible their denial is in comparison with the reasonableness and sublimity of belief. For example, one who is unable to accept vast truths of belief, such as the absolutely necessary Existence, Pre-eternity, and all-encompassing Attributes of God Almighty on account of their grandeur and sublimity, may form a creed of unbelief either by attributing the necessary Existence, Attributes, Pre-eternity and Creativity of God to uncountable material beings or atoms or nature or certain concepts such as chance; or like the foolish Sophists, they may even renounce reason by denying and negating both their own existence and that of the universe.

- **People vary in guidance and misguidance, and heedlessness has many degrees. Everyone cannot perceive completely this truth in all its degrees.**[112]

It may be said that both right guidance and misguidance have many degrees. However, since heedlessness numbs the senses, especially in the present age, the "civilized" are insensible to the acute pain of misguidance. However, the warnings of tens of thousands of deaths every day, which reminds people of the reality of death, may tear this veil of heedlessness asunder.

- **Each person must renew and refresh his or her belief, because both they and their personal worlds are renewed continually.**[113]

The Holy Prophet, upon him be peace and blessings, declares: "Refresh your belief with *There is no deity but God.*"[114] One of the many aspects of the meaning of this *hadith* is this: Each person must renew and refresh his or her belief, because both they and their personal worlds are renewed continually. Each individual acquires or is transformed into a different individual annually, monthly, daily, and even hourly. Given this, our transient world passes away and is replaced by a new one that opens its doors to us every day. Belief is the light of the life we acquire while

---

[112] *The Gleams*, "The Seventeenth Gleam", p. 167.
[113] *The Letters*, "The Twenty-sixth Letter", p. 347.
[114] Hakim, *al-Mustadrak*, 4:256; Ibn Hanbal, *al-Musnad*, 2:359.

alive, as well as the light of each world we inhabit. *There is no deity but God* is the key with which to obtain that light.

Also, we are subject to our carnal soul's constant influence. Our fancies and desires, when joined with Satan's seductiveness and enabled by our heedlessness, injure our belief and sever its light through evil doubts and suggestions. Furthermore, we are liable to frequent falling, and doing and saying certain things that are contrary to the Shari'ah. According to some leading scholars, these failings indicate unbelief (such as objecting to Divine judgments or displaying displeasure with Destiny and so on). Because of such and other reasons, we should constantly refresh our belief.

- **Reflecting (on creation and God's other signs in the universe or on humanity) is like light, for it removes or melts one's frozen heedlessness to and unawareness of God. However, when we reflect on ourselves (on our physical composition and inner world, our feelings, emotions, faculties, and conscience), we should reflect deeply, as the Divine Name "the Inward" wants us to do so. But when we reflect on the outer world, we should do so briefly; for we only need to understand the foundations upon which it is based; this is what the Name "the Outward" requires.**[115]

If we go deep in our inner world but make a brief and fast journey in the outer world, we can grasp unity in multiplicity. Individual parts acquire wholeness, compounds become composites, and composites become unified. From this unity issues the light of conviction of the Divine Unity. If we make a brief journey in the outer world, the splendor of Art becomes more evident and more dazzling when looked on and examined as a whole. However, if we only make a brief and superficial examination of our inner world while going into detail during our travels in the outer world, which is very spacious and has no shores, the diversity of things may engender confusion and doubt. If we dive into it, we may drown. This will strengthen our ego and ingrain heedlessness in us, developments that will make us incline to naturalism and, eventually, drowned in the diversity of things, to misguidance and denial. O God, do not include us among the misguided! Amen.

- **When associating partners with God in a veiled form arising from human egotism is solidified and condensed, it turns into associat-**

---

[115] *Al-Mathnawi al-Nuri*, "The Sixth Treatise", 202–203.

ing material causes with God as His partners. If this continues, it changes into attributing nothing to God with respect to one's life and all that is going on in nature. Beyond that, it changes—may God save us from such a state—into atheism.[116]

Human ego sees itself as the originator and the real cause of its successes, or attributes its successes only to itself. It does not tend to recognize a superior power above itself to govern its life and which bestows all its successes on itself. When it sees its incapacity to govern even its body and its impotence to meet even its vital needs, it attributes creativity to material or "natural" causes in order not to admit the Divine Being with absolute knowledge, will, and power. Then, it shares God's absolute power and dominion among all other things, and what it calls "forces" and "nature," and the things such as chance and matter. This ultimately leads to—May God save us from all such deviations—denial of God.

- **One of the reasons of unbelief is that the human carnal soul prefers an ounce of immediate pleasure to a ton of future pleasure, and shrinks in fear from an immediate slap more than it would from the thought of a year's future torment.**[117]

The Qur'an warns that people go to unbelief because they choose the present, worldly life in preference to the Hereafter.[118] This is because human beings seek ready payment and do not like the payment postponed. When desires and emotions prevail, people do not heed the judgment of reason. Under the influence of desires and whims, they prefer the slightest immediate delight to a vast, future reward. They keep away from some trivial present distress more than they fear some dreadful postponed torment. For desires, emotions, and whims are blind to the future. When the carnal soul gives them support, the heart, which is the seat of belief, and reason can no longer speak and are defeated. This is one of the cardinal reasons of unbelief.

- **As proclaimed in a Prophet Tradition,**[119] **a light like a fly's wing from the World of Eternity is, on account of its being eternal,**

---

[116] *Al-Mathnawi al-Nuri*, "The Eighth Treatise", p. 255.

[117] *The Gleams*, "The Thirteenth Gleam", p. 104.

[118] *Sura Ibrahim*, 14.3.

[119] al-Qurtubi, *al-Jami' li-Ahkam al-Qur'an*, 13:7.

equal to all the pleasures and bounties a person may receive from a whole worldly life.[120]

Despite this fact, since the human carnal soul prefers an ounce of immediate pleasure to a ton of future pleasure, and since evil is the way of destruction, passions and destruction are easy to follow, people can swiftly be driven towards sin and evil, and come to prefer the pleasures of this fleeting world to all of the pleasures of the everlasting world.

- **Unbelief is an evil, an act of destruction, an absence of affirmation. It may look like a single sin, but it implies an insult to creation, the debasement of all Divine Names, and the degradation of all humanity. It is a most horrible insult to the suns and moons of the heaven of humanity, namely more than one hundred Prophets, in whose lives not a single lie was witnessed, and millions of saintly scholars and saints.**[121]

Creation has a sublime rank and important task, for each part of it is a missive of the Lord, a mirror of His Glory, and a dutiful servant of His Divinity. Unbelief denies them this rank bestowed on them by virtue of these functions and reduces them to playthings of chance, and insignificant, useless, and worthless objects doomed to decay and eternal annihilation. It renders the entire universe worthless and futile, contradicts creation's witnessing to God's Existence and absolute Oneness.

Unbelief is also an insult to the Divine Names, Whose most beautiful inscriptions and manifestations are seen in the mirrors of all created forms throughout the universe. Furthermore, it casts humanity down to a level more wretched and weak, helpless and destitute, than the lowliest animal. It reduces us to an ordinary, perishable sign-board without meaning, confused and swiftly decaying. And this is when humanity, in reality, is a poetic work of Wisdom that manifests all Divine Names; a great miracle of the Divine Power that, like a seed, contains the Tree of Creation; and God-appointed ruler of the earth, who is superior to angels and higher than mountains, the earth, and heavens by virtue of the Supreme Trust we accepted.

By striking a match, a mischievous child can set on fire and burn down in one hour a magnificent palace which it took twenty men a few years to

---

[120] *The Gleams*, "The Thirteenth Gleam", p. 105.

[121] *The Words*, "The Twenty-third Word", 336; "The Twenty-sixth Word", 483; *The Rays*, "The Eleventh Ray", pp. 288–289; *The Gleams*, "The Thirteenth Gleam", 105.

build. While the health and survival of life is dependent on the existence of all the vital parts, even all the cells, of the human body and the vital conditions of existence, death is possible through the corruption of a single cell or disease of a single part of the body. Thus, because of its very nature, unbelief, even though apparently a single act, deserves eternal punishment. Just as killing a person in a minute deserves imprisonment for hundreds of thousands of minutes, as a limitless crime, unbelief deserves eternal punishment.

- **Islam is a pure monotheistic religion that rejects intermediaries between God and humanity like the Church, breaks egotism and establishes sincere worship, and denounces and rejects all false lordships from the carnal soul to nature and some human beings. Thus a pious member of the elite must give up egotism. Whereas Christianity, which accepts Divine sonship and begetting and therefore accepts intermediaries, inevitably ascribes creative power to causes and means. Rather than breaking egotism in the name of religion, it sacralizes the egotism of intermediaries by regarding them as holy representatives of Jesus.**[122]

It is because of this reality that members of the Christian elite who occupy high worldly positions can be pious. For example, Woodrow Wilson among the American presidents and Lloyd George among the British prime ministers, were as bigoted as any priest. But members of the Muslim elite who attain such high worldly positions must break their egotism to be pious Muslims perfectly conscious of God. This is why the Muslim elite could never use Islam to oppress and despise the masses, and why Islam protects and supports the weak, the poor and the oppressed. Also, In Islam, one joins either the elite or the masses through knowledge, God-consciousness, and piety.

- **O human being! It is a Qur'anic principle that you must not consider anything other than God Almighty as greater than you to the degree that you worship it. Nor must you consider yourself greater than anything and thus claim greatness before and dominion over it. For, just as all creatures are equally far from being the Object of Worship, they are also equal in being creatures.**[123]

[122] *The Letters*, "The Twenty-ninth Letter", p. 420.
[123] *The Gleams*, "The Seventeenth Gleam", p. 160.

All beings, including all of the Prophets such as Prophet Muhammad, Jesus and Moses, upon them be peace and blessings, and angels, are equal in being God's creatures and servants. It is only God Almighty Who creates and sustains, and Who is worthy of worship. Among all creatures, the one who is the greatest is he or she who is the greatest in God's sight and is therefore the most advanced in servanthood to Him.

- **The Qur'an concentrates on certain important points concerning its opponents and their evils—not because of their strength in the face of God's Power, but to display Divine Majesty and exhibit the opponent's wickedness. Sometimes it mobilizes the greatest and most powerful agents against the least and weakest thing to show the perfect order, infinite justice, boundless knowledge, and power of wisdom (displayed in it, the universe, and the human social system it builds). By doing so, the Qur'an also seeks to prevent injustice and aggression.**[124]

The wise Qur'an, for example, complains greatly of Satan and the people of misguidance, and frequently draws attention to them, threatening them severely. It is as if it were mobilizing armies against certain powerless creatures. It threatens them because of a single minor action, as if they had committed thousands of crimes. Even though they are essentially poor and miserable, with no claim to any of the possession or dominion of existence, the Qur'an deals with them as if they were aggressive partners of God in His Dominion, and complains of them. The reason for this and the wisdom in it is as follows:

Since Satan and those following him follow the way of misguidance, which is the way of destruction, and destruction is easy, they can cause great destruction with a minor action, and they can do many creatures great wrong with a small deed.

Consider that through some minor action or act of neglect of an insignificant duty, a man on a large, royal merchant ship of a sovereign can cause the efforts of all those who have a duty related to the ship to go to ruin. So, the illustrious owner of the ship complains of that rebellious one and severely threatens him on behalf of all his subjects that have some connection with the ship. And he severely punishes him, considering not

---

[124] *The Words*, "The Fifteenth Word", p. 198.

his insignificant action but its awful consequences, and not in his own illustrious name but in the name of the rights of his subjects.

Similarly, even with their apparently minor faults and rebelliousness, the people of misguidance, who are the party of Satan and exist on the ship of the earth together with the people of right guidance, can violate the rights of many creatures and cause their exalted duties to be fruitless. So it is pure wisdom and completely appropriate that the Eternal Monarch complains greatly of them and severely threatens them, frequently drawing attention to their destruction as if He were mobilizing great forces against them. Such a reaction is in no way an exaggeration, which would be wasting words.

It is a fact that the one who does not seek refuge in an exceptionally formidable stronghold—in the face of awful enemies causing great destruction with a small act—will suffer greatly. So, O people of belief! That heavenly stronghold of steel is the Qur'an. Enter it and be saved!

By doing so, God also draws the attention to the wickedness of misguidance and evil acts, and to the great worth and significance of belief and righteous acts.

- **In each sin is a path that leads to unbelief.**[125]

Each sin that we commit and each doubt that enters our mind causes wounds in our heart and our spirit. The wounds that arise from sins, the temptations and the doubts that arise from these wounds, inflict damage upon the inner dimension of the heart, which is the seat of belief, thus—we seek refuge in God from such a thing—harming our belief. They also prevent the spiritual joy which comes from religious recitations and acts of worship, thus causing the soul to turn away from recitation in aversion.

Sin penetrates to the heart, darkens and hardens it until it extinguishes the light of belief. Each sin has a path that leads to unbelief. Unless that sin is swiftly obliterated by seeking God's forgiveness, it grows from a worm into a snake that gnaws at the heart. It also rusts the heart, causing us to lose belief. This is what is stated in the verse, "*But what they themselves have earned has rusted upon their hearts.*"[126]

Also, when a person secretly commits a shameful sin and feels great shame, fearing that others may become aware of this misdeed, they find

---

[125] *The Gleams*, "The Second Gleam", p. 12.
[126] *Suratu'l-Mutaffifin*, 83:14.

the existence of angels and spiritual beings too much to endure. They then wish that there were some evidence to deny their existence. Similarly, if one who commits a major sin that deserves the punishment of Hell does not try to shield themselves from the sin by imploring God's forgiveness, they will then wholeheartedly wish for Hell's non-existence, and they dare to deny the existence of Hell if they find any encouragement.

Again, one who shows laziness in fulfilling his duty of servanthood, such as failing to perform the daily obligatory Prayers despite the repeated orders of the Sovereign of Eternity, will feel greatly distressed and wish there were no such duty of servanthood. In turn, there will arise from this wish a desire to deny God, which implies enmity towards Him. If some doubt concerning God's existence occurs in their heart, they will be inclined to cling to it as conclusive proof. Thus, a wide door to unbelief will be opened in front of them.

- **Muslim transgressors are not like the transgressors of other religions; the morality of Muslims subsists by their Religion. Those who leave the circle of Islam become like spoiled butter, which is no longer useful, while those who leave other religions become like spoiled milk, which can still be usable.**[127]

Muslim transgressors, those Muslims who are disobedient to God in some of His commandments, are usually immoral. Most of them are unfair and unscrupulous. An evil desire can only develop in a Muslim when the voice of belief has been silenced in their conscience. It is for this reason that the Religion of Islam recognizes a transgressor as a traitor or criminal; it rejects their testimony. It is for the same reason that Islam judges an apostate as lethal poison. However, it recognizes the life of a non-Muslim who belongs to a heavenly religion, so long as they follow the public law, or are not at war with it.

Suppose there is a palace, the central room of which has a large electric light. All other rooms have small lights connected to it. If someone turns off that large light, the palace is left in darkness. Another palace has small electric lights in each room that are not connected to its central light. If that palace owner turns off the central light, the other rooms remain illuminated. This allows its inhabitants to do their work and deter thieves.

---

[127] *Gleams of Truth*, pp. 112–113; *The Words*, "The Thirteenth Word", pp. 161–163; "The Twenty-fourth Word", pp. 382–383.

The first palace represents Muslims. Our Prophet, upon him be peace and blessings, is the large central light in the Muslims' heart. If they forget him or discard him from their heart, or do not obey him in the practice of Islam, they will be unable to believe in any other Prophet. Moreover, their spirit will have no room for any kind of perfection. They will not recognize their Lord, all their inner senses and faculties will be left in darkness, and their hearts will be ruined and invaded by despair and gloom. What will they be able to find to replace the resulting void and to find consolation in?

Christians and Jews are like the other palace. Even if they are not illuminated by the Prophet's light, they can manage with the "light" they think they have. Their form of belief in the Creator and Moses or Jesus, upon them be peace, can still be the means of some sort of moral perfection.

This parable explains that Muslim transgressors are like poison in a Muslim society. They are like decaying butter. They can no longer be governed by law. This also explains the confusion in Muslim lands at present and why transgressing people in Muslim societies do not love to obey the laws.

- **The punishment of Hell is in return for one's actions and pure justice, while Paradise is a pure Divine favor.**[128]

However insignificant and partial a free will they have, and even though their free will and action have no share in creation, human beings can cause awful destruction and evils. For destruction and evils are extremely easy and it is possible to bring them about with a slight action. Also, as their evil-commanding soul always inclines towards harm and evil, and it is human beings themselves who commit evils, human beings are responsible for the evils brought about as a result of any insignificant action. God never wills evil. He does not like evil, and never does He commit evil. In return for the limitless crimes that humanity commits, such as unbelief and injustice, they most definitely deserve eternal punishment.

As for good deeds, since they denote construction and existence and require the Creator to come into existence, human partial free will and action cannot be their creative cause. A human being cannot be their true agent. In addition, the carnal soul never desires good deeds; it is the Divine Mercy Which demands them and drives and enables human beings to do them, and the Divine Power brings them into existence. A human being can

---

[128] *The Gleams*, "The Thirteenth Gleam", pp. 114–115.

only claim to own them through belief and good intention. Besides, these good deeds and acts of worship are in fact thanks for all the limitless Divine bounties accorded to them before, like the bounties of existence and belief. So Paradise, promised by God, will be given purely as a favor of the All-Merciful One. Apparently it is a reward, but in reality it is a pure favor.

- **Creatures have no right to complain about God. If they have any "right" against the Necessarily Existent Being, it is to give thanks to Him for the favors God has bestowed on them.**[129]

Complaints arise from a right to complain. Creatures have no rights violated, nor have they been made to lose anything or been deprived of any right which would allow them to complain of God. Rather, there are numerous thanks that are obligatory for them, but they have not fulfilled them.

Consider: A person conducts a poor wretch to the top of a minaret. At every step he gives the wretch a different gift, a different bounty. Right at the top of the minaret he gives him the largest gift. Although he deserves thanks and gratitude in return for all those various gifts, the churlish wretch forgets the gifts he has received at each step, or considers them of no importance, and without offering thanks, looks above him and begins to complain, saying: "If only this minaret had been higher, I could have climbed even further. Why isn't it as tall as that mountain over there or that other minaret?" If he begins to complain like this, what a great ingratitude this is, what a great wrong!

If creatures have any "right" against the Necessarily Existent Being, it is to give thanks for the favors God has bestowed on them. Every human being comes into existence from nothing, and without being a rock or a tree or an animal, becomes human. Furthermore, being a Muslim is another great bounty. Most of the time, we enjoy good health and are honored with a great number of bounties. All of these and many other favors we enjoy are actual, concrete realities, whereas the greater favors we unjustly expect are only possibilities. There are infinite possibilities one above or below the other. For example, minerals cannot complain that they want to be plants, for there were infinite possibilities for them to have any level of existence. So they must thank their Creator for their mineral existence. Plants and animals cannot complain to God about why they were not granted a higher level. Plants must thank Him for being favored with existence and life, and

---

[129] *The Letters*, "The Twenty-fourth Letter", pp. 306–307; *The Gleams*, "The Twenty-fifth Gleam", pp. 303–304.

animals for being granted a precious gem of spirit as well as life and existence. So, we cannot look at others who are better off than us in enjoyment. We are rather charged with looking at those who are worse than us, and offering thanks. If our hand is broken, we should look at those whose hands have been severed. If we have only one eye, we should look at those blind, lacking both eyes. And offer thanks to God!

- **The denial of something which is not possible to specify in a particular place or position cannot be established.**[130]

For example, if I affirm the existence of something and you deny it, I can easily establish its existence by merely producing an example of it. But in order to establish the non-existence of the same thing, you will have to scour the entire world in order to deny it, even going so far as to examine the past thoroughly. Only when you have done this can you say: "It does not exist and has never existed."

Since those who negate and deny do not regard the actual reality, but judge rather according to their own perspective or their arbitrary opinion or knowledge, they can in no way strengthen or support each other. For the veils and causes which prevent seeing and knowing are various. Anyone can say, "I do not see it; therefore, in my opinion and belief, it does not exist." But no one can say, "It does not exist in actuality." If someone makes such a claim—particularly in matters of belief that pertain to the whole universe—it will be a lie as vast as the world itself and anyone who makes that claim will never be able to confirm it or have it confirmed by others.

In the case of affirmation or establishment, the result is one and every instance of affirmation supports and is supported by all other instances. But a denial or negation is based on personal, arbitrary opinions or perspectives, and is not supported by other denials. Since everyone who denies says, "In my view or opinion," or "according to my belief," the results multiply but do not corroborate each other.

- **Unbelief has kinds, all of which are in fact either arbitrary denial, ignorance, mistaken knowledge, sheer negation, or erroneous judgment based on no evidence.**[131]

---

[130] *The Rays,* "The Seventh Ray", pp. 115–116.
[131] *The Rays,* "The Seventh Ray", pp. 117–118.

The first kind of unbelief has no concern with the truths of Islam. It is a personal, erroneous conviction, a false belief, a mistaken acceptance and an unjust judgment.

The second kind opposes the truths of belief or faith, and fights against them. This kind of unbelief is itself of two kinds:

The first is non-acceptance. It consists simply of not affirming the truths of belief. It is a kind of ignorance—a sort of "non-judgment"—and as such is something which people fall into easily.

The second sort is the acceptance of non-being. To accept non-being means to confirm the non-existence of the Divine Being or another object of belief. This sort of unbelief is a judgment and a conviction, and involves taking up opposition to belief. Those who take up such opposition are obliged to affirm their unbelief or denial, which is, in reality, impossible,

As for this sort of denial or negation, again there are two types:

The first type is to deny the truth of any cardinal belief with respect to a particular matter, place, position, or time.

The second type consists of negating and denying the sacred, basic, and universal truths or matters of belief, which concern both this world and the Hereafter, and all times and places. This kind of negation or denial can in no way be substantiated, as explained above, for there must be a vision that is able to encompass and observe the whole universe, the Hereafter, and all of the past thoroughly, and even to probe into the whole existence.

In essence, unbelief that opposes and struggles against the truths of Islam is denial, ignorance, and negation. Even though it may appear to be an affirmation of some sort, it is in reality a negation, and thus devoid of any established facts. However, belief is knowledge and is based on established, observable facts: it is an affirmation and an objective judgment. Any aspect of belief which negates its opposites is either a description of a positive truth, or a screen upon which that truth is manifested. Even if, despite the extreme difficulties involved, the unbelievers who struggle against belief attempt to affirm their negative beliefs, or negation and rejection of belief in the form of the acceptance and affirmation of non-being (the non-existence of God, or the afterlife, or angels, or Prophethood and Revelation, for example), then their unbelief can be regarded as nothing more than a form of mistaken knowledge or erroneous judgment. But, non-acceptance and non-affirmation, both of which can be assented to easily and without thinking, are ignorance and a display of a complete lack of judgment.

- **Although unbelief is an attitude or judgment of the heart, certain practices which have gained the character of being a sign or symbol of unbelief can cause one to be judged an unbeliever.**[132]

The seat of both belief and unbelief is the heart. However, there are some practices which have gained the character of being a sign or symbol. For example, the Prescribed Prayers, Pilgrimage (to the Ka'ba), the Religious Festive Days, and the *adhan* (call to the Prayer) are among such signs or symbols of Islam. The rope girdle worn by the Christians and the Cross have been signs of Christianity, and so has the kippah been a sign of Judaism. Therefore, if one who wears the Christian girdle or the Jewish kippah without any coercion can be judged to be a Christian or Jew, if there is no clear sign showing that he is a Muslim.

- **An involuntary fancy of unbelief is not unbelief, just as an involuntary fancy of blasphemy is not blasphemy.**[133]

A fancy is not an act of judgment, whereas unbelief, which is a willful act, is. The words with which the heart is displeased and regrets mean not to come from the heart; rather, they come from "the tube of Satan," an inner faculty situated near the heart through which Satan whispers to it. The harm of involuntary evil fancies comes from imagining them to be harmful, for people think that a fancy not subject to judgment is reality. They ascribe Satan's work to their hearts by supposing that Satan's whisperings belong to their hearts, and thus think this is harmful and suffer harm.

- **Uttering a word which is regarded to be among the 'words of unbelief' does not mean unbelief unless it is certain that it issues from one's being an unbeliever.**[134]

There are some words which Muslim scholars have regarded to be among the 'words of unbelief,' as they carry the meaning of unbelief. However, if this word is uttered by one who is not an unbeliever, it cannot cause that one to be judged to be an unbeliever.

- **Belief is irreconcilable with unbelief, and since unbelief is the opposite of belief, the unbelievers are hostile to the believers.**

[132] *İşaratü'l-İ'caz*, "*Suratu'l-Baqara*", verse 6.
[133] *The Words*, "The Twenty-first Word", 288.
[134] *Sünuhat* (Occurrences to the Heart), in *Sünuhat, Tuluat, İşarat*, p. 21.

Unless the believers do not change not only their belief but also their way of life, the unbelievers will never love them.[135]

Belief and unbelief are opposite to and therefore irreconcilable with each other. While belief establishes brotherhood and sisterhood and affinity among all things, and the believers see even the strongest enemy as brothers or sisters in humanity, unbelief causes separation and alienation, which manifest in the unbelievers as strong feelings of greed, enmity and self-preference. This is why the unbelievers are hostile to the believers, and as the Qur'an declares, unless the believers follow the unbelievers in their creed and way of life, the unbelievers will never love and be pleased with the unbelievers.[136]

Religion cannot be bribed because of fear. Fear and weakness encourage external pressure and interference, and embolden one's enemies.[137]

Fear and weakness on behalf of Islam are futile and harmful to Muslims; they embolden external influences and draw them towards Muslims. A sure benefit should not be renounced for fear of potential harm. What we need is to take right action in the right time and place in the name of Islam; the outcome is with God.

- **One of the greatest miracles of the wise Qur'an and the clearest proof of its truth is that it contains and explains all degrees, varieties, and requirements of Divine Unity's manifestation and belief in such a perfectly balanced manner that it can address and satisfy all levels of understanding, and intellectual and spiritual development. Also, it maintains the perfect balance among all elevated Divine truths, contains all commandments and principles required by the Divine Names, and maintains exact and sensitive relationships among them. Furthermore, it holds together all the acts and essential characteristics of God's Divinity and Lordship with perfect balance.**[138]

This is very important in understanding Islam and the histories of the previous heavenly religions. The followers of the previous religions have not been able to preserve the equilibrium among the divisions and com-

---

[135] *Al-Mathnawi al-Nuri*, "The Fourth Treatise", p. 112; "The Fifth Treatise", p. 136.
[136] *Suratu'l-Baqara*, 2:120.
[137] *Gleams of Truth*, pp. 52–53.
[138] *The Words*, "The Twenty-fifth Word", p. 457.

mandments of Religion, and have therefore gone to extremes, dwelling on one or two points more than the others, and thereby destroying the balance and accurate relations among the truths.

Imagine a treasure under the sea. It is full of jewels. Many divers look for it but, since their eyes are closed, they search for it with their hands. One seizes a large diamond and concludes that he has found the whole of the treasure. When he hears that his friends have found other jewels, such as a round ruby or a square amber, he thinks that they are facets or embellishments of what he has found. Each diver has the same idea. For example, while the Jews have mainly dwelled on the outer aspect of the Religion, and destroyed the equilibrium of such basic tenets and requirements as love, mercy, and forgiveness, the Christians have neglected the Law and acts in favor of a self-claimed love. Even though some sects have appeared in Islam which have not been able to preserve the equilibrium or balance, the great majority of Muslims have preserved it. Some examples will be given below.

- **One of the reasons for deviating from the right course and going into extremes is confusing the decrees and acts of the Divine Name, "the All-Inward," with those of "the All-Outward," and expecting from the former what one should expect from the latter. One also confuses the necessities of Divine Power with those of Divine Wisdom, and seeks to see in the former what one should seek to see in the latter. Likewise, confusing the requirements of the realm where the law of causality has a certain role in God's Acts with those of belief in His absolute Unity, and the acts and ways of Divine Power's manifestation with the manifestations of certain other Divine Attributes, and trying to find the former's rules and laws in the latter can also cause error and deviation.**[139]

For example, our birth and growth in this world is gradual, but in the mirrors of the intermediate realms between this material realm and purely spiritual realms—as in dreams, for example—that development happens all at once. This is so because Divine Attributes vary in manifesting themselves, and creation and manifestation differ from each other.

Also, it is an error to want to see in the seed, which is an example of the manifestation of the Divine Name, the All-Inward, what one sees elaborately in the tree, which is an example to the manifestation of the Divine

---

[139] *Al-Mathnawi al-Nuri*, "The Fourth Treatise", p. 121.

Name, the All-Outward. Again, the Divine Power is absolutely able to do anything in an instant, but the Divine Wisdom usually requires, in this world, gradual creation based on the law of cause and effect. Because of this, this world has been called the realm of Wisdom, while the other world, where the Divine Power will act without the veil of the law of cause and effect, is designated as the realm of Power. In this world of Wisdom, we follow the requirements of the law of cause and effect in order to attain our goals, but we believe that it is God Who creates our acts and results, enabling us to attain our goals. Therefore, just as neglecting following the law of cause and effect in submission to God's being the sole Creator, the One Who creates results and enables our attainments, is a deviation, attributing our attainments and the results of our actions to ourselves, or the law of cause and effect, thus elevating us and the law of cause and effect to the position of creator, is another, grave deviation. This is confusing the realm of belief or creed with the realm of the law of cause and effect. This confusion is one the basic reasons of the emergence of the sects such as *al-Mu'tazila* and *al-Jabriyya*.

- **There is a grain of truth in every school of falsehood. Each has a particular situation; falsehood arises from a generalization that goes beyond this particular situation.**[140]

For example, since they over-trusted in their reason or intellectual ability, and therefore missed the balance between the truths of Islam and the acts or manifestations of the Divine Attributes, the *Mu'tazila* claimed that since God is the All-Just, He is obliged to put the pious believers in Paradise and the unbelievers and the sinful believers in Hell. Whereas God is not only the All-Just but He is also the One Who does whatever He wills. Therefore, He is not obliged to do anything, and He is also the One Who is not, and will never be, called to account for whatever He does. Also, He is the All-Compassionate and the All-Forgiving. Thus, He is not obliged to, for example, put the sinful believers in Hell. It is hoped from His Compassion and Forgiveness that He may forgive many sinful believers.

As another example, the past and its calamities, and the future and its sins, are not the same in the view and consideration of the Shari'ah. The past and its calamities are considered from the perspective of Divine Des-

---

[140] *Gleams of Truth*, pp. 39–40.

tiny; for this, the fitting word is that of the *Jabriyya*, (who refer every event to Destiny). Human accountability is taken into consideration about the future and sins; for this, the fitting word is that of the *Mu'tazila*, (who deny the role of Destiny in human actions). The *Mu'tazila* and *Jabriyya* are reconciled here. There is a grain of truth in both of these false schools. Falsehood arises from a generalization that goes beyond a particular situation.

Another example: The Shi'a developed from the love of the Prophet's Household, but went so far as to confuse love of them with hatred of others. That is, they hate the overwhelming majority of the Prophet's Companions, including, and especially, Abu Bakr and 'Umar, the two leading Companions, may God be pleased with them. Also, the Holy Prophet, upon him be peace and blessings, declared: "Whosever's master (*mawla'*) I am, 'Ali, too, is their master."[141] Based on this and certain other Prophetic Traditions, the Shi'a claim that the Caliphate was Ali's right after the Prophet, upon him be peace and blessings, and that an injustice was done to him. This they do because they include political leadership in the meaning of the word *mawla'*, whereas, in no place in the Qur'an is the word *mawla'* used in the meaning of political leadership. What is meant in the *hadith* is leadership in knowledge of the Religion and spirituality. Almost all the Companions and the greatest majority of the Muslims have admitted this high position of 'Ali, may God be pleased with him.

In conclusion, the generalization of something particular and destroying the balance in the truths of the Religion can cause deviations.

- **Absolute, unlimited truths cannot be comprehended by restricted minds and visions; it is only by the Qur'an's universal and all-encompassing vision that they can be seen in their infinitude.**[142]

The absolute, unlimited truths, such as those relating to God Almighty and His Attributes, and to eternity beyond time and space, and the eternal life, cannot be comprehended by all that is not the Qur'an. For this reason, we must study and learn about these truths in the Qur'an. However, we should not forget that even if we study them in the Qur'an, having restricted minds and capacities, we cannot comprehend them fully or in their entirety. We cannot be saved from going to extremes, dwelling on one or two points more than the others, and thereby destroying the balance and accurate rela-

---

[141] *at-Tirmidhi*, "Manaqib" 19; Ibn Maja, *Sunan*, "Muqaddima" 11; Ahmad ibn Hanbal, *al-Musnad*, 1:84, 118.

[142] *The Words*, "The Twenty-fifth Word", p. 457.

tions among the truths. We can only grasp some parts of them. Therefore, we must be careful while speaking and judging about these truths.

- **Misguidance came from uneducated ignorance in the past, and was therefore easy to remove. But it is caused by science and knowledge in our day, and it is difficult to remove.**[143]

In the past, misguidance coming from science and knowledge was very rare. However, in our day, misguidance is based on science, and those misguided through scientific knowledge are too arrogant to realize their ignorance. Science is the result of the discovery of what is called the laws of nature, which are in fact the usual Divine practices in creation and the direction of the universe. Therefore, in our day we should see and show in the light of the Qur'an that the Qur'an and the universe are God's two books of the same meaning—they are simply written in different materials. It is because of this that God uses the same word 'ayah (clear sign) for both parts of the Qur'an and all the phenomena in nature. So, we should see and show the correlations or correspondences between the Qur'an and nature, and interpret one in the light of the other.

- **Most Prophets appeared in the East, while most philosophers emerged in the West. This is a sign of the Divine Destiny showing that the main impulse for progress in the East is Religion and the "heart," not theoretical reason and philosophy.**[144]

- **The eye of Divine Messengership, and belief in God and His Oneness, view everything from the perspective of its Creator and Lord, and of the afterlife. However, human philosophy and modern science view it from the perspective of itself and the apparent reasons for its existence and life.**[145]

The Qur'an or Islam's view of everything is, first of all, from the perspective of God, the Creator and Lord, the afterlife, and human happiness—first in the next life and then in this world. In the view of the Qur'an, everything is a miracle of God, and a clear sign for both His existence and Oneness. However, modern science and human philosophy conceal the Divine Power's extraordinary miracles within veils of familiarity, and overlook them because of ignorance and indifference. For example, the Qur'an calls the

---

[143] *The Letters*, "The Fifth Letter", p. 31.
[144] *Al-Mathnawi al-Nuri*, "The Fifth Treatise", 152.
[145] *The Words*, "The Thirteenth Word", pp. 155–159; "The Nineteenth Word", pp. 255–256..

sun "a moving lamp," as in the verses, *"And He has made the sun as a lamp,"*[146] and *"The sun runs the course appointed for it..."*[147] By depicting the sun as a lamp, the Qur'an reminds people that the world is like a palace, the contents of which are decorations, provisions, and other necessities prepared for humanity and other living creatures, with the sun being a lamp to illuminate it. Thus, it implies the Creator's Mercy and Bounty.

By saying: *"And the sun runs the course appointed for it for a term to its resting-place for the stability of its system,"*[148] the Qur'an suggests the well-ordered disposition of Divine Power in the revolutions of the seasons, day and night, and so implies the Maker's Majesty. Whatever the reality of this running is does not harm the intended meaning, which is the observed order woven into the universe's structure. The Qur'an does not mention the sun for its own sake, but because it is the "mainstay" of order and the center of the solar system, and order and system are two ways of learning about the Creator.

Now consider how science and materialistic philosophy deal with the sun: "The sun is an enormous mass of burning gases. It causes the planets, which have been flung off from it, to revolve around it. It is of such and such size, and is of such and such qualities..." Such a description gives no perfection of knowledge to the spirit, but only a terrible dread and bewilderment.

We should also evaluate all the commandments of Islam first from the perspective of human happiness in the other life, and then from the perspective of their happiness in this world. Islam teaches us that the world is a tillage for the seeds of the afterlife. Therefore, Islam calls us to work in this world to be able to send acceptable petitions to God Almighty in the name of our eternal happiness in the other world. This is the way of our happiness in this world, too.

---

[146] *Sura Nuh*, 71:16.
[147] *Sura Ya-Sin*, 36:38.
[148] *Sura Ya-Sin*, 36:38.

Part 2

GENERAL PRINCIPLES RELATED TO BELIEF IN GOD, THE AFTERLIFE, DESTINY, AND THE METAPHYSICAL WORLD

General Principles Related
to Belief in God, the Afterlife, Destiny,
and the Metaphysical World

- **Absolute order, artistry, and value despite absolute abundance; absolute measure, balance, firmness, skill and perfection despite absolute ease and speed; absolute stability and firmness despite absolute facility; absolute beauty of art despite absolute heterogeneity and multiplicity; the absolute, firm harmony and coherence and perfect correspondence despite absolute distance; absolute distinction or individualization despite absolute compositeness, mixedness, multiplicity and world-wide distribution; and absolute, highest worth and value despite the infinite economy. These obvious qualities of existence are enough for a sensible person to admit that all these are the work of the Absolute Power, and that the One possessing that Power is absolutely the All-Knowing and the All-Willing.[1]**

Absolute abundance causes disorder and a lack of artistry and value, but there is an absolute order and artistry in everything in the universe, and everything is priceless. Almost all parts of the universe—from the sun to the earth, from air to water and soil, from days to seasons—give hand in hand for the formation of, for example, a single fruit, thus making it of the price of the universe. Also, everything occurs almost at absolute speed and easiness, which cause imbalance, infirmity, and awkwardness, but we see an ideal balance, measure, firmness and perfection in everything. Absolute heterogeneity and multiplicity cause ugliness and lack of art, but we see that there is a perfect art in everything. Everything occurs or comes into existence with absolute ease, which causes instability and

---

[1] *The Gleams* "The Twenty-ninth Gleam", p. 411; *Al-Mathnawi al-Nuri*, "The Third Treatise", pp. 49–51.

frailty, but everything is perfectly intact, firm, and stable. Despite world-wide distribution and vast distances, which cause incoherence and difference, a thing is of the same degree of beauty, artistry, and harmony, wherever it is in the world. Everything is formed of the same material, namely the atoms coming from earth, water, and air, and is composed of numerous parts, and can exist in all parts of the world; this causes disorder, disturbance, disarrangement, and dissimilarity, but we see absolute distinction, individualization, and perfectly harmonious formation. All these, and similar other qualities of existence, clearly show that everything is created by the One Who is the All-Knowing, the All-Powerful, the All-Willing, and the All-Seeing.

- **The existence and life of things demonstrate the existence of God, while their death and replacement by new ones show His ever permanence.**[2]

Consider: Bubbles on a mighty river reflect the sun's images and light, as do transparent objects glistening on the earth's face. Although the bubbles sometimes disappear (such as when passing under a bridge or through a tunnel), successive troops of bubbles continue to show the sun's reflections or images and display its light. This proves that the little images of the sun, which appear, disappear, and then re-appear in bubbles, point to an enduring, perpetual, single sun which continues to manifest itself from on high. Thus, just as through their appearance, those sparkling bubbles demonstrate the sun's existence, so through their disappearance and replacement by new ones, they display the sun's continuation and unity.

Similarly, through their existence and life, all beings and things continuously in flux testify to the Necessarily Existent Being's necessary existence and Oneness, while through their decay and death they bear witness to His eternity and permanence. The beautiful, delicate creatures that are renewed and recruited along with the alternation of day and night, summer and winter, and the passage of years, centuries and ages, show the existence, Unity, and permanence of an elevated, everlasting One. Their decay and death, together with the apparent causes for their lives, show that material or natural causes are only veils. This proves that these arts, inscriptions, and manifestations are the constantly renewed arts, changing inscriptions, and moving mirrors of an All-Beautiful One of Majesty, all of

---

[2] *The Words*, "The Twenty-second Word", pp. 318–319; *The Rays*, "The Fourth Ray", pp. 85–86.

Whose Names are sacred and beautiful. Also, they are His stamps that follow one after the other, and His seals that change through wisdom.

- **The All-Powerful Maker's Power creates the highest universal as easily as the smallest particular, and with the same artistic value. This can be explained with the assistance coming from Divine Unity, the facility originating in the unity of the center that governs the universe, and the manifestation of Divine Uniqueness or Oneness.**[3]

"His command when He wills a thing, is only to say to it 'Be' and it is..."[4] This declares that the Power of the All-Powerful One of Majesty controls everything and operates with utmost ease. The greatest and the smallest things are equal to the Divine Power. Creating a species is as simple as creating an individual, creating Paradise is as easy as creating spring, and creating spring is as easy as creating a flower.

Here is how to understand the assistance coming from Divine Unity: If one being owns and commands all things, such oneness enables him to concentrate the power of all things behind one thing, and so manage all things as easily as one thing. Thus, due to His Oneness, the unique Creator and Administrator of the universe—the universe's Maker—employs almost all things in the universe in the creation and administration of each and every thing. Through His Unity, He creates, controls, and administers all things as if they were one thing. This Divine Unity ensures that the universe and everything in it also is of the highest degree of art and value while also possessing the utmost abundance and variety.

The facility originating in the unity of the center: God's absolute Unity connects each specific thing to every other specific thing, and also connects each thing with everything, at the same time. Also, the entire universe is managed from one center, by one hand and one law. This is like thousands of fruits easily growing on a tree that depends on one law and one root. But if only one fruit could be grown on each tree, it would be as hard to produce a fruit as it is to grow a tree. It also would require the presence of all elements necessary for the tree to live.

The manifestation of Divine Uniqueness or Oneness can be understood as follows: As the Majestic Maker is not physical or corporeal, time and place cannot restrict Him; nor can space interfere with His encom-

---

[3] *The Letters*, "The Twentieth Letter", pp. 261–263.
[4] *Sura Ya-Sin*, 36:82.

passing all things at the same time, and witnessing all events; means and mass cannot veil His Acts. Both He and His Acts are free of fragmentation or division. His Acts do not impede one another, and so He performs innumerable Acts as if they were one act. Thus He makes an individual contain a world, just as He encapsulates a huge tree in its seed, and directs and controls creation as if it were one individual. So He does, like the sun's image being reflected in every burnished and shining object, for its luminosity makes it somewhat non-restrictable. Regardless of how many mirrors are held towards it, each one contains its complete, non-refracted image, without one preventing the other. Thus, the All-Majestic Maker of the universe has, due to His Uniqueness, such a manifestation through all of His Attributes and Names (Which are completely pure and immaterial) that He is ever-present everywhere and witnesses all things, although He is nowhere. He does every act at the same time, in all places, and without any difficulty or obstruction.

- **Small things are interconnected to larger things. The One Who arranged the flea's stomach is He Who arranged the solar system.**[5]

Certainly, the One Who has created the eye of a mosquito has created both the sun and the Milky Way. And the One Who has ordered the flea's stomach doubtlessly has set in order the solar system. Also, the One Who has given sight to the eye, and need to the stomach, has certainly adorned the eye of the sky with the kohl of light, and spread a feast over the face of the earth.

- **A particular which depends on God becomes a universal.**[6]

In its own right, a tiny transparent and glistening speck cannot contain a light larger than its own dimensions and mass. However, if that speck is open to the sun's manifestation, it can comprehend that immense sun, its (seven-colored) light and heat, and thus display a comprehensive manifestation of it. On its own, a speck's functioning is limited by its dimensions. But if it connects to the sun by facing it, and serving as a mirror, it can display examples of the sun's functioning to some degree.

Thus, if the existence of each being or particle is attributed a Single One of Unity, each particle becomes His officer through the resulting connection. This enables it to manifest Him somehow and, along with being

---

5   *The Words*, "Gleams of Truth", p. 711; *The Letters*, "Seeds of Truth", p. 445.
6   *The Letters*, "The Twenty-fourth Letter", pp. 268–269.

an object of His manifestation, depend on His Infinite Knowledge and Power. This relationship with the Creator's Power allows it to perform functions and duties far beyond its own power.

- **Those who submit to God's Will and pursue His good pleasure are served by everything; those who disobey God find everything turned against them.**[7]

Since everything is controlled by God Almighty, those who submit to His Will and pursue His good pleasure find everything at their service. This is also true for those who admit all that exists, without exception, belongs to Him, and is His property. He has created us surrounded by circles of need, and equipped us with devices that allow us, if we rely on our will and power, to satisfy only those needs in the smallest circle. Some of our other needs are related to an enormous circle stretching from the infinite past to the infinite future. To satisfy these needs, He has equipped us with prayer or supplication: *"Say: 'My Lord will not be concerned for you, were it not for your supplication.'"*[8] An infant calls its parents to provide what it cannot reach, and servants pray to their Lord for what they cannot obtain or overcome.

- **Just like the smallest beings or things, the greatest and most universals of creatures also glorify God according to the universality and greatness of each.**[9]

God declares: *"The seven heavens and the earth and all within them glorify Him."*[10]; *"We subdued the mountains to glorify (their Lord) along with him (David)."*[11]; and: *"We offered the Trust to the heavens and the earth and the mountains."*[12]

Glorification of God means believing and declaring, whether verbally or through action, that God is absolutely free from having any partners, and from having any defects or shortcomings. Each and every thing in the universe, through their existence, structure, maintenance, action, and every other state of their lives, demonstrate that God is One, with no partners, and that He is absolutely free from any defects and shortcomings.

---

[7] *Al-Mathnawi al-Nuri*, "The Fifth Treatise", p. 158.

[8] *Suratu'l-Furqan*, 25:77.

[9] *The Words*, "The Fourteenth Word", p. 181.

[10] *Suratu'l-Isra'*, 17: 44.

[11] *Sura Sad*, 38:18.

[12] *Suratu'l-Ahzab*, 33:72.

The bodies of even unbelievers make this glorification. Just as the heaven's words of glorification are the suns, moons, and stars, so animals, plants, and trees are words of the glorification of the earth. That is, each tree and star performs a specific form of glorification, while the earth and each of its parts—each mountain and valley, the land and the sea, and the firmament's spheres and heaven's constellations—all perform a universal form of glorification.

Also, if many things come together to form a collectivity, a collective personality comes into being. If such a collectivity forms a strong union, it will have a sort of collective spirit to represent it, as well as an appointed angel to perform its duty of glorification. For example, the earth, which possesses millions of heads, each of which carries its own language, has an angel appointed for it who translates and displays its flowers of glorification and fruits of praise in the World of Ideal Forms, and who represents and proclaims them in the World of Spirits.

- **The tree's seed (its essence) is contained by the fruit and, unless somehow impeded, grows by eternal Favoring into the tree and again is placed in its fruit. Thus, the fruit contains whatever the tree has. Similarly, the universe is a tree, and its branches are such basic elements as earth, water, air, and fire. Its leaves are plants, its blossoms are animals, and its fruits are human beings. So, the One Who creates the fruit is He Who creates the tree, and He is One and Single.**[13]

- **The conscience recognizes God through its attraction. It also recognizes Him through its sense of reliance and by asking God for help, for He is the One on Whom creatures rely and Who comes to the aid of creatures.**[14]

In the conscience there is an attraction, an infatuation; the conscience feels that it is constantly drawn by the pull of an attractive force. If the All-Beautiful, Gracious One, towards Whom the conscience feels attracted and Who attracts the conscience towards Himself, was to manifest Himself permanently without a veil, conscious beings would be overcome with ecstasy. The consciousness—the human conscious nature—testifies decisively to a Necessarily Existent One, One of Majesty and Beauty and

---

[13] *Al-Mathnawi al-Nuri*, "The Ninth Treatise", pp. 280–281.
[14] *The Words*, "The Thirty-third Word", p. 699; "Gleams of Truth", pp. 712–713.

Grace. The feeling of attraction is a testimony, and so too is the feeling of being attracted.

Moreover, searching for a point of support or reliance against count-less obstacles and hostilities in our infinite weakness and impotence, our conscience is always turned towards the Necessarily Existent Being. Besides, our infinite destitution and neediness compel us to look for a point of seeking assistance in order to realize our innumerable aims, and so our conscience has recourse to the Court of an All-Compassionate One, and we petition Him for our needs. Thus, with respect to our need for a point of support and a point of seeking assistance, two small windows open from each person's conscience onto the All-Compassionate, All-Powerful One's Court of Mercy, through which we can look to Him.

The Qur'an has many references to the human conscience. For exam-ple: "*It is He Who conveys you on the land and the sea. And when you are in the ships, and the ships run with their voyagers with a fair breeze, and they rejoice in it—until there comes upon them a tempest, and waves surge towards them from all sides, so that they are sure that they are encom-passed (by death, with no way out), and they call upon God, sincerely believ-ing in Him alone (as the only Deity, Lord, and Sovereign): 'If You save us from this, we will most certainly be among the thankful.'*"[15]

- **The innate disposition or God-given nature of things speaks the truth.**[16]

Like the human conscience, a thing's innate disposition or God-given nature does not lie; whatever it says is the truth. Given an inclination to grow, the tongue of the seed says: "I will sprout and yield fruit," and what it says is proven true. The inclination towards life murmurs in the depths of the egg: "If God wills, I will be a chick." What it says comes true.

If a handful of water intends to freeze inside an iron cannon-ball when it is cold enough, the inclination to expand within it says to iron: "Expand! I need more space." This command cannot be resisted. Strong iron sets out to work, and does not prove it wrong; the water's truthfulness and honesty split the iron.

All these inclinations are Divine creational commands and each is a Divine decree. They are all Divine laws of creation and life, all manifesta-

---

[15] *Sura Yunus*, 10:22.
[16] *The Words*, "Gleams of Truth", p. 713.

tions of Will. The Divine Will directs all beings in this way: all inclinations conform to the commands of the Lord.

- **The existence of something depends on the existence of all its parts, while its non-existence is possible through the non-existence of one part.**[17]

The existence, health and maintenance of a body depend on the existence, health and maintenance of all its parts. Thus, the existence of a single being and thing in the universe depends on the existence of the entire universe. Therefore, if beings and things are not attributed to the All-Independent, Single One of Unity, it would be necessary to collect all the particles to form a fly's body from all around the earth and the universal elements—quite simply, it would be necessary to sift the face of the earth to collect all the particles to create its body so full of art, and situate them in proper order in the mold of its body. Thus, the creation of a fly in this way would be as difficult as that of the universe; rather, completely impossible and inconceivable. When referred to causes and nature, the existence of each individual thing would require control or mastery over the entire universe, with all its material and immaterial realms.

Another result of this universal reality is that construction is difficult and destruction is easy. It is because of this that an impotent person does not incline to do or produce something positive or constructive that will show his power and capability; he acts negatively, and is usually destructive.

- **The Divine Grandeur and Dignity require that material or natural causes are, in the view of reason, a veil before the hand of the Divine Power; while the Divine Unity and Majesty require that natural causes have no hand in the coming into existence of the works of the Power.**[18]

The real agent acting in the universe is the Eternally Besought One's Power. The Divine Unity, Grandeur and Majesty, as well as our belief in them, require this. However, everything in the physical dimension of the universe has two faces. One looks to the visible, material world, resembling the mirror's dark face, while the other face is like the mirror's shining face and looks to the inner dimension of things, where Divine Power operates directly. In the apparent, material face of things, where opposites are min-

---

[17] *The Words*, "Gleams of Truth", p. 719; *The Gleams*, "The Thirteenth Gleam", pp. 450–452.
[18] *The Words*, "The Twenty-second Word", pp. 307–308; "Gleams of Truth", p. 710.

gled and such beings as humankind and jinn are allowed to have some part in certain events, there may be states that are seemingly incompatible with the dignity and perfection of the Eternally Besought One's Power. In this face, Divine Power veils His operations behind cause and effect so that those states may be ascribed to causes. But in reality, and with respect to the inner dimension of things, everything is beautiful and transparent. This dimension is fitting for the direct operation of the Divine Power. Whatever occurs in this dimension is not incompatible with Its dignity.

Another reason for apparent causes is that people tend to judge superficially. They raise unjust complaints and baseless objections about things or happenings that they find disagreeable. Almighty God, Who is totally just, has put causes in this material dimension of existence as a veil between such things or happenings and Himself, so that such objections and complaints should not be aimed at Him. The faults and mistakes that make things and events disagreeable essentially originate in people and things themselves.

Here is a meaningful illustration of this subtle point: Azrail, the Angel of Death, once said to God Almighty: "Your servants will complain about and resent me, for I take their souls." God Almighty told him in the tongue of wisdom: "I will put the veil of disasters and illnesses between you and my servants so that they will complain of them and not resent you." Thus illness is a veil to which people can attribute that which is disagreeable about death. However disagreeable in appearance, death in reality has many wise and beautiful aspects, and they are attributable to Azrail's duty. But Azrail is also an observer, a veil to the Divine Power; it is God Himself Who makes people die; He is the One Who Makes Die (*al-Mumit*).

In short: The Divine Dignity and Grandeur require that causes should be a veil before Divine Power's hand, while Divine Unity and Majesty demand that causes withdraw their hands from the true effect.

- **The law of rejection of interference prevails in existence. Sovereignty requires independence and rejects partnership and interference.**[19]

Authority and sovereignty do not allow rivalry, partnership, or interference. If a village had two headmen, its order and peace would be destroyed. A district or town with two governors would suffer great con-

---

[19] *The Words,* "The Thirtieth Word", pp. 695–696.

fusion, and a country with two kings (or governments) would be in constant turmoil. Since these pale shadows of absolute Authority and Sovereignty enjoyed by powerless people who are not self-sufficient reject rivalry and the intervention of their opposite, consider how strongly the true Sovereignty, in the form of a supreme, absolute Kingdom and Authority to the degree of Divine Lordship enjoyed by an Absolutely Powerful One, rejects interference and partnership. This means, Oneness and absolute Independence without partners is the most indispensable and constant requirement of Divinity and Lordship.

The universe's perfect order and most beautiful harmony testify to this. There is such a perfect order in the universe—from a fly's wing to the heavens' lamps—that our minds prostrate before it in amazement and admiration.

If there were any room for associating partners with God to interfere with Him, according to the meaning of: *"Had there been deities in them (the heavens and the earth) other than God, both would certainly have fallen into ruin..."*[20], order would be destroyed and the universe's form and shape would change. But, as stated in: *"Look yet again: can you see any rifts? Then look again and yet again, your sight will fall back to you dimmed and dazzled, and awed and weakened,"*[21] however hard we look for a flaw in creation, our gaze will return exhausted and inform our fault-finding reason: "I have exhausted myself in vain, for there is no flaw." This shows that the order is perfect, which means that this perfect order testifies to God's absolute Oneness.

- **The perfect order of the universe, the wise, mutual assistance and solidarity between things, and great beneficence and purposefulness in each and every thing is another proof for the existence and Oneness of God.**[22]

All of the Qur'anic verses that mention the universal order, and the purposes and benefits all the things serve within the fabric of the universe, are indicative of this proof. This proof is based on the fact that the perfect universal order takes into account beneficence and purposefulness. Whatever exists serves many benefits and purposes and has many instances of wisdom. As a corollary of this proof, any notion of chance or

---

[20] *Suratu'l-Anbiya'*, 21:22.
[21] *Suratu'l-Mulk*, 67:4.
[22] *Gleams of Truth*, pp. 175–176.

coincidence in the creation of beings is categorically rejected. Perfection or faultlessness is impossible without an all-encompassing knowledge and determining will. By showing the fruits and purposes that hang from the links of the chains of creatures, and the instances of wisdom, uses, and benefits concealed in the knots of the changes and transformations of conditions and states in existence, all the sciences that study the universe and witness its perfect order bear decisive witness to the Maker's purpose and wisdom. For example:

The sciences of botany and zoology bear witness to the fact that millions of plant and animal species came into existence at a point in time. Each of them ends in a father or mother-individual. What we call laws, the existence of which we deduce from the workings of the universe—and which are nominal, blind, and unconscious—are absolutely devoid of any capacity to originate, form, or develop these amazing chains of beings, or to appoint many wise purposes for them. Therefore, each individual and each species demonstrates and announces that they have been produced by the Hand of an All-Wise Maker's Power.

- **Creation or origination is another decisive proof for God Almighty's existence and Oneness.**[23]

Every species, and each member of that species, has been, and is, given an existence that accords with the function or purpose assigned to it, and the inherent capacity it possesses. Also, each and every thing is created together with the apparent, material causes of its coming into existence. Therefore, both the things themselves and the apparent causes of their existence are contingent and created.

In addition, no species is a link in a chain that stretches back to the eternity of the past so that it can also be the originator of the chain, for the existence of each species is contingent, not absolute. That is, there is a Will that makes a preference between the existence and non-existence of each thing, and a Power that gives it existence. Existence is clearly not timeless, but is contained in time and space, and therefore has a beginning. Something which has a beginning can be the originator of neither itself nor another thing. Something created cannot be a creator.

A truth, or an established reality, cannot become its opposite, nor can its nature change. Therefore, transformative mutations are no more than

---

[23] *Gleams of Truth*, p. 176.

myths. Hybrid species—like mules—which are the offspring of two different species, cannot reproduce. They are exceptions, and never mean the complete transformation of an established truth, which is impossible.

What people call matter is not separate from, or independent of, a changeable form, or the motions and changes which occur within time. Therefore, matter also has a beginning and is time-bound. Being accidental and time-bound, forces and forms cannot be the cause of the essential differentiation between species. Something accidental cannot be the original substance or essence. This means that all the links that form species and their distinguishing features originate from non-existence. The successive generation or reproduction in species is only among certain apparent, nominal conditions for their life and survival.

How strange a misguidance that those who cannot attribute to God His essential Attributes and manifestations, such as eternity and creativity, in their reason are able to ascribe them to lifeless, powerless, unconscious, and time-bound matter or atoms. How can the huge universe submit itself to the origination, control, and management of powerless, unconscious, and time-bound causes like nature, or matter, or what we call laws, or to certain notions such as chance and necessity.

- **Each science speaks of God, the Creator, and makes Him known in its own tongue and in the tongue of the laws on which it is based.**[24]

What we call the laws of nature are in fact the names we give to the results that we deduce from the regular workings of the universe. They are the usual Divine practices for the creation and operation of each and every thing. These laws teach us an important fact—that there can be no law where there is not a strict order. Thus, the universal order heralds purposes and therefore informs us of the existence of a Wise One Who has ordered the universe with whatever is in it, and appointed many wise purposes for them. So, each and every science, based on particular laws, is an eloquent tongue which manifestly speaks of the Divine Being.

Each science speaks of the Divine Being in its own tongue as well. For example, a well-equipped, well-designed pharmacy which has many medicines and pills composed of different precisely measured components certainly indicates an extremely skillful and learned pharmacist. In the same way, to the extent that it is bigger and more perfect than this

---

[24] *The Words*, "The Thirteenth Word", p. 170.

pharmacy, the pharmacy of the earth, which has countless life-giving cures and medicines implanted within all plant and animal species, shows and makes known even to blind eyes, through the sciences of medicine and pharmacology, the All-Wise One of Majesty, Who is the Pharmacist of the largest pharmacy on the earth.

Another example: A wonderful factory which weaves thousands of different cloths from a simple material undoubtedly makes known a manufacturer and skillful mechanical engineer. Likewise, to the extent that it is bigger and more perfect than this factory, with its countless parts, each having hundreds of thousands of machines, this traveling machinery or factory of the Lord which we call the earth shows and makes known its Manufacturer and Owner through the science of engineering. And so on.

- **Matter and the material world is subject to change. Anything subject to change has a beginning and came into existence within time and is time-bound. Anything that came into existence within time must have someone who brought it into existence. That being the reality, this universe has an Eternal Creator.**[25]

- **Everything in the universe is contingent. Contingency means equality between two possibilities. That is, if it is equally possible for something to come into existence or not, there must be one to prefer either possibility, one to create according to this preference, for contingent beings cannot create each other one after the other. Nor can they go back to eternity in cycles with the former having created the latter. Given this, there is a Necessarily Existent Being Who creates all.**[26]

- **The perfect correspondence and similarity in structure and form among species, and among the members of each species despite vast distances in time and space, demonstrate God's Unity, while it indicates His absolute Will and freedom that each creature, though generated from similar or even the same materials, has unique characters and features.**[27]

- **If material causes had creative effect in existence or actual agency in creation, they should have had universal knowledge, con-**

[25] *The Words*, "The Thirtieth Word", p. 696.
[26] *The Words*, "The Thirtieth Word", p. 697.
[27] *Al-Mathnawi al-Nuri*, "The Third Treatise", pp. 50–51.

sciousness and will-power, and due to their multiplicity and their variety in capacities, things would have had variable degrees in both structure and art.[28]

We clearly see that from the most distinguished to the most ordinary, and from the largest to the smallest, there is no fault or incongruity in things. Everything is perfectly firm and given the utmost care, and everything is given a perfect nature in accordance with its stature. This clearly shows that everything is created by a single Creator. Otherwise, due to their almost infinite multiplicity and their variety in capacities, things would have had variable degrees in both structure and art.

Human beings have been given partial will-power, and it is because of this that there are faults in their actions and works. That is, the lack of firmness in their actions and works shows that they are not compelled to do something by the Creator. However, everything in nature is of the same perfect nature and composition with no incongruity, infirmity, and defect. This clearly demonstrates that their Creator is the single One with absolute Will, Knowledge, and Power.

- **Divine Power creates the tiniest particle and the entire universe with the same ease. For It is intrinsic in the Divine Essence and inseparable from Him, so there can be no incapacity connected with It. Since impotence cannot be involved with Divine Power, It can have no degrees, for degrees in a thing's existence come about only through the intervention of opposites.**[29]

Degrees of temperature occur because of cold's intervention, and degrees of beauty exist because of ugliness' intervention. This is true of all qualities in the universe. Since contingent things and beings do not exist essentially of themselves and have no absolute qualities intrinsic in and inseparable from and originating in themselves, they contain opposites and degrees. Because of this, the contingent world is subject to change and transformation. However, the Eternal Divine Power contains no degrees—it is equally easy for It to create and operate particles and galaxies. Resurrecting humanity is as easy for It as reviving one person, and creating spring is as easy as creating a flower.

---

[28] *Gleams of Truth*, p. 100.
[29] *The Words*, "The Twenty-ninth Word", p. 544.

- **Such essential qualities in existence as transparency, correspondence and reciprocity, balance, orderliness, abstraction, and obedience help us to understand how the Divine Power creates everything, small or big, with the same ease.**[30]

Transparency. The reflection of the same sun on both the ocean's surface and in a drop of water has the same identity, and the multiplicity of things does not prevent it from illuminating and heating the earth and a piece of glass at the same time.

Correspondence and *reciprocity.* If we stand with a lit candle in the center of a large circle of people, each of whom is holding a mirror, each mirror will hold the same reflection without any one hindering any other.

Balance. If we weigh a pair of things—two stars or two eggs or two atoms—with a balance that measures each item with perfect precision, any extra force exerted upon either scale would disturb the balance.

Orderliness. We can steer a huge ship as easily as a small toy, for all the parts of its orderly system are interrelated.

Abstraction or *Incorporeality.* There is no difference of essence or character between a small and big creature belonging to the same species, for these incorporeal features are the same for both. For example, a minnow has the same essence or character as a basking-shark (both are fish), and a micro-organism has the same essence as a rhinoceros (both are living animals).

Obedience. A commander moves an army as easily as a single soldier by ordering it to march.

If defective, limited, weak, and non-creative contingencies display such effects in the face of these six features or phenomena, for sure, everything is equally susceptible to the Divine Power's order. This Power is infinite, eternal, and absolutely perfect. Nothing is difficult for It.

Note that the Divine Power cannot be measured in the scales of these features; they are mentioned only to have some grasp of the matter.

- **Each and every atom or molecule of air, a conductor of Divine Will and Command, is a reflection and proof of the Divine Oneness.**[31]

If several points are jumbled around one on a piece of paper, it is almost impossible for us to distinguish that point. If we do several jobs

---

[30] *The Words*, "The Twenty-ninth Word", p. 5445–546.
[31] *The Words*, "The Thirteenth Word", pp. 174–176.

simultaneously, we will be confused. If a living creature is loaded with many burdens at once, it will be crushed. If we listen to or say many words simultaneously, they become confused and muddled. However, although countless points, letters, words, and scenes are deposited in each air molecule—even in each atom—they are conveyed without confusion or irregularity. Also, the air performs all its duties simultaneously and without confusion. Each air molecule or atom bears heavy burdens without lagging behind or displaying any weakness. Also, countless words are carried into countless ears and come up to mouths with perfect order, and countless scenes are carried into countless eyes with perfect order and distinction without the least confusion. In performing all of these extraordinary duties, each atom or molecule of air says in the tongue of its being and functioning, in ecstasy and perfect freedom, and through its testimony: "There is no deity but He" and, "Say: He is God, the One." All of them travel among air-clashing waves like lightning and thunderstorms in perfect order and harmony, without one task of them hindering the other.

Given this, either each atom or molecule of air necessarily has infinite wisdom, knowledge, will, power, and all qualities needed to dominate all other atoms so that it can perform those functions—which is so absurd and inconceivable that not even Satan could imagine it—or air is used by the All-Majestic One with infinite Knowledge, Wisdom, Will, and Power.

- **There are three different kinds of reflections in something transparent like a mirror, which explain God's overall control of each and every thing at the same time, the Prophet's Ascension, and the appearance of some saintly or spiritually-progressive people in different places at the same time.**[32]

The first kind is the reflections of dense, material objects. Such reflections are "other" than the thing reflected, and so have a different identity. They are also lifeless, having no quality other than their lifeless appearance. A human being's reflection in a mirror is of this kind.

The second is reflections of material, light-giving objects. Such reflections are neither identical with, nor other than, the original. While not of the same nature as the original, they have most of its features and may be considered as living. For example, the sun is reflected in countless

---

[32] *The Words*, "The Sixteenth Word", pp. 210–212.

objects. Each reflection either contains its heat or light, together with its light's seven colors. If the sun were conscious, with its heat as its power, its light as its knowledge, and its seven colors as its seven attributes, it would be present in everything simultaneously, and able to rule over or make contact with each one freely and without one hindering the other. While we are distant from it, it would be nearer to us than ourselves.

The third kind is the reflections of pure spirits created from light and having their original purity. Such reflections are living and identical with the original. However, since they reflect or manifest themselves according to the receptive object's or mirror's capacity, the reflections are not wholly of the same nature as the original. For example, Archangel Gabriel could be with the Prophet in the form of Dihya (a Companion), prostrating in the Divine Presence before God's Most Exalted Throne, and be in innumerable other places relaying the Divine Commands simultaneously. Performing one duty does not block another. In the same way Prophet Muhammad, upon him be peace and blessings, whose essence is of *nur*, something more refined and penetrative than light, and whose identity is of *nur*, hears each member of his community in this world calling blessings upon him simultaneously. On the Day of Judgment, he will meet with all purified people at the same time. In fact, some saints who have acquired a high degree of purity and refinement are seen in many places and doing many things simultaneously. Just as glass and water reflect material objects, air, ether, and certain beings of the World of Ideas or Immaterial Forms also reflect and transport beings with the speed of light and imagination. This allows them to travel in thousands of pure realms and refined abodes at the same time.

Helpless and subjugated items like the sun, and creatures like matter-restricted spirit beings, can be present in many places at once because they are either light-giving creatures or created of light. Despite being particulars bounded by certain conditions, they become like absolute universals. With their limited power of choice, they can do many things at once.

God, the All-Holy, All-Pure Being, is wholly transcendent and free of matter, far above and exempt from any restriction and the darkness of density and compactness. All lights and luminous beings, whether light-giving or created of light, are dense shadows of His Names' sacred lights. All existence and life, as well as the World of Spirits and the World of Ideas or Immaterial Forms, are semi-transparent mirrors of His Beauty. His Attributes are all-embracing, and so are His essential Character or Qualities. What could escape or hide from His manifestation with all His Attributes, particularly His universal Will, absolute Power, and all-encompassing Knowledge? What could be difficult for Him? Who could be distant from Him? Who could draw close to Him without acquiring universality?

The sun's unrestricted light and immaterial reflection makes it nearer to us than our eyes' pupil, while our being bounded by certain conditions keeps us far from it. To draw near, we must transcend many restrictions and rise above many universal levels. Simply, in terms of spiritual transcendence, we have to become as large as the earth and rise as far as the moon. Only then could we directly approach, to a degree, the sun in its essential identity and meet with it without veil. In the same way, the All-Majestic One of Grace, the All-Gracious One of Perfection, is infinitely near to us, nearer to us than ourselves, while we are infinitely far from Him. If we have enough power of heart and sublimity of mind, we can try to see certain other realities in the other aspects of the comparison.

- **The Divine Power has numerous mirrors, one more refined and transparent than the other.**[33]

The Power of the All-Majestic One has numerous mirrors. They open up windows, each more transparent and subtle than the other, all looking onto the World of Representations or Ideal Forms. Various mirrors— from water to air, air to ether, ether to representations or ideal forms, ideal forms to spirits, spirits to time, time to imagination, and from imagination to the mind—all represent the manifestations of God's Acts. Turn your ear to the mirror of the air: a single word becomes millions! The Pen of Power makes copies in an extraordinary way.

- **Everything is equal before the Divine Power.**[34]

"Your creation and your resurrection are but as (the creation and resurrection of) a single soul."[35] The Divine Power is essential to and inherent in the Divine Essence; impotence cannot access It. There can be no degrees in Divine Power, nor can any impediment in any way obstruct It. Whether they be universal or particular, all things are the same in relation to It. Also, everything is interconnected to and interdependent on everything else; one who cannot make everything can make nothing.

---

[33] *The Words*, "Gleams of Truth", p. 716.
[34] *The Words*, "Gleams of Truth", p. 711.
[35] *Suratu'l-'Ankabut*, 31:28.

- **One who cannot hold the universe in his hand cannot create a particle.**[36]

If one does not have a hand that is powerful enough to lift the earth, the suns, and the stars—those innumerable bodies—and string them in order like prayer-beads, and place them on the head and breast of endless space, they cannot claim to create anything in the world; they have no right to claim to have invented anything.

- **The Supreme Divine Throne (*al-'Arsh*) is a combination of the manifestations of *He is the First and the Last, the All-Outward and the All-Inward*,[37] and encompasses the whole of creation.[38]**

Everything has both an outer and inner dimension. With respect to the outer dimension of existence, we are our heart's envelope; with respect to its inner dimension, we are its content. In the same way, in the sphere of the Divine Name the All-Outward (*az-Zahir*), the Supreme Divine Throne encompasses all things. In the sphere of the Divine Name the All-Inward (*al-Batin*), It is like the heart of creation. In the sphere of the Name the First (*al-Awwal*), It is pointed to by: "*His Supreme Throne was upon something fluid (like water).*"[39] In that of the Divine Name the Last (*al-Akhir*), It is symbolized by: "The ceiling of Paradise is God's Supreme Throne."[40]

- **The All-Majestic One, the Owner of the Supreme Throne, has four 'thrones' which He employs in conducting His commands and directing the creatures on the earth, the center of the universe and its heart and *qibla* (the direction faced).[41]**

*The first thron*e is the throne of preservation and life, which is soil. This is the manifestation of the Divine Names, the All-Preserving and the Giver of Life. *The second throne* is the throne of bounty and mercy, which is the element of water, and manifests the Divine Names, the All-Merciful and the All-Providing. *The third* is the throne of knowledge and wisdom, which is the element of light, and manifests the All-Knowing and the All-Wise. *The fourth* is the throne of command and will, which is the element of air, and manifests the All-Willing and the All-Directing.

---

[36] *The Words*, "Gleams of Truth", p. 712.
[37] *Suratu'l-Hadid*, 57:3.
[38] *Al-Mathnawi al-Nuri*, "The Fifth Treatise", p. 149.
[39] *Sura Hud*, 11:7.
[40] *al-Jami' as-Saghir*, hadith no. 3116, related by Ibn Maja and Ibn 'Asakir.
[41] *The Gleams*, "The Twenty-eighth Gleam", p. 378.

- **In the All-Majestic Maker's Art, motions have infinitely different degrees. For example, the speeds of electricity, spirit, imagination, and sound are quite different from each other. Also, the speeds of planetary movements are astonishingly different.**[42]

So why should it be unreasonable that Prophet Muhammad's body acquired a sort of refinement, accompanied his spirit in the Ascension, and moved at its speed? Sometimes you sleep for ten minutes but have a year's worth of experiences. If the words spoken and heard in a dream lasting for only a minute were collected, it would take a day and even longer to speak or hear them while awake. Thus a single period of time means a day for one and a year for another.

- **Just as the Divine Being has no rivals or opposites, according to, "*There is nothing like to Him, and He is the All-Hearing, the All-Seeing,*"[43] He has no form, likeness, or peer as well. Nothing resembles Him or is similar to Him. On the other hand, according to, "*And to Him applies the most sublime attribute in the heavens and the earth, and He is Exalted in Might, the All-Wise,*"[44] we can attempt to understand His Acts, Attributes, and Names by means of allegories and parables.**[45]

- **Just as the sun is nearer to us than ourselves through its light and heat but we cannot draw close to it, so too is the Divine Being nearer to us than ourselves, but we are infinitely far from Him. He is omnipresent everywhere, without being contained by any place.**[46]

- **When we turn to the Almighty supposing that He is known, He will become unknown. But if we turn to the Almighty, accepting Him as One existent but unknown, then rays of true knowledge of Him will be revealed, and the all-encompassing, absolute Divine Attributes manifested in the universe will appear in the light of this knowledge.**[47]

---

[42] *The Words*, "The Thirty-first Word", p. 591.
[43] *Suratu'sh-Shura*, 42:11.
[44] *Suratu'-Rum*, 30:27.
[45] *The Gleams*, "The Fourteenth Gleam", p. 138.
[46] *The Gleams*, "The Fourteenth Gleam", p. 139; "The Thirtieth Gleam", p. 476.
[47] *Al-Mathnawi al-Nuri*, "The Sixth Treatise", p. 185.

Our supposition of the Almighty Divine Being is usually based on a commonplace, imitative knowledge about Him. In most cases, such knowledge has nothing to do with truth. The meaning it conveys to our mind is far from explaining the absolute Divine Attributes. In addition, there is no limit to knowledge of God. Therefore, supposing that we know Him will be a veil before us which blocks our way to having more and more knowledge about Him. Therefore, we should always approach Him as One existent but unknown.

- **To create everything from one thing, and to make everything into one thing, is particular only to the Creator of all.**[48]

The Creator makes everything out of one thing, and one thing out of many things. He makes the countless members and systems of an animal's body out of the same simple substances like water and soil. Also, He transforms with perfect orderliness all substances contained in innumerable kinds of vegetable or animal food into particular bodies, weaving from them a unique skin for each and various bodily members. Countless beings eat the same kinds of food and are composed of the same elements, and yet each one has unique faces, fingerprints, characters, ambitions, feelings, and so on. This is irrefutable proof of the existence and Unity of an All-Knowing and All-Powerful Creator, Who has absolute Will and can do whatever He pleases in whatever way He wills.

- **Every village must have a headman, every needle a manufacturer and craftsperson, and every letter a writer. How could such a perfectly well-ordered land—the universe—have no creator and ruler?**[49]

- **As a letter indicates its writer, and an artistic inscription makes its inscriber known, how can then an Inscriber, a Designer, or a Decorator, Who inscribes a huge book in a single letter—Who inscribes a huge tree in its tiny seed or stone—and displays a thousand ornaments in a single ornament, not be recognized through His inscriptions and ornaments?**[50]

How can the One Who makes each human being identifiable through his or her DNA, fingerprints, and threads of hair be recognized?

---

[48] *The Words*, "The Tenth Word", p. 78; "The Twenty-second Word", p. 309.
[49] *The Words*, "The Tenth Word", p. 68.
[50] *The Words*, "The Twenty-second Word", p. 298.

- **God Almighty sets a special seal on each work of His Art, showing that He is the Creator of all things. He sets a special stamp on each of His creatures, demonstrating that He is the Artist or Artisan of all things.**[51]

Each and every thing is a work of the Divine Art and a creature of the Creator. When we look at something as a creature—something created—we should consider God as the Supreme Artist or Artisan so that we may not miss that everything is an artistic sign of God, making Him known to us in many respects. On the other hand, when we look at each and every thing as a work of the Divine Art, we should consider that it is a creation of God, or we should consider God as the Creator so that we may not attribute things to 'nature' and fall into naturalism. In short, when we look at something in the universe, we should consider all the Names of God which manifest themselves on it.

- **Many deviations about God and His Acts, especially about His creation and direction of each and every thing at the same time, issue from humanity's false suppositions and comparisons, particularly from their judging His Acts according to the standards they find in themselves or in others like themselves.**[52]

Human beings are usually unable to see or study something in its totality or as a complete entity. They tend to compartmentalize everything or divide it into parts, and then examine it. Human beings search for the standards of evaluating the thing with which they are occupied first in themselves and, if they cannot find it in themselves, then they search for the same in others like themselves. Even if they think about the Necessarily Existent Being, Who does not resemble any of the created in any way, they attempt to judge Him according to the particular standards they find in themselves or in others.

However, the All-Majestic Maker can never be "observed" or judged from the viewpoint of human beings. His Power has no limits at all. His Power, Knowledge, and Will encompass and penetrate everything. Consider that even the sun, which is a material body among numberless heavenly objects that have been created by God, Who has nothing in common with matter or being material, penetrates everything within the vast expanse of the reach of its light. We do not have anything with which we

---

[51] *Al-Mathnawi al-Nuri*, "The First Treatise", pp. 4–5.
[52] *The Reasonings*, "The Third Part", pp. 113–114.

can weigh or compare the All-Majestic Maker's Knowledge, Will, and Power. They simultaneously penetrate and encompass every single thing, no matter how vast or how minute. As they penetrate and encompass the universe as a whole, they also penetrate and encompass all individual parts of it at the same time. So, to compare the Necessarily Existent Being to any of the created entities is completely erroneous. Nevertheless, falling into this error, naturalists ascribe creativity to material causes or what they call nature and natural forces; the *Mu'tazilites* held that living beings were the creators of their own actions; the Muslim Peripatetic philosophers inserted what they called Ten Intellects between God and His creation, and asserted that Divine Knowledge does not encompass individual small entities or particles of existence; the Zoroastrians believed in two separate deities, one as the creator of good, and the other as the creator of evil. Some believers can be vulnerable to such false notions in the form of unintentional suggestions.

- **The reason why some people cannot understand God's creation from non-existence or giving existence to something non-existent is their false comparison of God's creation with the acts of the created.**[53]

Human beings conceive of God's creation of existence from non-existence, with nothing preceding Him, as if an imitation of the acts of the created. No creature is ever able to give existence to something that does not exist or to make something that is existent non-existent. What conscious, living beings can do is to imitate or bring the parts together to form a new composition or a complete entity, or divide a whole into parts.

Since human beings have never seen the like of the Divine Power in the universe, they cannot comprehend God's creation of existence from non-existence, or His causing something that exists to cease to exist. The rational arguments of human beings, and the conclusion they draw, are based on observations. They view the Creator's Acts and works from the perspective of the acts and works of the created, and make a misleading comparison between them. However, they should view the Creator's Acts and works with the consideration in mind of His limitless Power.

While thinking about the works of people, we should take their attributes into consideration; we should view their works from the perspective

---

[53] *The Reasonings*, "The Third Part", pp. 115.

of their personal attributes. If we view God's Acts and works from the perspective of the attributes (power, capacity, and knowledge) of the created, we can only arrive at a wrong conclusion. Everyday we witness innumerable instances of creation from non-existence. That material causes have a part in things or beings coming into existence should not deceive us, for they have no part in the giving of life, which is purely a gift of the Creator. In addition, every day many things occur, the causes of which science cannot explain. Despite these facts, those who see creation from non-existence as being impossible compare the Divine Being and His Attributes and Acts with the created, and want to see that which is essentially invisible.

- **Just as in logic theories are produced from premises, which are generally true rules or principles, so too do the "premises" in the works of the Maker suffice to see and explain the hidden points in His Art. This proves creation from non-existence.**[54]

That is, first we should recognize God with His limitless Attributes having no resemblance with those of the created, and then ponder on His Acts. If we attempt to know Him and His Acts from the perspective of our attributes and acts, this means that we think of the Divine Being as if a human being.

- **It is not necessary that a thing should be great in size in order to be great qualitatively. The scope of Divine Power rejects intermediaries and helpers.**[55]

A clock the size of a mustard-seed would be more eloquent than a clock the size of Ayasofya (Hagia Sophia). The creation of the fly is no less, indeed perhaps more, amazing than that of an imposing creature like the elephant.

For the All-Powerful One of Majesty, in relation to the scope of the control and operations of His Power, our sun is like a particle. In order to have some glimpse of the vastness of the control and operations of His Power in a single realm of beings, take the gravity between two atoms, and then go and put it beside the gravity between the sun of suns and the Milky Way. Bring an angel whose load is a snowflake to a sun-like angel who holds the sun; put a needle-fish beside a whale; then consider all at once the vast manifestation of the Eternal All-Powerful One of Majesty

---

[54] *The Reasonings*, "The Third Part", pp. 116.
[55] *Gleams of Truth*, pp. 72–73.

and the infinitely perfect "workmanship" in things, from the smallest to the greatest. Our earth resembles an animate being that displays signs of life. If, to suppose the impossible, it were reduced to the size of an egg, it would most probably become a tiny micro-organism. If a micro-organism were enlarged to the size of the earth, most probably it would be just like the earth. If the universe was reduced to the size of a human being, with its stars forming particles, it is possible it would become a conscious animal; reason does not deny this. This means, the world with all its parts is a glorifying servant of the Ever-Living Creator, the Eternal All-Powerful One, obedient and subservient.

- **A work's perfection points to the perfection of the act operating in the production of the work. The act's perfection points to the name's or title's perfection, which points to the attribute's perfection, which points to the essential capacity's perfection, which necessarily, intuitively, and evidently points to the perfection of the one with that essential capacity.**[56]

For example, a perfect palace's perfect construction, design, and adornments show the perfection of a master-builder's acts. The acts' perfection shows the perfection of the eminent builder's titles, which specify his rank. The titles' perfection shows the perfection of the builder's attributes, which are the origin of the art. The perfection of the art and attributes show the perfection of the master's abilities and essential capacity. The perfection of those essential abilities and capacity show the perfection of the master's essential nature. Similarly, the faultless works seen in the universe, about which the Qur'an asks: *"Can you see any flaw (or rift)?"*,[57] the art in the universe's well-ordered beings, points to an Effective, Powerful Agent's perfect Acts. The Acts' perfection point to the perfection of that All-Majestic Agent's Names. The Names' perfection points and testifies to the perfection of the Attributes of the All-Majestic One known with the Names. The Attributes' perfection points and testifies to the perfection of the essential Character and Qualities of the Perfect One qualified by those Attributes. The perfection of the essential Character and Qualities point to the perfection of the One having such Character and Qualities with such certainty that all types of perfections observed throughout the universe are but signs of His Perfection, hints of His Maj-

---

[56] *The Words*, "The Twenty-second Word", pp. 319–320.
[57] *Suratu'l-Mulk*, 67:3.

esty, and allusions to His Beauty in the forms of shadows when compared to His Perfection.

- **What materialists call nature is a Divine art, not the artist. It is something inscribed by the Lord, and it cannot be the scribe. It is a design, and it cannot be the designer. It is a register, and it cannot be the registrar. It is a law, and it cannot be the power. It is a pattern, and it cannot be the source. It is a passive recipient, and it cannot be the author. It is an order and it cannot be the orderer. It is a system of creation and it cannot be the establisher of the system.**[58]

If, to suppose the impossible, the tiniest animate creature was referred to nature and nature was told, "Make this," it would then be necessary for nature to possess perfect knowledge about the entire universe, including all that is in it and the relationships among all parts of it. It would then be required to provide molds, or rather machines, to the number of the tiny creature's members and bodily systems so that it could fulfill that task.

- **The Divine Power is the Agent, and the Divine Destiny appoints the pattern(s) upon which the Divine Power writes the 'book of meanings'.**[59]

The Qur'an specifically explains that everything is determined before and recorded after it comes into existence, as in: "*Not a thing, fresh or withered, wet or dry, but it is in a Manifest Book,*"[60] and many other verses. This is confirmed by the universe, this macro-Qur'an of the Divine Power, through its creational and operational signs like order, harmony, balance, form, shape, adornment and distinguishment. All seeds, fruit pits, measured proportions, and forms show that everything is predetermined before its earthly existence. Each seed or fruit pit is a case into which the Divine Destiny has inserted a tree's or plant's future life-history. The Divine Power uses the atoms, according to the measure established by the Divine Destiny, to cause the particular seed to grow miraculously into a particular tree. This means that the tree's future life-history is as though written in its seed.

Individuals and species differ, but they are formed from the identical basic materials. Plants and animals grow from the same basic elements, yet display such abundant diversity, and such harmony and proportion

---

[58] *The Gleams*, "The Thirtieth Gleam", p. 476.
[59] *The Words*, "The Twenty-sixth Word", pp. 487–488.
[60] *Suratu'l-An'am*, 6:59.

amid that diversity, that we can only conclude that each one has been given its unique form and measure by the Divine Power according to the measure established for it by the Divine Destiny or Determination. For example, consider how vast and innumerable are the inanimate atoms that shift, cohere, and separate so that this seed grows into this tree or that drop of semen grows into that animal?

A seed displays Destiny in two ways. The first is by showing the Manifest Book (*Kitabun Mubin*), another title for Divine Will and God's creational and operational laws of the universe. The second is by showing the Manifest Record (*Imamun Mubin*), another title for Divine Knowledge and Command. If we regard these two as different manifestations of the Divine Destiny, the former can be understood and referred to as "Actual Destiny" and the latter as "Formal (Theoretical) Destiny." The future physical form a tree will assume with all its roots, trunk, branches, leaves, blossoms, and fruits can be understood as its Actual Destiny. Its general (theoretical) form, represented by its seed and comprised of all the life stages it will pass through, is its Formal Destiny. Such manifestations of the Divine Destiny, so easily observed in a tree's life, illustrate how everything has been predetermined in a Record before its worldly existence.

On the other hand, all fruits (signs of the Manifest Book and Manifest Record), and all human memories indicating the Supreme Preserved Tablet (*Lawhun Mahfuz*), prove that just as everything has been prerecorded, everything's life-history has also been recorded. Each tree's life-history is recorded in each fruit, the outcome of its life. Humanity's life-history, including events occurring in the external world, is recorded in both human memory and on the 'tapes of creation.' Thus the Divine Power registers our deeds with the Pen of Destiny so that we will remember them and be called to account for them on the Day of Reckoning.

- **All such claims or statements as "Things are formed by themselves," "Causes have brought it about," or "Nature requires it to be so," are false.**[61]

We exist. So, according to the first statement, we are our own creatures. According to the second one, material causes have brought us about. According to the last one, some unconscious, deaf, and blind laws

---

[61] *Al-Mathnawi al-Nuri*, "The Sixth Treatise", pp. 199–200.

or forces attributed to nature, or lifeless things called "nature," required our existence. But the truth is that we are creatures of God, the Almighty.

As for the first statement, things cannot be formed by themselves, because each particle or atom forming our bodies would have to have an eye to see our whole bodies and all of creation, as well as consciousness to be aware of all the requirements of life and existence. Our perfect composition, the perfection of art in us, requires this, for all particles of existence are in vital and substantial relations with each other and with all creation.

To print a book, a printing house must have as many iron letters or keys as needed to print it. If we made ourselves, we must contain as many molds as the number of atoms in us, for they are in conscious relation and communication with one another. Our composition is uniform, meaning that all parts are in close interrelation with each other. Therefore, like the stones forming an arch or a dome, all our atoms or building blocks should be both dominant over and dominated by one another. They also should be like the manifestations of the Names and Attributes of the One Who rolls up the heavens like a scroll rolled up for books—both opposite and complementary to each other.

Causes cannot create anything by themselves. For example, if bottles containing medical ingredients fall off the shelf and become mixed on the floor, would the desired medicine be produced? Using the same analogy, could we be formed by chance or random causes? How could innumerable deaf, blind, and unconscious causes come together and create something that has perfect order? By coming together they only increase in deafness and blindness. Each human being is a perfect work of art: intelligent, conscious, and equipped with endless and extremely complex feelings, senses, and faculties, and feeling infinite need. How can that which is deaf, blind, and unconscious bestow hearing, sight, and consciousness on something else?

Assume that innumerable causes come together in a most orderly fashion and in exact measure to create a cell in our eyes. With the same amount of effort, then, the universe's basic parts or elements, including huge heavenly objects, should be able to assemble themselves in our palms or in each of our cells. Why? Because if we work in a house, this means the house contains us. All of the universe's parts and contents are related to humanity. So if causes created us, the entire universe should be able to operate within each of our bodies' parts and be contained by one of our cells. This is a most inconceivable sophistry.

Nature cannot create because it is something supposed to exist, a name given by those who do not know the real facts of the matter. However, in its true meaning, it is a Divine art, a painting by the All-Merciful.

"Natural forces" are only manifestations of the Power of the All-Merciful, All-Knowing, All-Aware, All-Willing. "Chance" is only a mistaken supposition put forward by those who are unaware of or deny the Single Maker. Could something restricted, solid, inanimate, whose existence or non-existence is equally possible (meaning that one must prefer its existence and create it), have woven the universe's garment? Could a gnat have participated in weaving these perfectly designed and adorned garments in which those words are dressed? The only explanation for our existence and that of creation is that everything that has been created is a creature of an Eternal Maker, and that they all testify to this fact.

- **Solid, material, and corporeal things are acted on and affected by immaterial things or things of light and refinement.**[62]

Look at sunlight and a mountain. The former comes from the sky and operates on the earth freely, while the latter, despite its huge size, can do nothing and has no effect on its environment. The subtler and the more refined something is, and the more light it contains, the more effective and active it is; the more material and solid something is, the more susceptible it is to being acted upon and affected. We can conclude from this that the Creator of causes and effects is He Who is the *Nur* of *Nur*: *"Nothing is like Him, He is the All-Hearing, the All-Seeing."*[63] *"Vision comprehends Him not, but He comprehends all vision. He is the All-Subtle, the All-Aware."*[64]

- **Matter is not essential. Therefore existence is not subject to or dependent on it. Rather, as a word is the mold of the meaning responsible for its existence, and therefore exists and subsists through that meaning, matter exists and subsists by means of a meaning. Existence does not serve matter so that everything could be ascribed to it. Rather, matter serves something immaterial, and that is life. Matter does not rule existence so that perfections should be sought from it. Rather, it is dominated, subject to the decree of an agent (life), and fashioned according to that decree's dictates. Matter is not the unchanged essence of exis-**

---

[62] *Al-Mathnawi al-Nuri*, "The Sixth Treatise", p. 202.
[63] *Suratu'sh-Shura*, 42:11.
[64] *Suratu'l-An'am*, 6:103.

tence; rather, it is a form and outer covering subject to disintegration. As matter becomes more refined, life's effects become more manifest and the spirit's light grows brighter. It is as though the more closely matter resembles the realm of spirit and consciousness, the more ethereal it becomes. This causes life's light to be manifested more brightly.[65]

- It is an established rule that a single, unique thing of particular individuality can only have issued from a single, unique source.[66]

If, in particular, a thing is a living one with a perfectly ordered and most sensitively balanced life, it will self-evidently display that it has not issued from numerous, different hands of different nature and quality, which would be certain to cause great confusion, conflict, and defect, but rather it has issued from the Hand of a single All-Powerful, All-Wise One. Furthermore, the random coming together of innumerable inanimate, ignorant, unrestricted, unconscious, blind, and deaf "natural" causes and elements for the existence of something would only cause the increase of their blindness and deafness amidst the limitless probabilities. Therefore, attributing any being, which has a unique, particular individuality formed of innumerable elements in perfect order and a most sensitively balanced way to such causes would be as unreasonable as accepting numberless impossibilities all at once.

- Even though, from the time of Adam, all human faces have had the same structure and organs and been made of the same elements, each has particular features distinguishing it from all others. This demonstrates an All-Knowing, All-Willing and All-Powerful One, Who has pre-knowledge of each and every human being and creates each human being with his or her particular, distinguishing features.[67]

- Absolute non-existence cannot exist where there is an all-encompassing Knowledge. Also, there cannot be room for chance where there is an absolute Will and Determination.[68]

As everything is contained or has a kind of existence or an ideal form within the infinite Divine Knowledge, there is no room for absolute non-

[65] *The Words*, "The Twenty-ninth Word", p. 531.
[66] *The Gleams*, "The Twenty-third Gleam", p. 254.
[67] *The Gleams*, "The Twenty-third Gleam", p. 264.
[68] *The Letters*, "The Fifteenth Letter", p. 98.

existence. Within the encompassing circle of Divine Knowledge, relative non-existence is, in essence, a nominal veil reflecting the manifestations of Divine Knowledge.

- **Attributing all beings to a Maker of Unity allows them to find salvation, and they find rest and contentment in the remembrance of One God. For if all those innumerable beings are not attributed to a Single Being, one thing must be ascribed to numberless causes. In which case, the existence of a single thing becomes as difficult as the whole creation; a fruit becomes as difficult as the universe—indeed, more difficult.**[69]

Consider this: If one soldier is commanded by a hundred officers, a hundred difficulties will arise. But if a hundred soldiers are commanded by one officer, they will be as easy to command as one soldier. This also is true in the case of creation, for the creation of one thing by multiple causes would face as many problems as there are causes. If an army's equipment is produced in one factory, through one law, and in one center, it is done as easily as equipping one soldier. But if each soldier's equipment is procured from many places, then equipping one soldier would require as many factories as needed for the whole army. Given this, belief in the Creator's Unity and knowledge or recognition of God will deliver us from the endless distress arising from the curiosity and desire to find the truth, which is inherent in our nature.

- **Everything in the cosmos is created and fashioned in perfect proportions, and perfect, pleasing, symmetrical orderliness, and it is maintained and preserved in a perfect order and balance.**[70]

These realities manifest that One Who has an all-encompassing Knowledge and Wisdom, Will and Power, creates and administers the entire cosmos with whatever is in it.

- **Each attainment, perfection, bit of knowledge, progress, and science has an elevated reality based on a Divine Name. By being based on a Name, Which has a great variety of veils and manifests Itself in various ways and levels, that particular branch of science**

---

[69] *The Words,* "The Twenty-Second Word", p. 302; "The Thirty-third Word", p. 675.
[70] *The Words*, "The Tenth Word", p. 93.

or art attains its perfection and becomes reality. Otherwise, it remains imperfect, deficient, and shadowy.[71]

For example, engineering's reality lies in the Divine Names the All-Just One Who gives everything a certain measure and due proportions and creates everything just in its place, and the All-Determining. Its final aim is to discover those Names and observe and reflect their wise and majestic manifestations. Medicine is an art and a science. Its reality and final rank lie in the All-Wise's Name the All-Healing, and it reaches its perfection by finding out a cure for every illness by discovering the merciful manifestations of that Name in the earth, His vast "pharmacy."

The science which discusses the reality of entities can be a true science, full of wisdom, only by discerning the regulating, directing, administering, sustaining, and all-embracing manifestations of the Divine Name the All-Wise in things, and in their benefits and advantages, and by being based on that Name. Otherwise it either become superstition and nonsense or, like naturalistic philosophy, causes misguidance. You can compare other sciences and attainments with these three examples.

By relating the miracles of the Prophets in the Qur'an, God Almighty marks the final point of the development of each science and urges people towards it.

- **All of the Divine Names manifested in the universe are manifested on humanity. However, the variety of the Names and their manifestations in different ways and degrees have caused variety among human beings, as they have caused differences in the forms of angels' worshipping, among the laws and missions of Prophets, the ways of saints, and the paths of purified scholars. For example, the All-Powerful was more predominant in Jesus, upon him be peace, than the other Names manifested in him. The All-Loving prevails in those who follow the path of love to God, and the All-Wise in those who follow the path of contemplation and reflection.**[72]

A sovereign has different titles by which he is known and mentioned in his government's various departments, different designations and attributes among his people's classes, and different names and signs for his rule's levels. For example, he is the supreme judge in the justice

---

[71] *The Words*, "The Twentieth Word", p. 275.
[72] *The Words*, "The Twenty-fourth Word", p. 354.

department, just ruler and chief administrator in the civil service, commander-in-chief in the military, and supreme teacher in the education department. Due to his public person and system of communication, he is present in every department. Through his laws, regulations, and representatives, he superintends all officials, watches all subjects, and is seen by them. Behind the veil at every level, he administers, executes his orders, and is watchful through his decree, knowledge, and power.

Similarly, the Lord of the worlds, the Sovereign of eternity, has at the levels of His Lordship's manifestations qualities and designations which are all different but correspond to each other. In the spheres of His Divinity, He has Names and marks which are all different but whose manifestations are concentric with each other. In His majestic execution of His rule, He has representations and appellations which are all different but resemble each other. In the operations of His Power, He has titles which are all different but imply each other. In the manifestations of His Attributes, He has sacred ways of revealing Himself that differ but point to each other. In His modes of acting, He has wise operations which are of numerous sorts but perfect each other. In His colorful artistry and varied works of Art, He has magnificent aspects of Lordship which differ but correspond to each other.

In every world and division of beings, each of His All-Beautiful Names is manifested individually. A particular Name is dominant in a particular sphere, with other Names being subordinate. In every level and division of beings, regardless of size, God has a particular display of Himself, a particular manifestation of Lordship, and a particular manifestation of a Name. Although the Name in question has a universal manifestation, It concentrates on something particular in such a way that we think It is exclusive to that thing. Therefore, it is surely necessary for one who recognizes Almighty God by one of His Names, Titles, or aspects of His Lordship not to deny His other Titles, Acts, and aspects of Lordship. If we do not move from the manifestation of one Name to the other Names, we are at a loss. For example, if we do not see the All-Knowing where we see the works of the All-Powerful and the Creator, we may fall into heedlessness and misguidance by regarding nature as self-originated.

Just as the title of just ruler belonging to the sovereign in the parable dominates in the department of justice and the other titles are subordinate, in each level of creatures and in each heaven, a Divine Title dominates and the others are subordinate to It. For example, in whichever heaven Prophet Muhammad met Prophet Jesus, upon them be peace and blessings, during his Ascension, who was distinguished with the manifestation of the Divine Name the All-Powerful, Almighty God is in constant manifestation in that heaven, primarily with that very Name. Again, in the sphere of the heaven which is the abode of Prophet Moses, God's Title the All-Speaking, with Which He distinguished Moses, upon him be peace, is predominant.

Finally, since Prophet Muhammad, upon him be peace and blessings, was honored with the manifestation of God's Greatest Name and of all His other Names as well as being given a universal Prophethood, he must be connected with all of His Lordship's spheres. Therefore, the Ascension's reality required Prophet Muhammad, upon him be peace and blessings, to meet with the Prophets whose seats are in those spheres, and pass through all of those levels.

- **The Divine Power has made everything movable and condemned nothing to immobility or inertia. Thus, the Divine Mercy did not bind, for example, the sun up in inertia, which is the brother of death and the cousin of non-existence. Therefore, the sun travels freely in obedience to the Divine law, on condition that it does not violate the freedom of others.**[73]

The Qur'an declares: "*And the sun runs the course appointed for it for a term to its resting-place for the stability of it(s system).*"[74] As the word 'moves' points to a style, the phrase 'the course appointed for it for a term to its resting place for the stability of it(s system)' demonstrates a reality. The sun travels and floats in the ocean of the heavens comprising ether and defined as a stretched and tightened wave in a Prophetic Tradition. Since the origin of the force of gravity is movement, the sun moves and quivers in its orbit. Through this vibration, which is the wheel of its movement, its satellites are attracted to it and preserved from falling and scattering. When a tree is shaken, its fruits fall. But when the sun shakes, its fruits—its satellites—are preserved from falling.

Eighty-four years after Bediüzzaman Said Nursi wrote this based on the Qur'anic verse above, solar astronomers have been able to observe

---

[73] *The Reasonings*, "The First Part", p. 73.
[74] *Sura Ya-Sin*, 36:38.

that[75] the sun shakes and continually rings like a well-hit gong. These vibrations of the sun reveal vital information about the sun's deep interior, its hidden layers, information which affects calculations of the age of the universe. Also, knowing exactly how the sun spins internally is important in testing Einstein's theory of general relativity. Like so many other significant findings in astronomy, this discovery about the sun was totally unexpected. Having discovered the quivering and ringing sun, some astronomers have commented that it is as if the sun were a symphony orchestra, with all the instruments being played simultaneously. All the vibrations combine at times to produce a net oscillation on the solar surface that is thousands of times stronger than any individual vibration.

- **The Divine Power, Which brings things into existence, does not leave them unattended and to their own devices. It brings them up or raises them under the supervision of the Divine Wisdom and has them maintained by the Divine Mercy and Provision or Providence.**[76]

This reality is pointed to in the Qur'anic verses: *"Glorify the Name of your Lord, the Most High, Who creates and fashions, and Who determines (a particular life, nature, and goal for each creature), and guides (it towards the fulfillment of this goal)."*[77]

- **The body is dependent on the spirit, and subsists and is animated through it; a word depends on its meaning, and is illuminated by it; form is based on substance, and acquires value through it. Now this visible, material world is like a body, a word, and a form, and it depends on the Divine Names that are behind the veil of the Unseen; it is from the Divine Names that it receives life and beauty. All of the instances of physical beauty originate in the immaterial beauties of the meanings and truths on which they are based. Their truths are illuminated and fed by the Divine Names and are, in a sense, their shadows.**[78]

This means that all of the different sorts of beauty in the universe are the manifestations, signs, and marks of a faultless, transcendent Beauty,

---

[75] Bartusiac, M. (1994), 'Sounds of the Sun', *American Scientist,* January-February, pp. 61-68.
[76] *İşaratü'l-İ'caz, "Suratu'l-Baqara, verse 20".*
[77] *Suratu'l-A'la,* 87:1–3.
[78] *The Rays,* "The Fourth Ray", pp. 88–90.

Which is manifested from beyond the veil of the Unseen through the Divine Names. However, the All-Pure and Holy Essence of the Necessarily Existent Being resembles absolutely nothing at all, and His Attributes are infinitely superior to the attributes of contingent beings. Consequently, His sacred Beauty does not resemble the beauty of creatures or contingent beings, but is infinitely more exalted. Certainly, an everlasting Beauty—a single manifestation of Which is a vast Paradise, together with all its exquisiteness and one hour's vision of Which makes the people of Paradise oblivious to where they are—can neither be finite nor have any like, equal, or peer. Clearly, everything has a beauty particular to itself and in accordance with its nature, and beauty has thousands of varieties, like the differences among species of beings. For example, the beauty perceived by the eye is not the same as the beauty perceived by the ear; an abstract beauty experienced by the mind is different from the beauty of the food tasted by the tongue. Similarly, the beauties perceived and appreciated by the faculties such as the heart, the spirit, and other internal and external senses are all different. For instance, the beauties of belief, truth, light, flowers, spirit, forms, affection, justice, and compassion all differ from each other. In the same way that the beauties of the infinitely Beautiful Names of the All-Gracious One of Majesty are different from one another, the beauties shared by beings also differ.

If you would like to observe one manifestation of the beauties of the All-Gracious and Beautiful One's Names in the mirrors of beings, look with the eye of your imagination so encompassing that will enable you to see the face of the earth as though it were a small garden, and be aware that terms such as mercy, compassion, wisdom, and justice refer to the Acts, the Names, the Attributes, and the Essential Character or Qualities of God Almighty.

Look at the sustenance of all living creatures, including humanity in particular, which arrives regularly from behind the veil of the Unseen, and see the all-gracious and beautiful countenance of Divine Mercy.

Then look and see how miraculously all infants are provided for, fed as they are by the sources of milk which hang over their heads in the breasts of their mothers, as delightful as the water of *Kawthar* (the heavenly fountain), and see the captivating countenance of the Divine Lordship's Compassion.

Then look and see the matchless, gracious countenance of Divine Wisdom, Which has made the entire universe into a mighty book of wisdom, every letter of which contains a hundred words, every word of which contains a hundred lines, every line of which contains a thousand chapters, and every chapter of which contains thousands of miniature books.

Then see the majestic beauty of a Justice Which holds the whole universe together with all its beings in exact balance, maintaining the equilibrium of all the heavenly bodies, whether large or small, providing symmetry and proportion—the most important elements of beauty. See how that Justice causes everything to be in its optimum state and gives the right to life to living beings, ensuring that their rights are preserved and their aggressors foiled and punished.

Then look at the countless different foods prepared by Mercy for the guests at the table of the earth of the All-Merciful and All-Compassionate One, Who is absolutely Munificent; consider their varied tempting aromas and dazzling colors, and their different delicious tastes, as well as the organs and members of all living creatures which facilitate their pleasure and enjoyment. Look at these and see the extraordinarily pleasant countenance and sweet beauty of the Bestowal and Munificence of Lordship.

As these examples show, each of the Divine Names has such a sacred beauty particular to It that a single manifestation of It makes the vast world and the species of beings that comprise innumerable members beautiful. You see the manifestation of the beauty of a Name in a single flower; yet, spring too is a flower, and Paradise is a flower that is yet to be seen. If you can visualize the whole of spring and see Paradise through the eye of belief, then look and understand how majestic that perpetual Beauty is. If you respond to that Beauty with the beauty of belief and the graciousness of worship, you yourself will become a most beautiful creature. But if you respond to it with the infinite ugliness of misguidance and rebellion, not only will you become one of the ugliest creatures on earth, but you will in effect become the object of hatred of all beautiful creatures.

- **The two parts of the affirmation of belief—I bear witness that there is no deity but God, and I bear witness that Muhammad is His servant and Messenger—attest to each other's truth. The first**

is the a priori argument for the second, and the second is the a posteriori argument for the first.[79]

The safest and the truest of the ways that lead to knowledge of God, which is the "Ka'ba" of perfections, is the soundest and most radiant one which was built by the holy resident of Madinatu'l-Munawwarah, upon him be peace and blessings. That resident, Prophet Muhammad, upon him be peace and blessings, is the spirit of right guidance, his heart is the lamp that illuminates the unseen worlds. His truthful tongue, which is the translator of his heart, is the most articulate and truest of the proofs of the Maker's existence and Oneness. His being and his words are both a light-diffusing proof. Prophet Muhammad, upon him be peace and blessings, is the most decisive and undeniable proof of the Maker, of the institution or mission of Prophethood, of the Resurrection and the afterlife, and of the truth.

- **Everything has two aspects: its visible form, which resembles a garment made specifically for the functions and purposes assigned to it, and its immaterial aspect, which comprises all forms it assumes during its life.**[80]

The second aspect is like a circle formed by something with light attached to one end spinning around itself at high speed. An item's immaterial aspect is, in one respect, its life-history determined by the Divine Destiny, which we call "fate" or the "destiny of things." Both aspects contain wise purposes for the item's existence and life. The material aspect requires Power, while Destiny determines its shape and growth. In other words, Destiny draws outlines or plans according to the purposes assigned to it by the Divine Wisdom, and the Divine Power builds it accordingly.

- **The perfect order and the meaningful arrangement things display and their stages of life prove the Divine Destiny or Determining.**[81]

The seeds and roots left by the last autumn, as well as the seeds and roots that will be left to future springs after this spring has ended—they all have life, just like spring, and are subject to the laws of life. In just the same way, all the branches and twigs of the tree of the universe each has a past and a future. They have a chain of existence that consists of their past and future states and stages. The various, multiple, perfectly ordered existences and states of each species and each member of each species,

---

[79] *The Reasonings*, "The Third Part", p. 120; *Gleams of Truth*, p. 5.
[80] *Al-Mathnawi al-Nuri*, "The Third Treatise", p. 48–49.
[81] *The Words*, "The Tenth Word", pp. 123–124.

which are contained in Divine Knowledge, form a chain of existences pertaining to or recorded in that Knowledge. All the states and stages of their material life occur according to the measures of the Divine Destiny or Determining in the Divine Knowledge.

- **The Manifest Record (**Imam Mubin—Lawhun Mahfuz**), which relates more to the World of the Unseen than to the visible, material world, is a book of Divine Knowledge, Commands, and Destiny that contains the origins, roots, and seeds of things, rather than their flourishing forms in their visible existence. While the Manifest Book (***Kitab Mubin***) relates more to the visible, material world than to the World of the Unseen, and more to the present than to the past and future. It expresses Divine Power and Will rather than Divine Knowledge and Command.**[82]

The Manifest Record and the Manifest Book point to the Divine Knowledge and Destiny or Determining and to the Divine Will and Power, respectively. The Manifest Record relates more to the World of the Unseen than to the visible and to the past and future than to the present. It is a book of Divine Knowledge, Commands and Destiny that contains the origins, roots, and seeds of things, rather than their flourishing forms in their visible existence.

By growing into their full bodies with perfect order and art, the origins, sources, and roots of things show that they are arranged according to a book of the principles contained in the Divine Knowledge. Likewise, the seeds, results, and fruits of things, which contain the indexes and programs of beings that will come into existence, demonstrate that each is a miniature register of the Divine Commands. For example, it can be said that a seed is the miniature embodiment of the program and index according to which a tree may be formed, and of the Divine principles or commands which determine this program and index. In short, the Manifest Record is an index and program of the tree of creation as a whole, which spreads its branches through the past and future and the World of the Unseen. In this sense, it is a book of Divine Knowledge and Destiny, or a register of its principles. Through the dictates of the Manifest Record, that is, through the decrees and instructions of the Divine Destiny, Divine Power uses atoms to create or manifest the chain of beings, each link of which is His sign, on the

---

[82] *The Words*, "The Thirtieth Word", pp. 565–566.

metaphorical or "ideal" page of time, which is called the Tablet of Effacement and Confirmation. Thus, atoms are set to move so that beings may be
transferred from the World of the Unseen to the material, visible world,
from (the Realm of) Knowledge to the (Realm of) Power.

The Manifest Book relates more to the visible, material world than to
the World of the Unseen, and more to the present than to the past and
future. It expresses Divine Power and Will rather than Divine Knowledge
and Command. Everything is specifically formed and given an appointed
measure and particular shape by the Divine Power according to the principles established by the Divine Destiny.

Curiously, the people of neglect, misguidance, and corrupt philosophy
name the Manifest Record "nature," thus making it completely meaningless.

- **A seed is like the page upon which the life-history of the future
  tree is inscribed, and the fruit growing on the tree is a miniature
  of the whole tree with its seed being the record of the whole life-
  history of the tree. This proves both the Divine Destiny and the
  afterlife.**[83]

A fruit is connected with all members of its species as well as the
whole earth. Therefore, by virtue of the greatness of its art and meaning,
the art of one fruit is as great as that of the earth. Thus the One Who creates a fruit with all of its art and meaning can create and govern the earth.

- **Destiny and human free will, which mark the final limits of belief
  and being a Muslim, are related to believers' inner experiences
  and spiritual states; they are not of the kind of theoretical matters to be discussed scientifically.**[84]

That is, believers attribute everything (and every act in the universe)
to God, even their actions and selves. However, in order that they should
not consider themselves to be free of responsibility and sins, human free
will confronts them and says: "You are responsible and under obligation,
therefore you are accountable for your actions." Then, so that they should
not feel proud of their good deeds, attainments, and personal perfections,
Divine Destiny stands before them and warns: "Know your limits, it is not
you who does these." Thus, marking the final limits of belief and being a
Muslim, Divine Destiny and human free will have been included among

---

[83] *Al-Mathnawi al-Nuri*, "The First and Third Treatises", pp. 12, 48.
[84] *The Words*, "The Twenty-second Word", p. 482.

the articles of belief to save the human carnal soul from conceit and unaccountability, respectively. They are not scientific matters which will provide grounds for obdurate evil-commanding carnal souls to attribute their evils to Destiny and clean themselves of their responsibility, and to become proud of the achievements bestowed on them.

- **God destines and decrees, executes His decrees and spares (forgives and withdraws His decree's execution).**[85]

In short, God's decree sometimes yields to His sparing. That is, something decreed is exempted from execution or a universal law that is the fate of a species or group is not enacted for some purpose or for a particular member. For example, a helpless infant survives a calamity that caused great death and destruction.

God has, in one respect, two or three main records or books: the Manifest Record or the Supreme Preserved Tablet (corresponding to Destiny or Divine Knowledge), the Manifest Book (corresponding to the manifest existence), and the Tablet of Effacement and Confirmation (corresponding to the reality of time). The Supreme Preserved Tablet never changes. However, *"He may change what He records in the Manifest Book: God effaces whatever He wills and confirms whatever He wills..."*[86]

Although we may not fully understand the reality of this effacement and confirmation, we frequently witness it in our lives. For example, one day we leave home with the intention of going to a place where sins are freely committed. However, out of His mercy and favor, God arranges for us to meet some good friends who persuade us to go to a good place. Likewise, we commit sins too freely and therefore are subject to misfortune. But instead of dealing with us by His justice, God, out of His grace, treats us with utmost grace and pardons us, thereby saving us from misfortune.

Divine grace or sparing exists so that we will not despair of being forgiven, so that we may turn to Him despite our sins. This is made explicit in the following verses: *"Whatever misfortune befalls you, is for what your own hands have earned, and for many (of them) He grants forgiveness."* [87] *"If God were to punish people for their wrongdoing, He would*

---

[85] *Al-Mathnawi al-Nuri*, "The Ninth Treatise", pp. 286–287.
[86] *Suratu'l-Ra'd*, 13:39.
[87] *Suratush-Shura*, 42:30.

not leave on the earth a single living creature; but He reprieves them to an appointed term."[88]

Many historical peoples, such as those of the 'Ad, the Thamud, and Pharaoh, deserved to perish because of their dissolute lifestyles, injustices, and atrocities. Thus, God eradicated them. However, Prophet Jonah's people turned to God with the utmost sincerity and deep repentance, and reformed themselves morally after they saw signs of impending destruction. As a result, God spared them the penalty of disgrace in the life of this world, and gave them comfort for a while: "*If only there had been a community that believed (just when God's decree of punishment was issued) and profited by their belief—there was none except the people of Jonah. When they came to believe We withdrew from them the punishment of disgrace in the life of this world, and We allowed them to enjoy life for a term.*"[89] Emphasizing this point, God's Messenger said: "Fear does not prevent misfortunes, but prayer and charity prevent them."[90]

Therefore, believers should never cease praying and giving charity. When they feel misfortune coming, they should immediately turn to God in prayer, repent, give charity, or perform some service for Islam.

- **A person's complaining about his misfortunes means criticism of the Divine Destiny and Decree, while his thanking God is submission or resignation to the Divine Judgment. No one has a right to complain about God for what befalls him.**[91]

Life is like capital; indeed, it is our greatest capital. If it yields no fruits, it is wasted. And if it passes in ease and heedlessness, it is short, bringing almost no profit. Through misfortune life is refined, develops and gains strength. Misfortune may transform each of the minutes of life into one hour's worship. For worship is of two sorts. One is that which is performed, the other is the sort which is not actually performed, but is suffered and thus leads to sincere supplication. Illnesses and disasters are examples of this sort.

We have not come to this world to live in ease and pleasure. Rather, possessing vast capital, we have come here to work for an eternal life by doing the required trade. Were it not for illness or other kinds of misfor-

[88] *Suratu'n-Nahl*, 16:61.
[89] *Sura Yunus*, 10:98.
[90] Muttaqi al-Hindi, *Kanzu'l-'Ummal*, hadith No. 3123.
[91] *The Gleams*, "The Twenty-fifth Gleam", p. 303.

tune, good health and ease would cause heedlessness, presenting the world as pleasant and making us oblivious of the Hereafter. But misfortune gives us awareness, and says to our bodies: "You are not immortal, and have not been left to your own devices. You have a duty. Give up haughtiness; think of the One Who has created you; know that you will enter the grave, and make the necessary preparation!" If this world were eternal, and if on our way to eternity there were no death, and if the winds of separation and death did not blow, and if there were no "winters" of the spirit in the calamitous and stormy future, we would wish only pleasures. However, death is inevitable. Therefore, before this life abandons us, we must try to abandon it in our hearts. Misfortune or suffering reminds us of this reality, saying, "Your body is not composed of stone and iron; rather it has been composed of various materials that are subject to partition and dissolution. Give up conceit, be aware of your innate impotence, recognize your Master, know your duties, and learn why you came to the world!" Thus, misfortune is an advisor that never deceives; and it is an admonishing guide.

The All-Majestic Maker—in order to display the embroideries of His All-Beautiful Names and indeed make us more and more beautiful—causes us to undergo numerous, different states and situations so that our capacities may develop into active abilities and our faculties may be refined, developed, and sharpened.

The disappearance of suffering is a pleasure, and the cessation of pleasure gives pain. Suffering or misfortune teaches us the delight and worth of health and other favors we enjoy, which lead us to thankfulness. It causes us to taste Divine favors or blessings more deeply, and increases them.

Like soap, misfortune or suffering washes away the dirt of sins and cleanses us. It is established in an authenticated *hadith* that illnesses are expiation for sins. God's Messenger, upon him be peace and blessings, says, "As ripe fruits fall from the tree when it is shaken, so the sins of a believer fall away with the shaking during illness."[92] Another *hadith* says: "A pious, God-revering believer who, due to illness, cannot do the invocations he does normally and regularly, receives an equal reward."[93] Illness substitutes for the supererogatory Prayers of the ill person who does

---

[92] *al-Bukhari*, "Marda'" 1, 2, 13; *Muslim*, "Birr" 14.
[93] *Abu Dawud*, "Jana'iz" 1; Ahmad ibn Hanbal, *al-Musnad*, 4:418.

their obligatory worship as much as possible, and shows patience in submissive reliance on God.

Misfortune or suffering induces respect and compassion, which are important and good for human social life. This saves people from conceited feelings of self-sufficiency, which drives them to unfriendliness and unkindness. For according to the reality stated in, *"No indeed, but the human is unruly and rebels, in that he sees himself as self-sufficient,"*[94] a carnal, evil-commanded soul which feels self-sufficient due to good health and well-being does not regard the many causes which warrant brotherhood and sisterhood. And they do not feel compassion towards the misfortune-stricken or ill, who should be shown kindness and pity. Yet, whenever they are struck with misfortune, they are aware of their own innate impotence and neediness, and feel respect towards their sisters and brothers who are worthy of it.

Certainly, there is significant reward for believers who help the suffering or unfortunate. Asking after the health of those who are ill and visiting them—provided it does not tax them—is a *sunnah* act, an act highly recommended by our Prophet, upon him be peace and blessings.[95] It is also expiation for sins. There is a *hadith* which says, "Receive the prayers of the ill, for their prayers are acceptable."[96]

If we have a father, mother, or relatives, their most pleasurable compassion towards us, which we may have long forgotten, will be awakened due to our suffering, and we will again see their kind looks which we received in childhood. In addition, the friends around us who have remained veiled and hidden will look again towards us with love through the attraction of misfortune. While our isolation and exile, together with our suffering, arouse sympathy in the hardest hearts and attract kindness and compassion to us, they will also attract the All-Compassionate Creator's compassion towards us, which is certain to be a substitute for the sympathy and compassion of everything else.

In the illnesses of innocent children there are many instances of wisdom pertaining to their worldly life. For instance, their illnesses are like exercises and drills for their delicate bodies, and the inoculations and

---

[94] *Suratu'l'Alaq*, 96:6–7.
[95] *al-Bukhari*, "Marda'" 4, 5; *Muslim*, "Salam" 47.
[96] *Ibn Maja* "Jana'iz" 1; al-Bayhaqi, *Shu'ab al-Iman*, 6:541.

training of the Lord, so that they may be able to withstand the tumults and upheavals of the world in the future.

God never wills evil or misfortune for His servants. He always wills good for them and directs them to it. So, whatever good thing happens to a person, it is because God has willed it for him and directs his free will toward it. This means that since God has willed it, He has directed a person's free will toward this action, enabling him to do it, and creating it; therefore, any good that happens to a person is solely from God. A person himself becomes the source and doer of whatever evil befalls them by preferring evil and doing it despite God's orienting their free will toward good. So, whatever evil befalls a person is from himself. The Qur'an declares: *"(O human being!) Whatever good happens to you, it is from God; and whatever evil befalls you, it is from yourself."*[97]

Any misfortune or calamity befalling believers paves the way for two rewards, one given immediately, the other later. It also causes the sin which attracts the calamity to be forgiven.

- **Knowing something's nature is different from knowing that it exists. The existence of many things is obvious to us, even though we do not understand their nature. Also, existence is not restricted to the number of things known to us, so our ignorance of something does not indicate its non-existence.**[98]

Everyone feels that he or she has free will and perceives its existence. We also know and experience the existence of our consciousness, although we do not know its nature. Our free will and the Divine Destiny are the things whose existences we continually experience.

- **Human free will does not contradict Divine Destiny; rather, Destiny confirms its existence. For Divine Destiny is in some respects identical with Divine Knowledge, Which parallels our free will, in determining our actions. Thus, It confirms free will.**[99]

God has pre-knowledge of everything, including what or how we will act, and writes them down. However, we do not do something or act in some way because God has pre-knowledge of it. Divine Destiny is a kind of knowledge, and knowledge is dependent on the thing known. God

---

[97] *Suratu'n-Nisa'*, 4:79.
[98] *The Words*, "The Twenty-sixth Word", p. 484.
[99] *The Words*, "The Twenty-sixth Word", p. 484.

knows our acts beforehand and writes them down. So God's pre-knowledge of our acts and our acting in the way He knows confirms our free will and shows its reconcilability with Destiny.

- **There are not two kinds of Destiny—one for the cause and one for the effect. Destiny is one. In the view of Destiny, cause and effect cannot be separated. This means that a certain cause is destined to produce a certain effect.**[100]

For this reason, it cannot be argued that, for example, killing someone with a gun is acceptable because the victim was destined to die at that time and would have died even if he or she had not been shot. Such an argument is baseless, for the victim actually is destined to die as a result of being shot. The argument that he or she would have died even without being shot means that the victim died without a cause. If this were so, we could not explain how he or she died.

- **Past eternity (azal) is not, as people imagine, just the starting-point of time so that God may be contained by time and has a relation with the divisions of time. God is beyond time and what we call past eternity (azal) is like a mirror that reflects the past, present, and future all at once.**[101]

Excluding themselves from time's passage, people tend to imagine a limit for past time that extends through a certain chain of things. They call this past eternity (*azal*). Such a method of reasoning is neither right nor acceptable. The following subtle point may clarify this matter. Imagine that you are holding a mirror. Everything reflected on the right represents the past, while everything reflected on the left represents the future. The mirror can reflect only one direction, since it cannot show both sides simultaneously while you are holding it. For it to do so, you would have to rise so high above your original position that just as left and right would become one in your mirror, there would no longer be any difference between first and last, beginning or end.

In some respects, Divine Destiny is identical with Divine Knowledge. It is described in a Prophetic Tradition as containing all times and events in a single point, where first and last, beginning and end, what has happened and what will happen are united into one. Neither we nor our

---

[100] *The Words*, "The Twenty-sixth Word", p. 485.
[101] *The Words*, "The Twenty-sixth Word", p. 485.

viewpoint and reasoning are excluded from It, so that we could imagine a final point for It in the past, and think of It like a mirror containing and reflecting only the space of the past. Therefore, there is no difference between God's pre-knowledge or pre-determination of something from His knowing or determining it at the present and in the future.

- **Although our free will cannot cause something to happen, Almighty God, the absolutely Wise One, uses it in the creation of our deeds. He in effect says: "My servant! Whichever way you wish to take with your will, I will take you there. Therefore, the responsibility is yours!"**[102]

For example, if a child riding on your shoulder asks you to take him up a high mountain, and you do so, he might catch a cold. How could he blame you for that cold, as he was the one who asked to go there? In fact, you might even punish him because of his choice. In a like manner, Almighty God, the Most Just of Judges, never coerces His servants into doing something, and so His Will considers our free will in our actions.

As human beings, we have a degree of free will. We must use it for our benefit by praying to God continuously. If we do so, we may enjoy the blessings of Paradise, a fruit of the chain of good deeds, and the attainment of eternal happiness. In addition to praying, we must always seek God's forgiveness so that we may refrain from evil and be saved from Hell's torments, a fruit of the accursed chain of evil deeds. Prayer and trusting God greatly strengthen our inclination to do good, and repentance and seeking God's forgiveness defeat our inclination to evil by breaking its transgressions.

- **The lack of firmness in the actions and works of human beings, and the perfection in the things that have no will-power and are directly willed and created by God, proves human free will and rejects fatalism.**[103]

It is worth observing that because of human partial will-power, a city built by human effort and intelligence is inferior to a beehive or a pomegranate and a pomegranate blossom in order and arrangement; the former can never be on a par with the latter. Human beings have been given partial will-power, and it is because of this that there are

---

[102] *The Words*, "The Twenty-sixth Word", p. 487.
[103] *Gleams of Truth,* p. 100.

defects and faults in their actions and works. Whereas we see perfection in the things that have no will-power and are directly willed and created by God. This shows that human beings are not compelled to do something by the Creator. Will-power is the base of their accountability for the deeds they commit.

- **In the sight of the Divine Power, the provision of beings has the same value as its life. Provision is produced by the Power, apportioned by the Destiny, and nurtured by the Grace or Favor. As life is the sure, certain outcome of particular circumstances and events, it is witnessed or visible in its totality. But provision is neither sure nor certain in the sight of living beings, for it is scattered and obtained over a certain time; it comes in uncertain degrees and leads people to contemplation and working to procure it.**[104]

It is as if the Divine Power works constantly to change and transform the world of death into that of life, and the dense into the transparent. Just as It scatters the gleams of life, even into the lowliest of substances, It also sows and stores up providence in everything. The dead atoms are set to move to meet with the light of life. Provision is sent to maintain life.

- **There are two sorts of sustenance. One is the sustenance that is absolutely essential to life. God has guaranteed this for every living being. The second sort is sustenance that is superfluous. God has not undertaken it.**[105]

The Qur'anic verses, *"Surely God—it is He Who is the All-Providing, Lord of all might, and the All-Forceful,"*[106] and *"No living creature is there moving on the earth but its provision depends on God,"*[107] declare that God the All-Providing provides the beings He creates with the required, lawful sustenance for survival. Unless people interfere with this sustenance by the misuse of their free will, their essential sustenance will find them. It remains in its place and says, "Come and search for me, take me!" However, through the abuse of our willpower, faculties, and neediness, inessential needs have become essential ones, and because of invented customs, we have become addicted to them. This sort of sustenance is not guaranteed by the Lord.

---

[104] *Gleams of Truth*, p. 62.
[105] *The Gleams*, "The Nineteenth Gleam", p. 199.
[106] *Suratu'dh-Dhariyat*, 51:58.
[107] *Sura Hud*, 11.6.

- **Lawful sustenance which God undertakes is not in direct proportion to power and will. It rather comes in proportion to one's need.**[108]

When utterly deprived of will and power in the womb before coming to the world, babies are given their provisions in such a way that they do not even need to move their mouths. Then when they come into the world, they still do not have power or will, but since they have some sort of capacity or potential senses, they need only to cry and move to fasten their mouths to the breast, and are provided through the fountains of the breasts with the perfect, the most nutritious, and easily digestible sustenance in the kindest and strangest fashion. As they grow in power and will, that fine, readily available sustenance starts to be gradually withdrawn from the infants. The fountains of the breasts dry up, and the child's sustenance comes from somewhere else. But since they still do not have enough will or power to obtain their sustenance, the All-Providing of Munificence sends their parents' care and compassion to their assistance. Whenever they feel they have enough power and will, then their sustenance is not sent to them in a readily available way.

In addition to the example of infants above, the weakest and simplest animals are the best fed; like fish and fruit worms. It is enough to compare fish with foxes, the new-born with wild beasts, and trees with animals, in order to understand that the procurement of fundamental, lawful food depends on neediness and impotence, rather than power, will, and skill.

- **Entrusting the accomplishment of a task to God without taking all necessary measures and making all necessary arrangements is laziness. Leaving the realization of the desired outcome to God after having done all that can be done is to put trust in Him. Contentment with one's lot or the result after having exerted one's greatest efforts is praiseworthy contentment, and encourages further effort, reinvigorating one's energy and industry. However, contentment with what one already has is a deficiency and means lacking in necessary endeavor or efforts.**[109]

- **Willing and committing evil deeds is evil, whereas creating them is not. Whatever God creates is good.**[110]

---

[108] *The Words*, "The Fifth Word", p. 30; *The Gleams*, "The Nineteenth Gleam", p. 199.
[109] *Gleams of Truth*, p. 15.
[110] *The Words*, "The Twenty-sixth Word", p. 482.

It is we ourselves who wish, cause, and commit evils, and therefore we are responsible for them. Just as some substances liable to decomposition go bad and putrefy in the pure, bright light of the sun—and this is because of their nature or disposition—, so our carnal soul wishes sins and evils, either through its nature and disposition, or through choice, and we commit them. As for their creation, it is good on account of many of its results, which are good. Although we derive great benefit from rain, those who have been harmed by it due to their faults cannot deny that rain contains God's grace for all people. Although there may be some evil in creating our evil deeds, creation is by its very nature absolutely good, and contains many instances of good (for the universe's general operation, life, and for the person who wills and commits that evil). **To abandon greater good for a minor evil becomes a greater evil.** Ugliness in our human acts lies in our will and potential, not in God's creating it.

- **As Divine Destiny is absolutely free of evil and ugliness in relation to results, it also is exempt from injustice on account of causes.**[111]

Divine Destiny always considers the primary cause, not the apparent secondary cause, and always does justice. On the other hand, we judge according to apparent causes and draw wrong conclusions. For example, a court may imprison an innocent person for theft. However, Divine Destiny actually passes this judgment because of that person's real crime, such as murder, that has remained unknown. So while the court unjustly jailed this person for a crime that he or she did not commit, Divine Destiny justly punished that person for his or her secret crime.

From this example, we see that Divine Destiny and creation are just, while we are liable to do injustice. Divine Destiny and Creation are absolutely free of evil and ugliness at the beginning and end of all events, and on account of cause and results.

- **As sending Prophets has caused many, or even most people, to become unbelievers because of Satan's seduction, creating evil things and acts is still good, and raising Prophets is a mercy for humanity.**[112]

---

[111] *The Words*, "The Twenty-sixth Word", p. 482–483.
[112] *The Letters*, "The Twelfth Letter", 72.

If someone is given a capital to do business and earn his life but he loses it in gambling, no one can claim that it is giving him the capital which is responsible for his misery.

Also, as quality is always far more important than quantity, we should consider qualitative values in making our judgment. To cite an example: 100 date-stones are worth only 100 cents until they are planted and grow into palm trees. But if only 20 grow into trees and the remaining 80 rot because of over-watering, how can we say it is an evil to plant and water them? Everyone would agree that it is wholly good to have 20 trees at the expense of 80 date-stones, since 20 trees will give 20,000 date-stones every year. Again, 100 peacock eggs are worth maybe 500 cents. But if she sits on the eggs and only 20 hatch, who can say it is an evil that 80 eggs were spoiled in return for 20 peacocks? On the contrary, it is wholly good to have 20 peacocks at the expense of 80 eggs, because the 20 peacocks will be worth far more than the eggs and will lay more eggs.

And so it is with humanity. Our being raised up by Prophets, as well as our fighting against Satan and our carnal soul, result in the loss of unbelievers and hypocrites (more in number but poorer in quality) in exchange for hundreds of thousands of Prophets, millions of saints, and billions of people of wisdom and sincerity—the suns, moons, and stars of the human world.

- **There are many instances of wisdom and good in that God allows innocent people like children and animals to suffer some misfortune and suffering.**[113]

No injustice can be attributed to God the All-Just and the All-Merciful, for He absolutely owns all of creation and so can do with it as He wills. Consider this analogy: A skillful designer pays you to serve as a model to display his artistry. He fashions the jeweled garment he has made you wear as he wills, and tells you to sit and stand. How can you say: "You cause me trouble by making me sit and stand. Also, you have damaged this cloth that makes me look beautiful." Such objections would be sheer impertinence.

God, the Majestic Creator, dresses us in an artistically fashioned garment (e.g., the body, jeweled with eyes, ears, a nose, and a tongue, etc.). To show His All-Beautiful Names' works, He makes us ill, hungry, and thirsty, and afflicts us with misfortune. He exposes us to various conditions so that we may develop intellectually and spiritually, be refined and

---

[113] *The Letters*, "The Twelfth Letter", 72–73.

perfected, and gain strength and resistance against ills. Thus, His All-Beautiful Names may be manifested. Given this, our objection will cause many instances of wisdom to silence us.

Monotony and inertia are a kind of non-existence, while activity and alteration mature life through suffering and misfortune. Life grows stronger and purer and develops fully through the Divine All-Beautiful Names' operation. Ultimately, life becomes the pen with which we determine and write our own fate. Thus we deserve their reward in the afterlife.

- **The purposes for the existence of things and ever-constant activity in creation relates not only to the creatures themselves but to God Almighty as well.**[114]

The incessant, amazing activity in the universe is caused by the Divine Names and done for three comprehensive purposes or results.

Firstly, every creature is active because it yearns for and takes pleasure in activity. It can even be said that every activity contains a kind of pleasure; moreover, activity itself is some sort of pleasure. Pleasure is turned toward perfection and is a kind of perfection. Since activity is turned toward perfection, and indicates pleasure and beauty, and since the Necessarily Existent Being, the Perfect One of Majesty, has all perfection in His Being, Attributes, Names, and Acts in a manner fitting to His Necessary Existence and Holiness, and in accordance with His essential independence and absolute Perfection and uniqueness, He has infinite sacred affection and love. Such affection and love will cause an infinite sacred enthusiasm, the origin of an infinite, sacred joy that is the source of infinite sacred pleasure. Due to this pleasure as well as His Compassion, the All-Merciful and All-Compassion-ate has infinite sacred gladness and pride when His creatures' realize their full potential and attain their relative perfection through their deeds by His Power. This sacred gladness and pride require creation's incessant, infinite whirl that, in turn, demands incessant change, renewal, and transformation. This incessant activity also calls for decay, death, and separation.

Secondly, God's All-Beautiful Names manifest themselves in countless ways and kinds. This causes multiplicity in creation and causes the Book of the Universe, with all its "sentences, words, and letters" to be renewed constantly. Each part of this Book, which is the manifestation of the

---

[114] *The Letters*, "The Eighteenth Letter", pp. 112–113; "The Twenty-fourth Letter", pp. 307–308.

Divine Names, is a sign of the Sacred Divine Essence so that conscious living beings can know Him; each creature is a Divine missive for conscious beings to study.

Thirdly, through their lives and activities, creatures present to God Almighty's view His Art's perfection, His Names' embellishments, His Wisdom's jewels, and His Compassion's gifts; they are mirrors reflecting His Grace, Beauty and Perfection. The Divine Power's actions, and the incessant flux of things they cause, are so meaningful that the All-Wise Maker causes all beings to speak through that flux. It is as if all active creatures in the heavens and on the earth, along with all their actions, are words of speech, and as if each movement is an act of speech. In other words, all creatures glorify God and proclaim His perfections through their movements, including their birth and death.

- **Everything has an aspect of true beauty, and is either beautiful in itself (beautiful by itself) or beautiful on account of its results (beautiful through others).**[115]

The Qur'an declares: *"(He) Who makes excellent everything that He creates."*[116] Even the things that appear to be the ugliest included, everything has an aspect of true beauty; there are the most radiant instances of beauty and order beneath that apparently ugly veil.

For example, beneath the veil of spring's stormy rains and muddy soil are smiles of innumerable beautiful flowers and well-ordered plants. Behind the veils of fall's harsh destruction and mournful separations are amiable small animals (friends of delicate, shy flowers) being discharged from their duties and preserved from winter's blows and torments. These are instances of Divine Majesty. Under the veil of winter, the way is prepared for a new and beautiful spring. Beneath the veil of storms, earthquakes, plagues, and similar events, are numerous hidden "immaterial flowers" that unfold. Seeds of many potentialities that have remained undeveloped sprout and flourish due to such apparently ugly events. It is as if upheavals, revolutions, and general changes function as "immaterial" rain.

- **Almighty God orders a thing and it becomes good. He prohibits a thing and it becomes bad.**[117]

---

[115] *The Words,* "The Eighteenth Word", pp. 242–243.
[116] *Suratu's-Sajda,* 32:7.
[117] *The Words,* "The Twenty-first Word", p. 290.

So, whether a thing is good or bad depends on the Divine command and prohibition. Therefore, a thing is good or bad for people according to whether they have done something ordered or prohibited or whether they have done it in accordance with the rules established by the Shari'ah. In addition, a thing is religiously good or bad not in respect to its apparent correctness and its apparent features, but with respect to the Hereafter.

- **Major cases and crimes are tried and judged in large centers, while minor ones are decided in small centers.**[118]

This is why Muslims, rather than unbelievers, are afflicted with disasters or heavenly blows in the world. Most of the punishment destined for unbelievers is postponed to the Last, Supreme Judgment, and that believers are partly punished in this world. Besides, those who abandon an abrogated and corrupted religion do not incur Divine wrath in the world to the extent of those who betray a true and eternal religion that will never be abrogated. These two points explain why Muslims suffer more than unbelievers in the world.

- **A general disaster coming as a result of the majority's wrongdoing, encompasses almost all people in the area without distinguishing between the guilty and the innocent.**[119]

A general disaster resulting from the majority's wrongdoing encompasses almost all people in the area because most of the people must have participated in the minority's sinful actions by giving them direct or indirect support or without trying to prevent them.

A general disaster does not usually distinguish the guilty from the innocent. The Qur'an declares: *"Beware of a trial that will surely not smite exclusively those among you who are engaged in wrongdoing."*[120] This means that this world is a field of trial and testing, a place of responsibility and struggle. Testing and responsibility require a veiling of the truth in certain matters so that the good and the evil may be distinguished from each other, with the result that while some rise to the highest rank, others fall to the lowest level. If the innocent were not touched by such disasters, everyone would have to submit in the same way. This would mean the door of testing and the spiritual progress through struggle being closed, and rendering our responsibility and testing meaningless.

---

[118] *The Words*, "The Fourteenth Word", p. 186.
[119] *The Words*, "The Fourteenth Word", p. 186–187.
[120] *Suratu'l-Anfal*, 8:25.

- **There is great mercy for the wronged behind the wrath and anger in a general disaster.**[121]

If Divine Wisdom requires that the wronged and wrong-doer suffer through the same disaster, what is the share of the former in Divine Mercy and Justice? For the wronged person, there is a kind of mercy behind the wrath and anger shown in the disaster. Just as an innocent person's lost property becomes like alms he gives to the poor and thereby gains permanence, his death in the disaster may be regarded as a kind of martyrdom through which he earns an eternal life of happiness. Thus, such people gain a great and perpetual profit from a relatively small and temporary difficulty and torment.

- **If there is greater good in something, it is not abandoned because of the lesser evil in it.**[122]

The world is the arena where opposites are mixed with each other. Even though there may be some apparent evil in certain events or things, if there is greater good in something, it is not abandoned because the lesser evil in it. If it is, then a greater evil occurs. Leaving many instances of good undone to avoid one evil is extremely ugly, contrary to wisdom and reality, and a fault.

- **If the strong and truthful defenders of belief and Islam are few or utterly defeated in a place, and the enemies of Islam have established an effective center of activity against Islam and its defenders, this may cause Divine wrath and punishment to descend there.**[123]

- **A reward or wage sometimes comes in advance, before one actually deserves.**

God knows beforehand how we will act and what we will do in the future. He also knows our desires and aspirations. Therefore, in order to encourage us, He may give the reward of some of our future deeds in advance before doing them. Bediüzzaman writes: "As the Creator knew before creating the Prophet that he would desire eternal happiness for humanity and all creation, and to be favored with the Divine Names' man-

---

[121] *The Words*, "The Fourteenth Word", p. 187.
[122] *The Words*, "The Fourteenth Word", p. 187.
[123] *The Words*, "The Fourteenth Word", p. 190.

ifestations, we may say that God answered his future prayers by creating the universe (where the eternal happiness would be gained)."[124]

- **The reason why God's Messenger, upon him be peace and blessings, asked his community to love his near relatives, including his household in particular ('Ali, Fatima, Hasan and Husayn—the latter two being his grandsons from Fatima and 'Ali) was because of the great service they and their descendants would provide for Islam until Judgment Day.**[125]

God declares in the Qur'an: "*Surely the noblest, most honorable of you in God's sight is the one best in piety, righteousness, and reverence for God.*"[126] So, superiority in Islam is by *taqwa* (piety and righteousness). However, God also orders His Messenger: "*Say: 'I ask of you no wage for it (for conveying God's Religion to you), but (I ask of you for) love for my near relatives.'*"[127] When considered together, these two verses explain that the extraordinary compassion which the noblest Messenger, upon him be peace and blessings, showed towards his household, particularly towards his daughter Fatima and grandsons Hasan and Husayn, was not because of a family relationship; his affection for them was rather because they would act as the origin, example, and index of an exceptionally important community that would carry on the religious duties which had been established through Prophethood.

- **The Shi'a consist of two groups: one are the Shi'a of sainthood, while the other are the Shi'a of Caliphate or politics. Although the second group are wrong in their stance, one which originates from their political, purposeful partisanship, the first group do not have any deliberate political attitude, and are sincere in their love of 'Ali and his descendants.**[128]

The Shi'a of politics or Caliphate, those who claim that 'Ali, may God be pleased with him, was uniquely entitled to the Caliphate after the Prophet, upon him be peace and blessings, and that the Prophet's Companions usurped his right, are totally wrong in their attitude. However, The Shi'a of sainthood, those Sunni saintly people who love 'Ali more than the other

---

[124] *The Letters*, "The Twenty-fourth Letter", p. 319.
[125] *The Gleams*, "The Fourth Gleam", pp. 34–35.
[126] *Suratu'l-Hujurat*, 49:13.
[127] *Suratu'sh-Shura*, 42:23.
[128] *The Gleams*, "The Fourth Gleam", p. 39.

Companions, including Abu Bakr and 'Umar, may God be pleased with them, and prefer him over them, can be excused because of two reasons. One is that they are people of love, and since 'Ali is regarded as the head of the ways of sainthood, they love him more. The second is that we should consider 'Ali, may God be pleased with him, from two perspectives. One concerns his personal perfections and rank, and the other concerns his representing the collective personality of the Prophet's Family. This collective personality manifests, in one way, the essential nature of the noblest Messenger, upon him be peace and blessings. This causes some to love 'Ali more, and prefer him over all the other Companions.

- **A less virtuous person may excel a more virtuous one in particular virtues.**[129]

When the personal excellences of Abu Bakr as-Siddiq and 'Umar al-Faruq, may God be pleased with them, and their accomplishments during their caliphates in carrying out the Islamic duties inherited from the Prophet, are weighed on the scales against the extraordinary personal excellences of 'Ali, may God be pleased with him, and his struggles for the Caliphate, which he was forced to undergo because of tragic events that were the result of certain distrust, the *Ahl al-Sunnah* perceive that Abu Bakr, or Umar, or 'Uthman Dhu'n-Nurayn weighed heavier, and so they perceive them as having a higher ranking.

Prophethood is such an elevated rank that when compared to sainthood, a minuscule manifestation of Prophethood is superior to a great manifestation of sainthood. From this perspective, the *Ahl al-Sunnah* have arrived at the conclusion that the success of Abu Bakr and 'Umar during their caliphates indicates that God gave them a greater share in the succession to the duties of Prophethood and the establishment and spread of Islam. Since the personal excellences of 'Ali, may God be pleased with him, did not transcend that greater share that came from succession to the most important duties of Prophethood, he acted as a *Shaykhu'l-Islam* (the greatest scholar and chief *mufti* of Islam) for Abu Bakr and 'Umar in the time of their caliphates, and he esteemed them. Let us make this truth clear through an example:

One of the three sons of a very rich man is given twenty coins of silver and four coins of gold from his father's inheritance, while another one is

---

[129] *The Words*, "The Twenty-seventh Word", p. 507; *The Gleams*, "The Fourth Gleam", pp. 41–42.

given five of silver and five of gold, and the third, three of silver and five of gold. Clearly, the last two receive less in quantity, but more in quality. That is, the extra one coin of gold given to the last two is more in value than the extra fifteen coins of silver the first one receives. As in this example, the little extra amount of the share of the *Shaykhayn*—Abu Bakr and 'Umar—in the gold of nearness to God which arises from succession to the duties of Prophethood and the establishment and spread of Islam, weighs heavier than the greater amount of 'Ali's share in the silver of nearness to God that comes from his perfections of sainthood and personal excellences. We should consider this point in comparison. But if they are compared with one another from the viewpoint of certain particular excellences such courage, knowledge, and sainthood, the results change.

- **The Battle of Camel, which occurred between 'Ali (on one side) and 'A'isha, Zubayr, and Talha (on the other), was a clash between absolute justice and relative justice. The war between 'Ali and Mu'awiya at Siffin was one between Caliphate and Sultanate. The struggle of Hasan and Husayn against the Umayyads was one of religion against nationalism or tribalism.[130]**

Imam 'Ali believed that it was his duty to make the absolute justice the rule, just as it had been during the time of Abu Bakr and 'Umar, while his opponents asserted that relative justice should prevail. They argued that prevailing conditions did not allow absolute justice to be enforced, because people's sincere beliefs and pure intentions had been muddied by the incomplete assimilation of new Muslims and the passage of time. Since both sides sought God's approval and acted for Islam's good, although 'Ali was more perfect in his opinions, all participants will enter Paradise, whether they killed or were killed. The Qur'an teaches us that there may be wars between Muslim believers even if they must be avoided, and these wars do not mean apostasy or leaving the sphere of Islam.[131]

Jurists who strive for the truth in those legal matters left open by the Qur'an and the Prophet will receive a double reward from God if the correct judgment is given. If an incorrect judgment is given, they will receive one reward and not be punished.

The war between 'Ali and Mu'awiya at Siffin (657) was one between Caliphate and Sultanate. Imam 'Ali defended purely religious command-

[130] *The Letters*, "The Fifteenth Letter", pp. 92–94.
[131] *Suratu'l-Hujurat*, 49: 9–10.

ments and Islamic truths against some principles of Sultanate and political expedience, preferring the world to come over the present life. Mu'awiya based his case on a dispensation from strict adherence to certain religious commandments so that he could reinforce Islamic social life through Sultanate.

The struggle of Hasan and Husayn against the Umayyads was one of religion against 'nationalism'. The Umayyads gave certain priority in administration to the bonds of kinship over those of Islam. This harmed the Muslim community in two ways: It annoyed and frightened the non-Arabs, and prevented serious, sincere thought about what was right and just. Racist rulers cannot practice justice, since they give priority to fellow nationals over co-religionists when dispensing rights and justice. Islam forbids this, as stated in a Tradition: "Islam forbids the racism of the Age of Ignorance and commands that there be no disparity between an (Abyssinian) black slave and a Qurayshi lord."[132] Thus, Husayn rightly fought the Umayyads to re-establish the religious bond, and consequently attained the rank of martyrdom.

• **The verse:** "Whoever slays a soul—unless it be for murder or spreading mischief in the land—will be as if he had slain humanity,"[133] **implying that no innocent person can be deprived of his or her right to life or sacrificed for the community's sake. This defines absolute justice. Relative justice means that the part can be sacrificed for the whole. It does not consider the individual's rights if these harm the community.**[134]

According to the absolute, pure justice, any right is a right in God's sight, and thus cannot be sacrificed for one considered greater. The right of an individual cannot be sacrificed for the supposed good of the community. Imam 'Ali, may God be pleased with him, wanted to continue establishing the Caliphate on absolute justice, while his opponents insisted on relative justice, saying that the other was no longer possible.

• **If 'Ali had become Caliph right after the Prophet's death, there probably would have arisen, as happened during his caliphate, a tendency in many persons and tribes to compete, and such com-**

[132] *Muslim*, "Imara", 53–54; *Abu Dawud*, "Adab" 111.
[133] *Suratu'l-Maeda*, 5:32.
[134] *The Letters*, "The Fifteenth Letter", pp. 92.

petition might have divided the believers at a time when they were more in need of agreement and unity than ever.[135]

The Holy Prophet's emigration to the other world was a shock for the young Muslim community. If at that time when the Companions were more in need of agreement and unity than ever 'Ali would have been elected as Caliph, this might have aroused, in some people, the feelings of competition—as happened during 'Ali's caliphate—and the Muslim community might have split into many factions. This would have meant the end, or corruption, of Islam during its infancy. If we consider the fact that those like Zubayr ibn 'Awwam and Abu Sufyan and the like who insisted on 'Ali's caliphate just after the Prophet fought against him during his Caliphate, it would be clearer that Abu Bakr's election as Caliph was a Divine blessing for Islam and the Muslims.

- **The Divine wisdom behind the bloody upheavals that happened to the earliest, most sacred Muslim Community was that they should cause Islam to found a magnificent civilization based on profound knowledge and spirituality, and indirectly served its establishment and maintenance on its basic pillars without any corruption.**[136]

A strong spring rain activates and develops predispositions inherent in vegetables, seeds, and trees so that each will bloom and flourish in its own fashion and realize its natural function. In the same way, upheavals during the time of the Companions and their successors activated various talents. Many people rose to preserve Islam, fearing that it was in danger. They shouldered a duty to be performed in the Muslim community and strove to fulfill it to the best of their ability. Each group performed a different function, such as striving to preserve the Prophetic Traditions, to protect the Shari'ah, to maintain and interpret the Qur'an and the truths of faith, and so on. This caused many branches of the religious and natural sciences to flourish, as well as many people of learning and deep spirituality to appear. The seeds of a brilliant civilization were scattered throughout the vast Muslim world, and half of the ancient world changed into "rose gardens." Nevertheless, certain "thorns" (deviant sects) also appeared in these rose gardens.

---

[135] *The Letters*, "The Nineteenth Letter", p. 128.
[136] *The Letters*, "The Nineteenth Letter", p. 129–130.

It was as if Divine Power shook that age through glory and majesty, turned it over vigorously, and thus electrified all people of zeal. Activated by that movement's centrifugal force, large numbers of illustrious jurists, enlightened Traditionists, blessed memorizers and interpreters of the Qur'an and Prophetic Traditions, and people of purity and chiefs of saints, dispersed throughout the Muslim world. Thus the Divine Power inspired Muslims with enthusiasm and awakened them to the Qur'an's treasures.

- **Love for somebody in God's Name or for God's sake is agreeable, whereas love for someone for his own sake is harmful.**[137]

The Qur'an declares: *"God has not made for any man two hearts within his body (one to be assigned for God and the other for others)."*[138] The human heart is regarded as God's throne or a mirror to Him. Therefore, it must be assigned for its true Owner, and whatever or whoever other than Him should be loved for His sake and in His Name. Otherwise, love becomes harmful.

There are two kinds of love. The first is loving somebody as a means to attain true love, which is love for God and in His Name. Such kind of love is agreeable. So we should and do love the Prophet's Family in the Name of God and His Messenger. Such love increases one's love of the Prophet and becomes a means to love God Almighty. Therefore it is lawful, its excess is harmless and not considered a transgression, and it does not call for reproach and enmity toward others.

The second takes the means as its real object. Such people "forget" God, devote their love to Jesus (the Christians), to 'Ali (the Rafidites) due to his heroic acts and perfections, and to Hasan and Husayn on account of their extraordinary virtues, regardless of whether they recognize God and His Prophet, upon him be peace and blessings. This love is not a means to love God and His Messenger. Rather, its excess leads to reproach and enmity toward others. The Christians have deified Prophet Jesus, upon him be peace. The Rafidites' excessive love for 'Ali caused them to reject the caliphates of Abu Bakr and 'Umar, deny their perfections, and eventually to deviate from the Straight Path. Such excessive and negative love causes spiritual ruin.

[137] *The Letters*, "The Nineteenth Letter", p. 134–135.
[138] *Suratu'l-Ahzab*, 33:4.

The "immaterial factories" producing the material world are in the celestial worlds, and its governing laws are determined or issue from them. The results of the acts performed by the earth's innumerable inhabitants, and the consequences of what is done by humanity and jinn, also assume form in those worlds.[139]

Together with the testimony of many indications and Prophetic Traditions, the Qur'an suggests, and the wisdom in the universe and the Divine Name the All-Wise require, that the good deeds done by humanity and jinn assume the forms of Paradise's fruits, while their evil deeds assume the forms of the bitter, poisonous fruits of the tree (*Zaqqum*) of Hell.

- **Creatures exist on the earth in great abundance and are constantly replaced by newer ones so that the world is filled and emptied of them continuously, and all the events taking place therein have their sources and origins in the universal laws and manifestations of Divine Names, which are first reflected in and received by the heavens.**[140]

To some degree simple and pure, each heaven is like a different world's roof, and represents a center for the administration of that world and regulation of its affairs. One of those worlds is the Garden of Refuge and Dwelling beside the Lote-tree of the farthest limit. The Truthful Reporter (the Holy Prophet) says the praises and glorifications of God performed on the earth assume the forms of that Garden's fruits. In other words, the storehouses containing the results or fruits of the works done here are located in those heavenly worlds; the harvest obtained here is sent there to "reap" on a predetermined day.

So how can an utterance, such as "All praise and gratitude are for God," which is lost in the air, can become embodied in a fruit of Paradise? Sometimes you say an agreeable word while awake and eat it in the form of a delicious apple in your dream at night. A disagreeable word said during the day returns at night as a bitter thing to swallow. If we stab someone in the back, they will make us eat its pain as decaying flesh. So whatever good or bad words we utter in this worldly sleep, we will eat them in the forms of fruits in the Hereafter, the world of being awake.

---

[139] *The Words*, "The Twenty-ninth Word", pp. 527–530.
[140] *The Words*, "The Thirty-first Word", pp. 600–601.

- **Seeing that the Eternal Power creates countless living beings from inert, solid substances and transforms the densest matter into subtle living compounds by life, thus radiating the light of life everywhere in great abundance and furnishing most things with the light of consciousness, the All-Powerful, All-Wise One would certainly not make such subtle forms of matter as light and ether, which are close to and fitting for the spirit, without life and consciousness. He has furnished all corners of the universe with living beings that are particular to each sphere.**[141]

God Almighty has not left any corner of the universe without life. He creates countless animate and conscious beings from light and darkness, ether and air, and even from meanings (conceived) and words (uttered). As He creates numerous animal species, He also creates different spirit creatures from subtle forms of matter. Some of these are angels, various spirit beings, and jinn. He has created countless varieties of angels and spirit beings, filling this universal mosque of existence with rows arranged in His worship.

Verena Tunniclife from Victoria University in Canada writes:

> All life requires energy, nearly all life on earth looks to the sun as the source. But solar energy is not the only kind of energy available on the earth. Consider the energy that drives the movement and eruption of the planet's crust. When you look at an active volcano, you are witnessing the escape of heat that has been produced by radioactive decay in the earth's interior and is finally reaching the surface. Why should there not be biological communities associated with the same nuclear energy that moves continents and makes mountains? And why could not whole communities be fuelled by chemical, rather than solar, energy?
>
> ... Most of us associate the escape of heat from the interior of the earth with violent events and unstable physical conditions, with extreme high temperatures and the release of toxic gases—circumstances that are hardly conducive to life. The notion that biological communities might spring up in a geologically active environment seemed fantastic. And until recently, few organisms were known to survive without a direct or indirect way to tap the sun's energy. But such communities do exist, and they represent one of the most startling discoveries of 20th-century biology. They live in the deep ocean, under conditions that are both severe and

[141] *The Words*, "The Twenty-ninth Word", pp. 527–530.

variable. Nearly 300 animal species, almost all them previously unknown, have been discovered living around hydrothermal vents which form when sea-water leaking through the ocean floor at spreading ridges is heated by the underlying magma and rushes into the cold ocean.[142]

So, science proves that God has innumerable creatures He has created from almost every material in the universe, and furnished all corners of the universe with living beings particular to each sphere. Some of these beings are angels and other kinds of spirit beings.

• **Like the earth, the heavens should have conscious or intelligent inhabitants particular to themselves.**[143]

For the earth, despite its small size and apparent insignificance when compared with the heavens, is continually filled with and emptied of conscious beings. This indicates that the heavens, which resemble decorated castles with awe-inspiring towers, are filled with living creatures, the light of the existence's light, and conscious, intelligent beings, who are the light of living creatures. These beings, just like jinn and humanity, are observers of this palace of the world, students and readers of this book of the universe, and heralds of the Lord's Sovereignty. Through their comprehensive and universal worship, they represent the glorifications of the creatures of universal nature or identity.

Also, the universe's infinite beauty and majesty calls for a response that must be of an infinite duty of reflection and worship. Since jinn and humanity can fulfill only a miniscule part of this duty, there must be countless varieties of angels and spirit beings to fill this universal mosque of existence with rows arranged in worship of the Creator. Indeed, there is a band or species of spirit beings and angels in every corner of the universe, each performing its own specific duty of servanthood. Some mobile, lifeless bodies—from planets to raindrops—serve as vehicles for some species of angels. They mount them by God's leave, and travel through the material world, spreading their glorifications.

• **Those who search for every truth in corporeality have their intellects in their eyes, when eyes are blind to spiritual things.**[144]

---

[142] *Discover (Magazine)*, October 1993.
[143] *The Words*, "The Twenty-ninth Word", pp. 527–528.
[144] *The Reasonings*, p. 16.

One who is very occupied in a subject is usually more insensitive to other subjects, and cannot understand these so well. For this reason, those who are greatly occupied in physical or material matters lack sufficient knowledge, or have only superficial understanding, of spiritual matters. Therefore, such people's opinions and judgments concerning spiritual matters carry little weight. If a patient seeks advice from an engineer rather than a physician, it means he has preferred to move to the hospital of the grave. Similarly, turning to materialists, or consulting their opinion in matters of spirituality, which are usually abstract, means that the heart, which is a faculty of faith and spirituality, will go into arrest while the intellect, which is a spiritual faculty, will atrophy.

- **The earth and the heavens are like two countries under one government, that conduct important relations and transactions. For example, things necessary for the earth like light, heat, blessings, and forms of mercy (like rain) are sent from the heavens. Also, angels and spirit beings descend to the earth from the heavens. Thus, we may deduce that there is a way for the earth's inhabitants to ascend to the heavens.**[145]

Just as people can travel to the heavens through their mind, vision, imagination, and even through certain vehicles, so, freed from or purified of their carnal and material being's gross heaviness, the spirits of Prophets and saints travel in such realms by God's leave; the spirits of ordinary believing people do so after death. Since those who are "lightened" and have acquired "subtlety" and spiritual refinement travel there, certain inhabitants of the earth and the air may go to the heavens if they are clothed in an "ideal" body, energetic envelope, or immaterial body or form, and are light and subtle like spirits.

- **Beings travel between the earth and the heavens, and important necessities for the former are sent from the latter. Given that pure spirits travel to the heavens, evil spirits attempt to do likewise, as they are physically light and subtle. But they are repelled with shooting stars.**[146]

We read in the Qur'an:

---

[145] *The Words*, "The Fifteenth Word", p. 194.
[146] *The Words*, "The Fifteenth Word", pp. 196–197.

But now when we sought to reach heaven, we found it filled with stern guards and flaming fires (shooting-stars). "We used to be established in position to overhear (its inhabitants); but now whoever attempts to listen finds a flaming fire in wait for him. We (being prevented from overhearing) did not know whether evil is intended for those who live on the earth, or their Lord wills for them right guidance and good."[147]

And, indeed, We have adorned the lowest heaven (the heaven of the world) with lamps (stars), and made (out of) them missiles to drive away devils; and for them, We have prepared (in the Hereafter) the punishment of the Blaze.[148]

Shooting stars are fired to prevent the jinn from reaching the heaven, or to repulse them from its doors.

Contact between fortune-tellers, jinn, or devils has a certain function in certain sorts of fortune-telling. The spying devils, who are representatives of the foulness and wickedness of the earth, attempt to soil the clean and pure realm of the heavens that are inhabited by pure beings, and spy on the talk of their inhabitants to mislead people, particularly through sorcerers, ill-willing mediums, and soothsayers. God allowed them to grab some pieces of information from their talks before the advent of His Last Messenger, upon him be peace and blessings. However, just prior to his advent, He shut the gates of the heavens to them completely. When they try to reach the heavens, they find it filled with strong guards who hurl missiles at them. If anyone from among them is able to grab something, they are pursued (and destroyed) by a shooting star dispatched by the angels on guard there.

- **Angels are not limited to one form. They can represent an entire species when they assume a particular form.**[149]

Created from *nur* (something immaterial, and more subtle and refined than light), angels, especially those who are the greatest among them like Gabriel, Michael, and Azrail, can be present in numerous places at the same instant and simultaneously assume many forms to do countless things according to the reflecting capacity or quality of the mirrors where they are present. For example, when the Companions saw him in the form of the Companion Dihya, Archangel Gabriel was present in thousands of places and in different forms while prostrating before God's Supreme Throne of

---

[147] *Suratu'l-Jinn*, 72:8–10.
[148] *Suratu'l-Mulk*, 67:5.
[149] *The Letters*, "The Twenty-eighth Letter", p. 362.

Honor with his magnificent wings stretching from east to west. Also, Azrail, the Angel of Death, can take the souls of numerous persons at the same time in different places. These angels have also many subordinates that both resemble, and are supervised by, them. Sometimes the subordinates of Azrail take souls. For example, the subordinate angel taking the souls of the righteous differs from the one taking the souls of the wicked.

• **Angels constitute a mighty community; many classes of them convey, represent, and embody Divine Commands of creation and order, which issue from the Divine Will and are known as the Shari'ah of creation and operation of the universe.**[150]

There are two kinds of Shari'ah (Divine sets of laws): those issuing from the Divine Attribute of Speech that regulate humanity's (a microcosm) deeds and states, and those that issue from the Divine Attribute of Will, and regulate the universe's (a macro-human) creation and operation. This second group is wrongly called nature.

Angels are God's honored servants who have subtle, luminous bodies. They are divided into classes, and do whatever He tells them to do. They obey the commandments issuing from the Eternal Will. Each heavenly body is a place of worship for them.

The worship of angels varies according to their nature and function as representatives of most species. Their services and praises differ in the different departments of Divine Lordship, as do the duties performed by a government's departments. For example, Archangel Michael superintends the growth of corn and provision upon the earth by God's permission and Power. If one may say so, he is the head of all farmer-like angels. Another great angel leads the "incorporeal shepherds" of all animals, by the All-Majestic Originator's permission, Command, and Power.

Since an angel represents each kind of creature and presents its service and worship to the Divine Court, the Prophet's descriptions of them are entirely reasonable and credible: "There are angels with forty thousand heads, each with forty thousand mouths, and forty thousand praises sung by forty thousand tongues in each mouth." This Prophetic Tradition means that angels serve universal purposes and that some creatures worship God with forty thousand heads in forty thousand ways. For example, the firmament praises the Majestic Creator through its suns and

---

[150] *The Words*, "The Twenty-ninth Word", pp. 532–534; *Gleams of Truth*, p. 17.

stars, while the earth worships with countless heads, each with countless mouths, and each mouth containing countless tongues. Thus this Tradition is said to refer to the angel representing the earth in the World of the Inner Dimensions of Things.

- **Although it seems to be ugly and revolting that Satan, or satans, who are pure evil, are created and allowed to attack believers, and that many people fall into unbelief and are condemned to Hellfire because of them, Satan's existence causes numerous universal good results and serves human attainment and perfection.**[151]

There are certainly some minor evils in the existence of Satan, but his existence causes numerous universal good results, and ultimately serves human attainment and perfection. However many degrees and ranks there are from a seed to a huge tree, the grades of human innate capacity are more numerous. Indeed, there are as many degrees as the reflections of the sun—from its reflection in a tiny shining object, or a bubble on the sea, to the sun itself. The development of these capacities or potentials requires action and work. What triggers the mechanism of the development is effort and struggle. This struggle is against satans, and other harmful agents and things. Otherwise, human beings would have had a constant spiritual station or rank like those of angels, and there would have been no gradations or differences in spirituality among humankind. It is contrary to wisdom and justice to forsake thousands of instances of good in order to avoid some minor evil.

It is true that the majority of people fall into misguidance because of Satan, but in general, something is important and valuable due to its quality, not due to its amount. Consider that if someone who has a thousand and ten seeds lets his seeds germinate under the earth, and ten become trees and a thousand rot, surely, the benefit the ten trees give to that man will reduce to nothing the loss that a thousand rotten seeds cause him. Similarly, through the struggle against the carnal, evil-commanding soul and the satans, the benefit, honor, and value humanity gains thanks to ten perfect people who, like stars, enlighten humanity, certainly diminish the harm caused by people of unbelief. This is why the Divine Mercy, Wisdom, and Justice have permitted the existence of Satan, and allow him to attack human beings.

---

[151] *The Gleams*, "The Thirteenth Gleam", pp. 96–97.

O people of belief! Your armor against those awful enemies is the utmost reverence for God and righteousness woven on the workbench of the Qur'an. Your shield is the elevated Sunnah of the noblest Messenger, upon him be peace and blessings. Your weapon is to seek refuge in God's protection and ask Him for forgiveness for your sins.

- **If believers follow God's way and serve Him, God Almighty makes Satan serve them and their cause.**

When the Muslims left Medina (624) in order to restore their stolen goods from the Meccan caravan of trade with only around three hundred, scantily armed people, Satan instigated the Meccans to attack these Muslims, thinking that it was just the time to overcome them. The Qur'an says: "*Satan decked out their deeds to be appealing to them, and said: 'Today, no power among humankind can overcome you and, for sure, I am your supporter.' But when the two hosts came within sight of each other, he turned on his heels to run away and said: 'Indeed I am quit of you; surely I see that which you do not see. Indeed, I fear God.' And God is severe in retribution.*"[152] When Satan perceived that the Muslim army was supported by angels, he chose to flee, as he feared receiving blows. His words "Surely I am quit of you," and, "In addition, I fear God," are only excuses for his flight. The Muslims defeated the powerful Meccan army at Badr and the leading figures of the idolatrous Meccans were killed at the battlefield. Thus, God employed Satan at the service of the Muslims by causing him to encourage the Meccans to attack the apparently weak Muslims. This was because the Muslims led by God's Messenger, upon him be peace and blessings, followed God's way strictly. If Muslims follow His way, God makes even Satan and other devils serve them and their cause.

- **One of the most abstruse deceits of Satan is that he causes his followers to deny his existence.**[153]

Those who have been confused by materialist philosophy are especially likely to hesitate despite the obvious evidence that points to Satan's existence.

Religions agree upon the existence of angels, who represent the Divine laws that are in force in good deeds, and supervise their application. Likewise, wisdom and reality require that there should be evil spirits or satans

---

[152] *Suratu'l-Anfal*, 8:48.
[153] *The Gleams*, "The Thirteenth Gleam", p. 111.

(devils) to represent the laws that are effective in evil acts. These satans have some part in these acts. Also, as humanity is a micro-universe (a microcosm), the universe is a macro-human being. This micro-universe is an index and summarized form of that macro-human. Thus, the macro-originals of models among human beings will necessarily exist in the macro-human. For example, the existence of human memory is a decisive proof of the existence of the Supreme Preserved Tablet. Likewise, everyone experiences that there is a center in one corner of the heart which functions as an instrument for evil suggestions, and a tongue which speaks under the influence of the power of groundless fear and fancy, and that when corrupted, the power of groundless fear and fancy may become like a small Satan, acting contrary to its owner's will and interest. All these are certain proof of the monstrous satans in the world. Functioning as an ear and tongue respectively, the satanic center in our heart, and the power of groundless fear and fancy, suggest the existence in the outer world of an evil being that blows in the heart and makes the tongue speak.

- **A decisive proof for the existence of jinn-satans is the existence of human-satans.**[154]

In the same way that there are corporeal evil spirits who function like Satan among human beings, it is also certain that there are incorporeal evil spirits among the jinn. If the latter were clothed in physical bodies, they would be the same as these evil human beings. If, on the other hand, the devils in human form were able to remove their physicality, they would be the same as the jinn-satans.

As is known, **when something of high quality is corrupted, it becomes more corrupt than something of less quality**. For example, when milk and yogurt go bad, they can still be eaten, but when butter goes bad, it can no longer be eaten; it even sometimes becomes like poison. Similarly, if human beings, the noblest, possibly the highest, of creatures, are corrupted, they become more corrupt than any other corrupted creature. Like vermin that receive pleasure from the stink of putrefied flesh and like snakes that take pleasure at biting and poisoning, they enjoy, and are proud of, the evil they commit and their corrupt morals in the marsh of misguidance, as well as the harm and injustices they inflict in the darkness of wrongdoing. It can be said that they take on the nature

---

[154] *The Gleams*, "The Thirteenth Gleam", p. 111.

of Satan. In short, a decisive proof for the existence of jinn-satans is the existence of human-satans.

- **Although the wise Qur'an declares, "The guile of Satan is ever feeble,"[155] it complains greatly of the people of misguidance, and frequently draws attention to them, threatening them severely, because Satan and his party follow the way of misguidance, and can therefore cause great destruction with minor actions, and do many creatures great wrong with small deeds.[156]**

Consider that through some minor action or act of neglect of an insignificant duty, a man on a large, royal merchant ship of a sovereign can cause the efforts of all those who have a duty related to the ship to go for nothing. So, the illustrious owner of the ship complains of that rebellious one and severely threatens him on behalf of all his subjects that have some connection with the ship. And he severely punishes him, considering not his insignificant action but its awful consequences, and not in his own illustrious name but in the name of the rights of his subjects.

Similarly, the people of misguidance, who are the party of Satan and exist on the ship of the earth together with the people of right guidance, can violate the rights of innumerable creatures and cause their exalted duties to be fruitless. So it is pure wisdom, completely appropriate, and perfectly eloquent that the Eternal Monarch complains greatly of them and severely threatens them, frequently drawing attention to their destruction as if He were mobilizing great forces against them.

- **It is pure wisdom that in the Books He sent, God Almighty repeatedly gives the glad tidings of a mighty reward like Paradise and warns of a tremendous punishment like Hellfire. In addition, He frequently calls us to guidance and encourages us to good and Paradise, and warns us against misguidance, threatening us with both Hellfire and other kinds of severe punishment. He also helps the believers in their struggle against Satan and his party. Despite such guidance, and despite following the Straight Path, people can be easily deceived by Satan, and believers may be defeated in the face of the feeble, repulsive ploys of Satan's party, which promises no real reward.[157]**

---

[155] *Suratu'n-Nisa'*, 4:76.
[156] *The Gleams*, "The Thirteenth Gleam", p. 98.
[157] *The Gleams*, "The Thirteenth Gleam", pp. 109–110.

Believers are not taken in by the deceit of Satan due to a lack of belief, or weakness in their belief. Those who commit major sins do not become unbelievers, contrary to the claims of the *Mu'tazilites* and some *Kharijite* sects that one who commits a major sin becomes an unbeliever or is in a state between belief and unbelief. Also, a believer who commits a major sin does not mean that he has undergone a contemptible degeneration and vileness. For Satan can throw people into perils through a paltry incitement that leads to destruction. Moreover, the human carnal soul always lends an ear to Satan.

Secondly, there is negligence and omission in all kinds of misguidance. Negligence and omission are quite easy, and they do not require any positive, constructive action. Misguidance means destruction, which is extremely easy and possible through minimal action. It also leads to aggression, and, therefore, can cause much harm. Because of this ease, and because of a tendency towards tyranny, and the fear this engenders in hearts, the leaders of misguidance hold a position of power in the eyes of the people. In addition to all this, humanity, which by nature is blind to consequences and addicted to easily available pleasures, has certain vegetable and animal powers that pursue pleasure, demand satisfaction, and are difficult to control. They cause human faculties such as the heart and reason to abandon their duties, which are required by true humanity, and which are related to the final end of humanity.

In contrast, the sacred way of the people of guidance, particularly the way of the Prophets, pursues existence, construction, and repair, and requires positive action, the observation of certain boundaries, the consideration of consequences, worship and servanthood, and strictly controlling the carnal soul, putting an end to its tendency to freely dominate human beings. Thus, due to the ease of Satan's deceptions, and since it is burdensome for people to discipline their soul, God Almighty encourages believers greatly, warns people of a tremendous punishment like Hellfire, and helps the believers in their struggle against Satan.

- **The way of misguidance is both easy and extremely difficult.**[158]

There are two types of unbelief and misguidance. One sort pertains to actions and is of a secondary degree, or particular. That is, it negates the

---

[158] *The Gleams*, "The Thirteenth Gleam", pp. 106.

parvfoRoute

articles of faith, or is a non-acceptance of the truth. This way of misguidance is easy to take.

The second sort of unbelief and misguidance is a judgment or conclusion of the heart and mind. It does not only comprise negation of belief but opens up a way that is opposed to belief. This means the acceptance of falsehood, and the willful admission of the opposite of the truth. It is not non-acceptance, but is the acceptance of non-existence, which can only be accepted by proving non-existence. According to the rule, "Non-existence cannot be proved," it is evidently not possible to prove it. Anyone with the slightest consciousness would not follow such a way.

- **Another of Satan's important schemes is that he calls on human beings not to admit their faults so that he can bar them from seeking forgiveness and refuge in God. He also provokes the egotism of the human carnal soul in order that the soul may defend itself like a lawyer, holding itself exempt from all faults.**[159]

An evil-commanding soul which heeds Satan does not want to see its faults. Even if it sees them, it explains them away in various ways. As stated in the adage, *The eye of contentment is blind to faults*, a person who considers his soul in approving terms does not see his faults. Since he does not see his faults, he does not admit them. Consequently, he neither implores God for forgiveness nor seeks refuge in Him, and so becomes a plaything of Satan. If a noble prophet like Prophet Joseph, upon him be peace , says, "*I do not claim myself free of error, for assuredly the human soul always commands evil, except that my Lord has mercy,*"[160] how can one trust one's carnal, evil-commanding soul?

One who accuses his own soul sees his own faults. One who sees and admits his own faults implores God for forgiveness. One who implores God for forgiveness seeks refuge in God from Satan. One who seeks refuge in God is saved from Satan's evils. Not seeing one's faults is a fault greater than the former ones committed. Non-admission of one's faults is a grave defect. If one sees a fault, then it ceases to be a fault. The one who admits his fault deserves forgiveness.

- **The spirit is some sort of law like the laws of "nature." However, while the laws of "nature" have only theoretical, or nominal,**

---

[159] *The Gleams*, "The Thirteenth Gleam", pp. 119.
[160] *Sura Yusuf*, 12:53.

invisible existence, the spirit has consciousness and a real, sensible existence.[161]

Like the enduring laws of creation, or "nature," the spirit also issues from the World of Divine Commands (*'Alam-i Amr*) and the Divine Attribute of Will. Divine Power clothes the spirit in an astral body or double (the etheric counterpart of the physical body) within a body of sensory organs. Both the spirit and the laws of "nature" are unchanging and permanent. If the Eternal Power had clothed laws with external existence, each would have been a spirit; if the human spirit were stripped of consciousness, it would become an immaterial law.

- **The spirit is a living, created entity which has permanence.**[162]

The spirit is a living entity created; it has permanence. The part in the human existence which tastes death is the soul, not the spirit.[163] Therefore, the spirit continues to live after death. All the proofs for the existence of angels and other spirit beings prove its permanence as well. We are too close to the souls of the dead—who are waiting in the Intermediate Realm to go to the Hereafter—to require proof of their existence. It is commonly known that some people can communicate with them, and almost everyone encounters them in true dreams.

Not only human spirits, but all creatures, even the most primitive, are created for some kind of eternity. Even the spiritless flower has a sort of post-death immortality in countless ways: its form is preserved in memories, and the law of its formation and life gains permanence via new flowers growing from its seeds. Since this law, which has the same significance for the flower as our spirit has for us, and the model of its form are preserved amidst turbulent events through its seeds by the All-Preserving, All-Wise One, the human spirit, which has a sublime and comprehensive nature and consciousness, and has been clothed with external existence, is far more deserving of permanence.

As mentioned before, the spirit is a living, conscious, luminous entity. It is a comprehensive, substantial law or command of God furnished with external existence and has the potential to achieve universality. Even "natural" laws, which are insubstantial when compared to the spirit, have stability and permanence. For all kinds of existence, although subject to

---

[161] *Gleams of Truth*, pp. 5–6.
[162] *The Words*, "The Twenty-ninth Word", p. 536.
[163] *Sura Al 'Imran*, 3:185.

change, possess a permanent dimension that remains unaltered through all stages of life.

- **The material existence of meaning (i.e., letters and words) may change and be effaced, but the meaning continues to exist. A covering may be rent, but its essence or kernel remains. Clothes are worn out and the body is ruined, but the spirit survives. Multiplicity and the multiple are divided and decay, but unity and the unitary remain permanent. Matter dissolves but life endures.**[164]

These realities show that the spirit will pass over the "ditch" of death and, freed from its hooks and stripped of its body, continue on to eternity, safe and sound.

- **God is All-Eternal and so are His Attributes. Therefore, these eternal Attributes require eternal manifestation, and the beings who will receive these manifestations become eternal.**[165]

The Glory of God's being the Lord and Divine Sovereign will certainly establish a reward for those who believe and perform good, righteous deeds, and punish the misguided who betray His purposes for creation.

Since the Lord and Ruler of this world has infinite Munificence and Mercy, some part of Which we observe especially in the sustenance of beings in the universe, and infinite Majesty and Dignity, His Munificence requires infinite giving, His Mercy requires favors worthy of Itself, and His Majesty and Dignity require punishing those who disrespect them.

The All-Majestic Being, Who manifests the sovereignty of His being Lord in the universe's order, purpose, justice, and balance, will surely show His eternal favor to believers who seek the protection of His being their Lord and Sovereign, who believe in His Wisdom and Justice, and act in conformity with them through worship. Also, He will punish those who, denying His Wisdom and Justice, rebel against Him and wrong others.

The unlimited Generosity, the inexhaustible riches and treasures, the unequalled eternal Beauty and Grace, as well as the everlasting Perfection, some part of Which we see in the universe adorned with so many beautiful objects and in the maintenance of beings, surely demand the existence of grateful supplicants, along with amazed and yearning onlookers who are destined to dwell permanently in an abode of blissful repose.

---

[164] *Al-Mathnawi al-Nuri*, "The Ninth Treatise", p. 271.
[165] *The Words*, "The Tenth Word", p. 80.

God is the All-Majestic Lord, to Whose command all beings—from suns and trees to atoms and molecules—are subdued like obedient soldiers. It is unthinkable that He should focus entirely upon the transient beings in this temporary world, and not create a permanent sphere of majesty and an exalted abode of Lordship where He will exercise His majestic Lordship. The majestic operations—like the changing of seasons, the awesome motions of gigantic planets, the amazing instances of subjugation such as making the earth our cradle and the sun our lamp, and vast transformations such as reviving and adorning a dead earth—show that a sublime Lordship rules with a splendid sovereignty behind the veil of what is seen. Therefore, that infinite, glorious sovereignty of Lordship requires subjects worthy of itself, as well as a fitting vehicle for its manifestation.

- **God, Who is the All-Answering of prayers and does not allow a prayer which He will not accept to be made, will certainly accept the first and foremost desire of all human beings, which is eternity, including especially the greatest petition of His foremost servant, his most beloved creature, namely Prophet Muhammad, upon him be peace and blessings.**[166]

Is it conceivable that a Lord of infinite compassion and mercy, Who most compassionately fulfills the least need of His lowliest creatures in the most unexpected fashion, Who answers the faintest cry of help of His most obscure creature, and Who responds to all petitions, would ignore the greatest petition of His foremost servant, his most beloved creature, by not granting his most exalted prayer? This servant pleads for the foundation of an everlasting world where its inhabitants will enjoy eternal happiness in thankfulness to Him, with such yearning and longing that creation is moved to tears and shares in his plea. The tender solicitude manifested in nurturing weak, young animals show that the Sovereign Lord of the universe exercises His being Lord with infinite mercy. Is it conceivable that such compassion and mercy in the exercise of Lordship would refuse the prayer of the most virtuous and beautiful of all creation?

- **The human conscience (conscious nature) indicates eternal happiness. Whoever listens to his or her alert conscience hears it saying eternity, again and again. Even if we were given the entire uni-**

[166] *The Words*, "The Tenth Word", pp. 86-87.

verse, we would not be compensated for the lack of eternity, for we have an innate longing, and were created, for it. Thus our natural inclination towards eternal happiness comes from an objective reality—eternity's existence and our desire for eternity.[167]

- **The end of pain is a sort of pleasure, and the end of pleasure is a sort of pain. Therefore, God Almighty is absolutely above making bitter the pleasures He causes His servants to taste in the world with the thought of their eternity, and causing eternal pain by not bringing the other, eternal world.[168]**

Inexhaustible treasures of Mercy require an everlasting abode of blissful repose that contains all desirable objects. They also require that those who enjoy it should dwell there eternally, without suffering the pain of cessation and separation. For the end of pain is a sort of pleasure, and the end of pleasure is a sort of pain. The Unlimited Generosity and Abundance desire to bestow infinite bounty and kindness, which require infinite gratitude. Thus, those who are to receive this bounty and give continual thanks in turn must live forever. A slight contentment, spoiled by its brevity or cessation, is incompatible with unlimited Generosity and Abundance.

- **Things are created for eternity, not for utter annihilation. Apparent annihilation (death) marks a completion of duty and a release from service, for while every transient thing progresses to annihilation in one aspect, it remains eternally in numerous other aspects.[169]**

Consider a flower, a word of God's Power. It smiles upon us for a while and then hides behind the veil of annihilation. Like a spoken word which goes but entrusts its thousands of copies to ears, and whose meaning remains in the minds of those who heard it, the flower disappears, but it leaves its visible form in the memories of those who saw it and its inner essence in its seeds. It is as if each memory and seed were a device to record the flower's adornment or a means for its perpetuation. As this is true for such a simple living entity, we can see how much closer we are attached to eternity, given that we are life's highest form and have an imperishable spirit. Again, from the fact that the laws, which resemble the spirit in one respect, and according to which flowering and fruit-bear-

---

[167] *The Words*, "The Twenty-ninth Word", p. 541.
[168] *The Words*, "The Tenth Word", p. 84.
[169] *The Words*, "The Tenth Word", p. 92.

ing plants are formed, and the representations of their forms are preserved and perpetuated in the most orderly manner in tiny seeds through all tempestuous changes of weather and seasons, we can easily understand how closely the human spirit is attached and related to eternity.

- **We have not been left to wander at will, like a loosely tethered animal pasturing where it pleases. Our deeds are "photographed" and recorded, with their consequences being preserved for the Day when we will have to account for them. The perfect preservation of everything in the universe and permanence in the same, subsequent forms points to an attribute of eternal preservation which unfolds all their deeds.**[170]

The Being Who administers this cosmos preserves all things in an order and balance, which manifest His Knowledge and Wisdom, His Will and Power. Have you not seen how the records of the deeds of all spring flowers and fruits, the laws of their formation, and the images of their forms, are all inscribed and preserved within minute seeds? The following spring, those records are opened—a bringing to account appropriate to them—and another vast world of spring emerges with absolute orderliness and wisdom. This shows the powerful and comprehensive exercise of the Divine Attribute of Preservation. The tapes on which our acts and voices are recorded also prove this universal recording and preservation. God the All-Preserving inscribes a compact life-history in a seed (that life's issue and outcome). Human memories, a tree's fruit, a fruit's kernel, a flower's seed—all manifest the law of preservation's universality and inclusiveness.

Considering that the issue of such transient, commonplace, and insignificant things is preserved, how could our deeds, which from the viewpoint of universal Lordship yield important fruit in the Unseen world, the Hereafter, and the World of Spirits, not be preserved and recorded as a matter of high significance?

- **The daily, weekly, monthly, seasonal, and yearly resurrections give the tidings of the Supreme Resurrection and Gathering.**[171]

The alternation of day and night, as well as spring and winter, atmospheric changes, our body's annual renewal, and our awakening and rising every morning after sleep all indicate a complete rising and renewal. Sec-

---

[170] *The Words*, "The Tenth Word", p. 93.
[171] *The Words*, "The Tenth Word", 95; "The Twenty-ninth Word, p. 539.

onds forecast minutes, minutes predict hours, and hours anticipate a day. The dials of God's great clock—the earth—point, in succession, to the day, the year, our lifetime, and the ages through which the world passes. As they show morning after night, and spring after winter, they intimate that the morning of the Resurrection will follow the death of creation.

- **The Supreme Decree says:** "Look upon the imprints of God's Mercy, how He revives the earth after its death. He it is Who will revive the dead (in a similar way). He has full power over everything."[172]

Indeed, the Almighty Disposer of this world's affairs continually creates on this finite, transient earth numerous signs, examples, and indications of the Supreme Gathering and the Plain of Resurrection. Each spring we see countless animal and plant species resurrected in a few days. All tree and plant roots, as well as certain animals, are revived and restored exactly as they were. Other animals are re-created in nearly identical forms. Seeds that appear so alike quickly grow into distinct and differentiated entities, after being brought to full vigor with extraordinary rapidity and ease, in absolute orderliness and harmony. Is it reasonable to ask how He can create the world anew and resurrect humanity with a single blast?

- **Would the All-Wise choose us to receive His direct and universal address; make us a comprehensive mirror to Himself; let us taste, measure, and get to know the contents of His treasuries of Mercy; make Himself known to us with all His Names; love us and make Himself beloved by us—and then not send us to an eternal realm, an abode of permanent bliss, and make us happy therein?**[173]
- **The Divine Wisdom, Justice, and Mercy never allow any wrongdoing and good to go unnoticed and forbid injustice, and therefore require the establishment of a supreme tribunal to reward good and punish evil.**[174]

There are two forms of justice, one positive and the other negative. The positive one consists in giving the right to the one who deserves it. Except for the injustices we commit in the realm where our free wills have a part, this form of justice is clearly observed throughout the world. For the All-Majestic Originator gives in definite measures, and according

---

[172] *Suratu'r-Rum*, 30:50: *The Words*, "The Tenth Word", 97.
[173] *The Words*, "The Tenth Word", 99.
[174] *The Words*, "The Tenth Word", p. 100; "The Twenty-ninth Word, p. 543.

to definite criteria, everything that is asked for in the tongues of natural need and absolute necessity. In other words, He meets all the requirements of everything's life and existence. Therefore, this form of justice is as certain as existence and life.

The negative form of justice involves punishing the unjust, and so giving the wrong-doers their due via requital and chastisement. Even though this form is not manifested fully here, countless signs suggest its existence. For example, the blows of punishment striking the rebellious peoples from 'Ad and Thamud to those of the present age show that a very exalted justice dominates the world. However, we also observe that cruel, sinful, and tyrannical persons usually lead a comfortable and luxurious life while godly, oppressed people live in poverty and difficulty. Death makes them equal, for both would have departed forever with their deeds unquestioned if there were no supreme tribunal. However, Divine Wisdom and Justice never allow any wrongdoing to go unnoticed and forbid injustice, and therefore require the establishment of a supreme tribunal to punish evil and reward good.

- **This world's adornments and pleasures are not merely for the sake of enjoyment. They are rather to instruct in wisdom, to arouse gratitude, and to encourage us to seek the permanent, eternal originals of which they are copies. They are like samples and forms of the blessings stored in Paradise by the All-Merciful's Mercy for people of belief.**[175]

You will understand that this world's adornments are not merely for the sake of enjoyment. As they are temporary, like our life being short, they give pain upon separation; they give us a taste, rouse our appetite, but never satisfy us. So, they are here only to instruct in wisdom, to arouse gratitude, and to encourage us to seek the permanent originals of which they are copies. In short, they are for exalted goals far beyond themselves.

The lifespan of all worldly things is short, whereas their worth and the subtleties in their fashioning are most exalted and beautiful. This implies that everything is only a sample to draw the viewer's gaze to its authentic original. Given this, we may say that this world's diverse adornments are samples of Paradise's bounties, made ready by the All-Merciful and All-Compassionate for His beloved servants.

---

[175] *The Words*, "The Tenth Word", pp. 90–91.

- **The Maker of this world has very important, amazing, and hidden perfections, which He wills to display via His miraculous arts. Hidden perfections long to be known by those who will gaze upon them with admiration and appreciation. Eternal perfection requires eternal manifestation, which in turn requires the eternal existence of those who will appreciate and admire it. The value of perfection diminishes in the view of its admirer if the latter is not eternal.**[176]

A celebrated beauty once rejected a common man who had become infatuated with her. To console himself, the man said: "How ugly she is!" and so denied her beauty. A bear once stood beneath a vine trellis and longed to eat the grapes upon it. Unable to reach the grapes or to climb the trellis, it said to itself, by way of consolation: "The grapes must be sour," and went on its way growling.

- **The human intellect, wisdom, experience, and deductive reasoning point out that nothing superfluous or vain occurs in creation. For the universe's All-Majestic Maker uses the best and easiest way in creation, and apportions many duties, purposes and results to each creature, no matter how insignificant it may appear. This indicates the existence of eternal happiness.**[177]

Since there is no waste and nothing in vain, there must be eternal happiness, for eternal non-existence would make everything futile and wasteful. The absence of waste in creation, particularly in human body, as testified to by several sciences, demonstrates that our countless spiritual potentialities, limitless aspirations and ideas, and inclinations will never go to waste. Our basic inclination toward perfection indicates perfection's existence, and our desire for happiness proclaims that an eternal happiness awaits us. If this were not so, all the basic features of our existence and nature, and all our sublime aspirations, would be wasteful and lose their essential meaning.

- **The human individual is like a species in the animal kingdom. For the light of intellect has given such breath to the aspirations and ideas of humanity that they encompass both the past and the future. Even if they consumed the entire world, they would not be satisfied. What will satisfy them is the eternal life.**[178]

---

[176] *The Words,* "The Tenth Word", p. 85.
[177] *The Words,* "The Twenty-ninth Word", p. 539.
[178] *The Words,* "The Twenty-ninth Word", p. 540.

In all other species, an individual's nature is particular, its value is personal, its view is restricted, its qualities are limited, and its pleasure and pain are instantaneous. Human beings, however, have a sublime nature and the greatest value, limitless perfection, and a more permanent spiritual pleasure and pain. Given this, the kinds of resurrection experienced by other species suggest that every human being will be resurrected completely on the Day of Judgment.

- **As this world is not exactly propitious for a complete development of human potentialities, we are destined to find realization in another world.**[179]

Humanity is endowed with unlimited potentialities that develop into unrestricted abilities. These, in turn, give rise to countless inclinations that generate limitless desires, which are the source of infinite ideas and conceptions. All of these indicate the existence of a world of eternal happiness beyond this material world. Our very nature, which is the origin of our innate inclination towards eternal happiness, makes one sure that such a world will be established.

Also, Our essence is comprehensive and is bound for eternity. As we have an extremely comprehensive nature, we can commit tremendous crimes and wrongdoings. Therefore, we cannot be left to our own devices without an order and discipline, nor can we be left to deteriorate into non-existence. Hell is waiting for us with a wide-open mouth, and Paradise is expecting us with open arms.

- **The All-Wise Originator usually restores to life that which is of great value. That is, He does not let valuable things perish permanently through the changes of seasons, years, and centuries; rather, He continually returns them to life.**[180]

Thus, based on this regular practice or law, we say: since sciences agree that humanity is the most perfect fruit of the Tree of Creation and has the greatest importance and value, and since each person is like a species of other living beings, then each person will be resurrected on Judgment Day with his or her exact identity and body, title and form.

[179] *The Words*, "The Twenty-ninth Word", p. 543.
[180] *The Gleams*, "The Seventeenth Gleam", p. 161.

- **The worldly recompense for evils proves punishment in the Here-after.**[181]

Everyone has experienced this at least once in their lifetime and concludes: "That person has done that evil and has met with what he deserves." This is a principle in life. This means that an evil, by virtue of its very nature, is subjected to and requires punishment. Minor evils are punished here, while major ones are referred to the Hereafter.

- **The repeated declarations of the Qur'an, "It is but a single blast,"[182] and "The matter of the Hour is but the twinkling of an eye, or even quicker,"[183] show that the Supreme Resurrection will happen in an instant.**[184]

This world is the realm of Wisdom; the Hereafter is the abode of Power. So, in accordance with the requirements of Divine Names such as the All-Wise, the All-Arranging, the All-Disposing, and the All-Nurturing, creation in the world is gradual and extends over a certain period of time. This is required by His Wisdom as the Lord. But given that Power and Mercy will be more evident than Wisdom in the Hereafter, creation in that realm will be instantaneous and free from anything related to matter, space, time, and duration. In order to show that what takes a day or a year to do here will be accomplished within an instant in the Hereafter, the Qur'an decrees: *"The matter of the Hour is but the twinkling of and eye, even quicker."*

- **If something is subject to the law of development, it must evolve to a final end. That which develops to a final end must have a limited lifetime and, therefore, a fixed natural end. That which has a fixed end inevitably dies.**[185]

Just as humanity is a microcosm subject to death, so the universe, a macro-human being, is also subject to death. Accordingly, it will perish and be resurrected on the morning of the Resurrection. Just as a living tree (a miniature universe) cannot save itself from annihilation, the universe (the branch of creation growing from the Tree of Creation) can not be saved from destruction and disintegration to be repaired and renewed.

[181] *Gleams of Truth*, pp. 60–61.
[182] *Sura Ya-Sin*, 36: 53.
[183] *Suratu'n-Nahl*, 16:77.
[184] *The Words*, "The Tenth Word", p. 124.
[185] *The Words*, "The Twenty-ninth Word", p. 546.

- **Water freezes to its detriment (loses its essential liquid form); ice melts to its detriment (loses its essential solid state); an item's essence becomes stronger at the expense of its material form; a language becomes coarse to the detriment of meaning; the spirit weakens as the flesh becomes more substantial, and the flesh weakens as the spirit becomes more illuminated. Similarly, the solid world is refined through life in favor of the afterlife.**[186]

The Creative Power breathes life into dense, solid, and inanimate substances through an astonishing activity. This suggests that the Power melts, refines, and illuminates that solid world to the advantage of the Hereafter through the light of life.

- **If there is a strong necessity that something possible should occur, and the power which will make it occur is able to do so, then it comes to be regarded as something that will certainly occur.**[187]

A close examination of what occurs in the universe shows that two opposite elements in it have spread everywhere and become rooted. Their clash accounts for good and evil, benefit and harm, perfection and defect, light and darkness, guidance and misguidance, belief and unbelief, obedience and rebellion, fear and love, and so on. Such ongoing conflict causes the universe to undergo continuous alteration and transformation in order to produce the elements of a new world. These opposed elements will eventually lead to eternity in two different directions, and materialize as Paradise and Hell. And the Power Which will realize this is absolutely able to do it.

- **Just a person has, in addition to her bodily existence, immaterial forms of existence such as mind, heart, spirit, imagination, memory, thought, consciousness, and free will, certainly the universe, which is the macro-human and of which humanity is the fruit, contains other worlds beside the physical one. Also each world, from the earth to Paradise, has a heaven.**[188]

Scientists generally agree that space is full of "ether." Such subtle and refined matters as light, electricity, and heat point to the existence of a more subtle and refined matter that fills space.

---

[186] *The Words*, "The Twenty-ninth Word", p. 547.
[187] *The Words*, "The Twenty-ninth Word", p. 548.
[188] *The Words*, "The Thirty-first Word", p. 589.

Just as fruits demonstrate the existence of the trees that bear them, flowers their flower-bed, shoots their field, and fish the sea, so do stars present the existence of their origin to the mind's eye. Since there are different formations in the celestial realm, and since different rules are enforced under different conditions, the heavens requiring the existence of those rules must be different.

- **Through its annual movement around the sun, the earth draws a large circle that will be the Place of the Supreme Gathering after the Resurrection.**[189]

In the annual orbit of the earth, there are innumerable creatures that exist but are invisible to us because they emit no light. It is like the moon when it is hidden from the sun's light—it cannot emit light and so becomes invisible to us.

The sublime wisdom displayed by the All-Wise Creator in everything (by attaching great wisdom to a small thing) is also manifested in the earth's revolution. It does not revolve aimlessly, but draws the periphery of a huge circle into which, through its revolution, it continually empties the outcomes of all events occurring within it. On the Day of Judgment, each person will see his or her life's outcome. All outcomes are continually transferred to the Place of the Supreme Gathering's registers or tablets. This plain, now behind the veil of the Unseen, will be visible on the Day of Judgment, and the earth's inhabitants will see it in their new Hereafter forms.

At the end of time, the earth—which is a field (of seeds to grow and be harvested for the Gathering), a stream (carrying our deeds), a measure of grain, a bushel (measuring and emptying the outcome of our deeds)—will have produced enough material to fill up the Place of the Supreme Gathering. The earth functions like a seed from which this plain will grow, like a tree, with all its contents. Just as a rapidly spinning, radiant dot produces a radiant circle, the rapid and purposeful movement of the earth, a small dot when compared to the universe, as well as its life's outcome, will be used to form the Place of the Supreme Gathering. *True knowledge is with God.*

---

[189] *The Letters*, "The First Letter", p. 6–7; "The Tenth Letter", p. 59.

- **If there were no Paradise, perhaps Hell would not be torment. If there were no extreme cold (besides its heat), Hell would not burn.**[190]

The degrees of heat are due to the existence of cold. The degrees of beauty come about through the intervention of ugliness. The apparent cause becomes as if the ultimate cause or raison d'être. Light is indebted to darkness, pleasure is indebted to pain; there is no consciousness of health without illness.

The Ever-Living Creator has demonstrated His Wisdom in the creation of opposites and His Majesty has become apparent. The Everlasting All-Powerful One has displayed His Power in the combining of opposites, and His Grandeur has become manifest. However, since the Divine Power is essential to and inherent in the Divine Essence, It comprises no opposites and therefore impotence cannot intervene in It; there can be no degrees in It; nothing can be difficult for It.

- **There is an absolute necessity for Hell. Many things going on in the world of humanity make one want to say: "Long live Hell!" Paradise does not come cheap, but rather at a very high price.**[191]

The Qur'an mentions Hell among the favors of God, the All-Merciful: *"This is Hell, which the disbelieving criminals deny. They will go round between it(s fire) and hot, boiling water. Then (O humankind and jinn), which of the favors of your Lord will you deny?"*[192] Hell is the result of the pure, absolute Divine justice, and justice is pure blessing.

- **According to the rule that "One is with whom he or she loves," each believer can have a part in the highest rank or position through closeness to the one with that position.**[193]

The Qur'anic love for the Prophets and saints will cause believers to benefit from their intercession in the Intermediate World of the grave and in the Place of the Supreme Gathering. They will also receive enlightenment from their elevated positions.

- **People of Paradise will be dressed, as the return of the deeds they did with each and every part of their bodies, in a fashion to display**

---

[190] *Gleams of Truth*, p. 58.

[191] *The Letters*, "The Twenty-ninth Letter",

[192] *Suratu'r-Rahman*, 55:43–45.

[193] *The Words*, "The Thirty-second Word", p. 662.

Paradise's beauties and blessings so that these beauties and blessings may please each sense and feeling, and satisfy each faculty.[194]

This is especially true for those who worshipped God with all their senses and faculties while in this world, for such people deserve all the pleasures of Paradise. As understood from the Prophetic Tradition, "*Houris* wear seventy celestial garments one over the other,"[195] the garments worn by the people of Paradise are not of the same kind. Every garment, from the most outer to the most inner, is of a different level so that all senses and feelings will receive their specific pleasures through specific beauties. In accord with wisdom and justice, the people of Hell will be clothed in garments that will cause each part of their bodies to suffer a special torment, for they sinned with their bodily organs, intellects, and so on, while alive. Each garment will be like a miniature hell.

- **The Qur'anic expression, "immortal children (of Paradise)"[196] point to the children of the believers who die before puberty, and indicate that they will remain immortal children in Paradise.[197]**

As the result of "lawful" love for parents and children—loving each other in God's Name and for God's sake—, Almighty God, the All-Merciful and All-Compassionate, will allow them to come together in Paradise and reward them with an eternal happy communion, even though the rank and place of each may be different. He will re-create children who died before puberty as the lovable and most beautiful immortal children of Paradise, in a form worthy of Paradise, and return them to their parents' arms so that they may enjoy eternally the pleasure of parenthood. Since Paradise is not the place of reproduction, some thought that the pleasure of having children would be absent there. But as Paradise contains every pleasurable thing in its highest degree, the pleasure of having children, at its best, will be there, by means of the children who died before reaching puberty. This is a good tiding for those parents whose prepubescent children have died.

- **God Almighty will show His justice and compassion in the Hereafter in judging people. If one's good (evil) deeds weigh more, God will reward (punish) him or her. Further, He judges good and evil**

---

[194] *The Letters*, "The Twenty-eighth Letter", pp. 375–378.
[195] *al-Bukhari*, "Bad' al-Khalq", 8; *at-Tirmidhi*, "Qiyama", 60.
[196] *Suratu'l-Waqia*, 56:17.
[197] *The Words*, "The Thirty-second Word", p. 661.

deeds according to quality, not quantity. Thus one good deed could outweigh a thousand evil ones and cause them to be forgiven.[198]

Since this is the way of Divine Justice, believers should not be condemned because of a few faults. Also, any Islamic institution should not be denounced and attacked because of the faults of some members of them.

- **Martyrs know that they are alive. Since they do not experience dying as death, they see that their lives, sacrificed for God's sake, are permanent, continual, and more refined.**[199]

The human life has five degrees. The first degree is as we live here and now, which is bound by certain conditions. The second degree is manifested in the lives of Khadr and Ilyas (Elijah?). To a certain extent it is free, for those who have it can be in different places at the same time, and are not bound by ordinary human life's necessities. The third degree is manifested in the lives of Prophets Jesus and Idris (Enoch?), upon them be peace, who live in heaven with their physical bodies.[200] Their bodies are not bound by human life's necessities and have acquired a sort of refinement and luminosity to the degree of astral bodies and an angelic type of life.

The fourth degree is the life of martyrs. Some Qur'anic verses state that martyrs enjoy a higher degree of life than deceased non-martyrs.[201] Since martyrs sacrifice their life in His cause, God Almighty grants them an intermediate life resembling worldly life without its pains and troubles. They do not feel the pangs of death or know that they are dead. Instead, they consider themselves transferred to a better world and enjoy perfect happiness.

The fifth degree is the deceased's spiritual life. Death is a changing of residence, and a discharge from worldly duties with the spirit set free, not a complete annihilation into non-existence.

---

[198] *The Letters,* "The Twenty-ninth Letter", p. 428.
[199] *Gleams of Truth,* p. 11.
[200] *Sura Al 'Imran,* 3:55; *Sura Maryam,* 19:57.
[201] *Suratu'l-Baqara,* 2:154; *Sura Al 'Imran,* 3:169.

Part 3

GENERAL PRINCIPLES RELATED TO BELIEF IN AND INTERPRETATION OF THE QUR'AN

General Principles Related to
Belief in and Interpretation of the Qur'an

- **The Qur'an, throughout all of its verses, aims mainly to establish and confirm four basic, universal truths: the existence and Oneness of the Maker of the universe; Prophethood; bodily Resurrection; and worship and justice.[1]**

The six pillars of the Islamic faith are interconnected and therefore believing in one of them requires believing in the others. So, believing in God and Prophethood requires believing in the Divine Books, the Divine Destiny and Decree, including human free will, and angels. Worship and justice encompass all the commandments of Islam.

- **The Qur'an contains all the truths in the previous Divine Scriptures revealed to different Prophets; all saints and purified, discerning scholars, following different ways of thought and paths to God, have derived their principles from the Qur'an, and all people of heart and intellect mention the Qur'an's laws and fundamentals in their books in a way that shows their affirmation. Besides, thousands of meticulous, learned scholars of high intelligence have written commentaries expounding the Qur'an, some of which consist of as many as seventy volumes, proving with clear evidence and arguments its innumerable qualities, characteristics, mysteries, subtleties and elevated meanings, and showing its numerous indications concerning every sort of hidden and unseen matter.[2]**

- **The Qur'an is luminous in each of its six aspects or sides, all of which point to its truthfulness and veracity. Beneath it lie the pillars of evidence and proof; above it shine the gleams of the stamp**

---

[1] *The Reasonings*, "The First Part", p. 11.

[2] *The Words*, "The Twenty-fifth Word", p. 389; *The Letters*, "The Nineteenth Letter", p. 207.

of miraculousness or inimitability; before it are the gifts of happiness in both worlds as its goal; behind it are the truths of the heavenly Revelation as its point of support; to its right is the well-documented and substantiated confirmation of innumerable sound and upright minds; to its left one sees the true satisfaction, sincere attraction and submission of sound hearts and pure consciences. These six, taken together, prove that the Qur'an is an extraordinary, firm, and unassailable heavenly citadel standing on earth.[3]

From these six aspects it is clear that the Qur'an is pure truth, that it is not a human word, and that it contains no errors at all. The Controller and Director of the universe, Who has made it His practice to always exhibit beauty in the universe, to protect goodness and truth, and to eliminate imposters and liars, has confirmed and set His seal on the Qur'an by giving it the most acceptable, highest, and most dominant place of respect and success in the world.

Also, the person who represented and communicated Islam and interpreted and explained the Qur'an throughout his life, upon him be peace and blessings, held it in greater respect than anything else. The words uttered by him outside the context of the Qur'an did not resemble the Qur'an and could never be on the same level. Despite being unlettered, with the Qur'an as his basis, he described, with complete confidence, many past and future events and numerous cosmic phenomena from behind the veil of the Unseen; as the supreme translator of the Qur'an, in whose behavior no trickery or shortcoming had ever been witnessed even by the sharpest eyes, he believed in and affirmed every pronouncement of the Qur'an with all his might, allowing nothing to shake him in his conviction. All of these facts serve to confirm, beyond doubt, that the Qur'an is the Divinely-revealed Word of his All-Compassionate Creator.

Moreover, all of the celebrated scholars in all branches of the religious sciences, the great interpreters of the Supreme Shari'ah in particular, together with the brilliant and exacting scholars of theology and the basic principles of the Religion, are able to exact from the Qur'an all the answers needed for their various disciplines. All of these facts confirm that the Qur'an is a source of truth, and a mine of reality.

---

[3] *The Words*, "The Twenty-fifth Word", p. 464; *The Letters*, "The Nineteenth Letter", p. 206

Furthermore, more than a fifth of humankind have been attached to the Qur'an with piety and rapture, paying heed to it eagerly in their desire to know the truth. In addition, each of the different classes of humankind, from the most simple and lowly to the most clever and learned, is able to take its share of the Qur'an's instruction, each according to their capacity.

Also, although the disbelieving ones among the Arab litterateurs, those who are most advanced in literature and eloquence, felt the greatest need to dispute the Qur'an, they have never been able to match it in eloquence by producing the like of even a single *sura*, despite the fact that eloquence is only one of the seven most prominent aspects of the Qur'an's miraculousness.

- **The value, superiority, and eloquence of a speech are based on the answers given to these questions posed with regard to it: "From whom has it come, for whom is it intended, and for what purpose?" In respect of these points, the Qur'an can have no peer, and none can reach it.**[4]

For the Qur'an is a speech and address by the Lord and Creator of all the worlds, and a conversation of His that is in no way derivative or artificial. It is addressed to the one who was sent in the name of all humanity and jinn, indeed of all beings, who is the most famous and renowned of humankind, the strength and breadth of whose belief gave rise to mighty Islam. It describes and explains matters concerning happiness in this world and the next, the results of the creation of the universe, and the purposes of the Lord within it. It also expounds the belief of its first and primary addressee, Prophet Muhammad, upon him be peace and blessings. His was the highest and most extensive belief, encompassing all of the truths of Islam. It shows every facet of the huge universe like a map, a clock or a house, describing it in a manner which befits the One Who made it. To produce a peer of the Qur'an is therefore not possible, nor can the degree of its miraculousness be attained.

The Qur'an is an eternal translation of the great Book of the Universe, and everlasting translator of its multifarious tongues, reciting the Divine laws of the universe's creation and operation; it is the interpreter of the books of the visible, material world and the World of the Unseen; the discloser of the immaterial treasuries of the Divine Names hidden on

---

[4] *The Words*, "The Twenty-fifth Word", pp. 388, 466.

the earth and in the heavens; the key to the truths lying behind events; the World of the Unseen's tongue in the visible, material world; the treasury of the All-Merciful One's favors and the All-Glorified One's eternal addresses coming from the World of the Unseen beyond the veil of this visible world; the sun of Islam's spiritual and intellectual world, as well as its foundation and plan; the sacred map of the worlds of the Hereafter; the expounder, lucid interpreter, articulate proof, and clear translator of the Divine Essence, Attributes, Names and essential Character or Qualities; the educator and trainer of the world of humanity, and the water and light of Islam, which is the true and greatest humanity; and the true guide of humanity that leads its followers to happiness.

For humanity, it is both a book of law, and a book of prayer, and a book of wisdom, and a book of worship and servanthood to God, and a book of command and call to God, and a book of invocation, and a book of thought and reflection. It is a comprehensive, holy book containing books for all of humanity's spiritual needs. It is a heavenly book that, like a sacred library, offers numerous booklets from which all saints, eminently truthful people, all discerning and verifying scholars, and those well-versed in knowledge of God, have derived their own specific paths, and which illuminate each way and answer their followers' needs.

- **The Qur'an has a different kind of miraculousness for everyone, and indicates this in the most perfect way.**[5]

To people of eloquence and rhetoric, it shows its miraculous eloquence; to poets and orators, it displays its miraculous and uniquely exalted style, one that cannot be imitated although it is liked by everyone. The passage of time does not alter its freshness, so it is always new. Its metrical and rhythmical style and composition have the greatest nobility and charm.

To foretellers, historians, and chroniclers, the Qur'an's miraculousness consists of the reports it gives about the Unseen and the information it relates about past nations, future conditions and events, and the Intermediate World and the Hereafter. To social and political scientists, it presents the miraculousness of its sacred principles, which comprise the Shari'ah. To those engaged in knowledge of God and the Divine laws of nature, the Qur'an shows its miraculousness in its sacred Divine truths

---

5   *The Letters*, "The Nineteenth Letter", p. 202.

that illuminate the path towards God. To those following a spiritual way to sainthood, it manifests the profound, manifold meanings in its verses that rise in successive motions like waves of the sea.

In short, the Qur'an shows its basic forty aspects of miraculousness to everyone by opening a different window. Even those who just listen to it and can derive a very limited meaning from it agree that the Qur'an sounds like no other book. This Qur'an is either below other books in degree—which is utterly impossible, and which even its enemies (and Satan) cannot—and indeed, do not—claim, or it is above them all, and therefore a miracle.

- **The wise Qur'an is the intellect of the head of the earth, and its power of thought. It is a chain, a "rope of God" which binds the earth to the sun, and the ground to the Divine Supreme Throne. It preserves the earth more than the law of general gravity.**[6]

If, God forbid, the Qur'an were to depart from the head of the earth, the earth would go insane. It is fair to say that with its head emptied of reason, it would collide with another planet and herald an apocalypse. Truly, if the gravity of the Qur'an, which is *the firm rope of God* that binds the earth to the sun and the ground to the Divine Supreme Throne, is broken, the tether holding the earth will come unfastened. The earth will consequently become dizzy and deranged: on account of the reversal of its usual motion, the sun will (be seen to) rise in the west. Through its collision with another planet, Doomsday will begin at the Divine command.

- **The Qur'an requires mirrors. Books and interpretations of Shari'ah should be mirrors of the Qur'an or telescopes through which the Qur'an is studied. That sun of miraculous exposition does not need shadows, or anyone to act on its behalf.**[7]

Rather than rational arguments, it is the sacredness of the source which encourages the mass of the Muslim Community to obey the Qur'an, and urges them to follow it. Ninety percent of the Shari'ah is comprised of the obvious, indisputable matters and essentials of Religion, each of which is a diamond pillar. The matters which are open to interpretation, controversial and secondary, only amount to ten percent. One who has

---

[6] *The Rays*, "The Fifth Ray", p. 368; "The Fourteenth Ray", p. 332; *Gleams of Truth*, p. 116.
[7] *Gleams of Truth*, pp. 32–33.

these ten gold pieces cannot own the ninety diamond pillars or put them in their purse, nor can they make them dependent on the gold pieces.

- **As stated in** "Not a thing, fresh or withered, wet or dry, but it is in a Manifest Book,"[8] **everything is found in the Qur'an, but not everyone can see everything in it, nor at the same level. For things are found at different levels in it. They are presented as seeds or nuclei or summaries or principles or signs, as well as explicitly or implicitly, allusively, vaguely or suggestively.**[9]

Depending on the occasion, one form is preferred to best convey the Qur'an's purposes and meet the context's requirements. For example, progress in science and industry has resulted in airplanes, electricity, motorized transportation, radio, telecommunication, and so on. Such things occupy a prominent position in our daily lives. As the Qur'an addresses humanity at all times, it does not ignore these developments; rather, it points to them either through the Prophets' miracles, or in connection with certain historical events, not directly and explicitly. For everything is found in it according to its degree of importance in God's sight especially with respect to guidance to the truth and the other world.

- **The Qur'an is so deep and infinitely comprehensive in meaning, and so interwoven in styles, that it considers each audience's level of understanding and temperament, and satisfies all levels in all times. There is not another word, Divine or not, which can be equal to the Qur'an.**[10]

Having come to us through 70,000 veils, the Qur'an penetrates the depths of hearts and spirits, and spreads its blessings through all levels of human society. Every era understands and knows it, every age acknowledges and accepts its perfection, every epoch makes friends with it and accepts it as its teacher, and every period needs and respects it to the degree it answers its specific needs. The Qur'an is not a superficial, shallow book; rather, it is a bottomless ocean, a shining sun, a profound guidance.

- **The Qur'an maintains the proportion or balance between all parts of the Tree of Creation, stretching from the beginning of creation to eternity, from the earth to the Divine Throne, from**

---

[8] *Suratu'l-An'am*, 6:59.
[9] *The Words*, "The Twentieth Word", pp. 265–266.
[10] *Al-Mathnawi al-Nuri*, "The Eighth Treatise", p. 260

particles to the sun, and between the pillars of faith and the commandments of Islam, and gives each part and fruit, each pillar and commandment, such a suitable form and place, and such rightful value, that all exacting and truth-seeking scholars have concluded: "What wonders God has willed. May God bless it. Only you, O wise Qur'an, solve the mystery of creation."[11]

If you want to see one of the Qur'an's highest degrees of miraculousness, consider the following parable: Imagine an extremely vast tree hidden behind a veil of the Unseen. You know that, just as between the members of a human body, there has to be, and is, a harmony and balance between various parts of a tree—between its branches, leaves, flowers, and fruits—and each part has its proper form and shape according to the tree's nature. If someone draws an exact replica of that hidden tree, correctly displaying all its parts, relationships, and proportions without seeing it, no one can doubt that the artist sees and depicts the hidden tree with an eye penetrating the Unseen.

In the same way, the Qur'an's explanations on the reality of things, namely, the reality of the Tree of Creation stretching from the beginning of creation to eternity, from the earth to the Divine Throne, from particles to the sun, maintain the proportion between all parts to such a degree, and give each part and fruit such a suitable form, that all exacting and truth-seeking scholars have concluded: "What wonders God has willed. May God bless it. Only you, O wise Qur'an, solve the mystery of creation."

The Qur'an describes the six pillars of faith with all their elements and furthest fruits and flowers with such proportion, observes their harmony to such a degree, and presents them in such a balanced and well-measured way, that we are amazed and scarcely able to grasp its beauty. It also observes the perfect relationship, complete balance, and amazing harmony among the five pillars of Islam and among its other commandments, which form a twig of the branch of faith, down to the finest details, the most insignificant points of conduct, the furthest aims, most profound wisdom, and most particular fruits.

- **Some of the verses of the Word of God—the Qur'an—all parts of which are interconnected, and which is therefore as if a single**

---

[11] *The Words*, "The Thirteenth Word", pp. 157–158; "The Sixteenth Word", p. 209.

paragraph, point to the gems of truth contained in other verses, and translate the secrets which lie in the hearts of their neighbors.[12]

The Qur'an allows each of its verses to be a sort of center to many of its other verses, and thus there is a connection among all verses within an encompassing context. It is as if each verse has an eye looking to most other verses, and a face turned towards them. Thus there are thousands of Qur'ans within the Qur'an, each being adopted by a different path or school in Islam. This is comparable to the way each star, apparently at random, extends, as if from a center, a line of connection to every other star in the surrounding area. Such a network also indicates the hidden relation between all creatures. It is as if, like the stars of Qur'anic verses, each star has an eye looking to and a face turning toward all stars. Reflect on the perfect order in apparent disorder, and take a lesson.

- **Everything related to the Qur'an and belief is, regardless of its apparent insignificance, of great significance. Since anything contributing to eternal happiness is significant, we should regard it as worthy of explanation.**[13]

- **Revelation, which aims at the guidance of people, is a form of Divine kindness and is described as "God's lowering His speech to the level of human capacity so that they can understand it." Since the great majority of people are common, it considers the understanding of common people, including those who are unlettered among them, but satisfies all levels at the same time.**[14]

Just as one uses appropriate words when addressing a child, the Qur'an uses a style appropriate to its audience's level from the lowest to the highest. By speaking in allegories, parables, and comparisons, it makes the most difficult Divine truths and mysteries understood by even the most common, unlettered person according to his or her capacity. For example: *"The All-Merciful has established Himself on the Supreme Throne,"*[15] shows Divine Lordship as though it were a Kingdom, and the aspect of His Lordship administering the universe as though He were a King seated on His Sovereignty's throne and exercising His rule.

---

[12] *The Reasonings*, p. 14.
[13] *The Letters*, "The Twenty-third Letter", p. 301.
[14] *The Rays*, "The Seventh Ray", p. 140.
[15] *Sura Ta-Ha*, 20:5.

- **Just as the Holy Prophet, upon him be peace and blessings, was a human being and, like all other human beings, subject to and dependent upon God's laws of life because he was a guide for humanity in all aspects of life, so does the Qur'an apparently follow the style of human speech and conversation as it addresses humanity to guide them to truth.**[16]

Our Prophet, upon him be peace and blessings, was a human being. All of his acts and attitudes, except for his miracles and states of Prophethood, originated in his humanity. Like all other human beings, he was subject to and dependent upon God's laws of life. He suffered from cold, felt pain, and so on. He was not extraordinary in all his acts and attitudes so that he could set an example to humanity through his conduct. If he had been extraordinary in all his acts and manners, he could not have an absolute guide in every aspect of life or a mercy for all through all his states.

In the same way, the wise Qur'an leads conscious beings, directs humanity and jinn, guides people of perfection, and instructs truth-seeking people. Thus it must follow the style of human speech and conversation. Humanity and jinn take their supplications and prayers from it, talk about their affairs in its terms, and derive their principles of good conduct from it. In short, every believer adopts it as the authorized reference for all their affairs. If, by contrast, it had been like the Word of God heard by Prophet Moses, upon him be peace , on Mount Sinai, no one could have borne it or used it as a reference. Even Moses, one of the five greatest Messengers of God, could endure to hear only a few pieces of that Word.

- **The wise Qur'an contains many particular events, each of which hides a universal principle and presents the tip of a general law.**[17]

For example: *"(He) taught Adam the names of all of them,"*[18] states that Prophet Adam, upon him be peace, was taught "the names" as a miracle to show his superiority over the angels in being favored with ruling the earth in God's Name. Although this seems a small and particular event, it constitutes a tip of the following universal principle: Due to its comprehensive nature, humanity was taught (or given the potential to obtain) a great deal of information, many sciences concerning all aspects of the universe, and vast knowledge about the Creator's essential Character or Qualities, Attri-

---

[16] *The Letters*, "The Twenty-sixth Letter", pp. 330–331.
[17] *The Words*, "The Twentieth Word", p. 260.
[18] *Suratu'l-Baqara*, 2:31.

butes, Names, and Acts. All of this made humanity superior to the angels, the heavens, the earth, and the mountains, for only humanity could bear the Supreme Trust. It also made humanity the earth's ruler in God's Name.

- **Just as the "Book of the Universe" is a complete entity, all parts of which are interrelated to one another whose verses therefore interpret one another, so too do the verses of the Qur'an interpret one another.**[19]

As mentioned before, the Qur'an allows each of its verses to be a sort of center to many of its verses and thus there is a connection among all verses within an encompassing context. It is as if each verse has an eye looking to most other verses and a face turned towards them. So, the verses interpret one another, and the first interpreter of the Qur'an is the Qur'an itself.

- **In regard to superiority, power, beauty, and fineness, a speech has four sources and should be viewed from the perspective of these sources: the speaker, the person addressed, the purpose, and the occasion on which it is spoken. In view of these sources, the Qur'an cannot be compared with other words and speeches, whether heavenly or not.**[20]

A speech derives its strength and beauty from these four sources, from the answers given to the questions "Who spoke it? To whom did he speak it? Why did he speak it? On what occasion did he speak it?" The one who speaks the Qur'an is God Almighty; the person addressed is the greatest of creation, namely Prophet Muhammad, upon him be peace and blessings. The Divine purpose for the revelation of the Qur'an is making God known, the guidance of humanity and jinn, and their worldly and eternal happiness. The Qur'an was revealed within twenty-three years in the darkest period of human history to illuminate all time and space. Therefore, from the perspective of these four sources, the incomparable, matchless degree of the Qur'an's eloquence, superiority, and beauty will be understood.

- **The Qur'an has challenged all of its opponents in eight degrees to produce a book similar to it, even similar to only one of its *suras*, no matter how short it is, but no one has ever been able to bring about a like of it, or even a like of one of its shortest *suras*.**[21]

---

[19] *The Reasonings*, "The Third Part", p. 116.
[20] *The Words*, "The Twenty-fifth Word", p. 449.
[21] *The Words*, "The Twenty-fifth Word", pp. 404–405.

The verse, "*If you are in doubt about (the Divine authorship of) what We have been sending down on Our servant (Muhammad), then produce just a sura like it and call for help from all your supporters, all those (to whom you apply for help apart from God), if you are truthful (in your doubt and claim),*"[22] directed to humanity and jinn, briefly means: (1) If you have doubt about the Divine authorship of the Qur'an and think a human being is writing it, let one of your unlettered people, as Muhammad the Trustworthy is unlettered, produce something similar. (2) If he cannot, send the most famous of your writers or scholars. (3) If he cannot either, let all of them come and work together and call upon all their history, "deities," scientists, philosophers, sociologists, theologians, and writers to produce something similar. (4) If they cannot, let them try—leaving aside its inimitable truths and the miraculous aspects of its meaning—to produce a work of equal eloquence in word order and composition.

By: "*Then produce ten suras like it, contrived,*"[23] the Qur'an means: (5) What you write does not have to be true; let it be fabrications or false tales. Neither need it match the Qur'an's length, just produce the like of its ten chapters. (6) If you cannot do that either, produce only the like of one chapter. (7) If you cannot do that, produce only the like of a short chapter. (8) If you cannot do that—which you cannot although you direly need to do it because such inability will put your honor, religion, nationality, lives, and property at risk, and you will die humiliated—then *fear the Fire, whose fuel is people and stones*[24]. You and your idols will spend eternity in Hell. Having understood your eight degrees of inability, what else can you do but admit eight times that the Qur'an is a miracle as the Word of God, the Lord of all the worlds?

- **As the Word of God, the Qur'an is a miracle—inimitable by anybody—in nearly two hundred aspects. Some of them are as follows:**[25]
  - The Qur'an is an eternal translation of the great Book of the Universe and of its multifarious tongues reciting the Divine laws of the universe's creation and operation; the interpreter of the books of the

---

[22] *Suratu'l-Baqara*, 2:23.

[23] *Sura Hud*, 11:13.

[24] *Suratu'l-Baqara*, 2:24..

[25] Please refer to the Twenty-fifth Word in *The Words* for detailed explanation with examples.

visible, material world and the World of the Unseen; the discloser of the immaterial treasuries of the Divine Names hidden on the earth and in the heavens; the key to the truths lying behind events; the World of the Unseen's tongue in the visible, material one; the treasury of the All-Merciful One's favors and the All-Glorified One's eternal addresses coming from the World of the Unseen, beyond the veil of this visible world; the sun of Islam's spiritual and intellectual world, as well as its foundation and plan; the sacred map of the worlds of the Hereafter; the expounder, lucid interpreter, articulate proof, and clear translator of the Divine Essence, Attributes, Names and essential Character or Qualities; the educator and trainer of the world of humanity and the water and light of Islam, which is the true and greatest humanity; and the true guide of humanity leading them to happiness. For humanity, it is both a book of law, and a book of prayer, and a book of wisdom, and a book of worship and servanthood to God, and a book of command and call to God, and a book of invocation, and a book of thought and reflection. It is a comprehensive, holy book containing books for all spiritual needs of humanity; a heavenly book that, like a sacred library, offers numerous booklets from which all saints, eminently truthful people, all discerning and verifying scholars, and those well-versed in knowledge of God have derived their own specific ways, and which illuminate each way and answer their followers' needs.

- The Qur'an is a miracle in eloquence, which originates in its words' beauty, order, and composition; its textual beauty and perfection; its stylistic originality and uniqueness; the superiority and clarity of its explanations; its meanings' power and truth; and its linguistic purity and fluency. Its eloquence is so extraordinary that its eternal challenge to the most brilliant people of letters of humankind, their most celebrated orators, and the most profoundly learned of them, to produce something like it, even if only a chapter, has yet to be answered. Instead, those geniuses who, in their self-pride and self-confidence, consider themselves so great as to touch the heavens have had to humble themselves before it.

- There is an extraordinary eloquence and stylistic purity in the Qur'an's word order or composition.

- There is miraculously comprehensive meaning.

- The Qur'an has unique, original styles that are both novel and convincing. Its styles neither imitate nor can be imitated.

- The Qur'an's wording is extraordinarily fluent and pure. As it is extraordinarily eloquent when expressing meaning, so also it is wonderfully fluent and pure in wording and word arrangement. For this reason:

- Even if the most beautiful poem or piece of music grows tiresome after singing or listening to it a few times, the Qur'an does not bore the senses but rather gives them pleasure, even if it is recited thousands of times. The more it is recited, the greater pleasure it gives.

- Even a child can memorize the Qur'an easily. There has never been, nor is, another book, heavenly or not, which can be memorized as easily as the Qur'an. Nor has a book been memorized by more people.

- Seriously ill people, even if troubled by a few words of ordinary speech nearby, feel relief and comfort upon hearing it.

- For dying people, it gives their ears and minds the same taste and pleasure as that left by the most tasteful water in their mouths and on their palates.

- The Qur'an feeds the heart, gives power and wealth to the mind, functions as water and light for the spirit, and cures the soul's illnesses.

- In all categories of expression and address, such as command and prohibition, promise and threat, encouragement and dissuasion, restraint and guidance, praise and censure, demonstration, explanation, argument, and narrative or parable, the Qur'an's expositions are of the highest degree.

- The Qur'an is infinitely comprehensive or rich in expressiveness and meaning. As pointed out in a *hadith*, each verse has outer and inner meanings, limits, and a point of comprehension, as well as boughs, branches, and twigs.[26] Each phrase, word, letter, and even an omission, has many aspects. Each person who hears it receives his or her share through a different door. Also, in addition to bestowing the necessary sources for exacting jurists, the illuminations of those seeking knowledge of God, the ways of those trying to reach God, the paths of perfected human beings, and the schools

---

[26] Abdu'r-Razzaq, *al-Musannaf*, 3:358; Abu Ya'la, *al-Musnad*, 9:278.

of truth-seeking scholars from the treasuries of its meaning, the Qur'an guides the students and scholars of all other branches of knowledge. Each of the different classes of humankind, from the most simple and lowly to the most intelligent and learned, is able to take its full share of the Qur'an's instruction and understand its most profound truths each according to their capacity.

- The Qur'an is extraordinarily comprehensive in the matters it deals with as well. It deals with humanity and its duties, the universe and its Creator, the heavens and the earth, this world and the next, and the past, future, and eternity. It explains all essential matters related to our creation and life, from correct ways of eating and sleeping, to issues of Divine Decree and Will, from the universe's creation to the functions of winds, and all other "natural" phenomena.

- The Qur'an explains all such essential and important matters in a way befitting an All-Powerful One of Majesty, Who administers the universe like a palace, opens and closes the world and the Hereafter like two rooms, controls the earth like a garden and the heavens like a lamp-adorned dome, and in Whose sight the past and future are like day and night or two pages, and all eternity (in the past and future) like a point of present time.

- The Qur'an is so wonderfully comprehensive in style that a single *sura* may contain the whole ocean of the Qur'an, in which the universe is contained. Its expressions are concise but all-inclusive. Its conciseness is like offering the ocean in a pitcher. Out of mercy and courtesy for ordinary human minds, it shows the most comprehensive and universal principles and general laws through a particular event on a particular occasion.

- The Qur'an contains all types of eloquence, all varieties of fine speech, all categories of elevated style, all examples of good morals and virtues, all principles of natural sciences, all indexes of knowledge of God, all beneficial rules of individual and social life, and all enlightening laws of creation's exalted reasons and purposes, and yet not a single trace of confusion is apparent in it.

- The Qur'an gives news of the past. Although communicated by an unlettered one, the wise Qur'an mentions in a solemn and powerful manner the important experiences of the leading Messengers from the time of Adam to the Age of Happiness, as well as the main aspects of their mission.

- For scholars of the inner aspects and innermost meanings of the Qur'an and creation, the Qur'an is full of true predictions concerning the near and distant futures.

- The Qur'an's explanations concerning Divine truths and its statements about the realities of creation, which solve the mystery of creation and unveil the talisman of the universe, are the most important and truest pieces of information about the Unseen.

- As an eternal discourse addressing all human beings, regardless of time or place and level of understanding, it should—and does—have a never-fading freshness. It so impresses each new generation that each one regards it as being revealed to itself, and receives its instructions therefrom. It demonstrates such freshness, youth, and originality that even though it has lived for fourteen centuries and been available to everyone, its vitality is such that one would think it has only just been revealed. Every century sees the Qur'an enjoying a new youth, as though it were addressing itself in particular. Similarly, even though they keep the Qur'an at their side constantly, in order to benefit from it and follow its method of exposition, scholars of every branch of learning see that the Qur'an continues to maintain the originality of its style and manner of explanation.

- The wise Qur'an addresses all people, regardless of time, place, or level of understanding, and calls them to and teaches them about belief, the highest and most profound science; about knowledge of God, the broadest and most enlightening branch of knowledge; and about the laws of Islam, the most important and elaborate of sciences. Therefore it has to—and indeed does—teach each group and level in an appropriate manner.

- The Qur'an is a book of perfect fluency, superb clarity and soundness, firm coherence, and well-established harmony and proportion. There is a strong, mutual support and interrelation among its sentences and their parts, and an elevated correspondence among its verses.

- Although the Qur'an was revealed over twenty-three years on different occasions, its parts are so mutually supportive that it is as if it were revealed all at once, on one occasion. Although the Qur'an came in answer to different and repeated questions, its parts are so united and harmonious with each other that it is as if it were the answer to a single question. Although the Qur'an came to judge diverse cases and events, it displays such a perfect order that it is as if it were the judgment delivered on a single case or event. Although the Qur'an was revealed by Divine courtesy in styles varied to suit innumerable people of different levels of understandings, moods, and temperaments, its parts exhibit so beautiful a similarity, correspondence, and fluency that it is as if it were addressing one degree of understanding and temperament. Although the Qur'an speaks to countless varieties of people, remote from each one in time, space, and character, it has such an easy way of explanation, pure style, and clear way of description that it is as if it were addressing one homogeneous group, with each different group thinking that it is being addressed uniquely and specifically. Although the Qur'an was revealed for the gradual guidance of different peoples with various purposes, it has such a perfect straightforwardness, sensitive balance, and beautiful order that it is as if it were pursuing only one purpose.

- The Qur'an is also miraculous in that it concludes most of its verses with a most succinct summary, which summarizes them in a way to show either the source of the truth it conveys, or the Divine Names on which it depends, or the message it communicates, or the result it will give—or which summarizes them with a call to reflection or taking a lesson, or with a promise or a threat or a warning or with a universal truth or reality or rule or principle.

- The Qur'an's explanations on the reality of things, or the reality of the Tree of Creation stretching from the beginning of creation to eternity, from the earth to the Divine Throne, from particles to the sun, maintain the proportion between all parts to such a degree, and give each part and fruit such a suitable form that all exacting and truth-seeking scholars have concluded: "How wonderful and incomparable they are!"

- The wise Qur'an also describes the truths of the Divine Names, Attributes, Essential Character or Qualities, and Acts in all of their ramifications and results in so harmonious, fitting, and appropriate a way that all those who have knowledge of these subjects cannot help but express their admiration. Also, the Qur'an describes the six pillars of faith with all their elements, furthest fruits, and flowers with such proportionately, and observes their harmony to such a degree, and presents them in such a balanced and well-measured way, that we are amazed and scarcely able to grasp its beauty. It also observes the perfect relationship, complete balance, and amazing harmony among the five pillars and all other commandments of Islam. All these are so because the Qur'an's explanations could not have issued from any human being's knowledge, especially from that of an unlettered person. Rather, its explanations rest on an all-comprehensive knowledge and the Qur'an is the Word of One Who sees all things together like a single thing, Who simultaneously observes all truths between two eternities.

- As well as bringing about a substantial, happy, and enlightening transformation in human social life, the Qur'an has brought about a revolution in the souls, hearts, spirits, and intellects of people, and in their individual, social, and political lives. Furthermore, it has perpetuated this revolution in such a way that, at every moment in the past fourteen centuries, its more than six thousand and two hundred verses have been read with the utmost respect by more than a hundred million people, training and refining their souls, and purifying their hearts. For spirits, it has been a means of development and advancement; for intellects, a guidance and light; and for life, it has been life itself, and felicity. Such a book is without doubt unparalleled in every respect. It is a wonder, a marvel and a miracle.

- **Just as the Qur'an, with all its aspects of miraculousness and truths that show its veracity, is a miracle of Prophet Muhammad, upon him be peace and blessings, Prophet Muhammad himself, with all his miracles, proofs of Prophethood and perfections of knowledge, is a miracle of the Qur'an, and a decisive proof of the Qur'an's being the Word of God.**[27]

- **The apparent repetitions in the Qur'an are another aspect of the Qur'an's miraculousness.**[28]

---

[27] *The Words*, "The Twenty-fifth Word", p. 462.
[28] *The Words*, "The Nineteenth Word", p. 255; "The Twenty-fifth Word", p. 468.

The Qur'an issues from the greatest and most comprehensive rank of the Eternal Speaker's universal Lordship. It is addressed, first of all, to the comprehensive rank of the one who received it in the name of the universe. Its purpose is to guide humanity from the time of its revelation until the end of time. It therefore contains entirely meaningful and comprehensive explanations concerning the Lordship of the Creator of the universe, and clarifications of the Divine laws which pertain to the administration of all creatures. This Divine discourse is so comprehensive and elevated, and therefore so inclusive and miraculous that even its most apparent, literal meanings which target the simple minds of ordinary people, who make up the majority of people, is enough to satisfy those among the people who have attained the highest and most sophisticated levels of understanding. The Qur'an addresses and is revealed to every age and all levels of understanding as a collection of universal principles. All these factors require the repetition of certain fundamental truths and principles from different perspectives.

The Qur'an shows that it is a book of prayer and invocation, a call to eternal salvation, and a declaration of God's Unity, all of which require reiteration. Consequently, it repeats this or that sentence or story, gives numerous meanings to many different groups or categories of addressees, and informs its readers about many complex and interrelated subjects. It relates some important events on different occasions for different purposes in a such a way that it presents universal principles, suggesting that those events function as though they were seeds, destined to produce numerous important fruits in all ages and all places.

The Qur'an is both a book of wisdom and law, and a book of prayer and worship, and a book of command and call to God, and a book of invocation and knowledge of God. It contains books for all of humanity's spiritual needs, and is like a sacred library offering booklets from which all saints, eminently truthful people, and all purified and discerning scholars have derived their own specific ways. Invocation requires reiteration to impress and enlighten hearts. Through repetition, prayer acquires and gives strength to hearts, and becomes ingrained therein. Commands and calls need restatement to be confirmed and enforced.

Not everyone can read the whole Qur'an whenever they want; usually they can read only one *sura* (chapter). This is why its most important purposes are reiterated in most of the longer chapters, each of which thereby can serve as a small Qur'an.

Certain purposes and themes like Divine Unity, Resurrection, and the story of Moses are repeated so that no one is deprived of their benefits. Also, spiritual tastes and needs vary like bodily ones. We need some of them at every breath. Just as the body needs air, the spirit needs *Hu–Huwa* (He–God). We need some others every hour, like *Bismillah* (In the Name of God). And so on. The reiteration of verses therefore arises from the recurrence of needs. The Qur'an reiterates to point out those needs, to make them deeply felt, and to stir our desire to satisfy them.

Furthermore, in its role as a founder, the Qur'an is the basis of a manifest religion and the foundation of the Islamic world. It came to change human social life and answer the recurring questions and needs of various classes of human society. A founder uses repetition to affirm, and reiteration to emphasize. A new establishment requires confirmation and strengthening, and therefore repetition.

The Qur'an speaks of such important matters and subtle truths that reiteration in different contexts is necessary to impress their different aspects on people's minds and hearts. However, such repetitions are merely apparent, for in reality each verse has manifold meanings, numerous benefits, and many aspects and levels. In each place, the words or verses occur in a different way and context, for a different meaning, purpose, and benefit.

- **The Qur'an is incomparable and miraculous in the moral training it offers and establishes for human individual and social life.**[29]

A comparison between the Qur'an's moral training and that of human irreligious philosophy: A sincere student of this philosophy is a Pharaoh-like tyrant who bows in adoration before the meanest thing, if he perceives it to be in his interest. That irreligious student is obstinate and refractory; but he is so wretched that he accepts endless degradation for one pleasure. He is unbending but so mean as to kiss the feet of devilish people for a base advantage. He is also conceited and domineering, but, unable to find any point of support in his heart, he is an utterly impotent and vainglorious tyrant. That student is a self-centered egoist who only strives to gratify his material and carnal desires; a

---

[29] *The Words*, "The Twelfth Word", pp. 146–147.

sneaky egotist who pursues the realization of his personal interests in certain national interests.

However, a sincere student of the Qur'an is a worshipping servant of God, but he does not degrade himself by bowing before even the greatest of the created. He is a dignified servant who does not take even a supreme benefit like Paradise as the aim of his worship; he aims at God's approval and good pleasure. He is modest, mild and gentle, yet he does not lower himself voluntarily before anybody other than his Originator, unless He allows him to do so. He is also aware of his innate weakness and need, but he is independent due to the other-worldly wealth that his Munificent Owner has stored up in him; and he is powerful because he relies on his Master's infinite Power. He acts and strives purely for God's sake and good pleasure, and to be equipped with virtue.

- **The Qur'an is also incomparable and miraculous in the social training it offers and establishes for human life.**[30]

An example of the social training of the Qur'an and human irreligious philosophy in human social life: Philosophy considers force or might to be the point of support in social life, and the realization of self-interest is its goal. It holds that the principle of life is conflict. The unifying bonds between the members of a community and communities are race and aggressive nationalism; and the fruits philosophy offers are the gratification of carnal desires and the continuous increase of human needs. However, force calls for aggression, seeking self-interest causes fighting over material resources, and conflict brings strife. Racism feeds by swallowing others, thereby paving the way for aggression. This is why humanity has lost happiness.

As for the Qur'anic wisdom, it accepts right, not might, as the point of support in social life. Its goal is virtue and God's approval, not the realization of self-interests. Its principle of life is mutual assistance and solidarity, not conflict. The only community bonds it accepts are those of religion, profession, and country. Its final aims are controlling carnal desires and urging the spirit to sublime matters, satisfying our exalted feelings so that we will strive for human perfection and true humanity. Right calls for unity, virtues bring solidarity, and mutual assistance means hastening to help one another. The Religion secures brotherhood and sisterhood, and

---

[30] *The Words*, "The Twelfth Word", pp. 147–148.

cohesion. Restraining our carnal soul and desires, and urging the spirit to perfection bring happiness in this world and the next.

- **Besides securing happiness in this world, the Qur'anic commandments basically serve and aim at the eternal happiness of humanity.**[31]

As the Qur'an's laws and principles transcend time and space, they do not become obsolete; they are always fresh and strong. For example, despite all its charitable foundations, institutions of intellectual and moral training, and severe disciplines and laws and regulations, modern civilization has been unable to contest the wise Qur'an even on the following two matters, and has been defeated by it:

"Perform the prescribed Prayer, and pay the Zakah,"[32] and, *"God has made trading lawful and interest and usury unlawful."*[33] The basic origin of all revolutions and corruption in human social life is one phrase, so is the cause and source of all vices and moral failings also one phrase: The first is: "I am full, so what is it to me if others die of hunger?" And the second: "You work so that I may eat."

A peaceful social life depends on the balance between the elite (rich) and common (poor) people. This balance is based on the former's care and compassion, and the latter's respect and compliance. Ignoring the first attitude, namely care and compassion, drives the rich to wrongdoing, usurpation, immorality, and mercilessness; ignoring the second attitude, namely respect and compliance, drives the poor to hatred, envy, and conflict with the rich. As this conflict has destroyed social peace for the last two or three centuries, it has also caused social upheavals in Europe due to the struggle between labor and capital.

Despite all its charitable societies, institutions of moral training, and severe laws and regulations, modern civilization has not been able to reconcile these two social classes, nor healed those two severe wounds of human life. The Qur'an, however, eradicates the first attitude and heals its wounds through the *Zakah*, and eradicates the second by outlawing interest and usury. The aforementioned Qur'anic verse stands at the door of the world and says to interest and usury: "You are forbidden to enter!" It decrees to humanity: "If you want to close the door of strife, close the door of interest and usury." It orders its students not to enter through it.

---

[31] *The Words*, "The Twenty-fifth Word", p. 429.
[32] *Suratu'l-Baqara*, 2:43.
[33] *Suratu'l-Baqara*, 2:275.

If humankind desires salvation and loves its life, it must impose *Zakah* and abolish usury and interest. Unfortunately, humankind has not heeded these commands of the Qur'an and has thus received two severe blows in the form of two world wars, the second being severer than the first. All of the savagery and crime of former times, all the cruelty and treachery, have been vomited in these wars all at once, and the world's stomach is still retching. Therefore, humankind should heed the Qur'an's call before receiving another, much severer blow.

- **The Qur'an's literary merits incomparably transcend all trends of human literature.**[34]

There are three arenas in which literature revolves. It roams within their bounds: either love and sorrow, or heroism and valor, or a depiction of reality. Modern literature does not seek the truth, or acclaim rightness in heroism; rather, it instills a desire for power by applauding the cruelties of oppressors.

As it regards sorrow and love, modern literature is not aware of true love; it injects into the soul a lust-driven thrill. In the matter of the depiction of reality, it does not look on the universe as Divine art; it does not see it as a painting of the All-Merciful. Rather, this literature approaches the universe from the point of view of "self-existent nature", or naturalism, and depicts it thus; it cannot free itself from this limitation. For this reason, what such literature inculcates is a false love of nature. It implants in the heart feelings associated with materialism, from which it cannot easily save itself.

Furthermore, this literature is only a sedative and narcotic for the distress of the spirit which arises from the misguidance resulting from materialism; it can provide no remedy. It has found a single remedy, and that is in novels and fiction. Books are animated corpses, movie pictures are moving corpses. The dead cannot give life! It has put a false, lying tongue in humankind's mouth, attached a lustful eye to its face, clothed the world in a scarlet dress, and does not recognize pure beauty.

If literature indicates the sun, it puts in the reader's mind a beautiful blonde actress; but it apparently says: "Dissipation is bad; it is not fitting for humanity." Literature indicates harmful consequences. But its depictions so incite dissipation that they make the mouth water and reason

---

[34] *The Words*, "Gleams of Truth", pp. 765–767.

lose control. They rouse appetite, excite desire, and thus, the emotions heed neither advice nor warnings.

The literature of the Qur'an, however, stirs up no such desires. It imparts love of, and attachment to, rightness, a passion for pure beauty and pleasure in it, and zeal to attain and establish the truth. It never deceives.

The Qur'an does not look at the universe from the point of view of "self-existent nature" or naturalism; it speaks of it as Divine art, as a painting of the All-Merciful. It does not confuse the mind. It inculcates the light of knowledge of the Maker. It indicates His signs in all things.

Styles of literature and rhetoric give rise to sorrow or joy. Sorrow is of two kinds: it comes from either the feeling of loneliness and lack of any protection and support, or separation from the beloved. The first is despairing and produced by the misguided, heedless, modern and naturalist civilizations. The second is lofty and exhilarating, and arouses a hope and eagerness for reunion. This is the kind given by the guiding, light-diffusing Qur'an.

Joy or eagerness is also of two kinds. The first incites the soul to animal desires; the carnal soul becomes excited, and fanciful desires are stimulated; there is no joy to the spirit. As for the Qur'an, it restrains the carnal soul and urges the human heart, spirit, intellect, and all inner senses and faculties to lofty things, and to reunion with the original, eternal abode and with friends who have passed on already. The Qur'an of miraculous exposition encourages this joy by arousing an eagerness to reach Paradise, eternal happiness, and the vision of God.

Indeed, in the view of those with sacred sorrow to whom it is addressed, the Qur'an becomes a gathering of friends. On every side there is mutual love and responsiveness, which causes no distress.

There is friendliness at every corner, giving the sorrowful in that society an elevated feeling, not a dejected grief.

- **The profound meaning and great truth contained in: "*Say: 'If humanity and jinn banded together to produce the like of this Qur'an, they would never produce its like, even if they backed one another,'*"[35] is pure truth and reality, which the long history of Islam has proved.[36]**

---

[35] *Suratu'l-Isra'*, 17:88.
[36] *The Words*, "The Twenty-fifth Word", pp. 429-430.

The challenge contained here has two principal aspects. One is that no work produced by humanity or jinn can resemble or equal the Qur'an's style, eloquence, rhetoric, wording, comprehensiveness, conciseness, and profundity. Nor can their most beautiful and eloquent words, all arranged in a volume by their most competent representatives, equal the Qur'an. The second aspect is that all human and jinn civilizations, philosophies, literatures, and laws, which are the products of the thought and efforts of humanity and the jinn, and even satans, are dim and helpless when faced with the Qur'an's civilization, commandments, wisdom, and eloquence.

- **The Qur'an holds the greatest rank among God's infinite words, including the previous Divine Scriptures.**[37]

Having come from God's Supreme Throne, originated in His Name with the most comprehensive manifestation, and issued from each Name's most comprehensive rank, the Qur'an is God's Word on account of God's being the Lord of the Worlds, and His decree on account of His having the title of Deity of all creatures. It is a discourse in the Name of the Creator of the heavens and the earth; a speech and conversation in regard to His absolute Lordship; an eternal sermon on behalf of the All-Glorified One's universal Sovereignty. It is also a register of the All-Merciful One's favors from the viewpoint of His all-embracing Mercy; a collection of messages or communications that sometimes begin with ciphers in respect of His Divinity's sublime majesty; and a wisdom-infusing holy Scripture that, having descended from the all-comprehensive realm of the Divine Name with the most comprehensive manifestation, looks over and surveys the circle surrounded by His Supreme Throne.

This is why the title "the Word of God" has been and will always be given to the Qur'an. As for other Divine Words, some of them are speeches coming as particular manifestations of a particular aspect of Divine Mercy, Sovereignty, and Lordship under a particular title and with a particular regard for a particular period of time to a particular people.

- **From Adam's time until the present, two great currents or lines of thought have spread their branches in all directions and in every class of humanity, just like two tall trees. One is the line of**

---

[37] *The Words*, "The Twelfth Word", p. 149.

Prophethood and Religion; the other is that of human irreligious philosophy.[38]

The line represented by Prophethood is the origin of pure worship and servanthood to God, for our selfhood knows that it is His servant. Selfhood realizes that it serves One other than itself and that its essential nature has only an indicative function. It understands that it bears the meaning of One other than itself and that it can be meaningful only when it points to that One upon Whom its existence depends. Selfhood believes that its existence and life depend upon that One's Creativity and Existence. Its feeling of ownership is illusory, for selfhood knows that it enjoys only an apparent, temporary ownership by the real Owner's permission and that it has only a shadow-like reality. It is a contingent entity, an insignificant shadow manifesting the true and necessary Reality. Its duty is consciously serving as a measure and balance for its Creator's Attributes and essential Character or Qualities.

The second line, represented by irreligious philosophy, regards selfhood as having an essential meaning of its own. It says that selfhood has an independent existence, is an index only to itself, and labors wholly on its own behalf. It considers selfhood's existence as necessary and essential, and falsely assumes that selfhood owns its being and is the real lord and master of its own domain. Philosophy supposes selfhood to be a permanent reality that has, as its duty, the quest for self-perfection for the sake of self-esteem.

- **Whenever the lines of Prophethood and the irreligious human philosophy agree and unite, whenever philosophy joins Religion in obedience and service to it, humanity has experienced brilliant happiness in both the individual and social sphere. But whenever they have followed separate paths, truth and goodness have accumulated on the side of Prophethood and Religion, whereas error, evil, and deviancy have been drawn to the side of philosophy.**[39]

According to the principles of human irreligious philosophy, power is approved. "Might is right" is the norm. Its maxims are: "All power to the strongest," "Winner takes all," and "In power there is right." It has given moral support to tyranny, encouraged dictators, and urged oppressors to

---

[38] *The Words*, "The Thirtieth Word", pp. 557–558.
[39] *The Words*, "The Thirtieth Word", pp. 555–562.

claim divinity. Whereas the principle of Prophethood says: "Right is might." It thus halts tyranny and secures justice.

According to one of Prophethood's principles concerning individual life, namely, the rule: "Be molded by Divine values," there is the instruction: "Seek distinction through Divine values and turn towards the All-Mighty with humility, recognizing your impotence and insufficiency, and be a servant in His Court, and thus find the source of the real power." But philosophy, due to its self-oriented principle of seeking human perfection in being like the Necessarily Existent Being, instructs: "Try to be like the Necessarily Existent Being." This is impossible, for while the Necessarily Existent Being is infinitely powerful, omnipotent, self-sufficient, and without need, our essence has been mixed with impotence, weakness, poverty, and need.

Among Prophethood's principles of social life's fundamental conditions are mutual assistance, solidarity, magnanimity, and generosity. These function in the reciprocal cooperation of all things—from the sun and the moon down to particles. For example, plants help animals, animals help people, and particles of food help the body's cells. Moreover, almost all parts of the universe come to the aid of a seed under earth so that it may grow into tree, and all parts of the body help one another. Philosophy, however, considers conflict to be life's fundamental condition. In fact, conflict springs from tyrants, brutes, and savages and wild animals misusing their innate dispositions because of the destruction of the ecosystem by human hands. Conflict is so fundamental and general to philosophy's line of reasoning that they absurdly claim that "life is conflict."

One sublime result and exalted principle of Prophethood about Divine Unity is: "That which has unity can proceed only from one (of unity)." That is, the unity and universal accord or harmony in existence is because of the Creator's Oneness. Whereas philosophy states that "Only one proceeds from one." Thus, as only one thing can proceed from one origin, everything comes from that one by means of intermediaries. This misleading principle opened the way to a most grievous polytheism. By presenting the absolutely All-Powerful and Self-Sufficient as needing impotent intermediaries, it gave all causes and intermediaries a kind of partnership in His Lordship and shared, in the view of Peripatetic philosophers, His creativity among an imaginary "Ten Intellects."

According to one of Prophethood's wise principles that *"There is nothing but it glorifies Him with His praise,"*[40] the purpose and wisdom in creation, particularly of living creatures, may have one aspect relating to the creature itself but many aspects relating to the Creator. For example, a fruit has as much wisdom and as many purposes involved in its creation as all fruits of a tree. However, according to philosophy's principles, which lack true wisdom, every living creature's purpose relates to itself or is connected with its benefits for humanity. This means that creation is so senseless that the purpose of a mountain-like tree is only to yield a tiny fruit, where it has numerous other meanings and functions with respect to God Almighty, the Creator and Lord of the worlds.

Philosophy also has attributed a creative effect to causes, and thereby attributes creative power to nature. Since it does not see the clear stamp upon everything signifying the Creator of all things, philosophy assumes nature to be the originator. It ignores the facts that nature, whose supposed power is ascribed to blind chance and necessity, is impotent, inanimate, unconscious, and blind. It attributes a part of creation to nature, although every element is but a missive from God, the Eternally Besought, relaying thousands of instances of exalted wisdom.

Moreover, philosophers did not find the door to the Resurrection and the Hereafter, which the All-Mighty (with all of His Names), the universe (with all of its truths), the line of Prophethood (with all of its verifications), and the revealed Books (with all of their verses) demonstrate. As a result, they denied bodily resurrection and ascribed pre-eternity to souls, even to matter. Indeed, the powers of evil have raised up and flattered the intellects of disbelieving philosophers as though with the beaks and talons of their egos, and thrown them into the abyss of deviation.

- **Some of the Qur'an's statements and commandments are decisive, unchanging, general and timeless, while others are restrictable, ambiguous, brief and specific.**[41]

The Qur'an addresses all times and places, and all peoples in every age and with different characters and capacities. Therefore, the Qur'an has different styles. Some of its commandments and expressions are decisive and timeless. Its principles or rules concerning the pillars of faith, human duty of worship, basic kinds of worship such as the Prescribed Prayers, fasting

---

[40] *Suratu'l-Isra'*, 17:44.
[41] *Sünuhat* (Occurrences to the Heart), in *Sünuhat, Tuluat, İşarat*, p. 20.

during the month of Ramadan, *Zakah*, and Pilgrimage, and its absolutely obligatory commandments and prohibitions are decisive However, both decisive commandments, and those which are brief and ambiguous and particular to certain times and conditions, need interpretation and explanation. Either the Qur'an itself or the Sunnah of the Holy Prophet make these interpretations and explanations. For example, the Qur'an decisively orders Muslims to pray properly, but nowhere does it explain how to do so. It is the Sunnah which teaches us how to pray. Also, the Qur'an lays down general principles of inheritance. For example, God's Messenger decreed that "The killer (of his testator) would be disinherited."[42] In other words, if someone kills his or her parents, brother (sister), or uncle (aunt), they cannot inherit from them. Thus the killer of his testator is excluded from the law of inheritance. This is a restriction of a general rule.

Some of the general commandments require specification or particularization. For example, the Qur'an commands: "*O you who believe! Consume not your goods among yourselves in vanity (through theft, usury, bribery, hoarding, and so on), except it be trade by mutual agreement.*"[43] Islam encourages trade as a way of making one's living, as long as it is carried out according to Islamic law. One condition, as stated in the verse, is mutual agreement. However, God's Messenger decreed: "Do not sell fruits until their amount is definite in the tree (so that the amount to be given as alms can be determined)"[44] and: "Do not go to meet peasants outside the market to buy their goods (Let them earn the market prices of their goods)."[45]

- **The Qur'an is a boundless treasury and all people, regardless of time, receive their share from its complementary, implicit truths without interfering with the shares of others after they acknowledge its principles and unchangeable commands.**[46]

Some people claim that the Qur'an's mysteries are unknown, and that its interpreters have not perceived its truths. This claim has two aspects, and those who make it fall into two groups. The first group comprises the people of truth and investigation. They say that since the Qur'an address-

---

[42] *at-Tirmidhi*, "Fara'id," 17.
[43] *Suratu'n-Nisa'*, 4:29.
[44] *al-Bukhari*, "Buyu'," 82; *Muslim*, "Buyu'," 51.
[45] *Muslim*, "Buyu'," 5:14–7.
[46] *The Letters*, "The Twenty-ninth Letter", p. 382.

es every level of understanding in every age, all people, regardless of level and time, can comprehend it according to their level.

The Qur'an becomes better understood over time and in more detail, and the dimensions of its meaning are clarified. However, this does not mean that we should doubt its literal, explicit truths expounded by our righteous predecessors, for belief in the certain and incontrovertible truths forming the fundamentals of the Qur'an and Islam is obligatory.

The second group comprises either single-minded friends who make matters worse while trying to help, or devilish enemies who oppose Islam's commands and the truths of belief. They want to make a way through the Qur'an's fortified *suras*, which are like a steel citadel around the Qur'anic truths. They spread their false claims to cast doubt upon the truths of belief and the Qur'an.

- **God Almighty swears by many things in the Qur'an. There are numerous mysteries and subtle points in these oaths.**[47]
- **The disjunct or abbreviated letters at the beginning of several Qur'anic suras** (al-hurufu'l-muqatta'at) **are Divine ciphers. In addition to the many other meanings they convey, God Almighty reveals some signs of the Unseen to His particular servant, Prophet Muhammad, upon him be peace and blessings, through them.**[48]

Much has been said and written about their meaning:

- Spelling letters means that people have just begun to learn how to read and write. So, the presence of these letters at the beginning of some *suras* shows that the Qur'an was sent down to an illiterate people.
- They imply that the Qur'an is a book composed of words and letters, which it is impossible for an illiterate person like Prophet Muhammad, upon him be peace and blessings, to have produced. As the Qur'an is a book, the universe is also a book. This is why Muslim sages call the former "the Revealed and Written Universe," and the latter "the Created Book." A letter has no meaning of itself; rather, it functions in a word and points to its writer in many ways. Each creature in the universe functions in a similar way by likewise pointing to its Creator.

---

[47] *The Letters*, "The Twenty-ninth Letter", p. 383.
[48] *The Letters*, "The Twenty-ninth Letter", p. 383, *İşaratü'l-İ'caz* (Signs of Miraculousness), pp. 32–34.

- The characters of the Arabic alphabet are variant forms, extended and curved, of the first letter *l* (*alif*), which is itself described as the extended form of the *nuqta*, or "point." This is a symbol of the reality that, like the letters, words and sentences of the Qur'an, and all the creatures of the universe originate in a single source and are inter-related. From this we may understand that, in order to be able to produce even a single atom in the universe or word in the Qur'an in its proper place, one must have the knowledge and power to produce the whole universe and the whole Qur'an.

- These letters are like ciphers between the Revealer—God—and the Messenger, the exact and complete meaning of which is known to the Messenger only. However, this does not mean no one else can grasp some of their meanings. Exacting scholars well-versed in the science of the mysteries of the letters have drawn many mysterious conclusions from them and discovered in them such truths that, in their view, these letters form a brilliant miracle.

- **A true and exact translation of the Qur'an is impossible. Its sublime style, an element of its miraculous meaning, cannot be imitated. Even explaining the truth and pleasure derived from its sublime style is impossible.**[49]

For example: "*Al-hamdu li-llah*" (All praise be to God) is a Qur'anic sentence meaning, according to Arabic syntax and semantics: "Every praise that has been or ever will be uttered by any being to anyone else is, in reality, for and deserved by the Necessarily Existent Being: God."

The meaning "every" derives from *al* (the). The meaning "by any being" derives from *hamd* (praise), for the original Arabic is in the infinitive form. The infinitive in Arabic expresses a general meaning if it has no subject. Besides, as this sentence contains no object either, although it is addressed to someone (or something) who is either present or absent, its meaning is also general. Besides, the word *hamd* cannot be translated literally into another language. For *hamd* denotes God Almighty with all His affirmative Attributes and, in one sense, answers the question Who is God? Saying "*Al-hamdu li'llahi*" is also a confession of belief in God in His absolute Oneness with all His affirmative Attributes describing Him.

---

[49] *The Letters*, "The Twenty-ninth Letter", p. 386–387.

"That has been or ever will be" comes from the rule that transitioning from a verb clause to a noun clause indicates persistence and duration. "For and deserved by" are expressed in the preposition *li* (to or for God), which specifies and expresses deserving. Since *Allah* is the Divine Being's Greatest Name or His Name with the most comprehensive manifestation, and since existence is essential and indispensable to the Divine Being and is a tableau to help reflect on the Majestic Being, *Allah* necessarily connotes the Necessarily Existent Being. If this is the explicit, briefest meaning of such a short sentence, which is agreed upon by linguists of Arabic, how can it be translated to another language with the same strength and miraculousness? How can the Qur'an's sacred words, revealed in Arabic and therefore having a syntax and comprehensiveness displaying an All-Encompassing Knowledge penetrating everything at the same time, be translated into other languages without losing their subtle meanings, allusions, and miraculous style? In reality, each letter in the Qur'an is such a rich treasure of truths that its explanation could cover at least one page.

- **What reliably interprets the Qur'an is primarily the Qur'an itself—its own sentences, expressions, and phrases; its meaning is in and of itself, like a pearl in an oyster—and the reliably narrated *Hadith*. Neither the Torah nor the Gospels, whose legal rules and decrees have been abrogated and narratives distorted, can be used to interpret the Qur'an.**[50]

The Qur'an is a miraculous Divine Word; it cannot be imitated and no one can produce even a single verse that resembles it. So, what will interpret the Qur'an is itself—its own sentences, expressions, and phrases. Its meaning is in and of itself, like a pearl in an oyster. Even if one intended to declare the truth and excellence of the Qur'an through an imagined agreement between the Qur'an and, say, Greek philosophy or another source like the previous Scriptures, again, it would be pointless. The Book, which is clear in itself and reveals all truth, is far removed from needing to be proven by such philosophy and reported knowledge, which itself is in need of the Qur'an to be proven and accepted. Conversely, if the Qur'an does not prove that knowledge, its testimony would not be worthy of attention.

---

[50] *The Reasonings*, "The First Part", p. 17.

- **Anything that is in a book of Qur'anic interpretation is not necessarily included in the meaning of the Qur'an, nor in the interpretation itself.**[51]

The meaning of the Qur'an and Shari'ah are not identical with the books written about them. It is not enough for a non-Muslim, in order to become a Muslim, merely to enter a mosque. Likewise, merely by being included in books of Shari'ah or interpretations of the Qur'an, matters pertaining to other sciences or to philosophy cannot be regarded as being included in matters of Shari'ah or the Qur'an.

For example, the famous interpreter Qadi Baydawi holds that the steep mountains mentioned in the verse—*(Dhu'l-Qarnayn said:) "Bring me blocks of iron." Then, after he had filled up (the space between) the two steep mountain-sides, he said: "(Light a fire and) work your bellows!" At length, when he had made it (glow red like) fire, he said: "Bring me molten copper that I may pour upon it."*[52]—are the mountains of Armenia and Azerbaijan. It would be unreasonable and illogical to accept this opinion of a great interpreter as the final truth. What led to him to this opinion was information he received from other sciences. The Qur'an is silent about which mountains those mentioned were. So, Baydawi's reading cannot be included as falling within the meaning of the Qur'an itself. But it would also be unjust to criticize this illustrious interpreter or shed doubt on his profound knowledge and comprehension in the science of Qur'anic interpretation because of this reading. One should accept it as one expert's opinion but realize that other opinions are also possible.

- **Every age needs a new interpretation of the Qur'an.**[53]

Each age has characteristics peculiar to itself and therefore has its own needs and demands. Time adds its own interpretation, and new events and developments especially in sciences cause many new meanings to be discovered. So, there should be convened a "parliament of scientists" that would consist of specialists in natural and religious sciences. This parliament should bring into being a new interpretation of the Qur'an, without at all neglecting to make reference to the classical interpretations. They should work on the acceptable elements in these, deep-

[51] *The Reasonings*, "The First Part", pp. 25–28.
[52] *Suratu'l-Kahf*, 18:96.
[53] *The Reasonings*, "The First Part", p. 20..

ening and developing them. Public opinion is an observer. **The consensus of scholars on a matter is a source of legislation in Islam.**

- **The explicit judgments to be found in any Qur'anic statements should be distinguished from those that are not explicit, without forgetting that it is obligatory to believe in the explicit ones.**[54]

For example, the explicit points in the Qur'an's answer to the question about Dhu'l-Qarnayn cannot be denied. According to this answer,[55] Dhu'l-Qarnayn was a person favored with God's confirmation and help. By God's leave and guidance, he built a barrier between two mountains in order to prevent the attacks and corruption of some savages—Gog and Magog are the names given to the two "tribes" that were engaged in corruption and disorder. When the Divine order comes, the barrier will be destroyed. These, and some other explicit truths that exist in the Qur'an's account of Dhu'l-Qarnayn, must certainly be considered as being true and confirmed. Denial of any of them means unbelief. However, as for the detail of what is narrated and meanings that it is possible to infer—the Qur'an is not clear about them. According to the rule that an expression employed to convey a general meaning does not necessarily constitute an argument or proof for some particular meaning incidental to that general meaning or alluded to, and the rule that whatever a statement states clearly with respect to its underlying and essential meaning is sufficient for it, it may be said that the Qur'an here does not necessarily indicate anything of detail. But since it does not categorically reject it, we can study and comment on it.

This means that all the interpretations, expositions, and analyses, other than the explicit meaning and the clear, apparent truths established by the explicit meaning, are only putative suggestions. They require corroboration by other indications. Interpreters can reason about them. They can be given different meanings. The differences of opinion among verifying scholars concerning them shows that the inferences and connotations—other than the evident, basic meanings—are putative.

- **There may be more than one judgment in a word, or several other judgments than the basic, intended one. However, they are of particular importance. Every one of these may issue from a dif-**

---

[54] *The Reasonings*, "The First Part", p. 60.
[55] *Suratu'l-Kahf*, pp. 83–98.

**ferent origin and bear a different fruit. One who cannot differen-
tiate between them remains devoid of the truth.**[56]

There are the following three judgments in a Qur'anic or Prophetic expression:

One: This expression is a word of God; if it is a *hadith*, it is a word of the holy Prophet, upon him be peace and blessings. This judgment about the *hadith* is based on the reliability of the chains of transmission.

The second: The meaning expressed in this Qur'anic or Prophetic word is true.

We must accept both of these judgments. Their denial means unbelief. However, the *hadith* whose denial is unbelief, must be a *mutawatir*—that is, it had to be transmitted through, at least, three reliable chains from the Prophet himself, upon him be peace and blessings.

The third: The judgment is what every qualified person deduces from it. This judgment cannot be reached through personal inclinations or desires or caprices. It should be based on true reasoning established on the necessary principles. One who is qualified to deduce a judgment from the Qur'an and the Prophetic Traditions (other than the explicit judgments addressing and understandable by everyone) is not obliged to follow another with the same qualifications. Differences of view occur in this third judgment. Phrases such as "So-and-so says," and "It is said," which we frequently come across in relevant books, bear witness to that. Those who have the necessary qualifications to deduce judgments from the Qur'an and the Prophetic Traditions do not commit a sin when, and if, they disagree with the judgment of others. The judgments—other than the explicit ones —must be in compliance with the basic principles and truths of the Religion, the rules of the Qur'anic language, and the rules of eloquence.

- **The apparent, basic meaning of a verse is one thing, and other meanings or connotations, inferred from it by scholars and the things that confirm it, are another. If one of the numerous connotations or meanings inferred cannot yet be confirmed, or appears to lack necessary evidence, the basic meaning cannot be denied.**[57]

- **The truth, falsehood, confirmation, or denial, cannot be gleaned from the apparent meaning of allusive and figurative expres-**

---

[56] *The Reasonings,* "The First Part", pp. 42–44.
[57] *The Gleams,* "The Twelfth Gleam", p. 86.

sions. **It is found in the purpose for which they are uttered, or what is meant by them.**[58]

For example, if we say that a tall person has a sword with a long handle, this is true even if that man does not have a sword, for what we have uttered is a figurative statement designed purely to indicate the height of the man. The Qur'an, the eternal Word of God addressing all times and conditions, and all levels of understanding, uses metaphors and certain other literary arts when necessary. Therefore, the true meaning in the expressions containing such arts should be searched in the purpose for which they are used.

- **The Qur'anic expressions such as the Best of Creators, the Most Merciful of the Merciful, the Best of Judges, and God is the Greatest cannot be meant to suggest the existence of other creators and judges, or other merciful and great ones comparable to God.**[59]

The Best of Creators means that the Creator has the highest rank of creativity. This does not suggest the existence of other creators for, like other Attributes, Creativity has ranks of manifestation. Thus this phrase means that He is the All-Majestic Creator, having the ultimate rank of creativity.

Secondly, such phrases as *the Best of Creators* relate to species of beings, or the variety of beings created, and mean that He is the Creator Who creates everything in the best and most appropriate fashion. This is the same meaning as that which is expressed by verses like *He Who makes excellent everything that He creates.*[60]

Thirdly, such phrases as *the Best of Creators, God is the Greatest, the Best of Judges*, and *the Best of the Benevolent* do not compare those Acts and Attributes of God that are manifested in the universe with those of creatures. First of all, it should not be forgotten that whatever beings have is a gift from God. We see because God is All-Seeing, and hear because He is All-Hearing. All perfections shared by humanity, angels, and jinn are only indistinct shadows in relation to His, which are beyond compare.

People, especially the misguided, cannot measure God properly and are usually forgetful of Him. For example, a private pays his corporal perfect respect and attributes to him whatever good he enjoys. He is oblivious of the king; even if he remembers him, it is still to the corporal that

---

[58] *The Reasonings*, "The First Part", p. 14.
[59] *The Words*, "The Thirty-second Word", pp. 633–635.
[60] *Suratu's-Sajda*, 32:7.

he shows gratitude in return for any good he receives. Such a private should be warned: "The king is greater and more benevolent than your corporal, so you must thank the king." This does not mean to compare the king's actual, magnificent commandership with the corporal's—such a comparison would be meaningless. What is meant is to warn the private who prefers the corporal in gratitude and forgets the king.

Similarly, means, nature, and causes blind heedless people to the True Bestower of bounties. They attribute the bounties which they receive to means and nature and creativity to causes, as if they were the actual sources, and praise and thank them. Therefore, the Qur'an warns: Almighty God is much greater and a far better Creator and Benefactor, actually meaning that He is the sole Creator and Benefactor. Regard Him and thank Him.

There are other meanings in such expressions, the explanations of which are outside the scope of this book.

- **The words and phrases the Qur'an uses and its styles of using them function as sources of numerous truths and judgments in the name of the Islamic sciences such as Theology, the Interpretation of the Qur'an, *Hadith*, and Jurisprudence, as well as of the Islamic thinking, belief, and life. They also show the profundity of the meanings every Qur'anic expression has.[61]**

Out of what We have provided for them they give as sustenance.[62]

The parts of the above sentence point to five conditions that make alms-giving acceptable to God.

First condition: While giving alms, believers must not give so much that they are reduced to begging. "Out of" expresses this.

Second condition: They must give out of what they have, not out of what others have. "We have provided for them" points to this.

Third condition: They must not remind the recipient of their kindness. "We" indicates this, for it means: "I have provided you with the thing out of which you give to the needy as sustenance. As you are giving some of that which belongs to Me, you cannot put the recipient under obligation."

Fourth condition: They must give to those who will spend it only for their livelihood, not in illicit ways. "They give as sustenance" points to this.

---

[61] *The Words*, "The Twenty-fifth Word", pp. 392–393.
[62] *Suratu'l-Baqara*, 2:3.

Fifth condition: They must give it for God's sake. "We have provided for them" states this. It means: You are giving out of My property, and so must give in My Name.

Together with those conditions, the word "what" signifies that whatever God bestows is part of one's sustenance or livelihood. Thus believers must give out of whatever they have. For example, a good word, some help, advice, and teaching are all included in the meaning of *rizq* (sustenance or provision) and *sadaqa* (alms). "What" (*ma*) has a general meaning and is not restricted here. Thus it includes whatever God has bestowed.

This short sentence contains and suggests a broad range of meaning for alms and offers it to our understanding. The word order of the Qur'an's sentences has many similar aspects, and the words have a wide range of relationships with one another. The same is true for the relationships between sentences.

Part 4

GENERAL PRINCIPLES RELATED TO KNOWING THE PROPHET AND TO HIS SUNNAH AND HADITH

General Principles Related to Knowing the Prophet and to His Sunnah and *Hadith*

- **Something's result or fruit is considered first. Thus the latest in existence is the first in meaning, consideration and intention. Since Prophet Muhammad, upon him be peace and blessings, is the most perfect fruit of the Tree of Creation, the means for valuing all other fruits, and the cause for realizing all purposes for the universe's creation, his nature is the first in creation.[1]**

The fruit is the purpose for the existence of a tree. We do whatever we do for a purpose, and do it according to our purpose. This means that in the existence of something, the purpose comes first. And every tree, which is grown for its fruit, grows from the seed in its fruit. This universe is, or has, the meaning of a tree. Just like a tree, it has numerous branches—immaterial and material worlds. Every world has twigs. For example, this world, which is a branch of the Tree of Creation, has the twigs of elements, and it has also leaves (plants), flowers (animals), and fruits (humanity) on its twigs. This Tree of Creation must have been formed from a seed, which must certainly have life like all other seeds.

These decisive realities of existence absolutely reject Darwinist evolution, which, based on the structural resemblances between species, claims the coincidental evolution of living species from each other. This claim means that first something is done purposelessly, and then a purpose and meaning are attached to it, or it gains a meaning and a purpose, as we see that there is nothing purposeless in existence. That is, for example, first we write some letters purposelessly; or rather, some letters appear by themselves purposelessly, and then they gain a purpose and meaning. Whereas

---

[1] *The Words*, "The Twenty-first Word", p. 600.

in the existence of something, the purpose comes first, and then comes the meaning, and then its plan. For example, when we write something, first we have a purpose; then we conceive of the meaning in our minds; and then we make a plan. The material existence comes last. Not a single word has ever been written by itself, so that all those countless creatures, all of which have explicit meanings and purposes for their existence, and perform purposeful and meaningful duties in the magnificent order of existence, may have appeared by themselves by chance.

God Almighty created this Tree of Creation so that He may be known and worshipped.[2] Those who will know and worship Him are the conscious beings. So, there must be one, or some, who will communicate with God to make Him known to conscious beings. Otherwise the creation of this meaningful universe would be useless. It was the Prophets who received Revelation from God and made Him known to people. Therefore, the Prophets were the brightest among the fruits of the Tree of Creation. However, there is one among the Prophets who made this duty universally—Prophet Muhammad, upon him be peace and blessings, while all other Prophets were sent to a particular people for a limited time. Therefore, Prophet Muhammad was the greatest and brightest fruit of the Tree of Creation, and he contained the seed of this Tree. This seed is his nature, which is called *Haqiqat Ahmadiya* (the Truth of Prophet Muhammad as Ahmad). Before his coming to the world as Muhammad, he was called Ahmad.[3]

- **Whatever Prophet Muhammad, upon him be peace and blessings, claimed is confirmed by all of the Prophets based on their miracles, and by all saints based on their good or marvelous works.**[4]

All the affirmations of Prophet Muhammad, upon him be peace and blessings, bear the seals of all perfected people during human history. If one hears him declaring *There is no deity but God*, thereby affirming Divine Unity, one will hear the same declaration from the past and the future, from the illustrious shining "suns"—Prophets—and stars—saints—of humanity. Despite their different approaches and temperaments, they agree with all of his affirmations, as if saying in unison: "You declare and speak the truth."

---

2   *Suratu'dh-Dhariyat*, 51:56.
3   *Suratu's-Saff*, 61:6.
4   *Al-Mathnawi al-Nuri*, "The Second Treatise", p. 20.

How can one object to what has been affirmed by innumerable witnesses, whose miracles and marvelous good works display their pure characters and truthfulness?

- **If we see the universe as a great book, we will see the nur (immaterial light) of Muhammad as the ink with which the Author of that book has written it. If we see the universe as a tree, we will see his nur as originally its seed, and consequently, its fruit. If we see the universe as an animate being, we will see his nur as its spirit. If we see the universe as a macro-human, we will see his nur as its intellect. If we see the universe as a flower garden, we will see his nur as its nightingale.**[5]

If we see the universe as a lofty, richly decorated castle with many rooms and apartments displaying the splendor of the Eternal Sovereign's sovereignty, the marvels of His Glory, the beautiful manifestations of His Grace, and the wonderful designs of His Art, we will see the *nur* of Prophet Muhammad as a spectator. He first views them on His behalf and then announces: "O people! Come and look at these pleasant sights. Hasten to receive your share in them—love, amazement, refreshment, appreciation, enlightenment, reflection, and many other lofty things." He shows all these to them; he observes them and has others observe them. As he himself is amazed by them, he causes others to be amazed by them. He loves their Owner and makes Him loved by others. As he is illuminated through them, he has others illuminated. He benefits from them and makes others benefit.

- **Just as Prophet Muhammad's mission of Messengership caused the creation of this world for trial and worship, so the prayer he makes as a requirement and dimension of his servanthood would cause the construction of the other world for reward and punishment.**[6]

How extraordinary! What does the Pride of Existence ask for, this man who stands with all the Prophets behind him and, raising his hand towards God's Supreme Throne, offers a supplication to which humanity and jinn say "Amen"? He intercedes with God for all beings. He asks for an eternal, happy existence, meeting with God, Paradise, and God's good pleasure. We see that the most insignificant petition is heard and

[5] *Al-Mathnawi al-Nuri,* "The Sixth Treatise", pp. 169–170.
[6] *The Words,* "The Tenth Word", p. 86; *Al-Mathnawi al-Nuri,* "The Second Treatise", p. 28.

answered most attentively. The prayer of every stomach is answered. Therefore, is it conceivable that a Lord of infinite compassion and mercy, Who most compassionately fulfills the least need of His lowliest creatures in the most unexpected fashion, Who answers the faintest cry of help of His most obscure creature, and Who responds to all petitions, would ignore the greatest petition of His foremost servant, his most beloved creature, by not granting his most exalted prayer?

- **As Prophet Muhammad's person is universal in nature, as well as his mission, the earth is his mosque, Mecca his place of worship as the leader in prayer, and Medina his pulpit. He leads all believers during history, who stand behind him in rows and follow his words on the principles of happiness in both worlds. The chief of all Prophets, he removes the lies and slurs leveled against them by their own people, and affirms them and the essentials of their religions, which Islam encompasses. The master of all saints and scholars, he guides and educates them via the light of his Messengership. He is the "pivot" around which turns a circle formed of the Prophets, the good, the truthful, and the righteous, who agree on his Message.[7]**

God's Messenger, Prophet Muhammad, upon him be peace and blessings, is matchless in the following points:

1. Prophet Muhammad, upon him be peace and blessings, has the meaning of the entire universe, which is the created Qur'an—and the Qur'an, which is the revealed universe, and contains all the truths that existed in the previous Scriptures. Together with the universe and the Qur'an, Prophet Muhammad is one of the three universal 'books' which make the Creator and Lord of the universe known to conscious beings. While all the other Prophets were sent to a particular people for a limited time, Prophet Muhammad was sent to the entire humankind and jinn.

2. While all the Books and messages of all the previous Prophets, which were particular to a particular people for a limited time, were corrupted during history, the Book—the Qur'an—which Prophet Muhammad brought from God and his Sunnah, the two unique sources of his Message, have been preserved intact. Also, the Qur'an contains, together with all the truths in the previous Scriptures, the eternal principles of

---

[7] *Al-Mathnawi al-Nuri*, "The Second Treatise", p. 20.

true thinking, sound belief and morality, and a happy individual and social life.

3. The Qur'an is the tongue of the worlds of the Unseen and the seen, the treasury of the eternal Divine Speech, and the eternal favors of the All-Merciful One. It is the foundation and plan, the sun of Islam's spiritual and intellectual world, and the map of the Hereafter. It is the expounder, lucid interpreter, articulate proof, and clear translator of the Divine Essence, Attributes, Names, and Acts. It is our educator and trainer, and the water and light of Islam, which is the true and greatest humanity. It is the true wisdom of humanity, the true guide leading us to the purpose of our creation.

The Qur'an is a book of law and wisdom, worship and servanthood to God, commands and invitations, invocations and contemplations. It is one book containing many books to answer our needs. It is like a sacred library of books and treatises from which saints, eminently truthful ones, purified and discerning scholars, and those distinguished with their knowledge of God derive their specific ways. It illuminates each way and answers their followers' needs.

4. The miracles of all the previous Prophets remained limited to their times, while the greatest miracle of Prophet Muhammad, upon him be peace and blessings,—the Qur'an—remains alive until Judgment Day. He was also affirmed by hundreds of other miracles he worked.

5. This most illustrious person is confirmed by both all the previous Prophets, and the millions of scholars and saints who have come after him. All of the earlier Divine Scriptures predicted his coming, and confirmed his Prophethood.

6. He is the most advanced in all praiseworthy characteristics and good morals. Like the sun showing itself through its light, heat, and other manifestations, all of the praiseworthy virtues concentrated in his person, as well as the merits and excellences he displayed while fulfilling his mission, confirm him as the greatest of creation.

He was also the most advanced in the six essentials of Prophethood, namely truthfulness, trustworthiness, communication of God's commands, intelligence, infallibility, and freedom from all bodily and mental defects. Also, his matchless courage, ability of administration, commandership, complete trust in God and utmost confidence in his mission and miraculous protection by God make him the greatest of all creations.

7. Prophet Muhammad is the greatest leader of history in all fields of life. He was both the greatest spiritual guide and a supreme teacher in all sciences; the most eminent statesman or president and diplomat; an invincible commander; the most compassionate leader of family; the most beloved and honored friend; the most articulate orator; the most eminent and just judge; the most competent educator; and yet he was also the most humble of all, and the most advanced in servanthood to God Almighty.

8. What stimulates him? Sacred power. Consider his accomplishments in that desert full of savages who adhered fanatically to their customs, their tribalism and hostility. They were so hard-hearted that they buried their daughters alive without remorse or grief. How did he remove such things from them so quickly, and equip them with high, laudable virtues? How did he make them teachers of humanity and masters of civilized peoples? Not by power and terror, as do most rulers, but by conquering hearts and minds. He subjugated spirits and egos, and became the beloved of hearts, the teacher of reason, the educator of selfhood, and the ruler of spirits.

9. It is very difficult even for a powerful, determined ruler or government to remove an established bad habit from a small community. The Prophet, upon him be peace and blessings, removed many established bad habits from vast communities of people who adhered fanatically to their customs and traditions. He did so with a small force, little effort, and very quickly. Moreover, he replaced them with praiseworthy virtues and exalted merits. Look at 'Umar ibn al-Khattab before and after his conversion to Islam, and see the differences in him, and the success of the Prophet, upon him be peace and blessings.

10. Almost all of the Prophet's accomplishments are extraordinary. Among the Prophets, Prophet Moses, peace be upon him, resembled Prophet Muhammad, peace and blessings be upon him, most in the inclusiveness of their missions. A similar movement launched by Prophet Moses, together with his brother Prophet Aaron, peace be upon him, was completed by Prophets David and Solomon in almost four centuries, despite the fact that their people were always led and governed by Prophets. However, the movement launched by Prophet Muhammad, peace and blessings be upon him, reached its goal within twenty-three years. In addition, Prophet Moses's mission was restricted for a limited time and for a particular nation, while Prophet Muhammad's mission was

universal, for all times and peoples. Besides, the powerful state founded and consolidated by Prophet David and Solomon, peace be upon them, was divided into two kingdoms just after Prophet Solomon. However, the state founded by Prophet Muhammad, peace and blessings be upon him, developed to the extent that it spread to an area as almost fifteen million km2 in a time as short as ten years after his death, and continued as the greatest power of the world for the next twelve centuries. Also, the Divine Religion upon which the state of David and Solomon was established was corrupted after Solomon; so, too, was the Old Testament. Likewise, the same Religion preached by Jesus, as well as the Book he conveyed, was altered just after him. Prophet Muhammad preached the same Religion in its universality, and both this Religion and its Book—the Qur'an—have been preserved intact. Whoever denies the exceptional accomplishments of Prophet Muhammad, peace and blessings be upon him, should go to the Arabian peninsula or another country or city of the world today, and see what they can accomplish there. Let them take a hundred philosophers, psychologists, sociologists, scientists, and pedagogues, and see if they can accomplish in a hundred years even one-hundredth of what the Prophet accomplished in a year.

Michael Hart, the writer of The 100, A Ranking of the Most Influential Persons In History (New York, 1978), has chosen him as the most influential person of human history. He explains the reason why he has done so as follows:

> My choice of Muhammad to lead the list of the world's most influential persons may surprise some readers and may be questioned by others, but he was the only man in history who was supremely successful on both the secular and religious level. ...It is probable that the relative influence of Muhammad on Islam has been larger than the combined influence of Jesus Christ and St. Paul on Christianity. ...It is this unparalleled combination of secular and religious influence which I feel entitles Muhammad to be considered the most influential single figure in human history.

11. This is the tribute of Alphonse de Lamartine, the French historian, to the person of the holy Prophet of Islam:

> Never had a man set himself, voluntarily or involuntarily, a more sublime aim, since this aim was superhuman: to subvert superstitions which had been interposed between man and his Creator, to render God unto man and man unto God; to restore the rational and sacred idea of divinity amidst the

chaos of the material and disfigured gods of idolatry then existing. Never has a man undertaken a work so far beyond human power with so feeble means, for he had in the conception as well as in the execution of such a great design no other instrument than himself, and no other aid, except a handful of men living in a corner of desert. Finally, never has a man accomplished such a huge and lasting revolution in the world, because in less than two centuries after its appearance, Islam, in faith and arms, reigned over the whole of Arabia, and conquered in God's name Persia, Khorasan, Western India, Syria, Abyssinia, all the known continent of Northern Africa, numerous islands of the Mediterranean, Spain, and a part of Gaul.

If greatness of purpose, smallness of means, and astounding results are the three criteria of human genius, who could dare to compare any great men to Muhammad? The most famous men created arms, laws, and empires only. They founded, if anything at all, no more than material powers which often crumbled away before their eyes. This man moved not only armies, legislation, empires, peoples, and dynasties, but millions of men (and women) in one-third of the then inhabited world; and more than that, he moved the altars, the gods, the religions, the ideas, the beliefs and the souls. On the basis of a Book, every letter of which has become law, he created a spiritual nationality which has blended together peoples of every tongue and of every race.

He has left to us as the indelible characteristic of this Muslim nationality, the hatred of false gods and the passion for the One and immaterial God. This avenging patriotism against the profanation of Heaven formed the virtue of the followers of Muhammad. The conquest of one-third of the earth to his creed was his miracle. The idea of the unity of God proclaimed amidst the exhaustion of fabulous theogenies, was in itself such a miracle that, upon its utterance from his lips, it destroyed all the ancient temples of idols and set on fire one-third of the world.

His life, his meditations, his heroic revilings against the superstitions of his country, and his boldness in defying the furies of idolatry; his firmness in enduring them for thirteen years at Makkah, his acceptance of the role of public scorn and almost of being a victim of his fellow-countrymen: all these and, finally his incessant preaching, his wars against odds, his faith in his success, and his superhuman security in misfortune, his forbearance in victory, his ambition which was entirely devoted to one idea and in no manner striving for an empire; his endless prayer, his mystic conversations with God, his death and his triumph after death; all these attest not to an imposture but to a firm conviction. It was his conviction which gave him the power to restore a creed. This creed was two-fold: the Unity of God and the immateriality of God. The former telling what God is; the latter telling what God is not. He was a Philosopher, Orator, Apostle, Legislator, Warrior, Conqueror of ideas, Restorer of rational dogmas, and of a cult without images. He was the founder of twenty terrestrial empires and of one spiritual empire. All that is Muhammad. As regards all standards by which human greatness may be measured, we may well ask: Is there any man greater than he?[8]

12. The Religion Prophet Muhammad, upon him be peace and blessings, preached became successful not only in being accepted by millions of people in a very short time but also in conquering hearts and minds to the extent that it defeated all the religions and philosophies that it encountered in the places it spread.

13. He had such sublime virtues in his blessed being, such exalted qualities in his Messengership, and such precious merits in the Religion and sacred Law that he preached, that even his most bitter enemies could find no fault with him. Since he combines theory and practice, Religion and life in his mission, and the most praiseworthy virtues in his personality, he is certainly the embodiment, master, and representative of all perfections and the high, laudable virtues found in creation.

13. He was so perfect a commander that he challenged the whole world with only a handful of followers. He repelled all who opposed his teachings and was never defeated, although he had no mortal teachers and never attended a military academy. He was so informed about science that he told his followers about almost all the major events that would occur until the Last Day. It was as if he were watching television or reading from an unseen tablet.

14. His Companions, may God be pleased with them, knew him and loved him very much. Their love for him was greater than their love for themselves. They were prepared to sacrifice their lives to protect him. He was so loved that his Companions would have given their lives if it meant that he could live forever. But, of course, he was mortal like other created beings. The appointed hour drew near and he had to say farewell to his friends of twenty-three years.

15. No one, whether before or after him, has taught about God the Lord, the Hereafter, the metaphysical realm, the principles of a happy life in both

---

[8] Alphonse de Lamartine, *History of Turkey*, New York, 1857, vol., 2, pp., 276–277.

worlds, and the meaning and interpretation of events and cosmic phenomena, as perfectly as him and in as perfect harmony and balance as he did.

16. He is also the most advanced in belief in, and worship of, God, including praying to Him. No one can match his love and awe of Him.

17. The life, actions, and sayings of no one other than Prophet Muhammad, upon him be peace and blessings, has ever been established, recorded, and transmitted through generations. Almost the whole life of God's Messenger was established, and his actions and sayings, and even his tacit affirmations, were recorded and transmitted through generations as the second foundation of the Religion.

18. Look at that most illustrious person from the viewpoint of his mission: He is the proof and lamp of the truth, the Sun of guidance, and the means of happiness. Look at him from the viewpoint of his person: He is the epitome of the All-Merciful's love of His creatures, the embodiment of the Lord's mercy upon them, the honor of humanity, and the most radiant and illustrious fruit of the Tree of Creation. Now look at him and see how the light of Islam has reached the east and the west with the speed of lightning, how one-fourth of humanity has accepted the gift of his guidance wholeheartedly.

19. Another dimension of Prophet Muhammad's exceptional position is the very concise nature of his speech. Remember that he is the leader, not only of those who lived during his lifetime, but of every believer to come. He was sent to address people of every level, from ignorant seventh-century bedouins to those of the highest intellectual and scientific achievements, until the Day of Judgment. No one has yet been able to disprove what he said. Ever since the beginning of his mission, billions of people have found in his words answers for their intellectual problems, cures for their spiritual diseases, and models for their behavior in all circumstances.

The enchanting, captivating, and informative words of God's Messenger that so enlightened his Companions intellectually, and revived them spiritually, have exerted the same influence on countless scholars, scientists, Qur'anic exegetes, Traditionists, jurists, spiritual guides, and specialists in science and humanities since the seventh century. Such people, the vast majority of whom have been non-Arab, have used the Qur'an and the Sunnah as the foundational sources of their academic studies and endeavors. Even today, one of his words is enough to cause people to reform themselves and embrace Islam. He acknowledged this as one of

God's blessings and, to emphasize it as a blessing, would sometimes say: "I am Muhammad, an unlettered Prophet. No Prophet will come after me. I have been distinguished with conciseness of speech and comprehensiveness of meaning,"[9] and: "O people, I have been honored with conciseness of speech and giving the final judgment in all matters."[10]

- **Prophets work miracles to prove their claim of Prophethood and to convince deniers, not to compel belief. If miracles somehow compelled everyone to see or believe in them, the All-Wise's wisdom in or the Divine purpose for creating us with free will and sending Religion, which entails that the ground be prepared for the mind's willing acceptance but the free choice not be negated or canceled, would be violated.[11]**

Some ask why the Prophet's splitting the moon in Mecca with a gesture of his finger print was not seen in the other parts of the world. There are reports that it was seen in India. Again, since this event occurred instantaneously at night while everyone was sleeping, it would certainly not be seen all over the world. Even if some people had seen it, they would not have believed their eyes. And even if it had made them believe, such a significant, miraculous event would not have been recorded by histories based on individual reports. Also, this miracle would certainly not be mentioned in Chinese, Japanese, and Native American historical accounts because, in addition to other obstacles, it was barely sunset in such European countries as Spain, France, and England (all enveloped in mists of ignorance), daytime in America, and morning in China and Japan when it happened.

However, whether it was seen or not, miracles were shown to convince those who heard the claim of Prophethood during the Prophet's time. Furthermore, if the All-Wise Originator had let the moon split for several hours so that everyone could see and record it in their historical records, it would have been only another astronomical event instead of an event unique to Muhammad's Messengership or an evidence of his Prophethood. Or it would have been so evident a miracle that everyone had been forced to believe, and free will would be annulled. Thus, the creation of humanity with a free will and with a special function and responsibility, as well as the

---

[9]   Muttaqi al-Hindi, *Kanzu'l-'Ummal*, 11.412.

[10]   *Ibid*, 11:425.

[11]   *The Words*, "The Thirty-first Word", pp. 606–607.

purpose for sending Revelation, would be negated. That is why this miracle was not shown worldwide so that it could be recorded.

- **Without the permission and help of God Almighty, Prophets can not work miracles nor can saints work wonders.**[12]

Miracles are evidence for Prophethood, while wonder-working is usually a favor of God for some of His beloved servants. Both miracles and wonders depend on the permission of God. Besides, if God does not enable them to work miracles or wonders, a Prophet cannot work a miracle nor can a beloved, saintly servant of God work wonders.

- **The sun cannot exist without emitting light, and Divinity cannot be thought not to reveal Itself by sending Prophets.**[13]

Could an absolute, perfect beauty not will to reveal itself through one who will demonstrate and display it? Or could the One of infinite essential Beauty not will to behold, and have others behold, in numerous mirrors, His Beauty's aspects and His Grace's dimensions? Could a perfectly beautiful artistry not will to make itself known through one who will draw our attention to it? Could the universal dominion of an all-embracing Lordship not will to make known its being One and the Eternally Besought to all levels of multiplicity and particularity through an envoy ennobled by his authority? Could He not do so by means of a beloved Messenger, who both makes himself loved by Him through his worship, and holds up a mirror to Him, making Him known and beloved by His creatures, and demonstrating the beauty of His Names?

Could the Owner of treasuries filled with extraordinary miracles and priceless goods not will to show His hidden perfections to an appreciative humanity via a master "jeweler," an eloquent describer? Could the One Who has adorned the universe with His artifacts that display His Names' perfections and so made the universe resemble a palace decorated with every variety of subtle, miraculous artistry not appoint a teacher and guide who will make those perfections known and teach people how to live in such a palace?

Could the Owner of the universe not resolve, by means of a messenger, our bewilderment over why there is constant change in the universe, and answer the questions in everyone's mind: What is our origin? Where are

---

[12] *The Letters*, "The Fifteenth Letter", p. 91.
[13] *The Words*, "The Tenth Word", p. 78.

we headed? What is our purpose here? Who is it Who has sent us here? What do life and death ask of us? Who is our guide in this life and to eternity? Could the All-Majestic Maker, Who makes Himself known to conscious beings through His fair creation and loved through His precious gifts, not send a messenger to convey to them what His Will demands from them in exchange? Could He create us with a disposition to suffer from multiplicity (this world and its charms) alongside an ability to engage in universal worship, without simultaneously wanting us to turn away from multiplicity toward Unity by means of a teacher and guide?

- **Prophethood is essential for humankind. The Divine Power, Which does not leave ants without a leader or bees without a queen, surely would not leave humankind without a set of laws and a Prophet.**[14]

The first reason why Prophets were sent is that they made God Almighty known to people with all His signs in the universe. Among the duties of Prophets or Messengers, God also sent them to guide people to the truth, and so they could be purified of falsehood and sin. Those who were enlightened by the Messengers found the way to the Divine Presence and attained the highest rank of humanity. Again, we were not created only to eat, drink, and reproduce; these are natural facts of our life, and natural needs. Our main purpose is to recognize and serve God. For this reason, all Prophets were sent to show us how to serve Him.

Another purpose for sending Prophets is to reveal Divine Commandments for a happy life in both worlds, teach people how to worship God, and convey the principles of justice and to establish it. Prophets also were sent to serve as examples. We are obliged to follow them consciously.

At a time when some people lived in monasteries and others drowned in luxury, Prophet Muhammad, peace and blessings be upon him, came with the Qur'anic instruction: "*Seek, amidst that which God has given you, the Last Abode, and do not forget your portion of the present world.*"[15] That is, all of the Prophets, upon them all be peace, came to establish balance between the material and spiritual life, reason and the soul, this world and the next, and indulgence and abstinence. Prophets also were sent so that people will not be able to plead ignorance in the Hereafter. Regard-

---

[14] *Gleams of Truth*, p. 30.
[15] *Suratu'l-Qasas*, 28:77.

ing this, the Qur'an says: *"Messengers bearing good tidings and warning, so that humanity might have no argument against God."*[16]

- **Prophet Muhammad, peace and blessings be upon him, is a clear proof not only for His Prophethood but also for God Almighty and all the truths of Islam.**[17]

  - This person, upon him be peace and blessings, possessed all possible laudable virtues and excellent characteristics; this was affirmed even by his enemies.

  - It has been reported through reliable channels of transmission that hundreds of miracles were performed by his hands.

  - Prophet Muhammad, upon him be peace and blessings, holds in his hand the Decree of the universe's Owner, namely the mighty, glorious Qur'an, which has been accepted and confirmed in every century by hundreds of millions of people.

  - Prophet Muhammad, upon him be peace and blessings, appeared with a Sacred Law, a Religion, a code of worship, a mode of prayer, a message, and a way of belief the like of which has never existed.

  - Islam, which originated in and is represented by the Prophet's deeds, sayings, states, and example, is also without peer. Regardless of time or place, it has served hundreds of millions of people as a guide and competent authority in their lives. It has taught and trained their minds, illuminated and purified their hearts, trained and refined their souls, and perfected their spirits.

  - Prophet Muhammad, upon him be peace and blessings, is the best example of the mode of worship that is prescribed by Islam; he is the most God-conscious and God-revering person of all.

  - His prayers and his knowledge of God are similarly unparalleled. He describes his Lord with such a degree of knowledge that no Prophet, saint, or gnostic has ever been able to achieve a similar degree

  - While conveying his message and calling his people to the truth, Prophet Muhammad, upon him be peace and blessings, displayed such steadfastness and courage that he never faltered or hesitated. And this was despite the hostilities of the surrounding powers and religions, as well as those of his own people and tribe, including even his uncle.

[16] *Suratu'n-Nisa', 4:165.*
[17] *The Rays*, "The Seventh Ray", p. 144–150.

- His belief was so extraordinarily strong and assured, so miraculously developed and ingrained in his heart, and so elevated and world-enlightening, that none of the ideas, beliefs, philosophies or spiritual teachings prevalent at the time could engender any doubt within him. Despite the opposition and hostility of his enemies, they were unable to shake him or make him unsure of his cause.

- Just as the consensus of the Prophets forms very strong proof of God's existence and Oneness, it also represents a sound testimony to that exalted person's truthfulness and Messengership. For history confirms that he possesses to the utmost degree all of the sacred attributes, miracles, and duties that indicate a Prophet's mission and veracity. Just as the previous Prophets predicted his coming by giving glad tidings of him in the Torah, the Gospels, the Psalms, and other Scriptures, they also confirmed him with their own missions and miracles, attesting to the truthfulness of this person, who is the most perfect in carrying out the mission and tasks of Prophethood, in effect putting their signature to his claims.

- Hundreds of thousands of people who have achieved sainthood on his way bear witness unanimously to the truthfulness and Messengership of that person, who is their master.

- Another hundreds of thousands of exacting, meticulous, purified, and truthful scholars and sages, all of whom have reached the highest station of learning through the teaching contained in the sacred truths that have been brought by that unlettered person, through the sublime sciences which he introduced, and through the knowledge of God which he had and taught—all prove and affirm with unanimity not only God's Oneness, which is the foundation of Prophet Muhammad's mission, but also the truthfulness of that supreme master and the veracity of his words. This is proof of his Messengership and truthfulness that is as clear as daylight.

- After the Prophets, the Family and Companions of Prophet Muhammad, upon him be peace and blessings, are the most elevated in insight, discernment, and perfection; they are the most renowned, respected, pious, and keen-sighted members of humankind. Having thoroughly scrutinized all of the Prophet's thoughts, and his hidden and apparent states and conditions, they have concluded unanimously that he was the noblest and most truthful and honest person in the world.

- This universe indicates the Maker, Author, Inscriber and Designer Who determined and fashioned it, and Who controls and administers it like a palace, a book, and an exhibition of marvels. Given this, there should therefore exist an exalted herald, a truthful revealer, an exacting master, and a veracious teacher who knows and makes known the Divine purpose behind the creation of the universe, who teaches others about the Divine wisdom that underpins the universe's purposeful motions and transformations, who declares its inherent value and the perfections of the creatures in it, and who expounds the meanings of this great cosmic book. The one—Prophet Muhammad, peace and blessings be upon him—carrying out such duties most perfectly is the most truthful in his cause, serving as the most trusted and exalted officer of the Creator of the universe.

- **Prayer has a great effect and always yields a result, especially when it is universal in nature. It may even be argued that prayer is one reason for the universe's creation. As the Creator knew before creating the Prophet that he would desire eternal happiness for humanity and all creation, and to be favored with the Divine Names' manifestations, we may say that God answered his future prayers by creating the universe.**[18]

Prayer is so significant and comprehensive. Therefore, it is not thinkable that the All-Merciful, Who answers the prayers of even the least of His creatures, will reject the prayer of His most beloved servant and Messenger and of countless Muslims and blessed people, as well as jinn, angels, and other spiritual beings, for the establishment of an eternal world. Prophet Muhammad, upon him be peace and blessings, has acquired, along with Prophethood and personal merits, an exalted rank far beyond humanity's powers of understanding and comprehension. So, as Muslims, we should consider how great an intercessor we may have on the Day of Judgment. If we desire his intercession, we must follow his Sunnah.

---

[18] *The Letters*, "The Twenty-fourth Letter", p. 319.

- **Following the Sunnah of the Prophet, upon him be peace and blessings, is of exceptional value. When one follows the Prophet, even in dealings of the least significance and in the practices of daily life such as eating, drinking, or sleeping, such ordinary transactions and natural acts become meritorious acts of worship and actions of Shari'ah.**[19]

Thus, one who appropriately follows the Sunnah as a way of life transforms even his habitual acts into worship, and can make his whole life fruitful and yielding of reward.

- **One who takes the Sunnah as the basis of one's path is on the way to the station of being a beloved of God under the guardianship of God's Beloved, upon him be peace and blessings.**[20]

Imam Rabbani, Ahmad Faruqi (d. 1624), may God sanctify him, says, "While passing through the ranks in my spiritual journeying, I saw the most brilliant, magnificent, appealing, sound, and reliable among the groups of the saints to be those who follow the Sunnah of the Prophet, upon him be peace and blessings, as the principle of their path. Even the ordinary saints of this group appeared to be more magnificent than the distinguished saints of other groups."

- **Like compasses used in ships to find the direction and to determine the course to follow, the principles of the elevated Sunnah of the Prophet, including even those that are concerned with good manners, are like electric switches along the innumerable hazardous, dark ways.**[21]

- **"All innovations in the Religion are misguidance, and all misguidance will be in Hellfire."[22] That is to say, according to the verse,** "This day I have perfected for you your Religion,"[23] **after the rules of the Shari'ah and the principles of the Sunnah have been completed, making new inventions or producing innovations in the Religion, which mean that one thinks these rules and principles are**

---

[19] *The Gleams*, "The Eleventh Gleam", p. 64.
[20] *The Gleams*, "The Eleventh Gleam", p. 64.
[21] *The Gleams*, "The Eleventh Gleam", p. 65.
[22] *an-Nasa'i*, "Iydayn" 22; at-Tabarani, *al-Mu'jamu'l-Kabir*, 9:97.
[23] *Suratu'l-Maeda*, 5:3.

defective and can be improved upon, is misguidance and deserves Hellfire.[24]

New inventions in the ordinances concerning Islamic worship mean innovation, and since innovation is opposed to the verse, *"This day I have perfected for you your Religion,"* they must be rejected. However, the regular recitations and invocations adopted by the sound Sufi ways, even if they are in various forms and manners, are not considered to be innovations, provided they are originally based on the Qur'an and the Sunnah and do not oppose the principles and fundamentals of the Shari'ah. Scientific and technological developments are not included in innovations as well.

- **There are degrees in the Sunnah. Some of its principles or decrees are imperative. The other degree of the Sunnah consists in supererogatory acts of worship and practices. Another category comprises the Prophet's practices that are regarded as good manners or good, commendable conduct.**[25]

The imperative acts and commandments of the Sunnah, such as those related to how we must worship, and to certain basic commandments of the Religion corcerning the religiously lawful and unlawful, cannot be ignored or abandoned. They are described in detail in the illustrious Shari'ah. They are among the established, unquestionable rules of the Religion and can in no way be altered.

The second group falls into two categories. One category is composed of the Prophet's supererogatory practices of worship, which are very meritorious and highly commendable for Muslims to perform. They are also described in the books of the Shari'ah. Changing them is innovation.

The third group, which consists of the daily practices of the Prophet regarded as good manners or good, commendable conduct, are mentioned in the books of *Hadith* and the Prophet's biographies. For example, there are numerous Prophetic practices showing good manners in speaking, eating, drinking, sleeping, and concerning social relationships. Not following them is not regarded as innovation, but it entails opposition to the Prophetic practices and good conduct, and causes deprivation of the light that derives from these acts and from the principles of good conduct or manners. One who follows these good manners in one's daily life

---

[24] *The Gleams*, "The Eleventh Gleam", p. 68.
[25] *The Gleams*, "The Eleventh Gleam", p. 69.

transforms his or her everyday practices into a form of worship, and they derive significant spiritual benefits from them. Observing the least of them recalls the noblest Messenger, upon him be peace and blessings, and imparts a light to the heart.

- **The most important rules and principles of the Sunnah are those which are the public symbols or marks of Islam (sha'air) such as the call to the Prayer, the Congregational Prayers of Friday and 'Iyd (religious festive) days, Sacrifice (nahr or dhabh) during 'Iyd al-Adha. These are acts of worship that the whole community of Muslims are required to perform, and are therefore included in the general social rights and duties.**[26]

If some among the community do them, the whole community benefits from it; by contrast, if none perform such actions, then the whole community becomes responsible. There can be no hypocrisy or ostentation in the performance of such indications of Islam, and they are openly proclaimed and performed. Even if some of them are included in the supererogatory acts of worship, they are socially more important than personal obligatory acts.

- **Every rule and practice of the elevated Sunnah indicates good conduct. There is nothing included in the Sunnah that does not bear a light, or teach good manners and conduct.**[27]

The noblest Messenger, upon him be peace and blessings, declared, "My Lord has taught and educated me, and how well He has taught and educated me!"[28] One who studies the Prophet's biography and knows his conduct will certainly understand that God Almighty collected all varieties of good conduct in His Beloved. One who abandons his Sunnah abandons good manners, and becomes the object of the saying, "An ill-mannered person is deprived of Divine favor." This means self-ruin.

- **The noblest Messenger, upon him be peace and blessings, had a perfect nature that was perfectly balanced, and he strictly obeyed the Divine order,** "Pursue, then, what is exactly right (in every matter of the Religion) as you are commanded (by God),"[29] **and his biography clearly demonstrates that he was always balanced and**

---

[26] *The Gleams*, "The Eleventh Gleam", p. 69.
[27] *The Gleams*, "The Eleventh Gleam", p. 70.
[28] al-Munawi, *Faydu'l-Qadir*, 1:225; al-Qurtubi, *al-Jami' li-Ahkami'l-Qur'an*, 18:228.
[29] *Sura Hud*, 11:112.

straightforward in all his actions and states. He continuously avoided going to all sorts of extremes.[30]

God's Messenger, upon him be peace and blessings, is a perfect representative of balance. For example, completely free of both stupidity and demagogy or sophistry, the extreme points of intellect that entail its corruption, the holy Prophet's intellect or power of reason always worked in accordance with wisdom; this is the point of balance, upon which uprightness is based. Likewise, his power or faculty of anger, completely removed from both cowardice and rage, the extreme points of this power which signify its corruption, always acted with blessed courage, which is the middle point. Similarly, his power of passion, absolutely purified of both frigidity and dissipation, which are the extreme points of this power, and therefore indicate its corruption, always strictly followed chastity, which is the middle way and the point of balance. And so on. In short, in all aspects of his Sunnah, his natural states and everyday practices, including his speech, eating, and drinking, and in all the ordinances of the Shari'ah, he always chose the balanced way and avoided all kinds of extremes and wastefulness, which entail wrongdoing and cause "darkness." Thousands of books have been written about the details of this matter.

- **The Prophet's sayings and practices, as well as the principles of Islamic law, are like stars that guide us among innumerable dark and misleading ways. Deviating from his way or Tradition (the Sunnah) makes one a plaything of devils, an object of illusion and suspicion, a target of fear, and a bearer of unbearable burdens. Deliverance from such things comes only from following the Sunnah.**[31]

The Sunnah's principles are also like ropes hanging down from heaven. Whoever holds fast to even a part of them can be elevated. Whoever opposes them and relies on their own, or even public reason, is like one who desires to obtain the means of traveling through the heavens' spheres in earthly vehicles. They are ridiculed like the Pharaoh, who said: "*O Haman. Build for me a tower to obtain the means (of traveling) in the heavens so that I may attain the ways, the ways of peering into the skies, and that I may have a look at Moses's God...*"[32]

---

[30] *The Gleams*, "The Eleventh Gleam", p. 78.

[31] *Al-Mathnawi al-Nuri*, "The Fourth Treatise", p. 118.

[32] *Suratu'l-Mu'min*, 40:36.

- **The verse,** "Say (to them, O Messenger): "If you indeed love God, then follow me, so that God will love you," **teaches us that in order to be loved by God, one must follow the Prophet.**[33]

The verse mentioned is a miracle of conciseness, for there are many sentences in this verse. Some of them are as follows:

The verse declares as follows: If you have faith in God, may His Majesty be exalted, you will certainly love Him. If you love God, then you will act in the manner He loves. Doing so means resembling the person whom God loves in his acts. Resembling that person is possible by following him. If you follow him, God will love you. You must love God so that He will love you.

All of these sentences form only a brief, concise interpretation of the verse. What is being said here is that the most important and exalted goal for human beings is being favored with the love of God Almighty. The verse decrees and shows that the way of achieving this most exalted goal is following God's Beloved, and following his elevated Sunnah. As required by His love, obeying God's commands and acting within the sphere of the things that please Him necessitate following the Prophet, for the perfect leader in obedience to God is Prophet Muhammad, upon him be peace and blessings.

- **The formidable stronghold in which the believers should, and do, seek shelter against the destruction of evil and misguidance is the Shari'ah of Muhammad, upon him be peace and blessings; it is his Sunnah.**[34]

Misguidance and evil are, for the most part, negative and destructive, and lead to extinction, while right guidance and good are always positive, constructive, formative and reformative, and lead to existence. As is known to all, a single man can destroy, in one day, a building which it took twenty men twenty days to build. While it is the All-Majestic Creator's Power Which creates and sustains human life, the survival of which He has made dependent on the existence of all the vital parts of the human body and the vital conditions of existence, by cutting off a part of the body, a tyrant may prepare the ground for death, which is non-being when considered in relation to life. For this reason, the saying, "Destruction is easy," has become proverbial.

---

[33] *The Gleams*, "The Eleventh Gleam", p. 74.
[34] *The Gleams*, "The Thirteenth Gleam", p. 96.

It is because of this reality that the people of misguidance sometimes triumph over the powerful followers of truth with only a weak force. But the followers of truth have such a formidable stronghold that when they take shelter in it, those terrible enemies cannot even approach them, and can do them no harm. Even if they cause some temporary harm, as stated in the Divine declaration, *"The final outcome is in favor of the God-revering, pious,"*[35] everlasting reward and profit compensate for that harm. This formidable stronghold in which to seek shelter is the Shari'ah of Muhammad, upon him be peace and blessings; it is his Sunnah.

- **The Divine Mercy can be reached through the Sunnah of the noblest Prophet, whom the Qur'an hails** as a mercy for all the worlds,[36] **and he can be reached by calling the blessings and peace of God upon him, for the intent of this prayer is also mercy.**[37]

Just as the light of the sun provides us with its reflection through our mirror although we cannot draw close to it, so too, does the light of God's Mercy make the All-Pure, All-Holy One, the Sun of Eternity, close to us, although we are infinitely far from Him. So, O human beings! Whoever finds this Mercy finds an eternal treasure of unfailing light. This Mercy can be reached through the Sunnah of the noblest Prophet, its most brilliant exemplar and representative, its most eloquent voice and herald, whom the Qur'an hails as *a mercy for all the worlds*, and he can be reached by calling the blessings and peace of God upon him, for the intent of this prayer is mercy.

- **Calling God's blessings and peace upon the Prophet is like answering the Bestower of bounties' invitation, Who spreads His blessings freely and has laid the table of His bounties on him whom He honored with Ascension.**[38]

When we ask God's blessings and peace upon the Prophet and mention an attribute of his, we should concentrate and reflect on the one whom we praise so that we may grow in zeal to call peace and blessings on him, over and over again.

- **There is no nation to which God Almighty has not sent a Messenger.**[39]

---

35 *Suratu'l-'Araf*, 7:128.
36 *Suratu'l-Anbiya'*, 21:107.
37 *The Gleams*, "The Fourteenth Gleam", p. 139.
38 *Al-Mathnawi al-Nuri*, "The Fifth Treatise", p. 135.
39 *The Letters*, "The Twenty-eighth Letter", p. 377.

The following verses of the Qur'an openly declare that God Almighty has sent a Messenger to each nation:

> We would never punish (a person or community for the wrong they have done) until We have sent a Messenger (to give counsel and warning).[40]
>
> How, then, will it be (with people on the Day of Judgment) when We bring forward a witness from every community (to testify against them and that God's Religion was communicated to them), and bring you (O Messenger) as a witness against all those (whom your Message may have reached)?[41]
>
> Every community has its Messenger: when their Messenger comes, (some believe in him and the others not, and) it is judged between them with absolute justice, and they are not wronged.[42]
>
> And certainly, We have raised within every community a Messenger (to convey the primordial Message): worship God alone, and keep away from false deities and powers of evil (who institute patterns of faith and rule in defiance of God).[43]

- **Members of an illustrious lineage, beginning with Abraham and resulting in God's Messenger, peace and blessings be upon them, must not have been indifferent to the true Religion's light, or overcome by unbelief's darkness.**[44]

Some Traditions relate that the ancestors of God's Messenger, upon him be peace and blessings, followed the remnants of Abraham's religion, which survived in some people despite the pervasive veils of heedlessness and spiritual darkness.

- **God holds His servants responsible for His Commands only after sending a Messenger.**[45]

According to significant scholars such as Imam Shafi'i and the Ash'ari School of *Ahlu's-Sunnah wa'l-Jama'ah*, based on the Qur'anic verse, "*We would never punish until We have sent a Messenger,*" people can be held responsible only if they are aware of belief and Divine commands. Even if God Almighty sent a Messenger to every people, there have surely been,

---

[40] *Suratu'l-Isra'*, 17:15.
[41] *Suratu'n-Nisa'*, 4:41.
[42] *Sura Yunus*, 10:47.
[43] *Suratu'n-Nahl*, 16:36.
[44] *The Letters*, "The Twenty-eighth Letter", p. 377.
[45] *The Letters*, "The Twenty-eighth Letter", p. 377.

in every age, numerous people who have left the world without being called to God's Message. They will not be punished.

- **There are many instances of Divine Wisdom in that Prophet Muhammad, peace and blessings be upon him, was raised as a Messenger when he was forty, which is regarded as the age of maturity, and died when he was sixty-three.**[46]

One of these instances of Wisdom is as follows: Prophethood is a great and heavy duty that can be performed only through the intellectual faculties' perfection and the spiritual potentialities' full development. The age of this development and perfection is usually forty. Youth is a time of carnal desire and worldly ambition and therefore not suitable for the holy and Divine duty of Prophethood, which is purely related to the Hereafter. However noble and sincere people may be before forty, fame-seekers might regard them as pursuing fame and glory. They cannot free themselves from such accusations easily, no matter how false they may be. But after they pass forty, they are nearer to the grave than the world, and so are more likely to be free of such accusations. Thus, people may free themselves from groundless suspicions.

One of the many reasons why he lived for sixty-three years is that believers must love and respect God's Messenger absolutely, and commend his manners without feeling any dislike. As old age is usually troublesome and humiliating, God sent him to the highest abode when he was sixty-three, the average lifespan of his community's members. Thus, God made him an example in this respect, also.

- **Throughout history, right and truth have always been found on the Prophet's side; misguidance, illusion, and extinction have been on the opposite side.**[47]

The Prophethood of Muhammad, upon him be peace and blessings, is the epitome of the perfection and good shared by humanity. His way and Religion are the most perfect expressions of happiness and pure beauty. We see in his life and Message superior perfection, articulate truth, distinguished good, and radiant beauty.

Out of the countless beauties and virtues that the Prophet brought, look at only this: The hearts and tongues of all believers in God's Unity are unit-

[46] *The Letters*, "The Twenty-third Letter", pp. 300–301.
[47] *Al-Mathnawi al-Nuri*, "The Seventh Treatise", p. 230.

ed on many occasions, such as the five daily Prayers, the Friday Congrega-tional, and Religious Festival Day Prayers. At these times, each believer responds to the illustrious and majestic address of God Almighty with the sounds of the hearts of all believers, and their supplications and recitations. This vast agreement and encompassing solidarity are like the entire earth speaking and praying, fulfilling the order: "*Perform the Prayer correctly*," which issued in all its awe from above the seven heavens.

By participating in the huge congregation of praying believers, weak and helpless human beings become servants loved by the Creator of the earth and heavens. They are honored with ruling on the earth in His Name, and become the head of all animate beings, as well as the final pur-pose for the universe's creation. If, as in the Unseen world, those count-less exalters of God would say, "God is the All-Great," at the same moment during and after the Festival Day Congregational Prayers, it would be equal to the earth's exaltation—as if it exalted as humanity does.

It would be as if the earth shook mightily on the Festival Day, exalting God with all its spheres and mountains, saying, "God is the All-Great," with its mouth of Mecca, with the sincerity of its heart of *qibla*—the Ka'ba. The words coming out of its caves—the mouths of believers scattered throughout it; or, rather, throughout the Intermediate World of Grave and the heavens—would rise in waves. May the Glory of Him Who has created the earth and made it like a cradle of brotherhood and sisterhood, and a place of prostration for His servants, be exalted and glorified.

- **There have always been two lines of thought and action in human history, of which the human selfhood's two aspects or faces are the origin. One face is represented by Prophethood, and the other by purely human thoughts or philosophies.**[48]

The face represented by Prophethood is the origin of pure worship and servitude to God, for our selfhood knows that it is His servant. Self-hood realizes that it serves One other than itself, and that its essential nature has only an indicative function. It understands that it bears the meaning of one other than itself and that it can be meaningful only when it points to that One upon Whom its existence depends. Selfhood believes that its existence and life depend upon that One's Creativity and Exis-tence. Its feeling of ownership is illusory, for selfhood knows that it

[48] *The Words*, "The Thirtieth Word", p. 558.

enjoys only an apparent, temporary ownership by the real Owner's permission, and that it has only a shadow-like reality. It is a contingent entity, an insignificant shadow manifesting the true and necessary Reality. Its duty is consciously serving as a measure and balance for its Creator's Attributes and essential Characteristics.

This is how Prophets, pure and righteous ones, and saints who follow the Prophets' line, perceive selfhood's nature. As a result, they resign sovereignty to the All-Majestic Sovereign and Master of creation and believe that He has no partner or like in His Sovereignty, Lordship, and Divinity. He does not need an assistant or a deputy. In addition, He possesses the key to and has absolute power over all things. "Natural" causes are but a veil of appearances, and that nature is the sum of His creation's rules, an assemblage of His laws, of how He displays His Power.

This radiant, luminous, beautiful face of Selfhood has always been like a living seed full of meaning. From it, the All-Majestic Creator has created the *Touba* (Paradisal) tree of worship, the blessed branches of which have adorned all parts of our world with its illustrious fruits. Through this face, the darkness over the past is removed and we understand that the past is not a domain of eternal extinction or a vast graveyard, as conceived by philosophy, but rather a source of light and a bright, shining ladder with many rungs from which all spirits traversing it may leap into the future and eternal happiness. It is also a radiant abode, and a garden for spirits that have left this world, cast off their heavy loads, and been set free.

- **The Prophet's every act and state bears witness to his Prophethood and faithfulness. But not all of them need to be miraculous, for he was sent by the All-Mighty as a human being to guide and lead human beings in their collective affairs and individual deeds to happiness in both this world and the next. If he were extraordinary in all of his acts, he could not guide human beings and instruct them through his acts, states, and attitudes.**[49]

Being supplied with some extraordinary phenomena to prove his Prophethood to obstinate unbelievers, God's Messenger, upon him be peace and blessings, worked miracles when necessary. But his miracles were never such that people were forced to believe against their will, as that would annul human free will in this world of test and trial. If this

---

[49] *The Letters*, "The Nineteenth Letter", pp. 121–122; "The Twenty-sixth Letter", pp. 330–331.

were not so, there would have been no choice, meaning that Abu Jahl would have believed as did Abu Bakr, and that no one could have been held responsible, in this life and the next, for their deeds.

Our Prophet, upon him be peace and blessings, was a human being. All of his acts and attitudes, except for his miracles and states of Prophethood, originated in his humanity. Like all other human beings, he was subject to and dependent upon God's laws of life. He suffered from cold, felt pain, and so on. He was not extraordinary in all his acts and attitudes so that he could set an example to humanity through his conduct. If he had been extraordinary in all his acts and manners, he could not have an absolute guide in every aspect of life or a mercy for all through all his states.

In the same way, the wise Qur'an leads conscious beings, directs humanity and jinn, guides people of perfection, and instructs truth-seeking people. Humanity and jinn take their supplications and prayers from it, talk about their affairs in its terms, and derive their principles of good conduct from it. In short, every believer adopts it as the authorized reference for all their affairs. Therefore, it must, and does, follow the style of human speech and conversation.

- **The true nature and true perfections of God's Messenger cannot be contained in accounts of his human qualities recorded in his biographies. To avoid falling into error about him, we must focus on his true nature and illustrious spiritual persona in his rank of Messengership. Otherwise we may risk showing him disrespect or entertain uncertainties about his persona.**[50]

Many history books and biographies describe the Prophet's behavior and characteristics. But most discuss his human nature, and thus ignore his spiritual persona and his being's sacred nature, both of which are very sublime and illustrious. For, according to the rule of "The cause is like the doer," the rewards of all Muslims' prayers are added to the accounts of his perfections from the day he declared his Prophethood until the end of time. Every day, he receives countless invocations by Muslims, as well as God's infinite mercy, which he draws in beyond measure.

Further, since he is creation's result and most perfect fruit, as well as the beloved interpreter of the Creator of the universe, his true nature and true perfections cannot be contained in accounts of his recorded human

---

[50] *The Letters*, "The Nineteenth Letter", pp. 125–126.

qualities. Certainly, the stature of one served by archangels Gabriel and Michael during the Battle of Badr cannot be sought in accounts of, for example, his bargaining over the price of a horse. Therefore, to avoid falling into error, we must focus on his true nature and illustrious spiritual persona in his rank of Messengership. Otherwise we may risk showing him disrespect or entertain uncertainties about his persona.

Consider the following analogies: Suppose a planted date-stone sprouts and becomes a tall, fruitful tree, growing upward and outward; or that a chick from an incubated peacock egg hatches, grows into a beautiful peacock, and, adorned with the Pen of Divine Power, grows bigger and prettier still. The date-stone or egg possess qualities, properties, and precisely balanced elements of the tree or the peacock in a compact form, but they are not as striking and significant as those of the tree and the peacock that grew from them. Given this, while describing the date-stone's and the egg's qualities along with those of the tree and the peacock, each item's qualities must be distinguished so that anyone following the description may find it reasonable. If this is not done (e.g., claiming that one date-stone and not the tree produces thousands of dates, or that the egg is already the prince of birds), people will be led to contradiction and denial.

The human nature of God's Messenger, upon him be peace and blessings, may be likened to that date-stone or egg, but his true nature, illumined with the Prophetic mission, is like the *Touba* tree or the Royal Bird of Paradise. Moreover, His true nature continues to grow more and more perfect. Given this, when one thinks of that exalted person bargaining with a Bedouin in the marketplace, he should gaze upon his illustrious essential nature, the one who rode the *Rafraf* during the Ascension, left Gabriel behind, and reached the Divine Presence. Otherwise, one risks showing insufficient respect to one's earth-bound soul of his true nature.

- **The Message of God's Messenger is based on the two kinds of Divine Revelation: explicit and implicit.**[51]

It is declared in the Qur'an: "*It is not for any mortal that God should speak to him unless it be by Revelation (into his heart) or from behind a veil, or by sending a messenger (angel) to reveal, by His leave, whatever He wills (to reveal). Surely He is All-Exalted, All-Wise.*"[52] So, Revelation to the Prophets is of two kinds, implicit and explicit. In the case of the explicit Revelation,

[51] *The Letters*, "The Nineteenth Letter", pp. 122–123.
[52] *Suratu'sh-Shura*, 42:51.

which comes in the last two ways described in the verse, the Messenger merely interprets and announces—he has no share in its content. The Qur'an and the Sacred Traditions (*hadith qudsi*)—the Prophetic sayings whose meaning and content belong to God exclusively, but whose wording belongs to the Prophet—are included here. In the case of implicit Revelation, which comes in the first way described in the verse, the essence and origin of which is based on Divine Revelation and inspiration, the Prophet is allowed to explain and describe them. When he does so, he relies either on direct Revelation and inspiration, or on his own insight. When giving his own interpretation, he either relies on the perceptive power bestowed upon him due to his Prophetic mission or speaks as a person conforming to his time's common usages, customs, and kinds of comprehension.

Thus, not all details of every Prophetic Tradition are necessarily derived from pure Revelation, nor are the sublime signs of his Messengership to be sought in all of his human thoughts and transactions. Since some truths are revealed to him in a brief and abstract form, and he describes them through his insight, and in accordance with normal understanding, the metaphors, allegories, or allusions he uses may need explanation or interpretation. Remember that the human mind can only grasp some truths through analogy. For example, once a loud noise was heard in the Prophet's presence. He said: "This is the noise of a rock that has been rolling down for seventy years and now has reached Hell's bottom."[53] An hour later, news came that "a notorious hypocrite who recently had reached the age of seventy died (and went to Hell)." This report showed the interpretation of the Prophet's eloquent parable.

- **A Prophetic Tradition related by numerous reliable authorities is indisputable. This form of relation (**tawatur**) has two kinds: obvious** tawatur **and** tawatur **with respect to meaning.**[54]

A Prophetic Tradition related by reliable authorities through numerous chains of transmission, at the beginning of which there is a Companion of the Prophet, is obvious *tawatur*. The second kind is *tawatur* with respect to meaning. This second one also has two kinds: those agreed upon by silence and those unanimously related by different people but with different words. In the first case, a Tradition related in the presence of others that is met with silence, or without engendering any dispute,

53 *Muslim*, "Janna" 31; Ahmad ibn Hanbal, *al-Musnad*, 3:341.
54 *The Letters*, "The Nineteenth Letter", p. 123.

enjoys an implied acceptance. If those remaining silent are interested in the narration and are known to be very sensitive to errors and lies, their silence implies acceptance with far more certainty. The second kind of *tawatur* with respect to meaning occurs when an incident is related unanimously by different people but with different words, as this also implies its actual occurrence.

Most of the Prophet's miracles and his Prophethood's proofs fall into either category. Although a few are related through only one chain of transmitters, they can be regarded as certain as if related through *tawatur*, since they have been accepted by confirmed authorities. Among such authorities were those who memorized more than 100,000 Traditions, and who were extremely God-conscious.

- **The leading Muslim Traditionists were so familiar with the Prophetic sayings and their exalted style that they could instantly spot and reject one false Tradition among a hundred reports.**[55]

Any Tradition accepted by those authorities after much scrutiny has the certainty of *tawatur*, even if it had only one chain of transmitters, for such people were so familiar with the Prophet's Traditions and exalted style that they could instantly spot and reject one false Tradition among a hundred reports. Like an expert jeweler recognizes a pure diamond, they could not confuse other words with those of the Prophet, upon him be peace and blessings. However, such meticulous authorities as Ibn Qayyim Ibnu'l-Jawziya were so excessive in their criticism that they unfortunately considered several authentic Traditions to be false.

- **A Tradition being regarded as fabricated does not always mean that its meaning is wrong; rather, it means that the wording does not belong to the Prophet, upon him be peace and blessings.**[56]

- **The relation of the Prophetic Traditions through chains of transmitters show the consensus of the truthful and reliable narrators, meticulous Traditionists, as well as the unanimity of the discerning authorities mentioned. Also, it shows that each scholar in the chain puts his seal on its authenticity.**[57]

---

[55] *The Letters*, "The Nineteenth Letter", p. 123.
[56] *The Letters*, "The Nineteenth Letter", p. 124.
[57] *The Letters*, "The Nineteenth Letter", p. 124.

- **The great majority of the holy Prophet's miracles were not transmitted with as great an emphasis as the Sharia's basic rules.**[58]

This point is also important in how we should approach and understand the Prophets and certain other distinguished peoples of missions. The Sharia's rules are used by people to guide their lives, and are applicable to everyone. Miracles, on the other hand, do not need to be known to everyone, and only need to be heard once. For example, some religious obligations (such as the Funeral Prayer) only need to be observed by a few people, and not the entire community. In the same way, only some people need to know about miracles. This is why a miracle, no matter how much firmer its establishment is than a Shari'ah rule, is transmitted by only one or two narrators, while a Shari'ah rule is transmitted by ten or twenty people.

- **The Messenger predicted some future events that are recurring, as opposed to isolated events having a particular significance in human history. They also have numerous aspects, each of which is explained through a different Tradition. A reporter combines these aspects as if a single narration, thereby making the Tradition appear to be at variance with reality.**[59]

For example, many narrations about the *Mahdi* (The Muslim Messiah) have different details and descriptions. But the truth of the matter is that God's Messenger, relying on Revelation, told of a *Mahdi* who would appear in every century to preserve believers' morale, prevent them from falling into despair over social upheavals, and secure their heart-felt devotion to members of the Prophet's Family (a most-illustrious lineage). He foresaw a *Mahdi* in every century similar to the Great *Mahdi* promised for the end of time. Some of the Caliphs or great scholarly saints, belonging to the Prophet's Family, had many of the Great *Mahdi*'s characteristics. So, narrations about the *Mahdi* differ due to confusing the Great *Mahdi*'s qualities with those great Caliphs or scholarly saints who came before him.

- **Since only God knows the Unseen, the Prophet did not know it by himself. He told his Companions whatever God, the All-Mighty, related to him about the Unseen.**[60]

---

[58] *The Letters*, "The Nineteenth Letter", p. 124.
[59] *The Letters*, "The Nineteenth Letter", p. 124.
[60] *The Letters*, "The Nineteenth Letter", p. 125.

The All-Mighty is also All-Wise and All-Compassionate. Thus His Wisdom and Compassion require the veiling of most future events, for as people consider many of them unpleasant, any prior knowledge of them would be painful. This is why we do not know when we will die and why the calamities we will experience remain behind the veil of the Unseen.

Divine Wisdom and Compassion also require that the Prophet not know the details of what will happen to his Household and Companions after his death because of his deep compassion and tenderheartedness. Nevertheless, the All-Mighty had a Divine purpose for telling him about some of them, albeit not in all their tragic aspects. He communicated pleasant events to the Prophet, either in outline or in detail, which he then related to his Companions.

Finally, his tidings were transmitted accurately to our own era by the great Traditionists who were at the height of piety, justice, and truthfulness, and who trembled with fear at such specific warnings as: "Whoever intentionally lies about me should prepare for a dwelling in the Fire,"[61] and "*But who does greater wrong than one who lies against God?*"[62]

- **Just as a patient goes to a doctor, engineers are consulted about engineering matters, and muftis are asked about religious issues, some scholarly Companions were entrusted with, and devoted themselves to, instructing the following generations in the Prophetic Traditions.**[63]

This is why some Companions like Jabir, Anas, and Abu Hurayra, and not, for example, Abu Bakr and 'Umar, related the Traditions. Abu Hurayra devoted his life to preserving Traditions, while 'Umar shouldered administrative matters and the Caliphate's problems. Thus 'Umar narrated only a few Traditions, for he had confidence in such people as Abu Hurayra, Anas, and Jabir, to instruct Muslims in the Traditions. In fact, a Tradition can be considered as established if it is reported by a well-known person belonging to the truthful, sincere, and trusted Companions. Given this, there is no need for it to be related by others. This is why some significant incidents have only one, two, or three channels.

- **There are many similar examples, most of which are narrated by Traditionists. Taken together, they represent a miracle having**

---

[61] Jalal al-Din al-Suyuti, *al-Jami'u's-Saghir*; related from 70 Companions.
[62] *Suratu'z-Zumar*, 39:32.
[63] *The Letters*, "The Nineteenth Letter", p. 157–158.

the **certainty of** mutawatir **in meaning, even if we were to regard each one as individual in nature and, accordingly, questionably reported.**[64]

Any incident reported in various ways is concluded to have happened, even though the separate reports are individually questionable. Suppose a loud noise is heard. One person says: "Such-and-such a house has collapsed." Another says: "A grocery has collapsed." A third reports the collapse of a prison, and so on. Each report may be questionable, and even untrue, but one thing is certain—a building did collapse. Even if we regard a narration as questionable, when taken together, many narrations indicating a miracle of the Prophet prove the occurrence of the miracle, just as the collapse of a building is certain in the above analogy.

- **Every species of creation recognizes, and is related to, God's Messenger, and therefore each displays a specific kind of his miracles.**[65]

Rocks, trees, the moon, and the sun recognize him and testify to his Prophethood, each demonstrating one of his miracles. In the same way, animals, the dead, jinn, and angels recognize him and testify to his Prophethood by becoming the objects of his miracles. This shows that Prophet Muhammad, upon him be peace and blessings, is the Messenger and envoy of God, the Creator and the Lord of creation. The field of his Messengership is far more comprehensive than that of all previous Prophets.

- **Prophet Muhammad, upon him be peace and blessings, was predicted in all the previous Divine Scriptures, as he is the heir to all the previous Prophets.**[66]

Tidings of Prophet Muhammad, upon him be peace and blessings, were given in the Torah, Bible, Psalms, and Scrolls or Scriptures sent to some among the previous Prophets, upon them be peace. It was fitting that they mentioned him, because he would testify to and convey all the truths in them, correct the faults interpolated in them in the course of history, and acquit the previous Prophets of the false accusations made against them over time.

---

[64] *The Letters*, "The Nineteenth Letter", p. 174.
[65] *The Letters*, "The Nineteenth Letter", p. 184.
[66] *The Letters*, "The Nineteenth Letter", p. 184–185. For a detailed study on the prediction of Prophet Muhammad, peace and blessings be upon him, in all the previous Scriptures see: Ali Ünal Harun Gültekin, *The Prophet Promised in World Scriptures* (2013), Tughra Books, Clifton.

- **Some of the Prophetic Traditions, like some Qur'anic verses, are allegorical and have meanings that can be understood only by distinguished, expert scholars.**[67]

For example, as mentioned before, once a rumbling was heard in the presence of God's Messenger, upon him be peace and blessings, he said: "This is the sound of a rock that has been rolling down for seventy years and now has reached Hell's bottom."[68] Those who do not know the context may reject this. However, about twenty minutes after the Prophet spoke, someone came and related that a well-known hypocrite had died twenty minutes ago. The Prophet had described most eloquently how the hypocrite's life of seventy years had been a continuous descent to the lowest of the low as a stone of Hell. Almighty God let the Prophet and Companions hear that rumbling. Discussion of such Traditions may be permissible for and among those qualified to discern the truth in them with clarity. They must know the degrees of Traditions, implicit Revelation, and categories of the Prophetic sayings.

- **While the Companions were alive, many Jewish and Christian scholars accepted Islam. Their former knowledge thus became "Muslim." Some of it, however, was contrary to the truth and, later on, was imagined to belong to Islam.**[69]

Some of the borrowings from the earlier non-Islamic, particularly Israelite, sources, and ancient Greek philosophy, infiltrated the sphere of pure Islam and, donning religious apparel, caused revolutions in some minds.

The Arabs were largely an illiterate people during the age of pre-Islamic ignorance. When the truth manifested itself among them, arousing their abilities, they saw that Islam was clear in itself, and that the truth had been revealed, opening the way to the entire truth; as a result, their efforts and inclinations were focused on learning the Religion. What motivated, informed, and trained their talented natures was the Qur'an. However, when they later began to take other peoples into their community, the information that came with these peoples became "Muslim." In particular, the conversion of some Jewish scholars, such as Wahb ibn Munabbih and Ka'bu'l-Ahbar, caused some excerpts from Israelite sources to find their

---

[67] *The Letters*, "The Twenty-eighth Letter", p. 361.

[68] *Muslim*, "Janna" 31; Ahmad ibn Hanbal, *al-Musnad*, 3:341.

[69] *The Words*, "The Twenty-fourth Word", p. 361; *The Reasonings*, "The First Part", pp. 16–17.

way into the minds of the Arabs. In addition, these borrowings received welcome from people because such scholars from among the People of the Book enjoyed great respect as they had converted and earned renown as Muslims. Since, in appearance, these borrowings were not contradictory to the fundamentals of Islam, and circulated in the form of narratives, they were accepted uncritically. Unfortunately, they later came to be accepted as criteria for certain truths and for understanding some verses of the Qur'an, giving rise to many doubts and misunderstandings.

These excerpts from Israelite sources could be used to understand some implications of the Qur'an and Sunnah. But they could never be taken as meanings or interpretations of the Qur'anic verses and Prophetic Traditions. Provided they were true, a place could be found for them in meanings of a secondary, even a third or fourth, degree. However, those who concentrated only on the literal meanings of the Qur'anic verses and who were lacking in, or did not look for, reliable sources to understand the verses, attempted to interpret some Qur'anic verses, as well as some Prophetic Traditions, in the light of the Israelite narratives. By contrast, what reliably interprets the Qur'an is primarily the Qur'an itself, and the reliably narrated *Hadith*. Neither the Torah nor the Gospels, whose legal rules and decrees had been abrogated and narratives distorted, can be used to interpret the Qur'an.

- **While relating Traditions, some narrators tended to make explanations and included meanings deduced from the Traditions. However, since we are not free of error, some erroneous explanations or deductions were later considered to be parts of Traditions and caused them to be branded as "weak."**[70]

There were some among Traditionists (scholars of *Hadith*) who were mentioned by the Prophet: "Among any community are those who are inspired."[71] Thus, the meanings obtained by some saintly Traditionists through inspiration concerning certain Traditions and communicated to others were considered Traditions in later times. However, due to certain obstructions, some inspirations may be defective and thus contrary to the truth. Therefore, such inspired, defective deductions or interpretations brought doubt upon certain Traditions.

---

[70] *The Words*, "The Twenty-fourth Word", p. 361.
[71] *al-Bukhari*, "Fada'ilu's-Sahaba" 6; *Muslim*, "Fada'ilu's-Sahaba" 23; *at-Tirmidhi*, "Manaqib" 17

- **Certain widely circulated narrations which came to be like proverbs over time and God's Messenger mentioned for the guidance of people cannot be a measure in judging about the Prophetic Traditions.**[72]

Certain widely circulated narrations come to be like proverbs over time. Their literal meanings and the words used are not important, for only the meaning and intent are considered. Thus the Messenger, upon him be peace and blessings, would sometimes mention such narrations in the form of comparisons or metaphors for the purpose of guidance. If there is any error in the original, literal meanings of such sayings, it is due to the people's customs and traditions, and to the way the sayings have been circulated.

- **Over time, and due to misunderstanding, many similes and parables assume the form of physical facts. Also, when passing from the hands of knowledge to the hands of ignorance, a metaphorical expression may change into a literal description, and open a door to superstition. These realities caused some Traditions to be misunderstood and rejected as weak or fabricated.**[73]

For example, two great angels who supervise land and sea animals, respectively, and are therefore called "The Ox" and "The Fish," and represented an ox and fish in the World of Representations or Immaterial Forms, were imagined to be a huge ox and a physical fish. As a result, the Tradition which says that the earth rests on an ox and a fish came to be taken with its literal meaning and was criticized. This Tradition has also other significant meanings as follows:

The bearers of the Divine Throne are sometimes called the Ox, the Vulture, the Man, or some other title. These are in fact angels. Therefore, the ox and fish mentioned in the Tradition in question could be referring to these angels. In addition, we learn from the Shari'ah: There is an angel appointed for each species of existence, and this angel manages the affairs of that species. The angel is called by the name of the species for which it is responsible and appears with its form in the world of the angels. For example, the angel responsible for the sun is called "the Sun," and is in the shape of the sun. So, the angel responsible for supervising land animals is in the form of an ox and called "the Ox," and the angel responsible for supervising sea animals is in the form of a fish and called

---

[72] *The Words*, "The Twenty-fourth Word", p. 362.
[73] *The Reasonings*, "The First Part", p. 23; *The Words*, "The Twenty-fourth Word", p. 362.

"the Fish." Thirdly, the ox is the most important animal for agriculture. Fish are the basic livelihood and fishing is the general business for those living in coastal regions in particular. If one asks us what keeps a state standing, we might answer, "The state depends on the pen and sword." The Prophet, who is the pride of creation, upon him be peace and blessings, could well have meant this when he said, "The earth stands on the ox and fish." If the one who asked him what the earth stood on was unable to understand a scientific answer, he would have been given the answer most appropriate to his level of understanding. That is, our Prophet, upon him be peace and blessings, may have been answering this person figuratively—meaning that the majority of people lived either by farming and agriculture, for which oxen were indispensable, or by fishing. Since a considerable portion of the population lived by the seashore, and their basic livelihood was fish, their world depended on fish.

- **The Traditions concerning certain future events, particularly certain important persons such as the** Mahdi **and** Dajjal, **are ambiguous and require interpretation.**[74]

In this world of testing and experience, the Absolutely Wise One hides certain vital things amidst a multiplicity of things: the Night of Destiny and Power in the month of Ramadan, the hour when prayers are not rejected in Friday, His favorite friends among the people, the appointed hour of death during a person's lifetime, and the time of Doomsday in the world's life. This causes Ramadan, Friday, the people, and a lifetime to be given due importance due to their vital parts kept hidden.

Also, this world is an arena of trial. A door is opened to reason, but human free will is not denied, nor ignored. For this reason, when those mighty individuals, even the terrible *Dajjal* (Anti-Christ), appear, most people (even himself) may not realize his true identity. These end-time individuals can be known only through the light of belief.

Another reason for the differences in the narrations about such end-time individuals as the *Mahdi* is this: The texts of some Traditions have been confused or even mixed with commentaries of interpreters with their own understandings and deductions. For example, the center of power when these Traditions had reached their widest circulation was Medina or Damascus. Thus, they thought that events connected with the

---

[74] *The Words*, "The Twenty-fourth Word", p. 363–364.

Mahdi and *Sufyan* (The *Dajjal* to appear among the Muslims) would take place there, or in neighboring places like Basra and Kufa, and interpreted them accordingly.

Furthermore, in every age, people feel a need for the meaning of the *Mahdi*, of one who will come to strengthen their morale and save them from despair. The time of such matters was left vague so that people would not heedlessly follow evil leaders or let the reins of their carnal souls go free out of indifference, and so that they would fear and hold back from terrible individuals who would come to lead the forces of disorder and hypocrisy. Also, in every age some *Mahdi*-like people have appeared and guided people in certain aspects of Islam, just as some *Dajjal* and *Sufyan*-like people have come to fight against the Divine Religion. In the Traditions concerning the *Mahdi* and *Dajjal* there are references to these people as well.

- **Personification of certain abstract truths or meanings, or attributing the qualities of a collective identity or community to individual persons, caused some Traditions to be misunderstood.**[75]

People tend to attribute the work of a community to its leader. Thus, certain mighty works belonging to the collective identity or community of the *Mahdi* or *Dajjal* have come to be attributed to the leader of either community, and thus regarded as unbelievable. This has brought doubt upon certain Traditions concerning them, although these Traditions contain miraculous information about future developments with many aspects of them.

One Tradition about the *Dajjal* says: "His first day is like a year, his second like a month, his third like a week, and his fourth like your normal days. When he appears, the world will hear. He will travel the world in forty days."[76] Some, saying this is impossible, deny the Tradition. However—the knowledge is with God—this Tradition must mean that an individual will appear in the north, where unbelief is strongest and at its peak. Leading a mighty current issuing from materialism, he will deny God and religion absolutely.

There is a subtle point here: In latitudes close to the North Pole, the whole year is a day and a night, each comprising six months. The expres-

---

[75] *The Words*, "The Twenty-fourth Word", pp. 364–365.
[76] *Muslim*, "Fitan" 110; *Abu Dawud*, "Malahim" 14; *at-Tirmidhi*, "Fitan" 59.

sion, "His first day is like a year," alludes to his appearance close to those latitudes, in the far north. "His second day like a month means" that coming south, there are latitudes where a summer day lasts a month. This means that the *Dajjal* will invade southward toward the civilized world. Coming south, there are places where the sun does not set for one week, and still coming further south, there are barely three hours between the sun's rising and setting.

The difficulty in understanding "the world will hear when the *Dajjal* appears," predicts and has been solved through new inventions in communication like radio. Also, it is now possible to travel the world in forty days. What was formerly considered impossible is now commonplace.

The mighty work being attributed to certain individuals is an allusion to the vast collective personality that those individuals represent. As an explanatory example, once, the Japanese Commander-in-Chief who had defeated Russia was photographed with one foot in the Pacific Ocean and the other foot in the fort of Port Arthur. The immensity of the collective personality is depicted in the person who represents it, through his pictures or the huge statues built to commemorate him.

- **According to the prevailing opinion among Tradition scholars, (scholars of *Hadith*) paraphrasing or narrating the Traditions with their meaning, though not with their exact wording, is permissible under certain conditions.**[77]

Although the literal narration of the Traditions with the exact words uttered by God's Messenger, upon him be peace and blessings, is better and always preferable, a narration of meaning is allowed if the narrator has an expert command of Arabic, if the word used is appropriate in the given context, and if the original has been forgotten. However, the Companions always tried to narrate Traditions literally, despite this permission.[78]

- **Although some Traditions about the virtues and rewards of certain religious acts were couched eloquently to encourage people towards good and away from evil, some consider them exaggerations. However, they are all pure truth and contain no exaggeration.**[79]

---

[77] *The Letters*, "The Nineteenth Letter", p. 117.
[78] M. Fethullah Gülen, *Muhammad: The Messenger of God* (2005), Tughra Books, p. 339.
[79] *The Words*, "The Twenty-fourth Word", p. 365–366.

First of all, the results of some issues of belief, or the rewards to be given for religious acts, are rarely concerned with this narrow and conditioned world; they are mostly related to the wide and unconditioned world of the Hereafter. For example, a most unfairly criticized Tradition relates: "If God valued this world as much as He does a fly's wing, unbelievers could not take even a sip of water from it."[80] This does not allude to the world, but rather to everyone's private world, which is limited to their short lives. It cannot equal an everlasting Divine favor to the extent of a fly's wing from the eternal world. "If God valued" refers to the eternal world. In other words, because it is everlasting, a light from the eternal world that is comparable in extent to a fly's wing, is greater than the amount of transient light that fills the earth.

Furthermore, the world has three facets. The first facet contains the mirrors that reflect Almighty God's Names. The second facet is concerned with the Hereafter. That is, this world is the arable field sown with the seeds of the Hereafter, the realm in which we might gain the eternal world. The third facet, looking to transience and non-existence, is the world of the misguided, of which God does not approve. This Tradition refers to the third facet with respect to the unbelievers—the world of the worldly, which is opposed to the Hereafter. It is not worth one everlasting particle out of what the believers will be rewarded with in the Hereafter. Thus, those who consider this Tradition an exaggeration are ignoring this most exact and serious truth.

- **Every letter of the wise, holy Qur'an brings a certain reward. However, God the All-Merciful may increase it as much as He wills, for whomever He wills, under certain conditions or in certain times.**[81]

Another category of Traditions that some consider exaggerated are the rewards for religious acts and virtues of some Qur'anic *suras*. For example, some Traditions relate that the reward for *Suratu'l-Fatiha* equals that for the Qur'an,[82] *Suratu'l-Ikhlas* equals one-third of the Qur'an,[83] *Suratu'l-Zilzal* equals one-fourth of the Qur'an,[84] *Suratu'l-Kafirun*

---

[80] *Muslim*, "Munafiqun" 18; *al-Bukhari*, "Tafsir Sura 18" 6; *Ibn Maja*," Zuhd" 3.
[81] *The Words*, "The Twenty-fourth Word", pp, 366–367.
[82] *al-Bukhari*, "Tafsir Sura 1" 1; *at-Tirmidhi*, "Thawabu'l-Qur'an" 1; *an-Nasa'i*, "Iftitah" 26.
[83] *at-Tirmidhi*, "Thawabu'l-Qur'an" 10; *Ibn Maja*, "Adab" 52; *Abu Dawud*, "Witr" 18.
[84] *at-Tirmidhi*, "Thawabu'l-Qur'an" 14; Ahmad ibn Hanbal, *al-Musnad*, 3:147.

also equals one-fourth of the Qur'an,[85]and *Sura Ya-Sin* equals ten times the Qur'an.[86] They base their criticism on the assertion that these more meritorious *suras* are contained within the Qur'an.

The truth of the matter is this: Imagine a field sown with 1,000 maize seeds. If we suppose that some seeds produce 7 shoots and each shoot 100 grains, a single seed equals two-thirds of the original 1,000 seeds. If 1 seed produces 10 shoots, and each shoot yields 200 grains, 1 seed is equal to twice the number of all the seeds originally sown. Many similar analogies can be made. In exactly the same way, if we suppose the wise Qur'an to be a sacred, luminous, heavenly field, each of its 300,620 letters, together with its original reward, is like a seed. Without considering the shoots these seeds may produce, the Qur'an may be compared with the *suras* and verses which bring multiple rewards mentioned by these Traditions.

Out of Divine Grace, the letters of some *suras* may sprout and yield 10, 70, or 700, like the letters of *Ayatu'l-Kursi*. Sometimes they yield 1,500, like the letters of *Suratu'l-Ikhlas*, or 10,000, like verses recited on the Night of Forgiveness (*Laylatu'l-Bara'ah*) and other blessed occasions. Sometimes they even yield 30,000, like verses recited on the Night of Destiny and Power (*Laylatu'l-Qadr*). These are like poppy seeds, each of which may produce 10 cones, each of which contains thousands of seeds. As the Qur'an considers the Night of Destiny and Power equivalent to 1,000 months,[87] one letter of the Qur'an recited on that night brings 30,000 rewards.

- **There are differences of virtue between the verses and *suras* of the Qur'an, as there are between times and places.**[88]

Given this, some *suras* and verses may bring multiple rewards, and be compared in certain circumstances with the whole Qur'an, when its letters are considered in their original merits and without producing a new crop of merits. For example, *Suratu'l-Ikhlas,* together with the *Basmala* (In the Name of God, the All-Merciful, the All-Compassionate) have 66 letters. Since this *sura* equals one-third of the Qur'an and the Qur'an has 300,620 letters, 3 times 66 is 196. Thus each letter of this *sura* has about

---

[85] *at-Tirmidhi*, "Thawabu'l-Qur'an" 9; Ahmad ibn Hanbal, *al-Musnad*, 3:147.
[86] *at-Tirmidhi*, "Thawabu'l-Qur'an" 7; *ad-Darimi*, "Fada'ilu'l-Qur'an" 21.
[87] *Suratu'l-Qadr*, 97:3.
[88] *The Words*, "The Twenty-fourth Word", p. 367

1,500 merits or rewards. Similarly, since *Sura Ya-Sin* equals 10 times the Qur'an, if all the letters of the Qur'an are multiplied by 10 and the result is divided by the number of the *sura*'s letters, we discover that each letter has about 500 merits or rewards. So, if you apply the others to this, you will understand what a subtle, true, and unexaggerated reality is related by these Traditions.

- **Sometimes under certain conditions a word or act of glorification opens up a treasury of happiness that one could not open before through a lifetime of Divine service.**[89]

In certain circumstances, one verse may earn as much reward as the whole Qur'an. This happens as such: As with most other species, certain people among humankind are extraordinary in their acts and achievements. If they excel in good deeds, they become the pride of humanity; otherwise they cause their own shame. They acquire a collective identity and become models for imitators. Since it is not certain who among people have this capacity, theoretically it is even possible that everyone could be like them. Also, as such people can emerge in any place, every place may have some of them.

It follows that any act has *the potential* to deserve the following reward: The Prophet, upon him be peace and blessings, declared: "The reward for two *rak'as* of Prayer performed at such and such a time equals the *Hajj* (pilgrimage to the Ka'ba)."[90] This means that all the two-*rak'a* Prayers performed at that time may earn a reward equal to performing the pilgrimage. The reward promised in such narrations is not actual, or for everyone at all times. Rather, as certain conditions must be fulfilled, it is possible that the reward will be earned.

Another Tradition says: "Backbiting is like murder."[91] This means that there is a sort of backbiting more harmful than deadly poison. Or, backbiting in certain circumstances may cause as much harm as murder. Again, for example: "A good word is equal in virtue to emancipating a slave, which is very meritorious."[92] By indicating the highest reward one may gain from a good deed, the Prophet sought to arouse eagerness for good and aversion to evil. Moreover, the things of the Hereafter can-

[89] *The Words*, "The Twenty-fourth Word", pp, 367–368.
[90] *at-Tirmidhi*, "Jumu'a" 59; at-Tabarani, *al-Mu'jamu'l-Kabir*, 77:40.
[91] ad-Daylami, *Musnadu'l-Firdaws*, 3:116.
[92] at-Tabarani, *al-Mu'jamu'l-Kabir*, 7:230; al-Bayhaqi, *Shu'abu'l-Iman*, 6:124.

not be measured on this world's scales, for the greatest thing in this world cannot equal the least thing in the Hereafter. Since rewards for good deeds are related to the Hereafter, we cannot grasp them fully with our narrow, worldly minds.

- **A king has two forms of speech and address. He either speaks on his private phone to a common subject regarding a minor matter or private need, or, in his capacity or position as the supreme sovereign, supreme head of the religious office, and supreme ruler, conveys his orders in the form of an exalted decree manifesting his majesty by means of an envoy or high official. Like this, the Creator of this universe, the Master of existence, the Lord of eternity, has two kinds of conversing and speaking, and two manners of favoring. One is particular and private, and done by the manifestation of one or two of His Names; the other is general or universal.**[93]

The first indicates sainthood, which is a particular, personal relationship with God, while the second refers to Messengership, which has a general or universal relationship with God. All the Prophets and Messengers before Prophet Muhammad, peace and blessings be upon him, had connection with God on behalf of their own peoples, while Prophet Muhammad, upon him be peace and blessings, had a universal connection and manner of relationship with Him as His being the Creator and Lord of the whole existence on behalf of the entire humankind and jinn. The Ascension of Prophet Muhammad, peace and blessings be upon him, is a sign of his position with the Creator and Lord of the universe.

- **In the All-Majestic Maker's Art, motions have infinitely different degrees. For example, the speeds of electricity, spirit, imagination, and sound are quite different from each other. Also, science has established that the speeds of planetary movements are astonishingly different. This explains how the Holy Prophet Muhammad's body acquired a sort of refinement, accompanied his spirit in the Ascension, and moved at its speed.**[94]

---

[93] *The Words*, "The Thirty-first Word", p. 581.
[94] *The Words*, "The Thirty-first Word", p. 591.

Sometimes, we sleep for ten minutes but have a year's worth of experiences. If the words spoken and heard in a dream lasting for only a minute were collected, it would take a day and even longer to speak or hear them while awake. Thus a single period of time means a day for one, and a year for another.

Consider this analogy: A clock measures the speed of a person, a cannonball, sound, light, electricity, spirit, and imagination. It has ten hands to show the hours, minutes, and seconds down to fractions of an hour to the tenth power. It also has ten circles, one around the other, and sixty times larger than it, respectively. If the circle with the hour hand is the size of a normal clock, the circle with the fraction-of-an-hour hand to the tenth power would have to be the size of the earth's annual orbit or much greater.

Suppose there are two people. One is mounted on the hour-hand and observes according to its motion, while the other is on the hand showing fractions of an hour to the tenth power. There would be a huge difference, as great as the proportion between a normal clock and the earth's annual orbit, with respect to what they could see during the same time period.

- **Just a human being—a micro or normo-cosmos—has, in addition to her bodily existence, immaterial forms of existence such as the mind, heart, spirit, imagination, and memory, certainly the universe, the macro-human and the tree of which humanity is the fruit, contains other worlds beside the physical one. Also each world, from the earth to Paradise, has a heaven.**[95]

The heavens are formed of "ether" and are the source of such subtle and refined matters, energies, or forces as light, heat, electricity, and gravity. As pointed to in the Tradition, "Heaven is a wave stretched and restrained." They were created in such a way that certain stars and planets can move easily within them. Wisdom and reason require that, from the Milky Way to the nearest planet, there should be heavenly levels of different formations, and a heaven as the roof of a world, be it the world of the earth to the Intermediate World (of the grave), or the World of Ideal Forms or Representations to the World of the Hereafter.

---

[95] *The Words*, "The Thirty-first Word", p. 589.

- **The Prophetic sayings (*hadiths*) say to the Qur'an's verses: It is not possible to reach you!**[96]

If you compare the Qur'anic verses and the *hadiths*, you will see clearly that even the most eloquent of humankind, the conveyor of the Revelation, could not attain the level of the Qur'an in eloquence.

The Qur'an does not resemble his sayings. That means that all the words issuing from Muhammad's tongue were not his. That is, apart from his own sayings (*hadiths*), Prophet Muhammad, upon him be peace and blessings, was also the conveyor of the Qur'an, revealed by God.

- **The Prophet's sayings are the mine of life, and inspire truths.**[97]

It is declared in the Qur'an: "*O you who believe! Respond to God and to the Messenger when the Messenger calls you (in the Name of God) to that which gives you life; and know well that surely God "intervenes" between a person and his heart (to cause his heart to swerve); and that it He is to Whom you will be gathered.*"[98]

This means that God's Messenger, upon him be peace and blessings, calls to pure life, and his sayings and actions are the source of this life.

- **A Prophetic Tradition contains three judgments:** One: **This Tradition belongs to the Prophet, upon him be peace and blessings.** The second: **What the Prophet means in this Tradition is true.** The third: **This is what the Prophet means by this Tradition.**[99]

The first judgment is based on the reliability of the chains of transmission. The second one is based on the fact that Prophet Muhammad, upon him be peace and blessings, is a Messenger of God, Who speaks not on his own; whatever he speaks (especially concerned with the Religion or his mission) is a Revelation revealed to him.[100] We must accept both of these judgments. One who denies the first commits a grave sin and is considered a liar. One who denies the second falls into misguidance and darkness.

The third judgment contained by the Tradition is what every qualified one deduces from it. One who has the necessary qualifications to deduce judgments from the Tradition says, "This is what was meant by this Prophetic saying; this is the pearl hiding in this oyster." This judgment can-

---

[96] *The Words*, "Gleams of Truth", p. 759.
[97] *Gleams of Truth*, p. 10.
[98] *Suratu'l-Anfal*, 8:24.
[99] *The Reasonings*, "The First Part", p.
[100] *Suratu'n-Najm*, 53:3–4.

not be reached through personal inclinations, desires, or caprices. It should be based on true reasoning established on the necessary principles. Differences of view occur in this third judgment. Phrases such as "So-and-so says," and "It is said," which we frequently come across in relevant books, bear witness to these differences. Those who have the necessary qualifications to deduce judgments from the Qur'an and the Prophetic Traditions do not commit a sin when, and if, they disagree with the judgment of others. There are many statements that contain several, and different, judgments.

Part 5

GENERAL PRINCIPLES RELATED TO WORSHIP, MORALITY AND ISLAMIC JURISPRUDENCE

General Principles Related to Worship, Morality, and Islamic Jurisprudence

- **We are on a long journey, which starts from the World of Spirits to all eternity, passing through the stages of the mother's womb, youth, old age, the grave, the Intermediate World, Resurrection, and the Bridge. Whatever we need along this journey has been given to us by our All-Munificent Host.**[1]

We are guests in this world of such a Munificent One that He has put His infinite treasuries of Mercy at our disposal and subjugated His unique works of creative Power and special servants to us. Also, He has prepared for our use, pleasure, and recreation such a vast arena that its radius is as far as sight, or even imagination, can reach.

If we rely on our physical and innate abilities, taking the worldly life as our goal and focusing on its pleasures in pursuit of our livelihood, we will suffocate within a very narrow circle. Moreover, our bodily parts, senses, and faculties will bring suit and witness against us in the Hereafter. But if we know that we are guests, and so spend our lives within the limits established and approved by our All-Munificent Host, we will lead a happy and peaceful life in a broad sphere, and gain a long, eternal life. We can rise to the highest of the high, and all of our bodily members and faculties will testify in our favor in the Hereafter.

Our wonderful faculties are not meant for this trivial worldly life; rather, they are for our eternal life, which is of great significance. For when compared with animals, we see that, regarding faculties and senses, we are far richer than animals, while in regard to worldly pleasures and animal life, we fall a hundred times lower. This is because every worldly pleasure we taste bears many traces of pain. Pains of the past, fears of the future, and the pains at the cessation of every pleasure spoil our enjoy-

---

[1] *The Words*, "The Twenty-third Word", p. 600.

ment. However, animals experience pleasure without pain, enjoyment without anxiety, and are neither wounded by the pains of the past or distressed by the fears of the future. They enjoy comfortable lives, and praise their All-Merciful Creator.

As mentioned above, our intellectual and spiritual faculties, feelings, and senses are much more developed than those of animals. For example, we can see all degrees of beauty, distinguish all the varieties of the particular tastes of foods, penetrate the many details of realities, yearn for all ranks of perfection, and so on. But animals, with the exception of a particular faculty that reaches a high state of development according to its particular duty, can realize only slight developments, if any.

We are rich in faculties because our senses and feelings have developed a great deal owing to our minds and intellects. Our many needs have caused us to evolve different types of emotions, and to become very sensitive to many things. Also, due to our comprehensive nature, we have been given desires that turn into several aims and objectives. Our senses and faculties have greatly expanded due to the diversity of our essential duties. Furthermore, since we are inclined and able to worship, we have the potential to realize all kinds of perfection.

Such rich faculties and abundant potentialities cannot have been given to us for an insignificant, temporary, worldly life. In reality, they were given to us because our essential duty is to perceive our obligations, which are directed toward endless aims; to affirm our impotence, poverty, and insufficiency in the form of worship; to study creation's glorifications with our far-reaching sight and penetrating understanding; and to bear witness to them; to discern and be grateful for the All-Merciful One's aid sent in the form of bounties; and to gaze, reflect upon, and draw warnings from the miracles of His Power as manifested in creation.

- **Belief in God is creation's highest aim and most sublime result, and humanity's most exalted rank is knowledge of Him. The most radiant happiness and sweetest bounty for jinn and humanity is love of God, contained within knowledge of God. The human spirit's purest joy and the human heart's sheerest delight is spiritual ecstasy contained within love of God.**[2]

---

[2] *The Letters*, "The Twentieth Letter", pp. 239–240.

All true happiness, pure joy, sweet bounties, and unclouded pleasures are contained within knowledge and love of God. Those who truly know and love God can receive endless happiness, enlightenment, and mysteries. Those who do not are afflicted with endless spiritual and material misery, pain, and fear. If any person were allowed to rule this transient world, despite his being powerless, miserable, and unprotected amid other purposeless people in this world, what would its true worth be?

People who do not recognize their Owner and discover their Master are miserable and bewildered. But those who do, and then take refuge in His Mercy and rely on His Power, see this desolate world transformed into a place of rest and felicity, a place of exchange for the Hereafter.

- **We are not sent to the world for a permanent residence. Rather, we are sent to the world to develop our capacities and abilities through learning and worship, and thus to do business in the name of the afterlife.**[3]

A decisive proof for this truth is the difference between how human beings and animals come into existence. Almost from the very moment of birth, an animal seems to have been trained, with its faculties perfected elsewhere. Within a few hours, days, or months, it can lead its life according to its particular rules and conditions. This means that an animal's basic obligation and essential role does not include seeking perfection through learning, progress through scientific knowledge, or prayer and petitioning for help by displaying its impotence. Rather, its sole purpose is to act within the bounds of its innate faculties, which is the mode of worship specified for it.

People, however, are born knowing nothing of life and their environment, and so must learn everything. As we cannot do this even within twenty years, we must continue to learn until we die. We are sent here with so much weakness and inability that we might need more than one year to learn how to walk. Only after fifteen years can we distinguish good and evil. Only by living in a society can we become intelligent and sensible enough to choose between what is beneficial and what is harmful.

Thus the essential and intrinsic duty of our existence is to seek perfection through learning, and to proclaim our worship of, and servanthood to, God through prayer and supplication. It is to seek answers for such

---

[3] *İşaratü'l-İ'caz*, "*Suratu'l-Baqara*", verse 16; *The Words*, "The Twenty-third Word", p. 332.

essential questions as: "Through whose compassion is my life so wisely administered? Through whose generosity am I being so affectionately trained? Through whose favors and benevolence am I being so solicitously nourished?" It is to pray and petition the Provider of Needs in humble awareness of our needs. In short, it is flying to the highest rank of being worshipful servants of God on the wings of learning and worship.

- **We resemble seeds which will grow into eternal, majestic trees whose branches extend into the Intermediate World and the World of Representations or Immaterial Forms, and which will be favored with countless bounties, and yield innumerable fruits of perfection in the next world and Paradise.**[4]

A seed is endowed with great potential by Divine Power, and a subtle program by Divine Destiny, so that it may germinate underground, emerge from that narrow world, and enter the spacious world of air. By asking its Creator in the tongue of its capacity to become a tree, it may attain a perfection particular to it. If, due to its malignant disposition, the seed abuses its potential to attract harmful substances, it will soon rot away in its narrow place. If it uses its potential properly, however, and in compliance with the creational commands of *"The Splitter of grain and fruit-stone,"*[5] it will emerge from its narrow place and grow into an awesome, fruitful tree. In addition, its tiny and particular nature will come to represent a great and universal truth.

In just the same way, our essence is equipped by the Divine Power with great potential, and is inscribed by Destiny with important programs. If we use our potential and faculties in this narrow world under the soil of worldly life to satisfy the fancies of our carnal, evil-commanding soul, we will, like a rotten seed, decay and decompose for an insignificant pleasure in a short life amidst hardships and troubles. Thus we will depart from this world with a heavy spiritual burden on our unfortunate souls.

But if we germinate the seed of our potential under the "soil of worship" with the "water of Islam" and the "light of belief" according to the Qur'an's decrees, and use our faculties for their true purposes, we will grow into eternal, majestic trees whose branches extend into the Intermediate World and the World of Representations or Immaterial Forms, and will be favored with countless bounties, and yield innumerable fruits

---

4   *The Words*, "The Twenty-third Word", pp. 337–338.
5   *Suratu'l-An'am*, 6:95.

of perfection in the next world and Paradise. We will, in fact, become the blessed, luminous fruit of the Tree of Creation.

True progress is possible only when we turn our faculties (e.g., intellect, heart, spirit, and even imagination) to the eternal life, and occupy them with its own kind of worship. What the misguided consider progress—being immersed in the life of this world and subjecting all our faculties to the carnal, evil-commanding soul to taste all worldly pleasures, no matter how base—is nothing but decline and degradation.

- **There are nine things in the human self of whose nature and consequences we live as if unaware.**[6]

First: Our body is like a fresh, pleasant, and enjoyable fruit in summer, but dried and rotten in winter.

Second: Our animal quality: see how quickly decay and death come to animals.

Third: Our human quality, which vacillates between corruption and extinction, and purification and permanence. Preserve that which is inclined to remain forever through constant remembrance of the Everlasting One.

Fourth: Our short and limited lifespan, which lasts only until the hour appointed for it, is neither antedated nor postponed. So we should not grieve for it, be anxious about it, or burden it with worldly ambitions that cannot be achieved during a whole lifetime.

Fifth: Our material existence is in the Hand of the True Owner of all things, Who cares for it much more than we do. If we interfere in it without His permission, we will harm it. Do we not see how avarice brings despair and disappointment, just as insistence on sleeping causes sleeplessness and restlessness?

Sixth: The calamities befalling us are not really bitter, for they disappear quickly. The pleasure of their disappearance is followed by delight and happiness. Besides, through the All-Permanent One, they cause us to turn from what is fleeting to what is permanent.

Seventh: We are guests wherever we are. Guests do not set their hearts upon what does not concern them or accompany them on their trip. We will depart from here soon, and from this town—we will either go out of it or be buried in it. We will leave this transient world, or be expelled from

---

6   *Al-Mathnawi al-Nuri*, "The Sixth Treatise", pp. 173–174.

it. So abandon and renounce it, with honor and dignity, before we are expelled in humiliation.

Eighth: We should sacrifice our material existence to the One Who has given it to us, for He buys it for a very high price. We should make haste to sell it—or, rather, to sacrifice it. For, first of all, it goes away for nothing. Second, it belongs to Him, and will ultimately be returned to Him. Third, our reliance on it causes us to fall into non-existence, for our existence is a door opened onto Him. If we open that door through renunciation, we will find permanent existence. Fourth, if we cling to it, only a point-sized part of it remains in our hand, and we will be enveloped by a thick darkness of "non-existence." If we blow off that part, the lights of existence will surround us.

Ninth: Worldly pleasure or enjoyment. Whatever Destiny has for us in store will come to us, so we should not worry about it. Sensible people do not set their hearts upon fleeting things. However our own particular world ends, we should renounce worldly pleasure. If it ends in happiness, we can attain happiness by renouncing pleasure. If it ends in misery, how can one waiting to be hanged get pleasure from decorated gallows? Even unbelievers who think they are headed for absolute non-existence—I seek refuge with God from such a supposition!—should renounce worldly pleasure, for the continual disappearance of such pleasure brings a continual feeling of the pain of the absolute non-existence they suppose to follow death. Such pain is much more acute than the pleasure they find in life.

- **Humanity, among the creatures, is much like a tender child. Our strength is in our weakness, and our power in our impotence. This lack of strength and power has caused creation to be subjugated to us.**[7]

So if we perceive our weakness and become humble servants of God through verbal and active prayer, and if we recognize our impotence and seek God's help, we will have shown our gratitude to Him for this subjugation of nature to us. Moreover, God will enable us to reach our goal and achieve our aims in a way far beyond our own capability. Sometimes we wrongly attribute a wish's attainment to our own power and ability, when in reality it has been obtained for us through the prayer offered by the tongue of our disposition. Consider how great a source of power is a chick's weakness, for it causes the mother hen to attack even a lion. A lion cub's

[7] *The Words*, "The Twenty-third Word", pp. 343–344.

weakness subjugates a great lioness, which will suffer hunger to feed its baby. How remarkable is the powerful appeal inherent in weakness, and what a spectacular manifestation of Compassion for importunate beings.

Tender, beloved children obtain their goals by weeping, wishing, or making sad faces, all of which can cause mighty people to serve them. If children rely on their own strength, in practical terms they can achieve nothing. Their weakness and powerlessness, as well as feelings of affection and protection, are so in their favor that a single gesture may allow them to subjugate powerful persons to themselves. Should such children arrogantly deny the care and affection shown to them, and claim to do all of this on their own, they would receive a sour face, and resentment. Our poverty is the source of Divine provision, our ignorance is compensated for by Divine inspiration, and our need draws Divine favors. Divine Mercy, Affection, and Wisdom, not our own power and knowledge, have empowered us with dominion over creation, and have put things at our disposal. It is the Divine Authority and Mercy Which, due to our weakness, enable us, beings so weak that we can be defeated by a blind scorpion and a footless snake, to dress in silk produced by a worm and to eat the honey produced by a stinging insect.

Since this is the reality, we should renounce arrogance and self-trust. Rather, we should declare and affirm our impotence and weakness in God's Court by asking for His help, and by praying and entreating Him. We should show that we are His true servants. Then we should say: *"God is sufficient for us. How excellent a Guardian He is!"*[8] and ascend to the higher ranks.

- **Our observed dominion in nature, and our advancement and progress in civilization and technology, are mainly due to our essential weakness and helplessness, which attract Divine aid.**[9]

A simple comparison between the memories of the people in the past and at present, and between their needs and conditions of life, is enough to prove this reality. God equips us with developments in sciences and technology to compensate our lack in certain essential capacities.

- **Every living being is a Divine palace. A human being, in particular, is the most beautiful and wonderful of palaces. Some of the jewels of this palace are gathered from the World of Spirits, some**

---

8 *Sura Al 'Imran*, 3:173.
9 *The Words*, "The Twenty-third Word", pp. 343.

from the World of Immaterial Representations or Ideal Forms and the Supreme Preserved Tablet, and others from the worlds of air, light, and elements. Therefore, the One Who has made this palace can only be the One Who has created, and governs, the entire universe.[10]

The One Who has made this palace can only be the One in relation to Whom the world and the Hereafter are just two dwellings for His creatures; the earth and the skies are each a page for His inscriptions, and He controls all time as though it were a single day. In this case, it is only He Who dominates the earth and the heavens, and holds the reins of the world and the Hereafter, Who has the right to be worshipped by human beings, and is the One in Whom human beings must seek refuge, and to Whom they must turn as the only Savior.

- **By virtue of the uniqueness of humanity, those who follow the way of servanthood to God will be rewarded, especially in the Hereafter, with all pleasures, blessings, and perfections acquired by, or allotted to, their parts, organs, limbs, systems, senses, feelings, and faculties. But if they follow the way of egoism, they will be the target of pain, suffering, and torment.**[11]

Those who recite God's Names, whether consciously or not, receive many benefits. Humanity is a very interesting creation. Each individual is a uniform being composed of many parts, simultaneously simple and complex, having organs, limbs, systems, senses, feelings, and faculties. Each of those have their own pains and pleasures, along with others related to, and coming from, the whole body. There is a swift, mutual sense of help and support among them. By virtue of this uniqueness, those who follow the way of servanthood to God will be rewarded, especially in the Hereafter, with all the pleasures, blessings, and perfections acquired by, or allotted to, their parts, organs, limbs, systems, senses, feelings, and faculties. But if they follow the way of egoism, they will be the target of pain, suffering, and torment. A toothache is different from an earache; the pleasure of the eyes is different from that of the tongue; and the pleasure and pain originating in touch, imagination, reason, and the heart differ from each other.

---

[10] *The Gleams*, "The Seventeenth Gleam", p. 187.
[11] *Al-Mathnawi al-Nuri*, "The Fifth Treatise", p. 134.

- **Our worship has two aspects. The first aspect concerns reflection on and consciousness of God's Acts and works. The second aspect is worship and prayer, done in His presence by addressing Him directly.**[12]

The first aspect is to obediently affirm the Sovereignty of His Lordship over creation and observe Its beauties and perfections in amazement; to draw attention to and herald the unique arts of creation; to study the pages of creation and the sheets of the heavens and the earth, each of which is a missive of Divine Power, and contemplate them in great admiration; and to gaze in amazement and admiration upon the subtle ornamentation and refined skills seen in creation, and to ardently desire to know their All-Beautiful and Gracious Originator, and to yearn to enter His Presence, where we hope to be received into His favor.

The second aspect of our worship is done in His presence by addressing Him directly. We pass from the works to their Producer and we see that an All-Majestic Maker wills Himself to be known through His Art's miracles, and in response we believe in Him and know Him. We see that an All-Compassionate Lord wills to make Himself loved through His Compassion's beautiful fruits, and in response we love Him and make ourselves loved by Him through devoting our love and adoration to Him. We see that an All-Munificent Provider nourishes us with the best and dearest of His material and spiritual favors, and we respond with gratitude and praise, expressed through our works, deeds, lifestyles, and, if possible, through all of our senses and faculties. We see that an All-Beautiful and Gracious One of Majesty manifests His Grandeur and Perfection, Majesty and Beauty, in the mirrors of beings, and draws attention to them, and in response, declaring, "God is the All-Great! All-Glorified is God!" we prostrate before Him in wonder and adoration, and in consciousness of our nothingness before Him. We see that One with Absolute Riches displays His limitless wealth and treasuries in an infinitely generous fashion, and, declaring our destitution, we respond by asking for His favors in praise and glorification. We see that an All-Majestic Originator has arranged the earth like an exhibition to display His matchless works, and in response we appreciate them by saying, "What wonders God has willed and created!"; confirm their beauty by saying, "God bless them!"; show our wonder by saying: "All-Glorified is God!" and express our admiration

---

[12] *The Words*, "The Twenty-third Word", pp. 345–346.

by saying, "God is the All-Great!" We see that the One who is absolutely Unique shows His Oneness throughout creation by His unique signs and specific decrees, and by His inimitable stamps and seals that He has put on each creature; that He inscribes signs of Unity on everything and raises the flag of His Unity throughout the world, proclaiming His Lordship. We respond to this with belief, affirmation, admission, and testimony to His Unity, and with devotion and sincere worship.

We may attain true humanity through such types of worship and reflection. We may show that we are of the best stature as the perfect pattern of creation and, by the grace of belief, become trustworthy rulers of the earth, worthy of bearing the Supreme Trust.

- **Like the sun's rising in the morning and setting in the evening, whatever happens to us, all our conditions have been predetermined by the Pen of Destiny and inscribed on our forehead. Our distress and depression will only increase if we criticize Destiny; this will be no different from willfully striking our head against an anvil. One who cannot penetrate the regions and depths of the heavens and earth must consent willingly to the Lordship of the One Who created everything and decreed its destiny.[13]**

This does not mean that humanity is like a dry leaf before winds. We have been equipped with free will and act by it. However, Destiny considers the human free will in predetermining whatever will happen to human beings. Therefore, having free will is not contrary to resignation to the Divine Destiny. We must use our free will in our actions in obedience to and trust in God Almighty, and resign to the results in reliance on Him.

Bediüzzaman also writes as follows:

> O helpless one, stop wailing over misfortune and trust God,
> For know this wailing is an error that causes trouble after trouble;
> If you have found Him Who makes you suffer, then know
> this suffering is a gift bringing peace and happiness.
> So, stop wailing and thank God, like nightingales:
> they are happy with the happiness of roses.
> But if you do not find Him, know that the whole world
> is a place of suffering, misfortune, and loss.

---

[13] *Al-Mathnawi al-Nuri*, "The Sixth Treatise", p. 176.

Why wail over a small misfortune
when you bear a worldwide responsibility,
Come, put your trust in God and smile at the face of misfortune
so that it may also smile, for as it smiles, it lessens and changes.[14]

- **Out of His perfect munificence, compassion, and justice, God Almighty has included in good deeds an immediate reward and, in bad ones, an immediate punishment. He has included in good deeds spiritual pleasures that recall the rewards of the Hereafter, and in bad ones, spiritual recompenses that recall the torments of Hell.[15]**

For example, love between believers is a good deed for the people of faith. Included in this good deed is spiritual pleasure, contentment, and exhilaration which recall the rewards of the Hereafter. Anyone who turns to their heart will feel this pleasure. While on the other hand, enmity and hostility between believers are evil, causing noble spirits to feel the torment of the conscience that is great enough to suffocate the heart and spirit.

Another example: Being respectful towards those who are worthy of respect, and compassionate to those who are worthy of compassion, and serving them are good deeds. There is such great pleasure and contentment in these good deeds that the rewards of the Hereafter are felt, leading one to show respect and compassion to the extent that they make one ready to sacrifice one's very life. The pleasure and reward a mother receives from the compassion she feels for her child are such that they may cause her to sacrifice her life. In the animal kingdom, the hen which attacks a lion in order to save her chick is an example of this truth. This means that there is an immediate reward in compassion and respect. Noble people of magnanimity and endeavor feel this, and thus they have a heroic character and attitude.

On the other hand, there is a punishment in greed and wastefulness—continuous complaints, dissatisfaction, worry, and heartache cause greedy, wasteful people to lose their senses. And in envy there is an immediate punishment that scorches the one who feels it. While in contentment and trust in God we find an immediate, pleasurable reward which removes all the tribulations and pains of poverty and neediness.

[14] *The Letters*, "The Sixth Letter", p. 36.
[15] *The Gleams*, "The Twenty-eighth Gleam", pp. 389–390.

As another example, pride and conceit are such heavy burdens that a proud person demands respect from everyone. Since they are despised because of this desire, they suffer constant torment. Respect is given; it is not to be sought.

Another example: The pleasurable reward in humility and the abandonment of egotism save one from the heavy, despicable burden of trying to make oneself liked. And the list goes on: all good and bad deeds, and good and bad morals, should be considered according to this standard.

- **The Religion does not consist only in belief; it also includes righteous action.**[16]

Is fear of imprisonment, or being seen and apprehended by a government detective, sufficient enough to prevent people from committing the kind of grievous sins and crimes which poison society, such as murder, adultery, theft, drinking, and gambling? If this were the case, there would have to be a policeman or detective stationed permanently in every house, or even at everyone's side, so that rebellious souls would restrain themselves from committing these despicable acts. However, the Religion places a permanent immaterial deterrent next to everyone—a deterrent which comes from belief and the duty to enjoin what is good and forbid what is illicit. By bearing in mind the existence of the awesome prison of Hell and Divine wrath, people are able to preserve themselves from evil.

- **The human conscious nature, which we call conscience, and which distinguishes between what is good and evil, which feels pleasure and exhilaration in what is good, and suffers from and is grieved by what is evil, consists of four basic elements, namely the spiritual intellect, willpower, the mind, and feeling. These four elements are also regarded as the senses of the spirit. In addition to their different duties and functions, each of these senses has an ultimate purpose for its existence. The ultimate purpose for willpower is worshipping God; for the mind, it is having knowledge of God; for feeling, it is love of God; and for the spiritual intellect, it is vision of God. What we call** taqwa **(piety and righteousness), which is the perfect form or degree of worship, is the result of the functions of all these four senses. The Shari'ah feeds them so that they develop, and it equips them with**

---

[16] *The Rays*, "The Twelfth Ray", p. 302.

the necessary materials, and directs them to the ultimate purposes for the existence of each.[17]

Even if reason abandons its essential duty and sees and judges wrongly, human conscience cannot forget its Maker. Even if it denies its own existence, the conscience thinks of Him, sees Him, and is turned to Him. Intuition, which is a power of quick, lightning-like grasp, continuously provokes it. Inspiration, which is doubled intuition, constantly illuminates it. Desire, which is doubled inclination, and yearning, which is doubled desire, and love of God always stimulate it towards knowledge of the All-Majestic One. The feelings of attraction felt in one's innate human conscience are due to the attractive power of this substantial truth.

• **After acquiring the necessary knowledge of belief, we must do good, righteous deeds. For, following belief, the Qur'an declares:** "Those who do good, righteous deeds."[18]

This short life suffices only for doing what is most important and necessary. Science and technology are necessary insofar as they help satisfy essential needs, human progress (both intellectual and spiritual), and human prosperity in both worlds. Whatever causes dissipation and sedition is harmful.

• **If qualities change places, their natures change. Because of this, the Qur'an generally mentions good works and piety and righteousness without defining them. By leaving them undefined, it alludes to the defining importance of circumstances; its conciseness is in fact a detailed explanation, and its silence, an expansive word.**[19]

In different places, one quality can sometimes be a demon, or it can sometimes be an angel; it is sometimes virtuous, sometimes wicked—some examples are as follows:

If an attribute which is regarded as dignity or self-respect for the weak is found in the strong or powerful (in the face of a weak one), it is pride and arrogance. If an attribute that is regarded as modesty for the strong or powerful is found in the weak, it is self-abasement and hypocrisy. In his office, the gravity of a person of authority is dignity, and his feeling of

---

[17] *Gleams of Truth*, p. 174.

[18] *Al-Mathnawi al-Nuri*, "The Fifth Treatise", 164.

[19] *Gleams of Truth*, p. 68.

self-nothingness is self-abasement. But in his house, his feeling of self-nothingness is modesty and his gravity, arrogance.

Forbearance or tolerance on one's own account is good and shows public-spiritedness; sacrifice (of one's own right) is also a good deed, a praiseworthy quality. However, when done on behalf of others or the nation, one's tolerance is treachery, and one's sacrifice is a wicked attribute or act.

Entrusting the accomplishment of an affair to God before taking all the necessary measures and making all necessary arrangements is laziness, while leaving the desired outcome's realization to Him after doing all that could be done is reliance on Him (*tawakkul*) as taught to us by the Shari'ah.

Contentment with one's lot or with the results after having exerted one's efforts is praiseworthy contentment, and it encourages further effort by reinvigorating one's energy. But contentment with what one already has is not desirable contentment; rather, it is lack of the necessary endeavor. There are numerous other examples.

- **Love is the cause of the universe's existence, the bond between all things, and the light and life of the universe. Since we are the most comprehensive fruit of existence, a love so overflowing that it can invade the universe has been included in that fruit's heart (its seed or core). One who deserves such an infinite love can only be one with infinite perfection.**[20]

The Qur'an declares: *"God has not made for any man two hearts within his body (one to be assigned for belief in and love and worship of Him, and the other to belief in and love and worship of others)."*[21] So, first we must love God Almighty and then love others only for the sake of His love and in Him Name.

However involuntary loving appears, we can direct it to a certain object. For example, by convincing ourselves that something beloved is ugly, or an obstacle to, or only a mirror for, an object worthy of true love, this feeling of love can be diverted to the true object of love.

For example, loving delicious foods and fruits because they are favors and bounties of Almighty God means loving the Divine Name the All-Mer-

---

[20] *The Words*, "The Twenty-fourth Word", p. 377; The Thirty-second Word", pp. 653–656.
[21] *Suratu'l-Ahzab*, 33:4.

ciful and Giver of bounties, and is a sort of thanksgiving. Love, when done in the All-Merciful One's Name, and not the carnal soul's name, is reflected by lawful earning, contentment with what is lawful, and consuming in gratitude and reflection and without extravagance.

Loving and respecting one's parents on behalf of the Divine Mercy and Wisdom that equipped them with affection and tenderness, are included in God's love. If done for Almighty God's sake, we must show our parents much more love, respect, and care when they can only cause us difficulty. The verse: "If either or both of them reach old age with you, do not say to them 'Uff!'"[22] tells children to love and respect their parents in five ways and degrees, shows how important parents' rights are in the eyes of the Qur'an, and how degrading and detestable filial ingratitude is.

Loving one's children with the utmost care and compassion because they are the All-Compassionate, All-Munificent One's gifts, is included in one's love of Almighty God. The sign that such love is for God's sake is to bring them up as sincere servants of God and show "becoming patience" at their death, and to not wail in despair and rebelliousness against Destiny.

A woman's greatest charm and beauty lie in her lovable good conduct accompanied with the kindness and grace particular to womanhood, and in her elevated, serious, and sincere compassion. That beauty of compassion and good conduct increase until she dies. It is through the love and respect for her compassion and good conduct that one can observe her rights to the end. If she is loved because of her physical beauty, she is deprived of her rights and the love and respect due to her at a time when she needs them most.

Loving virtuous people like Prophets and saints because they are approved servants of Almighty God, and in His Name and for His sake, are included in His love. If we love our life because it is a most valuable capital given by Almighty God to gain eternal life, a treasury containing the faculties with which to acquire all kinds of virtues and perfections, and if we spend it in His service, then this love is included in love of Almighty God, the All-Worshipped One.

- **There is some sort of love which leads the lover to perdition, even though this love is for Prophets and other beloved servants of God.**[23]

---

[22] *Suratu'l-Isra'*, 17:24.
[23] *The Words*, "The Thirty-second Word", p. 657.

Love for Prophets and saints or God's beloved servants, such as that found among Christians who believe in the Trinity, and the Rafidis (a Shi'a sect) who cherish enmity toward almost all Companions due to their love of 'Ali, is fruitless.

- **Any love in God's Name and in the Qur'anic manner yields good results in both this world and the Hereafter.**[24]

Loving delicious foods and fruits in God's Name makes them a favor and grace unmixed with pain, an ease that yields pure thankfulness.

Loving our carnal soul leads us to pity so that we will educate it and prevent it from harmful desires and fancies. When we do this successfully, our carnal soul cannot take us wherever it wishes and enslave us to its desires. On the contrary, we will mount it and guide it to truth, not drive it to passions.

If we love and have mercy for our spouses based on their good conduct, and their being mines of compassion and gifts of Divine Mercy, they will love and respect us. As we both age, this mutual love and respect will grow and increase our happiness. Carnal love based on physical beauty is fleeting. When it disappears, so do our mutual good relations.

Loving our parents for Almighty God's sake is an act of worship, and it increases as they age. With a most elevated feeling and endeavor, we pray for them to live long so that we may get more rewards because of them, and receive a pure spiritual pleasure by respecting and serving them. If we find their existence unbearable when they need us, and thus desire their deaths, we have descended to barbarism and will suffer a painful spiritual ailment.

Loving our children because they are Almighty God's lovable gifts that He has entrusted to us to raise and educate in an agreeable way is a love that brings happiness and blessing.

Loving virtuous people like Prophets and saints shows us that the Intermediate World of the grave, which appears to the heedless as a dark, frightening solitude, is actually a mansion illuminated by the existence of those blessed ones. We will not be afraid to go to that world. Rather, we will feel an inclination and eagerness to go there, and the pleasure we receive from our life will not be spoiled.

---

[24] *The Words*, "The Thirty-second Word", p. 657–659.

Loving this world in Almighty God's Name makes all of its creatures like amiable friends. Seeing it as a tillage for the Hereafter, we find in everything a capital that can be used for the good of our afterlife. Calamity does not scare us, and the transience of our life does not trouble us. We will stay in that guest-house peacefully until our appointed hour. But if we love the world as the heedless do, we will suffocate in a troublesome, calamitous, transient, and fruitless love.

- **A beloved who disappears is not beautiful, for one doomed to decline cannot be truly beautiful. It is not, and should not be, loved in the heart, for the heart is created for eternal love and is a mirror of the Eternally Besought One.**[25]

Prophet Abraham, upon him be peace , said: "I love not those that set."[26] Therefore:

> Want only One (the rest are not worth wanting).
> Call One (the others do not come to your assistance).
> Seek One (the others are not worth seeking).
> See and follow One (the others are not seen all the time;
> they become invisible behind the veil of mortality).
> Know One (knowledge other than that which does not add to
> your knowledge of Him is useless).

Mention One (words not concerning Him may be regarded as useless).

- **Our nature contains two faculties: the means of fear and the means of love. Such love and fear is felt for either the created or the Creator. Fear of the created is a painful affliction, and love of the created is a troublesome pain.**[27]

For we fear such things or persons that they show us no mercy or reject our request. If this is so, fear of the created is a painful affliction. As for love of the created, those we love either do not care for us and, like our youth and possessions, leave us without saying farewell. Or they disdain us because of our love. Ninety-nine percent of lovers complain of their beloved ones, for love of the idol-like worldly beloved from the bottom of one's heart, which is the mirror of the Eternally Besought One, is

---

[25] *The Words*, "The Seventeenth Word", p. 229.
[26] *Suratu'l-An'am*, 6:76.
[27] *The Words*, "The Twenty-fourth Word", pp. 377–378.

unbearable in the beloved's view. And so it is rejected, for human essential nature rejects and repels what is unnatural and undeserved.

In short, those we love either do not care for us, or they despise us, or they do not accompany us. Contrary to our desire, they leave us. So we should turn our fear and love toward such a One that our fear will be a pleasant humility and our love a happiness free of humiliation. Fearing the All-Majestic Creator means finding a way to His Compassion and taking refuge in Him. In fact, fear is a whip; it drives one into the embrace of His Compassion. A mother frightens her child away from something or someone, and attracts him or her into her arms. That fear is very pleasurable for children, for it draws them into the arms of care and compassion. However, the care and compassion of all mothers is only a ray from God's Compassion. This means there is a great pleasure in fear of God. Given this, we can understand what infinite pleasure can be found by loving Him. Furthermore, those who fear God are freed from the worrying, troublesome fear of others, and their love of created beings in God's Name causes no pain or separation.

- **Love is a very strong emotion. Feeling it for mortal beings either throws lovers into endless pain and sorrow or, since mortal beings are not worth so sincere a love, leads lovers toward seeking the Permanent Beloved One. In the latter case, it becomes real love.**[28]

Each of a person's thousands of feelings has two aspects: figurative and real. For example, everyone worries about the future even though they have no guarantee that they will be alive tomorrow. Then, they realize that they will die only at their appointed time. As a result, they stop worrying about their uncertain future here, and focus on their eternal future beginning with death. That is a future worth worrying about, especially for those who do not heed the Divine commandments.

In the same way, people feel great passion for wealth and position. But they soon understand that wealth, fame, and position are not worth it, for such things may remove their dignity, reveal such degrading attitudes as ostenation and hypocrisy, or cause them to bow and humble themselves before others. But above all, these things are temporary. In the end, such people incline towards the spiritual ranks and nearness to God, and busy themselves with good deeds so that they will have provisions for their

---

[28] *The Letters*, "The Ninth Letter", pp. 52–53.

eternal life. Their inordinate ambition to acquire transient things thus changes into acquiring what is eternal.

If people exploit their spiritual faculties to satisfy their sensual and worldly desires, and live in this world as if they would stay here forever, those faculties will lead to immoral qualities and cause much waste. But if people use them to prosper in the Hereafter, without neglecting life's essential needs, these faculties will lead to laudable moral qualities and happiness in either world in accordance with wisdom and truth.

One reason why preachers' advice is ineffective nowadays is that they invite people to change their nature. They advise: "Do not be envious or ambitious, do not feel enmity or be obstinate, do not love the world," and so on. Such advice is useless, for it is against human nature. Instead, these energies can and should be channeled into good deeds and directed towards positive aims. For example, love for the world can be channeled into love for the other world, enmity can be directed against one's carnal soul, and envy can become a means for competing to do good deeds.

- **The sphere of the needs of humanity is as extensive as sight, and extends as far as the imagination. We need whatever we do not have, and so our needs are limitless. Yet our power extends only as far as we can reach.**[29]

Thus our wants and needs are infinite, while our capital is minute and insignificant. So, what does that insignificant willpower signify when confronted with such need? We have to search for another solution. The solution is not to rely on our willpower and power, but to submit to the Divine Will and seek refuge in His Power by trusting in Him. "O Lord, since this is the way of salvation, I give up my free will on Your way and abandon my ego. I do this so that Your Grace may help and support me out of compassion for my impotence and weakness, that Your Mercy may take pity on me because of my want and need, and that It may be a support for me and open its door to me." Whoever finds the boundless sea of Mercy does not rely on his own free will, which is no more than a drop of water seen in a mirage. He does not abandon Mercy and resort to his will.

- **Alas! We have been deceived. We thought that this worldly life was constant, and thus lost it thoroughly.**[30]

---

[29] *The Words*, "The Seventeenth Word", p. 228.
[30] *The Words*, "The Seventeenth Word", p. 228–229.

Indeed, this passing life is but a sleep that passes like a dream. This life, having no foundation, flies like the wind. Those who rely on themselves and think they will live forever, will certainly die. They race towards death, and this world, humanity's home, falls into the darkness of annihilation. Ambitions are time-bound, but pains endure in the spirit.

Since this is the reality, come, my wretched soul that is fond of living and wants a long life, that loves the world and has boundless ambition and pain. Awaken and come to your senses. Consider that while the firefly relies on its own dim light, and always remains in night's boundless darkness, the honeybee finds the sun of daytime and observes its friends (flowers) gilded with sunlight because it does not rely on itself. In the same way, if you rely on yourself, and your being and self-confidence, you will be like the firefly. But if you dedicate yourself, your transient being and body on the way of the Creator Who gave it to you, you will find, like the honeybee, an endless life of being. Dedicate it, for your being and your body is no more than a Divine trust to you.

Moreover, it is the Creator's property; it is He Who gave it to you. So use it for His sake, unhesitatingly and without placing Him under obligation so that it will gain permanence or eternality. For a negation negated is an affirmation.

Thus if our non-being is negated (in favor of Being), our being finds true existence. The All-Munificent Creator buys His own property from us. In return, He gives us a high price like Paradise, looks after it for us, and increases its value. He will return it to us in a perfected and permanent form. So, my soul, do not wait. Do this business, which is profitable in five respects. As well as being saved from five losses, make a fivefold profit in one transaction.

- **The All-Originating One has equipped the human nature with such faculties that some of them would not be satisfied even if they could swallow the world. Some others cannot tolerate even a microscopic particle. Like the eye that is unable to bear the weight of a single hair while the head carries a heavy stone, these faculties cannot endure the weight of even a hair, that is, an insignificant state that arises from heedlessness and misguidance. They are sometimes even extinguished, and die.**[31]

---

[31] *The Gleams*, "The Seventeenth Gleam", p. 188.

So be alert and careful, always act with caution and in fear of sinking. Do not drown in a morsel, a word, a grain, a glance, a beckoning, a kiss! Do not cause your faculties, that are so extensive that they can contain the whole world, to drown in such a thing. For there are some small things which can in one respect swallow many large things. See how the sky and its stars are contained in a piece of glass, and most of the pages of your life history and actions are inserted in your memory, which is as small as a mustard seed. Thus, there are minute things which, in one respect, contain and swallow larger ones.

- **Considering the nature of the worldly, animal life and corporeal existence, be freed from animality, restrict your carnal appetites, and enter the level of the life of the heart and spirit!**[32]

Then, we will find a broader sphere of life than our imagined world and a realm of light. The key to that sphere and realm is to awaken the heart and spirit with the sacred pronouncement, *There is no deity but God*, which is the expression of Divine Oneness that uncovers the mysteries of knowledge of God, and makes them work.

- **As with every good action, courage, too, arises from belief in and loyal devotion to God. As with every bad action, cowardice arises from misguidance as well.**[33]

If the earth were to explode, those servants of God with truly illuminated hearts would not be frightened—they might even consider it a marvel of the Eternally Besought One's Power. A rationalist but unbelieving philosopher might tremble at the sight of a comet, lest it should strike the earth.

Our ability to meet our endless demands is negligible. We are threatened with afflictions that our own strength cannot withstand. Our strength is limited to what we can reach, yet our wishes and demands, suffering and sorrow, are as wide as our imagination.

Anyone not wholly blind to the truth understands that our best option is to submit to God, to worship and believe and have confidence in Him. A safe road is preferable to a dangerous one, even one with a very low probability of safe passage. The way of belief leads one safely to endless

---

[32] *The Gleams*, "The Seventeenth Gleam", p. 189.
[33] *The Words*, "The Third Word", p. 20.

bliss with near certainty; the way of unbelief and transgression, meanwhile, is not profitable and has a near certainty of endless loss.

- In a *hadith qudsi*, **God says: "I will treat My servants in the way they think of Me."**[34]

Good brings good, and evil brings evil. One who is well-mannered and a good character in belief in and devotion and submission to God thinks of the good and sees the good side of everything, so he is and will be treated in the way he thinks and sees. While the other who has an evil character and sees the bad side of everything in disobedience to God and complaint of everything also is and will be treated in the way he thinks and sees.

- **Is humanity to be left to its own devices? God forbid! Rather, humans are destined for eternity, and will certainly be met with either eternal happiness or perpetual misery. Whether small or great, they will be called to account for all deeds, and either be rewarded or punished.**[35]

The Qur'an declares: "*Whoever does an atom's weight of good will see it; and whoever does an atom's weight of evil will see it.*"[36] This indicates the most universal manifestation of the Divine Name, the All-Recording and Preserving. If we look at the pages of the Book of the Universe inscribed on the pattern of the Manifest Book—the Qur'an—we can see the most comprehensive manifestation of the Divine Name, the All-Recording and Preserving, and the examples of the truth expressed in the verses above.

Uncountable seeds of extremely different identities from almost infinitely various trees, flowers, and plants buried in the darkness of the simple and solid earth follow perfectly the commands of growth issued by the All-Wise Originator. It is as if they had perfect consciousness, perception, purpose, will, knowledge, and wisdom, they grow each into its own tree, flower, or plant when spring comes. There is no confusion, fault and error. They demonstrate the fact expressed in the Qur'anic statements, "*You do not see any fault or incongruity in the creation of the All-Merciful. Look yet again: can you see any rifts?*"[37] Through the manifestation and favoring of the Divine Name, the All-Recording and Preserving, each of the seeds preserves and displays, without confusion or error, the legacy

---

[34] al-Bukhari, "Tawhid" 15, 35; *Muslim*, "Dhikr" 2, 19; *The Words*, "The Ninth Word", p. 50.
[35] *The Gleams*, "The Seventeenth Gleam", p. 191.
[36] *Suratu'z-Zilzal*, 99:7–8.
[37] *Suratu'l-Mulk*, 67:3.

inherited from its parentage. This certainly indicates that the All-Record-ing and Preserving Being Who does this wonderful act of recording and preserving will display the more comprehensive manifestations of His preservation during the Resurrection. Such faultless and clear instances of recording and preservation of insignificant and temporary things and events is decisive proof that all the good and evil deeds, words, and works of humanity, who are the vicegerents on earth and who bear the Supreme Trust, —and whose deeds, words, and works have eternal effects and great importance—are precisely recorded and preserved, and will be subject to account.

- **The universe, with whatever is in it, has been created to know and worship God. Each species of creation has its own kind of worship. Glorifying (tasbih) and praising God (hamd) is the epito-me of worship.**[38]

It is declared in the Qur'an: "*I have not created the jinn and humankind but to (know and) worship Me (exclusively).*"[39] It is also declared: "*The seven heavens and the earth, and whoever is therein, glorify Him. There is nothing that does not glorify Him with His praise (proclaiming that He alone is God, without peer or partner, and all praise belongs to Him exclusively).*"[40]

As Divinity must be and is absolutely free from how the polytheists conceive it; and God, the Sole Deity, is infinitely exalted above having any partners, defects, needs, and opposites, and similarity to the created, the universe, with whatever is and occurs in it, demonstrates these truths. This means His glorification (*tasbih*). Also, God has many Attributes of Perfection, such as the Absolute Existence, Oneness, Eternity without beginning and end, Self-Subsistence by Whom all else subsist, and Life, Knowledge, Hearing, Sight, Will, and Power. It is He Who creates, sus-tains, maintains, and administers the whole universe with all that is in it. Furthermore, God is eternally worthy of praise and gratitude because He is God eternally, eternally Merciful, and the Lord of all creation. Whether His favors are recognized as such by His creatures or not, He must still be praised and thanked. Thanking is required by loyalty to God because of His favors, while praise is required by being sincere servants aware of

---

[38] *Isaharatu'l-I'jaz*, "*Suratu'l-Fatiha*", verse 2.
[39] *Suratu'dh-Dhariyat*, 51:56.
[40] *Suratu'l-Isra'*, 17:44.

Who God is and what servanthood means. This is His praise (*hamd*), and all praise is due to Him, and so the whole of creation praises Him exclusively. While conscious, believing beings praise Him consciously—verbally, actively, and by heart—all other things or beings praise Him through their lives, actions, and duties. The bodies of all human beings, whether believers or unbelievers, also praise Him through the satisfaction of their needs and contentment of their senses and faculties.

Praising God also means that it is God in Whom we seek refuge when we are in danger, to Whom we pray for help when we are in need, and Whom, alone, we adore and worship. In addition, wherever beauty, excellence and perfection occur, the ultimate source is God. No created beings, whether angels or humans, heavenly or earthly objects, have anything other than a dependent, relative excellence, beauty, or perfection. Where these qualities occur and whatever accomplishments creatures do, they are, in reality, simply favors from God. Thus, if there is one to Whom we should feel indebted and grateful, it is the Creator of everything, Who is in reality the Creator of that to which we respond with thanks, and not its apparent possessor.

- **Inanimate beings are like clocks telling the time without knowing their task or why they do it. Though plants and animals lack detailed knowledge about what duties they have, and for what sublime purposes they are employed, this does not mean that they are not employed in those duties and for those purposes.**[41]

The Qur'an states that everything in creation prostrates, worships, praises, and glorifies Almighty God according to their capacities and the Divine Names the manifestations of which they are favored with.[42]

The Lord of the Worlds, the All-Majestic Lord of the heavens and the earth, the All-Gracious Builder of this world and the next, uses angels, animals, inanimate objects, plants, and humanity in this palace of the universe, in this realm of causality. He does this not out of need, as He is the Creator of everything, but for certain instances of wisdom demanded by His Might and Honor, Grandeur and Lordship. He has charged these four classes with unique duties of worship.

---

[41] *The Words*, "The Twenty-fourth Word", pp. 372–377.
[42] *Suratu'l-Hajj*, 22:18.

The first class are angels. They are never promoted, for their ranks are fixed and determined. They receive a specific pleasure from the work itself and a radiance from worship, each according to their rank. In short, their reward is found in their service. Just as humanity is nourished by and derives pleasure from air, water, light, and food, so are angels nourished by and receive pleasure from the lights of remembrance, glorification, worship, knowledge, and love of God.

The second class are animals. God Almighty employs them in numerous duties and for many sublime purposes, without them being aware of these duties and purposes. Since animals also have an appetitive soul and a partial will, their work is not "purely for the sake of God" in the sense that, to some extent, they take a share for their selves. Therefore, since the All-Majestic and Munificent Lord of All Dominion is All-Kind and All-Generous, He gives them a wage as their share.

The third class of workers are plants and inanimate beings. They have no free will and receive no wages. Whatever they do is done purely for God's sake, by His Will and Power, and in His Name. However, as understood from their life cycles, they receive some sort of pleasure from carrying out the duty of, for example, pollination and producing fruits. But they suffer no pain, while animals experience both pain and pleasure because they have some degree of choice. The fact that plants and inanimate beings have no will makes their work more perfect than that of animals. Among animal creatures possessing some sort of choice, the work of those like bees, which are equipped with a kind of inspiration, are more perfect than those that rely on their own partial will.

Vegetable species pray and ask of the All-Wise Originator, each in the tongue of their beings and potentiality: "O Lord. Give us strength so that, by raising the flag of our species throughout the earth, we may proclaim Your Lordship's sovereignty. Grant us success so that we may worship You in every corner of the mosque of the earth. Enable us to grow in every suitable region, so that we may display the works of Your All-Beautiful Names and Your wonderful, invaluable arts." In response, the All-Wise Originator equips the seeds of certain species (e.g., many thorny plants and some yellow flowers) with tiny "wings of hair" so they can fly away and manifest the Divine Names on behalf of their species. He gives some species beautiful, delicious flesh that is either necessary or pleasure-giving for human beings. He causes us to serve them and plant them everywhere.

The All-Wise Originator, Who is the All-Powerful and All-Knowing, has created everything beautifully, and with perfect orderliness. He has equipped all beings with whatever they need, directs them towards agreeable aims, and uses them in the most proper duties. He causes them to worship and glorify Him in the best manner. So if you are truly human, do not deform these beautiful things by asserting that they were created by nature, chance, or necessity. Do not foul them with absurdity, purposelessness, and misguidance. Do not act in an ugly fashion, and do not be ugly.

The fourth class are human beings. Forming a working class among the servants, they resemble both angels and animals. They resemble angels in their extensive supervision and comprehensive knowledge, and in being the heralds of Divine Lordship. Indeed, we are more comprehensive in nature. Since we have an appetitive soul disposed towards evil (angels do not), we have the potential for almost boundless advance or decline. As we seek pleasure and a share for ourselves in our work, we resemble animals. Given this, we can receive two kinds of wages: one is insignificant, animal, and immediate; the other is angelic, universal, and postponed.

- **Worship of God is not an act through which to demand a Divine reward in the future, but rather the necessary result of a past Divine favor.**[43]

We have received our wages and, in return, are charged with serving and worshipping Him. For the All-Majestic Creator Who clothed us in existence, which is purely good, has given us a hungry stomach and, through His Name the All-Providing, has laid before us all edible things as a table of favors. Also, He has given us a life decked out with senses. It too demands its own particular sustenance, much like a stomach. All our senses are like hands before which He has laid a particular table of favors as vast as the earth. In addition, as He has made us human, which demands numerous immaterial favors, He has laid before us a table of favors within reason's grasp, and as multidimensional as the material and immaterial worlds. As He has also granted us belief and Islam, which is the greatest humanity, and thus demands endless favors and is nourished by the fruits of infinite Mercy, He has opened up for us a table of favors, happiness, and pleasures

---

[43] *The Words*, "The Twenty-fourth Word", p. 380.

which encompasses, together with the Sphere of Contingencies, the Sphere of His All-Beautiful Names and sacred Attributes. Moreover, by bestowing love on us, which is a light of belief, He has granted us yet another table of favors and pleasures. As we have received these and innumerable other wages already, we are charged with worship, which is an easy, pleasant, and eternally rewarding Divine gift.

- **It is worship which confirms and strengthens belief, and which makes the truths of faith an established ability. If the truths and judgments or conclusions of faith, which are experiences of conscience and affirmations of reason, are not reinforced and established through worship, their imprints and influences remain weak. Just as worship is a means of happiness in both worlds, it also leads us to regulate and order the worldly and otherworldly affairs. It also serves us to attain human perfections. Furthermore, it relates us to God Almighty as an elevated and honored bond.[44]**

- **Despite his or her restricted, particular thankfulness, a human being can respond to the universal, infinite favors of God Almighty through a universal intention, and through infinitely profound belief and devotion.[45]**

Suppose a poor man enters the king's presence with a cheap (in materialistic terms) present. There he sees expensive gifts sent by the king's favorites. He thinks: "My present means nothing, but this is what I can afford." Then suddenly he addresses the king, saying: "My lord! I offer all these precious gifts in my name, for you deserve them. If I could, I would offer double these." The king, who needs nothing but accepts his subjects' gifts as tokens of respect and loyalty, accepts the poor man's universal intention, desire, and deep feelings of devotion as though they were the greatest gift. Similarly, a poor servant says in his daily prescribed Prayers: "All worship and veneration is for God," by which he means: "In my name, I offer You all the gifts of worship that all beings present to you through their lives. You deserve all of them, and in reality far more than them." This belief and intention is a most comprehensive and universal thankfulness.

The seeds and stones of plants are their intentions to grow into elaborate plants. For example, with its hundreds of seeds, a melon intends:

[44] *Isaharatu'l-I'jaz*, "*Suratu'l-Baqara*", verse 21.
[45] *The Words*, "The Twenty-fourth Word", p. 381.

"O my Creator! I want to exhibit the inscriptions of Your All-Beautiful Names in many places of the earth." Having full knowledge of the future, Almighty God accepts its intentions as worship in deeds. The Prophetic saying: "A believer's intention is better than his action,"[46] expresses this reality. This is also why we glorify and praise Him with phrases expressing infinitude, like: "Glory be to You, and praise be to You to the number of Your creatures, and the things pleasing to You, and the decorations of Your Supreme Throne, and to the amount of ink of Your words. We glorify You with the sum of all the glorifications of Your Prophets, saints, and angels."

- **Just as a commander offers the king, in his name, all of his soldiers' services, humanity, the commander of all earthly creatures (including plants and animals), and acting in its own private world as if in the name of everyone, says:** "You alone do we worship and from You alone do we seek help,"[47] **thus offering the All-Worshipped One of Majesty, in humanity's name, all of creation's worship and entreaties for help. Saying: "Glory be to You with the sum of all the glorifications of all Your creatures and with the tongues of all things You have made," humanity makes all creatures speak in its own name.**[48]

Since we are the fruit of the Tree of Creation, we are a most comprehensive being and are related to all creation. We have within ourselves a heart that, like a fruit's pit, is the center in which all parts end and join together. We are mortal and inclined towards the world of multiplicity. But the worship of God is a line of union that turns us from mortality towards permanence, from the created towards the Creator, and from multiplicity towards unity. It is also a point of juncture between the beginning and the end.

- **God Almighty has not given to us His blessings of life, existence and body as personal properties so that we can use them however we wish. Rather, He has entrusted them to us, so we must use them according to the dictates of their Real Owner in order not to be treated as traitors.**[49]

---

[46] al-Munawi, *Faydu'l-Qadir*, 6:291.

[47] *Suratu'l-Fatiha*, 1:5.

[48] *The Words*, "The Twenty-fourth Word", p. 381–383.

[49] *Barla Lahikası* (Addendum of Barla), p. 311.

We are neither the owners nor masters of ourselves. We have been brought into existence, and whatever we have has been bestowed on us without the least part of our own. Therefore, we cannot claim that we can act in the world however we wish, and we can use all the gifts bestowed on us in whatever way we prefer.

- **Worship is carried out only as a Divine command and only to please Him. The Divine command requires worship, and its result is Divine good pleasure. The fruit and benefit expected of it pertain to the Hereafter.**[50]

However, provided that this is not the intention or the ultimate reason, the fruit and benefits accorded in the world, without expecting them, do not damage worship or the spirit of servanthood. They may even serve to encourage the weak. But if these worldly benefits are what is intended, and what is expected in return for worship, this in part invalidates worship. It may even render any act of worship completely fruitless.

- **A Prophetic Tradition says, "All may perish except the knowledgeable, and the knowledgeable may perish except those who practice, and those who practice may perish except the sincere, and the sincere are in grave danger."[51] So, the only means of salvation is sincerity.**[52]

It is of great importance to attain sincerity. A minute sincere act is preferable to masses of insincere ones. What will cause us to attain sincerity is that we must do our religious duties only because they are God's commands and in order to please God. We must never interfere in God's business.

Everything requires sincerity and everything must be done with sincerity. At the very least, even a small amount of sincere love is superior to tons of dutiful love for which some return is expected. Someone has described this sincere love as follows: "I do not demand return or reward for love, for love demanding a price is weak and transient."[53] Sincere love has been included in human nature and, especially, in all mothers. The

---

[50] *The Gleams*, "The Seventeenth Gleam", p. 181.

[51] al-Ajluni, *Kashf al-Khafa'*, 2:415; Abu Hamid Muhammad al-Ghazzali, *Ihya'u 'Ulumi'd-Din*, 3:414.

[52] *The Gleams*, "The Seventeenth Gleam", p. 183.

[53] This belongs to Abu Tayyib Ahmad ibn Husayn al-Mutanabbi (915–965), an Iraqi Arab poet.

compassion of mothers contains this sincere love to the utmost degree. Their sacrifice of their lives for their children clearly demonstrates that mothers demand no return for the love of their children. While the whole capital of a hen is its life, it sacrifices its own head in order to save the head of its chick from the jaws of a dog.

- **The limits of religiously permissible enjoyment are broad and adequate for our desire, and so you do not need to indulge in what is forbidden. The duties imposed by God are light and few. To be His servant and soldier is an honor beyond description.**[54]

The grave is there, no one can deny it. Whether they want or not, everyone will enter it. It is represented in three ways, there is not the fourth:

For believers, it is the door to a more beautiful world. For those who admit the next life but live a misguided, dissipated life, it is the door to solitary imprisonment that will separate them from their loved ones. Since they believe and confirm but do not live according to their belief, that is exactly how they will be punished. For unbelievers and the misguided who do not believe in the Hereafter, it is the door to eternal execution. Since they believe death to be an execution without resurrection, they will be punished eternally.

Death may come at any time without differentiating between young and old; its appointed hour is unknown. Such an awesomely threatening reality makes it our greatest, most urgent matter to search for a way to avoid eternal punishment and imprisonment, for a way to change the grave into a door opening onto a permanent world of light and eternal happiness.

Belief and worship change the grave into a door opening onto an eternal treasury, a palace of lasting happiness. Old age, illness, calamities, and numerous instances of death everywhere reopen our pain and remind us of death. Even if the misguided and the dissolute appear to enjoy all kinds of pleasure and delight, they most certainly are in a hellish state of spiritual torment. However, a profound stupor of heedlessness makes them temporarily insensible to it.

Obedient believers experience the grave as the door to an eternal treasury and endless happiness. Since the "belief coupon" they have causes them to have a priceless ticket from the allocations of eternal Divine Des-

---

[54] *The Words*, "The Sixth Word", p. 39: "The Thirteenth Word", pp. 159–161.

tiny, they expect the call "Come and collect your ticket" with profound pleasure and spiritual delight. If this pleasure could assume the material form of a seed, it would grow into a private paradise. But those who abandon this great delight and pleasure to indulge the drives of the carnal, evil-commanding soul, who choose temporary and illicit pleasures that resemble poisonous honey causing limitless pains fall far below even animals in the enjoyments of life.

So, those of you who are addicted to worldly pleasure, and in anxiety at the future, struggle to secure it and your lives. If you want pleasure and delight, happiness and ease in this world, be content with what is religiously lawful. It is sufficient for your enjoyment. You must have understood by now that each forbidden pleasure contains many pains. If the dissolute were shown their future—their states in fifty years from now—in the way past events are shown in the movie theater, they would be horrified and disgusted with themselves. Those who wish to be eternally happy in both worlds should follow the Prophet's instruction on the firm ground of belief.

- **One who is freely resigned to harm is not worthy of pity. Those who want to enjoy life should animate it with belief, adorn it with religious obligations, and maintain it by avoiding sins.**[55]

Life will definitely disappear. If we do not remain within the bounds of what is religiously lawful, it will be lost and, rather than pleasure, it will bring us suffering and calamities here, in the grave, and in the Hereafter. But if we adhere to Islamic discipline and spend it chastely, uprightly and in grateful worship to the blessings of youth, in effect, life will remain perpetually, and be the cause of eternal youth.

A life without belief, or with belief rendered ineffective by rebelliousness, only produces pain, sorrow, and grief that far exceed superficial, fleeting enjoyment and its resulting pleasure. This is because humanity has intelligence and, unlike animals, is connected to the past, present, and future, and derives both pain and pleasure from them. Whereas animals have no intelligence, and therefore their present pleasures are marred neither by past sorrows nor future anxieties. But such sorrows and anxieties plague the misguided and heedless, marring their pleasure and diluting it with pain. If this pleasure is illicit, it becomes like poisonous honey.

---

[55] *The Words*, "The Thirteenth Word", pp. 161–163.

Given this, we are far lower than animals when it comes to life's enjoyments. In fact, the lives of misguided, heedless people consist only of the day in which they find themselves, as is the case with their entire existence and world. According to their misguided belief, that which is past no longer exists. But their intellect, which connects them to the past and the future, produces only darkness, and their lack of belief in eternal life makes the future non-existent for them. It is this non-existence that makes separations eternal, and continually darkens their lives.

If you want to understand how so many of these lives end up in hospitals with mental and physical diseases, mainly because of the abuses in the period of youth especially; in prisons or hostels for the destitute due to their excesses; and in bars because of the distress provoked by their spiritual unease, go and ask at those places. As you will hear from the mute eloquence of hospitals' tongue the moans and groans of those who pursued youth's appetites, so will you hear from prisons the regretful sighs of unhappy people imprisoned mainly for illicit actions due to their youthful excesses. You will also understand that most torments of the grave are due to a misspent youth, as related by saints who can discern the life of the grave (the Intermediate Realm), and affirmed by all scholars of truth.

Further, consult the elderly and the sick. Most of them will answer you with grief and regret: "Alas! We wasted our youths in frivolity. Be careful not to do as we did!" Those who do not control the illicit passions of five to ten years' youth bring upon themselves grief and sorrow in this world, torment and harm in the Intermediate Realm, and the severe punishment of Hell in the Hereafter. Although they might be in a most pitiable situation, since they freely chose to pursue such a path, they are not worthy of pity. For one who is freely resigned to harm is not worthy of pity. May Almighty God save all of us from the alluring temptations of this age and preserve us against them. Amin!

In contrast, a life built upon belief results in the past and the future being illuminated, and acquiring existence through the light of belief. Such a life also provides exalted spiritual pleasures and lights of existence for their spirits and hearts.

- **If creatures have any "right" against the Necessarily Existent Being, it is to give thanks for the level of existence and other favors God has accorded on them.**[56]

O people of complaint! You are favored with existence and have experienced life's pleasures. Further, you enjoy a healthy human existence and enjoy innumerable blessings. O people of belief, you were favored with the blessing of Islam, and with being led out of misguidance. Complaining about God shows ingratitude. Be grateful for whatever level He has bestowed on you as a pure blessing, and do not show ingratitude by complaining that He did not favor you with still greater blessings to which you aspire passionately, though wrongly, since there are infinite possibilities everyone can aspire to.

Suppose people elevated to a high position, like being favored with a specific blessing at each step while climbing to a minaret's top, complain that they have not been elevated high enough. Even the most foolish people would see this as a great ingratitude and injustice on such people's part. Therefore, sensible people should try to be content and accept what they have. If they suffer abject poverty although they do what they can and must in lawful ways, they should turn to the All-Patient One and try to acquire a becoming patience. They should do so without complaining. If they want to find fault with someone, they should focus on their carnal souls and complain to God Almighty about that.

- **Impatience implies complaining of God by criticizing His Acts, accusing His Mercy, and disapproving of His Wisdom. Therefore we should not wail over calamities, but should complain to—not of—Him.**[57]

There are three kinds of patience, as follows:

- Piety and God-consciousness, or resisting the carnal soul's temptations and avoiding sins. Such patient people are included in: *"God is with the God-conscious and pious."*[58]

- Endurance during calamities by patient reliance on and total submission to God, Who numbers the patient among: *"God loves those who*

---

[56] *The Letters*, "The Twenty-fourth Letter", p. 306.
[57] *The Letters*, "The Twenty-third Letter", p. 300.
[58] *Suratu'l-Baqara*, 2:194.

rely on Him,"[59] and *"God loves the patient."*[60] Impatience implies complaining of God by criticizing His Acts, doubting His Mercy, and disapproving of His Wisdom. A weak, helpless person should not wail over misfortune, but should complain to—not of—Him, just as Prophet Ya'qub (Jacob) did: *"I complain of my anguish and sorrow unto God."*[61] It is futile, and even harmful, to encourage self-pity and complaining.

- Insistence on worshipping God. This elevates the patient person to the highest spiritual rank, that of being one of God's perfect and beloved servants.

- **It is mistaken to act as if more merciful or wrathful than God.**[62]

One should not feel or show greater mercy than God's, nor should one feel wrath greater than that of God. So leave matters to the All-Just, the All-Compassionate One, for excessive or inappropriate compassion causes pain, and excessive or inappropriate wrath is wrongful and blameworthy.

- **There are joyful manifestations of Divine Grace in the oppression that the Divine Destiny allows people to suffer.**[63]

Bediüzzaman Said Nursi says to himself as follows regarding the oppression he suffered at the hands of people and other calamities he was subject to:

> Divine Destiny, which is pure justice, has a large part in the oppression which these people are inflicting on you. You have food to eat in this prison; that provision of yours called you here. You should respond with contentment and resignation. The Wisdom and Mercy of the Lord also have a significant part in this situation: you should instruct those in this prison in Islamic truths and console them, so you might gain reward. Your response should be thousands of thanks and great patience. Your soul also has a part in this situation because of certain faults you may be unaware of. Your response should be repentance and seeking forgiveness, telling your soul that it deserved this blow. Also, some of your secret irreligious enemies have a part in it, through their deceitful intrigues that provoke certain ingenuous and suspicious officials to such oppression. In response to this, the powerful immaterial blows dealt by the *Risale-i Nur* to those hyp-

---

[59] *Sura Al 'Imran*, 3:159.
[60] *Sura Al 'Imran*, 3:146.
[61] *Sura Yusuf*, 12:86.
[62] *Gleams of Truth*, p. 60.
[63] *The Gleams*, "The Twenty-sixth Gleam", p. 360.

ocritical ones have sought your revenge completely. That is enough for them. Finally, the officials who were the actual means of bringing about this situation have a part in it. Your response should be—so that they may benefit from the *Risale-i Nur* through belief, whether they want to or not, and even if they came to it with the intention of criticizing it—to forgive them according to the rule, "*The God-revering, righteous ones—those who .... ever-restrain their rage (even when provoked and able to retaliate), and pardon people (their offenses);*[64] that would be an act of magnanimity.

He also writes:

Once in my old age I was released from the Eskişehir prison after serving a year's sentence. They exiled me to Kastamonu (in northern Turkey), where they kept me for two or three months as a guest in the police station. It may be understood how much distress someone like me suffered in a place like that; how difficult this was for one who prefers solitude, one who is wearied by meeting even loyal friends, and one who cannot endure the change of his classical, native dress. While in such tormenting conditions, Divine Grace suddenly came to the aid of my old age. The inspector and police officers in the police station became like faithful friends. They did not once warn me about how I dressed, and, as if they were my servants, they used to take me for trips around the town.

Then I took up residence in Kastamonu's "*Risale-i Nur Medrese*," opposite the police station, and started to write more of the *Risale-i Nur*.

Later they took us to Denizli prison, and put me into solitary confinement in a stinking, cold, damp cell. While struggling with old age, illness, and the unhappiness that arose from the troubles my friends were suffering because of me, as well as the grief and distress caused by the confiscations of the parts of the *Risale-i Nur* and the cessation in its activities, Divine Grace suddenly came to my aid. It changed that huge prison into a *Risale-i Nur Medrese*, proving it to be a School of Joseph. The *Risale-i Nur* started to spread through the diamond pens of the heroes of the *Medresetu'z-Zehra*... They began to conquer minds and hearts both within the prison and outside. This changed our losses in that disaster into great gains, and our distress into joy. It once again demonstrated the truth in the verse, "*It may well be that you dislike a thing but it is good for you, and it may well be that you like a thing but it is bad for you. God knows, and you do not know.*"[65]

---

[64] *Sura Al 'Imran*, 3:134.
[65] *Suratu'l-Baqara*, 2:216.

- **The more useful a species of creatures are and the greater duties they perform in the fabric of creation, the more populous God Almighty creates them. Whatever is of more vital importance for the human life God bestows it in greater amount, and more cheaply.**[66]

For example, the most vital need for life is air, and God gives it for nothing. Then comes water, which God sends for nothing as well. Bread is of the third degree of importance for life, and it exists in greatest abundance and is the cheapest for humanity. Whatever is more important for life God gives it more cheaply and in greater abundance.

This is an important reality to be considered, particularly by medicine. For life is the most valuable, and the greatest degree of life is the human life. Therefore, whatever serves human life must be easily available and cheap. This concludes that health and therefore medicine must be the cheapest for humanity.

- **All-encompassing provision does not exclude particular provision. God's bounties are not like the rain or water from which everyone can benefit without considering individual needs.**[67]

Thus, each individual needs to feel and should offer particular gratitude for their provision. The needs of individuals are not like homemade pots to be filled with the Divine bounties they expect to pour in like rain. Rather, the real Bestower of bounties considers each individual comprehensively, makes a particular pot, and then fills it with His bounties. Just as giving thanks is incumbent on everyone for general favoring, it is incumbent on each individual for these particular bounties as well.

- **Attachment to material causes and indifference to the Real Bestower engenders humiliation and rejection.**[68]

Consider this: Why are dogs, which should be considered blessed due to their many good qualities (notably their proverbial loyalty), considered ritually unclean? Why are other domestic animals (i.e., hens, cows, and cats) that feel no gratitude and loyalty in return for the good we do to them, considered blessed? This is because—provided it is not to back-bite dogs and break their hearts—dogs are greedy and so attached to

---

[66] *Lem'alar (The Gleams)*, "18. Lem'a (The Eighteenth Gleam), unpublished.
[67] *Al-Mathnawi al-Nuri*, "The Eighth Treatise", p. 260.
[68] *Al-Mathnawi al-Nuri*, "The Fourth Treatise", p. 114.

apparent causes that they cannot see the true Bestower of bounties. Thus they suppose the means to be truly effective in procuring their food, and so suffer the stigma of ritual impurity as punishment for their blindness and indifference to the true Owner and Bestower of bounties.

Blessed animals do not recognize means and causes, or give them any value or importance. Cats ask for food and, when they get what they want, behave as if they do not know you or you do not know them. They feel no gratitude towards you. Instead, they thank the true Bestower of bounties by saying: "O All-Compassionate, O All-Compassionate." By disposition, they recognize their Creator and worship Him consciously or unconsciously.

- **Branches offer fruit in the Name of the Divine Mercy.**[69]

Apparently, the branches of trees and those of the Tree of Creation extend the fruits of bounties to the hands of living beings on every side. But in reality it is a Hand of Mercy, a Hand of Power, Which holds out to us these fruits on those branches. Therefore, we should not receive the bounties that come to us at the hands of some worldly means or agents as if these means or agents were providing these bounties for us. If any means or agent is without consciousness and free will, like an animal or a tree for example, it gives the bounty directly on behalf of God Almighty. Since it gives in the Name of God, we should receive it, saying *In the Name of God*. If the agents have consciousness and free will, they should say while giving, *In the Name of God*; then we should receive it, and otherwise we should not. For apart from its explicit meaning, the verse, "*Do not eat of that over which God's Name has not been pronounced!*"[70] has also an implicit meaning, which is this: "Do not eat of any bounty which does not recall the True Bestower of bounties, and is not given in His Name."

Since this is so, both the one who gives and the one who receives should say, *In the Name of God*. If the one who gives does not say, *In the Name of God*, and we are in need, then we should say, *In the Name of God* while receiving it. We should see the Hand of Divine Mercy over their head, kiss that Hand in thankfulness, and receive it from them. That is to say, we should see the act of bestowing in the bounty, and consider the True Bestower of bounties in the act of bestowing. This consideration is an act of thanksgiving. Then if we wish, we pray for the agent or means, as the bounty has been sent to us with their hand.

---

[69] *The Gleams*, "The Seventeenth Gleam", pp. 183–184; *Gleams of Truth*, p. 88.
[70] *Suratu'l-An'am*, 6:121.

- **Every blessing has two aspects. The first pertains to the one on whom God has bestowed it. This blessing distinguishes one in a community. The second pertains to the Bestower of blessings. The blessing displays His Munificence and Mercy. What falls to humanity, in respect to the first aspect, is humility, while it is gratitude in respect to the second one.**[71]

Humility sometimes contradicts one's proclaiming God's blessings upon oneself, for doing so sometimes gives rise to pride and arrogance. Thus, avoid exaggeration and excessive description. The middle way in one's proclaiming God's blessings on him or her is as follows:

Every blessing has two aspects. The first pertains to the one on whom God has bestowed it. This blessing distinguishes one in a community, and may lead to pride and forgetting the One Who gave it. For people may arrogate the blessings or bounties to themselves, attributing them to their abilities or merits, and become haughty. Whereas what falls to humanity in the first case is humility, without appropriating the blessings coming to them.

The second aspect in the blessings or bounties pertains to the Bestower of blessings. They display His Munificence and Mercy. By bestowing blessings, the Bestower of bounties pronounces "verses" of His manifestations. Humility in this second case becomes denial of the Bestower's act of bestowing, and ingratitude. Therefore, we must attribute all the blessings we enjoy to God the All-Bestowing and His Munificence, and feel no self-pride. Our proclamation of God's blessings in attribution of them to Him is praiseworthy gratitude.

When we wear splendid clothes, people say to us: "How beautiful you are." We should respond, saying: "Beauty belongs to the clothes, not to me. It is God Almighty Who has bestowed it." This is both humility and a proclamation of the blessing.

- **A person can respond to the universal, infinite favors bestowed on her with her restricted, particular thankfulness through a universal intention and infinitely profound belief and devotion.**[72]

As mentioned before, suppose a poor man enters the king's presence with a cheap (in materialistic terms) present. There he sees expensive

---

[71] *Al-Mathnawi al-Nuri*, "The Ninth Treatise", p. 321.
[72] *The Words*, "The Twenty-fourth Word", p. 381.

gifts sent by the king's favorites. He thinks: "My present means nothing, but this is what I can afford." Then suddenly he addresses the king, saying: "My lord! I offer all these precious gifts in my name, for you deserve them. If I could, I would offer double of these." The king, who needs nothing but accepts his subjects' gifts as tokens of respect and loyalty, accepts the poor man's universal intention, desire, and deep feelings of devotion as though they were the greatest gift.

Similarly, a poor servant says in his daily prescribed Prayers: "All worship and veneration is for God," by which he means: "In my name, I offer You all the gifts of worship that all beings present to you through their lives. You deserve all of them, and in reality far more than them." This belief and intention is a most comprehensive and universal thankfulness.

The seeds and stones of plants are their intentions to grow into elaborate plants. For example, with its hundreds of seeds, a melon intends: "O my Creator! I want to exhibit the inscriptions of Your All-Beautiful Names in many places of the earth." Having full knowledge of the future, Almighty God accepts its intentions as worship in deeds. The Prophetic saying: "A believer's intention is better than his action," expresses this reality. This is also why we glorify and praise Him with phrases expressing infinitude, like: "Glory be to You, and praise be to You to the number of Your creatures, the things pleasing to You, the decorations of Your Supreme Throne, to the amount of the ink of Your words. We glorify You with the sum of all the glorifications of Your Prophets, saints, and angels."

- **Worship, in one respect, means declaring our failure and faults before the door of the All-Merciful's Mercy with "I ask God for forgiveness!" and "All glory be to God!"; our poverty with "God is sufficient for us!" and "All praise be to God!" and begging from Him; and declaring our impotence with "There is no power and strength save with Him," and "God is the All-Great," and asking Him for help.**[73]

With respect to our selfhood, we are imperfect and have limitless helplessness and poverty, need and desire. As we are given hunger and thirst in order to know and experience the pleasure of the Almighty's bounties, in the mirror of our failure and poverty, impotence and neediness, we should view the lofty works of the All-Glorified's Perfection. We should use our poverty to measure His Wealth and Mercy; our impotence,

---

[73] *Al-Mathnawi al-Nuri*, "The Ninth Treatise", p. 312.

His Power and Grandeur; and our need, the variety of His bounties and favors.

- **Just as there are many stages and degrees between a date-palm's stone and the fully grown tree, praying and benefiting from our Prayers are characterized by possibly even more numerous degrees and stages. However, the basis of that luminous truth is present in each degree or stage.**[74]

Never say: "My Prayers mean almost nothing when compared with the reality of what Prayer should be." For just as the date-palm stone encapsulates and contains the tree itself (the difference is only between the summary and the fully evolved or elaborated form), a great saint's Prayer is fully evolved while that of ordinary people like us (even if we are unaware of it) has a share in that Divine light, and a mystery in its truth. However, our perception of and illumination by that truth varies according to our degrees.

- **Praying five times a day should never cause us weariness and boredom. Rather, far from causing boredom or weariness, spending one twenty-fourth of our life on a fine, agreeable, easy, and gracious act of service, which is the means to happiness in the real, eternal life, actually arouses vigor and gives pleasure.**[75]

Weariness in praying five times a day comes from our fancy that we will live forever. We complain as though we will remain here forever in eternal enjoyment. If only we understood that our life is short and passes in vain, we would understand that, far from causing boredom or weariness, spending one twenty-fourth of it on a fine, agreeable, easy, and gracious act of service, which is the means to happiness in the real, eternal life, actually arouses vigor and gives pleasure.

Secondly, every day we eat, drink and breathe; do these cause us boredom? They do not, because these needs recur and so give pleasure when satisfied. Thus the five daily Prayers should not bore us, for they attract and conduct the needs of our companions in the house of our body—the sustenance of our heart, the water of life of our spirit, and the air of our spiritual intellect.

Thirdly, is it at all sensible to think today of the hardship or difficulties of past worship and troubles of past calamities and so to be distressed,

---

[74] *The Words*, "The Twenty-first Word", p. 287.
[75] *The Words*, "The Twenty-first Word", p. 283–286.

and to imagine the difficulties of future worship or Prayer and the pain of future misfortune, and so display impatience? Past troubles are now a mercy. Their pain has gone, while their pleasure remains. Hardships have changed into blessings, and trials and toils into rewards. So why should we be weary? Rather, we should feel a new eagerness and a fresh zeal, and make a serious effort to continue praying. Also, the future has not come yet, so why should we worry about it? This is as ridiculous as complaining now about future hunger and thirst, of thinking of them now and feeling bored and wearied. Since this is the reality, we should consider only today when it comes to matters of worship. We should say: "I am spending one hour out of twenty-four on pleasant and elevated acts of service, the reward for which is great, and whose trouble is little." Our bitter disappointment will change into a pleasurable endeavor.

We are charged with three types of perseverance: in worship, in refraining from sin, and in the face of calamities. We should use our God-given power of perseverance in the proper way, without scattering it for past and future troubles; we should concentrate it on the present one.

Fourthly, is this duty of worship so fruitless and its reward so little that we feel weary? Whereas if someone offers us money or threatens us, he would make us work until evening, and we would work without respite. So, are the five daily Prayers in vain while they are our weak heart's "food" in this guest-house of the world, sustenance and light in our grave (a station to eternal life), a document and warrant on the Day of Judgment, and a light and a mount on the Bridge, which everyone has to cross?

Is the Prayer's reward so little? If someone promised us a present of a hundred dollars, he would make us work for several days. Though he may go back on his word, we would trust him and work without respite. So if One Who never breaks His promise says that He will reward us with something like Paradise and a gift like eternal happiness, and employ us for a very short time in a most agreeable duty—if we leave that service undone or act reluctantly as if being forced and in a manner to accuse Him of His promise or belittle His gift, would we not deserve a severe reprimand and a terrible punishment? While we work without slacking at the most difficult jobs in this world out of our fear of imprisonment, does the fear of an eternal imprisonment like Hell not give us zeal for so light and pleasant an act of service as the Prayers?

Fifthly, were we created only for this world, so that we should spend all our time on it?

We know that we are superior to all animals regarding our potential, but even a sparrow can do a better job than us when it comes to satisfying our daily needs. Why do we not understand from this that our duty as human beings is not to labor only for worldly aims, like animals, but to work for the real, everlasting life? Besides, most worldly concerns are trivial and useless matters from which we derive no benefit. Yet, leaving aside the most essential things, we waste our time in numerous useless things.

In short: Yesterday has left us, and we have no guarantee that we will be alive tomorrow. Our life consists of today. So we must set at least one hour aside for the Prayer mat. Think of it as a savings box and reserve fund for the Hereafter. We should set this hour aside for our real future, which is eternal.

- **There is no difficulty in religion. Since the four Schools of Law are on the right path, and since realizing a fault which leads to seeking forgiveness is preferable (particularly for those afflicted with scruples) to seeing deeds as good, as the latter leads to pride, it is better for such people to see their deeds as faulty and ask God's forgiveness rather than seeing them as good and becoming proud.**[76]

A kind of involuntary fancy arises from seeking a religious deed's best form. This can be better called a scruple. If people suppose it to be a true or pure piety, it becomes more vigorous and makes the resulting condition more severe. It can reach such a degree that, while searching for even better forms of the deed, such people fall into what is forbidden. Sometimes seeking after what is commended in worship causes people to neglect what is obligatory therein. Pausing over whether the act of worship was canonically acceptable or not, they repeat it. This state continues, and they soon fall into despair. Satan takes advantage of this state to wound these people. What follows is the cure for this wound.

Such a scruple may be right for the *Mu'tazilites*, who argue: "Deeds and things for which the Religion holds humanity responsible are either, of themselves and in regard to the Hereafter, good and therefore commanded, or bad and therefore prohibited." Thus, from the point of view

---

[76] *The Words*, "The Twenty-first Word", p. 290–291.

of reality and the Hereafter, things are good or bad in their essence, and the Divine command and prohibition are dependent on this. Following this school of thought, a scruple arises in every act of worship: "Have I been able to perform this act in the good way that in essence it is?"

However, the *Ahlu's-Sunnah wal-Jama'ah* (people representing the great majority of Muslims following the way of the Prophet and his Companions) argue: "Almighty God orders a thing and it becomes good. He prohibits a thing and it becomes bad." So, whether a thing is good or bad depends on the Divine command and prohibition. Therefore, a thing is good or bad for people according to whether they have done something ordered or prohibited, and whether they have done it in accordance with the rules established by the Shari'ah.

For example, you performed *wudu'* (ritual ablution) or Prayer according to the rules of each. But there was a cause that of itself would invalidate them. However, you were completely unaware of it. Your ablution and Prayer are therefore sound and good. But the *Mu'tazilites* argue: "In essence they were bad and unsound. But they may be accepted due to your ignorance, which is an excuse." According to the *Ahlu's-Sunnah wal-Jama'ah*, you should not indulge in scruples about a deed you did in conformity with the rules of the Shari'ah; do not worry about whether it was sound or not. Rather worry about if it was accepted, and do not become proud and conceited.

- **Those who are heedless and indifferent in belief and the practice of the Religion should not be indulged with dispensations; they should rather be warned strictly and aroused with heavier responsibilities and greater care.[77]**

The way to dispensation can be shown to those who are extremely scrupulous in the practice of the Religion, but those who are negligent in and indifferent to performing the essentials and the basic injunctions of Islam should be warned strictly and aroused with heavier responsibilities and greater care.

- **Imagining or reflecting on unbelief is not unbelief, and picturing or reflecting on misguidance is not misguidance. For imagina-**

---

[77] *Gleams of Truth*, p. 16.

tion, conceptualization, picturing, and reflection are different from confirmation by reason and acceptance by the heart.[78]

Some suffer scruples in the form of what they think are doubts in matters of belief. Sometimes they confuse a passing fancy with a conceptualized idea, mistakenly considering this doubt to arise from themselves and therefore possibly harmful to their belief. They may think that such a doubt impairs their rational, conscious confirmation of the essentials of belief, or that thinking of something related to unbelief has made them unbelievers. That is, they confuse the use of reflection, study, and objective reasoning on the causes of unbelief with being contrary to belief. Frightened by these suppositions, which result from Satan's whispering, they believe that their hearts have become corrupted and their belief impaired. Unable to put these mostly involuntary states right by their free will, they give in to despair.

The cure is as follows: Imagining or reflecting on unbelief is not unbelief, and picturing or reflecting on misguidance is not misguidance. For imagination, conceptualization, picturing, and reflection are different from confirmation by reason and acceptance by the heart; they are voluntary to certain degree. It is hard for the free will to control them so that we should be answerable for them.

Confirmation and acceptance are deliberate, for they depend on certain criteria and intentional reasoning. In addition, just as the former are not the same mental activities as confirmation and acceptance, neither are they the same as doubt and hesitation. Therefore, they are not given importance. They may pave the way to doubt if they are repeated unnecessarily and become established. Especially if people continually support the opposing side on the pretext of objective reasoning or fairness, they may favor it involuntarily and thereby fall into danger. Gradually, their state of mind becomes fixed, and they become officious advocates of Satan or the enemy. Secondly:

- **What is theoretically possible should not be confused with what is reasonably likely. A theoretical possibility does not negate certain knowledge of a present reality or contradict the demands of reason.**[79]

---

[78] *The Words*, "The Twenty-first Word", pp. 291–292.
[79] *The Words*, "The Twenty-first Word", p. 292

The most characteristic scruple here is that one confuses the theoretically possible with the reasonably likely. This violates a principle of reasoning or logic: A theoretical possibility does not negate certain knowledge of a present reality or contradict the demands of reason. For example, it is theoretically possible that the Black Sea could sink into the ground right now. However, we know and judge with certainty that it has not done so. The theoretical possibility of its being otherwise causes no real doubt and does not impair our certainty about the present reality.

Theoretically, the sun might not set today or rise tomorrow. But this possibility does not impair our certainty or engender any real doubt. Such baseless suspicions about the truths of faith, such as the death of this world and the resurrection of the dead in the Hereafter, which are among the truths of belief, do not impair the certainty of belief. Moreover, one of the established principles of the sciences of the methodology of Islamic law and the foundations of Religion states that a possibility based on no evidence is not worth considering.

- **God's Messenger declared: "When God wills a people well, He makes them watchful of their defects."[80] Also, the Qur'an narrates that Prophet Joseph said: "I do not claim that my soul is always innocent; surely, the soul of humanity incites to evil."[81] Those who rely on and trust in their carnal souls are unfortunate, while those who see their own defects are fortunate. But sometimes, despite the carnal soul's being refined and becoming the "self-accusing soul," or even "the soul at rest," it moves its attack to the nerves.[82]**

As a result, those people cannot be free of anger and irritation until they die. Many pure and saintly people complain of their souls' temptations and wail over spiritual ailments, even though their souls were at rest and their hearts were illuminated and pure. What they actually complain of is not having an evil-commanding soul, but the transferal of those evil commands to the nerves. Their spiritual ailments are imaginary. It is not their carnal, evil-commanding souls or spiritual diseases that afflict them, but they are rather suffering from nerves, so that they may continue their struggle to make spiritual progress.

---

[80] al-Ajluni, *Kashfu'l-Khafa'*, 1:81.
[81] *Sura Yusuf*, 12:53.
[82] *The Letters*, "The Twenty-sixth Letter", p. 343.

- **Those who recognize and obey God are prosperous, even if they are in prison, while those who forget Him are like wretched prisoners, even if they live in palaces.**[83]

A human being is a living machine, subject to many sorrows and capable of knowing many pleasures. Although totally impotent, we have innumerable physical and spiritual enemies. Although completely destitute, we have infinite internal and external needs, and we suffer continuously from the blows of gradual decay and separation. But if, through belief and worship, we can establish a connection with the All-Majestic Sovereign, we will find a source of support against all of our enemies, and a source of help for all of our needs. Everyone takes pride in the honor and rank of those in high places with whom they enjoy a connection. Given this fact, if one establishes a connection through belief with the infinitely Powerful and Compassionate Sovereign, if one enters His service through worship, he will change even his private world into a sort of Paradise before entering Paradise, even though his private world is a prison.

Once, a wronged but fortunate man—fortunate on account of his belief and ensuing martyrdom—said to the wretched wrongdoers who were executing him: "I am not being executed; rather, I have been discharged from my duties, and am going forward to eternal happiness. However, I can now see that you are condemned to eternal punishment; this suffices as my revenge upon you." And saying "There is no deity but God," he died a happy man.

- **Those who pursue this transient life place themselves in hell, even though they stay in what appears—to them—as a paradise on the earth. Those who seek the eternal life find peace and happiness in both worlds. Despite all the troubles they may suffer in the world, they show patience and thank God, as they see the world as the waiting room for Paradise.**[84]

- **Whoever relies on God finds that God is sufficient for her. So, say: "God is sufficient for me, what an excellent guardian He is." God is absolutely perfect. Absolute perfection is loved for its own sake, and great things are sacrificed for it. Since He is loved for His own sake, He is the true beloved, and love requires sacrifice.**

---

[83] *The Rays*, "The Eleventh Ray", pp. 236–237.
[84] *The Words*, "The Eighth Word", p. 53.

He is the Necessarily Existent One. The lights of existence originate in His nearness, while absence from Him brings the darkness of extinction or non-existence, and causes the human soul incurable pain by extinguishing its aspirations. He is the refuge of the human spirit suffocated within material existence's narrow confines, suffering from the world's deceit, crushed by the pain arising from its affection for creation. He is the Everlasting, by Whom things become permanent and without Whom things decay and are extinguished, which cause grief and sorrow. Without Him pain accumulates in the human spirit, whereas light pours from everywhere over one who finds and trusts in Him. He is the All-Wealthy and the Bestower of wealth, and in His Hand are the keys to everything.[85]

He is the sole Owner of existence. He wants to bear our burdens of life and bodily existence that He has entrusted to us, as we cannot carry them and suffer if we think we own them. If we desire their permanence and His continued favoring, we should not be grieved when He takes them from us. Bubbles containing the sun's images do not grieve when they disappear, and gladly sacrifice their apparent forms for the renewal of the sun's reflections. Fruits do not grieve when they are separated from their tree, and seeds do not grieve over the fruit's disintegration in the ground, for its disintegration means the growth of a new tree that will yield many fruits. We are also a fruit, an embodiment of His favoring.

If we become His sincere servants and then look at the universe, we will see our Master's sovereignty and magnificence, and find relief. We will come to view the universe as if it were our property that we own without trouble, and the disappearance of which would not grieve us. A sincere servant of the Sovereign who is annihilated in His love becomes proud of whatever belongs to Him.

He is the Lord of all Messengers and Prophets, saints and God-conscious people, all of whom are happy in His mercy. If we have a sound, uncorrupted heart, our knowledge of their happiness must give us happiness and pleasure.

---

[85] *Al-Mathnawi al-Nuri*, "The Sixth Treatise", pp. 185–186.

- **Belief is both light and power. Those who attain true belief can challenge the universe and, in proportion to their belief's strength, be relieved of the pressures of events.**[86]

Relying on God, they travel safely through the mountainous waves of events on the ship of life. Having entrusted their burdens to the Absolutely Powerful One's Hand of Power, they voyage through the world comfortably until their last day. The grave will be a resting place, after which they will fly to Paradise to attain eternal bliss. If, however, they do not rely upon God, their worldly life will force them down to the lowest depths.

- **Belief requires affirming Divine Unity; affirmation of Divine Unity requires submitting to God; submission to God requires relying on God; and reliance on God yields happiness in both worlds.**[87]

- **Entrusting the accomplishment of an affair to God before taking all necessary precautions and making all necessary arrangements is laziness. Leaving the desired outcome's realization to God, after doing all that can be done, is to trust in Him. Contentment with the result after exerting one's efforts is a laudable virtue that encourages further effort and reinvigorates one's energy and industry. Contentment with what one already has destroys endeavor.**[88]

Reliance on or having trust in God does not mean ignoring cause and effect, and complete negligence of the means to attain a goal. Rather, it means that one should think of causes or means as a veil before the Power's hand. One observes them by seeking to comply with the Divine Will, which is a sort of prayer in action. However, such desire and seeking is not enough to secure a particular effect. We must understand that, in accordance with right belief, the result is to be expected only from God, the All-Mighty. As He is the sole producer of effects, we should always be grateful to Him.

The one who relies on God and one who does not are like the two men in the following parable:

Once, two people boarded a royal ship with heavy burdens. One put his burden on the deck immediately after boarding and sat on it to keep it safe. The other one, even after being told to lay his burden down, refused to do so and said: "I won't put it down, because it might get lost.

[86] *The Words*, "The Twenty-third Word", p. 330.
[87] *The Words*, "The Twenty-third Word", p. 330.
[88] *The Words*, "The Twenty-third Word", p. 331; *Gleams of Truth*, p. 15.

Besides, I'm strong enough to carry it." He was told: "This reliable royal ship, which carries us, is stronger and can hold it better. You will most probably get tired, feel dizzy, and fall into the sea with your burden. Your strength will fail, and then how will you bear this burden that gets heavier every moment? If the captain sees you in this state, he will think either you are insane, or that you do not trust them and make fun of them. Your vanity reveals your weakness, your arrogance reveals your impotence, and your pretension betrays your humiliation."

- **Prayer and trusting in God greatly strengthen our inclination to do good. Repentance and seeking God's forgiveness defeat our inclination to evil, and break its transgressions.**[89]

Although our free will cannot cause something to happen, Almighty God, the absolutely Wise One, uses it to bring His will into effect and guides us in whatever direction we wish. He in effect says: "My servant! Whichever way you wish to take with your will, I will take you there. Therefore, the responsibility is yours!" He, the Most Just of Judges, never coerces His servants into doing something, and so His Will considers our free will in our actions.

In sum, as human beings, we have a degree of free will. Although it is so limited that it makes almost no contribution to our good acts, it can cause deadly sins and destruction. So we should use our free will for our benefit by praying to God continuously. If we do so, we may enjoy the blessings of Paradise, a fruit of the chain of good deeds, and attain eternal happiness. In addition to praying, we should always seek God's forgiveness so that we may refrain from evil and be saved from Hell's torments, a fruit of the accursed chain of evil deeds.

- **Belief requires prayer for attainment and perfection, and our essence needs it. God Almighty says:** "Say (O Muhammad): 'My Lord would not concern Himself with you but for your prayer.'"[90] and: "Pray to Me and I will answer you."[91]/[92]

- **Praying is a mystery of servanthood to God through worship. Worship is done solely to please God, and for His Sake. We should affirm and display our poverty and weakness, and seek refuge in**

---

[89] *The Words*, "The Twenty-sixth Word", p. 487.
[90] *Suratu'l-Furqan*, 25:77.
[91] *Suratu'l-Mu'min*, 40.60.
[92] *The Words*, "The Twenty-third Word", p. 333.

Him through prayer. We must not interfere in His Lordship, but rather let God do as He wills. We must rely on His Wisdom and not accuse His Mercy.[93]

Every creature offers its unique praise and worship to God. What reaches the Court of God from the universe is prayer.

One kind of prayer is that which is done through the tongue of potential. Plants pray through the tongue of their potential to achieve a full form and manifest certain Divine Names. Another kind of prayer is expressed in the tongue of natural needs. All living beings ask the Absolutely Generous One to meet their vital needs, as they cannot do so on their own.

Yet another kind of prayer is done in the tongue of complete helplessness. A living creature in difficult circumstances takes refuge in its Unseen Protector with a genuine supplication, and turns to its All-Compassionate Lord. These three kinds of prayer are always acceptable, unless somehow impeded.

The fourth type of prayer is the one done by humanity. This type falls into two categories: active and by disposition, and verbal and with the heart. For example, acting in accordance with the law of cause and effect or fulfilling the prerequisites is an active prayer. We try to gain God's approval by complying with the law of cause and effect or fulfilling the prerequisites, for causes or means alone, or the fulfillment of prerequisites, cannot produce the result—only God can do that. For example, plowing the soil is an active prayer, for this means knocking at the door of the treasury of God's Mercy. Such a prayer is usually acceptable, for it is an application to the Divine Name the All-Generous.

The second type of prayer humanity performs is done with the tongue and the heart; this is the ordinary one. This means that we ask God from the heart for something we cannot reach. Its most important aspect, and finest and sweetest fruit, is that we know that God hears us, is aware of our heart's contents, that His Power extends everywhere, that He can satisfy every desire, and that He comes to our aid out of mercy for our weakness and inadequacy.

- **An answered prayer does not necessarily mean its acceptance. There is an answer for every prayer. However, accepting the**

---

[93] *The Words*, "The Twenty-third Word", p. 334.

prayer and giving what is requested depends upon the All-Mighty's Wisdom.[94]

For example, a sick child asks a doctor for a certain medicine. The doctor will give either what is asked for or something better, or he will not give anything. It all depends upon how the medicine will affect the child. Similarly the All-Mighty, Who is the All-Just and Omnipresent, answers His servants' prayer and changes their loneliness into the pleasure of His company. But His answer does not depend on the individual's fancies; rather, according to His Wisdom, He gives what is requested, what is better, or nothing at all. Moreover, prayer is a form of worship, and worship is rewarded mainly in the Hereafter.

- **If He did not will to give, He would not give the desire to want.**[95]

That is, if He allows and enables us to pray to Him, this means that He will answer it in the way which is the best and most appropriate for us.

- **Worldly needs and purposes are only causes or occasions for prayer.**[96]

For example, praying for rain is a kind of worship occasioned by the lack of rain. If rain is the prayer's only aim, the prayer is unacceptable, for it is not sincere or intended to please God and obtain His approval.

Sunset determines the time for the evening Prayer, while solar and lunar eclipses occasion two particular kinds of worship. Since such eclipses—the veiling of two luminous signs of day and night—are two means of manifesting Divine Majesty, the All-Mighty calls His servants to perform a form of worship—the Prayer of Eclipse—particular to these occasions. This Prayer has nothing to do with causing the eclipse to end, for this is known already through astronomical calculations. Similarly, drought and other calamities are occasions for certain kinds of prayer. At such times, we best realize our impotence, and so feel the need to take refuge in the high Presence of the Absolutely Powerful One through prayer and supplication. If a calamity is not lifted despite many prayers, we should not say that the prayer has not been accepted. Rather, we should say that the time for prayer has not yet ended. If God removes the calamity because of His endless Grace and Munificence, this is light upon

---

[94] *The Words*, "The Twenty-third Word", p. 333.
[95] *The Letters*, "The Twenty-fourth Letter". 321.
[96] *The Words*, "The Twenty-third Word", p. 333.

light, profit upon profit, and marks the end of the special occasion for prayer.

- **The blessing and help of saints and the enlightenment they diffuse are a sort of prayer done either actively or through disposition, for the One Who actually guides and helps is God. Each person has an innermost sense or faculty that, if he or she prays through it, the prayer will be answered regardless of spiritual condition. If they swear by God through it that (something will happen), God does not disprove them.**[97]

It is declared in the Qur'an: "*O you who believe! Keep from disobedience to God in reverence for Him and piety, and seek the means to come closer to Him, and strive in His cause, so that you may prosper (in both worlds)."*[98] The Prophets, scholars, saints and others like them are means for guidance and to come closer to God. It is God Himself Who guides and brings His servant close to Him.

- **Happy is the person who knows his limits and does not exceed them.**[99]

The sun is reflected in a piece of glass, and drop of water, and a pool, and a sea, and the moon, and all other planets. Each of these contains the sun's image according to its capacity, and each knows its limits. In accordance with its capacity, a drop of water says, "I have an image of the sun," but it cannot say, "I am a sea-like mirror to the sun." In just the same way, saints have different ranks according to the capacity of each to reflect the manifestations of the Divine Names. Each of the Divine Names has manifestations like those of the sun, from each person's heart to the Divine Supreme Throne. Every heart is a throne, but it cannot say, "I too am the Divine Supreme Throne."

Those who, instead of knowing their essential powerlessness, destitution, faults, and defects, which form the basis of worship and servanthood, and so prostrating before the Divine Court in entreaty, but who rather attempt to proceed on the way to God with great expectations from God, and pride in their acts of worship, hold their tiny hearts equal to the Divine Throne. They confuse their drop-like stations with the ocean-like stations of great saints. In order to show themselves fitting for

[97] *Al-Mathnawi al-Nuri*, "The Tenth Treatise", p. 358.
[98] *Suratu'l-Maeda*, 5:35.
[99] *The Gleams*, "The Seventeenth Gleam", p. 182.

those high stations, they stoop to artificiality, affectation, and meaning-less self-promotion, causing themselves many difficulties.

- **Those who rely on and trust in their carnal souls are unfortunate, while those who see their own defects are fortunate.**[100]

- **The qualities or merits of a delicious bunches of grapes should not be sought in their dry stalks. With respect to their accomplishments, human beings are like those dry stalks.**[101]

Just as the dry stalks cannot appropriate the delicious grapes hanging from them, so too, it is not human beings themselves who must appropriate the achievements God creates through them. It is God Who favors them with these achievements.

- **There is the seed of unbelief in the essence of sins, especially frequently committed ones.**[102]

For such sins make people indifferent. These sins can become addictions that only abandonment can cure. Such people hope that there will be no punishment for their sins, and so unconsciously look for an excuse to believe in the non-existence of torment in the eternal world. This continues until they deny the abode of punishment. As the shame arising from sinning is not followed by remorse and asking forgiveness from God, sinners begin to deny that their sins are really sins, and then begin to deny the existence of those—like guardian angels—who oversee them and are aware of their sins. Due to this intense shame, they hope that there will be no reckoning in the other world. When they encounter even a false argument for its non-existence, they take it as strong proof and deny the final reckoning. Consequently, their hearts become even darker. May God save us from such a consequence! Amen.

- **Prayer (**Salah**) stands for praising, glorifying, and thanking God Almighty.**[103]

We glorify Him by saying *Subhana'llah* (All-Glorified is God) by word and action in awareness of His Majesty. We exalt and magnify Him by saying *Allahu akbar* (God is the All-Great) through word and action in awareness of His Perfection. We offer thanks to Him by saying *Al-hamdu*

---

[100] *The Letters*, "The Twenty-sixth Letter", p. 343.

[101] *The Letters*, "The Twenty-ninth Letter, the Seventh Part".

[102] *Al-Mathnawi al-Nuri*, "The Sixth Treatise", p. 180.

[103] *The Words*, "The Ninth Word", pp. 57–58.

li'llah (All praise and gratitude are for God) with our heart, tongue, and body, in awareness of His Grace. That is to say, the heart of Prayer consists of glorification, exaltation, praise, and thanksgiving. Thus, these three seeds are present in all words and actions that constitute Prayer. Further, following each Prayer, they are repeated 33 times each to confirm and complete the Prayer's objectives. The meaning of Prayer is pronounced consecutively with these concise utterances.

- **Each appointed Prayer time is the beginning of a vital turning point, and a reminder of greater revolutions or turning points in the universe's life. Through the awesome daily disposals of the Eternally Besought One's Power, the Prayer times remind us of the Divine Power's miracles and the Divine Mercy's gifts regardless of time or place. So the prescribed Prayers, which are an innate duty, the basis of worship, and an unquestionable obligation, are most appropriate and fitted for these times.**[104]

The time for *fajr* (before sunrise) corresponds to spring's birth, the moment when sperm takes refuge in the mother's womb, and to the first of the six consecutive "days" during which the heavens and earth were created. It recalls how God disposes His Power and acts in such times and events.

The time for *zuhr* (just past midday) corresponds to the middle of summer, the completion of adolescence, and to the period of humanity's creation in the world's lifetime. It also points to God's manifestations of mercy, and a profusion of blessings in those events and times.

The time for *'asr* (afternoon) resembles autumn, old age, and the happy time of the Last Prophet, upon him be peace and blessings. It calls to mind the Divine acts and the All-Merciful's favors in them.

The time for *maghrib* (sunset) reminds us of many creatures' decline at the end of autumn, and also of our own death. It thus forewarns us of the world's destruction at the Resurrection's beginning, teaches us how to understand the manifestation of God's Majesty, and wakes us from a deep sleep of neglect.

The time for *'isha* (nightfall) calls to mind the world of darkness veiling all daytime objects with its black shroud, and winter covering the dead earth's surface with its white shroud. It also brings to mind the remaining works of the dead being forgotten, and points to this testing

---

[104] *The Words*, "The Ninth Word", pp. 57–58.

arena's inevitable, complete decline. Thus *'isha* proclaims the awesome acts of the All-Overwhelming One of Majesty.

Night reminds us of winter, the grave, the Intermediate World, and how much our spirit needs the All-Merciful's Mercy. The late-night *tahajjud* Prayer reminds and warns us of how necessary this Prayer's light will be in the grave's darkness. By recalling the True Bestower's infinite bounties granted during these revolutions, it proclaims how worthy He is of praise and thanks.

The next morning points to the morning following the Resurrection. Just as morning follows night, and spring comes after winter, so the morning or spring of the Resurrection follows the intermediate life.

- **Weariness of the five daily Prayers comes from the fancy that we will live forever. We complain as though we will remain here forever in eternal enjoyment. If only we understood that our life is short and passes in vain, we would understand that, far from causing boredom or weariness, spending one twenty-fourth of it on a fine, agreeable, easy, and gracious act of service which is the means to happiness in the real, eternal life actually arouses vigor and gives pleasure.**[105]

Every day we eat, drink and breathe; do these cause us boredom? They do not, because these needs recur and so give pleasure when satisfied. Thus the five daily Prayers should not bore us, for they attract and conduct the needs of our companions in the house of our body—the sustenance of our heart, the water of life of our spirit and the air of our spiritual intellect.

The food and strength of a heart exposed to endless grief and pain, and inclined to infinite pleasure and ambition, may be obtained by knocking on the One All-Compassionate and Munificent's door through supplication. Also, for a spirit connected with most beings and moving quickly to the other world amid cries of separation, the water of life may be imbibed by turning, through the five daily Prayers, towards the spring of the Everlasting Beloved, the All-Permanent Worshipped One, Who suffices and substitutes for everything.

Further, a conscious inward sense, a luminous and infinitely delicate faculty, and a subtle mirror to the Eternal Being, which by nature desires

---

[105] *The Words*, "The Twenty-fifth Word", pp. 283–284.

the eternity for which it was created, is most needy of "air," of relief and relaxation, so that it can deal successfully with the distressing, crushing, and suffocating conditions of worldly life. It can breathe only through the window of Prayer.

- **Fasting during Ramadan, being one of Islam's foremost pillars and greatest symbols, is a comprehensive and ordered response of servanthood to God's being the All-Merciful, the All-Compassionate, and the Lord.**[106]

God the All-Munificent displays His Lordship's perfection and His being the All-Merciful and All-Compassionate upon the earth's surface, which He has designed as a table to hold His bounties in a way beyond human imagination. Nevertheless, people cannot perfectly discern this situation's reality due to heedlessness and causality's blinding veil. But during Ramadan, like an army waiting for its marching orders, believers display an attitude of worship towards the end of the day as if they expect to be told to help themselves to the banquet prepared by the Eternal Monarch. Thus they respond to that magnificent and universal manifestation of Divine Mercifulness with a comprehensive and harmonious act of collective worship.

- **Fasting during Ramadan is the key to a true, sincere, comprehensive, and universal thanksgiving.**[107]

Many people cannot appreciate most of the bounties they enjoy, for they do not experience hunger. For example, a piece of dry bread means nothing to those who are full, especially if they are rich. However, the believers' sense of taste testifies at the time of breaking fast that it is indeed a very valuable bounty of God. During Ramadan, everyone is favored with a heartfelt thanksgiving by understanding the value of the Divine bounties.

While fasting, believers think: "These bounties do not originally belong to me, and so I cannot regard them as mere food or drink. Since the One owns and grants them to me, I should wait for His permission to eat them." By thus acknowledging food and drink as Divine gifts, believers tacitly thank God. This is why fasting is a key to thanksgiving, which is a fundamental human duty.

---

[106] *The Letters*, "The Twenty-ninth Letter", p. 390.
[107] *The Letters*, "The Twenty-ninth Letter", p. 391.

- **Fasting, related to humanity's collective life, is a Divine invitation to the rich to help the poor.**[108]

  Human beings have been created differently in regard to livelihood. So God invites the rich to help the poor. Without fasting, many rich and self-indulgent people cannot perceive the pain of hunger and poverty, or to what extent the poor need care. Care for one's fellow beings is a foundation of true thanksgiving. There is always someone poorer, so everyone must show care for such people. If people do not experience hunger, it is nearly impossible for them to do good or to help others. Even if they do, they can do so only imperfectly because they do not feel the full extent of a hungry person's condition.

- **Fasting shatters the illusory lordship of the carnal soul and enables it to admit its servanthood and perform its real duty of thanksgiving.**[109]

  The carnal soul desires —and considers itself—to be free and unrestricted. It even wishes, by its very nature, for an imagined lordship and free, arbitrary action. Not liking to think that it is being trained and tested through God's countless bounties, it swallows up such bounties like an animal and with the greed of a thief or robber, especially if its wealth and power is accompanied by heedlessness.

  During Ramadan, the carnal soul understands that it is owned by One Other, not by itself; that it is a servant, not a free agent. Unless ordered or permitted, it cannot do even the most common things, like eating and drinking. This inability shatters its illusory lordship, enabling it to admit its servanthood and performing its real duty of thanksgiving. Fasting during Ramadan prevents the carnal soul from rebelling and adorns it with good morals.

- **Fasting, especially during the month of Ramadan, breaks the haughtiness of the human carnal soul and leads it to take refuge in the Divine Court in complete helplessness and destitution, rising to knock at the door of Mercy with the hand of tacit thanksgiving.**[110]

---

[108] *The Letters*, "The Twenty-ninth Letter", pp. 391–392.
[109] *The Letters*, "The Twenty-ninth Letter", pp. 391–392.
[110] *The Letters*, "The Twenty-ninth Letter", p. 392.

A person's carnal soul forgets itself through heedlessness. It neither sees nor wants to see its inherent infinite impotence, poverty, and defects. It does not reflect on how it is exposed to misfortune and subject to decay, and that it consists of flesh and bone that disintegrate and decompose rapidly. It rushes upon the world with a violent greed and attachment, as if it had a steel body and would live forever, and clings to whatever is profitable and pleasurable. In this state it forgets its Creator, Who trains it with perfect care. Being immersed in the swamp of immorality, it does not think about the consequences of its life here or its afterlife.

Fasting, especially during the month of Ramadan, causes even the most heedless and stubborn souls to feel their weakness and innate poverty. Hunger becomes an important consideration and reminds them of how fragile their bodies really are. They perceive their need for compassion and care and, giving up haughtiness, want to take refuge in the Divine Court in complete helplessness and destitution, rising to knock at the door of Mercy with the hand of tacit thanksgiving—provided, of course, that heedlessness has not yet corrupted them completely.

- **Ramadan transforms the Muslim world into a huge mosque in which millions recite the Qur'an to the earth's inhabitants.**[111]

Displaying the reality of, *"The month of Ramadan, in which the Qur'an was revealed,"*[112] Ramadan proves itself to be the month of the Qur'an. While some in the vast congregation in the great mosque of the Muslim world listen to its recitation with solemn reverence, others prefer reciting it individually. It is most disagreeable to forsake that heavenly spiritual state by obeying the carnal soul, and thus eating and drinking in the sacred "mosque," for this provokes the whole congregation's hatred. It is also most disagreeable and must provoke the Muslim world's dislike and contempt to counter and defy those Muslims who fast during Ramadan.

- **Ramadan is the most proper time for a profitable trade in the afterlife's name. It is like a most fertile field to cultivate for the afterlife's harvest. Its multiplication of rewards for good deeds make it like April in spring. It is a sacred and illustrious festival for the parade of those who worship His Lordship's Sovereignty.**[113]

[111] *The Letters*, "The Twenty-ninth Letter", p. 393.
[112] *Suratu'l-Baqara*, 2:185.
[113] *The Letters*, "The Twenty-ninth Letter", p. 394.

The rewards for good deeds done during Ramadan are multiplied by a thousand. One Tradition states that ten rewards are given for each letter of the Qur'an. Reciting one letter means ten good deeds and brings forth ten fruits of Paradise. But during Ramadan, this reward is multiplied by a thousand and even more for such verses as the "Verse of the Supreme Seat."[114] The reward is even greater on Ramadan's Friday nights. Furthermore, each letter is multiplied thirty thousand times if recited during the Night of Power and Destiny (*Laylatu'l-Qadr*). One Ramadan may enable believers to gain eighty years' worth of reward, for the Qur'an declares the Night of Power and Destiny, which is in Ramadan, to be more profitable than eighty years having no such night.[115] Thus, during Ramadan the Qur'an becomes like a huge blessed tree producing millions of permanent fruits of Paradise. In fact, Ramadan contains and causes believers to gain, through fasting, a permanent life after a short period in this world.

- **Fasting also enables people to abandon sins committed by their bodily senses or members, and to use them in the acts of worship particular to each.**[116]

Those who fast should stop their tongue from lying, backbiting, and swearing by busying it with reciting the Qur'an, glorifying God, seeking His forgiveness, and calling His blessing upon Prophet Muhammad, upon him be peace and blessings. They should prevent their eyes from looking at, and their ears from listening to, forbidden things; rather, they should look at things that give a spiritual lesson or moral warning, and listen to the Qur'an and its truths. When the factory-like stomach is stopped from working, other members (small workshops) can be made to follow it easily.

- **Observing the fast of Ramadan breaks the carnal soul's illusory lordship and, reminding it that it is innately helpless, convinces it that it is a servant. As the carnal soul does not like to recognize its Lord, it obstinately claims lordship, even while suffering. Only hunger alters such a temperament.**[117]

---

[114] *Suratu'l-Baqara*, verse 255.
[115] *Suratu'l-Qadr*, 97:3.
[116] *The Letters*, "The Twenty-ninth Letter", p. 395.
[117] *The Letters*, "The Twenty-ninth Letter", p. 395.

God's Messenger, upon him be peace and blessings, relates that God Almighty asked the carnal soul: "Who am I, and who are you?" It replied: "You are Yourself, and I am myself." However much God punished it and repeated His question, He received the same answer. But when He subjected it to hunger, it replied: "You are my All-Compassionate Lord; I am Your helpless servant."

- *Zakah* **(the Prescribed Alms) is one of Islam's most important pillars, a means of being blessed with abundance and fertility, and of repelling misfortune. Those who neglect it lose an equal amount of wealth either through spending on useless things or suffering misfortune.**[118]

Zakah is due to those Muslims who have the sufficient amount of wealth; it is the right of those who are entitled to receive it. Therefore, not paying the *Zakah* means usurpation of their right.[119] Bediüzzaman writes:

> I had a true, highly interesting dream during the fifth year of WWI. In it, I was asked the reason for this hunger, financial loss, and bodily trial afflicting the Muslims. I replied: "From the wealth He grants to us, God Almighty requires, as *Zakah*, either a tenth or a fortieth so that we may benefit from the poor people's grateful prayers and avoid their rancor and envy. As our greed did not allow us to pay, God Almighty removed its accumulated amount: three-fourths where a fortieth was owed, and four-fifths where a tenth was owed..."

- **All immorality and disturbances in human social life proceed from two sources or two attitudes: "Once I am full, what do I care if others die of hunger?" and "You work and I will eat."**[120]

These attitudes are perpetuated by the prevalence of usury and interest and the abandonment of *Zakah*. The only remedy is to implement *Zakah* as a universal principle and duty and then ban usury. *Zakah* is a most essential pillar for individuals, particular communities, and humanity to live a happy life. Humanity usually comprises two classes: the elite and the masses. Only *Zakah* can arouse the elite's compassion and generosity towards the masses, and the masses' respect for the elite. Without *Zakah*, the elite cruelly oppress the masses and thereby often engenders

---

[118] *The Letters*, "The Twenty-second Letter", p. 291.
[119] *Suratu'l-An'am*, 6:141; *Suratu'Dh-Dhariyat*, 51:19; *Suratu'l-Ma'arij*, 70:24–25.
[120] *The Letters*, "The Twenty-second Letter", p. 292.

grudge and revolt. Such a development gives rise to a constant struggle and conflict, finally resulting in labor and capital confronting each other, as in Russia at the beginning of the twentieth century.

- **Through its numerous principles of compassion, such as mandating the Prescribed Alms (*Zakah*) and prohibiting interest and usury, Islam protects the masses. Through its many warnings, like: "Will you not exercise your reason?"; "Will they not contemplate and reflect?"; "Do they not ponder?", it considers intellect and science as proofs for its truths, and protects and encourages (true) scientists to conduct research. Since it is the citadel of the masses and scientists, no one should regret being a Muslim.**[121]

- **If you please your Creator by abstaining from sin, obeying His commands, and doing righteous deeds, this is sufficient.**[122]

If the created are pleased with you on behalf of the Almighty, you will benefit; if they are pleased on behalf of themselves, there is no benefit, for they are impotent—just like you. Choosing the first alternative pleases your Lord; choosing the second causes you to associate partners with God.

- **Public attention and respect cannot be demanded, but may be given by people themselves. If it is given, one should not be pleased with it. If one admits it with pleasure, one loses sincerity, and ostentation takes its place.**[123]

If public attention and respect come in return for seeking fame and public honor, it is not a reward but a reproach and punishment for a lack of sincerity. Harmful to sincerity, which is the life of all good deeds, fame and public attention are only a temporary, slight pleasure that lasts until the door of the grave, but takes on the form of torment in the grave. Therefore, one should not seek public attention or respect, but be wary of it and flee from it. Be warned, all you who are fame-seekers and who pursue public attention and respect!

- **One should take as a principle the altruism of the Companions or the quality of preferring others to one's own self, which the Qur'an praises. One should prefer others to one's own self in**

---

[121] *The Letters*, "The Twenty-sixth Letter", p. 340.
[122] *Al-Mathnawi al-Nuri*, "The Eighth Treatise", p. 256.
[123] *The Gleams*, "The Twentieth Gleam", p. 210.

receiving gifts and alms, and not seek any worldly return for religious service.[124]

No wages should be demanded or received in return for religious service. All the Messengers declared unanimously: "*I ask of you no wage for that (for conveying God's Message); my wage is due only from the Lord of the worlds.*"[125] Demanding any worldly return for religious service causes a loss of sincerity. The community should provide for people of religious service in need and poverty, who have the right to receive a share from the *Zakah*. But they should not demand it. If it is given without having been asked for, it should not be regarded as a reward for the service done. Rather, one should act in perfect contentment, and prefer others who are qualified for the same service and who are more deserving of the reward to one's self.

- **In this world, and particularly in the services done for the eternal afterlife, a most important foundation, and a greatest power, and a most acceptable intercessor, and a firmest point of reliance, and a shortest way to the truth, and a most answerable prayer, and a most blessed and marvelous means of achieving one's goal, and a most sublime virtue, and a purest form of worship is sincerity, or doing something good or any religious deed purely for God Almighty's sake.**[126]

- **Good deeds acquire vitality through sincere intention, and are corrupted through show, ostentation, and hypocrisy.**[127]

The feelings for and natural tendencies towards good ingrained in one's conscience lose their purity through conscious or purposeful intention. Intention is the life of deeds, while purposeful intention is the death of natural states. For example, the intention to be humble spoils humility, the intention to be great provokes contempt, the intention to have relief causes relief to disappear, and the intention to be sad decreases sadness.

- **Islam differs from other religions because it is founded upon pure monotheism and so denies any intermediary or intermediate causal creative or formative effect, and thus breaks egotism.**[128]

---

[124] *The Gleams*, "The Twentieth Gleam", p. 210–211.
[125] *Suratu'sh-Shu'ara'*, 26: 109, 127, 145, 164, 180.
[126] *The Gleams*, "The Twenty-first Gleam", p. 225.
[127] *Al-Mathnawi al-Nuri*, "The Ninth Treatise", p. 279.
[128] *The Letters*, "The Twenty-ninth Letter", pp. 419–421.

Christianity admits such influences, for it allows saints and elders a certain partnership in the manifestation of God's Sovereignty by saying that God has begotten a son: *"They have taken as lords beside God their rabbis, monks, and the Messiah son of Mary, when they were commanded to serve but One God. There is no God but He, be He glorified from their associating partners with Him."*[129] Christians who rise to the highest worldly posts can remain Christians. They even become, like the late American president Wilson, bigoted and full of egotism. Their Muslim counterparts, however, are expected to renounce egotism and pride in order to be good Muslims. Followers of pure monotheism, Muslims who cannot do so either become indifferent to Islam or even lose their belief.

- **Islam does not condemn the world categorically. In fact, the world has three facets. The first relates to God's Names. With respect to its second facet, the world is the arable field of the Hereafter. These two facets are beautiful. The third facet, which is condemned, relates directly and exclusively to the world itself, and is where people pursue the gratification of their bodily desires and seek to meet the needs of this transient worldly life.**[130]

The world has three facets. The first facet contains the mirrors that reflect Almighty God's Names. The second facet is concerned with the Hereafter. That is, this world is the arable field sown with the seeds of the Hereafter, the realm in which we might gain the eternal world. Loving these two facets of the world is a means of perfection. The more profound one is in appreciating and loving these two facets of the world, the deeper one is in worship and knowledge of God. Considering the world an arable field of the Hereafter, Muslims sow it with seeds to grow in the Hereafter. Also, they see all creatures as mirrors reflecting the Divine Names and observe them lovingly. The world is evil in its mortal facet which looks to our animal appetites. This third facet, looking to transience and non-existence, is the world of the misguided, of which God does not approve.

- **A constant spring is greater than a lake with no inlet. It is exactly the same with the earth. The earth, despite its small size and insignificance when compared with the heavens, is the universe's heart and center with respect to the meaning and art it contains,**

---

[129] *Suratu't-Tawba,* 9:31.

[130] *Al-Mathnawi al-Nuri,* "The Fourth Treatise", p. 121; *The Words,* "The Twenty-seventh Word", p. 513.

and that it is the cradle and dwelling place of humankind, which is the fruit of the Tree of Creation.[131]

God Almighty has created the earth to exhibit the works of His Art and manifest His Names, and as a garden where His Mercy flowers and as a field to cultivate the seeds of Paradise. It functions as a measure to fill and empty the universe of countless worlds of creation, and resembles a spring flowing into the "seas" of the past and the World of the Unseen. Consider the "shirts" woven of creatures in countless forms that the earth changes each year, and the ever-renewed worlds with which the earth is filled each time and then pours into the past and the world of the Unseen. It is the speedily operating workshop for eternal textiles, the fast-changing place of copies of eternal scenes, and the narrow, temporary field and tillage rapidly producing seeds for permanent gardens in the Hereafter.

It is because of this greatness of the earth with respect to its meaning and its importance in regard to art, that the wise Qur'an puts it on par with the heavens, although it is like a tiny fruit of a huge tree when compared with the heavens. It places the earth in one pan of a pair of scales and the heavens in the other, and repeatedly mentions them together, saying, the "Lord of the heavens and the earth."

- **Focusing only on the world with respect to its third facet changes a great pleasure into a grievous pain.**[132]

Imagine that there are two people in this village. Ninety-nine out of every hundred of one's friends have moved to Istanbul, where they are living happily. He will shortly join them, and he so longs for and thinks of Istanbul. When he is told he can go there, he will be overjoyed and go happily. The second person, facing the same situation, thinks that some of his friends have perished and that the others have gone where they do not see and cannot be seen. Imagining that they have gone to utter misery, he seeks consolation in his only remaining friend, who is about to depart. He wants to compensate for the heavy pangs of separation through that friend.

O my soul! God's Beloved above all, Prophet Muhammad, upon him be peace and blessings, and all your friends are on the other side of the grave. One or two remain here, but they also will go there. So do not fear death or the grave, or avert your attention from death. Look at it bravely

---

[131] *The Words*, "The Fifteenth Word", p. 195.
[132] *The Words*, "The Fourteenth Word", p. 184.

and listen to what it seeks. Laugh in its face and see what it wants. And be sure that you are not like the second person.

- **A sensible person neither rejoices at something he gains nor grieves or complains about anything he loses in relation with the world.**[133]

This world is decaying, as we and our own world are. We are not created to stay here permanently, nor are we made of iron or wood so that we can stay longer. We are made of ever-renewed flesh, blood, and delicate limbs, and we are vulnerable to everything. One part or component of us breaks, another freezes, and still another dissolves through its atoms' disintegration. The dawn of old age has broken on our head and has covered half of our head like a white shroud. The diseases visiting and intending to dwell in us are forerunners of death and destroyers of this life's pleasures. The eternal life is before us. Although our comfort and happiness in the Hereafter depend on what we do here, our avarice is so great that we think we can stay here forever. We must awake before the throes of death awaken us.

- **Everyone has a private world, the nature of which depends on one's heart and deeds, contained in this world.**[134]

Just as a magnificent palace reflected in a mirror assumes the mirror's color and quality, just as an uneven mirror shows the finest things to be coarse, so do we change our own world's appearance through our heart, mind, deeds, and attitudes. We may cause it either to testify for or against us. If we pray and turn towards the All-Majestic Maker, our private world will be illuminated suddenly. Prayer resembles a powerful electric light switched on by our intention to pray. It disperses our world's darkness and spreads over our heart a light from the illuminated verse: "*God is the Light of the heavens and the earth.*"[135]

- **This world is a guest-house. All who die confirm and testify that death is a reality. Since we cannot destroy it and contradict those testimonies, death calls us to believe in and rely on God. In place of God, nothing can illuminate the eternal darkness before those who are dying, and change their despair into hope.**[136]

---

[133] *Al-Mathnawi al-Nuri*, "The Sixth Treatise", p. 185.
[134] *The Words*, "The Twenty-first Word", p. 287.
[135] *Suratu'n-Nur*, 24:35.
[136] *The Letters*, "The Twenty-ninth Letter", p. 422.

Can technology or weaponry illuminate the eternal darkness before those who are dying and change their despair into hope? Since death is inevitable and the grave awaits us, and since this transient life gives way to the permanent life, we should mention God 1,000 times and mention other things such as science and technology only once. However, technology and weaponry lead to God when used in the cause of God and operate and cease in His Name in the lawful way.

- **Although death appears to be decomposition, seems to extinguish life's light and cause a living body to rot away, though it seems to destroy pleasures, verses such as** "He has created death and life that He may try which of you is best in conduct..."[137] **imply that death is created, like life, and is thus a blessing for living beings.**[138]

Death is a discharge from this worldly life's duties, a changing of residence, a transferal of the body, and an invitation to and the beginning of an everlasting life. The world is continually enlivened through acts of creation and Divine determination, and yet it is also continually stripped of life through other cycles of creation, determination, and wisdom. The dying of plants, the simplest level of life, is a work of Divine artistry, as is their living—but more perfect and better designed. This is so because when a fruit seed dies, it seems to decompose and rot away into the soil. But in reality, it undergoes a perfect chemical process, passes through predetermined states of re-formation, and grows again into an elaborate new tree. Thus the seed's "death" is a new tree's beginning, and death, which is something created, like life, is as perfect as life.

As the death of fruits and animal flesh in people's stomachs raises them to the degree of human life, this death can be regarded as more perfect than their lives. Since a plant's death is so perfect and serves so great a purpose, each person's death must be much more perfect and serve a still greater purpose, for humanity is life's highest level. After going underground, each of us will be brought into eternal life.

Death is a blessing for many reasons such as those that follow:

First: It discharges us from life's hardships, which gradually become harder through old age. It also allows us to meet again the ninety-nine percent of our friends who have already died.

---

[137] *Suratu'l-Mulk*, 67:2.
[138] *The Letters*, "The First Letter", pp. 5–6.

Second: It releases us from worldly life, which is a turbulent, suffocating, narrow dungeon of space, and admits us to the wide circle of the Eternal Beloved One's mercy, where we enjoy a pleasant and everlasting life without any suffering.

Third: It frees us from old age and similar conditions that make life unbearable. For example, if your old parents and grandparents were living in misery in front of your eyes, you would see death as a great blessing and life as an unendurable pain. Besides, the autumnal death of insects (lovers of lovely flowers) is a mercy for them, for they do not have to live through winter's harshness and severity.

Fourth: Sleep is a time of repose and relief, and thus a mercy, especially for the sick and afflicted. Similarly, death (the "brother" of sleep) is a blessing and mercy especially for those afflicted with such misfortune that they might contemplate suicide. As for the misguided, both life and death are torment within torment, and pain after pain.

Fifth: Death is also an occasion to receive the wage to be bestowed by the All-Compassionate and Merciful One's generosity for services rendered to Him.

- **The earth is the universe's heart and soil is the earth's heart. The quickest way to the target is through "soil," by way of the gate of humility and self-annihilation. Soil is nearer to the Creator of the heavens than even the highest heaven, for nothing else equals soil in receiving manifestations of Divine Lordship and the Names the All-Living and Self-Subsistent, displaying Divine Creativity, and being the object of Divine Power's activities.**[139]

As the Divine Throne of Mercy is on water, the Throne of Life and Revival is on soil, which is the most comprehensive mirror (reflecting the manifestations of life). However transparent the mirror of a dense thing is, it shows that thing more clearly. However dense the mirror of a luminous thing is, the manifestation of that thing on it is more complete. Air receives only a dim light from the sun's radiance, and water cannot reflect the sun's colors, although it shows the sun to you with its light. Through its flowers, soil shows whatever is in the sunlight. Compared with the Eternal Sun's Light, the sun is only a dense, shining drop. Soil's adornment and display of its spring finery—its flowers of various forms

---

[139] *Al-Mathnawi al-Nuri*, "The Tenth Treatise", p. 359.

and colors, and its beautiful animals testifying to the Divine Lordship's perfection—are witnesses to the Creator. Look at a violet, and see how the Hand of the All-Wise Maker disposes, colors, and adorns it.

- **If you want a friend, God is sufficient. If you want a companion, the Qur'an is sufficient. If you want wealth, contentment is sufficient. If you want to feel enmity, your evil-commanding soul and Satan are sufficient. If you want counsel, death is sufficient.**[140]

Indeed, if God is a friend to us, so is everything. Imagine yourself with the Prophets and angels mentioned in the Qur'an, and study their experiences and become intimate with them. The content become thrifty, and the thrifty are blessed with great wealth. The self-conceited obtain grief; the humble obtain care and peace. One who thinks of death gets rid of his or her love of the world, and strives for the next life.

- **Everything related to the Qur'an and belief is, regardless of its apparent insignificance, of great significance. Since anything contributing to eternal happiness is significant, we should regard it as worthy of study, understanding, and explanation.**[141]

- **Forgetting is also a bounty; it allows one to suffer the pains of only the present day; it makes one forget accumulated sorrows.**[142]

- **Every calamity contains degrees of Divine Favor. Be mindful of the greater calamity, thereby being thankful for the favor of the lesser calamity. Concentrating on and exaggerating a calamity increases it, and this exaggerated reflection in the heart or imagination makes it real and troublesome.**[143]

Your likeness, when stricken with a misfortune thrown by Destiny, is that of sheep trying to enter a public pasture. The shepherd seeks to turn them aside by throwing stones at them. The sheep struck by the stones turn back, as if saying: "We are under the shepherd's command. He knows us better than ourselves, so we must return." Know, O my soul, you are not more astray than the sheep. When stricken with misfortune, say: "We belong to God and are bound to return to Him."

---

[140] *The Letters*, "The Twenty-third Letter", p. 301.
[141] *The Letters*, "The Twenty-third Letter", p. 301.
[142] *Gleams of Truth*, p. 14.
[143] *Gleams of Truth*, p. 15.

- **There are two causes for every event. One is the apparent cause: people base their judgments on this and frequently do wrong or go astray as a result. The other is the truth of the matter, according to which the Divine Destiny judges: It acts with justice in all events in which humans do wrong.**[144]

As Divine Destiny is absolutely free of evil and ugliness in relation to results, it also is exempt from injustice on account of causes. Divine Destiny always considers the primary cause, not the apparent secondary cause, and always does justice. On the other hand, we judge according to apparent causes and draw wrong conclusions. For example, a court may imprison a person unjustly for a theft that he has not committed. However, the Divine Destiny actually passes this judgment because of that person's real crime, such as murder, that has remained unknown. So while the court unjustly jailed this person for a crime that he did not commit, Divine Destiny justly punished that person for his secret crime. In short, Divine Destiny and creation is just, while we are liable to do injustice. Divine Destiny and creation is absolutely free of evil and ugliness at the beginning and end of all events, and on account of causes and results.

- **Genuine and harmful misfortune is that which affects the Religion and one's religious life. One should always seek refuge, in tears, at the Divine Court from misfortune in matters of Religion. They should cry out for help.**[145]

However, any misfortune that does not affect the Religion or one's religious life is not a misfortune from the perspective of truth. Some such misfortunes are merciful warnings from the All-Merciful One. Consider the shepherd who throws a stone at his sheep when they trespass on another's field; the sheep, feeling that the stone is intended as a warning to save them from a harmful action, turn back gladly. Similarly, there are many apparent misfortunes that are in reality Divine warnings and admonitions; some others serve for atonement for and forgiveness of sins, while yet others arise from heedlessness of religious duties, and remind us of our human helplessness and weakness, thus giving us some sort of peace and serenity. Diseases regarded as misfortune are not misfortune in truth, but rather a favor from God and a means of purification. There is a Prophetic Tradition

---

[144] *The Words*, "The Twenty-sixth Word", pp. 482–483; *The Rays*, "The Thirteenth Ray", p. 312.

[145] *The Gleams*, "The Second Gleam", pp. 16–17.

which says, "Just as a tree drops its ripe fruit when shaken, so, too, do sins fall away through the shivering of a fever."[146]

- **Physical misfortunes grow when they are seen to be great, and shrink when they are seen to be small.**[147]

For example, we think we see something at night. If we concentrate on it as if it were a real thing, it grows bigger, but if we do not, it disappears. As another example, if we attempt to ward off an attacking swarm of bees, they will become more aggressive, but if we go on without paying them any attention, they will disperse. In the same way, physical misfortunes, when perceived as great and given attention, grow, and worry causes them to penetrate the body and take root in the heart. However, if the worry is removed through resignation to the Divine Decree and reliance on God, the physical misfortune will gradually decrease, dry up and disappear, just like a tree whose roots have been severed.

- **Whatever is beneficial to human beings, such as good health, appetites, and pleasures, leads human beings to offer thanks, prompts their machine of being to carry out its functions in many respects, and thus a human being becomes a factory that produces gratitude. Likewise, afflictions such as illness, pain, and other things that provoke suffering and trouble set in motion other mechanisms in that machine, working the mines of helplessness, weakness, and poverty that are inherent in the human nature. They put human beings in a state where they are ready to seek help and refuge in God Almighty, but not only with a single tongue but with the tongue of all its members. Thus a human being becomes like a moving pen that consists of thousands of different pens due to those afflictions.**[148]

- **To keep the balance between this world and the next and to let people live between hope and fear, living and dying must be possible at any moment.**[149]

For this reason, in addition to many others as well, God has hidden the time of death and the Resurrection.

---

[146] al-Bukhari, *al-Jami'u's-Sahih*, "Marda" 2; Ibn Maja, *as-Sunan*, "Tibb" 18.

[147] *The Gleams*, "The Second Gleam", pp. 17–18.

[148] *The Gleams*, "The Second Gleam", p. 19.

[149] *The Words*, "The Twenty-fourth Word", p. 362.

- **God Almighty owns everything—from the earth to the Supreme Throne of God, from the ground to the sky, and from the minutest particles to all heavenly bodies, as well as everything within both past and future eternity and within this world and the Hereafter. He has the highest and most comprehensive degree of ownership of everything.**[150]

O soul! Do not imagine that you own yourself, for you cannot administer your own affairs. You cannot maintain your spirit and body by meeting their needs and securing them against calamity. You cannot avoid exhaustion and aging, because you are subject to time and other erosive factors. Also, this world that you love, to which you are connected, belongs to an All-Powerful and Compassionate One. So return it to its Owner and leave it to Him. Mind your own duty and do not interfere with His Acts. Do not be troubled by what you cannot overcome. Whenever you are afraid, say like Ibrahim Haqqi: "Let's see what the Master does; whatever He does is always best..." and observe His Acts with complete trust.

- **God Almighty is sufficient for us. Since He exists, everything exists. Since this is so, those who have left this world do not go to non-existence. They are traveling to another of His realms. To replace them, that Owner of the Supreme Throne sends others from among His innumerable creatures.**[151]

Those who have entered the cemetery have not been utterly annihilated. They are on the way to another realm. He sends others who are duty-bound in their place. He substitutes for everything. All things cannot be equal to a single manifestation of His favor and regard.

- **The outer world seeming to be stable and perpetual should not give us the illusion that we are also stable and perpetual. For we and our own world are decaying every moment.**[152]

- **A sensible person does not set his heart on what will abandon him when he dies and will not accompany him on his journey to eternity, and has no care for what perishes during the revolutions of the Hereafter, the continuously changing conditions of**

---

[150] *The Letters*, "The Twentieth Letter", p. 241.
[151] *The Gleams*, "The Eleventh Gleam", p. 67.
[152] *The Gleams*, "The Seventeenth Gleam", p. 161.

the intermediate world of the grave, and the world's tumults and convulsions.[153]

- **A single second spent in God's good pleasure gains immortality. A hundred years spent in this world by people heedless of Divine truths and orders are in fact only a second.**[154]

In this world, time has extremely diverse effects on the death and decay of things. Although things and beings exist one within another like concentric circles, they differ greatly in decay and death.

Just as the hands of a clock counting the seconds, minutes, and hours resemble one another in appearance, but differ in respect of speed, so too do the spheres of the body, soul, heart, and spirit in a human being differ from each other. For example, while the body has a life, existence, and endurance restricted to each day, or even the hour, and although it has no consciousness of the past or the future, the heart has a wide sphere of existence and life that extends through many days, including the past, the present, and the future. As for the spirit, its sphere of life and existence extends from years before the present day to the years following it.

Considering this reality, when time is spent in worship of the All-Merciful, All-Glorified God, embedded with knowledge and love of Him, pursuing His approval and good pleasure, which is the source of the life of the heart and spirit, our transient life in this world encapsulates the seeds of and results in an everlasting life. It takes on the effect of an eternal life.

Truly, one second spent for the good pleasure of the Truly Everlasting One in knowledge of and love for Him is equivalent to a year. If it is not lived for His sake, a year lasts no longer than a second. It can even be said that a single second spent for His good pleasure gains immortality. A hundred years spent in this world by people heedless of Divine truths and orders are in fact only a second.

- **Anything turned to the Everlasting One receives the manifestation of immortality.**[155]

So we should spend our life on the way of the Truly Everlasting One. For since everyone passionately desires a long life and yearns for immortality, and since there is a means of transforming this transitory life into

---

[153] *The Gleams*, "The Seventeenth Gleam", p. 160.
[154] *The Gleams*, "The Third Gleam", p. 26.
[155] *The Gleams*, "The Third Gleam", p. 27.

an everlasting life, surely anyone who still preserves her humanity will seek out that means and try to transform that possibility into a reality, acting accordingly. The means in question are as follows: We should do whatever we should for God's sake, meet with others for God's sake, and work for God's sake. We should act within the sphere of "for God, for God's sake, and on account of God." If we follow these steps, all the minutes of our life will become like years.

- **Worship consists of two kinds, positive and negative. What is meant by positive is the worship we perform regularly. As for negative worship, this is when one who is afflicted with misfortune or disease perceives his own weakness and helplessness, turning to and seeking refuge in his All-Compassionate Lord, concentrating upon Him, and entreating Him, and thus offers a pure form of worship.**[156]

Hypocrisy cannot penetrate this second kind of worship. If one endures patiently, concentrating on the rewards to be given in return for misfortune, and offers thanks, then each hour that passes will count as a whole day spent in worship.

This world is the realm of testing, the abode of service. It is not the place of pleasure or being rewarded for things that were performed in God's cause. So diseases and misfortunes—as long as they do not harm the Religion and are patiently endured—conform fully to service and worship, and even strengthen it. Since such diseases and misfortunes make each hour's worship equivalent to that of a day, one should offer thanks instead of complaining.

- **Just as it is pure lunacy to eat and drink continually today out of the fear that we will probably be hungry and thirsty in the future, so too, is it foolish to think at this present moment of past and future pains—pains which do not exist—and, as a result, to grow impatient, to ignore one's faulty soul, and to act as though one is complaining about God. If we do not waste our precious stores of patience on worrying about the past and the future, neither of which exists, it will cause our existing pain to decrease tenfold.**[157]

---

[156] *The Gleams*, "The Second Gleam", pp. 13–14.
[157] *The Words*, "The Thirteenth Word", p. 166.

- **Illness is not a loss for people, but a gain, a sort of cure. For it makes the capital of life yield huge profits.**[158]

For life departs like capital. If it yields no fruits, it is wasted. And if it passes in ease and heedlessness, it is short, bringing almost no profit. Illness makes the capital of life yield huge profits. Moreover, it prevents life from being short; it holds it back, lengthening or expanding it, so that it may depart after yielding its fruits.

- **Illness substitutes for the supererogatory Prayers of the ill person who does their obligatory worship as much as possible and shows patience in submissive reliance on God.**[159]

It is stated in a *hadith*, "A pious, God-revering believer who, due to illness, cannot do the invocations he does normally and regularly, receives an equal reward."[160]

- **Illness reminds people of their innate impotence and weakness, and causes them to pray both verbally and through the tongue of their state.**[161]

God Almighty has created human beings with impotence and weakness so that they continually seek refuge in the Divine Court and pray and supplicate. Since, according to the verse, "*My Lord would not care for you were it not for your prayer,*"[162] the value of humankind lies in sincere prayer, and as illness leads people to such prayers, rather than complaining about illness, we should thank God.

- **Sins are real illnesses; they are perpetual illnesses with respect to the eternal life. They are also illnesses for the heart, conscience, and spirit in this worldly life. Material illnesses wash away the dirt of sins and cleanse the ill if they show becoming patience without complaint.**[163]

It is established in an authenticated *hadith* that illnesses are expiation for sins. It says, "Just as a tree drops its ripe fruit when shaken, so, too, do sins fall away through the shivering of a fever."

---

[158] *The Gleams*, "The Twenty-fifth Gleam", p. 289.
[159] *The Gleams*, "The Twenty-fifth Gleam", p. 297.
[160] *Abu Dawud*, "Jana'iz" 1; Ahmad ibn Hanbal, *al-Musnad*, 4:418.
[161] *The Gleams*, "The Twenty-fifth Gleam", p. 298.
[162] *Suratu'l-Furqan*, 25:77.
[163] *The Gleams*, "The Twenty-fifth Gleam", p. 294–295.

If we persevere and do not complain, we are being saved from numerous perpetual illnesses through that temporary illness. But if we do not worry about sins, or are not aware of the afterlife, or do not recognize God, we have such an illness that it is a million times worse than our present illness.

- **One who does not recognize God is afflicted with a worldful of tribulations, while the world of one who recognizes God is full of light and spiritual joy.**[164]

Everyone is aware of this according to the strength of their belief. The pain of physical illnesses melts away under the spiritual joy, healing, and pleasure that come from belief.

- **Humankind has not come to this world for enjoyment or pleasure. Rather, possessing vast capital, humankind has come here to work for an eternal life by doing the required trade. The capital given to them is their life.**[165]

Were it not for illness, good health and ease would cause heedlessness, presenting the world as pleasant and making people oblivious of the Here-after. By distracting them from the thought of death and the grave, good health and ease cause them to waste the capital of life on trifles. But illness suddenly gives them awareness, and says to the body: "You are not immortal, and have not been left to your own devices. You have a duty. Give up haughtiness; think of the One Who has created you; know that you will enter the grave, and make the necessary preparation!" Thus, from this perspective, illness is an advisor that never deceives; and it is an admonishing guide.

- **Illness is a Divine favor especially for some people, a gift of mercy.**[166]

Bediüzzaman writes as follows:

For these last eight or nine years, a number of young people have visited me to pray for them because of their illnesses. I have noticed that compared to those of the same age, any unwell young person I have met has begun to think of the Hereafter. They are no longer in the typical intoxication of youth, and have saved themselves to a degree from the animal

---

[164] *The Gleams*, "The Twenty-fifth Gleam", p. 295.
[165] *The Gleams*, "The Twenty-fifth Gleam", p. 291.
[166] *The Gleams*, "The Twenty-fifth Gleam", p. 292, 299.

desires that are embedded in heedlessness. For instance, from among my friends there were two youths, may God have mercy on them. I used to note with amazement that although these two were illiterate and could not serve by copying the *Risale-i Nur*, they were among the foremost in sincerity and the service of belief. After their deaths I understood that both had suffered from a serious illness. Guided by that illness, unlike other heedless youths who did not carry out the obligatory worship, they had great reverence for God, and performed the most valuable services, attaining a state beneficial to the Hereafter. God willing, the trouble of two years' illness was the means to the bliss of millions of years of eternal life. If, like some young people, they had trusted in their youth and good health and let themselves fall into heedlessness and dissipation, and if death, which is always on the watch, had grasped them right in the midst of the filth of their sins, their graves would have been the lairs of scorpions and snakes, instead of that treasury of lights.

Since death can come at any time, if it captures the human being in heedlessness, it may cause great harm to their eternal life. But illness dispels heedlessness, makes people think of their afterlife and reminds them of death and thus prepares them for the Hereafter.

• **Since the world will one day say to us, "Now, it is the time of departure!" and close its ears to our cries, warned by illnesses, we must give up our love of it before it drives us out. Before it abandons us, we must try to abandon it in our hearts.**[167]

Illness reminds us of this reality and says, "Your body is not composed of stone and iron; rather it has been composed of various materials that are subject to partition and dissolution. Give up conceit, be aware of your innate impotence, recognize your Master, know your duties, and learn why you came to the world!" Illness says this secretly in the ear of the heart.

• **Illnesses and calamities cause us to taste deeply the real pleasure of life and health, and thus lead us to preserve health and give God continual thanks.**[168]

O you who are ill and have lost the pleasures of health! Your illness does not ruin the contentment of the Divine blessing in health; rather, it causes you to taste it more deeply, and increases it. For if something continues uninterruptedly, it loses its effect. Also, things are known through

---

[167] *The Gleams*, "The Twenty-fifth Gleam", p. 293.
[168] *The Gleams*, "The Twenty-fifth Gleam", p. 294.

their opposites. Therefore, without illnesses, health and appetite would be without pleasure.

- **People fear and are distressed by illness because it sometimes leads to death. Since death is frightening to the superficial, heedless view, illnesses that may lead to it cause fear and worry. However, the appointed hour of death is certain and does not change. Also, death is not frightening; rather, it is the door to Divine mercy.**[169]

It has many times occurred that the healthy ones weeping beside the seriously ill have died, while the seriously ill have been cured and continue to live. Secondly, death is not frightening; it is not as it appears to be. For people of belief, death is a discharge from the hardship of the duties of this life; a respite from worship, which is a drill and training in the arena of trials in this world; and a means of reunion with ninety-nine relatives and beloved ones who have already emigrated to the other world. It is also a means of entering the true homeland and eternal abode of happiness. In addition, it is an invitation from the prison of the world to the spacious gardens of Paradise. And it is the door to Divine mercy, and the time when one receives a wage from the grace of the All-Compassionate Creator in return for one's services. Only for the people of misguidance is it the door to the pit of eternal darkness and tribulation.

- **Although illness causes some suffering, all the former illnesses have produced an immaterial contentment for one's spirit resulting in recovery from them, and a spiritual pleasure arising from the reward received for enduring them. The present illness will function the same.**[170]

- **If a believer loses her sight and enters the grave blind, she may, in accordance with her degree, gaze on the world of light to a much greater extent than the other people of the grave.**[171]

Just as in this world we see many things that blind believers do not see, if they go from this world with belief, they see to a greater extent than the other people of the grave. As if looking through the most powerful telescopes, they can, in accordance with their degree, see and gaze on the gardens of Paradise as on a movie screen.

---

[169] *The Gleams*, "The Twenty-fifth Gleam", p. 295–296.

[170] *The Gleams*, "The Twenty-fifth Gleam", p. 297.

[171] *The Gleams*, "The Twenty-fifth Gleam", p. 300.

- **There are some illnesses which, if they lead to death, are like a sort of martyrdom. They cause one to gain some certain degree of sainthood.**[172]

For example, like the believing women who die during or because of childbirth, those who die from pains in the abdomen, and by drowning, burning, or the plague,[173] are considered as martyrs. Furthermore, since illness lessens the love of the world and attachment to it, it lightens the pain of parting from the world, which is extremely grievous for worldly people. Sometimes it makes such a departure desirable.

- **Illness induces respect and compassion, which are most important and good for human social life. This saves people from conceited feelings of self-sufficiency, which drives them to unfriendliness and unkindness.**[174]

According to the reality stated in, *"No indeed, but the human is unruly and rebels, in that he sees himself as self-sufficient,"*[175] a carnal, evil-commanding soul which feels self-sufficient due to good health and well-being does not regard the many causes which are deserving of brotherhood or sisterhood. And they do not feel compassion towards the misfortunate or ill, who should be shown kindness and pity. Yet, whenever they become ill, they are aware of their own innate impotence and neediness, and feel respect towards their sisters and brothers who are worthy of it. They pay respect to their believing brothers and sisters who visit or help them. And they feel human kindness, which originates in fellow-feeling and compassion for the disaster-stricken—a most important Islamic characteristic. Comparing others to themselves, they empathize with them, feel affection for them, and do whatever they can to help them. At the very least they pray for others and pay them a visit of consolation, which is a *Sunnah* act according to the Shari'ah,[176] thus earning reward.

- **It is illness that opens the door of the most sincere of good works. Illness is a most important means of continuously gaining reward for the sick person and for those who are looking after them for**

---

[172] *The Gleams*, "The Twenty-fifth Gleam", p. 301.
[173] al-Bukhari, "Jihad" 30; Muslim, "'Imara" 164.
[174] *The Gleams*, "The Twenty-fifth Gleam", p. 301.
[175] *Suratu'l-'Alaq*, 96:6–7.
[176] Muslim, "Birr" 40; Abu Dawud, "Jana'iz" 7; at-Tirmidhi, "Jana'iz" 2.

the sake of God; it is, in addition, a means for supplications to be accepted.[177]

Certainly, there is significant reward for the believers who look after the sick. Asking after the health of those who are ill and visiting them—provided it does not tax them—is a *sunnah* act, an act highly recommended by our Prophet, upon him be peace and blessings.[178] It is also expiation for sins. There is a *hadith* which says, "Receive the prayers of the ill, for their prayers are acceptable."[179]

Especially if the person who is ill is a relative, in particular, parents, looking after them is an important form of worship which yields great, significant rewards. To please an invalid person's heart, and to console him, is like giving alms. Fortunate is the one who pleases the easily-touched hearts of their father and mother when they are ill, and receives their prayer.

- **Worry doubles the burden of illness; in addition, it causes an immaterial illness in the heart. Through submission, resignation, and thinking of the wisdom and benefits inherent in illness, worry vanishes and one of the important roots of the illness will thus be severed.**[180]

- **No one has a right to complain of God. For we have no rights violated, nor have we been made to lose anything which would allow us to complain. Rather, there are numerous thanks that are obligatory for us, but we have not fulfilled them.**[181]

Without performing our duties towards God Almighty, which are His rights over us, we are complaining as if we are demanding rights in a manner that is not righteous. We cannot look at others who are better off than us in health and complain. We are rather charged with looking at those who are worse than us in health, and offering thanks. If our hand is broken, we should look at those whose hands have been severed. If we have only one eye, we should look at those blind, lacking both eyes. And we must offer thanks to God!

- **Among created things, the most subtle and beautiful, and the most comprehensive mirror that reflects God's being the Eternally**

---

[177] *The Gleams*, "The Twenty-fifth Gleam", p. 302.
[178] *al-Bukhari*, "Marda'" 4, 5; *Muslim*, "Salam" 47.
[179] *Ibn Maja* "Jana'iz" 1; al-Bayhaqi, *Shu'ab al-Iman*, 6:541.
[180] *The Gleams*, "The Twenty-fifth Gleam", p. 296.
[181] *The Gleams*, "The Twenty-fifth Gleam", p. 303.

Besought is life. Therefore, whatever befalls life, from the viewpoint of truth, is good, because it exhibits the beautiful imprints of the All-Beautiful Names, which are all good and beautiful. Calamities and illnesses refine, perfect, and polish the mirror of life.[182]

If life passes monotonously with permanent health and appetite, it becomes a deficient mirror. Indeed, in one respect, it suggests non-existence and nothingness, and causes weariness. It reduces the value of life, and changes the pleasure of life into distress. With the intention of passing their time quickly, out of boredom people let themselves fall into either dissipation or into distractions. They become hostile to their valuable life as if it were a prison sentence, and want to kill it, and make it pass quickly. By contrast, a life that revolves in change and action and different states makes its value felt, and enables us to recognize its importance and pleasure. Even if it is a life of troubles and misfortune, one with such a life does not want life to pass quickly. They make no complaints out of boredom.

- **In addition to refining and purifying life, calamities and illnesses strengthen and develop it, increasing its capacities of resistance and immunity.**[183]

- **Illness is of two kinds. One kind is real; the other is imaginary. As for the real kind, the All-Wise Healer of Majesty has stored up in His mighty pharmacy of the earth a remedy for every illness. Without illness, those remedies could not have been known and enjoyed. So, illnesses serve the development of the sciences of medicine and pharmacology.**[184]

The Religion requires that medicines should be used in treatment, but we should know that their effect and the cure are from God Almighty. It is He Who gives the cure, and it is He Who provides the medicine.

- **Illnesses attract and awaken the most pleasurable, long forgotten compassion of parents, relatives and friends.**[185]

You, brother or sister in faith or humanity, who are sick! You are suffering physical pain because of your illness, but a significant spiritual pleasure which will remove the effect of your physical pain surrounds you. For if you

---

[182] *The Gleams*, "The Twenty-fifth Gleam", p. 305.

[183] *The Gleams*, "The Twenty-fifth Gleam", p. 306.

[184] *The Gleams*, "The Twenty-fifth Gleam", p. 306.

[185] *The Gleams*, "The Twenty-fifth Gleam", p. 307.

have a father, mother, or relatives, their most pleasurable compassion towards you, which you have long forgotten, will be awakened and you will see again their kind looks which you received in childhood. In addition, the friends around you who have remained veiled and hidden will look again towards you with love and compassion through the attraction of illness. In the face of these, your physical pain is infinitesimal. In addition, since you have attracted towards yourself the empathy and human tenderness of people, you have found many helpful friends and kind companions who expect nothing in return. Again, you have received from your illness the order to rest from many exhausting duties, and you are taking a rest. Certainly, in the face of these spiritual pleasures, your minor pain should lead you to thanksgiving, not to complaint.

- **Illnesses arouse sympathy in the hardest hearts and attract kindness and compassion to the ill; certainly they also attract the All-Compassionate Creator's compassion, which is certain to be a substitute for the sympathy and compassion of everyone else.**[186]

It is He Who presents Himself to us at the start of all but one of the *suras* of the Qur'an with the Attributes of "the All-Merciful and the All-Compassionate." Through one gleam of His Compassion, He causes all mothers to nurture their young with wonderful tenderness, and through one manifestation of His Mercy every spring, He fills the face of the earth with bounties. Also, with all its wonders, Paradise, which is the abode of eternal happiness, constitutes a single manifestation of His Mercy. Thus, our relation to Him through belief, and our recognition of Him and entreating Him through the voice of helplessness that is found in illness, will surely attract His mercy towards the ill.

- **Severe illnesses such as paralysis is regarded as blessed for the believers. For they are saved through them from the great dangers that this world poses to the spiritual life and the attainment of the eternal happiness, and these illnesses function as austerity, religious exercises, and asceticism.**[187]

In order to obtain the approval and good pleasure of God Almighty and to attain perfection, the people of God have chosen to follow two principles:

---

[186] *The Gleams*, "The Twenty-fifth Gleam", p. 308.
[187] *The Gleams*, "The Twenty-fifth Gleam", p. 307–308.

The first is contemplation of death. Thinking of the world as transitory and realizing that they, too, are transient guests in the world, who have many duties, help people to work for eternal life.

The second: In order to be saved from the dangers of the carnal, evil-commanding soul and its blind passions, they have tried to kill the evil-commanding soul through austerity, religious exercises, and asceticism. The believers suffering severe illnesses such as paralysis have been given these two principles, which are the cause of happiness, so that their bodies continually warn them against the fleeting nature of the world and remind them that human beings are mortal. The world cannot drown them anymore, nor can heedlessness close their eyes. And certainly, the carnal, evil-commanding soul cannot deceive someone in this state with vile lust and animal appetite; that person is quickly saved from the trials of the evil-commanding soul. Thus, through belief in and submission to God, and reliance on Him, a believer can benefit in a short time from a severe illness like paralysis, without having to undergo the severe trials of the saints. Thus a severe illness becomes an exceedingly modest exchange for these gains.

- **Attending innocent, sick children or the elderly (who are like innocent children) is an important trade for the Hereafter. Not only looking after relatives who are elderly or innocent children, but also willingly serving a sick person, especially if that one is in need, is a requirement of being a Muslim.**[188]

There are many instances of wisdom pertaining to worldly life in the illnesses of innocent children. For instance, their illnesses are like exercises and drills for their delicate bodies, and the inoculations and training of the Lord, so that they may be able to withstand the tumults and upheavals of the world in the future. As is accepted by verifying scholars, like expiations for sins in adults, the illnesses of innocent children are also inoculations which will serve their spiritual life, and their spiritual purification and development in the future or in the Hereafter. In addition, the merits ensuing from such illnesses are recorded in the notebook of the good deeds of the parents, and particularly of the mother who, out of compassion, prefers the health of her child to her own.

---

[188] *The Gleams*, "The Twenty-fifth Gleam", pp. 309–310.

As for looking after the elderly, it is accurately reported from our Prophet, upon him be peace and blessings, and has been established by many historical events, that in addition to bringing mighty rewards, receiving the prayers of the elderly, and especially that of parents, and making their hearts happy and serving them faithfully is the means to happiness both in this world and in the Hereafter.[189]

- **A most beneficial, truly pleasurable and sacred medicine, which is the cure for every illness, is belief, and repentance and seeking God's forgiveness for the sins committed, and the five daily Prayers, and other duties of worship.[190]**

- **"The best of your young people are those who are like your old people, and the worst of your old people are those who are like your young people."[191]**

This is related as a Prophetic saying. It means that the best young people, like an old person, think of death and, without being captivated by youth's fancies, strive for the next life. The worst old people are those who, trying to imitate the young in worldly aspirations by ignoring the Divine commands, obey their carnal soul's temptations.

- **The mercy of the All-Compassionate Creator is the greatest hope and most powerful light especially for the old. This mercy can be attained by forming a connection with and adhering to the All-Merciful through belief and by obeying Him, particularly by performing the daily Prayers.[192]**

- **We are leaving; there is no use in deceiving ourselves. Even if we close our eyes to it, we will not be allowed to remain here. There is mobilization. The land of the Intermediate Realm of the grave, which we are leaving for, is the meeting place of friends. It is the realm where we will meet with, foremost, God's Beloved, Prophet Muhammad, upon him be peace and blessings, and with all our friends. The means of being entitled to that person's intercession, profiting from his light, and being saved from the darkness of the**

---

[189] al-Bukhari, "Adab" 1–6,; Muslim, "Birr" 1–6, 9, 10; at-Tirmidhi, "Da'awat" 110.
[190] The Gleams, "The Twenty-fifth Gleam", p. 310.
[191] The Letters, "The Twenty-third Letter", p. 301.
[192] The Gleams, "The Twenty-sixth Gleam", p. 315.

Intermediate Realm is to follow his noble example or way (Sunnah).[193]

- The Maker of Majesty, Who has created this world as a most perfectly ordered city or palace, certainly speaks to His most important guests and friends—humanity—in that palace. And since He has made this palace or city as a fine guesthouse and place of trade for us, He will certainly have a book that demonstrates His relations for us and what He wants from us. The most perfect of such sacred Books is the Qur'an of miraculous expression. In it is a cure for every ill, a light for every veil and kind of darkness, and a hope for every instance of despair. The key to this eternal treasury is belief and submission to God, listening to the Qur'an and accepting and reciting it.[194]

- As there is the Hereafter and it is everlasting, and it is a realm much better than this world, and as the One Who has created us is both All-Wise and All-Compassionate, we should not complain of or regret our old age. On the contrary, since old age is a sign of reaching the age of maturity in belief and worship, and signals a discharge from the duties of life and departure for the world of mercy in order to rest, we should be pleased with it.[195]

- Denial is negation; that is, it is a claim of non-existence, and therefore it cannot be proved. Since the denial of the afterlife and Paradise is such a negation, and therefore impossible to be proved, it has no value at all.[196]

It may be realized from the following comparison how easy it is to prove an already existing thing or clear fact and how hard it is to deny it. If someone says: "Somewhere on this earth is a wonderful garden that provides canned milk in the form of fruit," and others dispute this, the first person only has to show the garden or some of its produce. Deniers, however, must inspect and display the whole world to justify their negation. Similarly, the testimony of two truthful witnesses is enough to establish the truth of something. Thus, the testimony of two Prophets, who never lied, for the existence of the afterlife and Paradise suffices for

---

[193] The Gleams, "The Twenty-sixth Gleam", p. 316.
[194] The Gleams, "The Twenty-sixth Gleam", pp. 317–318.
[195] The Gleams, "The Twenty-sixth Gleam", p. 318.
[196] The Words, "The Tenth Word", pp. 129–130.

the establishment of their existence. Deniers must examine, explore, and sift the infinite cosmos, and travel throughout infinite and eternal time before they can prove Paradise's non-existence. Therefore, understand how secure and sound it is to believe in the Hereafter.

A *hadith* says that one hundred and twenty-four thousand Prophets,[197] who are the most eminent and distinguished among humanity, have been sent. All of these Prophets, based on Divine Revelation and their own spiritual observation, unanimously and in complete agreement, gave news that the Hereafter does exist, that human beings will be sent there, and that the Creator will bring it as He promised. In addition, one hundred and twenty-four million scholarly saints, with spiritual illumination, discovery, and observation have confirmed the reports of the Prophets with the degree of certainty arising from knowledge, and testified to the existence of the Hereafter.

Also, all the Names of the All-Wise Maker, through their manifestations in this world, show the absolutely necessary existence of an everlasting realm. For example, the Eternal Power, Which every spring restores to life innumerable corpses of dead trees on the face of the earth with the command of "Be! and it is," and Which revives hundreds of thousands of species of plants and animals as samples of the resurrection of the dead, most clearly necessitates the existence of the Hereafter. Likewise, the infinite, Eternal Wisdom, Which allows nothing to be in vain or purposeless, and the Eternal Mercy and Perpetual Favor, Which, with perfect compassion and in an extremely wonderful fashion, provide the sustenance of all living beings that are in need of it, and for a brief time in spring allow them to display their manifold varieties of adornment and decoration, require the Hereafter. Furthermore, humanity is the most perfect fruit of the universe or the Tree of Creation and its Creator's most beloved creature, and among all beings, humanity is the most closely and deeply connected and concerned with the other beings in the universe. The intense, unshakable, and constant love of eternity and ambition for permanence that are innate in the human nature prove the existence of a permanent realm, an everlasting abode of happiness that will follow this transient world so decisively that they necessitate the acceptance of the Hereafter with the same certainty as we accept the existence of this world.

---

[197] Ahmad ibn Hanbal, *al-Musnad*, 5:265; Ibn Hibban, *as-Sahih*, 2:77.

Since one of the most important things the wise Qur'an teaches us is belief in the Hereafter, and since this belief is so powerful and provides such hope and solace that if a single person were overwhelmed by old age a hundred thousand times over, the consolation arising from this belief would be sufficient to face it, then surely we who are elderly should say, "All praise be to God for perfect belief," and love our old age.

- **Since we have a Compassionate Creator, there can be no exile for us. Since He exists, everything exists for us. Since He exists and has angels, the world is not empty. Lonely-seeming mountains and apparently empty deserts are full of God Almighty's servants. Apart from His conscious servants, His stones and trees also become like familiar friends when viewed through His light and on His account. They may converse with us and give us contentment.[198]**

Evidence and testimonies to the number of beings in the universe and to the number of the letters of this vast book of the universe affirm the existence of our All-Compassionate, All-Munificent, All-Intimate, and All-Loving Creator, Maker, and Protector. They show us His Mercy to the number of the living creatures, and of the provision and favors they enjoy, all of which are the instruments of His Compassion, Mercy, and Grace, and point the way to His Court. The most acceptable intercessor at His Court is impotence, weakness, and neediness. And the greatest time of impotence, weakness, and neediness is old age. So we should not resent old age, which is an acceptable intercessor at this Court, but welcome it.

- **As belief illuminates the six sides of us—the front, the back, the right, the left, the past, and the future—and since it means a connection with God Almighty, it gives the limited human faculty of willpower a document through which one relies on an infinite Power and can be connected to a limitless Mercy, and thus can gain Paradise.[199]**

Indeed, belief itself is that document in the hand of human willpower. Though this human instrument of willpower is in itself both short-range, feeble, and deficient, yet—just as when a soldier uses his limited capacities on behalf of the state, he performs duties far exceeding those capacities—through belief, if that limited willpower is used in the name of God

---

[198] *The Gleams*, "The Twenty-sixth Gleam", p. 321.
[199] *The Gleams*, "The Twenty-sixth Gleam", p. 324.

Almighty and in His cause, it may also gain an arena in Paradise as broad as five hundred years of walking.

- **As declared in the Qur'anic verse, "**Every soul is bound to taste death,**"[200] humankind is a soul, so it will die in order to be resurrected; the earth is a soul, so it will die in order to assume an eternal form; and the world, too, is a soul, so it will die in order to assume the form of the Hereafter. The sole consolation, hope and light in the face of these deaths is the glad tidings in the Qur'an for the believers.[201]**

- **If youth, which is in fact the most powerful and pleasant means of doing good works in the name of the eternal life, is not spent in uprightness, modesty, and God-consciousness, it ruins eternal happiness and the life in this world. Indeed, in return for the pleasures of a few years of youth, many years of grief and sorrow are caused in old age.[202]**

- **Everyone has his own particular world within this world. It is as if there are worlds, one within the other, equal to the number of human beings. The pillar of everyone's private world is his own life. When his body is destroyed, his world collapses on his head, and it is doomsday for him.[203]**

Since the heedless do not realize that their world has such a nature, which is bound for such speedy destruction, they suppose it to be perpetual as the general world appears to be, and they adore it.

For believers, the world is a temporary market set up on the road to eternity, a guesthouse filled and emptied every day, an ever-renewed notebook of the Eternal Inscriber, in which He continuously writes and erases; every spring is a gilded letter of His and every summer a well-composed ode. It is formed of mirrors reflecting the ever-renewed manifestations of the All-Majestic Maker's Names. It is a seedbed of the Hereafter, a flowerbed of Divine Mercy, and a temporary workshop producing tablets that will be displayed in the Realm of Eternity.

I offer a hundred thousand thanks to the Creator of Majesty, Who has made the world in this way. I understood that while humankind has been

---

[200] *Sura Al 'Imran*, 3:185.
[201] *The Gleams*, "The Twenty-sixth Gleam", p. 325–326.
[202] *The Gleams*, "The Twenty-sixth Gleam", p. 327.
[203] *The Gleams*, "The Twenty-sixth Gleam", p. 327–328.

endowed with love for the beautiful, inner faces of the world, which look to the Hereafter and Divine Names, many have wasted that love on its transient, ugly, harmful, heedless face, and so realized the meaning of the *hadith*, "Love of this world is the source of all errors."[204]

- **Just as the most powerless and weakest of living beings are the young or babies, and it is babies who are favored with the sweetest and most beautiful manifestation of Mercy, so are the weakness and powerlessness of old age means for attracting Divine grace and mercy.**[205]

And so, elderly men and women! Know that the weakness and powerlessness of old age are means for attracting Divine grace and mercy. Just as I have observed this in myself on numerous occasions, the manifestation of mercy on the face of the earth demonstrates this truth clearly.

The powerlessness of a young bird in the nest at the top of a tree employs its mother like an obedient soldier as a manifestation of mercy. Its mother flies all around and brings it food. As soon as its wings grow strong and the nestling forgets its powerlessness, its mother says, "Go and search for your own food by yourself!" and no longer listens to it. It is in the same way that infants are sent their sustenance in a wonderful fashion by Divine Mercy because of their impotence, flowing forth from the springs of their mothers' breasts. Just as this reality of mercy is in force for the very young, so too is it in force for the elderly, who are like the young in weakness and impotence. The sustenance of the believing elderly, who have acquired innocence, is sent in the form of miraculous abundance. The part of a *hadith* which says, "Were it not for the elderly with their bent backs, calamities would descend on you in floods,"[206] makes clear that a family's source of abundance is its elderly, and it is the elderly who preserve the family from calamities.

- **Elderly people certainly enjoy—in place of the temporary physical pleasures roused by the appetites of youth—substantial, continual mercy and respect from Divine Grace, innate human feelings of tenderness, and the contentment of spirit that arises from such respect and compassion.**[207]

---

[204] al-Bayhaqi, *Shu'ab al-Iman*, 7:338; al-Mundhiri, *at-Targhib wa't-Tarhib*, 3:178.

[205] *The Gleams*, "The Twenty-sixth Gleam", p. 330.

[206] at-Tabarani, *al-Mu'jamu'l-Kabir*, 22:309; Abu Ya'la, *al-Musnad*, 11:287.

[207] *The Gleams*, "The Twenty-sixth Gleam", p. 331.

- **Death is a reunion with the beloved ones who have left behind their worn-out dwellings, some traveling about the stars and some through the levels of the Intermediate Realm. Like the seeds a farmer scatters over the earth, the All-Compassionate Creator temporarily takes that beloved creature of His—humanity—under the ground, which is a door of mercy, in order to produce shoots in another life.[208]**

- **Seeing we are mortal regarding our bodies, what good can come from the mortal to a mortal one? Seeing we are powerless, what can be expected from the powerless to a powerless one? What we need is an All-Powerful, Everlasting One Who will provide a remedy for our ills.[209]**

- **Since God Almighty exists, He is sufficient in place of everything else. Since He is Everlasting, He is surely sufficient. A single instance of His Grace substitutes for the whole world. And one manifestation of His Light gives life to the three vast corpses, showing that they are not corpses, but rather they have completed their duties and have left for other worlds.[210]**

Everyone is at the head of three vast corpses: Our bodies are renewed twice a year. So the first corpse is the totality of one's bodies mixed with earth. The second corpse is the vast corpse of all our fellow human beings who have died since the time of Prophet Adam, upon him be peace, and who have been buried in the grave of the past. The third corpse is the whole world which will one day die like human beings and the worlds that travel through it every year. These corpses have left for the other world to be resurrected on Judgment Day. Therefore they do not go to eternal non-existence.

- **Like the new fruit of a tree taking the place of those that have been harvested, death and separation, in humankind, are in fact renewal and refreshment. From the perspective of belief, they are a renewal which should not cause painful sorrow due to the want of friends, but a sweet sorrow that arises from parting in order to meet again in another, better place.[211]**

---

[208] *The Gleams*, "The Twenty-sixth Gleam", p. 332–333.
[209] *The Gleams*, "The Twenty-sixth Gleam", p. 334.
[210] *The Gleams*, "The Twenty-sixth Gleam", p. 342.
[211] *The Gleams*, "The Twenty-sixth Gleam", p. 350.

- **The bounty of the light of belief shows the two realms of the world and the Hereafter as being full of bounties and mercy, from which every believer can rightfully benefit using their numerous senses developed by the leave of their Creator.**[212]

So, those who rely on the Mercy of the All-Merciful and All-Compassionate One through belief and are aware of their relation with Him certainly find such a source of help that even its least degree provides for innumerable ambitions that extend as far as eternity, enabling their realization.

My elderly brothers and sisters! There is a *hadith* which says, "Divine Mercy is ashamed to leave unanswered the prayers offered to the Divine Court by an elderly believer of sixty or seventy years."[213] Since Divine Mercy holds you in such respect, be respectful towards this respect by worshipping Him!

- **Our innate love of permanence arises from a manifestation in our being of a Name of the One of Perfection and Majesty, Who is naturally loved because of His absolute Perfection, and should therefore be directed towards the Essence, Perfection, and Permanence of that Absolutely Perfect One.**[214]

- **One who has a connection to the All-Powerful through belief and relies on His infinite Power has found such a moral strength that he can feel he has enough power to challenge the entire world.**[215]

- **One who declares "God is sufficient for us!" in dependence on His absolute Power and Wealth also gives voice to the testimony to the absolute Oneness of God of all other beings who pronounce the same in the tongue of their disposition.**[216]

Bediüzzaman writes:

> I at once looked and saw that innumerable birds and flies (which are miniature birds) and innumerable animals, plants and trees were, like me, reciting, *God is sufficient for us; how excellent a Guardian He is!* through the tongue of their disposition. They recall to everyone the following fact: that they have such a Guardian Who guarantees all their essential necessities of life that before our eyes, and particularly in the spring, His vast and all-

---

[212] *The Gleams*, "The Twenty-sixth Gleam", p. 348.
[213] at-Tabarani, *al-Mu'jamu'l-Awsat*, 5:270.
[214] *The Gleams*, "The Twenty-sixth Gleam", p. 352.
[215] *The Gleams*, "The Twenty-sixth Gleam", p. 353.
[216] *The Gleams*, "The Twenty-sixth Gleam", p. 354.

majestic Power creates in utmost abundance, with the greatest ease, on a vast scale, with the greatest art, and in balanced and well-ordered fashion, and in forms all different from one another, with no defect, fault, or confusion at all, from eggs, drops of fluids, grains, and seeds that look very much like each other and whose component elements are the same, a hundred thousand species of birds, hundreds of thousands of animals, hundreds of thousands of types of plants, and hundreds of thousands of varieties of trees. The similarity and resemblance among all these beings, despite the infinite difference, demonstrate to us His Unity and Oneness, and inform us that there cannot be any interference or participation in those acts of His Lordship and Creativity. Those who want to understand my personal identity and human nature as a believing man, which is like that of all believers, should look at the meaning of the 'I' included in the first person plural 'us' in *God is sufficient for us*. What is my apparently insignificant, needy being, or that of any believer? What is life? What is humanity? What is Islam? What is certain, verified belief? What is knowledge of God? How should love be? They can find the answers to all these questions.

- **If our life looks to us in one respect, it looks to the All-Living and the Self-Subsisting in a hundred. And if, out of its results, one looks to us, a thousand look to our Creator. Therefore, one instant of its endurance within the bounds of God's good pleasure and approval is sufficient; a long time is not required.**[217]

The more life is grasped, causing it to look to the All-Living and the Self-Subsisting, and the more belief becomes the life and spirit of life, the more it becomes perpetual and yields enduring fruits. It also becomes so elevated that it receives the manifestation of eternity. Whether life is long or short ceases to be a consideration.

- **Mirrors, pieces of glass, transparent objects, and bubbles manifest the various hidden beauties of the sun's light and the seven colors in its spectrum; and through their disappearance, renewal, and replacement with new ones possessing different capacities and refractions, they cause the renewal and re-manifestations of these beauties. In the same way, in order to act as mirrors to the sacred Beauty of the All-Gracious, Beautiful One of Majesty, the Eternal Sun, and to the permanent beauties of His All-Beautiful Names, and to cause the ever-renewal of their manifestations,**

---

[217] *The Gleams*, "The Twenty-sixth Gleam", p. 355.

all the creatures, these lovely beings arrive and depart in a constant flux. They demonstrate that the beauties manifested by them are not their own property, but the signs, indications, gleams, and manifestations of an eternal, transcendent, sacred Beauty Which wants to become manifest.[218]

- As paternal affection for children is a sublime reality of worldly life, filial gratitude is a most urgent and heavy duty. Parents lovingly sacrifice their lives for their children. Given this, children who preserve their humanity and have not become monsters of ingratitude should try to please their parents and gain their approval by showing them sincere respect and serving them willingly.[219]

> *Your Lord decrees that you worship only Him and be good to (your) parents. If one or both of them reach old age with you, do not say even a single word of contempt to or chide them, but speak to them in terms of honor. Lower unto them the wing of humility out of mercy, and say: "My Lord, have mercy on them, as they took care of me when I was young." Your Lord knows best what is in your minds (hearts). If you are righteous, He is All-Forgiving to those who are patient.*[220]

You who are unaware of filial responsibility toward parents, whose house contains an elderly parent, a helpless and invalid relative, or a brother or sister in faith unable to earn a living. Heed these verses and see how they insist in five ways that you show filial affection.

As paternal affection for children is a sublime reality of worldly life, filial gratitude is a most urgent and heavy duty. Parents lovingly sacrifice their lives for their children. Given this, children who preserve their humanity and have not become monsters of ingratitude should try to please them and gain their approval by showing them sincere respect and serving them willingly. Islam assigns uncles and aunts the same honorable value as parents.

Know, you who neglect such duties, how terribly disgraceful and unscrupulous it is to be bored with their continued existence and to hope for their deaths. Know this and come to your senses! Understand what an injustice it is to desire the deaths of those who sacrificed their lives for you.

O you immersed in earning your livelihood! Know that your disabled relative, whom you consider a burden, is a means of blessing and abun-

[218] *The Gleams*, "The Twenty-sixth Gleam", p. 356.
[219] *The Letters*, "The Twenty-first Letter", pp. 275–277.
[220] *Suratu'l-Isra'*, 17:23–25.

dance. Never complain about the difficulty of making a living, for were it not for the blessing and abundance bestowed upon you due to them, you would face even more hardship.

I swear by God that this is a reality that even my devil and evil-commanding soul accept. All existence can see that the infinitely Merciful and Compassionate Creator of Majesty and Munificence sends children here along with their sustenance: their mother's breast milk. He sends sustenance for the elderly, who are like children and even more worthy and needy of compassion, in the form of blessing and unseen, immaterial abundance. He does not load their sustenance onto mean, greedy people.

The truth expressed in: *"God is the All-Providing, the Possessor of Strength and the Steadfast,"*[221] and *"How many an animate creature bears not its own provision, but God provides for it and you,"*[222] is proclaimed by all living creatures through the tongue of their disposition. So not only is the sustenance of elderly relatives sent in the form of blessings, but also that of pets, created as friends to people who feed and take care of them.

O people, you are the creature most esteemed, noble, and worthy-of-respect. Among people, believers are the most perfect. Among believers, the helpless and elderly are the most worthy and needy of respect and compassion. Among the helpless and elderly, relatives deserve more affection, love, and service than others. Among relatives, parents are the most truthful confidants and the most intimate companions. If an animal is a means of blessing and abundance when it stays as a guest in your house, consider how invaluable a means of blessing and mercy your elderly parents are if they stay with you. The following Tradition shows what an important means for removing calamities they are: "Were it not for the elderly with their bent backs, calamities would descend on you in floods"[223]

So come to your senses. If you have been assigned a long life, you also will grow old. If you do not respect parents, then, according to the rule that one is rewarded or punished in accordance with one's action, your children will not respect you. Further, serious reflection on your afterlife shows that gaining your parents' approval and pleasing them through service is a precious provision for your afterlife. If you love this worldly life, please them so that you may lead a pleasant life. If you consider them a burden, break their easily offended hearts, and desire their deaths, you will be the object of the Qur'anic threat: *"He (She) loses both the world and*

---

[221] *Suratu'dh-Dhariyat*, 51:58.

[222] *Suratu'l-'Ankabut*, 29:60.

[223] al-Ajluni, *Kashfu'l-Khafa'*, 2:163.

the world to come."[224] So, those who wish for the All-Merciful's mercy must show mercy to those entrusted to them by God.

- **Veiling is natural for women and their innate disposition demands it.**[225]

Women are weak, gentle and delicate in nature, and feel in need of protection and help. Also, they do not want to show their age and be known to be unattractive. In addition, they are afraid of being subjected to aggression or aspersion, and do not want to be accused of unfaithfulness by their husbands. Furthermore, it is a fact that most women are made uncomfortable at, and hurt by, the gaze of men. By nature, they are fearful of men who are strangers. All these and similar other factors naturally lead them to veil themselves.

- **The substantial and strong relationship, and the love and interest between men and women do not arise only from the needs of this worldly life. Indeed, a woman is not a companion of her husband only in the world; she is his companion also in the eternal life, and he is hers. As she is so, she certainly should not attract the looks of others besides her husband, her everlasting companion, to her beauty, and should not offend him and arouse his jealousy.**[226]

How happy is the husband who sees his wife's good religious life and follows her, becoming a pious one in order not to lose her companionship in the eternal life. How happy is the wife who sees her husband's good religious life and becomes a pious, righteous one in order not to lose her eternal friend. Alas for the man who indulges in dissipation, which will lose him his righteous wife forever. How unfortunate is the woman who does not follow her God-revering, pious husband, and loses her eternal, blessed friend.

- **Happiness in family life is possible and continuous through mutual confidence, sincere respect, and love between the husband and wife. Immodest dress and indecency destroy this mutual confidence, respect, and love.**[227]

- **The main purpose for marriage is an increase in population. Immodest dress excites the carnal appetites and desires of men**

---

[224] *Suratu'l-Hajj*, 22:11.
[225] *The Gleams*, "The Twenty-fourth Gleam", p. 276.
[226] *The Gleams*, "The Twenty-fourth Gleam", p. 277.
[227] *The Gleams*, "The Twenty-fourth Gleam", p. 277.

and leads to much abuse, waste, the weakening of young generations, and a loss of strength. Besides, since it is not possible for
the continuously aroused appetites to always find satisfaction,
this also causes psychological problems, and is one of the main
causes of violence towards women.[228]

- **Women are heroes of compassion, and since the self-sacrifice
contained in this compassion means true sincerity and demands
nothing in return, this shows that women are capable of great
heroism. By developing this heroism, they can serve Islam and
the salvation of both themselves and their children in both lives.[229]**
- **There is no means other than the Islamic religious education that
will secure our happiness in the Hereafter, as well as in this
world, and save our innate elevated qualities from corruption.[230]**

If a woman sees bad conduct and faithlessness in her husband, and
just to spite her husband, breaks her loyalty to him and destroys his confidence in her, the factory of the family is utterly destroyed. The woman
should rather try her hardest to reform her husband's faults so that she
can save her friend for eternity. If she unveils herself in an attempt to
show herself to others and make herself attractive to them, she will harm
herself in every respect. For the one who abandons faithfulness suffers its
recompense in this world, too. Just as women are not like men in their
heroism of compassion and sincerity, and men cannot be equal to them in
this respect, so, too, can innocent women not compete with men in vice.

- **A lie is a word of unbelief. Unbelief is a lie, while belief or faith is
truth.[231]**

One grain of truth burns a million lies. A grain of reality destroys a castle of dreams. Truthfulness is a supreme principle, a shining jewel.

Truthfulness is the very foundation of Islam, and the core of Islamic
social life. Ostentation is a deceitful act; sycophancy and pretension are a
very mean kind of lying. Hypocrisy is the most harmful kind of lying.
Lying is slandering the Power of the All-Majestic Maker.

---

[228] *The Gleams*, "The Twenty-fourth Gleam", p. 279.
[229] *The Gleams*, "The Twenty-fourth Gleam", p. 281.
[230] *The Gleams*, "The Twenty-fourth Gleam", p. 284.
[231] *Gleams of Truth*, pp. 41, 131, 161.

With all its shades, unbelief is a lie, while belief is truthfulness. For this reason, there is an infinite distance between lying and truthfulness, so they must be kept infinitely far from each other; they can never exist together. Prophet Muhammad, upon him be peace and blessings, rose to the highest of the high through truthfulness and opened with this the treasures of the truths of belief, and the truths of the universe of creation, while Musaylima the Liar, and those like him, fell into the lowest of the low through lying. For this reason, truthfulness was the most valued and desired property in the marketplace of the social life of the Prophet's Companions. This is why they never knowingly became customers of lies or sullied themselves with false-hoods. Their justice and truthfulness became a standard in the science of *Hadith*. No one now can attain the level of the Companions.

- **Whatever you say must be true, whatever judgment you give must be right, but you have no right to voice all that is true.**[232]

If speaking the truth may cause harm, silence can be preferred; but there is never a place for lies, even if they appear to have some use. Whatever you say must be right, but you have no right to say everything that is right. For if you are not sincere in saying it, it may cause an evil result, and thus right comes to serve wrong.

- **Take what is clear and untroubled, leave what is turbid and dis-tressing. See the good side of things, so that you will have good thoughts. Know things to be good and think of them as good, so that you will find pleasure in life.**[233]

- **In life, hope and thinking well of things is life itself; boredom and distress are the teachers of dissipation; despair, pessimism and evil-suspicion or thinking ill of others are the destroyers of hap-piness and killers of life.**[234]

Despair is a most terrible disease which has infiltrated the heart of the Muslim world. Muslims have found a pretext for their laziness in one another's indifference and loss of energy, saying, "Everyone is bad like me," or "Has the reformation of things been left to me?" and abandoned Islamic zeal and the responsibility to serve Islam, which is required by belief. We should smash its head with *"Do not despair of God's Mercy!"*[235]

---

[232] *Gleams of Truth*, pp. 42.
[233] *Gleams of Truth*, pp. 42.
[234] *Gleams of Truth*, pp. 16, 42, 71.
[235] *Suratu'z-Zumar*, 39:53.

and break its waist with the truth of the Islamic principle, "If something cannot be obtained entirely, it is not to be abandoned entirely."

Despair is the most terrible disease, a cancer, for nations. It blocks the way to perfection and is contrary to the truth of God's pronouncement, "I am with my servant in the way he thinks of Me."[236] It is the characteristic of the ignoble, cowardly, and impotent. It can never be at one with Islamic valor and the spirit of endeavor. God willing, all Muslim peoples should go hand in hand with each other in perfect solidarity and unity, and hoist the flag of the Qur'an all over the world.

- **Backbiting means speaking about absent people in ways that would repel and annoy them if they were present. If the words are true, it is backbiting; if they are not, it is both backbiting and slander, and thus doubly loathsome. Backbiting is the weapon of the weak and the low, and the Qur'an induces an aversion to backbiting in six miraculous ways and shows how disgusting this practice is.**[237]

The verse: *"Would any of you like to eat the flesh of his dead brother?"*[238] induces an aversion to backbiting in six miraculous ways and shows how disgusting this practice is.

The *hamza* (the interrogative) at the beginning of the original Arabic sentence penetrates the verse like water, so that each word carries an interrogative accent. Thus the first word following the *hamza* asks: "Do you have no intelligence with which to ask and answer, to discriminate between good and bad, so that you cannot perceive how abominable such a thing (backbiting) is?"

The second word *like* asks: "Is your heart, with which you love or hate, so spoiled that you love such a repugnant thing?"

Third, the phrase *any of you* asks: "What has happened to your sense of social responsibility and civilized life, which derives its meaning and energy from living together as a community, that you dare to accept something so poisonous to social life?"

Fourth, the phrase *to eat the flesh* asks: "What has happened to your sense of humanity that you tear your friend to pieces with your teeth like a wild animal?"

---

[236] al-Bukhari, "Tawhid" 15; *Muslim*, "Tawba" 2, *at-Tirmidhi*, "Zuhd" 51.
[237] *The Letters*, "The Twenty-second Letter", pp. 293–294.
[238] *Suratu'l-Hujurat*, 49:12.

Fifth, the phrase *of your brother (sister)* asks: "Do you have no human tenderness, no sense of kinship, that you sink your teeth into an innocent person tied to you by many links of brotherhood or sisterhood? Do you have no intelligence that you so senselessly bite your own limbs?"

Sixth, the word *dead* asks: "Where is your conscience? Is your nature so corrupt that you commit so disgusting an act as eating the flesh of your dead brother or sister who deserves great respect?"

In its totality, this verse shows that slander and backbiting are repugnant to one's intelligence, heart, humanity, conscience, human nature, and religious and social unity. Its six degrees of condemnation in the Qur'an are very concise and precise, and restrain people from them in six miraculous ways.

- **The All-Merciful Creator's most important command is to give thanks. Proclaiming that not doing so means denying bounties, He reproaches the unthankful severely, in** Suratu'r-Rahman, **no less than thirty-one times: "Then which of your Lord's bounties do you deny?" Thanksgiving is recognized by contentment and thrift, consent and gratitude; not giving thanks is recognized by greed and waste, ingratitude and consuming without regard for what is lawful and unlawful.**[239]

Humanity has the greatest need for provision. God Almighty created humanity as a mirror to reflect His Names, as a miracle of His Power able to weigh and recognize the contents of His Mercy's treasuries, and as a vicegerent on the earth able to measure His Names' most subtle manifestations. Given this, humanity needs all kinds of material and spiritual provisions. Having such a comprehensive nature, people can attain the highest of the high (being creation's "best pattern") only through thanksgiving. Without it, they commit a most dire sin, and fall to the lowest rank.

- **The All-Compassionate Creator demands thankfulness in return for the bounties He has bestowed on humankind. Wastefulness is contrary to thankfulness and implies a slighting of the bounty in a manner that will cause loss. Frugality, however, means worthwhile respect for the bounty.**[240]

---

[239] *The Letters*, "The Twenty-eighth Letter", pp. 371–373.
[240] *The Gleams*, "The Nineteenth Gleam", pp. 195–196.

Truly, frugality is both a form of thankfulness and respect for the Divine mercy that comes in the form of bounties, as well as being a certain cause of abundance, an abstinence-like means of health for the body, a source of honor that rescues one from the disgrace of what is nothing more than begging, and an effective means of feeling and tasting the pleasure in bounties that some may not find delectable. As for wastefulness, since it means running counter to these instances of wisdom, it has grave consequences.

- **"One who observes economy does not suffer a shortage in livelihood for their family."**[241]/[242]

- **Out of His perfect Munificence, God Almighty makes a poor person aware of the pleasure of His bounty the same as a rich one, and a deprived one the same as a king. Indeed, the pleasure a poor person receives from a dry piece of black bread due to satisfaction and frugality is greater than that a rich one receives from the choicest baklava he eats with a lack of appetite that comes from excess and frequent eating.**[243]

It is really surprising that some extravagant, self-indulgent people accuse the thrifty of being stingy. God forbid! Frugality is dignity and true generosity. Stinginess and meanness are the hidden, true side of the apparent nobility of the people of extravagance and self-indulgence.

- **Wastefulness causes greed, and greed has three results: discontentment, disappointment and loss, and the damaging of sincerity in the deeds related to the afterlife.**[244]

The first is discontent. Discontent destroys enthusiasm for work and endeavor, and causes complaints instead of thankfulness, and leads to laziness. It also causes the discontent person to pursue easy gain, even though this is unlawful, instead of a lesser gain that is legitimate. Such a person loses his credit, and even his honor.

The second result of greed is disappointment and loss. Greedy people miss their target, subject themselves to disregard, and are deprived of assistance. They are a confirmation of the proverb, "The greedy person is condemned to disappointment and loss."

241 Ahmad ibn Hanbal, *al-Musnad*, 1:447.
242 *The Gleams*, "The Nineteenth Gleam", p. 198.
243 *The Gleams*, "The Nineteenth Gleam", p. 200.
244 *The Gleams*, "The Nineteenth Gleam", pp. 203–204.

The third result of greed is that it damages sincerity and injures the deeds done for the sake of the Hereafter. If a pious, righteous person is greedy, they will seek the acceptance and respect of people. One who considers the acceptance and respect of people cannot have complete sincerity or purity of intention. This result is worthy of great attention.

- **Greed, a great disease that is harmful to Islam's individual and social life, causes disappointment, sickness, humiliation, deprivation, and misery, while seeking one's provisions with contentment and trust in God is a means to tranquillity, and displays its good effects everywhere.**[245]

- **Greed causes deprivation, especially for believers; trusting God the All-Providing, and contentment are the means to Divine mercy.**[246]

Divine Wisdom arranges everything according to a certain deliberation. For example, a loaf of bread is made only after tilling the field, harvesting the crop, taking the grain to a mill, and baking the loaf. If we do not comply with this deliberation, and neglect to follow all the arranged steps, we cannot achieve the desired result.

Just as it takes a year to obtain or produce a loaf of bread following certain steps, Divine Wisdom arranges everything according to a certain deliberation. And just as with the loaf of bread, if you do not comply with this deliberation and neglect to follow all the arranged steps, you cannot achieve the desired result.

Also, think of a person who is greedy of sleep. Being over-anxious to sleep and striving to do so in the middle of the night causes one to lose sleep and reach the morning wakeful. Again, there are two beggars, one greedy and importunate, the other contented, shy, and retiring. It is to the latter that one wants to give charity, not to the former. Thus does the Divine order urge or punish. There are many other examples like these, demonstrating the universality of this law.

- **God is with the patient; He helps the patient and makes them successful, so patience is a means of relief. Whereas greed is subject to disappointment and loss.**[247]

---

[245] *The Letters*, "The Twenty-second Letter", pp. 289–290.
[246] *Gleams of Truth*, pp. 108–109; *The Letters*, "The Twenty-second Letter", pp. 289–291.
[247] *The Letters*, "The Twenty-third Letter", pp. 299–300.

As mentioned above, God's Name the All-Wise requires the establishment of an order, a definite procedure, for things to come into existence. Impatient people are not deliberate—either they overleap and fall, or omit some steps and fail to reach their goal. This is why greed causes deprivation, and patience is a key to solving problems. As a proverb says: "Greed is subject to disappointment and loss, but patience is a means of relief."

God Almighty helps the patient and makes them successful. There are three kinds of patience, as follows:

- Piety and God-consciousness, or resisting the carnal soul's temptations and avoiding sins. Such patient people are included in: *"God is with the God-conscious and pious."*[248]

- Endurance during misfortune by patient reliance on and total submission to God, Who numbers the patient among those he loves best: *"God loves those who rely on Him,"*[249] and *"God loves the patient."*[250] Impatience implies complaining about God by criticizing His Acts, accusing His Mercy, and disapproving of His Wisdom. A weak, helpless person should not wail over misfortune, but should complain to—not of—Him, just as Prophet Ya'qub (Jacob) did: *"I complain of my anguish and sorrow unto God."*[251] It is futile and even harmful to encourage self-pity and complaining.

- Insistence on worshipping God. This elevates the patient person to the highest spiritual rank, that of being one of God's beloved servants.

- **Just as modesty or humility is a praiseworthy quality which superficially resembles self-degradation or humiliation, but which is completely different, and dignity is another praiseworthy quality that is apparently similar to haughtiness, but utterly different, frugality, which was among the exalted virtues of the Prophets and is one of the foundations of the universal order based on Divine wisdom, has nothing to do with stinginess, which is a mixture of baseness, meanness, greed, and avarice.**[252]

What follows is an incident corroborating this:

'Abdullah ibn 'Umar, may God be pleased with him, who was one of the most distinguished scholars among the Prophet's Companions, once had

---

[248] *Suratu'l-Baqara*, 2:194.

[249] *Sura Al 'Imran*, 3:159.

[250] *Sura Al 'Imran*, 3:146.

[251] *Sura Yusuf*, 12:86.

[252] *The Gleams*, "The Nineteenth Gleam", pp. 201–202.

a heated dispute in the marketplace over something worth only a few *dirhams* for the sake of economy and trustworthiness, which is one of the pillars of commercial life. A Companion saw him, and thought the manner of the son of the illustrious Caliph 'Umar, who had ruled over a third of the old world, was an odd sort of stinginess. He followed Ibn 'Umar to his house. He witnessed that the illustrious Imam stayed for some time with a poor man who was standing at his door. Then he saw him again sitting for a while with another poor man whom he encountered at another door of his house. Curious now, the Companion, who was watching from afar, advanced and asked the two poor men, "The Imam halted for a while with you. What did he do?" Each of them replied, "He gave me a gold piece." The Companion thought to himself, "All-Glorified is God! How is it that he heatedly argued over a few *dirhams* in the marketplace and gave away coins worth hundreds of *dirhams* in complete happiness and contentment without letting anyone know?"

He left and found 'Abdullah ibn 'Umar, and said, "O Imam! Explain it to me! In the market you did that, but in your house you did this!" The Imam replied, "In the marketplace it was what is required by economy, good sense, and the preservation of reliability and truthfulness, upon which commercial life is based. It was not stinginess. And what I did in my house was due to compassion, magnanimity, and the duty of brotherhood. The former was not stinginess, nor was the latter excessiveness."

The following words of Imam Abu Hanifa are an explanation of this fact: "There can be no excess in doing good, as there is no good in wastefulness."[253]

- **The door to** ijtihad **is open, but certain obstacles block the way to it. For instance, during a winter storm or a flood, when even smaller holes are closed, to open new and larger ones is unreasonable and dangerous. Likewise, under the onslaught of a mighty flood, making openings in a wall to repair it leads to being drowned. So, at the time of the un-Islamic and even anti-Islamic practices, the onslaught of foreign un-Islamic customs, the legion of religious innovations and the destruction of misguidance, any attempt to make** ijtihad **in a manner to open new holes and invasion routes in the citadel of Islam is a crime against Islam.**[254]

[253] al-Ghazzali, *Ihya'u 'Ulumi'd-Din*, 1:262; al-Qurtubi, *al-Jami' li-Akhami'l-Qur'an*, 7:110.
[254] *The Words*, "The Twenty-seventh Word", p. 499.

- Ninety percent of the Shari'ah consists of the essential and incontestable rules of Islam, and may be likened to diamond pillars. The remaining ten percent, which is open to interpretation and is to be determined by Islam's legal authorities, may be likened to gold pieces. Ninety diamond pillars cannot be put under the protection of ten gold pieces. Rather, the religious books and judicial arguments and judgments should help us to understand the Qur'an better. They should serve as binoculars to see and as mirrors to reflect its meanings, not to veil or replace it.[255]

- The essentials of Islam are not subject to ijtihad. They are specified and definite, and are like basic food and sustenance without which life is impossible. What must be done at the time they are abandoned and neglected is to strive to restore and revitalize them with all our strength. The principles which early generations of Islam established for deduction of new rules from the main legal sources and the rules they deduced with perfect authority and pure intention are adequate for almost all times and places. Therefore, abandoning them and seeking new ones in an indulgent and fanciful fashion is a harmful innovation and a betrayal of Islam.[256]

- The tendency towards expansion in a person who sincerely confirms and completely complies with the essentials and the basic injunctions of Islam is a tendency toward perfection. Yet the same tendency in another who is outside the sphere of obedience to Islamic essentials and who is indifferent to them is a tendency towards corruption and destruction. The right course of action during times of "storms" and "earthquakes" is not to open the door of ijtihad—that is to attempt to derive "new" laws from the Qur'an and Sunnah; rather, it is to close the doors and shutter the windows (against innovations). Those who are heedless and indifferent in belief and the practice of Religion should not be indulged with dispensations; rather, they should be warned strictly, and aroused with heavier responsibilities and greater care.[257]

- Various products are sought in the marketplace according to season and demand. This is also true of humanity's social life and civ-

[255] *Gleams of Truth*, p. 6.
[256] *The Words*, "The Twenty-seventh Word", p. 500.
[257] *Gleams of Truth*, p. 16–17.

ilization as well. During the early generations of Islam, the most sought-after "product" was learning from the Word of the Creator of the heavens and the earth what He approves of and wants from us, and how to obtain eternal happiness in the world of the Hereafter, the doors of which had been opened so widely by the light of Prophethood and the Qur'an that they could not be closed. However, in our age people seek to secure their worldly life, and pursue materialistic philosophies and politics, and the conditions of modern life scatter minds and hearts, which are estranged from spiritual issues, and divide efforts and cares. Therefore, capacities have grown too dull to qualify for being a *mujtahid*.[258]

- It is an established principle of the methodology of Islamic jurisprudence (*Fiqh*) that one who is not a trained and qualified faqih—a jurist, a specialist in the Islamic Law—even though he may be an expert in the methodology of *Fiqh*, is not counted among the faqihs. Such a person is only an ordinary person in relation to *faqihs*.[259]

- One qualified to make *ijtihad* may deduce a new law for himself, but he cannot be a law-giver.[260]

Anyone who has the competence to practice *ijtihad* may deduce new laws for himself in matters about which there are no explicit verdicts in the Qur'an or Sunnah; these are binding on that person, but not on others. He cannot make laws and call on the Muslim Community to obey them. His conclusions are regarded as belonging to the Shari'ah, but they cannot be included in the Shari'ah as being binding on all Muslims. He may be a *mujtahid*, but he cannot be a law-giver. It is only the consensus of the majority of scholars which legislates in the name of the Shari'ah. The first condition for calling on others to accept an idea is acceptance by the majority. Otherwise, such a call is innovation and must be rejected; it is kept in the throat, and must not be uttered!

- So long as there is no evidence to its being contrary to the basic principles and truths of the Religion, the general acceptance of Muslim people counts as a sort of proof in the framework of 'urf or ma'ruf (things generally accepted and practiced by the majority of Muslims).[261]

[258] *The Words*, "The Twenty-seventh Word", p. 501–502.
[259] *The Reasonings*, "The First Part", p. 25.
[260] *Gleams of Truth*, p. 34.
[261] *The Gleams*, "The Sixteenth Gleam", p. 147.

- **The majority of common people (the masses) are drawn by the sacredness of authority, rather than the strength of proofs.**[262]
- **The religious judgments and deductions cannot be founded upon changing conditions and realities; they are rather based on constant facts.**[263]
- **After the Prophets, the Companions of Prophet Muhammad, peace and blessings be upon him, who constitute the best community among humankind, are the most virtuous people.**[264]

The Qur'an declares about the Companions:

> Muhammad is the Messenger of God; and those who are in his company are firm and unyielding against the unbelievers, and compassionate among themselves. You see them (constant in the Prayer) bowing down and prostrating, seeking favor with God and His approval and good pleasure. Their marks are on their faces, traced by prostration. This is their description in the Torah; and their description in the Gospel: like a seed that has sprouted its shoot, then it has strengthened it, and then risen firmly on its stem, delighting the sowers (with joy and wonder), that through them He fills the unbelievers with rage. God has promised all those among them who believe and do good, righteous deeds forgiveness (to bring unforeseen blessings) and a tremendous reward.[265]
>
> You are the best community ever brought forth for (the good of) humankind, enjoining and promoting what is right and good, and forbidding and trying to prevent evil, and (this you do because) you believe in God. If only the People of the Book believed (as you do), this would be sheer good for them. Among them there are believers, but most of them are transgressors.[266]

There are some narrations from the holy Prophet, upon him be peace and blessings, that at a time when religious innovation is widespread and heresy is on the attack, some righteous God-conscious believers who try to conform to God's laws of Religion and life may attain to the Companions' rank or even be more virtuous. The authentic ones among such narrations refer to particular virtues, not virtuousness in general. A less vir-

---

[262] *Gleams of Truth*, p. 6.
[263] *Barla Lahikası* (Addendum of Barla), p. 366.
[264] *The Words*, "The Twenty-seventh Word", pp. 506–507.
[265] *Suratu'l-Fath*, 48:29.
[266] *Al 'Imran*, 3:110.

tuous person may excel a more virtuous one in certain particular virtues. As regards general superiority, however, no one can equal or better the Companions, whom God describes as having praiseworthy qualities, and whom the Torah and Gospel predicted and praise highly.

- **Companionship with the Greatest of creation, upon him be peace and blessings, and being taught by him is such an elixir that one honored with it for even a minute may receive as much enlightenment as that which another person receives only after years of spiritual journeying. Companionship and the Prophet's education cause one to be "colored" with the Prophet's "color" and receive his reflections. Following the Prophet and being illumined by the greatest light of the greatest of Prophets enables a person to rise to the highest spiritual level. This is like a great king's servant who, through servanthood and absolute allegiance to the king, reaches the rank that an ordinary king cannot.**[267]

His conversation and companionship was such an enlightening elixir that when a wild and hard-hearted Bedouin who had murdered his daughter by burying her alive was honored with an hour of his companionship, he would become so compassionate and tender-hearted that he no longer even trod on an ant.

- **Most of the Companions attained the highest degrees of human perfection under the guidance and instruction of the greatest Teacher of creation, upon him be peace and blessings. Since Islam revealed good and truth in their full beauty and evil and falsehood in their full ugliness, witnessing the Beloved of God as the highest example, sample and herald of human perfections, truth, right, and good, their pure characters impelled them to exert all their strength and effort to follow him.**[268]

- **The Companions, whose accomplishments proved them to be the community who had he greatest capacities in all levels of life in human history and whose senses were awakened to the utmost degree and faculties fully alert, experienced and performed the Islamic rituals in the highest degree and derived their shares in them with all their faculties.**[269]

---

[267] *The Words*, "The Twenty-seventh Word", p. 507.
[268] *The Words*, "The Twenty-seventh Word", pp. 507–508.
[269] *The Words*, "The Twenty-seventh Word", p. 509.

In the mighty social revolutions brought about by the Qur'an's lights, opposites were completely separated from each other. Evil with all its darkness, details, and consequences and good and perfection with all their lights and results stood face to face. Thus in that exciting, stimulating time, all levels of the meaning of words and phrases of recitation, praise, and glorification were revealed in their full freshness and originality. This stirred up and awakened the feelings and spiritual faculties of those fully experiencing all stages of this mighty revolution, and even caused such senses as fancy and imagining to wake up fully, receive, and absorb these meanings based on their own perception.

Besides, everything in the name of Islam was new and ever fresh for the Companions. Therefore they tasted them with all their faculties in all their originality and benefited from them to the utmost degree. For these and some other reasons, no one is ever able to reach them.

- **Compared to sainthood, Prophethood is like the sun in relation to its images in mirrors. Thus, however much superior Prophethood is to sainthood, the Companions, the servants of Prophethood and the planets around that sun, must be and indeed are comparatively superior to the righteous, saintly ones. And to what extent Prophet Muhammad, upon him be peace and blessings, is greater than all the other Prophets, his Companions are greater than all other communities to the same extent.**[270]

- **No one can equal the Companions in** ijtihad **(deducing God's ordinances and what He approves of from the Qur'an and Sunnah).**[271]

For the mighty Divine revolution at that time sought to learn and understand God's commandments and the things of which He approves. All minds were concentrated upon deducing Divine ordinances, and all hearts wondered what their Lord wanted from them. All events and circumstances impelled people towards that goal. Conversations, discussions, and stories taught Divine ordinances and what He approves of in His servants. These all perfected the Companions' capacities and enlightened their minds.

Moreover, since their potentials to make deductions and exercise *ijtihad* were as ready to ignite as matches, even if we had their level of intelligence and capacity we could not attain in ten or even a hundred years

---

[270] *The Words*, "The Twenty-seventh Word", p. 509.
[271] *The Words*, "The Twenty-seventh Word", p. 509–510.

the level of deduction and *ijtihad* they attained in a day or a month. For at present, people consider worldly happiness rather than eternal happiness and so concentrate on worldly aims. Since the struggle to make a living and not relying on God have bewildered and stupefied spirits, and naturalistic and materialistic philosophy have blinded intellects, the social environment only scatters and confuses people's minds and capacities in exercising *ijtihad*.

- **No one can reach the Companions in merits of deeds, rewards for actions, and virtues pertaining to the Hereafter.**[272]

A soldier guarding a dangerous point under perilous conditions for an hour can gain the merits of a year of worship, and a soldier who achieves martyrdom in one minute can attain the rank of a type of sainthood that others can reach only after at least forty days. The Companions' services in establishing Islam, spreading the Qur'an's commandments, and challenging the world for Islam's sake were so meritorious and rewarding that others cannot gain in one year the merits they acquired in a minute. It can even be said that every minute of theirs equals the minute of that soldier martyred while in that sacred service. Every hour of theirs is like the hour of watch of a self-sacrificing soldier under perilous conditions.

- **Since the Companions were the first line in establishing Islam and disseminating the Qur'an's lights, according to the rule of "The cause is like the doer," they share in all Muslims' rewards, regardless of time or place.**[273]

Muslims invoke God's peace and blessings on the Companions, saying: "O God, bestow blessings and peace on our master Muhammad, his Family, and Companions," thereby showing that the Companions share in all Muslims' rewards (without causing any reduction in the Muslims' rewards). Muslims in all times also pray for them that God may be pleased with them.

Just as an insignificant characteristic in a tree's roots assumes a great form in its branches and is larger than the largest branch, just as a small amount at the beginning becomes a large mass, and just as a little point in the center forms a wide angle in the circumference, the Companions' actions were multiplied and their service acquired a huge consequence. They formed the roots of the blessed, illustrious tree of Islam, were

[272] *The Words*, "The Twenty-seventh Word", p. 511.
[273] *The Words*, "The Twenty-seventh Word", p. 511.

among the Muslim community's leaders and first in establishing its traditions, and were the nearest to the center of the Sun of Prophethood and
the Lamp of Truth, upon him be peace and blessings.

- **Even though some of the Companions, may God be pleased with
  them, indulged in the world and enjoyed it to great extents, their
  interest in the world was due to its facets that look to the Hereafter and the manifestation of God's Names.**[274]

As mentioned before, loving the two facets of the world that look to
the Hereafter and manifest God's Names is a means of perfection. The
more profound one is in appreciating and loving these two facets of the
world, the deeper one is in worship and knowledge of God. The Companions concerned themselves with these two facets. Considering the world
an arable field of the Hereafter, they sowed it with seeds to grow in the
Hereafter. They saw all creatures as mirrors reflecting the Divine Names
and observed them lovingly. The world is evil in its mortal facet which
looks to our animal appetites.

- **The Shari'ah has two spheres: individual rights and public law.
  This latter group contains Islam's "public symbols or rituals" or
  "banners." Even the minor ones among them, such as *adhan*, are
  just as important as Islam's most fundamental matters. Also, the
  Shari'ah matters related to worship are independent of human
  reason, and the cause for their performance is God's command.
  The Divine wisdom for their legislation and the legislation of the
  public symbols cannot be restricted to their known benefits.**[275]

- **Islam's fundamentals and incontrovertible principles are not
  subject to dispute or alteration. The commands and principles of
  the Shari'ah cannot be changed, for they are like the body or at
  least the skin of Islam's essentials—they are organically molded
  to each other in such a way that they cannot be separated.**[276]

- **Historical arguments against (the historical) Christianity do not
  work with Islam, for Islam protects the people and has been a
  shelter and stronghold for the masses; has brought no internal
  wars of religion; constantly urges people to reason and investi-**

---

[274] *The Words*, "The Twenty-seventh Word", p. 513.
[275] *The Letters*, "The Twenty-ninth Letter", pp. 389–390.
[276] *The Letters*, "The Twenty-ninth Letter", p. 419.

gate; gives people of reasoning and knowledge a very high and important position, never demanding blind imitation and faith; and first of all, Islam is a pure monotheistic religion that rejects means and intermediaries, breaks egotism and rejects all false lordships from the carnal soul to despotic rules and nature.[277]

- The Shari'ah has, from one perspective, two kinds of commands. One kind consists of those which the Shari'ah itself has legislated; the other kind comprises those which the Shari'ah has amended and left their best form or abolishment to future developments in human social life. Slavery falls in this second category.[278]

- If the existence of numerous ills and cures is a rightful reality, the multiplicity of the fields of specialty in medicine is right. The variation of needs and foods is right, and right becomes diverse. The multiplication of capacities and education is right, and this right will also multiply. The same water functions in five different ways when given to five different people. It will cure the first person's illness, and so it is necessary. It will be like poison for the second person, and is therefore medically forbidden. It will be slightly harmful for the third person, and therefore should be avoided. It will be beneficial for the fourth person, and thus medicine advises it. It will be neither harmful nor beneficial for the fifth person, and because he can drink it with good health it is medically permissible. Thus all five approaches are valid. Similarly, Divine Wisdom requires that Divine ordinances of secondary importance should differ according to time, conditions and those who follow them. This results in different schools of law, all of which are right.[279]

---

[277] *The Letters*, "The Twenty-ninth Letter", p. 420.
[278] *Gleams of Truth*, p. 178.
[279] *The Words*, "The Twenty-seventh Word", p. 504; *Gleams of Truth*, pp. 56–57.

Part 6

_____

GENERAL PRINCIPLES RELATED TO KNOWLEDGE OF GOD, ISLAMIC SPIRITUAL LIFE, AND "SUFISM"

General Principles Related to Knowledge of God, Islamic Spiritual Life, and "Sufism"

- **Sufism** (Tasawwuf) **is a lovely, light-giving, spiritual truth known under various terms:** tariqah **(spiritual order or way), sainthood** (vilayah—**being God's friend), initiation, and following a spiritual order or way** (sayr u suluk). **Sufism is the name of the spiritual way by which initiates** (salik) **seek knowledge of God and attain full perception of the truths of belief and the Qur'an. This way aims to elevate initiates, at the end of the spiritual journeying and under the auspices of the Prophet's Ascension, to the rank of the perfect person** (al-insanu'l-kamil).[1]

- **Sainthood proves Divine Messengership, and the way or spiritual order** (tariqah) **testifies to the Shari'ah. Saints experience the truths of belief communicated by the Messenger with the certainty of seeing, and confirm them through the witnessing of their hearts and the spiritual pleasure they derive. Such confirmation proves the truth of Divine Messengership.**[2]

Sufis are convinced, through the pleasure and enlightenment received and the ability of spiritual discovery acquired, that the Shari'ah's commands and principles are of Divine origin, and true. As sainthood and Sufism prove the truth of Messengership and the Shari'ah, they also express Islam's perfections, are among the sources of its light, are means for humanity's spiritual progress, and serve as sources of enlightenment through their connection with Islam.

---

[1]   *The Letters*, "The Twenty-ninth Letter", p. 429.
[2]   *The Letters*, "The Twenty-ninth Letter", pp. 430–431.

Despite this great truth, some deviant sects deny it. Themselves deprived of Sufism's lights, they want to deprive others of them, too. Unfortunately, certain superficial or literalist scholars among the *Ahlu's-Sunnah wa'l-Jama'ah* also oppose it due to some Sufis' abuses and mistakes. But every order or system has its faults! If incompetent and unqualified people are admitted, some abuse will occur. But God Almighty will show His Lordship's justice in the Hereafter by judging what people have done. If one's good or evil deeds weigh more, God Almighty will reward or punish them accordingly. Further, He judges good and evil deeds according to quality, not quantity. Thus one good deed could outweigh 1,000 evil ones and cause them to be forgiven.

Since this is the way of Divine Justice, Sufism should not be condemned because a few of its members abuse it. Also, following a *tariqah* or a spiritual way according to the Sunnah is always greater than its evils. A most decisive proof of this is that Sufis preserve their belief at the most critical times when the people of misguidance attack all religious values.

Sufism must not be condemned because of the evils of some self-proclaimed orders, or some schools that have broken with the sphere of piety—or even with Islam itself. Apart from its very significant religious, spiritual, and Hereafter-related fruits, Sufism has always exerted a strong influence on developing, and then causing, the sacred bond of Muslim unity.

- **The way of sainthood is paradoxical: easy and difficult, short and long, precious and desirable yet also risky, broad and narrow. Such paradoxes sometimes cause adherents to drown or lose their way. Sometimes people turn back and cause others to deviate.**[3]

Sufis can follow either of two ways: travelling in the inner world or in the outer world. Members of the first group begin from the carnal soul and head straight for the heart. They pierce and smash egotism and self-conceit and, by making a way through the heart, reach the truth. Then they set off in the outer world to witness the truth that they have seen in the inner world. Most spiritual orders that invoke God's Names silently follow this way.

The other travelers start from the outer world and, after observing the manifestations of God's Names and Attributes in all objects, enter the inner world. In their hearts, they witness to some extent the same lights

---

3   *The Letters*, "The Twenty-ninth Letter", pp. 431–434.

that they observed in the outer world and follow the quickest way into the heart. They attain their goal only after perceiving that the heart is the mirror of God, the Eternally Besought One.

If followers of the first way cannot destroy their carnal souls, abandon whim and fancy, and break egotism and self-conceit, they abandon thanksgiving for self-pride, and then vanity. If they are in a state of ecstatic love, or are spiritually intoxicated because of feeling attracted by God, they make exaggerated claims, such as disregarding God's threats and chastisements, belittling Paradise, or seeing their own rank as above everybody else's. And so they harm themselves and others. Those captivated by such a state should judge according to the Shari'ah. They should follow the guiding principles laid down by the scholars of religious methodology, as well as the instructions of such scholarly saints of meticulous research and truth-seeking as Imam al-Ghazzali and Imam Rabbani. Also, they should reproach their carnal souls continually, ascribing to them nothing but defect, helplessness, and poverty.

- **One important Sufi school is that of the Unity of Being (**Wahdatu'l-Wujud**). This doctrine almost denies the universe's essential existence in the name of the Necessarily Existent Being, and even regards apparently existing creatures as imagined mirrors reflecting the Divine Names' manifestations.**[4]

This school is based on an important truth: In the eyes of saints of very high ranks and ecstasies, and due to their strong conviction of and absorption in the Necessarily Existent Being's existence, the existence of contingent beings is so insignificant that, in the Name of God, they deny the existence of all creatures, which seem to them no more than mere illusions.

This doctrine has certain risks, the foremost being that there are six fundamentals of belief or faith: Belief in God, the Day of Judgment, angels, Prophets, Divine Scriptures, and Divine Destiny. Each of these requires the existence of contingencies. As these fundamentals are substantial, they cannot be based on illusion or imagination. Thus saints belonging to this school should not act according to its requirements when returning to the world of realities from a state of spiritual intoxication. Being based

---

[4] *The Letters*, "The Twenty-ninth Letter", pp. 434–435.

on the experiences of the heart, and on spiritual pleasure and ecstasy, this school should not be regarded as rational or scientific.

In addition, such experiences and pleasures should not be mentioned in this world of realities, for this school is not in accordance with the intellectual principles, scientific laws, and theological rules coming from the Qur'an and the Sunnah. As the Four Rightly-Guided Caliphs and the greatest jurists and righteous scholars of Islam's early centuries did not mention or suggest it, it cannot be the most exalted school of Sufism. Although it is considerably exalted, it has defects. It is important but risky, difficult but very pleasant. Those who enter it for its pleasures do not like to leave it and, if they are haughty, suppose it to have the highest rank.

One important risk is as follows: The way envisioned by the Unity of Being is a sound way based on direct experience of some elite among exalted saints who, in a state of spiritual intoxication, transcend causality, renounce everything except God, and have nothing to do with contingency. But to offer it as a way to those immersed in causality and fond of this world, who want to cling to material and natural philosophy, would cause them to drown in the swamp of materialism and naturalism. In other words, it would make them deviate from the truth. Those who love this world and are enveloped within causality wish to give a kind of permanence to this transient world. Unwilling to renounce the beloved (the world), they use this doctrine to imagine an unimagined eternity for this world, even going so far as to deny God in the world's name.

Materialism is now so widespread that some people ascribe everything to matter. Even if some distinguished believers may assert the Unity of Being on the grounds of the insignificance of material existence, it is highly probable that materialists may adopt this concept on matter's behalf, in the form of monism, naturalism, or pantheism, although the Unity of Being is the school furthest removed from such currents or philosophies. Its adherents are so deeply absorbed in Divine Existence through their strong belief that they deny the universe's existence on its behalf, whereas materialists, pantheists, and monists attribute existence exclusively to matter or other created things, and deny God in the universe's name. How far are the latter from the former!

- **The most beautiful, straightest, and brightest way of sainthood is following the Sunnah and obeying the Shari'ah as strictly as possible.**[5]

Such adherence transforms one's ordinary deeds, actions, and natural movements into a form of worship. It reminds people of the Sunnah and the Shari'ah and causes them to think of the Prophet, which in turn calls God Almighty to mind. This remembrance gives a kind of peace and contentment. Thus, one's whole life can be counted as spent in continuous worship. In addition to being the broadest highway, it is the way of the Companions and their righteous followers, who truly represented the succession to the Prophetic mission.

- **Prophethood is such an elevated rank that when compared to sainthood, a minuscule manifestation of Prophethood is superior to a great manifestation of sainthood.**[6]

- **The most comprehensive, direct, and safest of the ways leading to God Almighty, a way defined by and depending on the Qur'an, is based on our perception and admission of our innate impotence, helplessness, and poverty before God's Might and Riches, and on affection and reflective thought.**[7]

This way is as sure as the way of love. It might even be safer, for it elevates you so as to be loved by God on account of sincere devotion to Him. Our perception and admission of our impotence leads us to the Divine Name the All-Merciful. Affection is more effective than love, and leads to the Name the All-Compassionate. Reflective thought is brighter and more comprehensive than love, and leads to the Name the All-Wise. Let it not be misunderstood. This way means and demands the sincere admission of one's innate impotence, poverty, and sinfulness before God; it does not mean making a show of one's impotence, poverty, and sinfulness before people.

Our way consists of four steps and is the truth (*haqiqah*), rather than a Sufi way (*tariqah*). It is the Shari'ah. Its fundamental principles consist in following the Sunnah, performing the religious obligations, avoiding the major sins, performing the prescribed Prayers properly and carefully,

---

5   *The Letters*, "The Twenty-ninth Letter", pp. 435–436.
6   *The Gleams*, "The Fourth Gleam", p. 42.
7   *The Words*, "The Twenty-sixth Word", pp. 494–496.

and saying words of praise, glorification, and exaltation of God after every Prayer. It consists of the following four steps:

- The first step is expressed by: *"Do not justify and hold yourselves pure."*[8]

- The second step is indicated by: *"Be not like those who are oblivious of God—and so He has made them oblivious of their own selves."*[9]

- The third step is pointed to by: *"Whatever good happens to you is from God; whatever evil befalls you is from yourself."*[10]

- The fourth step is shown by: *"Everything is perishable (and so perishing) except His Face (and His good pleasure)."*[11]

The following is a brief explanation of these four steps.

First step: We should never regard ourselves as infallible and sinless. As human beings, we love our own selves before all else, so much so that we sacrifice anything for ourselves. We praise ourselves as if praising an object of worship, and hold ourselves free of faults and defects. We exploit the faculties given to us to praise and thank God by using them to glorify ourselves and resemble him who is mentioned in: *"Who has taken his lusts and fancies for his deity."*[12] We praise, rely on, and admire ourselves. To be purified of such attitudes, we should never hold ourselves pure; instead, we should regard ourselves as fallible and susceptible to error.

Second step: Contrary to what the verse, *"Be not like those who are oblivious of God—and so He has made them oblivious of their own selves,"* teaches, we are oblivious and unaware of ourselves. We do not want to remember death, while we always consider others mortal. We hold back when confronting hardship and rendering service, but believe that we should be the first one rewarded when it is time to collect the wages. Purifying ourselves at this step involves carrying out our responsibilities, being prepared for death, and forgetting ourselves when it comes to pleasures, ambitions, and collecting wages.

---

[8] *Suratu'n-Najm*, 53:32.
[9] *Suratu'l-Hashr*, 59:19.
[10] *Suratu'n-Nisa'*, 4:79.
[11] *Suratu'l-Qasas*, 28:88.
[12] *Suratu'l-Furqan*, 25:43.

Third step: Contrary to what the verse, *"Whatever good happens to you is from God; whatever evil befalls you is from yourself,"* teaches, our evil-commanding soul always ascribes good to itself and feels conceited. In reality, we should perceive our defects, insufficiencies, impotence and poverty and then thank and praise God for whatever good we can do and whatever virtue we have. According to the meaning of, *"He is indeed prosperous who has grown it in purity,"*[13] our purification at this step consists of knowing that our perfection lies in confessing our imperfection, our power in perceiving our helplessness, and our wealth in accepting our essential poverty and inadequacy.

Fourth step: Contrary to what the verse, *"Everything is perishable except His Face (and His good pleasure),"* teaches, the carnal, evil-commanding soul considers itself completely free and existent in its own right. It even claims Lordship for itself and harbors hostile rebelliousness against its Creator, the All-Worshipped. We can save ourselves from this perilous situation only by perceiving the truth that everything, with respect to its own self, is essentially non-existent, contingent, ephemeral, and mortal. But in respect of being like a letter in a word to signify something other than itself, and in respect of being a mirror reflecting the All-Majestic Maker's Names and entrusted with various duties, it is existent, experiencing, and experienced.

Here, we can purify ourselves by perceiving that our existence lies in acknowledging our essential non-existence. If we abandon pride and egoism and recognize that we are only a mirror in which the Real Creator manifests Himself, we attain infinite existence. One who discovers the Necessarily Existent Being, the manifestations of Whose Names cause all things to come into existence, is counted as having found everything.

This way is the way of recognizing our innate impotence and poverty, as well as that of affection and reflective thought. This four-stage way leads to its objective rapidly, since it is the easiest and most direct way. Recognizing our incompetence or impotence leads us to be freed from our evil-commanding soul's influence and to rely on the All-Powerful One of Majesty alone. This way is safer than other ways, for it enables us to recognize our limits, and find within us nothing other than impotence, poverty, and defect, and it saves us from high-flown claims.

---

[13] *Suratu'sh-Shams*, 91:9.

This way is a main highway, very broad and more universal, for it allows us to attain a constant awareness of God's presence without denying or ignoring the universe's actual existence, as demanded by the followers of the Way of the Unity of Being (*Wahdatu'l-Wujud*) or the Unity of the Witnessed (*Wahdatu'sh-Shuhud*), respectively. Instead, it admits the universe's actual existence, as proclaimed in the Qur'an, but it ascribes it directly to the All-Majestic Creator. It admits that all things consist in the manifestations of Divine Names, devoted to His service, and are charged with being mirrors reflecting them. It saves us from heedlessness by allowing us to travel to Him through everything, by making us always aware of His presence.

- **Affection, one of the sweetest and most beautiful manifestations of Divine Compassion, is a kind of water of life that leads humanity to God more quickly than love.**[14]

While love for temporal beings can change into love for God only after much difficulty, affection can make one's heart sincerely devoted to God, but without as much difficulty. It is keener, purer, and more sublime than love. It is also graceful and deeply felt. In addition, affection is so comprehensive that people's affection for their own children makes them feel some affection for all children and all living beings. They can become comprehensive mirrors in which the Divine Name the All-Compassionate manifests Itself. Furthermore, affection is a sincere feeling with no ulterior motive and seeking no return. The tears caused by love demand such a return, while even the lowest type of sincere affection (such as that felt by animals for their young) proves that affection does not demand any return.

- **When the human carnal soul, like those of the Companions, is refined and purified, and is honored with and elevated through numerous varieties of worship and praise, it can be used for glorification and thanksgiving with its multiple inborn faculties. This is the way of the Companions, who were favored with all kinds and dimensions of worshipping God, using their intellects, spirits, and souls. However, the worship of the saints following a Sufi way becomes simple and one dimensional after they completely annihilate their carnal, evil-commanding soul.**[15]

---

[14] *The Letters*, "The Seventeenth Letter", p. 103.
[15] *The Words*, "The Twenty-seventh Word", pp. 510–511.

One can acquire nearness to God Almighty in two ways. The first way is through God's favor to make one near to Him and to make one realize His nearness. Through companionship with and succession to the Prophet, upon him be peace and blessings, the Companions were endowed with this sort of nearness. The second way is through continuous promotion to higher ranks until finally being honored with nearness to God. Most saints follow this way, and make a long spiritual journey in their inner world and through the outer world.

The first way is a gift of God. Nearness in this way is realized through the All-Merciful One's attraction and being beloved by Him. This way is short but extremely elevated and sound, perfectly pure and free of obstacles. The other is long and has obstacles. Even if the latter is endowed with miracle-like wonders, this way is inferior to the former in acquiring nearness to God Almighty. Consider this example: One can experience yesterday once more in two ways. Without following the course of time, one rises by a sacred spiritual power to a position from which all time is seen as a single point. Or, following the course of time, one lives a whole year and reaches the same day next year. Despite this, one cannot preserve yesterday or prevent it from passing.

Similarly, one can pass from the external observation of religious commandments to the realization of their truths in two ways. Without entering the intermediate world of religious orders, one submits to the truth's attraction and finds it directly in its external aspect. In other words, one experiences the external and the internal combined into a single unity. Or, one is initiated into a spiritual way and continually promoted to higher ranks. However successful those following this second way are in self-annihilation and killing their carnal, evil-commanding souls, saints cannot reach the Companions, who were purified, had refined souls, and were honored with all varieties of worship and sorts of praise and thanksgiving with the soul's multiple inborn faculties. The worship of the saints who completely annihilate their carnal soul becomes simple and one dimensional.

- **The most important basis of sainthood and Sufism is sincerity (purity of intention), for this saves one from any implicit form of associating partners with God. Whoever has not acquired sincerity cannot travel in those ways.**[16]

---

[16] *The Letters*, "The Twenty-ninth Letter", p. 436.

The only means of salvation is sincerity. It is of great importance to attain sincerity. A minute sincere act is preferable to masses of insincere ones. In the services done for the afterlife, the most important foundation, and the greatest power, and the most acceptable intercessor, and the firmest point of reliance, and the shortest way to the truth, and the most answerable prayer, and the most blessed and marvelous means of achieving one's goal, and the most sublime virtue, and the purest form of worship is sincerity, or doing something good or any religious deed purely for God Almighty's sake.

- **This world is the abode of wisdom and service, not of wages and reward. Everything happens in accordance with God's Wisdom, and people will be rewarded in the Hereafter for their good deeds and services. Thus the fruits of good deeds done for God's good pleasure should not be sought here.**[17]

If some fruits of good deeds are given in this world, they should be accepted with sorrow, for it is unreasonable to use up here the fruits that will be given in Paradise eternally and replaced right after they are eaten. Eating them here is like exchanging a lamp giving permanent light for one that is extinguished in a minute.

- **The final station of all spiritual journeying is to attain the full perception of the truths of belief. Even one matter of belief being known in plain terms is preferred to attaining thousands of spiritual pleasures and ecstasies and working wonders.**[18]

According to Imam Rabbani (1564–1624), one of the most outstanding figures in the Naqshbandi order, there are three kinds of sainthood: that known to everybody (minor), that of a medium degree, and that of major sainthood (the greatest one), which can be attained through direct succession to the Prophetic Message. This greatest one paves the way to the truth without entering the intermediate realm of spiritual orders. One can progress in the Naqshbandi way by having a firm belief in the pillars of belief and performing the religious duties. Neglect of or deficiency in either makes this way impossible to follow.

This means that the Naqshbandi way encompasses three kinds of mission. The first and greatest is directly serving the truths of belief without

---

[17] *The Letters*, "The Twenty-ninth Letter", p. 437.
[18] *The Letters*, "The Fifth Letter", pp. 29–30.

having to follow a Sufi order. Imam Rabbani entered into such service, especially in the closing years of his life. The second is to try one's hardest to perform and promote the obligatory religious duties and the Sunnah of the Prophet by following a spiritual order. The third is to purify oneself of spiritual diseases by following a Sufi way. The first is obligatory, the second is necessary, and the third is supererogatory.

- **The Shari'ah, that collection of Divine religious principles, commands, and prohibitions, is the result of the direct Divine address to humanity through the Prophet and from the point of His absolute Oneness and Lordship. Therefore, all** tariqah **rules and ranks, including the greatest, are parts of the Shari'ah. All** tariqahs **are means to reach the Shari'ah's truths, and all results are included in the Shari'ah's confirmations.**[19]

Unlike the misconceptions of some Sufis, the Shari'ah is not a mere outer covering with Sufism being the inner part or *haqiqah* (the truth), the kernel or essence. The Shari'ah flourishes according to a person's spiritual level, for it contains all levels suitable to those who understand and practice it. People elevate their levels by understanding, practicing, and tasting it more perfectly. So we should not think that the ordinary people's understanding and practice of Islam is the Shari'ah, and consider the saints' practice of the Shari'ah as Sufism and *haqiqah*. In essence, Sufism is a discipline or technique that allows people to practice the Shari'ah in a better way. It has numerous degrees of understanding and practice. The most advanced Sufis are the most devoted, attached, and obedient to the Shari'ah.

- **Sufism is only a means. If it is taken as the aim or end, the Shari'ah's commands and the Sunnah's principles are reduced to mere ceremonies for outward performance, and the heart is turned directly toward Sufism.**[20]

Such people attach more importance to reciting God's Names in dervish circles than to performing the daily prescribed Prayers, concentrate more on daily supererogatory recitations than on religious obligations, and are more careful to avoid opposing Sufism's good manners than the major sins.

---

[19] *The Letters*, "The Twenty-ninth Letter", pp. 434–435.
[20] *The Letters*, "The Twenty-ninth Letter", p. 435.

Since all religious obligations are among the Shari'ah's established commands, not all of the *tariqah*'s daily supererogatory recitations can compensate for even a single one of them. The *tariqah*'s recitations and good manners are only a means of consolation for being unable to derive true pleasure from religious obligations, not the real source of that pleasure. Thus recitations and manners in the Sufi lodge are means for the pleasure and exact performance of the prescribed Prayers in mosque. Those who perform the prescribed Prayers in mosque as if they were a formality and then run to the lodge to get true pleasure and attain spiritual perfection are in loss and deviance.

- **Besides numerous benefits of it, there are some risks that a Sufi initiate may face in a Sufi way.**[21]

Some of the benefits:

First benefit: By following the Sufi path correctly, one attains a certain degree of perception of the truths of belief and is favored with their manifestations to the degree of their certainty of seeing.

Second benefit: Sufism allows the heart, our center and spring, to work, and thereby directs the other human faculties to their creative functions. This enables one to attain true humanity.

Third benefit: Sufism serves believers to join *tariqah* and become friends of the saints following it on their way to the Intermediate World and the Hereafter. This relieves believers of solitude and lets them benefit from the saints' company in respect of both worlds.

Fourth benefit: Sufism serves believers to feel inwardly the truths contained in religious duties. The resulting spiritual alertness and remembrance of God causes them to perform those duties willingly and enthusiastically, instead of like slaves forced to do so.

Fifth benefit: By experiencing the pleasure of knowing God via belief, and love of God coming from the knowledge of Him, believers are relieved of solitude and loneliness.

Sixth benefit: Sufism serves believers to attain the station of reliance on and submission to God, and the rank of being approved and loved by Him.

---

[21] *The Letters*, "The Twenty-ninth Letter", p. 437–440.

Seventh benefit: Sufism allows people to achieve a sincere and pure intention, which protects them from the disguised association of partners with God, and such degrading attitudes as showiness and pretense.

Eighth benefit: Through the reflective thought of the mind and remembrance of God by the heart, *tariqah* serves believers to acquire spiritual peace, awareness of God's ever presence, and sound intentions.

Ninth benefit: Through this journey of the heart and the constant struggle against Satan and the carnal, evil-commanding soul, and via the resulting spiritual progress attained, believers strive for perfection.

Some of the risks:

First risk: Some initiates who do not follow the Prophet's Sunnah strictly may prefer sainthood to Prophethood, even though Prophethood is far higher than and superior to sainthood.

Second risk: They might regard some saints of excessive views as superior to the Companions and even as equal to the Prophets. A saint, how great he or she is, can never attain the rank of a Prophet and a Companion.

Third risk: Some fanatical Sufis prefer the *tariqah*'s daily recitations and secondary principles over those of the Sunnah, and even abandon the Sunnah in favor of the *tariqah*'s recitations. Whereas the reward or degree acquired by observing one religious obligation is higher than 1,000 Sunnah commands. Thus, one practice of the Sunnah is preferable to 1,000 practises of the *tariqah*.

Fourth risk: Some excessive followers consider the inspiration coming to saints and the Divine Revelation coming to Prophets as equal. However, the Divine Revelation is incomparably higher, more comprehensive and sacred than inspiration.

Fifth risk: Some self-proclaimed Sufis, unaware of Sufism's truth, become engrossed in the spiritual pleasure, enlightenment, and wonder-working granted—without being desired—to followers to reinforce the weak, encourage those lacking in zeal, and lighten the tedium and troubles that may come from acts of worship. They gradually prefer those over acts of worship, daily recitations, and service. However, this world is the realm of serving, and not of receiving wages. Those who demand their wages here reduce the everlasting fruits of Paradise to the dying, transient fruits of this life.

Sixth risk: Some initiates who are not people of verification and truth confuse sainthood's real and universal ranks with their particular examples and shadows. However, the sun is multiplied through its reflections, which, despite having light and heat like the sun itself, are very faint in comparison with their origin. The ranks of Prophets and great saints also have shadows and reflections. When initiates find themselves under these shadows or receive some of these reflections, they see themselves as greater than the greatest saints, and even the Prophets. To avoid this, one must always use the essentials of belief and the Shari'ah's fundamentals as guiding principles and condemn any visions or experiences that oppose them.

Seventh risk: Some people of enthusiasm and spiritual pleasure prefer vanity, airs, and graces, and desire to gain people's love and become a resort for them. Whereas, the greatest spiritual rank is servanthood, and Prophet Muhammad, upon him be peace and blessings, is the most beloved in God's sight because he was the most advanced in servanthood to God. Such servanthood is founded upon thankfulness, entreaty, supplication, pious reverence, perception of human poverty and helplessness, and indifference to people's belongings, love, and attention. Although some great saints sometimes displayed the defects mentioned before God, but unintentionally and for a temporary period, they are not to be followed intentionally in this matter. They are not guides in this respect, even though, in general terms, they were guided.

Eighth risk: Some initiates may utter words incompatible with the Shari'ah and confuse the standards of this world with the worlds beyond. Therefore, in the Sufi way the rules, standards and principles of the Shari'ah must be strictly observed.

- **Just as a traveler passes by many stops and places during his or her travel, a traveler to God also passes through many stations, and there are conditions special to each station.**[22]

Those traveling to God should adopt an attitude particular to each station, rank, and veil that they either pass by or through, and to each state they are to experience. Whoever confuses these with one another makes mistakes. They would be like those who hear a horse neighing in a barn at a village and then, hearing a nightingale singing in a palace in a town, confuse the two animals with each other, or expect the nightingale to neigh like a horse.

---

[22] *Al-Mathnawi al-Nuri*, "The Sixth Treatise", p. 189.

- Like saints, the Prophets as well are mirrors reflecting God's manifestations—that is, they reflect the light that emanates from the Eternal Sun. They are only containers into which the honey of Divine vision is poured; people then take this honey from them.[23]

Neither the saints nor the Prophets, who guide people on the way towards God, ever know themselves to be the sources of the light of guidance; it should be realized that the guide is a mortal one—and therefore it is impossible for such to be the source of the light. It is also because of this that initiation into a spiritual way is based on humility or modesty, and continues along the path of self-denial until it ends in annihilation before God's Existence. The stations of the spiritual journey begin at this point.

- The characteristics of sainthood and greatness are humility and modesty. They are not arrogance and domination. One who feels arrogant is one who feigns sainthood, or feigns being a spiritual guide. Such a person should not be treated as a great one.[24]

- A true spiritual guide must, first of all, have sincerity or purity of intention. He must exert himself to fight, first, against his own soul—the major jihad, which he should teach his disciples as well. He must also abandon pursuing his personal interests and lead an austere life, which is their distinguishing mark. Guides must love each other, which they always claim and advise, and which is the essence of an Islamic disposition, and serve the unity of Muslims.[25]

- God's use of His servant to perform a wonder (karamah) differs from His gradually leading another servant to perdition by enabling him or her to do extraordinary things (istidraj).[26]

Karamah is an act of God. Those through whom it is done know that it originates from the All-Glorified One, that the Almighty oversees and protects them, and wills them good. This strengthens their certainty about and reliance on Him. Although they are sometimes conscious of the *karamah* and how it takes place, it is safer for them and their belief that they remain unaware that it is God Who does this through them. For example, God may cause them to say unconsciously what occurs to another person's heart or mind, or reveal scenes from the Unseen so that others may

---

[23] *Gleams of Truth*, pp. 101–102.

[24] *Gleams of Truth*, pp. 146–147.

[25] *Gleams of Truth*, pp. 166.

[26] *Al-Mathnawi al-Nuri*, "The Ninth Treatise", p. 322.

be guided to the Straight Path. These beloved servants are unaware of what God does for His servants through them.

As for *istidraj*, for example, some things from the Unseen may appear to heedless or misguided people. They may even perform wonders. Attributing these to their own power or ability, they grow in conceit, vanity, and distance from God. They say, "*I have been given it only on account of knowledge I possess,*[27] and it happened because of my purity and my heart's enlightenment."

Those who are half-way in their spiritual journey confuse *karamah* and *istidraj*. Those who have attained the highest ranks and realized self-annihilation may be made aware of some things belonging to the Unseen with their external senses, which function as a means for God to execute His decrees. Since their inner world is perfectly illumined and illuminates their outer world, they distinguish clearly between *karamah* and *istidraj*.

- **If one's purpose is to combine the Islamic light of heart with the light of mind, if his way is based on love and characterized by humility or modesty, if the distinguishing mark of his way is selflessness and avoidance of pursuing personal interests, and if one acts out of Islamic zeal and for the victory of Islam—then we may hope that such a person is a true guide.**[28]

However, if one's way is characterized by criticizing others to show himself as meritorious and virtuous, by trying to inculcate his love by cherishing hostility toward others, and by bias or partiality, which causes divisions of power; and if his love depends on hostility toward others, which gives rise to backbiting, then such a person is a seditious, misguiding claimer of guidance, and a wolf in pursuit of plunder. Such people drum on the spiritual way with their hands instead of playing the drum so that they may be tipped and receive gifts. They attempt to hunt the world with Religion. They have been deceived by either a poisonous pleasure, a lowly fancy, or a wrong reasoning and deduction; thus they suppose themselves to be great and have opened the way to having an ill-opinion of truly great guides and holy persons.

- **Deviant ways in Sufism have appeared because their leaders who, having set out into the inner dimension of existence and spiritual**

---

[27] *Suratu'l-Qasas*, 28:78.
[28] *Gleams of Truth*, pp. 167–168.

journeying, have turned back halfway, relying on their findings. **They have obtained something but lost many things, and they themselves have gone astray and led their followers astray.**[29]

- **The blessing and help of saints, and the enlightenment they diffuse, are a sort of prayer done either through disposition or actively, for the One Who actually guides and helps is God.**[30]

Each person has an innermost sense or faculty that, if he or she prays through it, the prayer will be answered regardless of spiritual condition. If they swear by God through it that something will happen, God does not disprove them.

- **Just as giving the property of a community to one person is a wrong, and one who lays hands on the property of a charitable foundation commits a wrong, so, too, attributing the product of a community's labor or the honor and merits resulting from the good deeds of all its members to the leader or teacher of the community is a wrong committed against both the community and the leader or teacher.**[31]

Doing so flatters the leader's or teacher's ego, and encourages their arrogance. It may even lead them to wronging themselves by stirring up ostentation or hypocrisy, which is a kind of concealed association of partners with God.

Indeed, the commander cannot claim the booty, victory, or glory that belongs to the battalion that has conquered a castle. In the same way, a guide or teacher should not be considered to be the source or origin of the favors coming to their pupils. Guides or teachers should be known only as mirrors reflecting these favors. For example, if you attribute the heat and light of the sun coming to you through a mirror to the mirror itself, in heedlessness of the sun, and are grateful to the mirror instead of the sun, this would be foolishness, even lunacy. The mirror should be preserved, because it receives and reflects the favor. The spirit and heart of the guide is a mirror; it receives the lights or effusions that emanate from God Almighty and is the means of their being reflected to the pupils. So, such a teacher should not be ascribed a higher rank than that of being a means for spiritual or intellectual illumination. It sometimes may even

---

[29] *Al-Mathnawi al-Nuri*, "The Sixth Treatise", p. 191.
[30] *Al-Mathnawi al-Nuri*, "The Tenth Treatise", p. 358.
[31] *The Gleams*, "The Seventeenth Gleam", p. 185.

happen that a teacher or guide who is considered to be a source is neither a source nor a mirror. Pupils suppose the illumination or effusions they receive due to the purity of their intention, sincerity, and the strength of their loyalty to and concentration on their teacher as having come from the mirror of the teacher's spirit. It sometimes occurs that a sincere pupil of a deficient *shaykh* may be more advanced than the *shaykh*. The pupil then guides the *shaykh* and so becomes the *shaykh* of his *shaykh*.

- **The people of sainthood cannot know by themselves the things pertaining to the Unseen unless they are shown to them by God Almighty. Therefore, the denial of a saint by another saintly one does not damage his sainthood. However, sainthood cannot be an excuse for the approval or neglect of any act contrary to the clear commandments of the Shari'ah, or based on an evidently wrong ijtihad.**[32]

- **There are two kinds of sainthood: minor and major. The minor sainthood usually is attained by strictly following a Sufi order (tariqah). An initiate is sometimes favored by God with unexpected wonders in return for overcoming human instincts and animal desires. As for the major sainthood, it is attained through a direct inheritance of the Prophetic mission and, without having to follow a Sufi order, by full observance of the Shari'ah, penetrating to the truth, and ultimately gaining nearness to God. Such sainthood, though much greater and more valuable than the minor one, is rarely favored with wonder-working.**[33]

The Companions enjoyed the rank of major sainthood. Such sainthood, though much greater and more valuable than the minor one, is rarely favored with wonder-working. Therefore it is safer; wonder-working can lead saints to attribute wonders to themselves, and thus bring about spiritual desolation. Without having to follow a Sufi order's discipline for many years, the Companions attained the rank of major sainthood through the grace and elixir of the Prophet's presence and guidance.

This can be explained by an analogy: The sun is near to us, even nearer to us than ourselves, through its reflected light and heat, or its image in the mirror in our hand, despite our great distance from it. If we feel its nearness in its reflections, and perceive its identity and relation to us

---

[32] *Kastamonu Lahikası* (Addendum of Kastamonu), p. 164; *The Letters*, "The Fifteenth Letter", p. 91.

[33] *The Letters*, "The Fifteenth Letter", pp. 89–91.

through its reflected form in our mirror, we draw nearer to it and establish nearer relations. But if we try to reach and know it from our remote starting-point, we must make a long journey of thought and research. In other words, we will need a very demanding, long scientific study of its formation, heat, light, and seven colors. Even after this study, we cannot acquire as much and experienced knowledge of it as we know it through its direct reflection.

In just this way, sainthood attained through direct inheritance of the Prophet's mission enables people to draw nearer to God because of this direct, unrestricted relation. Accordingly, major sainthood is much greater than minor sainthood, which can be attained only through long years of spiritual discipline within an order.

- **According to the rule that "One will be with whom he or she loves," each believer can have a part in a high rank or position through closeness to the one who has this position.**[34]

Therefore our Qur'anic love for the Prophets and saints will cause us to benefit from their intercession in the Intermediate World of the grave and in the Place of Supreme Gathering. We also will receive enlightenment from their elevated positions.

- **Whether in spiritual training or the practice of Religion, following one spiritual way and one school of law is sufficient. Following more than one way or more than one school of law means following none of them.**[35]

The greatest guide and teacher is the Qur'an and the Sunnah. However, everyone cannot be able to follow the Qur'an and the Sunnah without a guide or teacher. Therefore, in order to obey and follow the Qur'an and the Sunnah, we must follow a teacher, guide, or a school of law. God Almighty orders us to pray to Him in every *rak'ah* of every Prayer to guide us to the way of those whom He has favored (with guidance and the mission of "guiding" others),[36] and points us towards some persons He has chosen among people. He describes them as those whom He has favored. He presents the Straight Path as their way, and He publicizes their identity as follows:

---

[34] *The Words*, "The Twenty-second Word", p. 662.
[35] *The Letters*, "The Twenty-eighth Letter", p. 365.
[36] *Suratu'l-Fatiha*, 1:6–7.

Whoever obeys God and the Messenger (as they must be obeyed), then those are (and in the Hereafter will be in Paradise) in the company of those whom God has favored (with the perfect guidance)—the Prophets, and the truthful ones (loyal and truthful in whatever they do and say), and the witnesses (those who see the hidden Divine truths and testify thereto with their lives), and the righteous ones (in all their deeds and sayings and dedicated to setting everything right). How excellent they are for companions![37]

One who sincerely searches for such people finds them, because they shine in the spiritual and intellectual "heaven" of humankind.

- **The people following a spiritual way have tried to acquire knowledge of God in their inner world or in the outer world. They have found the most direct and sound way to be the human inner world. Scholars of truth have also followed two ways in order to be able to rise to the most secure and certain level of faith: they have preferred the way of either studying the book of the universe or creation, or the map of the truth of humanity or human nature.[38]**

If we were no more than a heart, we would have to renounce everything other than God and follow only a spiritual way. In reality, however, we have many senses and intellectual and spiritual faculties (e.g., the intellect with its many faculties, such as imagination, conceptualization, reflection, reasoning, plus we have the spirit, soul, and several other innermost faculties). Each of these faculties has particular duties and functions, and specific needs to satisfy. Perfect people are those who, using each sense and faculty for its particular type of worship, strive to reach the truth. With their hearts serving as the commander, and the other faculties as soldiers, they advance heroically like the Companions in a broad sphere and in a manifold way towards their goal. For the heart to leave its soldiers in order to save itself and proceed on its own is a cause of distress, not of pride.

- **Suspicion or ill-opinion of others causes people to think that others suffer the same defects and vices that they do. This view causes them to condemn everyone, and blind themselves to the virtues of present and past illustrious people, from whom they could derive some benefit. Thus they turn daylight into night for**

---

[37] *Suratu'n-Nisa'*, 4:69.
[38] *Emirdağ Lahikası* (Addendum of Emirdağ), vol. 1.

themselves. May God save us from despair, self-admiration, vanity, and suspicion. Amen.[39]

The Qur'an declares:

> O you who believe! Let not some people among you deride another people; it may be that the latter are better than the former. Nor let some women deride other women; it may be that the latter are better than the former. Nor defame one another (and provoke the same for yourselves in retaliation); nor insult one another with nicknames (that your brothers and sisters dislike). Evil is using names with vile meaning after (those so addressed have accepted) the faith (doing so is like replacing a mark of faith with a mark of transgression). Whoever (does that and then) does not turn to God in repentance (giving up doing so), those are indeed wrongdoers. O you who believe! Avoid much suspicion, for some suspicion is a grave sin (liable to God's punishment); and do not spy (on one another), nor let some of you backbite others. Would any of you love to eat the flesh of his dead brother? You would abhor it! Keep from disobedience to God in reverence for Him and piety. Surely God is One Who truly returns repentance with liberal forgiveness and additional reward, All-Compassionate (particularly toward His believing servants).[40]

- **First and foremost, the Prophets, scholars, saints, and all believers must be mentioned with good words, designations or descriptions, and with petitionary prayers.**[41]

The best petitionary prayer for believers is that which accords with the conditions of acceptability. A prayer is answered if certain conditions are met. First, we should cleanse ourselves by seeking God's forgiveness. Then we should call God's blessing on Prophet Muhammad, upon him be peace and blessings, as an intercessor before and after prayer, for calling God's blessing on our Prophet is acceptable, and a prayer said between two acceptable prayers is usually acceptable. Also, such a prayer should be said in the absence of the believer in question and be of the kind mentioned in the Qur'an and the Traditions. For example, we should prefer such comprehensive prayers as: "O God, I ask forgiveness of You, for me and him (her), and soundness in the Religion, in this world, and in the Hereafter. Our Lord, grant us good in this world and in the Hereafter, and guard us against the punishment of the Fire."

---

[39] *Al-Mathnawi al-Nuri*, "The Fourth Treatise", p. 87.

[40] *Suratu'l-Hujurat*, 48:11–12.

[41] *The Letters*, "The Twenty-third Letter", pp. 298–299.

Pray from your heart with sincerity, religious seriousness, and solemn reverence. Do so after the five daily Prayers and, particularly, after the early morning Prayer and in such blessed times as Friday—especially during the hour when prayer is absolutely accepted, in the three blessed months, particularly on the special nights, during *Ramadan*, and most particularly on the Night of *Qadr* (the Night of Power and Destiny).

Further, try to supplicate in mosque. God is expected, through His Mercy, to accept petitions meeting such conditions. He either answers it here, or causes the one in whose name it is made to benefit from it in the Hereafter. So if you do not obtain the desired result, consider your prayer as having received a better acceptance.

It has become a preferred tradition to say of a Companion, "May God be pleased with him (or her)." Although this prayer has been a tradition to say of the Companions, it may, even should, be said of people who, like the founders of the four legal schools, as well as 'Abdu'l-Qadir al-Jilani, Imam Rabbani, and Imam al-Ghazzali, were approved by God through succession to the Prophetic mission (the greatest rank of sainthood). Nevertheless, according to the common usage of religious scholars, we tend to say: "May God be pleased with him (or her)" when mentioning a Companion; "May God have mercy upon him (or her)" of those belonging to the two succeeding generations after the Companions; "May God forgive him (or her)" of those who followed them; and "May God sanctify him (or her)" for saints.

- **What some saintly people of vision see has a reality, but they may err in interpreting and naming their visions. People of vision cannot interpret their visions while in a trance-like state, just as people cannot interpret their dreams while dreaming. Their visions can be interpreted only by pure, saintly scholars who are true heirs of the Prophetic mission (asfiya'). When such people of vision attain the rank of pure, saintly scholars and become aware of their mistakes in the light of the Qur'an and Sunnah, they correct them.[42]**

Consider the following parable: Two pious shepherds milked their animals and collected the milk in a wooden bowl. They laid their flutes across the bowl, and one of them went to sleep. While he was sleeping,

---

[42] *The Letters*, "The Eighteenth Letter", pp. 108–109.

the other noticed that something like a fly flew from his friend's nose and, after buzzing around the milk for a while, went through one of the flutes and disappeared into a hole at the foot of a gum-tree. Shortly afterwards, the fly-like thing came out of the hole, passed through the flute, returned to the sleeping shepherd's nose, and caused him to wake up.

After he woke up, the shepherd related his strange dream. "May God turn it to goodness," his friend said, and asked him what he had seen. The man replied: "I saw a milky lake across which stretched a strange covered bridge with windows. Passing along the bridge, I saw a place covered with tipped bushes, at the foot of which was a cave. I went into the cave and found a treasure therein." His wise friend interpreted the dream: "The milky lake is that wooden bowl, and the strange bridge is the flute lying across it. The bushes are that gum-tree over there, and the cave is that small hole. Now fetch the ax so I can show you the treasure." They dug up the tree and found the treasure, which made them both happy in this world.

Although what the sleeping shepherd saw is not unreal, he cannot make his vision correspond literally to reality, since he might confuse the non-material world with the material one. The shepherd who stayed awake can interpret the dream, because he can distinguish between the two worlds. Thus in order to reach the reality, one must distinguish between the material and spiritual worlds.

In conclusion, this reveals that the rank of spiritual vision is lower than that of belief in the Unseen. Thus a saint's conclusions reached through spiritual discovery carry little weight when compared with those witnessed by pure scholarly people of truth and verification, who rely on the Qur'an and Sunnah. In other words, all spiritual states, visions, and conclusions reached via contemplation, intellectual intuition, or spiritual discovery should be judged according to the principles of the Qur'an and the Sunnah, and the standards derived from them by pure scholarly people of truth.

- **If saintly, true lovers of God err in following their way or in their interpretations, or in describing Him, they are forgivable; but if the saints who are distinguished in knowledge of God err in following the way or in their vision or in their speech, they are not excused.**[43]

---

[43] *Gleams of Truth*, pp. 102–103.

Those endowed with knowledge of God (*ma'rifatu'llah*) are not like lovers; they are awake, aware of themselves and what they are doing, and they act with their free will. Besides, if they err, they mislead both themselves and others. However, lovers of God usually go into ecstasies or trance-like state, and they are excusable for their acts and words while in this state. For it is ecstatic love, not their free will, which dominates and directs them.

It is because of this that certain words of some from among those with knowledge of God—their words implying heresy have led them to misguidance and eventually to execution, because such words issuing from them were not open to interpretation and were therefore not tolerated. But lovers of God—even when some of them have explicitly uttered the same heresy-implying words, and not allusively, have continued to be respected by the Muslim Community, which has in no way punished them. Even though the heresy-implying words of Muhyiddin, Mulla Jami', Ibnu'l-Farid and Ibnu's-Sab'in resembled one another, they were not perceived as being the same and were therefore not treated as the same.

- **If the Shari'ah judges a word or deed to be unbelief and that a believer cannot therefore utter or do it, it means that this word or deed cannot be compatible with belief. One who has uttered or done it has committed an act of unbelief, but we cannot therefore judge that person to be an unbeliever.**[44]

For he has many other attributes that arise from his belief and which prove that he is a believer. A word or deed uttered or done in certain circumstances or in a different state or mood, and which is open to interpretation, cannot annul his attributes that demonstrate that he is a believer. We can judge that person to be an unbeliever only when we are certain that that word or deed has arisen from his unbelief; that is, we can only make such a statement when an attribute of unbelief observed in them is the result of unbelief, not of something else.

- **A person's habitual deeds and established attributes that indicate belief prove that he is a believer; suspicion cannot be a basis of judgment.**[45]

---

[44] *Gleams of Truth*, pp. 104–105.
[45] *Gleams of Truth*, pp. 105.

Doubt cannot always cancel judgment when it is based on certainty. One cannot be accused of unbelief due to a word or deed that can be attributed to forgetfulness or an unintentional error or confusion.

- **If certain rituals that have taken the form of worship in some spiritual ways have been adopted with good intentions, and meet the following three conditions, they may not be harmful: They must not be contrary in any way to the decorum and solemnity of Divine remembrance, nor to the manners that must be adopted in God's presence. The second condition is that there must never be a religiously forbidden act in them; if there is one, such ways cannot be tolerated. The third condition is that these acts or actions must not be carried out as part of the worship.**[46]

For worship is remembrance itself, while other excusable acts or rituals can be a means of encouragement. The Qur'an has not stipulated any form of remembrance; it has placed no restrictive definitions on a permissible form. The acts of remembrance may not resemble the acts of worship appointed by the Shari'ah. For the acts appointed by the Shari'ah are like fruit where both the meat and peel are edible. Whereas the rituals included in Divine remembrance are like walnuts. Their shells are only hard coverings and not edible.

- **Sufism is not possible outside the Qur'an and the Sunnah, or the Shari'ah. The words and attitudes of some saints contrary to the Shari'ah have issued from them when they have been under the complete influence of the states of spiritual intoxication.**[47]

Sa'di al-Shirazi says: "Sa'di, it is inconceivable for one who does not follow the way of the Messenger to find the truth's lights." As the Messenger is the Seal of the Prophets and the addressee of God on humanity's behalf, humanity must follow his broad highway and remain under his flag.

On the other hand, people in trance, ecstasy, or spiritual absorption are not considered responsible for disobeying the Shari'ah. People are not asked to account for their opposition to religious commands when under the influence of senses or faculties that their willpower and reason cannot control. Thus ecstatic saints do not lose their sainthood while in such states.

---

[46] *Gleams of Truth*, pp. 105.
[47] *The Letters*, "The Twenty-ninth Letter", pp. 438–439.

Sufis outside the Sharia's sphere fall into two categories. The first consists of those overcome by trance or ecstasy, spiritual absorption and intoxication, or under the influence of senses or faculties that cannot be controlled by reason and willpower. Such people may sometimes leave the Shari'ah unintentionally. They do not intentionally deny or contradict any commandment conveyed by the Prophet, and any neglect comes from their ignorance or spiritual intoxication, trance, or ecstasy.

The second comprises those who, fascinated by Sufism's splendid pleasures, consider the Shari'ah's truths to be tasteless and mere ceremonies, and thus become indifferent to them. Considering the Shari'ah a superficial covering, and being content with what they find in Sufism, they consider the latter as the real object and thus abandon the Shari'ah. The "sober" ones among those are held responsible for their un-Islamic actions, and may fall to the lowest level, and are ridiculed even by Satan.

- **The image or reflection in a mirror is one of several sorts: it is either only the identity or the physical form of the thing reflected; or the identity together with the essential, living attributes; or both the identity and a ray from the thing's nature; or both the nature and the identity. Examples are a human being, the sun, and an angel. This explains many truths, such as how God is present everywhere while being nowhere, and knows, provides, and controls each and every creature at the same time. It also explains the presence of angels and Prophets and angelic saints in many places at the same time.[48]**

The images of solid things in mirrors are moving but dead forms. Such reflections are other than the thing reflected, and so have a different identity. They are also lifeless, having no quality other than their lifeless appearance.

The images of a luminous body reflected are living and connected to it; even if it is not identical to it, they are none other than this. While not of the same nature as the original, they have most of its features, and may be considered as living. For example, the sun is reflected in countless objects. Each reflection either contains its heat or light, together with its light's seven colors. If the sun were conscious, with its heat as its power, its light as its knowledge, and its seven colors as its seven attributes, it would wil-

---

[48] *The Words*, "The Sixteenth Word", pp. 210–212; *Gleams of Truth*, pp. 33–34.

fully and consciously be present in everything simultaneously, and able to rule over or make contact with each one freely and without one hindering the other. It also would be able to meet with all of us via our mirrors. While we are distant from it, it would be nearer to us than ourselves.

The reflections of pure spirits and of those that have gained purity are living and identifiable with the original. However, since they reflect or manifest themselves according to the receptive object's or mirror's capacity, the reflections are not wholly of the same nature as the original. For example, Archangel Gabriel could be with the Prophet in the form of Dihya (a Companion), prostrating in the Divine Presence before God's Most Exalted Throne, and be in innumerable other places relaying the Divine Commands simultaneously. Performing one duty does not block another. Also, God knows how many places Azra'il—the Angel of death—can be present in simultaneously, taking the spirits of the dying. In the same way Prophet Muhammad, upon him be peace and blessings, whose essence is 'light' (*nur*) and whose identity is of 'light,' hears each member of his community in this world calling blessings upon him simultaneously. On the Day of Judgment, he will meet with all purified people at the same time. In fact, some saints who have acquired a high degree of purity and refinement (*abdal*: substitutes) are seen in many places and doing many things simultaneously.

- **Just as glass and water reflect material objects, so do many 'mirrors, one more subtle than the other, just as air, ether, and certain things or beings of the World of Representations or Ideal Forms reflect and transport spirit beings and the like with the speed of light and imagination. This allows them to travel in thousands of pure realms and refined abodes at the same time. Also, a word multiplies millions of times in the mirror of air. The Pen of Divine Power accomplishes this in an amazing way.**[49]

Helpless and subjugated items like the sun, and creatures like matter-restricted spirit beings, can be present in many places at once because they are either light-giving creatures or created of light. Despite being particulars bounded by certain conditions, they become like absolute universals. With their limited power of choice, they can do many things at once.

---

[49] *The Words*, "The Sixteenth Word", pp. 211–212; *Gleams of Truth*, p. 7.

The All-Holy, All-Pure Being is wholly transcendent and absolutely free of matter, infinitely far above and exempt from any restrictions, or the darkness of density and compactness. All lights and luminous beings, whether light-giving or created of light, are dense shadows of His Names' sacred lights. All existence and life, as well as the World of Spirits and the World of Representations or Ideal Forms, are semi-transparent mirrors of His Beauty. His Attributes are all-embracing, and His essential Qualities are universal. What could escape or hide from His manifestation with all His Attributes, particularly His universal Will, absolute Power, and all-encompassing Knowledge? What could be difficult for Him? Who could be distant from Him?

The sun's unrestricted light and immaterial reflection makes it nearer to us than our eye's pupil, while our being, bounded by certain conditions, keeps us far from it. To draw near, we must transcend many restrictions and rise above many universal levels. Simply, in terms of spiritual transcendence, we have to become as large as the earth and rise as far as the moon. Only then could we directly approach, to a degree, the sun in its essential identity and meet it without veil. In the same way, the All-Majestic One of Grace, the All-Gracious One of Perfection, is infinitely near to us, while we are infinitely far from Him. In order to be able to get near to Him, we must transcend almost innumerable stations and gain universality. For example, if we want to draw near to Him only through His Name of the Creator, we must connect with Him first on account of His being our creator, and then on account of His being the Creator of all human beings, then His being the Creator of all living creatures, and then the Creator of all beings or the entire universe with whatever is in it. Otherwise, we will remain in shadow and only find a particular manifestation. Everyone has his or her own degree of nearness to, or distance from, Him.

- **There is no collision and repulsion between the worlds of light, heat, air, electricity, and gravitation, and those of ether, representations, ideal forms, and the Intermediate World of the grave. They exist together with us wherever we are, without one preventing and being mixed with the other. Similarly, although much more spacious or larger than this narrow world, many of the unseen worlds can exist together. Also, air and water do not prevent us from journeying, from going on or through them, just as glass does not stop light from passing through it, and a solid** object does not hinder the penetration of X-rays, the intellect's light, and an angel's spirit. Iron cannot block heat's permeation and electricity's conduction. Nothing can stop gravity's penetration, the spirit's movement, and the intellect's light. Likewise, this solid, material world does not stop or prevent spirit beings from circulating, jinn from moving around, Satan from infiltrating and penetrating, and angels from journeying.[50]

- The Single, Eternally Besought One, Who is the Sun without beginning and the Lord of eternity, manifests Himself in the nature of humanity in two forms that comprise innumerable degrees. The first manifestation occurs in the heart's mirror through one's relationship with the Lord. The second is that since we have a comprehensive nature and are the most enlightened fruit of the Tree of Creation, we can reflect all Divine Names in the mirror of our spirits. Thus Almighty God manifests Himself and all His Beautiful Names most comprehensively in humanity's best and greatest representative. This form of manifestation occurred during the Ascension of Prophet Muhammad, upon him be peace and blessings.[51]

A person holds a mirror up to the sun. According to its capacity, the mirror receives what it can from the sun's seven-colored light. That person has a relation with the sun through the mirror and according to its ability to reflect the sun. If he or she directs the mirror's shining side towards his or her dark house or small, private, covered garden, he or she can benefit only according to the mirror's capacity, not in proportion to the sun's value.

Another person puts down the mirror and, facing the sun directly, sees its splendor and comprehends its grandeur. He or she then climbs a very high mountain and faces the sun without veil, witnessing the majesty of its broad dominion. Coming back, this person tries to have a direct connection with the sun's constant light by making large windows in his or her house or garden's roof, and obtains other means of benefiting from the sun directly. Facing it, that person may say in indebtedness: "O amiable sun, beauty of the world and darling of the skies, who gilds the earth's face with light and makes it and all flowers smile in joy and happiness! You have illuminated and heated my house and garden, as you

---

[50] *Al-Mathnawi al-Nuri*, "The Fourth Treatise", p. 192.
[51] *The Words*, "The Thirty-first Word", pp. 581–582.

illuminate the world and heat the earth's face." The first person cannot say this, for the sun's reflection in his or her mirror is restricted to the mirror's capacity.

Likewise, the Single, Eternally Besought One, Who is the Sun without beginning and the Lord of eternity, manifests Himself in the nature of humanity in two forms that comprise innumerable degrees. The first manifestation occurs in the heart's mirror through one's relationship with the Lord. Everyone may receive a manifestation of the Eternal Sun's light and conversation in certain degrees in accordance with his capacity, the character of his spiritual journey towards sainthood, and his ability to receive manifestations of Divine Names and Attributes. As a result, the kind of sainthood which is attained through journeying within the shade of some particular Name(s) or Attribute(s) contains innumerable degrees.

The second is that since we have a comprehensive nature, and are the most enlightened fruit of the Tree of Creation, we can reflect all Divine Names in the mirror of our spirits. Thus Almighty God manifests Himself and all His Beautiful Names most comprehensively in humanity's best and greatest representative. This form of manifestation occurred during the Ascension of Prophet Muhammad, upon him be peace and blessings.

Sainthood contains veils between one's heart and the Divine Names' manifestations, as in the case of the first person in the second comparison above. Messengership contains no veils, as in the case of the second person in the second comparison, for it is connected directly with the All-Majestic Being's manifestation with all His Names, in a single being.

- **Like Prophet Yusuf's (Joseph) dream, the kernel of** Sura Yusuf, **such verses as,** "We have appointed the night for you as a rest,"[52] **show that sleep and dreams contain important truths. God's Messenger says in an authentic narration that true dreams are one of Prophethood's forty-six aspects.**[53] **Therefore, they contain some truths and have some connections with the Prophetic mission.**[54]

There are three kinds of dreams. Two are included in the Qur'anic category of "jumbles of dream images."[55] Either the imagination gives form

---

[52] *Suratu'n-Naba'*, 78:9.
[53] *Muslim*, "Ru'ya" 1; *at-Tirmidhî*, "Ru'ya" 1.
[54] *The Letters*, "The Twenty-eighth Letter", pp. 357–360.
[55] *Sura Yusuf*, 12:44.

to a bad temper's deviations, or the mind remembers an exciting event and gives it a new form. Both are worthless.

The third kind are true dreams. As the dreamer's senses that are connected with the outer, material world do not function during sleep, the innate, inner spiritual faculty can find an opening to the Unseen World. Looking at impending events through that opening, it meets a manifestation of the Guarded Tablet or an example of the "letters" of Destiny, and sees real events. But since the imagination "colors" what the spiritual faculty sees, the dreamer does not see an accurate reflection.

A true dream is the result of a presentiment being highly developed. Among pious people and saints, such presentiment develops to the point of becoming a source of wonders. Ordinary people with a kind of sainthood can grasp something of the future or the Unseen World in true dreams. Just as sleep is like a rank of sainthood regarding true dreams, it is a time or space of recreation in which magnificent Divine moving pictures are shown. People of good conduct think of what is better, and see beautiful tablets, whereas those of evil conduct think of what is worse, and see ugly tablets.

True dreams make sleep a window opening on the Unseen World, a field of release and freedom for human beings (who are confined in a restricted area), a theater having a kind of permanence, and a realm in which only the present exists (past and future are united). True dreams especially concerning the Unseen, and/or the future, prove that the Divine Destiny encompasses everything.

- **With respect to traveling towards God and the attainment of truth, there are basically three groups: The first group consists of thinkers; those who strive for their particular level of perfection via the physical senses and intellectual faculties only, and those who, keeping their egotism, are preoccupied with and study the physical existence in its elaborate multiplicity and try to reach the truth through deduction and reasoning only. The second group comprises saints and saintly scholars; those who strive through using the mind and refining the soul, and those who search through reason, religious learning, and by acquiring knowledge of God. The third group comprises Prophets; those who pursue the truth through certified belief, submission, and purifying the heart, and those who travel to the truth swiftly**

through certified belief and the Divine Scripture, worship, and acknowledgment of their poverty and neediness before God.[56]

This is also the answer to many such vital questions as follows:

Why did the early Prophets not elaborate on some pillars of belief as much as the Qur'an? Why were they content with a brief exposition?

Why, among saints well-versed in the knowledge of God, have only some advanced in affirming Divine Unity? They have attained total certainty coming from direct experience in the truths of belief, yet apparently neglected some pillars of belief. This has caused later followers to pay less attention to those pillars, which, in turn, has caused some to deviate. Although true perfection is attained through full development in all pillars of belief, why have the people of truth advanced greatly in some while remaining backward in others? What is the reason for all these differences while the noblest Messenger, who was endowed with the greatest manifestations of all Divine Names and was the prince of Prophets, as well as the wise Qur'an, the most luminous chief of all sacred Divine Scriptures, described all pillars of belief in detail, clearly, and in a most emphatic way?

Humanity is created with a capacity to be able to receive the manifestations of all Divine Names and attain all perfections. However, we search for truth amid thousands of veils and barriers and with a partial will, a slight power, and variable desires and different degrees of abilities. For this reason, insurmountable barriers intervene while we are trying to discover the reality and find out and comprehend the truth. Abilities and levels of understanding differ. Some abilities cannot encompass certain pillars of belief with all their dimensions. Furthermore, the Names' manifestations assume different colors according to the people who receive them. Some can receive them in their universal and original forms, while others can do so only in their partial and shadowy forms. In some people, only one Name predominates and prevails over the others.

Secondly, heed the following comparison: Imagine a luxuriant flower, a living drop of water in love with the moon, and a simple dew drop that looks to the sun. Each is conscious and has some goal of perfection to attain. Together with pointing to many other truths, they allude to the journey of the soul, mind, and heart on the way of truth, and correspond to the three basic types of people searching for truth. Each group also has

[56] *The Words*, "The Twenty-fourth Word", pp. 355–360.

three subgroups, each in every group being mixed with the others to certain extents. Thus, the three things given in the comparison as representatives of the three groups correspond to nine categories.

The first group consists of thinkers. They are those who strive for their particular level of perfection via their physical senses and intellectual faculties only, and those who, keeping their egotism, are preoccupied with and study the physical existence in its elaborate multiplicity and try to reach the truth through deduction and reasoning only. Since they cannot be saved from engagement with the physical world and depend on their intellectual ability, they cannot transcend the sphere of causality; and since there are as many degrees in the intellectual ability as the number of human beings, they differ in their findings and conclusions both in respect to quantity and quality. The members of this group resemble flowers in their connection or relationship with the sun.

The second group comprises saints or saintly scholars. They are those who strive through using the mind and refining the soul, and those who search through reason and religious learning, and by acquiring knowledge of God. Since the members of this group cannot open their hearts and spirits fully to the sun and are restricted by their spiritual capacities, their refinement and knowledge of God are also in different degrees, natures, and qualities. With respect to their relationship with God Almighty and the truth, they resemble drops or bubbles of water in their connection with the sun.

The third group comprises Prophets. They are those who pursue the truth through certified belief, submission, and purifying the heart, and those who travel to the truth swiftly through belief and the Divine Scripture, worship, and acknowledgment of their poverty and neediness before God. With respect to their relationship with God and the truth, they resemble a dew drop in its connection or relation with the sun. Although they are wholly agreed on the fundamentals of their Messages, since some of them were given a Divine Scripture containing a Shari'ah, and some a Scripture without a Shari'ah, and some others received only Divine Revelation but were not given a Scripture, they represented, practiced, and communicated the Divine Message in parts, and not in Its totality, addressing all times and peoples. Only Prophet Muhammad, upon him be peace and blessings, was sent to all peoples, regardless of time and place. The Book given to Him—the Qur'an—contains all the truths of the

Divine Religion, which he received, represented, practiced, and communicated in its universality. While the previous Prophets, peace be upon them, each focused on the part of the Divine Message relating to their own time and people, Prophet Muhammad, upon him be peace and blessings, represented and communicated it in a perfect balance.

- **The view of heedlessness and philosophy in its "sleep" cannot be the criterion for the truths of Prophethood.**[57]

Those who are awake can interpret a sleeping person's dream, and sometimes those who are sleeping can hear the conversations of those who are awake and interpret their words according to their world of sleep. In the same way, O unfair one stupefied in the sleep of heedlessness and false reasoning! Do not deny in your "dream;" rather, interpret the vision of the one who always and truly was awake, and about whom God declared, "*His eye never wavered nor swerved,*"[58] and himself said, "My eye sleeps, but my heart sleeps not."[59] If a mosquito bites someone who is sleeping, he may dream that he has been severely wounded. If questioned, he would reply: "I've been wounded. They fired guns and rifles at me." Those sitting by him would laugh at his anguish in sleep. Thus the view of heedlessness and philosophy in its "sleep" cannot be the criterion for the truths of Prophethood.

- **Three great and universal things make our Lord known to us: the Book of the Universe; Prophet Muhammad, upon him be peace and blessings, the Seal of the Prophets, who is the supreme sign in the Book of the Universe; and the glorious Qur'an. There are numerous other witnesses or evidences of knowledge of God, which fall in three categories.**[60]

The witnesses or evidences of the first category are like water. We can feel and see them, but cannot hold them with our hands. We should not examine them with the fingers of criticism; if we do so, they flow away and are lost. The water of life cannot remain between fingers.

Those of the second category are like air. We can feel them, but cannot see or seize them. We should breathe them in with our spirit rather than

---

[57] *The Words*, "The Twenty-fourth Word", p. 370.

[58] *Suratu'n-Najm*, 53:17.

[59] *al-Bukhari*, "Tahajjud" 16; *at-Tirmidhi*, "Adab" 86; *Abu Dawud*, "Tahara" 79.

[60] *The Words*, "The Nineteenth Word", p. 247; *The Gleams*, "The Seventeenth Gleam", p. 177.

responding to them with our hands of criticism stretched out to seize them. Otherwise they will disappear. These witnesses and evidences cannot be held in our hands.

Those of the third category are like light. We can see them, but cannot touch or receive them. We should turn to them with the eyes of our heart and with the sight of our spirit. Light cannot be held in the hand nor sought out with the fingers. It can be hunted only with the light of insight.

- **There are four ladders or ways to acquire knowledge of the Creator, which is the highest point that human beings can reach: The first is the way of the scholarly Sufis; the second is the way of the scholars of Islamic theology; and the third way belongs to the people of wisdom or the believing philosophers; and the fourth is the way of the Qur'an.**[61]

The way of the scholarly Sufis is based on purification of the soul, refinement of the heart, and intuition or inner observation. The way of the theologians is founded upon two arguments. The first is that the existence of the universe is possible, but not necessary. This is because it is contained in time and space, or is accidental or contingent. So there must be One Who willed its existence and brought it into existence. The second argument is that the universe is not timeless or without beginning; it has a beginning, and this requires the existence of a timeless One Who brought it into existence. Both of these ways are derived from the Qur'an, but human thought has given them their own forms, and therefore elaborated on them.

The third way which belongs to the people of wisdom or the believing philosophers is open to controversy and the attack of whims or suspicion.

The fourth way, which is that of the Qur'an, is the most direct and the clearest of ways, one which shows the peerless eloquence of the Qur'an and is possible for everyone to follow. This way or ladder basically has two important steps, which are as follows:

The first is the argument of assistance, beneficence, and purposefulness. All the Qur'anic verses that mention the benefits of things and the purposes they serve indicate or are comprised of this argument. This argument is based on the fact that the perfect universal order takes into account beneficence and purposefulness. Whatever exists serves many

---

[61] *The Reasonings*, "The Third Part", pp. 107–111.

benefits and purposes and has many instances of wisdom in the perfect universal order. This categorically rejects and negates the assertions of chance or coincidence.

The second basic Qur'anic argument for God Almighty's existence and Oneness is that of creation or origination. Its summary is as follows:

Every species and all members of every species have been given an existence according to the function or purpose assigned to each, and the capacity accorded to each. In addition, no species is a link in a chain that stretches back to the eternity of the past, for their existence is contingent or accidental, not absolute. There is a Will that makes a choice between their existence and non-existence, and a Power that gives them existence. Existence is clearly not timeless, but is contained in time and space, and therefore has a beginning.

A truth cannot become its opposite, nor can its nature change. There cannot be any intermediary species between existing species. For every species has its own nature, upon which its structure based. Therefore, the transformation or evolution of a species into another means the complete transformation of an established truth, which is impossible.

Every species came into existence separately and has an original ancestor. Besides, neither the material causes, nor nature, nor any other "law," supposed, nominal, or real, can have any creative part in the things that come into existence. Every species and every member of a species is created by the All-Wise Maker, individually and separately. The All-Majestic Maker has put on the forehead of everything the stamps of "contingency" and "having a beginning" or "being contained in time and space."

With respect to their essence, species are different from one another. Neither the forms nor the forces, which are claimed to be produced through the motion of atoms, nor the nuclei of cells, can be responsible for this essential difference. For all of these are accidental to the essence; they themselves are the results of the differences of the essence. This shows that all the species, with their differences, were brought into existence separately by a Creator, Who does whatever He wills however He wills. If you desire further explanations concerning the argument of creation or origination, you can enter the paradise of the Qur'an, where you can find every truth, either in the form of blossoming flowers or as buds or as seeds.

Human conscious nature categorically rejects those who attribute eternity to matter or force or movement when explaining the origin of existence by ignoring the perfect order of the universe; it rejects those who maintain that all is coincidence or chance, despite the amazing, miraculous art and embroidery in every single thing and in the entirety of creation; it rejects those who ascribe creativity to material causes and what they call laws, in spite of sound thought and reasoning and an unbiased scientific approach; and it rejects those who think that they have found consolation in attributing existence to nature because of the regularity in things and events, despite the opposite judgment of their conscience.

Matter cannot be thought of as being separate from the changing form and the movement which appears and disappears over time. So it is not eternal; it is contained in time. How ridiculous then that there are those who cannot accept the existence and eternity of the Maker, Whose existence is absolutely necessary for the universe to come into existence and for it to continue to exist, yet, at the same time, they can attribute eternity and creativity to matter, which is lifeless, unconscious, and absolutely devoid of knowledge and will-power. How strange it is that some, who although members of humanity, cannot ascribe the universe, which is wonderful in all its parts and in its totality, to the Maker, Who has all the attributes of perfection, but rather ascribe it to lifeless, unconscious, and blind chance, and to the motion of atoms, which are also lifeless, blind, and unconscious.

As for what they call "nature" or "forces of nature," God Almighty has a collection or an assembly of His laws called "the laws of creation and the operation of the universe," which are in fact God's Acts of creating, regulating, putting in order and maintaining the corporeal world with whatever is in it and the functions of its "members" and "organs." This assembly of the laws of the creation and the operation of the universe is like an immaterial Divine printing machine, but they call it nature. What they call "the laws of nature" are those Acts of God or the sum of their effects; and what they call "the forces" are the ways they are carried out. The regularity of their execution or the formation of a collective, imaginary body in the mind that is caused by their execution, or by the incessant, rapid movement of their execution that cannot be observed, causes people to attribute external existence to this assembly of laws and the effects of their implementation. What they call nature is this imagined external existence.

Those things they call nature and natural forces are not able to be the origin of existence, nor can they be accepted as such by a sound mind or by the truth. But the obstinacy of not accepting the existence of the Creator and the regularity of His Acts which are responsible for the creation and operation of the universe may lead some to attribute these amazing works of the Divine Power to what they call nature. However, nature is, in fact, a print; it is not the printer; it is a tune, not the composer; it is a design, not the designer; it is a recipient, not the agent; it is an order, not that which gives the order. It is a collection of laws established by the Divine Will, not a power.

- **When we turn to the Almighty supposing that He is One known and recognized, He will become unknown and unrecognized, for our supposition is based on a commonplace, imitative knowledge about Him. In most cases, such knowledge has nothing to do with truth. The meaning it conveys to our mind is far from explaining the absolute Divine Attributes. But if we turn to the Almighty, accepting Him as One existent but unknown, then rays of true knowledge of Him will be revealed and the all-encompassing, absolute Divine Attributes manifested in the universe will appear in the light of this knowledge.[62]**

- **Every living thing receives the manifestations of numerous Names. For example, the Names the Creator, the All-Shaping, the All-Seeing, the All-Hearing, the All-Arranging, the All-Providing, the All-Sustaining, the All-Healing, and many others manifest themselves on the same being. Like the seven colors in sunlight, though each Name has Its own beauty and imprints, they work to the same effect in each individual thing, even cells, and show many other Names in Its own mirror.[63]**

This manifest reality shows that the One Who has these Names is one and the same being: The All-Living Creator of something is also its Shaper, Provider, and Sustainer; the One Who provides something is the Creator of the sources of provision; and its Creator is He Who knows and has dominion over everything. That is, although some Divine Names (like the All-Knowing) encompass all things, the Divine Names manifested in the universe cooperate in the creation, life, and working of all its parts down to the minutest particles. Like sunlight's seven colors, they work to

---

[62] *Al-Mathnawi al-Nuri*, "The Sixth Treatise", p. 186.
[63] *Al-Mathnawi al-Nuri*, "The Fourth Treatise", pp. 73, 77.

the same effect. Although each has Its own manifestation and produces Its own effects, they ultimately produce an integrated entity. This demonstrates that the Being called by those Names is one. In the language of the coordination and solidarity among the Names manifested in it, the universe testifies that there is no deity but God.

- **Since the Names and Attributes of God manifest themselves one within and together with another, it is surely necessary for one who recognizes Almighty God by one of His Acts or Names or Attributes not to deny His other Acts, Names and Attributes and consider them together.**[64]

The Lord of the worlds has at the levels of His Lordship's manifestations qualities and designations which are all different but correspond to each other. In the spheres of His Divinity, He has Names and marks which are all different but whose manifestations are concentric with each other. In His majestic execution of His rule, He has representations and appellations which are all different but resemble each other. In the operations of His Power, He has titles which are all different but imply each other. In the manifestations of His Attributes, He has sacred ways of revealing Himself that differ but point to each other. In His modes of acting, He has wise operations which are of numerous sorts but perfect each other. In His colorful artistry and varied works of Art, He has magnificent aspects of Lordship which differ but correspond to each other.

In every world and division of beings, each of His All-Beautiful Names is manifested individually. A particular Name is dominant in a particular sphere, with other Names being subordinate. In every level and division of beings, regardless of size, God has a particular display of Himself, a particular manifestation of Lordship, and a particular manifestation of a Name. Although the Name in question has a universal manifestation, It concentrates on something particular in such a way that we think It is exclusive to that thing. Therefore, it is surely necessary for one who recognizes Almighty God by one of His Names, Titles, or aspects of His Lordship not to deny His other Titles, Acts, and aspects of Lordship. If we do not move from the manifestation of one Name to the other Names, we are in loss. For example, if we do not see the All-Knowing where we see the works of the All-Powerful and the Creator, we may fall into heedlessness

---

[64] *The Words*, "The Twenty-fourth Word", pp. 352–353.

and misguidance by regarding nature as self-originated. Or if we see the Creator but do not see the Maker with perfect art, we ignore things as signs or mirrors of God and see them as mere objects with no meaning and art. On the other hand, if we see the perfect art in things but do not see the Creator, we may fall into the pit of materialism. So we always should recite "He" and "He is God," and in unison with all creation, we should proclaim: "There is no deity but He." The Qur'an, clear in itself and clearly showing the truth, through the declaration, "*God, there is no deity but He. His are the All- Beautiful Names,*"[65] points to these truths.

- **Divine Unity (***Wahidiya***: which demonstrates Itself through the manifestation of the Divine Names throughout the universe) is evident in the boundless multiplicity of individualized creatures. So as not to overwhelm our minds in the all-encompassing manifestation of these Names, the Qur'an, being a miracle of exposition, constantly reiterates the manifestation of Divine Absolute Oneness (***Ahadiya***) within Unity—the concentrated manifestation of certain Divine Names on beings individually.**[66]

Consider this analogy: The sun encompasses innumerable things in its light. Therefore, to hold the totality of the sun with its encompassing light in our minds, we would need a vast conceptual and perceptual power. So lest the sun be ignored and forgotten, each and every shining object reflects its properties (light and heat) as best as it can and so manifests the sun, and those properties (heat, light, and the color spectrum) encompass the objects that the sun faces.

Similarly—*to God applies the most sublime attribute*[67]—just as God's Oneness, His being Eternally Besought, and His Divine Names are manifested in everything, particularly in living things and especially in our mirror-like nature, each Divine Name related to creatures encompasses all creatures through Divine Unity. Thus, the Qur'an constantly draws our attention to the seal of Divine Oneness (through the Divine manifestation on each individual being or thing or on particulars) within Divine Unity (through the Divine manifestation on the entire universe or on the

---

[65] *Sura Ta-Ha*, 20:8.

[66] *The Gleams*, "The Fourteenth Gleam", pp. 133–134.

[67] The Qur'an, 16: 60. This verse is mentioned because although God is beyond all comparisons, we may need comparisons to explain abstract truths for Him and His Acts. However the most sublime comparisons should be made to explain Divine truths.

wholes), lest our minds be overwhelmed by Unity and our hearts become heedless of the Pure and Holy Essence. *Basmala* (In the Name of God, the All-Merciful and the All-Compassionate) indicates this reality.

- **If you want to acquire knowledge of the truth and true wisdom, try to attain knowledge of God. For all truths and realities of creation consist in the rays of the Divine Name al-Haqq—the Ultimate Truth and Ever-Constant—and the manifestations of His Names and Attributes. The reality of each human being and every existence, whether material or spiritual, substantial or accidental, originates in the light of one of His Names. Otherwise they would be mere forms without any substantial reality and truth.**[68]

Each science even originates in, and is based on, one or more Divine Names. For example, the science of medicine originates in the Name the All-Healing, and engineering in the Name the All-Just and Designing, and geometry in the All-Wise and Determining, and so on. Therefore, each science, in fact, continuously speaks of God, the Creator, and makes Him known in its own tongue.

- **The most evident and powerful sign for the existence of something is speech. The Divine Eternal Speech is a Divine Attribute like the Knowledge and the Power, and therefore infinite and limitless. It functions like the Power and therefore the Qur'an says,** "When He wills a thing to be, He but says to it 'Be!' and it is..."[69] **when speaking about God's creation. Just as the Divine Speech has words, so do the Knowledge and Power have their own words, which are all things, beings and events. The words of God are limitless and cannot be computed.**[70]

- **The act of bestowing is discerned and the All-Merciful's favor is perceived in each bounty. If you discern this act through what is bestowed, you will find the All-Bestowing One. Each work of the Eternally Besought One points out the All-Majestic Maker's Names like a missive.**[71]

Every item that exists is a word of embodied meaning, and shows many of the All-Majestic Maker's Names. Since beings are words of Divine Power,

[68] *The Words*, "The Twenty-sixth Word", p. 492.
[69] *Sura Ya-Sin*, 36:82.
[70] *Lem'alar*, "Yirmisekizinci Lem'a (The Twenty-eighth Gleam)", (unpublished).
[71] *The Words*, "The Seventeenth Word", pp. 230–231.

casting the letters or shells left without meaning into the wind of transience, we should understand their meanings and place them in our heart.

- **Alas! We have been deceived. We thought that this worldly life was constant, and thus lost it thoroughly. Indeed, this passing life is but a sleep that passed like a dream. This life, having no foundation, flies like the wind. Those who rely on themselves and think they will live forever will certainly die. They race towards death, and this world, humanity's home, falls into the darkness of annihilation. Ambitions are time-bounded, but pains endure in the spirit.[72]**

Since this is the reality, come, my wretched soul that is fond of living and wants a long life, that loves the world and has boundless ambition and pain. Awaken and come to your senses. Consider that while the firefly relies on its own dim light and always remains in night's boundless darkness, the honeybee finds the sun of daytime and observes its friends (flowers) gilded with sunlight because it does not rely on itself. In the same way, if you rely on yourself, and your being and self-confidence, you will be like the firefly. But if you dedicate yourself, your transient being and body on the way of the Creator Who gave it to you, you will find, like the honeybee, an endless life of being. Dedicate it, for your being and your body is no more than a Divine trust to you.

Moreover, your being is the Creator's property; it is He Who gave it to you. So use it for His sake unhesitatingly and without placing Him under obligation so that it will gain permanence. For a negation negated is an affirmation. Thus if our non-being is negated (in favor of the True Being), our being finds true existence. The All-Munificent Creator buys His own property from you. In return, He gives you a high price like Paradise, looks after it for you, and increases its value. He will return it to you in a perfected and permanent form. So, my soul, do not wait. Do this business, which is profitable in five respects. As well as being saved from five losses, make a fivefold profit in one transaction.

- **If you desire permanence in this transient world, permanence is born out of transience and annihilation. Annihilate your evil-commanding soul so that you may gain permanence.[73]**

---

[72] *The Words*, "The Seventeenth Word", pp. 228–289.

[73] *The Words*, "The Seventeenth Word", p. 230.

Free yourself of bad morals, the basis of worldly adoration, and realize self-annihilation. Sacrifice your wealth in your possession and control for the True Beloved's sake. See the end of beings, which marks extinction. For the way leading from this world to permanence passes through self-annihilation.

- Surely, this exalted, universal act of cleansing, which keeps the palace of the universe clean, is the manifestation and requirement of the Divine Name the All-Holy. As the act of ordering and order, which are a manifestation of the Divine Attribute of Wisdom and the Divine Name the All-Wise, and the act of making balanced and balance, which are a manifestation of the Attribute of Justice and the Name the All-Just, and the act of equipping and benevolence, which are a manifestation of the Names the All-Gracious and the All-Munificent, and the act of rearing, nurturing and bestowal, which are a manifestation of the Names the Lord and the All-Compassionate, are each a single truth and a single act observed throughout the universe, they demonstrate the necessary existence and Unity of a Single Being. In exactly the same way, the act of purifying and making clean, which is a manifestation of the Name the All-Holy, demonstrates, like the sun, the existence of the Necessarily Existent One, and His Unity like daylight.[74]

- The perfect, all-embracing justice, order, balance and harmony in the universe issue from the most comprehensive manifestation of the Divine Name the All-Just, and are among the most evident and powerful evidences of God's existence and Oneness.[75]

The universe is such a palace that in it is a "city" which is being continuously shaken by destruction and repair. And in the city there is a "country" which is incessantly plagued by war and emigration. And within the country is a "world" which is constantly revolving amidst death and life. But such an astonishing balance, equilibrium, and act of ordering prevail in the palace, city, country, and world that it obviously proves that all the changes, the incomings and outgoings which occur in these innumerable beings, are measured and weighed on the scales of a Single Being Who every moment sees and supervises the whole universe with what-

---

[74] *The Gleams*, "The Thirtieth Gleam", pp. 429–430.
[75] *The Gleams*, "The Thirtieth Gleam", pp. 429–430.

ever is and takes place in it. For considering that, for example, a single fish lays around a thousand eggs at one time and a single flower like a poppy produces around twenty thousand seeds, if causes—all creatures—were free and unrestrained, they would be able to destroy the balance and overrun everything through the onslaught of incessant changes and the elements flowing in floods. If they were under the control of aimless, purposeless "chance," anarchic blind forces, or unconscious dark nature, then the balance in beings, or the balance of the whole universe, would have been so utterly destroyed that within a year, indeed within a day, there would have been chaos.

Thus, everything in the universe from the cells of an animate body to the red and white corpuscles in the blood, from the transformations of minute particles to the proportion and relationship between the body's organs, from the water coming in and out of the seas to the income and expenditure of springs under the earth, from the birth and death of animals and plants to the destruction of autumn and the reconstruction of spring, from the duties and motion of the universal elements and the stars to the alternations, struggles and clashes of death and life, light and darkness, and heat and cold... the universe is ordered and weighed with such a sensitive balance, so fine a measure, that the human mind can nowhere see any waste or futility, just as sciences see and indicate the most perfect order and beautiful balance everywhere. Indeed, sciences, based on "laws" deduced from the perfectly well-ordered and regular operation of each and everything, are manifestations, interpretations and evidences of that order and balance.

- **The all-embracing manifestation of the Divine Name the All-Wise has made the universe into such a book that hundreds of books have been written on every page of it, and hundreds of pages have been included in every line of it, and there are hundreds of lines in every word of it, and every letter of it contains hundreds of words, and a short index of the book is to be found in every point. The book's pages and lines, down to the very points, demonstrate its Inscriber and Author in hundreds of respects with such clarity that an observation of that book of the universe establishes the existence and Unity of its Scribe to a degree that is hundreds of times greater than the proof of the book's own existence. For if a single**

letter exhibits its own existence to the extent of a letter, the same letter exhibits its Scribe to the extent of a line.[76]

One page of this macro-book is the face of the earth. In spring, as many books as there are plant and animal species can be seen written on this page, one within the other, together, at the same time, without error, and in the most perfect form.

One line of the page is a garden. We see with our eyes that, on this page, there are written well-composed odes to the number of flowers, trees, and animals in the garden. They are written all together, one within the other, and without error.

One word of the line is a tree which has blossomed and put forth its leaves in order to yield its fruit. This word comprises meaningful passages that laud and praise the All-Wise One of Majesty to the number of its orderly, well-proportioned, and adorned leaves, flowers, and fruit. It is as if, like all other trees, this tree is also a well-composed ode, singing the praises of its Inscriber.

It is also as though the All-Wise One of Majesty wants to look with thousands of eyes on His wonderful, venerable works, thus displaying them in the exhibition of the earth.

And it is as though the bejeweled gifts, decorations, and uniforms accorded to the tree by that Eternal Monarch have been made with such incredibly adorned, well-proportioned, orderly, and meaningful forms in order that they might be presented to His view in spring, the tree's particular festival and parade, that each of these gifts, decorations, and uniforms—the flowers, leaves, and fruits—bears witness to the existence and Names of the Inscriber in numerous ways and with many proofs, one within the other.

For example, each blossom or fruit displays a perfect organization and balance. The balance is maintained through an unceasing and ever-renewed act of ordering; the act of ordering follows perfect art and decoration, and this art and decoration is combined with exceptional scents and purposeful tastes. Thus, each blossom indicates the All-Wise One of Majesty to the number of the blossoms on the tree.

The tree, which is itself a word, grows from a seed, which is a letter. This letter is a small coffer containing the future content and program of

---

[76] *The Gleams*, "The Thirtieth Gleam", pp. 436–445.

the entire tree. And so on. To continue the same analogy, the manifestation of the Name the All-Wise not only makes every page of the book of the universe, but it also creates its lines, words, letters, and points, as miracles; thus even if all the causes—living or non-living—should gather together, they would not make the like of a single point, nor could they dare to compete with it. And so on...

- **The Divine Name the All-Independent, Single One has placed a stamp of Divine Unity on the universe as a whole and on each species of creature in it, and on each individual being, thus making the universe a single, indivisible, unitary entity.**[77]

Here, only three stamps will be indicated:

The first stamp: The manifestation of Divine Independence and Oneness has placed such a seal of Unity on the face of the universe that it has made it an indivisible whole. One who does not have the power of control or disposal over the entire universe cannot be the true owner of any part of it. The stamp is the following:

Like the perfectly well-ordered parts of a factory, the parts and species of beings that comprise the universe help one another, and work to complete one another's functions. Through their solidarity and cooperation, and through their hastening to the aid of one another, embracing one another and being one within the other, they form such a united existence that, like the organs of the human body, they cannot be separated from one another. One who takes the reins of one part or element in their hand cannot maintain their control over it unless they take the reins of the whole of the universe.

Thus, this universal cooperation, solidarity, mutual response, and embracing one another form a most brilliant supreme stamp of Divine Unity.

The second stamp: Through the manifestation of the Name the All-Independent, Single One, such a brilliant seal of Divine Oneness and a stamp of Unity are shown on the face of the earth and the countenance of spring that it proves that one who cannot administer all the living creatures on the earth, together with all their individuals and conditions and states, and who does not know or see them all together, and cannot create them, cannot possibly have any part in creation. The stamp is the following:

---

[77] *The Gleams*, "The Thirtieth Gleam", pp. 446–459.

Disregarding the most orderly, yet hidden, stamps of the mineral substances, the elements, and the inanimate creatures of the earth, consider the following stamp that is woven with the threads of hundreds of thousands of animal species and hundreds of thousands of plant species: we see with our own eyes that on earth in spring, despite having different duties and different forms, and being one within the other and all mixed up together, all things are given their sustenance and equipment without confusion or error, with complete distinction and differentiation, with extremely sensitive balance, without difficulty, at exactly the right time, from unexpected places. This situation, this planning, this administration forms such a seal of Divine Unity and stamp of Oneness that one who cannot create all these creatures at once from nothing and administer them all together can have no part at all in Lordship or creation. If they were to have a part, the all-embracing balance of administration would have been spoilt. However, humans apparently serve the fine application of these laws of Lordship by God's leave and command.

The third stamp: This stamp of Divine Oneness is on the human face. Rather, the human face itself is such a stamp of Divine Oneness that one who does not hold in their view all the human beings who have come and who will come from the time of Adam until the end of the world, and who cannot place on each face hundreds of distinguishing marks, indeed, who cannot make each face a distinguishing mark for each individual human being, can have no part at all in the creation of even a single face with its particular, distinguishing features. The One Who places the stamp in question on each individual human being's face must surely hold within His view, and encompass with His Knowledge, all the members of the human species. For although all faces resemble one another in respect of their basic features like eyes and ears (and all are made of the same material), they are all different and distinguishable from one another. While the fact that the faces of human beings are all alike in respect of their basic features and their structure or composition is a stamp of Unity that shows that the Maker of the human species is One, many wise differences—unlike in other species—distinguish one individual human from another so that they should not be confused, and that the rights of each human being should be preserved demonstrate the Maker's absolutely free choice or will. In addition, these differences make each face a subtle stamp of Divine Unity, which shows that one who cannot create all humans and animals, indeed, the whole universe, cannot impress this stamp.

- **Life, a comprehensive manifestation of the Divine Names the All-Living and the Giver of Life, is the greatest result of the universe, as well as its most comprehensive aim and most valuable fruit, and therefore has a great aim and result as vast as the universe. When life enters a thing, it makes it like a world; if it is a part, it makes it like a whole; if it is something of a particular nature that belongs to an indivisible whole, it gives it the comprehensiveness of that whole. Indeed, life is of such a nature that it is a comprehensive mirror that reflects God's Oneness on particular things in the concentrated manifestations of many of His Names.[78]**

  Life is:

  - the most important aim of the universe, and
  - its greatest result, and
  - its most brilliant light, and
  - its subtlest and most pleasant leaven, and
  - a pure extract distilled from it, and
  - its most perfect fruit, and
  - its most elevated perfection, and
  - its most beautiful countenance, and
  - its most beautiful adornment, and
  - the secret of its unitary nature, and
  - the bond of its unity, and
  - the source of its perfections, and
  - something that has spirit and which is most extraordinary in respect to art and nature, and
  - a miraculous reality that makes the tiniest creature like a universe, and
  - a miracle of Divine Power which, as though the universe were situated in a tiny living creature, shows in that creature some sort of index of the huge universe, and connects the creature to other things and beings; and
  - it is a wonderful Divine art which makes a tiny part as great as the whole, and that allows parts of a whole represent the whole itself,

---

[78] *The Gleams*, "The Thirtieth Gleam", pp. 459–473.

showing that in respect of the Lordship over it the universe is an indivisible whole or a universal entity interconnected with all its parts and which allows no participation; and

- life is the most brilliant, the most decisive, the most perfect of proofs testifying to the necessary existence and Oneness of the All-Living and Self-Subsistent One; and

- among Divine works of art life is both the most hidden and the most apparent, and the most valuable and the most inexpensive, and it is the purest, most shining, and most meaningful embroidery of the Lord's Art; and

- life is a graceful, refined, delicate manifestation of the Mercy of the All-Merciful which makes other beings serve itself; and

- it is a most comprehensive mirror of the essential Qualities that are indispensable to His Essence; and

- it is a wonder of the Lord's creation that comprises the manifestations of numerous All-Beautiful Names, such as the All-Merciful, the All-Providing, the All-Compassionate, the All-Munificent, and the All-Wise, subjecting to itself many realities like provision, wisdom, grace, and mercy, and it is the source and origin of all the senses like sight, hearing, and touch; and

- life is such a transformation machine in the vast workshop of the universe that it continuously cleans and purifies everywhere, allowing progress and illumination. And it makes living bodies, which are its dwellings, guesthouses, schools, or barracks for the caravans of atoms so that they may be refined and brought up to perform their duties. Quite simply, through the machine of life, the All-Living One, the Giver of Life, beautifies, makes pleasant, and illumines this dark, transient, lowly world, and gives it a sort of permanence, preparing it to go to another, everlasting world; and

- both of the two faces of life—that is, both its outer and inner faces —are bright, sublime, unsoiled, and without defect. It is an exceptional creature in the creation of which the direct operation of the Divine Power has not been veiled by physical causes, so that it can clearly be shown that it has emerged directly without veil or means from the hand of the Lord's Power; and

- the reality of life relates to the six pillars of belief, supporting them in meaning and indirectly. That is to say, it is a luminous reality which relates to, and proves, the absolutely necessary, eternal existence of the Necessarily Existent One, the Hereafter and eternal life, and the existence of angels, and other pillars of belief;

- also, just as life is the purest essence of the universe, distilled from all of it, so too is it a mighty mystery generating thanksgiving, worship, praise, and love, which are the most important Divine purposes for the existence of the universe and the most important results of the world's creation.

So consider all these significant, valuable merits and properties, and these elevated, comprehensive duties of life, and then look and see the magnificence of the Name the All-Living behind the Name the Giver of Life. And understand from these immense properties and fruits of life how comprehensive a Divine Name is the Name the All-Living.

Also understand that since life is the greatest result of the universe, as well as its most comprehensive aim and most valuable fruit, it must have an aim and result as vast and great as the universe. For as the tree's result is its fruit, the fruit's result, too, by means of the seed, is a future tree. Indeed, just as the aim and result of this life is eternal life, so too, one of its fruits is thanksgiving to the One All-Living and Giver of Life, and worship and praise of Him, and love for Him. And just as this thanksgiving, love, praise, and worship are the fruit of life, so too are they the aim of the universe. Understand from this how ugly ignorance is, and what a blasphemy, paramount to unbelief, lies in the claim of those who say that the aim of life is to live comfortably, enjoy oneself heedlessly, and indulge oneself in pleasure, degrading and insulting the most valuable bounty of life, the gift of consciousness, and the bounty of reason; what appalling ingratitude they display.

- **The Majestic Creator of the universe is Self-Subsistent; that is, He subsists and eternally exists by Himself. All things subsist, continue, and have permanence by Him. If the universe's connection with His being the Self-Subsistent by Whom all subsist was severed for even a fraction of a second, the universe would be utterly destroyed.**[79]

Besides being the Self-Subsistent by Whom all subsist, as the Qur'an of mighty stature decrees, the All-Majestic Being is also *"the One like Whom*

---

[79] *The Gleams*, "The Thirtieth Gleam", pp. 475–479.

there is nothing whatever."[80] That is, neither in His Essence, nor in His Attributes, nor in His acts has He either a like, equal, peer, or partner. Indeed, it is inconceivable that there be any like, equal, partner, or peer for the All-Holy One, Who holds in the grasp of His Lordship the entire universe with whatever is or happens in it, and Who administers, sustains, and nurtures it with perfect order as though it were a house or a palace.

He is such an All-Living, Self-Subsistent One of Majesty that the creation of the stars is as easy for Him as that of particles, and the greatest thing is subservient to His Power in the same way as the most minute thing is, and His doing one thing can in no way prevent Him from doing another thing, and innumerable things are present before His View, all at the same time, as if a single thing, and He hears all voices simultaneously and is ever able to answer the limitless needs of all simultaneously, and, as testified to by the order and balance in all corners of the universe, there is nothing, no action or state, that is outside the sphere of His Will, and although absolutely not limited by space, He is omnipresent everywhere with His Power and Knowledge, and although everything is infinitely distant from Him, He is infinitely close to all things. Certainly, such an All-Living, Self-Subsistent One of Majesty can in no way have any like, equal, partner, deputy, opposite, or peer; it would be impossible. We can only consider His sacred essential Qualities and Attributes through parables and metaphors.

The act of creation and subsistence observed in beings is such that it clearly demonstrates that it proceeds from a Power and Will that see and know all things simultaneously, and know and secure each and every living creature's relationship with the entire universe. It thus demonstrates that it can in no way be the act of causes, which are material, and which are not all-encompassing. It is due to God Almighty's Self-Subsistence that even a most particular creative act bears the supreme quality that indicates that it is directly the act of the Creator of the entire universe. For example, an act pertaining to the creation of a bee demonstrates that it is peculiar to the Creator of the universe in two respects.

The first respect: The fact that all the other bees throughout the world display the same act at the same time demonstrates that the particular act displayed by an individual bee and all bees is the tip of a comprehensive act which embraces the entirety of the earth. Therefore, whoever is

---

[80] *Suratu'sh-Shura*, 42:11.

the author of that comprehensive act must also be the author of the particular act.

The second respect: In order to be the author of an action connected with the creation of the bee in question, there must be a power and will that are encompassing enough to know and secure conditions for the life of the bee, and all its members, and its relationship with the universe. Therefore, only the one who authors the particular act will be able to perform it so perfectly by having authority over the entire universe.

- **When viewed with the light of belief, lawful pleasures in the world and bounties in the Hereafter form a virtuous circle. The disappearance of pleasures or separation from bounties does not cause pain, for the pleasures of belief and thankfulness are permanent. But without belief, pleasures change into pain for the decay of those pleasures; even thinking of their decay causes pain. Unbelief views each pleasure as an end in itself, and its disappearance causes pain.[81]**

- **The world's pleasure and beauty, in the absence of knowledge about our Creator, Owner, and Lord, are no more than a hell, even if they were as great as those of Paradise. With true knowledge of Him, a blessing like compassion becomes so pleasing and sweet that it may make one indifferent to whatever is in the world, even to Paradise.[82]**

- **Existence based on the human ego ends in non-existence, whereas self-annihilation or annihilation of the ego results in existence, and leads to the Necessarily Existent Being. If you desire existence and find it, try to annihilate your ego.[83]**

- **Whoever relies on God finds that God is sufficient for him or her. So, say: "God is sufficient for me, what an excellent guardian He is."[84]**

First: God is absolutely perfect. Absolute perfection is loved for its own sake, and great things are sacrificed for it.

---

[81] *Al-Mathnawi al-Nuri*, "The Fourth Treatise", p. 114.
[82] *Al-Mathnawi al-Nuri*, "The Fifth Treatise", p. 148.
[83] *Al-Mathnawi al-Nuri*, "The Fourth Treatise", p. 113.
[84] *Al-Mathnawi al-Nuri*, "The Sixth Treatise", p. 185–186.

Second: Since He is loved for His own sake, He is the true beloved, and love requires sacrifice.

Third: He is the Necessarily Existent One. In His nearness originate the lights of existence, while absence from Him brings the darkness of extinction or non-existence, and causes the human soul incurable pain by extinguishing its aspirations.

Fourth: He is the refuge of the human spirit suffocated within material existence's narrow confines, suffering from the world's deceit, crushed by the pain arising from its affection for creation.

Fifth: He is the Everlasting, by Whom things become permanent and without Whom things decay and are extinguished, which causes grief and sorrow. Without Him pain accumulates in the human spirit, whereas light pours from everywhere over one who finds and trusts in Him.

Sixth: He is the sole Owner of existence. He wants to bear your burdens of life and bodily existence that He has entrusted to you, as you cannot carry them and suffer if you think you own them. If you desire their permanence and His continued favoring, do not be grieved when He takes them from you. Bubbles containing the sun's images do not grieve when they disappear, and gladly sacrifice their apparent forms for the renewal of the sun's reflections. Fruits do not grieve when they are separated from their tree, and seeds do not grieve over the fruit's disintegration in the ground, for its disintegration means the growth of a new tree that will yield many fruits. You are also a fruit, an embodiment, of His favoring.

Seventh: He is the All-Wealthy and Bestower of wealth, and in His Hand are the keys to everything. If you become His sincere servant and then look at the universe, you will see your Master's sovereignty and magnificence and find relief. You will come to view the universe as if it were your property that you own without trouble, and the disappearance of which would not grieve you. A sincere servant of the King who is annihilated in His love becomes proud of whatever belongs to Him.

Eighth: He is the Lord of all Messengers and Prophets, saints and God-conscious people, all of whom are happy in His mercy. If you have a sound, uncorrupted heart, your knowledge of their happiness must give you happiness and pleasure.

- **A beloved who disappears is not beautiful, for one doomed to decline cannot be truly beautiful. It is not, and should not be,**

loved in the heart, for the heart is created for eternal love and is a mirror of the Eternally Besought One.[85]

I am mortal, so I do not want the mortal.

I am impotent, so I do not desire the impotent.

I surrendered my spirit to the All-Merciful, so I desire none else.

I want only one who will remain my friend forever.

I am but an insignificant particle, but I desire an everlasting sun.

I am nothing in essence, but I wish for the whole of creation.

- **Perfections in the world are usually judged by way of contrast. Pleasure's perfection cannot be perceived without pain, light cannot be recognized without darkness, and union gives no pleasure if there is no separation. However, any virtue, perfection, or superiority that manifests itself in comparison to, or in contrast with, others is of relative value and significance. Losing its opposite causes it to lose its value. Therefore, true pleasure, love, perfection or virtue do not show themselves in comparison with others, or in proportion to their opposites' degree—they are by and of themselves, and so are substantial and constant realities.**[86]

For example, existence, life, love, knowledge (especially knowledge of God), belief, permanence, mercy, compassion or affection, as well as light, sound sight and hearing, eloquence, munificence, good conduct or moral virtues, and appropriate form are all virtues by their very nature. With or without opposites, they are virtues and perfections in themselves. Neither they themselves, nor their pleasure and beauty, need comparisons or opposites to be perceived and appreciated. Their opposites can only serve in recognizing and perceiving them better and more effectively. Thus, all perfections of the All-Majestic Maker, the All-Gracious and Beautiful Originator and the Creator of Perfection are true in and of themselves. Whatever other than Him can have no effect on Him. The perfections in creation are only their reflections according to the capacity of each being. In *Sharhu'l-Mawaqif*, Sayyid Sharif al-Jurjani writes: "The cause of love is either pleasure or benefit or sexual or natural inclination or perfection. Perfection is loved because of itself." So, as they are true,

---

[85] *The Words*, "The Seventeenth Word", pp. 229, 235.
[86] *The Words*, "The Thirty-second Word", pp. 633, 635–636.

indisputable, and infinite, all of Almighty God's Perfections and His All-Beautiful Names are loved because of themselves.

- **With their nature, identity, and heart, human beings are like mirrors, and the love of permanence and eternity implanted in their nature is, in essence, not for the mirror. Rather, it is felt for the Everlasting One of Majesty, Whose manifestations are reflected in the mirror according to its capacity. However, due to our foolishness, we direct the mirror to other, fleeting objects, and thus misuse our love of permanence.[87]**

There are some foolish people who, because they do not recognize the sun, start to love it when they see its image in a mirror. They try to preserve the mirror with intense attachment to it so that the sun's image in it may not be lost. But if they understand that the sun does not perish or disappear when the mirror does, they will direct their love only to the sun itself. The image in the mirror does not depend on the mirror for its permanence; rather, the mirror's permanence depends on the sun. The permanence of the mirror's "liveliness" and its shining (with the sun in it) are possible only through the permanence of the sun's manifestation and the mirror's facing the sun.

O human being! With your nature, identity, and heart you are like that mirror, and the love of permanence implanted in your nature is, in essence, not for the mirror. Rather, it is felt for the manifestation of the Everlasting One of Majesty, which is reflected in the mirror according to its capacity. However, due to your foolishness, you direct the mirror to other objects. This being the case, say, "O the Everlasting, You are the Everlasting!" That is to say, "Since You exist and are everlasting, those who are transient and mortal may do what they want to do with us; let them do it, for I do not mind whatever befalls us."

- **The spiritual heart is a spiritual faculty in human beings whose sensations and feelings are reflected in conscience, and whose thoughts are echoed in the mind. There is such a relationship between this spiritual faculty and the biological heart that the former has the same meaning, function and importance for the**

---

[87] *The Gleams*, "The Seventeenth Gleam", pp. 187–188.

intellectual and spiritual life of a human being as the latter means for his or her material life.[88]

- His body and what maintains it has been bestowed on a human being by God. He does not own them, and so cannot control them as he wishes.[89]

A person can control or dispose of what has been given to him only if He consents, just as a guest cannot waste or dispose of something belonging to the host without the latter's approval.

- If it is a just claim that a tiny seed is the agent of all the fruit on a fig tree, or it is a dry branch of the vine which produces bunches of grapes on it, and that those who benefit from them must respect and praise the branch and the seed, a person might have the right to be proud and conceited about the gifts given to him or her.[90]

O foolish soul delighted with self-pride, enamored with fame, fond of praise, and peerless in egotism. In reality, you deserve only to be chided constantly because you are not like the seed and the branch even. Since the tree growing from the seed and the grapes growing on the vine are more perfect than your works. Also, since you have free will, you reduce these gifts' value through your pride, damage them through your conceit, nullify them through your ingratitude, and usurp them by appropriating them to yourself. Your duty is being thankful to God, instead of taking pride in yourself. What is fit for you is not fame, but humility and feeling shame (for your deficiencies). Your right is not praise, but repentance and seeking forgiveness, and your perfection lies not in self-centeredness but in attributing every good to God Almighty.

- The human ego or carnal soul (the source of all defect and lust), in order to maintain the dominion it claims in its own realm, does not wish to admit or conceive of something proceeding from itself as less valuable than that created by the Creator's Power. As long as the ego does not regard itself as the least creature or as nothing in essence, one cannot avoid secretly denying the Creator's Attributes or associating partners with God.[91]

---

[88] İşaratü'l-İ'caz, "Suratu'l-Baqara, verse 7".
[89] Al-Mathnawi al-Nuri, "The Fifth Treatise", p. 155.
[90] The Words, "The Eighteenth Word", pp. 241–242.
[91] Al-Mathnawi al-Nuri, "The Fourth Treatise", pp. 122–123.

- Due to vanity or conceit, and therefore seeing his knowledge and accomplishment as sufficient, a person remains deprived of the blessings and benefits to come from the good deeds, perfections, and virtues of others, and this deprivation causes him to be exposed to whims, suspicions, and fancies.[92]

- Indifference to the True Owner, the All-Glorified and Majestic, causes people to claim absolute independence and ownership of their self. Such a mistaken belief leads one to imagine a realm of personal dominion. Then, after comparing other people and material causes to themselves, they share the rest of God's property or dominion among them.[93]

However, the Almighty has given us a (human) ego for a totally different purpose: to allow us to measure or compare Divinity's Attributes so that we may comprehend them. For example, a person who sees himself equipped with the limited powers of sight, hearing, and learning and therefore his works as defective may conclude that the Creator must be All-Seeing, All-Hearing, and All-Knowing because there are no defects in His works. Also, one's poverty, helplessness, and mortality may lead one to discover that the Creator is absolutely Wealthy, Powerful, and Permanent. Unfortunately, we abuse our powers or faculties, attempt to oppose the Divine Commandments, and contend against the Creator's Destiny and Decree.

People can learn subtle truths, particularly abstract ones, through comparison, and infinite things can be perceived by imagining limits to them. So the human ego, rooted in each one of us through the "water" of indifference to the True Owner of creation, was given to us to serve only as a point of comparison by which we can perceive the Attributes of the Creator, Who has no partners, and none to contend against Him in His Sovereignty, Lordship, or Divinity.

The ego does not own itself or its body. Its body is not something found on the way, the result of chance, or self-formed. Rather, it is an extremely complex, intricate, and amazing Divine machine or factory in which the Pen of Divine Power continuously works in the hand of Destiny and Decree.

O selfhood or ego! Give up such a false claim. Submit the "property" (the body) to its Owner, and be a reliable trustee in fulfilling your respon-

---

[92] *Al-Mathnawi al-Nuri*, "The Fourth Treatise", p. 87.
[93] *Al-Mathnawi al-Nuri*, "The Fourth Treatise", p. 88–89.

sibility towards the body with which you have been entrusted. When people claim ownership of even one particle, they begin to share God's property with fellow beings and then with material causes. Herein lie the roots of many kinds of associating partners with God in the creation and rule of the universe.

O selfhood or ego! People do not own themselves. They do not make or create their bodies. Material causes cannot claim to own them either. How can people make their own bodies, seeing that basically they do not differ from sheep? People and sheep are made of the same elements and do not have the least part in creating themselves. How can a sheep claim it has made its body? There is a close affinity between a sheep and a pomegranate. How can a pomegranate's dye make its seeds? How can a fruit placed at the top of a tree create the tree? If a sheep can make itself, if a pomegranate can create its tree, then a human being can own him or herself.

Each creature proclaims: "I was made, in accordance with precise measures, by an All-Knowing, All-Wise, All-Hearing, and All-Seeing One." Material causes are blind, deaf, and lifeless. Their intermingling only increases their blindness and deafness. Preparing a certain medicine requires proficiency in the relevant medical sciences and pharmacology, and accurate knowledge of the ingredients and the amounts needed. If these are all placed on a roof and a wind blows them down and then mixes them, can the required medicine be formed by itself or chance?

Materialists and naturalists attribute creation to itself, causes, or nature. If a given medicine can create itself in the circumstances outlined above, one can claim that creation is either self-created or the product of chance and causes. The beginning of creation and the origin of things and life are awesome questions to be answered. Thus, attributing creation to someone or something other than an All-Knowing, All-Wise, and All-Powerful Creator with an absolute Will is sheer, arrogant folly.

- **Each person has a world particular to himself or herself, one which is very spacious and founded upon personal aspirations, relationships, and needs. Its main pillar is the individual's life. However, this pillar is weakened by time, events, and diseases. In other words, it is unsound and subject to decay and sudden or gradual collapse.**[94]

---

[94] *Al-Mathnawi al-Nuri*, "The Fourth Treatise", p. 89.

The human body is not long-lasting, for it is not composed of iron or rock, but of flesh, bone, and blood, all of which are ready to disintegrate at any time. Its decomposition means the destruction of that individual's world.

Look at the past—apparently a large grave containing the ruined worlds of the dead; the future is a grave waiting to be filled. All of us stand between two large graves: yesterday became my father's grave, and tomorrow will be mine. Although the world we live in is one, it contains as many worlds as the number of the people living in it. One's death means the end of one's world.

- **This world and its pleasures are a heavy burden. No one except the corrupt in spirit and conscience is contented with it.**[95]

Rather than suffering from dependence on almost the whole universe, being needy of all means and causes, and appealing to contending deaf, dumb, and blind masters, people should seek refuge in a single, All-Hearing, and All-Seeing Master. If they place their trust in Him, He is enough for them.

- **The world has, from one perspective, two aspects: Its first aspect is that outwardly it is partly and temporarily attractive but inwardly it is eternally horrible. Its second aspect is that outwardly it is partly horrible while inwardly eternally beautiful.**[96]

The Qur'an draws attention to the second aspect, which relates to the Hereafter. The first aspect is connected with eternal annihilation, as opposed to eternal afterlife.

- **Intention changes ordinary acts and customs into acts of worship. It is a penetrating and pervading spirit through which inanimate states and deeds acquire life and become "living" acts of worship. It is also through a special quality of intention that evil changes into virtue or good deeds.**[97]

Intention is a "spirit" that causes ordinary deeds and customs to become "living" acts of worship. Its "soul" is sincerity or acting solely for God's sake. Salvation is found only in sincere actions done in His cause. Sincerity multiplies an action's worth, and through it one can reach Paradise with a little action and in a short life.

---

[95] *Al-Mathnawi al-Nuri*, "The Fourth Treatise", p. 89.
[96] *Al-Mathnawi al-Nuri*, "The Fourth Treatise", p. 113.
[97] *Al-Mathnawi al-Nuri*, "The Fourth Treatise", p. 113.

- **Worldly bounties and pleasures have two aspects. Their first aspect is that we confess that the bounties consumed are conferred by the "hand" of the Mercy and Favor. Thus we pass from bounties to the Divine act of giving bounties, and the pleasure received therein increases. The second aspect is that we pursue pleasure only to gratify bodily desires. The Divine act of giving bounties is not recalled; rather, we concentrate on the bounty and pleasure themselves as something falling to our lot for nothing, and do not consider how or why they have been bestowed.**[98]

In the first case, the "spirit" lasts when its pleasure disappears. By thinking "the Bestower of bounties' mercy does not forget me," we feel an unbreakable connection with the Bestower of bounties. This is not true for the second aspect, however, for the "spirit" disappears when the pleasure is gone. But the pleasure's "smoke"—sins arising from ingratitude and unlawful ways of obtaining and consuming bounties—remains.

When viewed with the light of belief, lawful pleasures in the world and bounties in the Hereafter form a virtuous circle. The disappearance of pleasures or separation from bounties does not cause pain, for the pleasures of belief and thankfulness are permanent. But without belief, pleasures change into pain for the decay of pleasure; even thinking of their decay causes pain. Unbelief views each pleasure as an end in itself, and its disappearance causes pain.

- **The repetition of** "Which of the blessings of your Lord do you deny?" **in** Suratu'r-Rahman **at the end of the revealed verses pointing to diverse "natural" phenomena—each is a sign of Divine existence and Oneness— indicates that humanity's and the jinns' disobedience to God's commands, rebelliousness, and ingratitude arise mainly from their blindness to the Divine act of bestowing bounties and their heedlessness of the One Who bestows. Therefore, they attribute bounties to causes and chance, and deny God's blessings.**[99]

Given this, believers must say "In the Name of God, the All-Merciful, the All-Compassionate," when they begin to use or consume a bounty. This means that it is from God and is received in His Name and for His sake, not for the sake of means and causes. To Him belongs all praise and gratitude.

---

[98] *Al-Mathnawi al-Nuri*, "The Fourth Treatise", p. 113–114.
[99] *Al-Mathnawi al-Nuri*, "The Fifth Treatise", p. 142.

- **There are significant lessons for human beings in plants and animals. Consider this: Why are dogs, which should be considered blessed due to their many good qualities, notably their proverbial loyalty, are considered ritually unclean, while other domestic animals, i.e., hens, cows, and cats, which feel no gratitude and loyalty in return for the good we do to them, are considered blessed? This is because—provided it is not to backbite dogs and break their hearts—dogs are greedy and so attached to apparent causes that they cannot see the true Bestower of bounties. Thus they suppose the means to be truly effective (in procuring their food) and so suffer the stigma of ritual impurity as punishment for their blindness and indifference to the true Owner and Bestower of bounties. For attachment to material causes engenders humiliation and rejection.**[100]

Blessed animals do not recognize means and causes, or give them any value or importance. Cats ask for food and, when they get what they want, behave as if they do not know us or we do not know them. They feel no gratitude towards us. Instead, they thank the true Bestower of bounties by saying: "O the All-Compassionate, O the All-Compassionate!" By disposition, they recognize their Creator and worship Him, consciously or unconsciously.

- **We are guests in this world. Guests do not set their hearts upon what does not concern them or accompany them on their trip.**[101]

We will depart from here soon, and from this town—we will either go out of it or be buried in it. We will leave this transient world or be expelled from it. So we should abandon and renounce it, with honor and dignity, before we are expelled in humiliation.

- **The soul contains an important, obscure knot that causes something to give birth to its opposite, and by which the soul regards what is against it as in its favor.**[102]

For example, the sun puts out its "hand" to us and either caresses or slaps us. But we cannot put out our hand to it and influence it. It is nearer to us than ourselves, despite our great distance from it. If we think our distance from it is so great that it cannot exert any influence on us, or so

---

[100] *Al-Mathnawi al-Nuri*, "The Fourth Treatise", p. 114.
[101] *Al-Mathnawi al-Nuri*, "The Sixth Treatise", p. 172.
[102] *Al-Mathnawi al-Nuri*, "The Fourth Treatise", p. 118–119.

near to us that we can affect it, we are mistaken. Likewise, if the carnal soul views its Creator as distant, despite His being nearer to it than itself, it is misguided.

When the carnal soul encounters a great reward, it says: "If only I had done the same. If only I had behaved that way." However, when it comes across a terrible punishment, it consoles itself by ignoring or denying it.

The Acts of the Almighty are, first of all, concerned with Him, not with the carnal soul and its narrow mind. The "wheel" of creation does not revolve according to the carnal soul's fancies, and it did not witness His creation of the universe. Surely, Imam Rabbani told the truth: "The gifts of the Sovereign can be borne only by those qualified for them."

- **The area where the human heart and mind move is so broad that it cannot be encompassed. Paradoxically, it is so narrow that it cannot contain a needle. Although we sometimes put the whole world before our eyes and include all creation in our intellect, aspiring to see the Necessarily Existent Being, at other times, we travel and drown within a minute particle, float in a drop, and imprison ourselves in a dot. Sometimes we become smaller than a minute particle or greater than the heavens, or we enter a drop or include everything that exists.**[103]

Bediüzzaman also writes as follows:

> The All-Wise Originator has implanted within your nature a strange characteristic: Since the world cannot contain you, you frequently utter, as if in a suffocating dungeon, a sound of disgust. Yet something as small as a mustard seed, a cell, a memory, or a minute of time so absorbs you that you are lost in it and are passionately attracted to it. Your mind and heart, which cannot be contained by the huge world, are contained by that smallest thing.
>
> Also, the All-Originating One has equipped your nature with such faculties that some of them would not be satisfied even if they could swallow the world. Some others cannot tolerate even a microscopic particle. Like the eye that is unable to bear the weight of a single hair while the head carries a heavy stone, these faculties cannot endure the weight of even a hair, that is, an insignificant state that arises from heedlessness and misguidance. They are sometimes even extinguished and die.

---

[103] *Al-Mathnawi al-Nuri*, "The Fifth Treatise", pp. 141–142.

So be alert and careful, always act with caution and in fear of sinking. Do not drown in a morsel, a word, a grain, a glance, a beckoning, a kiss! Do not cause your faculties that are so extensive that they can contain the whole world to drown in such a thing. For there are some small things which can in one respect swallow many large things. See how the sky and its stars are contained in a piece of glass, and most of the pages of your life history and actions are inserted in your memory, which is as small as a mustard seed. Thus, there are minute things which in one respect contain and swallow larger ones.[104]

- **His small bodily size cannot be an excuse for the insignificance of a human being's sins. For a negligible amount of darkness or hardness in our heart may extinguish all the stars of our particular world.**[105]

Everyone has a particular world identical with the outer world, except that its center is that particular individual and not the sun. Its keys are in that person's hands, and are connected with his or her senses and faculties. This world takes its color from the individual and, based on this same individual, is either prosperous and beautiful, or ugly and dark. Just as a garden's reflection and the changes it displays depend on the mirror where it is reflected, every person's world depends on its owner's views and characteristics. Your small bodily size is not an excuse for the insignificance of your sins. For a negligible amount of darkness or hardness in our heart may extinguish all the stars of our particular world.

- **All the instruments—the feelings like compassion, love and fear, and all the senses, faculties, and organs—have been given to human beings so that they may know God Almighty and love and worship Him with each of them according to its nature and thus gain eternal happiness in the afterlife. Negative and harmful-seeming faculties and feelings have also been given for the same purpose by canalizing them into certain virtues, such as canalizing jealousy into emulating those who are more advanced in virtue and good deeds. Acting otherwise causes wretchedness, misery, pain, corruption of nature and character, and discord in family and social lives.**[106]

[104] *The Gleams*, "The Seventeenth Gleam", p. 188.
[105] *Al-Mathnawi al-Nuri*, "The Sixth Treatise", pp. 171.
[106] *The Words*, "The Twenty-third Word", p. 337; "The Twenty-second Word", pp. 650–651.

Human beings have two faces. The first face looks to this worldly life because of our selfhood. Here our capital consists of a free will as feeble as a hair, a power restricted to a most limited talent with respect to positive, constructive acts, a life or lifespan as short as a flash of light, and a material existence bound to decompose swiftly. In this state, we are no more than a feeble member of one species among countless others spread throughout the universe.

The second face looks to the eternal life because of our nature as God's servants charged with and in need of worshipping Him. Our perception of helplessness and insufficiency as God's servants needy of Him make us extremely important and inclusive beings. For the All-Wise Originator has implanted an infinite impotence and poverty in our nature so that each of us may be a comprehensive mirror reflecting the boundless manifestations of an All-Compassionate One of infinite Power, an All-Munificent One of infinite Richness.

We resemble seeds. A seed is endowed with great potential by Divine Power, and a subtle program by Divine Destiny, so that it may germinate underground, emerge from that narrow world and enter the spacious world of air. Asking its Creator in the tongue of its capacity to become a tree, it may attain a perfection particular to it. If, due to its malignant disposition, the seed abuses its potential to attract harmful substances, it will soon rot away in its narrow place. If it uses its potential properly, however, and in compliance with the creational and administrational commands of *"The Splitter of grain and fruit-stone"*,[107] it will emerge from its narrow place and grow into an awesome, fruitful tree. In addition, its tiny and particular nature will come to represent a great and universal truth.

In just the same way, our essence is equipped by the Divine Power with great potential, and is inscribed by Destiny with important programs. If we use our potential and faculties in this narrow world under the soil of worldly life to satisfy the fancies of our carnal, evil-commanding soul, we will, like a rotten seed, decay and decompose for an insignificant pleasure in a short life amidst hardships and troubles. Thus we will depart from this world with a heavy spiritual burden on our unfortunate souls.

But if we germinate the seed of our potential under the "soil of worship" with the "water of Islam" and the "light of belief" according to the Qur'an's decrees, and use our faculties for their true purposes, we will

---

[107] *Suratu'l-An'am*, 6:95.

grow into eternal, majestic trees whose branches extend into the Inter-mediate World and the World of Representations or Ideal Forms, and which will be favored with countless bounties and yield innumerable fruits of perfection in the next world and Paradise. We will, in fact, become the blessed, luminous fruit of the Tree of Creation.

True progress is possible only when we turn our faculties (e.g., intel-lect, heart, spirit, and even imagination) to the eternal life and make occu-py them with our own kind of worship. What the misguided consider progress—being immersed in the life of this world and subjecting all our faculties to the carnal, evil-commanding soul to taste all worldly plea-sures down to the basest—is nothing but decline and degradation. It is only the wise Qur'an that takes us out of the lowest pit and raises us to the highest rank through belief and righteous deeds. It fills the deep pit with the steps of intellectual, moral, and spiritual progress, and the means of perfection.

- **Fame is identical with show and ostentation, and it is poisonous honey that kills the heart. Only those who wish to be slaves to human beings seek it. If it happens to one, he should say: "Surely we belong to God and are returning to Him."**[108]/[109]

- **O human soul or selfhood! Do you remain obstinate, conceited, and proud, when in reality you are weak and impotent, destitute and abject? A tiny microbe can defeat you completely.**[110]

The sun—the lamp of the world—can enter and illuminate a gnat's eye via manifestation. However, a flame produced by lighting a match cannot do this, for its flame would blind the eye. In the same way, a min-ute particle can manifest the Names of the Eternal "Sun," even though it contains nothing truly effective and operative in creation. Therefore, a human being is as great as the universe when he can become like a trans-parent drop of water or a dew-drop before God. For then God's Attributes and Names will be manifested in us.

- **Humans, like the Pharaoh, who rebelled against the All-Compel-ling Lord of the heavens and the earth in reliance on his power, tend to be proud of themselves in heedless reliance on their**

---

[108] *Suratu'l-Baqara*, 2:156.

[109] *Al-Mathnawi al-Nuri*, "The Sixth Treatise", p. 124.

[110] *Al-Mathnawi al-Nuri*, "The Fifth Treatise", p. 132.

accomplishments. However, when pierced in the heart, a seed cannot grow into a tree and be proud of itself. Likewise, when ego's hard grain is pierced with the rays and burning "flames" of the regular recitations (of the Divine Names, and of God's glorification and praise), it cannot grow and become strengthened to be proud of itself.[111]

Naqshbandi saints have opened up the heart's grain and found a short way to ignite the rocky mountain of ego and smash the head of the conceited soul with the "drill" of silent recitations. The loud recitations destroy the idol of philosophical naturalism that attribute existence to nature.

- **Human beings have numerous faculties, among which are those which attract the Divine blessings and effulgence from even the unconscious recitations of the Divine Names and God's glorification, praise and extolment. Therefore, even unconscious recitations do not remain devoid of blessing and effulgence.[112]**

Those who recite God's Names, whether consciously or not, receive many benefits. Humanity is a very interesting creation. Each individual is a uniform being composed of many parts, simultaneously simple and complex, having organs, limbs, systems, senses, feelings, and faculties. Each of those have their own pains and pleasures, along with others related to and coming from the whole body. There is a swift, mutual helping and support among them. By virtue of this uniqueness, those who follow the way of servanthood to God will be rewarded, especially in the Hereafter, with all pleasures, blessings, and perfections acquired by, or allotted to, their parts, organs, limbs, systems, senses, feelings, and faculties. But if they follow the way of egotism, they will be the target of pain, suffering, and torment. A toothache is different from an earache, the pleasure of the eyes is different from that of the tongue, and the pleasure and pain originating in touch, imagination, reason, and the heart differ from each other.

The blessed phrases—*Subhana'llah, al-hamdu li'llah*, and *Allahu akbar*—are recited repeatedly after the daily Prayers to establish and confirm their meanings, which support each other, in our minds and hearts. For example, throw a stone into the center of a large pool and see how larger circles are formed one after the other. Similarly, we recite *Subhana'llah, al-hamdu li'llah*, and *Allahu akbar* repeatedly after the five

[111] *Al-Mathnawi al-Nuri*, "The Fifth Treatise", p. 145–146.
[112] *Al-Mathnawi al-Nuri*, "The Fifth Treatise", p. 133.

daily Prayers to establish and confirm their meanings and to obtain the fruits expected of their recitation.[113]

- **The regular recitation of certain Divine Names and certain phrases of Divine glorification, praise, and extolment, are marks or signs of Islam. The signs of Islam are too exalted for the "hand" of ostentation and hypocrisy to reach. The repeated recitation of the formula of Divine Unity—There is no deity but God—isolates the heart from inner relations with whatever separates one from God and false objects of worship.[114]**

For the one who recites this formula has many faculties and senses, each of which should be convinced of the Divine Unity and absolutely isolated from polytheistic attitudes particular to itself.

- **It makes no difference whether we send as a gift the reward of reciting, say, *Suratu'l-Fatiha*, to one person or millions of people, as there is no difference between one person and millions in hearing a spoken word.[115]**

Immaterial things multiply or spread very rapidly, without one copy hindering any other, like a light reflected in one or in millions of mirrors.

- **Calling blessings and peace upon the Holy Prophet, upon him be peace and blessings, is like answering the Bestower of bounties' invitation, Who spreads His blessings freely and has laid the table of His bounties on him whom He honored with *Mi'raj* (Ascension), upon him be peace and blessings.[116]**

When we call blessings and peace upon the Prophet and mention a good attribute of his, we should concentrate and reflect on the one whom we praise so that we may grow in zeal to call peace and blessings on him over and over again.

- **It is through the work of Divine Mercy that all creatures receive instruction in the glorification and prayer particular to each. They respond with glorification to the manifestations of the Majestic Maker's Names; they perform a graceful chant.[117]**

---

[113] *Al-Mathnawi al-Nuri*, "The Fourth Treatise", p. 97.
[114] *Al-Mathnawi al-Nuri*, "The Fourth Treatise", p. 134.
[115] *Al-Mathnawi al-Nuri*, "The Fourth Treatise", p. 134.
[116] *Al-Mathnawi al-Nuri*, "The Fourth Treatise", p. 134.
[117] *The Words*, "The Seventeenth Word", pp. 235–237.

O Lord, all living creatures hasten from everywhere to gaze on You, on Your Beauty.

From every corner they emerge and look on the face of the earth, which is a work of Your Art.

Emerging from above and below, they cry out like heralds.

Those herald-like trees dance in pleasure at the beauty of Your inscriptions.

Filled with delight at Your Art's perfection, they are joyful and sing sweet melodies.

It is as if the sweetness of their melodies fills them with renewed joy and makes them sway coyly.

At last they have started dancing and are seeking ecstasy.

It is through the work of Divine Mercy that all living creatures receive instruction in the glorification and prayer particular to each.

After receiving instruction, each tree stands on a high rock and raises its head towards the Divine Throne.

Each stretches out hundreds of hands to the Divine Court and assumes an imposing position of worship.

They make their twigs curl like dancing love-locks, and arouse fine ardor and exalted pleasures in those who are watching.

As if the most sensitive strings were touched, they sing love songs at a high pitch, and make even the dead hear their eternal tunes arising from the sweet sorrow caused by touching.

The spirit understands from this that things respond with glorification to the manifestations of the Majestic Maker's Names; they perform a graceful chant.

The heart reads the meaning of Divine Unity in this exalted, miraculous spectacle from these trees, each of which is like an embodied Qur'anic verse.

In other words, there is so wonderful an order, art, and wisdom in their creation that if all "natural causes" were conscious agents able to do whatever they wished, they could not imitate them even if they joined all their forces.

On seeing this, the soul thinks that the earth is revolving in a clamorous tumult of separation and seeks an enduring pleasure.

It has received the meaning: "You will find it by abandoning your adoration of the world."

From such chanting of animals, plants, trees, and air, the mind discerns a most meaningful order of creation, inscriptions of wisdom, and a treasury of secret truths. It concludes that everything glorifies the All-Majestic Maker.

The desirous soul receives such pleasure from the murmuring air and whispering leaves that it forgets mundane pleasures, the basis of its life, and seeks to realize self-annihilation in this pleasure of truth.

The imagination beholds the scene as if angels appointed for trees were embodied in each tree, from whose branches hang many flutes.

It is as though the Eternal Monarch clothed these angels in trees for a magnificent parade accompanied with the sounds of countless flutes. So the trees show themselves to be conscious and meaningful.

The flutes' tunes are pure and touching, as if issuing from an elevated heavenly orchestra.

The mind hears the grateful thanks offered to the All-Living, Self-Subsistent One for His Mercy, and praises for His sustaining.

Since the trees are bodies and their leaves are tongues, a breeze makes each tree to recite with its thousands of tongues: "He, He (meaning God)." As the glorification and praise of their lives, they proclaim their Maker to be the All-Living and Self-Subsistent.

All things form a universal circle to proclaim God's Unity: "There is no deity but God," and perform their duties.

In the tongue of disposition, they often declare "O Ultimate Truth," and ask for their vital needs from His treasury of Mercy. Through the tongue of being favored with life, they continuously recite His Name: "O All-Living One."

O All-Living, O Self-Subsistent! For the sake of Your Names, the All-Living and Self-Subsistent, endow this wretched heart with life, and show this confused mind the right direction. Amin.

Part 7

GENERAL PRINCIPLES RELATED TO SOCIAL MATTERS AND ISLAMIC ACTION

General Principles Related to Social Matters and Islamic Action

- **Islam is peace and reconciliation; it wants no dispute or hostility within.**[1]

O World of Islam! Your life lies in unity, and if you want unity, your guiding principle should be the following: You should adopt the principle, "This is true," rather than "This alone is true;" and "This is the best," rather than "This is what is exclusively good."

Every Muslim can say about their own school and way: "This is true; I do not interfere with others. Even if the others are good too, mine is the best." They should not say: "This alone is true, the others are all false. Only mine is good, the others are all wrong and unpleasant."

The mindset of exclusiveness arises from self-love. It eventually becomes a disease and leads to dispute.

- **If the existence of numerous ills and cures is a rightful reality, right will also multiply. The variation of needs and foods is right, and right becomes diverse. The multiplication of capacities and education is right, and this right will also multiply. A single substance is both poison and the antidote.**[2]

The truth is not fixed in the secondary matters of the Religion; it is relative and compounded according to the differences of temperament and circumstance. The founders of the schools of law or spiritual orders made judgments in non-specific terms, leaving the specification of the limits of their schools or orders to the various temperaments that followed.

Bigoted attachment to a school or order causes the rulings of that school or order to be generalized, and partisanship arising from this leads to conflict.

---

[1] *Gleams of Truth*, pp. 56.
[2] *Gleams of Truth*, pp. 56–57.

The deep rifts between the classes of humanity before Islam, and the great distance between peoples and places demanded the existence of numerous Prophets at any one time, and a variety of Shari'ahs, and numerous sects. Islam caused a revolution among humankind, and peoples drew closer to each other. The different Shari'ahs were summed up in a single Shari'ah, and there was one Prophet. But the levels of humankind were not the same, so the schools of law and ways of spiritual training multiplied. If a single system of training and education were sufficient and proper for all, then the schools could unite.

- **Islamic "politics" should proceed from Islam itself; this sort of politics should not be instrumental for worldly purposes; partisanship causes hearts to be divided, not united. It is always necessary to take action to serve Religion. However, what urges one to come forward in the name of Religion should be love of Islam and religious zeal. If the motive is politics and partisanship, it is dangerous. If we err in the first case, it will be forgivable, but even if we succeed in the second case, we will be responsible for the consequences.**[3]

Political madness is the product of a Byzantine (i.e. deceitful and clandestine) mindset. The political divergences here go in opposite directions, and they have no point of intersection in the country; it is not possible for them to come together anywhere on the entire face of the wide earth.

- **Whoever prefers their transgressing, sinful fellow-partisan to their religious political opponent due to political pretexts, their motive is politics. Also, if due to a monopoly of views, one presents the Religion, to which all Muslims belong, as restricted to fellow-partisans, it will arouse opposition to the Religion in a powerful majority and cause the Religion to be disfavored. This shows that the motive is politics. One can serve the Religion by guiding people to it, encouraging them to observe it, and reminding them of their religious duties. Accusing some people of irreligion means pushing them to attack the Religion. The Religion should not be used for negative motives or negative ends especially within a Muslim land.**[4]

---

[3] *Gleams of Truth*, pp. 53–54, 168.
[4] *Gleams of Truth*, pp. 53–54, 168.

Even the least negative use of Religion in the homeland yields a terrible result. Muslims are bound to come out of this as losers.

- **Those who suppose the Religion and life to be separable are the cause of disaster. The Religion is the very life of life, its light and its foundation. The revival of Muslim nations is possible only through the revival of the Religion.**[5]

Those who do not know that our Religion is the basis of our life and think that the nation and Islam are different from each another harm Muslims. Time has shown that the system of civilization outside the Religion is harmful. The Religion is the very life of life, its light and its foundation. The revival of Muslim nations is possible only through the revival of the Religion.

In contrast to the nations of other cultures and traditions, the Muslim nation is able to progress to the extent that we adhere to our Religion. It has declined to the degree we have neglected it. This is a historical fact, which we have pretended to forget.

- **The value of human beings is proportional to the nature and greatness of their ideals and the exertion of their efforts to realize them. Whoever lives and endeavors for the happiness of their nation is a nation by themselves.**[6]

God Almighty says of Prophet Abraham, upon him be peace:

> Abraham was an exemplary leader, (whose self-dedication to the good of his nation made him) as if a nation, sincerely obedient to God as a man of pure faith (free from any stain of unbelief and hypocrisy), and he was not of those who associate partners with God.[7]

Europeans have taken from us some of our elevated moral values and some of our lofty characteristics in social life. They have used these as a means for their development and in return we have borrowed from them their vices and evil characteristics.

For example, due to a national characteristic they have borrowed from us, one of them says, "Even if I die, let my nation survive, for I have a permanent life in my nation." They have borrowed this lofty characteristic from us and made a most formidable foundation for their develop-

---

[5] *Gleams of Truth*, pp. 50–51.
[6] *The Reasonings*, "The Third Part", p. 113; *Gleams of Truth*, p. 136.
[7] *Suratu'n-Nahl,* 16:120.

ment. This characteristic issues from the true Religion, and from the truths of belief. It belongs to the people of belief. Whereas due to an evil characteristic, which has come to us from foreigners, a selfish man from among us says, "If I die of thirst, let rain no more come down on the world. If I cannot be happy, let the world become corrupted in whatever way it will." This foolish, evil attitude issues from irreligion; it comes from ignorance of the Hereafter. It has entered us from abroad and poisons us. A person from Europe gains as much value as his nation due to his national and patriotic zeal. For a person is valuable to the extent of his intentions and endeavors. Whoever lives and endeavors for the happiness of their nation is a nation by themselves. Whereas, whoever pursues only his personal interests cannot be counted as a human being, because human beings are civilized by nature; a human being is obliged to care about his fellow human beings. His personal life can continue within social life. For example, in order to obtain a loaf of bread, one needs the cooperation of numerous hands. You can compare to bread the clothes one wears. A person cannot live with skin like animals, and therefore we have to be interrelated with our fellow human beings. One who restricts himself to his personal interests is no longer a human being; such have been reduced to cannibalistic animals.

- **The absence of an objective or ideal strengthens egotism. If people have no goals to pursue, or if the main objective is forgotten or neglected, the mind turns to individual ego and revolves around it.**[8]

The ego thus becomes inflated, sometimes swelling with anger; it is not "pierced" or deflated so that it might become "we." Those who love themselves love no other.

- **The most important mechanism of virtuous progress in humankind is competition in virtue which, in turn, arises from belief. Virtue can be removed from humanity only by changing human nature, extinguishing the power of reason, killing the heart, and destroying the spirit. Virtue arising from belief cannot be the cause of oppression or despotism. Oppression and despotism issue from a lack of virtue. The people of virtue prefer participat-**

---

[8] *Gleams of Truth*, pp. 8, 37, 164.

ing in human social life through humility, love of humanity, and social solidarity.[9]

> Every people have a direction towards which they turn (a goal they turn to in life). So strive together, as if in a race (O community of believers), towards all that is good. Wherever you may be, God will bring you all together. Surely God has full power over everything.[10]
>
> We have sent down to you (O Messenger) the Book with the truth (embodying it, and with nothing false in it), confirming (the Divine authorship of, and the truths that are still contained by) whatever of the Book was revealed before it, and guarding over (all the true teachings in) it. Judge, then, between them by what God has sent down (to you), and do not follow their desires and caprices away from the truth that has come to you. For each (nation to which a Messenger was sent with a Book), have We appointed a clear way of life and a comprehensive system (containing the principles of that way and how to follow it). And if God had so willed, He would surely have made you a single nation (following the same way of life and system surrounded by the same conditions throughout all history); but (He willed it otherwise) in order to test you by what He granted to you (and thereby made you subject to a law of progress). Strive, then, together as if competing in good works. To God is the return of all of you, and He will then make you understand (the truth) about what you have differed on.[11]
>
> And (rather than competing for the things of this world) race with one another to forgiveness from your Lord, and to a Garden the vastness of which is as the vastness of heaven and earth, prepared for those who truly believe in God and His Messengers. That is God's bounty, which He grants to whom He wills. God is of tremendous bounty.[12]

- **Whoever wishes a lasting success must follow the way established by God and know His way of acting in the universe or in the creation and administration of things. Otherwise, God's way of acting, which manifests itself in "nature", will respond by causing any attempt to go to waste, and condemn those who oppose it to extinction in the deserts of nothingness.**[13]

---

[9]   *The Gleams*, "The Twenty-second Gleam", pp. 242–243.

[10]   *Suratu'l-Baqara*, 2:148.

[11]   *Suratu'l-Maeda*, 5:48.

[12]   *Suratu'l-Hadid*, 27:21.

[13]   *The Reasonings*, "The Third Part", p. 135; *The Gleams*, "The Twenty-second Gleam", pp. 242.

If those who launch a new way in human social life do not act in conformity with the Divine laws of the creation and the operation of the universe, they cannot be successful in their attempts at progress and in doing good things. Rather, their actions only serve evil and destruction. For example, one can be successful in realizing absolute equality among human beings only by changing the basic nature of humanity and abolishing the Divine wisdom in its creation. We should rather sincerely adopt the principle of the equality of rights before the law. We should oppose wrongdoing, despotism and oppression of every kind, and support absolute justice.

Basic human nature and the wisdom in the creation of humanity are not in conformity with absolute egalitarianism. For the All-Wise Originator, Who in order to show the perfection of His Power and Wisdom makes a single thing yield a great result or fulfill numerous duties, and Who has numerous books written on a single page, causes humankind to carry out the duties of thousands of species. It is for this significant reason that God Almighty has created humankind with a nature that would divide it into as many "classes" or "divisions" as there are animal species. He has not restricted by birth the powers, faculties and feelings of humanity as He has restricted those of animals, but has equipped humanity with the capacity to rise to the limitless ranks of progress and accomplishment. Because of this, while being a single species, humanity has become like thousands of species and has been appointed as the ruler of the earth— the species which should work for the prosperity of the world in accordance with the Divine laws—and become the fruit of the universe, or the final result of creation and the monarch of living beings.

Also, based on this fact, see and consider what subtle, genuine, and sensitive truths and realities there are, on which the rules of the Shari'ah are based, and how impossible it is for human reason to discover these, and how sensitively the Shari'ah preserves the balance among what exists in the existing laws of creation and the operation of the universe.

The Shari'ah has preserved its genuineness and validity through so many centuries and revolutions, developments, and clashes in human history. This shows that the way of God's noble Messenger, upon him be peace and blessings, is based on eternal truths.

- **An unlawful way leads to the opposite of what is intended. Islam stipulates that both the aim and its execution must be lawful.**[14]

The murderer cannot inherit (from the one whom he has murdered): this is a very significant principle. Someone who follows an unlawful way (in Islam) to reach his goal generally attains in retribution the opposite of what they intended.

Love of the corrupt face of modern civilization is not a lawful love in view of the Shari'ah; it is a blind imitation and disagreeable friendliness. Its recompense is the tyrannical hostility of the beloved, and its crimes.

The sinner condemned to loss will find, in the end, neither pleasure nor salvation.

- **An attempt to obtain everything means abandoning much of everything. God has established the law of development towards perfection, applicable to both the creation and the life of the universe. He is pleased with the division of labor that occurs when this law is followed.**[15]

A person cannot be expert in many disciplines. One with an extraordinary capacity may be expert at most in four or five branches of science. An attempt to obtain everything means abandoning much of everything. Every discipline has its own nature, form of subject matter and discourse, and specialization.

God Almighty has established the law of development towards perfection, applicable to both the creation and the life of the universe. He is pleased with the division of labor that occurs when this law is followed. Acting in compliance with this principle of division of labor is compulsory upon every individual; yet we have not fully observed it. It is as follows:

The Divine wisdom which requires a division of labor has sown different abilities and tendencies in human nature, and has enabled human beings to carry out the duty of establishing sciences and developing technology. The fulfillment of this duty is obligatory upon humanity as a whole, though not on every individual. However, as Muslims, we have misused these abilities and tendencies, and have dampened the zeal which gives strength to our tendencies with inappropriate, destructive ambitions, and the individual desire to be superior to others, which is the

---

[14] *Gleams of Truth*, p. 39.
[15] *The Reasonings*, "The First Part", pp. 25–27.

source of ostentation. Evidently, one who rebels deserves hellfire. So, as we have not observed the Divine laws of creation and the operation of the universe, we suffer the hellfire of ignorance as a punishment. What will save us from this torment is observing the law of the division of labor. The generations that preceded us observed this and subsequently rose to the heaven of knowledge.

- **Curiosity is the teacher of knowledge, and density or multiplicity of population triggers need, which gives rise to research, the invention of new crafts, and an increase in learning. These factors lie in scientific and technological progress.**[16]

There are two cardinal causes for the development and present dominion of Europe, one material, the other immaterial.

The first, material cause is the physical condition of Europe, which is the "church" of all Christians, and the source of their life. Europe is a narrow continent, "naturally" beautiful. It has important rivers and vast sources of iron, is surrounded by seas on three sides, and has a meandering coastline.

Although Europe covers nearly one-fifteenth of the land on earth, it has attracted one-fourth (now nearly one-thirteenth) of the world population with its "natural" beauty and rich resources. It is a fact that the density of population is the cause of the multiplicity of need; the more people, the greater the need. Particularly when need increases due to certain reasons such as traditions, modernism, or civilization, it cannot be satisfied through the "natural" productivity of the land. It is for this reason that need opens the way for new crafts and, together with curiosity, urges learning.

The narrowness of the European continent and the possibilities of travel and transportation via the seas and rivers have encouraged and facilitated tourism and mutual acquaintance, which in turn have led to continental trade. Mutual assistance or cooperation has resulted in partnership, mutual contact, and relations, which in turn have given rise to the exchange and development of ideas, while rivalry has brought about competition. In addition, since Europe is very rich in iron, which is the source of industry, iron has equipped its civilization with such a weapon that Europeans have plundered all the remnants of ancient civilizations throughout the world, thus destroying the balance of world power.

[16] *Gleams of Truth*, pp. 16, 138–140.

Furthermore, continental Europe is relatively cold, and this climate causes people to adopt everything late and abandon it late. This has gained Europeans firmness and steadfastness in their endeavors, and caused their civilization to endure. Moreover, the formation of their states based on science, the constant collisions between them, the hardships and harassment caused by their former, cruelly despotic systems, the pressure of religious fanaticism, as represented by the Inquisition, which in turn gave birth to significant reactions, and the competition between the more modest elements, have developed the capacities of Europeans and awakened in them certain meritorious and nationalist tendencies.

The second, immaterial cause is their point of reliance. When any Christian attempts to attain any of their successive or combined goals, they turn back and see a powerful point of reliance which lifts their morale. They find in themselves a power that will combat even the hardest and greatest of matters. An example of this point of reliance is the intriguing, sophisticated fanaticism of the Inquisition, which was ever ready to feed the roots of life of many Christians, and to cut off the life-veins of Muslims. Moreover, European civilization has become the barrack or church of a mass that has been armed with the intoxicating pride of the victory of their civilization.

- **It will be in contradiction of the Divine laws of creation and life if a person abandons something for which he has a talent and attempts to do something which he is not qualified to do. Everyone is expected to develop his talents by applying them in a task for which he is qualified, following the rules of the craft or job at which he is skilled.**[17]

Misuse of such talents, and acting contrary to the rules of any craft or job, causes distortion and corruption. Any incompatibility between a natural skill or capacity and a task performed will give rise to confusion.

- **Divine Wisdom has arranged everything according to a certain deliberation. If we do not comply with this deliberation and neglect to follow all the arranged steps, we cannot achieve the desired result.**[18]

---

[17] *The Reasonings*, "The First Part", p. 48.
[18] *The Letters*, "The Twenty-second Letter", p. 291.

For example, a loaf of bread is obtained only after tilling the field, waiting for the passage of winter and coming of spring and summer, harvesting the crop, taking the grain to a mill, and baking the loaf. Negligence of any of these steps results in failure.

- **Entrusting the accomplishment of an affair to God before taking all necessary precautions and making all necessary arrangements is laziness. Leaving the desired outcome's realization to God, after doing all that can be done, is to trust in Him. Contentment with the result after exerting one's efforts is a laudable virtue that encourages further effort and reinvigorates one's energy and industry. Contentment with what one already has destroys endeavor.[19]**

- **The cure for one ailment may be harmful to another; what is an antidote for one becomes poison for another. If the cure is taken to excess, it causes illness and becomes fatal.[20]**

- **Justice must be implemented in the name of the Religion, so that together with the soul, the mind, heart, and conscience can submit to and abide by it.[21]**

If a law is promulgated only in the name of the public or political order, it can only rouse fear or apprehension in the heart. The law can then effect the mind only through apprehension; if one is inclined to commit a crime, one only then considers the formal penalty. He fears the whip of punishment only if it is proven that he is a criminal.

Or he may refrain from a crime fearing that people may reprove of him. Equally, he may find comfort in the hope that his crime will remain hidden from people.

It is because of the neglect of the Religion in the execution of justice that justice is no longer respected or effective. Even though it is implemented in full, justice that is not implemented in the name of the Religion is like a Prayer which is carried out without intention, without facing the direction of the Ka'ba, or without doing the obligatory preparatory ablution—this is Prayer that is not acceptable because some of the obligatory rites are missing.

---

[19] *The Words*, "The Twenty-third Word", p. 331; *Gleams of Truth*, p. 15.
[20] *Gleams of Truth*, pp. 12, 54.
[21] *Gleams of Truth*, p. 112.

- **Those who apply the laws should apply them first to themselves and then to others. By not applying a principle to themselves which they impose on others, they are first of all violating and opposing their own principles and laws.**[22]

One of the basic reasons why Prophet Muhammad, upon him be peace and blessings, was exceptionally successful in his mission is that he believed in the pillars of faith more than anyone, and he devoutly practiced the Religion he communicated. He is the foremost practitioner of the worship prescribed by Islam and the most God-conscious person. He worshipped with the utmost care and attention to even the minutest details, even during times of great peril and throughout a life of constant struggle and activity. He manifested God's Divinity at the highest level and in the most brilliant fashion through the most perfect and comprehensive way of worship. He possessed all laudable virtues and excellent characteristics in the highest degree, as affirmed even by his enemies.

Those who do not obey the laws they themselves have made, and do not practice what they advised others to follow, are senseless and devoid of understanding: "*Do you enjoin upon people godliness and virtue but forget your own selves, (even) while you recite the Book (and see therein the orders, prohibitions, exhortations and warnings)? Will you not understand and come to your senses?*"[23]

- **Authority and sovereignty do not allow rivalry, partnership, or interference. If a village had two headmen, its order and peace would be destroyed. A district or town with two governors would experience great confusion, and a country with two kings (or governments) would be in constant turmoil.**[24]

While these pale shadows of absolute authority and sovereignty enjoyed by powerless people who are not self-sufficient reject rivalry and the intervention of their opposite, consider how strongly true Sovereignty, in the form of supreme, absolute Kingdom and Authority at the degree of Divine Lordship enjoyed by an Absolutely Powerful One, rejects interference and partnership. This means, Oneness and absolute Independence without partners is the most indispensable and constant requirement of Divinity and Lordship. The universe's perfect order and most

[22] *The Gleams*, "The Twenty-second Word", p. 244.
[23] *Suratu'l-Baqara*, 2:44.
[24] *The Words*, "The Thirtieth Word", p. 696.

beautiful harmony testify to this. There is such a perfect order in the universe, from a fly's wing to the heavens' lamps, that our minds prostrate before it in amazement and admiration, declaring: "All-Glorified is God! What wonders God has willed! God bless it!"

Principles of wisdom and laws of right have no effect upon ordinary people unless the former are combined with the law of the state and the latter with the rules of force.

- **If the principles of wisdom, laws of the state, precepts of right, and rules of force do not help or support one another, they will neither be fruitful nor effective among the people. They will no longer be a point of support for people in their affairs, and people will no longer have confidence in, or rely upon, them.**[25]

- **The reward, demand, and attention which public view assigns to something is not due to its essential value, but to the common people's need for it.**[26]

A watchmaker's earning more than a great scholar proves this. If, therefore, the essential religious needs of the Muslim community had been directed towards the Qur'an, if Muslim peoples had understood that they needed the Qur'an more than anything else, this holy Book would have been much more in demand than anything else, and as a result of such a need, the Qur'an would have received much more attention.

- **Strangely enough, sometimes a person or even the majority of a community falls in a filthy marsh and, in order to deceive themselves out of vanity or ideological or political partisanship, mistake its dirt and filth for musk and ambergris.**[27]

What falls to others to do in such a case is to show them to the true path to lead them out.

- **Weakness is sometimes tyrannical.**[28]

Despair and suspicion cause a weak spot in the heart. For example: a person so affected sees that the blows of a tyrant hurt the oppressed one. The blows are terrible; the pains of the oppressed one are reflected in the heart of that weak-hearted one, and sadden him. Sorrows are hurtful and

---

[25] *Gleams of Truth*, p. 36.

[26] *Gleams of Truth*, p. 155.

[27] *Hutbe-i Şamiye* (The Sermon of Damascus), p. 150; *The Letters*, "The Thirteenth Letter", p. 83.

[28] *Gleams of Truth*, p. 107.

difficult for a weak heart to endure. He wants to be saved from them, so in order to have ease of heart, he deceives himself into saying that the oppressed one deserves the blows. He tries to find an excuse; for example: "What business has that lowly one in a place where he will be beaten?" Thus one becomes wrongful and helps the tyrant.

- **If an idea addressed to the public does not acquire sacredness, it will soon decline and die.**[29]

Bediüzzaman commented on socialism when it appeared as follows:

Socialism is a new idea, both calamitous and useful, which is turned towards the public. It surely needs permanence, and its permanence depends on its acceptance by the public. Acceptance by the public requires that there is sacredness. That which can give it sacredness must be a religion that considers the public mercifully. It cannot be Christianity, for Christianity can neither accept it nor respond to it. So it needs Islam, which is the sincere friend of the poor and labor. However, since at the present, people, especially of the West, mean Christianity by religion, and socialism has discovered that the present Christianity has been its enemy, it has never made peace with religion. Thus it will inevitably resort to Islam for a reconciliation, or it will die.

Just as Bediüzzaman commented, socialism was not able to establish a secure footing, especially among Muslims, due to its hostile stance against religion, and it died.

- **Rather than instruction in its theoretical matters, it is necessary to remind people of Islam's explicit, incontestable essentials.**[30]

Islam is not only knowledge; it as also a practice and experience. Also, the essentials of Islam, the explicit, incontestable matters of the Shari'ah, consist of almost ninety percent of it. Therefore, people should be continually reminded of them, and made fully conscious of them.

- **Like degrees in heat, every calamity contains degrees of Divine favor. Be mindful of the greater calamity, thereby being thankful for the favor of the lesser calamity. Concentrating on and exaggerating a calamity increases it, and this exaggerated reflection in the heart or imagination makes it real and troublesome.**[31]

---

[29] *Gleams of Truth*, pp. 114–115.
[30] *Gleams of Truth*, pp. 114–115.
[31] *Gleams of Truth*, pp. 13, 15. 57–58.

- **There is great wisdom in the combination of opposites, and perfections in the created world are judged by way of contrast. Pleasure's perfection cannot be perceived without pain, light cannot be recognized without darkness, and union gives no pleasure if there is no separation.**[32]

The Divine Power manifests Itself in the combining of opposites. There is pain in pleasure, evil within good, ugliness within beauty, harm within benefit, trouble within bounties, fire within light. It is this way so that relative truths may be established, and so there may be many things within a single thing, and numerous incidents of existence become apparent.

There must be relative truths so that seeds may sprout in this world. These constitute the clay of the universe, the bonds of its order, and the connections among its inscriptions.

The degrees of heat are due to the existence of cold. The degrees of beauty come about through the intervention of ugliness. Light is indebted to darkness, pleasure is indebted to pain; there is no consciousness of health without illness. If there were no Paradise, perhaps Hell would not be torment. Hell cannot exist without extreme cold. If there were no extreme cold (besides its heat), Hell would not burn.

The Ever-Living Creator has demonstrated His Wisdom in the creation of opposites and His Majesty has become apparent. That Everlasting All-Powerful One has displayed His Power in the combining of opposites, and His Grandeur has become manifest.

- **Sometimes opposites contain opposites, or conceal their opposites within them.**[33]

Sometimes opposites conceal their opposites within them. In the language of politics, the words are the opposites of their meanings. Tyranny has donned the cap of justice. Treachery has found a cheap dress in patriotism. *Jihad* and war for God's sake have been labeled aggression and a violation of human rights. Enslavement to animal passions and the despotism of Satan have been called freedom.

Things have become their opposites, forms have been exchanged, names have been swapped, positions and ranks have changed places.

---

[32] *Gleams of Truth*, pp. 57–58.
[33] *Gleams of Truth*, p. 36.

- **Politics based on self-interest is bestial.**[34]

The politics which are based on self-interest are like a rapacious beast. If you show love to a ravenous beast, you will not attract its compassion, but will rather sharpen its appetite. Then it will turn on you and demand payment from you for the use of its claws and teeth.

Since human faculties have not been restricted in creation, their crimes are great.

Unlike animals, the faculties of human beings have not been restricted in creation; and the evil that proceeds from them especially knows no limits. If the selfishness that issues from one faculty and the egotism that proceeds from another are combined with haughtiness and obstinacy, the sins that will be committed are so great as to not have a name. As these sins are proofs of the necessity of Hell, so, too, can their penalty only be Hell.

For example, in order to justify just one of his lies, a man desires, from his heart, the downfall of Islam. The present time has shown that Hell is not unnecessary and Paradise is not cheap.

- **Sometimes good leads to evil.**[35]

While in reality the merits of the elite should give rise to modesty and self-effacement, regrettably, they have often led to arrogance and oppression. And while the destitution of the poor and the poverty of the common people should serve (as they do in reality) as means to arouse compassion and graciousness, they have often resulted in the abasement and servitude of the common people.

If honor and merit result from something, it is offered to the elite and leaders. But if vice and evil proceed from it, it is divided and distributed among the common people, or among employees and servants.

If a victorious tribe has won some honor, congratulations are offered to its chief; but if some harm is obtained thenceforth, every curse is poured upon the members of the tribe. This is a sorry evil among humankind!

- **Physical wounds will eventually heal, but the wounds inflicted upon the dignity of Islam and national honor are too deep to heal. The most severe of blows are those which are delivered to the spiritual and moral values.**[36]

---

[34] *Gleams of Truth*, p. 36–37.

[35] *Gleams of Truth*, p. 37.

[36] *Gleams of Truth*, pp. 9, 40.

- **Any extremity in human behavior or moral standard destroys human potential, which, in turn, causes purposelessness and vanity. Purposelessness and vanity are absolutely contrary to the Divine universal wisdom, which is clearly observed to attach purposes and benefits to everything in the universe, from the smallest to the greatest.**[37]

- **Humanity desperately needs a Divine Law, which will enable people's spiritual, intellectual, and physical happiness both in this world and the next.**[38]

The laws and systems made by human beings cannot satisfy the perennial needs and expectations of humanity, nor properly restrict people's innate aggressions, properly train their faculties, or correctly guide their potential and disposition to their highest development or progress. Also, human laws and systems are lifeless and do not last. Even though they are based on the accumulated knowledge and experiences of humanity over the course of history, they are unable to cause the seeds of potential in humanity to grow properly or to yield sound fruit. For this reason, humanity desperately needs a Divine Law, which will enable people's spiritual, intellectual, and physical happiness both in this world and the next. This Law must also guide humanity along the way to the attainment of human perfection through the realization of its potentials. It is the Prophets who bring us this living, life-endowing, everlasting Divine Law.

If it is argued that those who do not follow the Divine Religion may enjoy a healthy order, the answer will be as follows:

If there is any order in their way, this is due to the affirmed or non-affirmed guidance and the effect of the Divine Religion and religious leaders. There has never been a community left completely devoid of the guidance of a Prophet, so even though many people reject the Divine guidance and Religion, they are not able to remain unaffected by Religion. Any approvable, lasting order observed in any community has its basic source or roots in Divine guidance. With respect to other aspects that are incompatible with Divine guidance, the order of irreligious people or of those who do not follow the Divine Religion is bound to collapse, even though such an order may appear to have brought some sort of worldly happiness to certain people. In addition, a good order must be one which

---

[37] *The Reasonings*, "The Third Part", p. 126.
[38] *The Reasonings*, "The Third Part", p. 125.

brings true, lasting happiness to an overwhelming majority of humanity. An order which brings only an apparent, transient, superficial happiness to a small minority in the world, while hurling others into subjection and humiliating misery, cannot be regarded as a good, approvable order.

- **There must be a universal mind or intellect that has the perfect knowledge of humanity, encompassing all their dimensions. It can be the mission of this intellect only to establish the order and laws for the life of humanity. This is the Religion which God the Creator, Who creates and knows, has sent. There must also be a power which can dominate the spirits and consciences of human beings, and thus implement the required justice and rules in human life. This power must have superiority over others. This power is the institution of Prophethood, which was founded by the Creator of the universe Himself. It is He Who chose the Prophets and made them distinguished in many respects.**[39]

Humanity has an inborn tendency to live in a way befitting the essential human nature. Human beings must not, and cannot, live like animals. They must lead a life befitting their essential honor. It is because of this inborn tendency that human beings need to improve and decorate their dwelling places, clothes, and foods, and use sciences and crafts. It is not possible for an individual to have sufficient knowledge about all such sciences or crafts. Therefore, human beings need to live together, cooperate with one another, and exchange their products among themselves. The satisfaction of this need requires justice and the existence of certain rules, as the desires, potentials, and faculties of humanity are not restricted from birth, and so can be the cause of limitless aggression and injustice. Any individual mind or intellect is unable to establish the nature of this justice or these rules, as human beings are neither their own creator nor do they have true, all-embracing, or universal knowledge about themselves, their environment, and their future. They lack sufficient knowledge, accurate viewpoints, and the ability to know themselves in all aspects and dimensions of their existence, and they lack the ability to lead their lives in a proper way that will enable their happiness in both their individual and collective spheres. In addition, they suffer whims, fancies,

---

[39] *The Reasonings*, "The Third Part", pp. 124–125.

and errors, and are often defeated by their carnal impulses, which require discipline to control.

In conclusion, there must be a universal mind or intellect that has this knowledge. This is the Divinely revealed Religion. There must also be a power which can dominate the spirits and consciences of human beings, and thus implement the required justice and rules. This power must have some sort of superiority over others. This power is the institution of Prophethood, which was founded by the Creator of the universe Himself. It is He Who chose the Prophets and made them distinguished in many respects.

A Prophet inculcates the Creator's grandeur in the minds and spirits of human beings. The Divinely revealed Religion he communicates requires regular worship, which enables people to continuously and increasingly feel the Creator's grandeur. Worship directs thoughts and feelings to the Creator, which, in turn, leads to obedience to Him. Obedience to the Creator, Who is also the Supreme Author of the universal, magnificent order, secures the perfect public order in human life. This perfect public order is based on God's Wisdom. The essence of God's Wisdom is that nothing in the universe is purposeless and meaningless. The universal order, beauty, and harmony bear witness to this Wisdom.

- **If it is impossible to obtain something totally, it is also not permissible to forsake it totally.**[40]

- **If there is greater good in doing something, it should be done. Otherwise, a complete evil will emerge. Also, since not doing a necessary good is evil, instances of evil would be committed to the number of the good effects it will produce. Leaving many instances of good undone to avoid one evil is extremely ugly, contrary to wisdom and reality, and a fault.**[41]

- **After finding what is right, do not cause discord for the sake of something better. If there is consensus concerning what is good and true, and seeking what is better and truer causes disagreement and discord, then what is true is truer than what is truer, and what is good is better than what is better.**[42]

---

[40] *İşaratü'l-İ'caz*, "İfadetü'l-Meram" (Introduction), p. 6.
[41] *The Words*, "The Fourteenth Word", p. 187.
[42] *Gleams of Truth*, pp. 13, 56, 164.

So say: "My way is good and true," but never say: "My way is the only way, the truest and best."

In order to remove the differences and disagreements in the Muslim world, we should first of all concentrate on the basic points of agreement. Our God is one, our Prophet is one, our Qur'an is one, and we are all agreed on the essentials of the Religion. Disagreement on the secondary matters and details cannot and must not shake this unity. Secondly, if "loving for God's sake" is adopted as a principle, and love of truth directs our attitudes and behavior, our differences and disagreements can be directed into accurate, straight channels. Regrettably, when the main objective is forgotten or neglected, the minds turn to individual egos and revolve around them.

The various parts of an institution should be in harmony with one another. Personal merits and capabilities should not give way to disagreement and discord. Individual egos should be torn apart and a collective "we" should emerge.

- **A lesser evil is preferred to avoid a greater evil (in the absence of good).**[43]
- **A sure benefit should not be renounced for fear of potential harm.**[44]
- **Timidity and weakness embolden the enemy and encourage external pressure and interference.**[45]
- **Do not appear important, or you will be degraded.**[46]

In human society, in the social structure of the human community, everyone has a window, known as status, through which to see and be seen. If the window is higher than a person's height (real stature or worth), he will, through pride, try to appear as tall (or taller). But if the window is lower than his height (his stature or the extent of his endeavors for God's sake and for people), he will bend and bow down out of modesty. In human beings, the measure of greatness is to know oneself as low-ranking or modest, and the measure of a true low-ranking is to feign greatness or conceit.

---

[43] *The Letters*, "The Fifteenth Word", p. 92.
[44] *Gleams of Truth*, p. 53.
[45] *Gleams of Truth*, pp. 11, 52.
[46] *Gleams of Truth*, pp. 11, 52

- **If qualities change places, their natures change.**[47]

In different places, one quality is sometimes a demon, sometimes an angel, sometimes virtuous, sometimes wicked—some examples are as follows:

Weak people's self-respect or dignity in the face of the strong or powerful is arrogance when assumed by the latter. Powerful people's modesty before weak people becomes self-abasement when assumed by the latter. In his office, the gravity of a person of authority is dignity, and his feeling of self-nothingness is self-abasement. But in his house, his feeling of self-nothingness is modesty and his gravity is arrogance. Forbearance and sacrifice on one's own account are good and virtuous, but are bad and treacherous when done on behalf of others or the nation. People may bear patiently what has been done to them personally, but cannot bear patiently what is done to the nation on behalf of the nation. Pride and indignation on the nation's behalf are commendable, but are reprehensible on one's own behalf.

Entrusting the accomplishment of an affair to God before taking all the necessary measures and making all necessary arrangements is laziness, while leaving the desired outcome's realization to Him after doing all that should and can be done is reliance on Him as taught to us by the Shari'ah. Contentment with one's lot or with the results after having exerted one's efforts is praiseworthy contentment, and encourages further effort, reinvigorating one's energy. But contentment with what one already has is not desirable contentment; rather, it is lack of the necessary endeavor. There are numerous other examples.

The Qur'an generally mentions good works and piety and righteousness without defining them. By leaving them undefined, it alludes to the defining importance of circumstances; its conciseness is in fact a detailed explanation, and its silence is an expansive word.

- **Human happiness in social life lies in economy, labor, and contentment, and the rich and the poor can make peace in these values. However, the modern Western civilization, which does not give ear to the heavenly Religion and has made human beings to be wage-earners, has both made the overwhelming majority of people poor and increased their needs, and replaced economy and**

---

[47] *Gleams of Truth*, pp. 15, 68.

contentment with waste, greed and avarice, opening ways to wrongdoing, injustice, exploitation and religiously forbidden acts.[48]

- There are two Europes. One Europe is that which, benefiting from the religion of Jesus and Islamic civilization, serves human social life and justice through its scientific and technological inventions. The other is that which is based on naturalistic and materialistic philosophy and, supposing the evils of civilization to be virtues, has driven humankind to vice and misguidance.[49]

- Those who break their ties with Islam cause great harm to the Muslim social life; it is as if they are a fatal poison. Apostates go completely bad, and become like poison to social life. For this reason, unlike followers of other revealed religions living among Muslims, those who commit major sins openly and without shame are treated like traitors. Their testimony is not accepted in court, for their consciences are guilty and corrupt.[50]

However, do not be deceived by the great numbers of transgressors. For transgressors are not pleased with their transgressions. They usually find themselves in them. Almost all transgressors want to be pious and devout Muslims, to see their superiors as pious and righteous, only except those—May God save us from such corruption!—whose consciences have been corrupted through apostasy and receive pleasure from poisoning, like snakes.

- While urging Muslims to strive for worldly life and material progress, due care should be shown that the ropes by which they are connected to the Religion are not broken.[51]

- What causes the economic degradation of Muslims is usually greed, for "The greedy are subject to loss and disappointment," has become proverbial; greed is the cause of loss for Muslims.[52]

- It is always the error of the majority which causes general disasters. The calamity of world wars is the calamity of all humankind.[53]

---

[48] *Emirdağ Lahikası* (Addendum of Emirdağ), vol. 2, pp. 88–89.
[49] *The Gleams*, "The Seventeenth Gleam", p. 162.
[50] *The Gleams*, "The Seventeenth Gleam", p. 170.
[51] *The Gleams*, "The Seventeenth Gleam", p. 170.
[52] *The Gleams*, "The Seventeenth Gleam", p. 170.
[53] *Gleams of Truth*, p. 47.

Humankind's misguided thinking, Nimrod-like obstinacy, and Pharaoh-like haughtiness, grew and grew on earth until they reached the heavens. Humanity also offended the sensitive mystery of creation. It caused the tragedy of the world wars to pour down from the heavens like the plague and deluge; it caused a heavenly blow to be dealt to the infidel.

This means, the calamity was the calamity of all humankind. The common cause, inclusive of all humankind, was the misguided thinking that arose from materialism—bestial freedom, the despotism of carnal desires and fancies.

- **Since the majority of Muslims did not obey both of God's Shari'ahs or sets of laws—the Shari'ah of life, or of creation and operation of the universe, which proceeds from the Divine Attribute of Will, and the well-known Shari'ah, which proceeds from the Attribute of Speech—they fell behind the West in the economic and military fields, and lost in the First World War. The deed causes the punishment of its kind. The punishment is of the same as the deed.**[54]

The Creator the All-Exalted wanted from us one hour out of the twenty-four. He ordered us, willed that we, for our good, assign one hour for the five daily Prayers. But out of laziness we gave them up, neglected them in heedlessness. So we received the following punishment: He made us perform Prayers of a sort during these last five years through a constant, twenty-four hour drill and hardship, keeping us ceaselessly moving and striving.

He also demanded of us one month a year for fasting, but we pitied our carnal souls, so in atonement He compelled us to fast for five years through hunger and poverty during the war.

He wanted us to pay as *Zakah* either a fortieth or a twentieth or a tenth of the property He gave us, but out of miserliness we did wrong: we mixed the unlawful with our property, and did not give the *Zakah* voluntarily. So He had our accumulated *Zakah* taken from us, and saved us from what was unlawful in our property. The deed causes the punishment of its kind. The punishment is of the same as the deed.

The neglect of the *Hajj* and its wisdom drew Divine Wrath, and the punishment it incurred was not atonement for our sins but an increase in our sins. It was the neglect of the elevated Islamic policy, which exists in

---

[54] *Gleams of Truth*, pp. 47–49.

the *Hajj* and brings unity of views through mutual acquaintance and cooperation through mutual assistance, and it was the neglect of the vast social, economic, and political benefits contained in the *Hajj* which prepared the ground for the enemy to employ millions of Muslims against Islam and themselves. Instead of hastening to the *Hajj* eagerly, which is pure good, millions of Muslims were made to make long journeys under the enemy flag, which is pure evil. Ponder on this and take heed!

- **"The truth prevails" is true both in itself and in respect of the consequences, and the final happy outcome or the final triumph is for the truth.**[55]

A questioner once asked: "As 'The truth prevails' is the truth, why are the unbelievers triumphant over Muslims, and force or might triumphant over right?"

I replied: Consider these four points and your difficulty will be resolved. *The first point* is this. Every means to every truth and right may not be true and rightful at all times. Similarly, not every means of every falsehood has to be false. The result is a means which (falsehood employs and) is true prevailing over a false means (which truth or right uses). In which case, a truth is overcome by falsehood. But this has occurred temporarily and indirectly, not essentially or permanently. However, the final triumph is always that of the truth. It should also not be forgotten that force possesses a truth, and there is a purpose and meaning in its creation.

The second point is this: While it is obligatory that all attributes of all Muslims are Muslim, in reality this may not always be so. Similarly, not all the attributes of all unbelievers have to be connected to unbelieving or arise from their unbelief. In the same way, all the attributes of all sinful transgressors may not be sinful, nor do they need always arise from sinfulness. This means that an unbeliever's Muslim attribute prevails over a Muslim's irreligious attribute. Indirectly and due to the means, the unbeliever can prevail over the believer. Furthermore, **in this world the right of life is all-embracing**. Life—that meaningful manifestation of the universal Mercy—has an instance of wisdom, which unbelief cannot impede.

The third point is this: Two of the All-Majestic One's Attributes of perfection give rise to two sets of laws. One is the Shari'ah of life or of the creation and operation of the universe, which proceeds from the Attribute of

---

[55] *Gleams of Truth*, pp. 69–70.

Will; and the other, the well-known Shari'ah, proceeds from the Attribute of Speech. Just as the commands or laws of the well-known Shari'ah are obeyed or disobeyed, so, too, do people obey or disobey the Shari'ah of life. The reward and punishment for the former is received mostly in the Hereafter, while the penalties and rewards of the latter are suffered mostly in this world. For example, the reward of patience is success, while the penalty for laziness is privation; and the reward of labor is wealth. The reward of steadfastness is triumph. The punishment of poison is illness and the reward of its antidote is health.

Sometimes the commands of both Shari'ahs are in force in a single thing; it has aspects pertaining to each. That means, obedience to the rules of life is a truth, and obedience prevails, while disobedience to it is a false attitude. If a truth has been the means to a falsehood, when it prevails, it will be the true means to a falsehood. This is an example of truth being defeated by a falsehood owing to the means. It is not the defeat of the truth itself by falsehood.

In consequence, "The truth prevails" means: "The truth is triumphant essentially or in itself." Also, the end or consequence is intended.

The fourth point is this: A truth has remained in potential or it is powerless, or adulterated, or contaminated. It needs to be developed or given fresh strength. In order to improve and brighten it, falsehood is temporarily allowed to attack it, so that however much pure gold of truth is needed will emerge unadulterated.

Even if in the beginning falsehood is victorious in this world, it cannot win the war. *"The final (happy) outcome is in favor of the God-revering, pious,"* will strike it a blow!

So falsehood is defeated. The truth of "The truth prevails" inflicts punishment on it. See: the truth is triumphant.

- **Good, righteous acts are of two sorts: one positive and voluntary, the other negative and enforced. All pains and calamities are good deeds, but they are negative and enforced. The *hadith* that tells us of this[56] offers consolation.[57]**

---

[56] The Pride of humankind says: "In whatever circumstance a believer is, it is to his good. This is not so for anyone other than believers. For if something happy happens to him, he thanks God, and this is to his good. If some harm touches him, he remains patient, and this also is to his good." (*Muslim*, "Zuhd" 64; *ad-Darimi*, "Riqaq" 61.)

[57] *Gleams of Truth*, p. 49.

This sinful nation has made its ablutions in blood; it has repented with deeds. Muslims have two rewards in return for a calamity. As an immediate reward, four million, a fifth of this nation, were raised to the degree of sainthood through the rank of martyrdom or warring for God's sake; this wiped out their sin. The world-wide victory of Islam will be its later reward.

- **Major cases and crimes are tried and judged in large centers, while minor ones are decided in small centers. God's wisdom requires that most of the punishment destined for unbelievers be postponed to the Last, Supreme Judgment, and that believers be partly punished in this world.**[58]

For example, those (like the communist Russians) who abandoned and abrogated and corrupted religion do not incur Divine wrath (in the world) to the extent of those who betray a true and eternal religion that will never be abrogated. Thus the quaking earth shows its anger towards believers and leaves the others unpunished, at present.

- **Destruction is easy, thus the weak are destructive.**[59]

The existence of something depends on the existence of all its parts, while its non-existence is possible through the non-existence of one of its parts; thus, destruction is easy. It is because of this that the impotent never incline to do or produce something positive or constructive that will show their power and capability; they act negatively, and are always destructive.

- **An insignificant private who serves a great ruler's laws and commands can achieve more than an insignificant ruler's chief general.**[60]

If asked: "Who are you to challenge these famous philosophers? While you are like a fly, how dare you challenge the flight of eagles?" I would reply: "I have an eternal teacher like the Qur'an, and so, in matters of the truth and knowledge of God, I do not need to attach as much value as a gnat's wing to such eagles, who were students of a misguided philosophy and deluded reason. However inferior I am to them, their teacher is far more inferior than mine. With the help of my 'teacher'— the Qur'an—nature and materialistic tendencies that led them to drown

---

[58] *The Words*, "The Fourteenth Word", p. 186.
[59] *Gleams of Truth*, p. 36.
[60] *The Words*, "The Thirtieth Word", p. 563.

cannot even wet my toes. An insignificant private who serves a great ruler's laws and commands can achieve more than an insignificant ruler's chief general."

- **Every winter is followed by spring and every night by the morning.**[61]

We Muslims, who are the students of the holy Qur'an, follow proof and accept the truths of belief with our reasons, intellects, and hearts. Unlike some members of other religions, we do not abandon proof or blindly imitate religious leaders. Therefore, in the future, when reason, science, and knowledge will dominate, it will be the Qur'an, the decrees and propositions of which are all confirmed by reason, that will certainly rule.

No period of history, from the Age of Happiness until the present time, tells us of a Muslim who has preferred another religion over Islam, based on sound reasoning, and entered that religion based on a sound proof. It is true that there have been some who have left Islam; but this has been through imitation and is of no importance. If we demonstrate the perfections of Islamic morality and the truth of Islam through our acts, the followers of other religions will continue to enter it in greater numbers; even some whole regions and countries of the earth will accept it.

Look, time does not move in a straight line so that its beginning and end grow distant from one another. Rather, like the movement of the earth, time moves by drawing a circle. It sometimes displays progress as an embodiment of spring and summer and sometimes displays decline as an embodiment of winter and a season of storms. So, just as every winter is followed by spring and every night by the morning, so too humankind will, God willing, also live a new morning and spring. From the Divine Mercy we can expect to see the true civilization marked by a general peace in the sun of the truth of Islam.

- **A fine but tarnished diamond is always preferable to a piece of glass, no matter how well polished.**[62]

The guidance of Islam has rusted, while the genius of the present civilization has been gilded with desires and passions. Even if a peerless diamond has rusted, it is always preferable to a gilded piece of glass. That diamond has been engraved with a heavenly inscription; the eyes of

[61] *Sünuhat* (Occurrences to the Heart), in *Sünuhat, Tuluat, İşarat*, p. 93.
[62] *Gleams of Truth*, pp. 10, 49.

materialists do not see that peerless inscription, nor can they read it. Materialists seek everything in matter; their intelligence is in their eyes, they are blind to whatever is spiritual, for bodily eyes are blind to that.

- **An unlawful way leads to the opposite of what was intended.**[63]

One who follows an unlawful way (in Islam) for a lawful objective generally attains the opposite result of what he intended. For example, *The murderer cannot inherit* (from the one whom he has murdered); this is a very significant principle: "Someone who follows an unlawful way (in Islam) to reach his goal generally attains the opposite of what he intended in retribution." This is very important especially in acting in the name of or to serve Islam.

Also, the reward for an un-Islamic love, like that of (the second) Europe, is the beloved's pitiless enmity. Love of (the second) Europe is not a lawful love in view of the Shari'ah; it is a blind imitation and disagreeable friendliness. Its consequence and recompense is the tyrannical hostility of the beloved and its crimes.

The sinner condemned to loss will find, in the end, neither pleasure nor salvation.

- **Politics based on personal interest is bestial.**[64]

The politics of the present, which is based on self-interest, is a rapacious beast. If you show love to a ravenous beast, you will not attract its compassion, but will rather sharpen its appetite. Then it will turn on you and demand from you payment for the use of its claws and teeth.

- **A faultless government is impossible. Demanding what is impossible is to do oneself evil. Especially a government whose parts are composed of sins cannot be faultless.**[65]

Demanding what is impossible is to do oneself evil. One who takes off from a mountain in order to fly is smashed into pieces. People wish for an innocent, faultless government. But it is not possible, even for an individual, to remain or become faultless. How, therefore, can a government, especially if its parts are composed of sins, become faultless? So we should consider whether the good of the government outweighs its evils. If those who wish for an innocent government were to live a thousand

[63] *Gleams of Truth*, pp. 9, 39.
[64] *Gleams of Truth*, pp. 8, 36.
[65] *Gleams of Truth*, pp. 145–146.

years and see every form of government, they would not be satisfied. They would try to destroy any form with the inclination to destruction that arises from their fancy.

- If a heart or conscience has not been equipped with Islamic virtues, it cannot be expected to have true patriotism, loyalty, and justice. However, since righteousness and being skillful are different things, for example, a transgressor in the Religion can be a competent shepherd. A drunkard can make a good watch when he is not drunk. Therefore, righteousness is not enough in the jobs where skill and knowledge are necessary. What is better and preferable is that righteousness and competence should be combined. If this is not possible, competence should be preferred in the jobs or works where it is absolutely necessary.[66]

- Depending on politics usually leads to two perilous consequences: Believers either despair of God's Mercy, due to successive disappointments, and are condemned to punishment by, "Do not despair of God's Mercy,"[67] or feel forced to support every party decision or activity in some way, whether it conforms to Islam or not, and thus face the threat of, "And do not incline toward those who do wrong, lest the fire should touch you."[68]/[69]

Bediüzzaman answers as follows to the questions put to him about why he is so indifferent to politics, Turkey's political situation in particular, and that of the world in general:

> Serving the Qur'an caused me to abandon politics, even to forget to think of it. Basing myself on the Qur'an's light, I say that humanity has reached a marsh in this century. Whole caravans of humanity are trying, with great difficulty, to advance in this putrid marsh. A small minority follows a safe way and some have extricated themselves, but the majority continues to flail around in the dark. Although 20 percent of this majority seems quite happy with this struggle, mistaking its dirt and filth for musk and ambergris, the other 80 percent knows that it is in a filthy marsh but cannot see the safe path (leading them out).

---

[66] *Münazarat* (Discussions), pp. 20–21.
[67] *Suratu'z-Zumar*, 39:53.
[68] *Sura Hud*, 11:113.
[69] *The Letters*, "The Thirteenth and Sixteenth Letters", pp. 82–84.

We must bring that majority out of the marsh. To do so, we must either use a mace to knock the 20 percent back to its senses or provide the 80 percent with a light to see a way to safety. I see that most people hold maces, but almost no one gives light to the helpless 80 percent. If some still have light, they are not trusted because they also carry maces. People are afraid of being beaten after being drawn to the light. Besides, the light may be extinguished if the mace is broken.

This marsh represents the modern corrupted social life of misguided people. The intoxicated 20 percent are those who willingly indulge in life's material pleasures and stubbornly resist the light. The great majority, who are bewildered in the marsh, dislike deviation but cannot get out of it. The maces represent political trends and movements, while the light is the Qur'an's truths. No one should oppose and feel hostile towards the light, for only Satan hates it. Thus I took refuge in God from Satan and politics, threw the mace of politics away, and held tightly to the light. Many of those involved in political trends love the light. No one should turn away from or accuse the Qur'anic lights and truths, which are offered sincerely and without ulterior political motives and aspirations, unless they are human devils who favor irreligion in the name of politics.

I thank God that abandoning politics prevented me from reducing the Qur'an's diamond-like truths to pieces of glass under the accusation of exploiting them for political ends. On the contrary, these diamonds continue to grow in value in the eyes of more and more people from every social stratum.

In addition, believers cannot serve their cause through politics in such stormy circumstances. Whatever service is rendered for Islam through politics eventually benefits the dominant anti-Islamic system, because foreign powers control the reins of political life. Engaging in politics also divides Muslims into opposing political factions that have a negative impact upon individual hearts and collective life—some people are so obstinate that even Muslims may label angelic brothers or sisters as satans, or a satanic party member as an angel, depending upon whether or not they support a certain political party. When I saw a learned man severely reproach a good, virtuous man who did not share his political views and then praise a corrupt member of his political faction, I became dismayed by the evils of politics and completely withdrew, saying: "I take refuge in God from Satan and politics."

Another important reason for my indifference to politics is that eternal happiness can be attained only through belief or faith. One without belief is unhappy in both worlds and is doomed to suffer the greatest suffering.

Therefore, regardless of their personal belief or unbelief, piety or impiety, sincerity or insincerity, no one but Satan has the right to oppose serving belief.

Furthermore, belief is Islam's very foundation or spirit, and manifests itself in each particle of Islam. The more established people are in belief, the more successful they can be in other areas of the Religion. Depending on politics usually leads to two perilous consequences: Believers either despair of God's Mercy, due to successive disappointments, and are condemned to punishment by, "*Do not despair of God's Mercy,*" or feel forced to support every party decision or activity in some way, whether it conforms to Islam or not, and thus face the threat of: "*And do not incline toward those who do wrong, lest the fire should touch you.*"

- **The eye of obstinacy perceives an angel as a devil.**[70]

Obstinacy causes one to behave in this way: if a devil helps or supports one or their side, they hail him as "an angel" and call down blessings upon him. But if they see an angel on the opposing side, they view him as a devil in the guise of an angel, and they call down curses on him out of enmity.

- **An enemy is more harmful when he is unknown, more cruel and evil when he is deceitful, more severe in corruption when he is dishonest, more destructive when he is internal.**[71]

This is why at the beginning of *Suratu'l-Baqarah* the Qur'an elaborates on hypocrites with thirteen consecutive verses after it praises the believers with three verses and condemns the unbelievers with two verses.

- **The Qur'an does not mention the hypocrites by names. If it had disclosed their identities, the believers would have felt ill-suspicious of themselves due to the temptation of the carnal soul. Ill-suspicion leads to fear, fear to ostentation, and ostentation to hypocrisy. It is possible that an evil remaining concealed may disappear gradually.**[72]

- **Deception and sedition have power so long as they remain under veil. They lose power and are extinguished when they are unveiled.**[73]

---

[70] *Gleams of Truth*, p. 54.

[71] *İşaratü'l-İ'caz*, "*Suratu'l-Baqara*, verse 8."

[72] *İşaratü'l-İ'caz*, "*Suratu'l-Baqara*, verse 8."

[73] *Hutuvat-ı Sitte* (Six Steps), "The Sixth Step", p. 27.

- **If there is not a sound or sincere unity in a community, it will weaken as its numbers increase through mere population growth. This is like the multiplication of fractions. The number grows less in proportion to how many times they have been multiplied.**[74]

Multiplying by or adding whole numbers leads to a greater number, whereas multiplying by fractions leads to a smaller number. Four times four makes sixteen. But when a fourth is multiplied by a fourth, the result is a sixteenth. In just the same way, if there is not a substantial, sincere unity in a community, its increase in number only causes it to become smaller, disintegrating and losing value.

- **Dispute, discord, partisanship, obstinacy, and envy, which cause rancor and enmity among believers, are distasteful, vile, harmful and wrongful for personal, social, and spiritual life, and from the viewpoint of truth, wisdom, and Islam, which is supreme humanity. Moreover, they poison human life.**[75]

A believer may be compared to a house or a ship belonging to God. Such a person has not nine, but as many as twenty innocent attributes such as belief, Islam, and neighborliness. If we cherish rancor and enmity for him (or her) because of one criminal attribute we do not like, which means desiring the destruction of that ship or house, our crime would be most atrocious.

- **Unity in belief requires unity of hearts, and unity in following the same principles of creed and action demands social agreement and solidarity.**[76]

If we are in the same squadron as someone else, we will feel friendly towards him and so form a mutually friendly relation because we are commanded by one commander. We also will experience a fraternal relationship with another due to being from or living in the same town. Given this, there are ties of unity, bonds of accord, and fraternal relationships generated by the light and consciousness of belief and as many as the Divine Names to which it shows us. For example:

As Muslims, we all serve the same One Creator, Sovereign, Object of Worship, Provider... so there are as many ties between us as there are

---

[74] *Gleams of Truth*, p. 55.
[75] *The Letters*, "The Twenty-second Letter", p. 281.
[76] *The Letters*, "The Twenty-second Letter", p. 282–283.

Divine Names. Our Prophet, religion (Islam), and *qiblah* are one and the same, and the number of such ties amounts to almost a hundred. Our town, country, and state is one, and tens of things are one and the same for us. These ties require unity and oneness, union and concord, love and brotherhood and sisterhood. Such immaterial chains are strong enough to link all planets together. If, despite all this, we prefer things as frail and trivial as a spider's web and that cause dispute, discord, and rancor, and cherish enmity and grudges towards fellow believers, we must understand—unless our heart is dead and our intelligence extinguished—how great is our disregard for those ties of unity, and how seriously we are offending those causes of love and transgressing against those brotherly and sisterly relationships!

- **Like light and darkness, love and hostility cannot exist together. If hostility wins, love changes into flattery and hypocrisy; if love overcomes, then hostility is transformed into pity and compassion. A Muslim's way is loving love and being hostile to hostility. What a Muslim loves most in the world must be love, and what he or she resents most must be hostility.**[77]

Believers should love—and indeed do love—their brothers and sisters in faith and should be pained by any evil seen in them. They should try to help them reform themselves only with gentleness, for a Prophetic Tradition states: "Believers should not be angry with each other, nor refuse to speak to each other for more than three days."[78]

- **As the attribute of love deserves to receive love, enmity deserves to receive enmity.**[79]

What is most fitting for and worthy of love is love, and what is most worthy of hostility is hostility. That is, the attribute of love, which enables a happy human social life, most deserves love; while hostility, which ruins human social life, is an ugly, harmful attribute most deserving of hostility and hatred.

The time of hostility has come to an end. The two world wars have shown how evil and devastatingly wrong hostility can be. It is manifestly clear that evil has not the least benefit for humankind. For this reason, unless evil acts are in the form of aggression, such acts on the part of our

---

[77] *The Letters*, "The Twenty-second Letter", p. 282; *Gleams of Truth*, p. 167.
[78] *al-Bukhari*, "Adab," 57; *Muslim*, "Birr," 23; *Abu Dawud*, "Adab," 47.
[79] *The Letters*, "The Twenty-second Letter", p. 284; *Gleams of Truth*, pp. 133–134.

enemies should not drive us to hostility. Hell or God's punishment is enough for them.

Arrogance and selfishness sometimes wrongly lead believers to feel hostility towards their brothers or sisters-in-religion. Even though they may see themselves as rightful, hostility towards believers means belittling the powerful reasons for loving them such as belief, being Muslim, and being a fellow human. This is paramount to lunacy; preferring the pebble-sized reasons for hostility over the mountain-sized reasons for love. That is, the reasons for love are the luminous, powerful chains and the spiritual castles such as belief, being Muslim, and being human, while the reasons for hostility towards believers are no more than pebbles. Therefore, hostility towards believers is as great a wrong as disparaging the mountain-like reasons for love.

In short: Brotherhood, sisterhood, and love are the characteristics of Islam and of bonds between Muslims. The people of hostility are like mischievous children, who desire to cry and therefore seek a reason to cry. They make a thing that is as petty as the wing of a fly a pretext for crying. They are also like an unfair, pessimistic man who does not have a good opinion of others as long as it is possible to have an ill opinion. He covers ten instances or acts of good with a single evil. Islamic characteristics, fairness, and the rule of having a good opinion of others counter this attitude.

We must not nurse anger and hostility towards believers to please our harmful soul. If we cannot remove this enmity, there are many unbelievers and heretics deserving enmity.

- **If we want to defeat our enemy, we must meet evil with good, for responding with evil increases enmity. Even though outwardly defeated, such people nurture rancor and enmity in their hearts. If we respond with good, they will repent and become our friends.**[80]

If you say: "But I have no choice, for enmity is part of my nature. Moreover, these things anger me and so I cannot overlook them," I respond: "If you do not act badly such as backbiting, or under the influence of such impulses towards those for whom you cherish enmity, and if you are conscious that you err, it is harmless. For awareness of your error and admis-

---

[80] *The Letters*, "The Twenty-second Letter", p. 282.

sion that your evil impulse is wrong means repenting and seeking God's forgiveness, which will deliver you from its evil consequences."

• **According to** "Every soul earns only to its own account; and no soul, as bearer of burden, bears, and is made to bear, the burden of another,"[81] **which expresses absolute justice; nurturing rancor and enmity for believers is like condemning all of their innocent attributes on account of one criminal attribute—a very great injustice indeed!**[82]

Despite this Qur'anic eternal principle, *"People are much given to wrongdoing,"*[83] and *"Man is indeed prone to doing great wrong and misjudging, and acting out of sheer ignorance..."*[84] the source of human capacity to do terrible wrong and injustice is this: unlike animals, human beings are not restricted in creation in respect of their innate powers or inclinations. For this reason, unless they are guided and trained to do so, human beings do not encounter any limits to wrongdoing or egotism. When egotism, self-centeredness, selfishness, arrogance, and obstinacy are added to the human inclination to wrongdoing, human beings invent such monstrous offenses and sins that they have not yet been able to name them all. As these are proofs for the necessity of Hell, their punishment can only be Hell. Consider the following:

A human being has numerous attributes or characteristics. If one of these attracts enmity, the first verse cited above (6: 164) requires that enmity should be restricted to only this characteristic or attribute. Having many other good attributes, that human being should only be pitied and not be a target of injustice or transgression.

However, out of untrained inclination towards wrongdoing and acting out of sheer ignorance, human beings extend enmity to all the attributes of that human being and indeed his very person. Not being content with this, they nurture enmity towards his relatives and even colleagues. However, since something may be the result of many reasons, the sinful or wrongdoing attribute deserving enmity may result from an external factor, not from the corruption of the heart. Therefore, even if this attribute is wrongful, that person cannot be considered a wrongdoer.

---

[81] *Suratu'l-An'am*, 6:164.
[82] *The Letters*, "The Twenty-second Letter", p. 283.
[83] *Sura Ibrahim*, 14:34.
[84] *Suratu'l-Ahzab*, 33:72.

We see that the present, modern civilization has given humankind such an unjust, pitiless principle that it reduces all its virtues to nothing, and explains how *"Man is indeed prone to doing great wrong and misjudging, and acting out of sheer ignorance."* It permits the destruction of a village with all the innocents in it if a traitor has taken refuge there, or the annihilation of a whole community with all its innocents, children, women, and the elderly, if one rebel is among them, or the devastation of a sacred building of immeasurable worth, such as Ayasofya (Hagia Sofia), if one who does not obey the wrongful laws of this society seeks refuge there.

If a person is not accountable in the view of the Ultimate Truth for the sin of their brother or relative or colleague, how can it be that thousands of innocent people are treated as responsible for the rebellion of one unruly person in a place where there may always be ill-disposed revolutionaries?

- **A believer pays respect to their elders, has compassion for those younger than them, and love and magnanimity for their peers.**[85]

A ship cannot be sunk because there is a single criminal among its passengers. Similarly, a believer who has many innocent attributes cannot be shown enmity because of a single criminal attribute or act. In particular, noble attributes, such as belief, confirmation of Divine Unity, and submission to God, which are all means of love, are like Mount Uhud. By contrast, the faults that are means of enmity are like pebbles. What great foolishness and lunacy it is to consider pebbles as being weightier than Mount Uhud! It is equally mercilessness for a believer to feel enmity towards another believer. Weighed on the balance of feelings, enmity in believers is contrary to Islam and the security and peace it entails. A Muslim can only feel pity towards their Muslim brothers or sisters for their faults, and can feel no rancor at all. In sum: Islam demands brotherhood and sisterhood, and love is essential to belief.

- **When we know our way to be right and our opinions to be true, we may be justified in saying: "My way is right and better." But we cannot say: "Only my way is right."**[86]

According to the principle, "The eye of contentment is too dim to perceive faults, whereas the eye of anger exhibits all vice," our unjust view

[85] *Gleams of Truth*, p. 112.
[86] *The Letters*, "The Twenty-second Letter", p. 284.

and distorted opinion cannot judge between the ways, and should not condemn another's way as wrong.

• **Whatever we say should be true, but we have no right, nor is it true, to say (carelessly and on every occasion) whatever is true. For those who are not sincere may be irritated by our advice and react unfavorably.**[87]

If we want to nurse our hostility, we must direct it against the enmity in our heart and try to remove it. Also, we should be an enemy to our evil-commanding soul and its fancies and try to reform it, for it is our most dangerous enemy.

• **Those who indulge in rancor and enmity serve to transgress their own souls, fellow believers, and Divine Compassion. For they condemn their souls to torment whenever they see their enemies obtain a blessing or advantage, and suffer pain because they fear their enemies. Enmity arising from envy is the severest torment, for envy consumes and destroys the envious while leaving the one envied untouched or largely untouched.**[88]

If those ensnared in such envy want to be cured, let them ponder the fate of what or who engenders such envy. Doing so will cause them to see that the physical beauty and strength, and the worldly rank and wealth, which they see their enemies have, are transient. Their benefit is slight, but the trouble they cause is great. If we envy others because of their merits with respect to the Hereafter, we are either hypocrites who want to use up here the rewards to be paid in the Hereafter, or unjustly consider the object of our envy a hypocrite or ostentatious.

If we rejoice when those we envy suffer misfortune and grieve when they receive a bounty, we are being offended by the good done to them by Destiny and Divine Compassion, and thus indirectly criticize and object to them. Those who criticize Destiny mean they strike and break their heads on an anvil; those who object to Compassion are deprived of it.

• **Obstinacy and partisanship only harm social life. If one's conduct is not based on exalted principles, "Loving for God's sake; disliking for God's sake; judging for God's sake," dispute and discord**

---

[87] *The Letters*, "The Twenty-second Letter", p. 284.
[88] *The Letters*, "The Twenty-second Letter", p. 285.

will result. If one ignores these principles, attempts to do justice will result in injustice.[89]

A *hadith* says: "Difference among my community is a mercy."[90] The difference intended in the *hadith* is a positive difference. That is, it allows each side to promote and propagate its own argument, to improve and reform a competing view instead of destroying it. The Prophet, upon him be peace and blessings, rejects a negative difference, for it seeks to destroy another side because of partisan bias and hostility. Those who are at each other's throats cannot act positively towards each other.

If partisanship is in the name of truth, it can be a refuge for those seeking their rights. But the biased and self-centered partisanship is only a refuge and a focus of support for the unjust. If Satan appears to support those engaged in biased partisanship, such partisans will call God's blessings upon him. Moreover, if angelic people join another side, the same partisans will call God's curses upon them.

If people argue in the name of truth, this is only a difference of means. In reality, it is an agreement on the basis of the matter and the basic purpose. Such an argument can reveal all aspects of truth, and so serves justice and truth. But a confrontation between biased, partisan opinions driven by egotism and fame-seeking, one engendered by a tyrannical, carnal soul, can only bring forth the flames of dissension. Failing to agree on a purpose, opposing views of this kind cannot find a point of convergence anywhere on the earth. Since they do not differ in the name of truth, they split into extremes and give rise to irreconcilable divisions.

- **A harmonious social life requires that internal enmities be forgotten and abandoned, especially when the nation is confronted with foreign enemies.**[91]

While even the most unsophisticated people recognize and practice this, why do those who claim to be serving the Muslim community fail to forget their petty hostilities at a time when numerous enemies are taking up positions to attack, one after the other? This failure thereby prepares the ground for the attacks of the enemies. This is nothing less than corruption, barbarity, and treachery directed against the social life of Islam!

[89] *The Letters*, "The Twenty-second Letter", pp. 286–287.
[90] al-Munawi, *Faydu'l-Qadir*, 1:210.
[91] *The Letters*, "The Twenty-second Letter", pp. 287–288.

- **Enmity and rancor towards or between believers spoils spiritual life and worship, for they spoil sincerity and purity of intention— the means of salvation.**[92]

Biased partisans seek superiority over their opponents while performing good deeds and so do not act purely for God's sake. Slanting their judgments and dealings towards their supporters, they cannot be just. Their intention becomes impure, and their justice becomes injustice, both of which void their good deeds.

- **Those who perform the same duty in the same way or for the same ideal are accounted as the same as each other.**[93]

Differences of time and place cannot hinder friendly conversations of brothers-in-truth. Even if they are as far apart as east and west, past and future, this world and the Hereafter, they may be considered as being together and engaging in conversation. In particular, those who perform the same duty for the same purpose are accounted as the same as each other.

- **Just as the disagreement of the people of truth does not come from their lack of the truth, so too the agreement of the worldly people who are heedless of Divine guidance is not based on following the truth.**[94]

Rather, modern social life demands a division of labor and has caused the formation of social classes, professional groups, and political parties, each of which has its own particular duties, wages, renown, and popular respect. So, there is almost no point of rivalry, conflict, and dissension. It is for this reason that however evil the way that each follows may be, the worldly people can come together for their interests.

However, as for religious people, particularly scholarly ones, and those following Sufi ways, their duties are concerned with the whole people, and there are no worldly wages determined for them, nor do they have a specified place, or share of fame, or popular acceptance. Many may demand the same position, and many hands may be stretched out for the same material and immaterial reward. This may cause conflict and rivalry, and discord and disagreement may take the place of concord and agreement. The cure for this dreadful disease is sincerity. People can gain sincerity by preferring

---

[92] *The Letters*, "The Twenty-second Letter", p. 289.
[93] *The Letters*, "The Twenty-third Letter", p. 297.
[94] *The Gleams*, "The Twentieth Gleam", pp. 210–211.

attachment to the truth to self-love, and by always holding the truth over selfish motives, and following the Prophetic rule, "*My wage is only due from God,*"[95] by remaining indifferent to any material or immaterial wage that comes from people. Also, in accordance with the principle, "*What rests with the Messenger is only conveying the Message,*"[96] they should know that it is God Who will bestow popular respect and acceptance if He wills, and that obtaining popular respect and acceptance is not included in religious duties.

- **This world is the place of working for the Hereafter, of fulfilling religious responsibilities to get the reward in the Hereafter. There must be no rivalry and jealousy, for such things point to insincerity and an impure intention.**[97]

At the time of working or rendering service for God's sake, feelings of rivalry and jealousy remain quiet. Sharing the work and responsibility lightens the burden and lessens the difficulty, and the weak appreciate the strong, and the lazy love the hard-working. However, when it comes to receiving wages or sharing the profit, feelings of rivalry and jealousy begin to stir. This world is the place of working for the Hereafter, of fulfilling religious responsibilities to get the reward in the Hereafter. There must be no rivalry and jealousy, for such things point to insincerity and an impure intention. Such people, by looking for such worldly rewards as material wages or appreciation and praise, invalidate their good deeds, make others partners with God in giving reward, and are condemned by others.

- **Sincerity is never fruitless, even if it is for the sake of evil. Whatever one seeks with sincerity, God will grant it to him or her.**[98]

- **The misguided people agree and cooperate because of their abasement, while the rightly-guided people disagree because of their dignity.**[99]

That is to say, since the worldly people of heedlessness and misguidance do not base themselves on the truth, they are weak and abased. Because of their abasement, they need to find strength and power. This need leads them to hold fast to alliances with and the help to come from

[95] *Sura Yunus*, 10:72.
[96] *Suratu'n-Nur*, 24:54.
[97] *Al-Mathnawi al-Nuri*, "The Ninth Treatise", pp. 320–321.
[98] *The Gleams*, "The Twentieth Gleam", p. 211.
[99] *The Gleams*, "The Twentieth Gleam", pp. 211–213.

others. It is as if they find some sort of partisanship of truth in wrongfulness, sincerity in misguidance, a religious fanaticism in irreligion, and concord in hypocrisy and dissension, which make them successful in their cause. For sincerity is never fruitless, even if it is for the sake of evil. Whatever one seeks with sincerity, God will grant it to him or her.

However, religious or rightly-guided people, including, in particular, scholarly ones and those who follow the spiritual ways, base themselves on the truth and rely on God's help. Because of certain differences on the paths they follow, they do not feel in need of any help that may come from these other paths or alliance with their followers. If, in addition, they have a certain degree of egotism or self-centeredness, supposing themselves to be right and their opponents wrong, discord and rivalry will take the place of concord and love. This causes a loss of sincerity and failure in the fulfillment of duties.

The cure for blindness to the critical consequences of this dreadful state lies in the following nine principles:

- We should always act positively. That is, we should act out of love for our own way, and not allow enmity towards or criticisms of other true ways.
- We should consider that, irrespective of the particular paths within the general sphere of Islam, there are certainly numerous points of agreement and bonds of unity in Islam that generate and require love, brotherhood and sisterhood, and concord.
- On condition that they do not criticize the paths of others, everyone who follows a true path has the right to say, "My path is true and more beautiful," but they cannot imply the falsity or ugliness of the paths of others by saying, "Only my path is true," or "The beautiful path belongs only to me."
- We should consider that agreement with the people of truth attracts Divine help and success, and is a means of dignity in religious life.
- Realizing that even the most powerful individual resistance is subject to failure in the face of the attacks of the collective force of the people of misguidance and wrongdoing, the people of truth should form a collective force through agreement in order to preserve right and justice.
- We must save the truth from the assault of falsehood. Therefore,

- We should renounce self-centeredness and egotism, and
- Abandon the mistaken concept of self-esteem, and
- Give up worthless feelings of rivalry.

- **The disagreement among the people of truth does not emanate from a lack of zeal or aspiration, nor does the agreement of misguided people arise from having lofty ideals or great endeavors for the same. Rather, the disagreement of the rightly-guided arises from the misuse of the endeavor for their lofty cause, while the agreement of the misguided comes from weakness and impotence that arises from not having an elevated cause and endeavoring for the same.**[100]

What causes the rightly-guided to misuse their endeavors for their cause and therefore leads to discord and rivalry among them is their extreme aspiration for eternal reward and the fulfillment of the duties pertaining to the Hereafter, which is regarded as a praiseworthy quality from the viewpoint of the eternal life. However, with the thought of "I will gain this reward; let me guide these people; let them listen to me," they take up a position of rivalry to their true brothers and sisters who are in real need of their love, assistance, and brotherhood or sisterhood. The egotism of scholarly people, which engenders in them the feelings, "Why do my pupils go to him for learning and guidance? Why do I not have as many pupils as he has?", causes them to seek the favor of others or to chase positions of powers. This egotism is an evil quality, and causes them to lose sincerity, opening to them the door of ostentation.

The cure for this error, this wound, this appalling spiritual disease, is as follows: One can gain God's good pleasure through sincerity, not through a multiplicity of followers or great success. It even sometimes happens that a single word may result in one's salvation and obtaining God's good pleasure. Therefore, quantity should not be given much importance. For the guidance of a single person may sometimes be as pleasing to God as the guidance of a thousand. In addition, sincerity and attachment to the truth require that we should earnestly desire Muslims to benefit from anyone or any school or path of guidance they can. Thinking, "Let them take lessons from me and cause me to gain reward!" is a trick of the carnal soul and egotism.

---

[100] *The Gleams,* "The Twentieth Gleam", pp. 213–214.

- **While lowly and heartless worshippers of the carnal soul and the world can sincerely come together around immediate worldly pleasures and instant benefits, although guided by what is true and right, the people of right guidance may fail to preserve sincerity and straightforwardness and thus fall into disagreement.**[101]

The people of misguidance, under the influence of the carnal soul and lust, and driven by desires and impulses which are blind to consequences and prefer an ounce of immediate pleasure to a ton of future pleasure, can come together in powerful, sincere alliances for the sake of instant benefits and immediate pleasures. Indeed, lowly and heartless worshippers of the carnal soul can sincerely come together around immediate worldly pleasures and benefits. However, since the people of right guidance cannot preserve straightforwardness and perfect sincerity to form a powerful, selfless unity and since they cannot be fully freed from egotism and self-centeredness, they lose their agreement, which is a sublime source of power, and their sincerity is shattered.

The cure for this grave disease is, with the guidance of the principle of *loving for God's sake*, proudly accompanying those who follow the Straight Path, deferring leadership to them, renouncing egotism with the thought that whoever is following the Straight Path may be better than oneself, and thus gaining sincerity, knowing that an ounce of deeds done with sincerity is preferable to tons of deeds done without sincerity, and preferring being a follower to leadership, which brings responsibility and therefore is risky.

- **The weak form powerful unities because they desperately need alliances and agreements. But since the powerful do not feel this need much, their unity is weak. Therefore, the disagreement of the rightly-guided people arises from their feeling of being powerful due to reliance on God, while the agreement of the people of heedlessness and misguidance comes from their weakness and impotence that results from the fact that they can find no point of support in their hearts.**[102]

The weak form powerful unities because they desperately need alliances and agreements. But since the powerful do not feel this need much, their unity is weak. Lions do not need union, nor do foxes, and therefore they live

---

[101] *The Gleams,* "The Twentieth Gleam", p. 215.
[102] *The Gleams,* "The Twentieth Gleam", pp. 216–217.

as individuals, whereas wild goats and oxen and antelopes form herds to protect themselves against wolves and lions. This means that the community and collective personality of the weak is strong, while the community and collective personality of the powerful is weak. Powerful women's organizations are an example of this in the human sphere. The Qur'an makes a subtle allusion to this fact. Although the feminine form of the verb should have been used for the community of women where there are two instances of femininity (women is a feminine noun, and as a plural subject requires the feminine form of the verb in Arabic), it uses the masculine form of the verb in, "*And women in the city said,*"[103] while in "*The desert Arabs said,*"[104] the feminine form of the verb for the community of men is used. This usage delicately implies that the community of weak, feeble, and tender women gains strength, toughness, and sternness with togetherness, and so acquires some sort of manliness. By contrast, since strong men, particularly those of the desert Arabs, rely on their own individual strength, their community suffers from weakness. This is why their community takes on a kind of femininity and requires the feminine form of verb; so the Qur'an has used this form most appropriately.

Thus, due to their submission to and trust in God, which is provided by belief in God, and which is a most powerful point of reliance, the people of truth do not display neediness before others or ask for their help. Even if they sometimes feel needy, they do not need to hold fast to this help. But since the worldly people are neglectful of the true source of support for humanity in worldly affairs, they suffer weakness and impotence, and therefore cooperate sincerely and even with self-sacrifice when in dire need of external help and support. The cure for this disease of the people of truth is to adopt as guidance in life the powerful Divine prohibition in, "*Do not dispute with one another, or else you may lose heart and your power and energy desert you,*"[105] and the wise Divine command for social life in, "*Help one another in virtue and goodness, and righteousness and piety.*"[106] We should also consider how harmful to Islam disagreement is, and how it facilitates the triumph of the misguided people over the people of truth, and join the caravan of the people of truth sincerely

---

[103] *Sura Yusuf*, 12:30.
[104] *Suratu'l-Hujurat*, 49:14.
[105] *Suratu'l-Anfal*, 8:46.
[106] *Suratu'l-Maeda*, 5:2.

and self-sacrificingly in awareness of our innate powerlessness as human beings. Also, renouncing self-centeredness and forgetting individual selfish interests, we should be freed from ostentation and pretension, and thus acquire sincerity.

- **The people of truth and right guidance must adopt the good manner described in the holy Criterion's verse,** "When they happen to pass by anything vain and useless, they pass by it with dignity."[107]/[108]

O people of truth! O truth-loving followers of the Divine way of life and true spiritual paths! Counter this awful disease of discord and disagreement by overlooking each other's faults and closing your eyes to each other's shortcomings. The people of truth and right guidance must adopt the good manner described in the holy Criterion's verse, "*When they happen to pass by anything vain and useless, they pass by it with dignity.*" Abandoning internal disputes while you are subject to external attacks and regarding the deliverance of the people of truth from decline and humiliation as your primary, most urgent and important duty that pertains to your afterlife, realize the brotherhood and sisterhood, the love and cooperation among you, for they are enjoined by hundreds of Qur'anic verses and Prophetic Traditions. Establish with all your powers a much stronger unity with your fellows and brothers and sisters in religion than that which exists between the worldly people, and allow no disagreement or discord among you!

- **The disagreement and rivalry among the people of truth comes from being unable to maintain magnanimity among themselves and zeal for endeavor, both of which originate in the truth and the praiseworthy form of competition in doing good on the way of the truth. As for the people of worldliness and heedlessness, in order not to lose the benefits to which they are so attached, and not to offend the leaders and companions they adore for the sake of their benefits, in their humiliation, cowardliness, and due to the lack of a sublime goal or endeavor for the same, they form unity at all costs, and sincerely come together with their partners in whatever way may be for their common interest.**[109]

---

[107] *Suratu'l-Furqan*, 25:72.
[108] *The Gleams*, "The Twentieth Gleam", p. 218.
[109] *The Gleams*, "The Twentieth Gleam", pp. 219–221.

O disunited, calamity-stricken people of truth! Since at this time of calamity you have lost sincerity and been unable to make God's good pleasure your sole aim, you have caused all the people of truth to suffer the present humiliation and defeat. In matters relating to the Religion and the afterlife there should be no rivalry or jealousy, and indeed there cannot be either from the viewpoint of the truth. For jealousy and the ensuing rivalry arise from the conflict, dispute and competition that are caused by many hands being stretched out to obtain the same object, or many eyes being fixed on the same position, or many stomachs demanding the same food. Since in the world many desire and apply for the same thing, and the world is too narrow and temporary to satisfy the limitless desires of humanity, people fall into rivalry. However, there is no cause for rivalry in the Hereafter, where each individual will be given a Garden where every one of the people of Paradise will be fully satisfied with his or her share.

Therefore, there can be no rivalry or jealousy about good deeds done to gain eternal happiness in the Hereafter. One who shows jealousy is either a person of ostentation, who is pursuing worldly results in the fulfillment of good deeds, or an ignorant devotee who does not know the reason why good deeds should be done, or does not perceive that the spirit or essence of good deeds is sincerity. By feeling some sort of enmity towards God's beloved servants because of this rivalry, such a person takes up a position by which they deny the limitless vastness of God's Mercy.

- **Serving the truth is like carrying and preserving a great, heavy treasure. The greater the number of powerful hands that rush to the aid of those who carry it on their shoulders are, the happier and more pleased they will be.**[110]

Far from being jealous, while one should proudly and lovingly applaud the superior strength, effectiveness and assistance of the true brothers/sisters and self-sacrificing helpers who come forward to offer their help, why do we respond to them with rivalry, thus losing sincerity? Why in the eyes of the worldly, misguided people, whose way is lower than ours, do we expose ourselves to appalling accusations such as earning the world by misuse of the Religion, exploiting the knowledge of truth to earn our livelihood, and ambitiously and greedily competing for worldly interests?

---

[110] *The Gleams,* "The Twentieth Gleam", pp. 221–222.

The sole remedy for this disease is condemning one's own soul and taking the side of the fellows against one's soul. One should also follow the following principle adopted and established by scholars in the art of debate: "A person who desires, in debate on a subject, his own thesis to be true and is happy with its turning out to be right and the opposing side to be wrong and mistaken, is an unfair one." Such a person is also in loss, for when he wins the debate, he has learned nothing new; rather, his probable pride may cause him further loss. But if the truth turns out to be on the opposing side, he will have learned something previously unknown to him and thereby acquired something beneficial, as well as having been saved from probable pride. Therefore, a fair, truth-loving one wounds the pride of his carnal soul for the sake of the truth. When he sees the truth in the hand of his opponent, he willingly accepts it and support it.

If the people of the Religion, the truth and knowledge, and the followers of spiritual paths take this principle as a guide, they will attain sincerity, and succeed in their duties pertaining to the Hereafter. They will also be saved through God's Mercy from the present tragic decline and wretchedness.

- **In this world, and particularly in the services done for the afterlife, a most important foundation, and a greatest power, and a most acceptable intercessor, and a firmest point of reliance, and a shortest way to the truth, and a most answerable prayer, and a most blessed and marvelous means of achieving one's goal, and a most sublime virtue, and a purest form of worship is sincerity, or doing something good or any religious deed done purely for God's sake.**[111]

- **Numerous harmful obstacles appear before works of great good. Satans strive very much against those who try to do these works. We should rely on the strength of sincerity against these obstacles and satans. We must avoid things that harm sincerity to the same degree that we avoid snakes and scorpions.**[112]

As declared by Prophet Joseph, upon him be peace , "*Yet I do not claim myself free of error, for assuredly the human carnal soul always commands evil, except that my Lord has mercy,*"[113] the carnal, evil-commanding soul

---

[111] *The Gleams,* "The Twenty-first Gleam", p. 225.
[112] *The Gleams,* "The Twenty-first Gleam", p. 226.
[113] *Sura Yusuf,* 12:53.

should not be trusted. We should not let egotism or the carnal soul deceive us!

- **Just as sainthood has its wonders, so does a pure intention or sincerity have wonders. Especially serious, sincere solidarity between the brothers and sisters who have come together within a sphere of brotherhood and sisterhood purely for God's sake, produces numerous wonders. In fact, the collective personality of such a community may become like a perfect saint, and attract Divine favours.**[114]

- **We should pursue God's good pleasure in our actions. If He is pleased with us, even if the whole world is displeased, it is of no consequence.**[115]

If He approves, it has no effect even if all others reject our ideas and actions. When He is pleased and approves, even if we do not seek the approval of others, should He will it to be so and His Wisdom requires it, He will make others accept it and be pleased with us. For this reason, it is absolutely necessary to aim at God Almighty's good pleasure in the service of the Qur'an and belief.

- **We should not criticize our brothers and sisters in their service of the Qur'an or belief, and do not provoke their envy by making a display of our virtues.**[116]

For a person's hands do not compete with each other, nor do their eyes criticize one another, nor does their tongue oppose their ears, nor does their heart see the faults of the spirit. Rather, the members of his body complete the deficiencies of one another, veil one another's shortcomings, assist one another in meeting their needs, and help one another with their duties. Otherwise, the life of that person's body would be extinguished, their spirit would go away, and their body would decompose. So, we should be like a living organism at the service of the Qur'an and belief or faith.

- **If you have any merits or qualities, let them remain under the soil of concealment, so they may flourish.**[117]

---

[114] *The Letters*, "The Twenty-eighth Letter, Seventh Issue".
[115] *The Gleams*, "The Twenty-first Gleam", p. 226.
[116] *The Gleams*, "The Twenty-first Gleam", pp. 226–227.
[117] *Gleams of Truth*, pp. 59–60.

O one of renowned qualities! Do not be oppressive by exhibiting yourself; if you remain under the veil of concealment, you will be a source of favors and blessings for your brothers. Also, you brothers will benefit from or have a share in your merits; it is even possible that every brother of yours will become like you—this will attract respect to each of them.

The veil of concealment drawn over an exceptional individual within his community enhances the value of the entire community and makes it appreciable. For example, saints among humankind and the appointed hour of death within a lifetime are unknown, indefinite. Concealed within Friday is an hour when prayers are accepted. Hidden in the month of Ramadan is the Night of Power and Destiny. Concealed among the All-Beautiful Names of God is the elixir of the Greatest Name or the Name with the most comprehensive manifestation. It is their being undefined that brings splendor, in these examples, to the whole of humanity thanks to the saints among it, the whole day of Friday due to the hour when prayers are accepted, and the entire month of Ramadan due to the Night of Power and Destiny. The appointed hour of death being undefined maintains the balance between fear and hope, working for the next world and for this. And the imagined permanent existence imparts a pleasure to life.

If you emerge from concealment and exhibit yourself, although respected and magnanimous under it, you will become an oppressor in the open. There you were a sun, here you will overshadow others. You will cause your brothers to lose respect. That means, self-manifestation and being distinguished individually are despotic attitudes. If this is true of the manifestation of genuine qualities, what place remains for acquiring fame through lying, artifice, and hypocrisy?

- **All power lies in sincerity and truth. Indeed, power lies in truth and sincerity. Even those who are wrong may have power through sincerity despite being wrong.**[118]

- **Believers should take pride in the merits and virtues of their brothers and sisters-in-religion as if it were they who possess them, and be thankful to God for them.**[119]

The Sufis circulate among themselves such terms as "annihilation in the guide," and "annihilation in the Messenger." Like this, as the believers

[118] *The Gleams,* "The Twenty-first Gleam", p. 228.
[119] *The Gleams,* "The Twenty-first Gleam", p. 229.

at the service of the Qur'an and faith or Islam, we should have this principle among ourselves as "annihilation in the brothers and sisters." This is called, among the brothers and sisters, "mutual annihilation." It means the brothers and sisters being annihilated in one another. That is to say, oblivious of their own merits and the pride which may arise from them, each person lives with the merits and feelings of his brothers and sisters in his mind.

- **One of the most influential means of attaining sincerity and preserving it is "contemplation of death."**[120]

While long-term worldly ambitions damage sincerity and cause ostentation and worldliness, the "contemplation of death" leads one to abhor ostentation and gain sincerity. By never forgetting death and always considering the transient nature of this worldly life, one can be saved from the tricks of the carnal soul. The Prophetic saying, "Frequently remember that which dispels pleasures and makes them bitter,"[121] urges us to such contemplation.

- **Rivalry in material benefits gradually destroys sincerity. It also harms the results of any service done, and causes the loss of the desired material advantage.**[122]

In order to have great wealth and power, the worldly people, and even some politicians, committees, and certain manipulators of social life, have adopted the principle of participation in or corporate ownership of wealth. Despite all the disadvantages and misuses such a practice can cause, they can also obtain an amazing power and benefit. If unity and agreement in worldly affairs yield such great results, the believers in the service of Islam can correlate this with how profitable it would be to join efforts in deeds that pertain to the Hereafter, the reward of which is not divided and is given to each participant wholly by Divine Grace. This huge profit should not be lost out of rivalry and insincerity.

- **Another thing which destroys sincerity is flattering the ego and giving a lofty position to the evil-commanding soul by pursuing public attention and acceptance in the name of fame, renown, or status in people's eyes.**[123]

---

[120] *The Gleams*, "The Twenty-first Gleam", p. 230.
[121] *at-Tirmidhi*, "Qiyama" 86; *an-Nasa'i*, "Jana'iz" 3.
[122] *The Gleams*, "The Twenty-first Gleam", pp. 231–233.
[123] *The Gleams*, "The Twenty-first Gleam", p. 233.

This is the most perilous of spiritual diseases, one that leads to ostentation and self-centeredness, which is regarded as a hidden association of partners with God.

The way of those in the service of the wise Qur'an is based on truth and requires true brotherhood and sisterhood. Brotherhood and sisterhood requires self-annihilation among the brothers and sisters, and preferring others to oneself. Therefore, there should not be rivalry among them that arises from seeking status in people's eyes. This is totally contrary to the way of serving Islam. Every individual can and should enjoy the total honor of all brothers and sisters.

- **Since destruction and evils are extremely easy, and it is possible to bring them about with a slight action, weak, insignificant, and ostentatious people take on a position against the people of truth to be able to show themselves as powerful with a little action, and to gain status for themselves by intimidating and terrorizing others and causing harm.**[124]

Such people seek to gain fame by causing destruction, which comes not from their power or ability, but from their lack of the true power and ability that is necessary for an approvable attainment. It has become proverbial that one such fame-seeker sullied a place of worship so that people might talk about him. His fame-seeking caused him to welcome the curse of people.

- **One of the Satanic plots which corrupt human social life is that Satan causes people to veil all the merits of a believer because of a single evil committed by the believer.**[125]

The unfair ones who heed this scheme of Satan feel enmity towards that believer. However, when God Almighty weighs up the deeds of the responsible beings with absolute justice on Judgment Day, He will judge by measuring the goods deeds against their evil deeds. Furthermore, since there are many more causes that lead to evil and committing such acts is easier, He may sometimes eliminate many evils because of one single good deed.

So, we should act in this world in accordance with that Divine justice. If a person's good deeds or merits are greater than their evil acts, either in

---

[124] *The Gleams,* "The Thirteenth Gleam", p. 117.
[125] *The Gleams,* "The Thirteenth Gleam", p. 119–120.

terms of quality or quantity, that person is worthy of love and respect. More than that, we should consider them with an attitude of forgiveness on account of any one single merit they may have. However, due to the innate tendency to injustice in their nature and through the incitement of Satan, some people can forget a hundred merits of a person because of one single evil, and feel hostility towards their Muslim brother or sister, thus earning a grave sin. Like a fly's wing which covers the eye, concealing the mountain from it, due to their feeling of hatred and grudge, they become blind and forget the virtues of other believers, be they as great as a mountain, because of an insignificant evil act, and are hostile towards them, becoming instruments of corruption and disorder in human social life.

- **Just as giving the property of a community to one person is a wrong, and one who lays hands on the property of a charitable foundation commits a wrong, so too, attributing the product of a community's labor or the honor and merits resulting from the good deeds of all its members to the leader, teacher, or guide of the community is a wrong committed against both the community and the leader, teacher, or guide.**[126]

Doing so flatters the leader's or teacher's ego and encourages their arrogance. While only a doorkeeper, it causes them to suppose that they are kings. Furthermore, it may even lead them to wronging themselves by stirring up ostentation or hypocrisy in them, which is a kind of concealed association of partners with God.

- **Human devils seek to delude the Qur'an's self-sacrificing servants through love of fame, post, and position, hoping that this will cause them to abandon that exalted service and spiritual holy struggle.**[127]

Everyone has some ambition for fame, love of position, or desire to acquire status. They may even sacrifice their lives if they can gain some fame thereby. This desire is dangerous for the people of the afterlife, and destructive for the people of this world. It engenders many bad morals and is the weakest point in the human character. By exciting this desire for public recognition, human devils can subdue people and attach them to themselves.

---

[126] *The Gleams,* "The Thirteenth Gleam", p. 185.
[127] *The Letters*, "The Twenty-eighth Letter", pp. 399–400.

O fellow servants of the Qur'an, tell such intriguing worldly agents, heralds of misguidance, and disciples of Satan: "God's approval, the All-Merciful's compliments, and the Lord's acceptance is so great a station or position that, in comparison, people's favor and commendation mean almost nothing. If God likes and approves us, people's approval or commendation may be accepted—provided it reflects God's approval. Otherwise it should not be desired, for it will not benefit us at the grave's gate."

- **Fear is a most basic human emotion. Wrongdoers, agents of the worldly, and heralds of misguidance play upon fear to inculcate anxiety within ordinary people, and particularly within religious scholars. Worldly people cause Muslims to sacrifice many important things by arousing groundless fears and anxieties.**[128]

God Almighty has placed fear in our nature so that we might preserve our life, not ruin it. He did not give us fear to make life an unbearable burden full of pain and torment. If there is a risk of 1:2 or 1:3 or 1:4, or at most 1:5 or 6, it may be permissible and tolerable to fear and avoid the risk. But to fear a chance of 1:20, 1:30, or 1:40 is groundless suspicion, a sort of paranoia that changes life into a torment.

Therefore, dear brothers and sisters! If sycophants and unbelievers use fear to tempt you into abandoning your struggle in His cause, say: "We are people of the Qur'an, and, according to God's declaration: '*We sent down the Qur'an and We will guard it,*'[129] we are within its stronghold. God is sufficient for us. How good a Being He is to trust in and rely on, and our trust is a strong citadel around us. Your urging us to fear a danger, even though there is only a 1:1,000 chance that it will affect us during this short transient life cannot lead us to follow a way that is 100 percent harmful to our eternal life in the Hereafter."

- **Greed deceives many people. As is clear in decisive statements from the Qur'an, lawful provision comes according to one's poverty, impotence, and need, not one's capacity and willpower.**[130]

For example, trees are living creatures that need provision. As they are stationary, their needed provision comes to them. Animals are not provided with food in such a perfect manner, because they seek their food impatiently. Fish are fed perfectly and usually become fat, although

[128] *The Letters*, "The Twenty-eighth Letter", pp. 401–402.
[129] *Suratu'l-Hijr*, 15:9.
[130] *The Letters*, "The Twenty-eighth Letter", pp. 401–402.

they are the least intelligent animals, whereas such clever and strong animals as apes, foxes and wolves are mostly weak due to insufficient nutrition. This also shows that provision is based on need or destitution, not power or ability.

Animal and human infants are fed very well and extraordinarily via their mother's breast milk, the best food and sweetest gift of Mercy's treasury. It is bestowed on them in an unexpected way out of His concern for their weakness and incapability. In contrast, wild animals usually have to be content with the scarce food they obtain through tiring effort.

The poverty of many literary figures and scholars and the richness of many ignorant people also shows that weakness and need, and not intelligence and ability, attract provision. Other ways of attracting provision are relying upon God and petitioning Him verbally and through one's disposition and lawful effort. The verse, *"God is the All-Provider, the Possessor of Strength, the Steadfast,"*[131] is so strong and firm a proof that all vegetation, animals, and babies announce it. Every living species needing provision recites it through the tongue of their disposition.

Since God Almighty, the All-Compassionate and All-Munificent, supplies all provision, it is extreme folly to humble oneself in a way that derides His Mercy and belittles His Munificence, or to offer one's conscience and sacred things in return for some wealth. Worldly people, especially the misguided, loan money to get a high return. In exchange for some wealth that might contribute to a year's livelihood, they may cause people to lose the Hereafter's eternal life. Unfortunately, there are always some who attract Divine wrath through their disgusting greed and by trying to please the misguided.

Dear followers! If those who fawn on misguided worldly people and hypocrites seek to capture you through greed, know that only thrift and contentment—not wages or salaries—allow you to preserve your life. If they lend you unlawful money, they will demand a high rate of return. Your involvement in their world may hinder your serving the Qur'an, each hour of which can open the gates of an eternal treasury. Being deterred from this service is so great a loss that no salary or wage can ever be a sufficient compensation.

---

[131] *adh-Dhariyat*, 51:58.

- **Supporters of the misguided desire to use human egotism to separate the Muslims who serve the Qur'an and faith from each other and their teachers or guides. A person's most dangerous temperament and weakest spot is egotism. By exciting this sentiment, they urge people to do very bad things.**[132]

Dear brothers and sisters, do not let them captivate you through egotism. Know that the people of misguidance, carried by their ego, have gone astray. The people of truth must forsake their ego to serve the truth, for using their ego will make them resemble the people of misguidance. Serving the Qur'an, which is our purpose, has no room for egotism; rather, it demands cooperation in sincere unity.

- **Those at the service of the Qur'an and faith should take pride and spiritual pleasure in each other's merits, instead of entering into rivalry with each other.**[133]

Envy is egotism's most harmful aspect. If our service is not purely for God's sake, envy intervenes and adulterates it. Just as your hands are not envious of each other, and your eyes do not envy your ears, and your heart does not compete with your intellect, each of us is like a member or a sense of our collective body.

- **Knowledge is the greatest wealth, which usually leads its owner to egotism. Some scholars may boast of their knowledge. Even if they are humble, they find it hard to get rid of the egotism caused by being knowledgeable.**[134]

However devout and faithful scholars are in heart and intellect, their carnal souls want others to know that they are knowledgeable and to be aware of their merits. Moreover, they may be jealous of each other. Therefore, the scholars direly need spiritual training and purification.

- **One who has an uneducated and unpurified carnal soul, and who loves and appreciates oneself, cannot love others. Even if they apparently love someone, they cannot do so sincerely. They love only the benefits and advantages that come to them from or through the others.**[135]

---

[132] *The Letters*, "The Twenty-eighth Letter", pp. 401–402.
[133] *The Letters*, "The Twenty-eighth Letter", p. 412.
[134] *The Letters*, "The Twenty-eighth Letter", p. 412.
[135] *The Gleams*, "The Twenty-eighth Gleam", pp. 399–400.

Such people always try to make themselves liked, and do not ascribe faults to themselves; rather, they defend themselves like a lawyer and claim to be free of error. By praising and exalting themselves through exaggeration, and even lying to justify themselves, they make themselves subject to the condemnation of the verse, *"Who has taken his lusts and fancies for his deity."*[136]

Such self-praise and trying to make oneself loved have the reverse effect, and cause a person to be despised and treated coldly. They also lose the sincerity and purity of intention in their actions that pertain to the Hereafter, and are tainted with hypocrisy.

- **We feel indebted to the one who informs us of the scorpion on our neck; so we should be more indebted to those who warn us against our faults and sins.**[137]

A scorpion may cost us at the most this short, fleeting worldly life, but faults and sins are the scorpions which threaten our eternal life.

- **There are several true or right ways to follow in serving Islam. We should follow one of these ways and its master, without being busied with what the followers of the other true or right ways do.**[138]

- **Out of His perfect Mercy, God the Ultimate Truth has included part of the reward for service in serving, and part of the reward for action in acting itself.**[139]

Thus even lifeless creatures obey God's commands of creation and the operation of the universe with perfect zeal and pleasure. Everything, from bees, flies, and chickens, to the sun and the moon, carries out its duties with perfect pleasure particular to each. This means that they receive pleasure from their work so that they perform it perfectly, even though unconsciously and without considering the consequences.

- **Negative nationalism or racism in the guise of nationalism is a combination of heedlessness, ignorance, misguidance, ostentation, and wrongdoing that support and strengthen one another. Racists make a fetish of their race. We seek refuge in God from**

---

[136] *Suratu'l-Furqan*, 25:43.
[137] *Emirdağ Lahikası* (Addendum of Emirdağ), Vol. 1, p. 44.
[138] *The Letters*, "The Twenty-eighth Letter", p. 365.
[139] *The Gleams*, "The Seventeenth Gleam", p. 171.

such deviation. As for the zeal for Islam, it is a bright light coming from belief.[140]

God Almighty declares in the Qur'an as follows:

> O humankind! Surely We have created you from a single (pair of) male and female, and made you into tribes and families so that you may know one another (and so build mutuality and co-operative relationships, not so that you may take pride in your differences of race or social rank, or breed enmities). Surely the noblest, most honorable of you in God's sight is the one best in piety, righteousness, and reverence for God. Surely God is All-Knowing, All-Aware.[141]

Racism is one of the severest problems of our age. When God's Messenger, upon him be peace and blessings, was raised as a Prophet, the attitudes behind racism were prevalent in Mecca in the guise of tribalism. The Quraysh considered themselves (in particular) and Arabs (in general) as being superior to all other peoples. God's Messenger, upon him be peace and blessings, came with this Divine message and proclaimed it, explaining: "No Arab is superior to a non-Arab, and no white person is superior to a black person;"[142] and, "If a black Abyssinian Muslim is to rule over Muslims, he should be obeyed."[143]

Zayd ibn Harithah, a slave emancipated by God's Messenger, upon him be peace and blessings, was his adopted son before the Revelation banned adoption as a legal procedure. The Prophet, upon him be peace and blessings, married him to Zaynab bint Jahsh, one of the noblest (and non-black) among the Arab Muslim women. In addition, he chose Zayd as the commander of the Muslim army that was sent against the Byzantine Empire, even though it included such leading Companions as Abu Bakr, 'Umar, Ja'far ibn Abi Talib (the cousin of God's Messenger, upon him be peace and blessings), and Khalid ibn Walid (even then famed for his genius as a military commander).[144] Further, the Prophet, upon him be peace and blessings, appointed Zayd's son Usama to command the army he formed just before his death. Included therein were such leading Companions as Abu Bakr, 'Umar, Khalid, Abu 'Ubayda, Talha, and Zubayr. This

---

[140] *Al-Mathnawi al-Nuri*, "The Fifth Treatise", p. 160.
[141] *Suratu'l-Hujurat*, 49:13.
[142] Ibn Hanbal, *al-Musnad*, 5:441.
[143] *Muslim*, "'Imara," 37.
[144] *Muslim*, "Fada'il as-Sahabah," 63.

established in the Muslims' hearts and minds that superiority is not by birth or color or blood, but by righteousness and devotion to God.

- **The illustrious tree of Islam, which is deeply established in and has sent out roots through creation's or the universe's truths, is not to be implanted in racism's dark, barren, arid, unstable, and easily scattered dust-like soil. It is heretical, destructive, and unreasonable to try to do so.**[145]

- **Such trends as nationalism and racism are temporary; they sweep over the earth like a strong wind and disappear. Islam's enduring and eternal nationality cannot be grafted onto racism. Any attempt to this end will corrupt Islam but cannot maintain racism. Although at first it may give a temporary pleasure, it will endure too briefly and end in catastrophe.**[146]

Separatist movements usually lead to internal conflicts almost impossible to heal, for each side will break the other's power and thereby exhaust the nation's overall strength. As a result, any foreign power will be able to manipulate the nation easily, for the force of a small stone can manipulate two mountains of the same weight when put on the scales. This explains the method of foreign powers summed up in, "Divide, separate, and govern."

- **Only the incapable seek solace in impotence and complaints.**[147]

If you want a life of ease of mind, you should not seek solace in displaying impotence in what you can do or find a solution for, nor should you lament over what you cannot do or find a solution for.

- **Sometimes opposites hide their opposites within them, which demonstrates how the wheel of time rotates in the opposite direction.**[148]

They attribute to Christianity the virtues of civilization which are not its property, while Islam is accused of encouraging backwardness, something which Islam is opposed to and fights. Especially in the language of politics, the words are the opposites of their meanings. For example, tyranny has donned the cap of justice. Treachery has found a cheap dress in

---

[145] *The Letters*, "The Twenty-ninth Letter", p. 422.
[146] *The Letters*, "The Twenty-ninth Letter", p. 423.
[147] *Gleams of Truth*, pp. 9, 40.
[148] *Gleams of Truth*, pp. 10, 360.

patriotism. *Jihad* and war for God's sake have been labeled aggression and a violation of human rights. Enslavement to animal passions and the despotism of Satan have been called freedom. Things have become their opposites, forms have been exchanged, names have been swapped, positions and ranks have changed places.

- **If there is deep, strong devotion and sensitive care at the beginning of a way, it usually leads to or ends in slackness, while dispensation in the beginning leads to or ends in strong devotion and care.**[149]

Examples are the Hanafi school of law and the Hanbalis, in some aspects. Also, while the early supporters of the House of the Prophet, who were careful and strong in their adherence, have partly given way to the sect of Rafidites, the careless Umayyads finally joined the *Ahlu's-Sunnah wa'l-Jama'ah*. This historical reality teaches us that we should preserve the middle way, without going into extremes. Any extremity cannot usually be saved from going into its opposite—that is, the opposite extremity.

- **The child of the imperfect one from among the two scholars may sometimes become perfect, while the child of the perfect one may become faulty and imperfect.**[150]

- **Humankind has an inclination towards renewal. If the succeeding generation sees the preceding one as perfect, since they cannot find anything to add, they find the satisfaction of their inclination in other ways. It even happens that the perfection in the preceding generation causes reaction in the succeeding one, driving them to act in reaction or even opposition.**[151]

As a striking example, almost the sons of no Companion were able to reach the degree of their father in the practice and service of Islam.

- **One should follow the majority of Muslims if he seeks salvation and security.**[152]

O seeker of salvation and security! A *hadith* indicates that we should follow and keep the company of the majority of Muslims.[153] The Qur'an also declares:

---

[149] *Sünuhat* (Occurrences to the Heart), in *Sünuhat, Tuluat, İşarat*, pp. 33–34.
[150] *Sünuhat* (Occurrences to the Heart), in *Sünuhat, Tuluat, İşarat*, p. 34.
[151] *Sünuhat* (Occurrences to the Heart), in *Sünuhat, Tuluat, İşarat*, p. 34.
[152] *Gleams of Truth*, pp. 13, 55–56.
[153] *Muslim*, "'Imara" 59; *at-Tirmidhi*, "Fitan" 7; *Abu Dawud*, "Salah" 46.

While whoever cuts himself off from the Messenger after the guidance (to what is truest and best in thought, belief, and conduct) has become clear to him, and follows a way other than that of the believers (for whom it is impossible to agree unanimously on a way that leads to error), We leave him (to himself) on the way he has turned to, and land him in Hell to roast there: how evil a destination to arrive at![154]

The Umayyads were, in the beginning, not careful to follow the Religion, but after they joined the majority of the Muslim Community, they were eventually included among the *Ahlu's-Sunnah wa'l-Jama'ah*. The Shi'ah were careful and steadfast in adherence to the Religion in the beginning, but a great portion of them who were in the minority eventually formed the sect of Rafidites. This is a significant, noteworthy reality. Remaining in minority usually also causes harmful reaction and opposition.

- **General circumstances and the majority of people are considered when establishing general rules and laws, even though there are exceptions to every rule and every general situation. However, exceptions are not ignored, and a good legal system has a ground for exceptional rules.**[155]

As the laws and principles of the Qur'an, which God the Almighty has established as the Creator and Lord of humanity, transcend time and space, they do not become obsolete; they are always fresh and strong. Despite all its foundations, institutions of intellectual and moral training, and severe disciplines and laws and regulations, modern civilization has been unable to contest the wise Qur'an on establishing rules and laws for the administration of human societies. For it is God Who creates, and therefore knows, as declared in the Qur'an: *"Is it conceivable that the One Who creates should not know?"*[156]

Human beings who manufacture something prepare a manual to describe how it must be used, and we use it according to that guide. This means that one who manufactures it knows it best, and that only one who truly knows can manufacture it. So God, being the All-Knowing, creates; and, being the Creator, He knows all that He creates. Thus, we must conclude that the One Who knows and creates is entitled to and should control and govern it, because only the One Who creates and knows can gov-

---

[154] *Suratu'-Nisa'*, 4:115.

[155] *The Words*, "The Sixteenth Word" p. 17; "The Twenty-fifth Word", p. 428.

[156] *Suratu'l-Mulk*, 67:14.

ern what He creates in the best way. However, it shows the injustice and ignorance of humankind that while they claim authority over what they make or manufacture, they deny God's authority over what He creates.

- **The basic purpose for and wisdom in marital relations is reproduction. The resulting pleasure is a small payment in advance determined by Divine Mercy to realize this duty.**[157]

The laws and rules concerning marriage and marital and family relations should consider this fundamental fact.

- **The corrupt aspect of modern civilization has opened a door to such an enormous, disgusting show of hypocrisy that, in the name of fame and reputation, hypocrisy rules the individual and the nation.**[158]

The mass media makes "famous" people known to everyone, and, as modern concepts of history and recently written history books acclaim them, they urge others to follow them. Whereas, fame is identical with show and ostentation, and it is poisonous honey that kills the heart. Only those who wish to be slaves to human beings seek it.

- **When men become womanish through focusing on worldly whims and fancies, women become masculine through crudity and impudence. If a beautiful woman enters a gathering of "brothers," ostentation, rivalry, and envy are aroused. Unveiling women and allowing them to mix freely with men to whom they are not related, encourages vices or bad morals.**[159]

- **Pictures, especially obscene ones, have an important part in people's present sinfulness and ill-temper. Statues, prohibited by Islam, are either petrified tyranny, or solidified passion, or embodied hypocrisy.**[160]

- **The main origin of all revolutions and corruptions in human history is one phrase; so, too, are all vices and moral failings caused by one phrase: The first is: "I am full, so what is it to me if others die of hunger?" And the second: "You work so that I may eat." The Qur'an eradicates the first attitude and heals its wounds through**

---

[157] *The Words*, "The Twenty-fifth Word", p. 428.
[158] *Al-Mathnawi al-Nuri*, "The Eighth Treatise", p. 259.
[159] *Gleams of Truth*, p. 16.
[160] *Gleams of Truth*, p. 16.

the *Zakah*—"*Perform the Prescribed Prayer, and pay the Zakah,*"[161] **and eradicates the second by outlawing interest and usury**—"God has made trading lawful and interest and usury unlawful."[162]/[163]

A peaceful social life depends on the balance between the social and economic classes. This balance is based on justice and mutual respect and compassion, especially on the wealthy's care and compassion, and the poor's respect and accord. Ignoring the first attitude drives the rich to wrongdoing, usurpation, immorality, and mercilessness; ignoring the second attitude drives the poor to hatred, grudge, envy, and conflict with the rich. As this conflict has destroyed social peace for the last two or three centuries, it has also caused social upheavals in Europe due to the struggle between labor and capital.

Despite all its charitable societies, institutions of moral training, and severe laws and regulations, modern civilization has neither reconciled the social classes nor healed those two severe human wounds. The Qur'an, however, eradicates the first attitude and heals its wounds through the *Zakah*, and eradicates the second by outlawing interest and usury. The second one, from among the above-mentioned Qur'anic verses, stands at the door of the world and says to interest and usury: "You are forbidden to enter!" It decrees to humanity, "If you want to close the door of conflict, close the door of interest and usury," and orders its students not to enter through it.

- **If humankind prefers life, it must put to death usury of every sort.**[164]

The bond of human relationships that extends from the elite to the common people has been severed. The cries of revolution arise from below, from the lower social strata. They shout for revenge, and scream of grievance and envy. From above descend fires of tyranny and scorn, the thunder of arrogance, and the lightning of oppression. What should arise from below are love, respect, and accord. And from above should descend compassion and assistance, kindness and consideration. If humankind desires these, it should hold fast to the *Zakah* and abandon usury and interest. The Qur'anic justice stands at the door of the world,

---

[161] *Suratu'l-Baqara*, 2:43.
[162] *Suratu'l-Baqara*, 2:75.
[163] *The Words*, "The Twenty-fifth Word", p. 427.
[164] *Gleams of Truth*, pp. 38–39.

saying to usury and interest: "No entry! You have no right to enter!" They should retreat from this door and disappear from the world.

Humankind has not heeded this command and has thus received severe blows (world wars); people should heed this call now before receiving another, severer blow.

- **The pure, perfect justice of the Qur'an does not sacrifice the life of an innocent person even for the whole of humanity. In the sight of Divine Power and Justice, an individual's life is equal to the life of humanity. Yet some people can be so selfish that they would destroy everything and annihilate all of humanity, even the whole world if they could, if it seems to be an obstacle to the fulfillment of their desires.**[165]

- **In the sight of Divine Power, provision or sustenance is as important as life. Provision is produced by Power, apportioned by Destiny, and nurtured by Grace or Favor. As life is the sure, certain outcome of particular circumstances and events, it is witnessed or visible in its totality. But provision is neither sure nor certain, for it is scattered and obtained over a certain time; it comes in uncertain degrees and leads people to contemplation.**[166]

- **The Power that created every thing with its own disposition has restrained humanity and animals through their need, in particular hunger, and put them in a certain order. It has also prevented total disorder and confusion in the world and, by making need a motive for civilization, secured progress.**[167]

- **The most miserable, distressed, and wretched person is the one who is idle. For idleness is the nephew of non-existence, whereas exertion or working hard is the life of the body and the waking state of life. Boredom and distress are the teachers of dissipation; despair, misguidance in thought, and darkness in the heart are the mines of distress and depression.**[168]

- **Imagine that you have two pieces of food of equal nutritional value. One costs a hundred cents and the other costs ten dollars.**

---

[165] *Gleams of Truth*, p. 11.
[166] *Gleams of Truth*, p. 14.
[167] *Gleams of Truth*, p. 16.
[168] *Gleams of Truth*, p. 14.

If you prefer the latter solely for the few seconds of pleasure it will give your sense of taste, the inspector or doorkeeper of your body, then is this not the meanest form of waste?[169]

- **When pleasure calls, one should say, "It is as if I have eaten it (Sanki yedim)." One person who followed this principle could have eaten the equivalent of a mosque called** Sanki Yedim, **but he did not.**[170]/[171]

- **An easy life may be appealing when most Muslims are not hungry. But when most Muslims are hungry, no Muslim can choose such a life.**[172]

- **Since human faculties have not been restricted in creation, their crimes are great.**[173]

Unlike animals, the faculties of human beings have not been restricted in creation; the evil and destruction in particular that they cause know no limits. If the selfishness that issues from one faculty and the egotism that proceeds from another are combined with haughtiness and obstinacy, such sins will be committed that no name has as of yet been found for them. As these sins are proofs of the necessity of Hell, so too their penalty can only be Hell.

For example, in order to justify just one of his lies, a man desires, from his heart, the downfall of Islam. The present time has shown that Hell is not unnecessary and Paradise is not cheap.

- **Sometimes good leads to evil.**[174]

While in reality the merits of the elite should give rise to modesty and self-effacement in them, regrettably they have led to arrogance and oppression. And while the destitution of the poor and the poverty of the common people should serve (as they do in reality) as means to arouse

---

[169] *Gleams of Truth*, pp. 16.17.

[170] There is a mosque in Istanbul called *Sanki Yedim* (It Is as if I Have Eaten It). Whenever the one who funded the building of this mosque wanted to eat something expensive, he would say, "It is as if I have eaten it," and saved the money he might have otherwise spent. He finally had a mosque built with the money which he saved in this way.

[171] *Gleams of Truth*, p. 14.

[172] *Gleams of Truth*, p. 14.

[173] *Gleams of Truth*, p. 37.

[174] *Gleams of Truth*, p. 37.

compassion and graciousness towards them, unfortunately they have now resulted in the abasement and servitude of the common people.

If honor and merit result from something, it is offered to the elite and leaders. But if vice and evil proceed from it, it is divided and distributed among the common people, or employees and servants.

If a victorious tribe has won some honor, congratulations are offered to its Hasan Agha (the chief); but if some harm is obtained thenceforth, every curse is poured upon the members of the tribe. This is a sorry evil among humankind!

- **The same age and status or social standing cause rivalry and conflict. Being complementary and congruous is the basis of solidarity. An inferiority complex provokes arrogance. A weak character is the source of haughtiness. Impotence gives rise to opposition. Curiosity is the teacher of knowledge.**[175]

- **Tell a mad person repeatedly, "You are well," and it is not unusual that he becomes cured. And tell a good one repeatedly, "You are bad," and it is not rare that he become bad.**[176]

- **One reason why preachers' advice is ineffective nowadays is that they invite people to change their nature. They advise: "Do not be envious or ambitious, do not feel enmity or be obstinate, do not love the world," and so on. Such advice is useless, for it is against human nature. Instead, these energies can and should be channeled into good deeds and directed towards positive aims.**[177]

For example, love for the world can be channeled into love for the other world, enmity can be directed against one's carnal soul, and jealousy can become a means for competing to do good deeds.

- **The light of conscience is religious sciences, and the light of reason or intellect is physical sciences. The truth is manifested from their fusion. The endeavor of students soars on these two wings. When they remain separate, the religious sciences cause bigotry, while the physical sciences give rise to doubt, deception and denial.**[178]

---

[175] *Gleams of Truth*, p. 16.
[176] *Gleams of Truth*, p. 12.
[177] *The Letters*, "The Ninth Letter", p. 53.
[178] *Gleams of Truth*, p. 157.

Another wisdom in studying these two kinds of sciences together is that such study will save the intellectual reasoning from the darkness of the fallacies that result from four corrupted analogies or comparisons and remove the sophistry to which philosophical approaches have given rise in parasitic imitators. These fallacious comparisons are these: (1) comparing the material or physical with the spiritual and accepting the modern, European view and position as the norm in spiritual matters, and accepting the views of some famous people in a field of science as proof in other sciences as well; (2) rejecting the view of religious scholars who have no knowledge of physical sciences in religious sciences; (3) trusting in oneself in religious matters out of arrogance resulting from their knowledge of physical sciences; (4) comparing earlier generations with new ones and the past with the present, and raising wrongful objections to the Religion.

Part 8

GENERAL PRINCIPLES RELATED TO ELOQUENCE OR CORRECT AND EFFECTIVE USE OF LANGUAGE

General Principles Related to
Eloquence or Correct and Effective Use
of Language

- **The life of eloquence or the philosophy of effective language lies in the imitation of the truths in creation or the order of the universe.[1]**

Eloquence finds its life in, or the wisdom of speech lies in, taking the laws that operate in nature as one's guide. That is, there are laws upon which all the truths that are manifested as nature or in nature are dependent. These laws are unchanging, while their effects or results change either with their identities or nature. For example, the flowers, leaves, and fruits of a tree in the present year are not the same in identity as those in the other years, but they are the same in nature. Eloquence finds life by applying these laws to the meanings that arise in the mind, taking into consideration the changes undergone by their effects. This means that eloquence, like a mirror, dons and displays the rays of the truths that are reflected from the outer world. It is as if it wants to imitate creation and nature with the art of imagination and the embroidery of words. Even if a word or speech is not identical with the truth itself, it should receive help from the truth and the order it shapes in the outer world, and grow from the seed of truth. That is, a word or speech should use the basic truths that are manifested as nature as the seeds to grow from. Every seed grows into a shoot, plant, or tree peculiar to itself. A seed of wheat cannot grow to be a tree. For this reason, if the philosophy of speech is not considered, eloquence produces only superstition, and imagination only hallucination.

---

[1] *İşaratü'l-İ'caz*, *"Suratu'l-Baqara*, verses 23 and 24"; *The Reasonings*, "The Second Part", p. 92.

- **Like speech, grammar also has a philosophy. This philosophy, like nature, displays the Creator's wisdom. The philosophy of grammar is based on the relationship between the words, phrases, clauses, and sentences.**[2]

For example, in Arabic, any modifiable word is modified only by the modifier that is placed right in front of it. The interrogative particle, *Hal*, wants to immediately join the verb which it modifies. The word functioning as the subject is powerful and appropriates the vowel mark *u*, which is also powerful. In short, the laws operating in languages are like the reflections of the laws operating in nature.

- **Eloquence requires speaking (or writing) in accordance with the requirements of the situation.**[3]

Some ask how it is reasonable in accordance with its perfectly balanced and proper eloquence and styles that the wise Qur'an complains greatly of Satan and the people of misguidance, and frequently draws attention to them, threatening them severely. Even though they are essentially poor and miserable, with no possession or dominion of existence, the Qur'an deals with them as if they were aggressive partners of God in His Dominion, and complains of them.

The reason and wisdom is this: since Satan and those following him follow the way of misguidance and destruction, they can cause great destruction with a minor action, and they can do many creatures great wrong with a small deed. Consider that through some minor action or act of neglect of an insignificant duty, a man on a large, royal merchant ship of a king can cause the efforts of all those who have a duty related to the ship to go for nothing. So, the illustrious owner of the ship complains of that rebellious one and severely threatens him on behalf of all his subjects that have some connection with the ship. And he severely punishes him, considering not his insignificant action but its awful consequences, and not in his own illustrious name but in the name of the rights of his subjects.

Similarly, even with their apparently minor faults and rebelliousness, the people of misguidance, who are the party of Satan and exist on the ship of the earth together with the people of right guidance, can violate the rights of many creatures and cause their exalted duties to be fruitless.

---

[2]   *The Reasonings*, "The Second Part", pp. 92–93.
[3]   *The Gleams*, "The Thirteenth Gleam", p. 98.

So it is pure wisdom and completely appropriate and perfectly eloquent that the Eternal Monarch complains greatly of them and severely threatens them, frequently drawing attention to their destruction as if He were mobilizing great forces against them. And it is in accordance with the requirements of the situation, which is the basis of eloquence; rather, it is eloquence itself as eloquence is defined as speaking (or writing) in accordance with the requirements of the situation. Such a reaction is in no way an exaggeration, which would be wastefulness in words.

- **Presenting abstract truths at a level at which human beings can understand with the use of literary devices is a requirement of eloquence. Since the general public cannot easily understand the abstract truths in their abstractness, those truths should be conveyed to them in concrete forms. This requires the use of some literary devices, such as comparisons, similes, personifications, and metaphors, which we find contained in the allegorical statements of the Qur'an.**[4]

The Qur'an has made these literary devices binoculars for the general public so that they can observe the abstract truths. Even though it is possible for some to be entangled in these devices and the apparent meanings of the verses containing them, and thus misunderstand some Divine truths—such as attributing a body, time, and space to the Divine Being, and comparing Him to the created—careful observation can easily penetrate the truths behind these devices. For example, when thinking on the verse, "*The All-Merciful has established Himself on the Supreme Throne,*"[5] a person can see the truth that God is the sole Ruler of the universe. The verse establishes in our minds God's supreme authority and dominion, and that God is not just the Creator of the universe, but also is its absolute Sovereign and Ruler. Having created the universe, He has not detached Himself from it, and has not become indifferent to His creation. On the contrary, He effectively rules the universe as a whole, as well as controlling every small part of it. All power and sovereignty rest with Him. Everything in the universe is fully in His grasp and is subservient to His Will and Power. In order to establish this truth in our minds, the Qur'an speaks at the level of the general public and presents to their view a sovereign's rule of His country from His

---

[4]   *The Reasonings*, "The Third Part", pp. 141–142.
[5]   *Sura Ta-Ha*, 20:5.

throne. This style of the Qur'an is described as "God's lowering His speech to the level of human understanding."

- **It is completely contrary to eloquence and guidance to throw minds into confusion by burdening them with what they cannot bear. "Speak to the people according to their mental capacities!" is a principle of wisdom.**[6]

The four basic purposes of the Qur'an are establishing in the mind God's existence and Oneness, the Prophethood, the bodily Resurrection, and justice and worship. Therefore, the Qur'an refers to the facts of creation, which are the subject matter of physical sciences and can only be known through scientific study, parenthetically for the sake of its basic purposes. While mentioning the facts observable by everyone in every age clearly, it refers to others allusively and in broad terms, leaving their clarification to scientific studies over time and encouraging humankind to study them.

- **It is a rule of both eloquence and guidance that the evidence should be clearer than the thesis and known prior to it.**[7]

For this reason, the apparent meanings of some Qur'anic verses relate to the impressions sensed by the majority of people. However, these verses are not intended to provide evidence for those impressions. As well as serving for the establishment in the minds of people of the four basic purposes of the guidance of the Qur'an, they contain such subtle truths that they attract the attention of researchers and truth-seeking people. The verses of the Qur'an, clear in themselves and clearly showing the basic truths, interpret one another; some verses uncover the jewels of meanings contained in their siblings. Therefore, we should try to see those more important meanings that lie under their apparent, literal meanings. If in order to draw attention to God's existence and Oneness the Qur'an clearly mentioned electricity, the law of gravity, the daily or annual movements of the earth, the formation of chemical compositions with more than a hundred elements that have been discovered, and the sun's movement, then the proofs would have been more hidden and in need of explanation than the thesis itself. For this reason, the Qur'an uses a language that is comprehensible for every level of understanding and never throws its audience into confusion, taking into consideration the level of the

---

[6] *The Reasonings*, "The Third Part", p. 143.
[7] *The Reasonings*, "The Third Part", pp. 143–144.

majority of the people without ever neglecting the elite, and referring to certain subtle realities that will be discovered over time through metaphors, comparisons, and similes.

- **Just as the temperament of a people is the source of their feelings, in the same way, a language reflects those feelings and sentiments. Every group of people has a temperament particular to itself. Likewise, every language has a capacity for eloquence that is different from others.**[8]

According to logic, analogies in the form of comparisons do not offer certainty. But one type of analogy is stronger than logical proof and gives greater certainty than induction: You point to the tip of a universal truth through a particular analogy based on concrete facts, and base your conclusion on that truth. To teach that mighty truth and deal with particular incidents and realities in accordance with it, you show the general or universal law on which the truth is based in a certain, particular thing or event.

For example, through the analogy that the sun is a single body that can be present in all shining objects at once because it emits light, we show the law of a truth: Light and things of light are not restricted. Distance, size, and quantity make no difference to such items, and they cannot be contained in space. Another example: A tree's flowers, leaves and fruits are formed easily and perfectly at the same time and in the same center through a law of Divine Command. This shows the tip of a mighty truth and a universal law, and proves that truth and law. Like a tree, this vast universe is the result of that law and the manifestation of oneness.[9]

- **According to the science of eloquence, a metaphor is a word or phrase used to suggest or express a meaning other than its literal one. In such statements, the metaphorical (and not the literal) meaning is considered. If the metaphorical meaning conforms to reality, you are saying the truth.**[10]

For example, height can be conveyed by the phrase: "The sheath of so-and-so's sword is long." If that man is tall, this statement is true whether or not he has such a sword. If he is not tall, this statement is false even if he has such a sword, for the phrase is only figurative in meaning.

---

8   *The Reasonings*, "The Second Part", p. 80.
9   *The Words*, "The Thirty-second Word", p. 632.
10   *The Words*, "The Thirty-second Word", pp. 632–633.

- **Using metaphors is permissible provided they conform to the rules of rhetoric and linguistics. Otherwise, there is the risk that we will interpret or use a metaphor as reality or vice versa. This adds to the oppressive power of ignorance.**[11]

Going to extremes by considering everything to be a metaphorical usage and looking for the truth in the inner dimension of the words and making an esoteric interpretation of every verse, even giving rise to a school of esotericism, is harmful. On the other hand, going to the opposite extreme by making an exoteric interpretation and looking for the truth only in the literal meaning of the words is also harmful. The middle, safe way, which prevents going to extremes, is the spirit of the Shari'ah, and the science of eloquence, reason or logic, and wisdom. Wisdom (which is based on the Prophetic practice of the Qur'an, and also includes a rational approach to it) is pure good.

- **A truth is not to be sought in all aspects of a metaphor. However, there is and must be a grain of truth in every metaphor and it is this truth in which the metaphor originates and flourishes. There is no waste or futility in creation, and the Qur'an reflects this, choosing the most direct way in its expressions. So, it is not only that which prevents a truth from being understood plainly which leads to the use of a metaphor, but it is in order to adopt the most direct and understandable way as well. This is why the Qur'an uses metaphors.**[12]

- **When passing from the hands of knowledge to the hands of ignorance, a metaphorical expression may change into a literal description, and open a door to superstition.**[13]

Thus, whenever the dark hand of ignorance usurps a metaphor or simile from the luminous hand of knowledge, it may be taken for a reality. Also, whenever a metaphor or simile enjoys a long life, it loses its freshness and taste.

The transparency of a metaphor displays the glint of truth. But if a metaphor is taken for a reality, it then becomes dense and masks the truth it is meant to display. Actually, this change is something that has taken place throughout history and so can be regarded as natural. Consider how a language undergoes changes over the course of time. Since

---

[11] *The Reasonings,* "The First Part", pp. 24–25.

[12] *The Reasonings,* "The First Part", pp. 70, 74.

[13] *The Reasonings,* "The First Part", pp. 23–24.

many words, expressions, narratives, and meanings that were addressed to the comprehension of earlier generations have gradually grown old and lost their luster and attraction, new generations, which do not see them as suited to their appetites and tastes, dare to make changes in them or even coin new ones to replace them. This occurs not only in language but also in images, meanings, and narratives. This teaches us that we should not judge everything according to its appearance. One who searches for truth should be like a diver, freed of the effects of time, able to dive into the depths of the past, weigh ideas on the scales of reason, and discover the source of everything. What led me to this conclusion is the following event: once during my childhood there was an eclipse of the moon. I asked my mother about it. She answered that a snake had swallowed the moon. I asked why I could still see it then. She explained, "The snakes of the sky are semi-transparent."

See how a simile taken for a reality conceals the truth! For ancient astronomers the word "snake" referred to an indistinct shape that somewhat resembles a snake during the lunar eclipse. Over time the common people took this term of science, a simile to describe a reality, and thought that there really was a snake in the sky that sometimes swallowed the moon!

- **Exaggeration or exaggerated praise is implicit denigration. It also causes disorder. Seeing and showing someone or something as having more than what God has favored them with is, essentially, not a favor to them. Anything that enters a community should not destroy the order of the community.**[14]

It is characteristic of human beings that, since they tend to magnify the pleasure they receive from something, inflate what they are describing, and use exaggeration in their narratives, they mix reality with the imagination. Even if one intends to do good, to act in this way is in fact doing an evil or harmful thing. What they call reform becomes deforming, and what they consider as good and praiseworthy is in fact evil and disparaging. Such behavior unknowingly destroys the beauty that arises from balance and proportion. Just as taking a higher dose of medicine than is required simply because it tastes good or makes one feel good turns something that is beneficial into something harmful, exaggeration

---

[14] *Gleams of Truth*, p. 50; *The Reasonings*, "The First Part", pp. 22–23, 29.

intended to encourage or discourage, despite the fact that the truth does not require this—for example, regarding urination while standing as great a sin as unlawful sex, or deeming a few dollars of charity as meritorious as carrying out pilgrimage, in fact means that the crime of unlawful sex has lost some of its gravity and pilgrimage has been degraded.

In short, whoever loves the Religion and truth should be content with the original value and proportion of everything and not go beyond that through exaggeration. Such exaggeration means slandering the Divine Power and being discontent with the beauty and perfection that exists in creation; such behavior led Imam al-Ghazali to say, "It is not probable that there could be a universe more beautiful than the present one."

Attributing to anything or anyone more good than God has attributed to them is not a positive move, nor does it mean that you have done them any good. A single grain of truth is preferable to a bumper harvest of false imaginings. We must be content with defining something or someone with the good God has accorded them in creation and the virtues they have. Anything that enters a community should not destroy the order of the community. The honor of a thing lies in itself, not in its lineage. Fruit displays the nature and quality of the roots. Any produce, no matter how valuable it is, added to someone else's produce usually damages the latter's worth, and may even cause it to be sequestrated.

Based on all these criteria, I also say: It is sheer ignorance and a great fault to attribute some fabricated Traditions to the distinguished Companions, such as 'Abdullah ibn 'Abbas, in order to encourage people to do the religious acts or to discourage them from indulging in prohibited things. Truth is "wealthy" enough not to need such attributions, and its light is enough to illuminate hearts. Authentic Traditions are sufficient for us to interpret the Qur'an, and we are content with accurate narratives weighed on the scales of reason.

- **As light may be mistaken for fire, forceful eloquence may sometimes be mistaken for exaggeration. Repetitions in the Qur'an are an example of this fact.**[15]

Sometimes fire is seen in light. Repetition to reinforce a message, repeated reminders to establish the message, and reiteration to draw attention are all devices that linguists, rhetoricians, and orators make use

---

[15] *Gleams of Truth*, pp. 13, 97–99.

of. Just as at every instant human beings are in need of air, and of food every day, of light every night, and medicine every year, the recurrence of causes (like need) requires the recurrence of effects (like satisfaction).

So too, the intelligence of human beings, which is their most precious means, and their conscience and other deep faculties, need the truth. And they need it at every instant. Every moment, they eagerly desire it and passionately seek Divine manifestations. They also feel needy of Divine remembrance every hour, and pursue Divine knowledge every day. Since those needs are repeated, the Qur'an guides them to light through repetitions.

The repetitions in the Qur'an are serious reminders and refreshments. Certainly, there are other contexts where repetition could be seen to be a defect; it is only an added decoration for the things that give only pleasure (and not instruction). For example, repeated consumption of a food gives desirable familiarity with it if it is nourishment essential to the body. Human disposition always seeks the food which it needs and is familiar with. But if the food is of fruit or sweet, repeated consumption of it leads to boredom and disgust with it. For any essential, unchanging truth that a word contains, for one that is able to grow—repetition will cause it to be understood more clearly and to become established; this, too, is something the mind wants. Styles—the form or garment of the word—become worn, so they require variation and renewal, which are agreeable to linguists and rhetoricians.

The Qur'an is thoroughly the food of the heart and the source of power for the conscience; it has so great a stature that it reaches the heavens. It is also the food for spirits and a cure for minds. Its repetitions and reiterations are verification that establishes its truths, and enlightenment that reinforces and perfects its guidance. Some of its reiterated truths are the extracts of its food, something that is vitally required by human beings. The more they are necessary, the more they are repeated. The *Basmala* is an example, for which there is, as for air, constant, vital need.

Since the Qur'an is a true and a luminous truth, it is not consumed; rather it gives brighter and brighter light, and guides us to the cure for our "illnesses."

- **One of the Qur'an's miraculous aspects is its eloquence. Even though eloquence can be comprehended by only a few scholars,**

the Qur'an has a different kind of miraculousness for everyone, and indicates this in the most perfect way.[16]

For example, to people of eloquence and rhetoric, it shows its miraculous eloquence; to poets and orators, it displays its miraculous and uniquely exalted style, one that cannot be imitated although it is liked by everyone. The passage of time does not effect its freshness, so it is always new. Its metrical and rhythmical prose and its verse have the greatest nobility and charm.

To many, including especially soothsayers and foretellers, the Qur'an's miraculousness consists of the reports it gives about the Unseen. To historians and chroniclers, its miraculousness is the information it relates about past nations, future conditions and events, and the Intermediate World and the Hereafter. To social and political scientists, it presents the miraculousness of its sacred principles, which comprise the Shari'ah. To those engaged in knowledge of God and the Divine laws of nature, the Qur'an shows its miraculousness in its sacred Divine truths. To those following a spiritual way to sainthood, it manifests the profound, manifold meanings in its verses that rise in successive motions like waves of the sea.

In short, the Qur'an shows its 40 aspects of miraculousness to everyone by opening a different window. Even those who just listen to it and can derive a very limited meaning from it agree that the Qur'an sounds like no other book. Any ordinary person who listens to it says: "This Qur'an is either below other books in degree—which is utterly impossible, and which even its enemies and Satan cannot claim—or above them all, and therefore a miracle."

- **Another important aspect of eloquence is that since abstract truths cannot be understood by the overwhelming majority of people in their abstraction, they are offered in concrete forms or particular "dresses."**[17]

All human beings are not of the same level of understanding, nor are they specialists in every branch of science. Therefore, God Almighty speaks in the Qur'an in a way understandable to everyone. Those of a higher level of understanding and having expert knowledge can benefit from anything that is addressed to all people. But when a work addresses

---

[16] *The Letters*, "The Nineteenth Letter", pp. 201–202.
[17] *The Reasonings*, "The First Part", pp. 41–42.

only the scholarly, things may become difficult for common people to understand. People often find it hard to deal with abstractions, but find it easier to understand things when expressed with metaphors and similes as these are closer to everyday life. For this reason, truths are usually presented in familiar terms or forms, and thereby effectively presented for guidance. The Qur'an of miraculous exposition has considered how people can easily understand it and has used styles that are suitable to be presented in this way. The Qur'an is God's address to human beings in a form that they can understand.

- **A conclusion from a text is built upon the relationship between the main theme of that text and the underlying meaning that it carries. Further studies of the text and additional explanations do not necessarily have to be based on or originate from the science which gives rise to the text. They can be related to other sciences with which the text has some connection.**[18]

It is not enough for a non-Muslim, in order to become a Muslim, merely to enter a mosque. Likewise, merely by being included in books of the Shari'ah or interpretations of the Qur'an, matters pertaining to the natural sciences or to philosophy, geography, history, and so on, cannot be regarded as being included in matters of the Shari'ah or the Qur'an. Also, only when they are specialists in their fields can interpreters of the Qur'an or jurists have a definitive say in the interpretation of the Qur'an or jurisprudence, respectively. Their opinions on the matters parenthetically included in the books of these sciences are not to be regarded as definitive evidence or rulings.

Anything that is in a book of Qur'anic interpretation is not necessarily included in the meaning of the Qur'an, nor in the interpretation itself. It is among the self-evident realities that one who is a specialist in a discipline like engineering can be quite ignorant in another discipline like medicine. It is an established principle of the methodology of Islamic jurisprudence (*Fiqh*) that one who is not a trained and qualified *faqih*—a jurist, a specialist in the Islamic Law—even though he may be an expert in the methodology of *Fiqh*, is not counted among the *faqihs*. Such a person is only an ordinary person in relation to *faqihs*.

---

[18] *The Reasonings*, "The First Part", pp. 25–28.

- **There may be more than one judgment in a word, just as a single oyster may contain several pearls. Each of these judgments arises from a different source and yields different fruit.**[19]

All of the judgments are not based on personal inclinations or desires or caprices. Rather, they are reached by those who have the necessary qualifications to deduce them. One who is qualified to deduce a judgment from the Qur'an and the Prophetic Traditions (other than the explicit judgment[s] addressing and understandable by everyone) is not obliged to follow another with the same qualifications.

- **It is widely accepted that an expression employed to convey a general meaning does not necessarily constitute an argument or proof for some particular meaning incidental to that general meaning, or alluded to or required by it.**[20]

For example, the famous interpreter Qadi Baydawi holds that the steep mountains mentioned in the verse—"*(Dhu'l-Qarnayn said:) 'Bring me blocks of iron.' Then, after he had filled up (the space between) the two steep mountain-sides, he said: '(Light a fire and) work your bellows!' At length, when he had made it (glow red like) fire, he said: 'Bring me molten copper that I may pour upon it.'*"[21]—are the mountains of Armenia and Azerbaijan. It would be unreasonable and illogical to accept this opinion of a great interpreter as the final truth. What led to him to this opinion was information he received from other sciences. The Qur'an is silent about which mountains those mentioned were. So, Baydawi's reading cannot be included as falling within the meaning of the Qur'an itself. But it would also be unjust to criticize this illustrious interpreter or shed doubt on his profound knowledge and comprehension in the science of Qur'anic interpretation because of this reading. One should accept it as one expert's opinion but realize that other opinions are also possible.

- **The answer to a question may not always exactly conform to the aim of the questioner in asking his question.**[22]

For example:

---

19 *The Reasonings*, "The First Part", p. 43.
20 *The Reasonings*, "The First Part", p. 28.
21 *Suratu'l-Kahf*, 18:96.
22 *The Reasonings*, "The First Part", p. 58.

> They ask you (O Messenger) about the new moons (because of the month of Ramadan). Say: "They are appointed times (markers) for the people (to determine time periods) and for the Pilgrimage."[23]

The waxing and waning of the moon attracted people's attention in the pre-Islamic era, as it still does today, and some fanciful ideas and superstitions were associated with it. Secondly, propriety and good sense should control curiosity, so that it does not become, nor lead to, idle or vain preoccupations. When a question is put, the teacher or leader should give an answer that will, rather than satisfying curiosity of any kind, direct curiosities towards more worthy or useful matters. Curiosity needs to be disciplined so that it approaches what is unknown through questions that can be answered intelligibly, in a way that sustains the questioning— questions that, if asked and answered truthfully, increase the stock of human knowledge and strengthen the pillars of faith in the knowledge and wisdom of the Almighty Creator, Who made this world and made it intelligible, and made human beings, within certain limitations, capable of understanding it. The answer should also be the most useful for the questioner.

As to the questions put to the Messenger about the waxing and waning of the moon, the worthwhile, useful element of the questioners' curiosity is indicated in the response of God: it is necessary for them to know the beginning and end of months and the periods between, so that the time of the great religious rites can be determined by reference to phenomena literally visible or knowable by all human beings, but not the special privilege of a particular caste of people. That tells us what the waxing and waning is for, and how the knowledge thereof helps us. It also tells us that such knowledge should be useful.

- **The rivers of thoughts and feelings find their natural course in the composition or arrangement of meanings. The composition of meanings is based on the principles of logic. Logic has its source in truths that are based on and corroborate one another, as well as in the thoughts that lead to these truths. The thoughts that lead to such truths penetrate the most subtle points of the natures of existent things. The most subtle points of natures are the links in the chain of the perfect order of the universe. The**

---

23 *Suratu'l-Baqara*, 2:189.

perfect order of the universe has a whole, abstract beauty which is the source of all the beauty of existence. This abstract beauty is the "natural" park of eloquence called literary merit and style. This park is constituted in the tunes of the nightingales—called poets—who travel in the gardens of creation and are the lovers of flowers. What gives a spiritual, effective tone to the tunes or songs of the nightingales is the composition of meanings.[24]

- Just as a fondness for wording is a disease, so also is over-concentration on form, style, simile, and rhyme a disease; and for the sake of all of these meaning is sacrificed.[25]

In our time, many literary people have written about bizarre things for the sake of a fine point or rhyme. I admit that there should be artistry in wording, but only in a manner that serves the meaning. Styles should be as attractive as possible, but remain within the frame of the meaning and the purpose of the speech or writing. Literary arts should certainly be used, but on condition that they support the truth and not damage it.

- A word comes to life and grows when the meaning is clothed in a form and breathes speech into lifeless things through the power of imagination. Every imagining should contain a seed of reality, and what makes a speech beautiful is how close the images it contains are to reality.[26]

- The fascinating garment or mold of a speech is woven on the loom of style. The beauty of speech lies in its style.[27]

What I mean by style is the form of the word. Different people can use different words to describe the same thing. The benefit of a style is that it solders the separate statements together, forming a unity. According to the rule, "Something is established through the existence of all its parts," styles set the whole into movement by setting even only one part into movement. When a piece of writing or speech demonstrates the accomplishment of style in even a part of it, the reader or listener can sense that style throughout, albeit dimly.

---

[24] *The Reasonings*, "The Second Part", p. 80.
[25] *The Reasonings*, "The Second Part", p. 81.
[26] *The Reasonings*, "The Second Part", pp. 80—82.
[27] *The Reasonings*, "The Second Part", pp. 84, 98.

Style consists of three kinds, for the most part: The first is the simple, straightforward style, like the styles of Sayyid Sharif al-Jurjani and Nasiru'd-Din at-Tusi. The second is the ornate style, like the bright, splendid style of 'Abdu'l-Qahir al-Jurjani in his *Dala'ilu'l-I'jaz* ("Intimations of Inimitability") and *Asraru'l-Balagha* ("Secrets of Eloquence"). The third is the elevated or lofty style, like some of the magnificent writings of as-Sakkaki, az-Zamakhshari, and Ibn Sina (Avicenna). If you write about theology and methodology, you should not abandon the elevated or lofty style, which has intensity, awe, and vigor. If you aim to persuade the audience and use an oratorical style, do not abandon the ornate style, which contains encouragement, discouragement, luster, and vivid descriptions. But you should avoid affectation. If you write and speak on the matters included in or discussed by instrumental sciences, such as logic, mathematics, and linguistics, and the sciences of human relationships, prefer the simple, straightforward style.

- **A word derives its power from the mutual support of its elements and from their being turned towards the basic themes.**[28]

All the elements of the word should conform to the principle expressed in the adage:

> Our statements diverge, but your beauty is one;
> Each statement indicates that beauty.

A word's basic theme should be like a pool, with its elements being the streams or rivers flowing into it from all directions, so that minds will not become confused.

- **Just as a speech is composed in a way to express the basic idea for which it has been made, so too, its beauty and depth of meaning lie in setting secondary or additional meanings and purposes to act with the help of the style that contains such literary arts as allusion, indirect reference, simile, suggestion, and indication.**[29]

With all its elements, the style stirs up the faculty of the imagination to move in various directions, and arouses feelings of appreciation in distant corners of the heart or mind. Allusions, suggestions, and indications are not intended to be the main focus; they are not made to serve the basic purpose. For this reason, a speaker is not held responsible for what allusions, suggestions, and indications are brought to mind.

---

[28] *The Reasonings*, "The Second Part", p. 85.
[29] *The Reasonings*, "The Second Part", pp. 86–87.

- **The fruits of a word or speech exist in its various layers of meaning, as well as in both its denotative and connotative meanings.**[30]

Those who are familiar with chemistry know that when a precious metal, like gold, is obtained, the heap of earth which contains the ores is boiled down in large containers in a factory, and the matter formed is passed through many filters in the different stages of the process. In a similar way, a word has various, different meanings, which give rise to different understandings.

- **Just as each official in a government department should be paid a salary according to their capacity, the work they do, their rank, and years of service, so too, the meanings in a speech that arise from different ranks should be given attention according to the relation of each to the basic purpose for the speech and the contribution it makes to that purpose.**[31]

In this way the justice in this division can give rise to an order, order gives rise to proportion, proportion gives rise to mutual aid and solidarity, and mutual aid and solidarity can provide a just measure for the beauty and excellence of speech. Otherwise, those whose job is cleaning or running errands, or those who have a childish temperament, grow haughty because of the high rank they are given and destroy the proportion and solidarity, causing confusion. So, the capacity of each element in a speech should be considered. For despite their individual beauty, components such as the eyes or nose can make the face ugly if they are greater or smaller than the norm.

- **A marshal may not be able to undertake the same tasks that an ordinary soldier does—for example, reconnaissance work—and a great scholar may not be able to realize the same remarkable achievement that a student can; everyone is great in their own field. Similarly, it sometimes occurs that among a multitude of meanings, a seemingly insignificant one becomes the most important and thus gains value.**[32]

The duty of such a one is important for the following reason:

---

[30] *The Reasonings*, "The Second Part", p. 88.
[31] *The Reasonings*, "The Second Part", pp. 90–91.
[32] *The Reasonings*, "The Second Part", p. 91.

The basic element in a speech becomes either too apparent to draw any attention, or too weak to serve the main purpose of the speech. Or perhaps there is no audience to lend an ear to or accept that element; or perhaps it is not compatible with the state or conditions of the speaker; or it does not serve the speaker's need or intent in making the speech; or perhaps it is not in agreement with the character or honor of the speaker; or perhaps it appears to be foreign to the main purpose of the speech, or to its secondary meanings and purposes; or perhaps it is not suitable for the preservation of the purpose, or the procurement of the elements that are necessary. Consequently, each of these factors may gain precedence in certain circumstances. But if all of them are present in accord with one another, they elevate the value of the speech to the highest rank.

- **One of the virtues of eloquence is that it suggests the craft that the speaker is most occupied with.**[33]

For example, the hoopoe of Prophet Solomon, upon him be peace, described God Almighty as one *who brings to light what is hidden in the heavens and the earth.*[34] Like the Bedouin diviners who, through their insight, amazingly discovered the places where water was to be found in the Arabian deserts, as a diviner among birds and other animals, Prophet Solomon's hoopoe was a blessed bird who served Prophet Solomon as a diviner. It considered God Almighty from the viewpoint of its own craft, and stated that God has the exclusive right to be worshipped and prostrated before because He makes known the things hidden in the heavens and earth.

- **When the meaning in a word belonging to an eloquent one is too apparent to be known to everybody, the basic purpose for the word is to be sought in the meaning required by the apparent meaning.**[35]

For example: *"He begets not, nor is He begotten"*[36] in *Suratu'l-Ikhlas* is obvious and self-evident, therefore the intended meaning is this: "Those having parents and children cannot be God." So, in order to declare that neither Prophet Jesus or Prophet Uzayr (Ezra), upon them be peace, nor the angels, nor the celestial bodies, nor any other objects deified by any people can be God, the verse emphasizes God Almighty's being absolutely

---

[33] *The Gleams*, "The Twenty-eighth Gleam", p. 386.
[34] *Suratu'n-Naml,* 27:25.
[35] *The Gleams*, "The Twenty-eighth Gleam", pp. 391–392.
[36] *Suratu'l-Ikhlas*, 112:3.

free from any limits of time and space or other attributes particular to creation. Likewise, by saying that the All-Providing of Majesty, Who is our sole object of worship, does not want provision from us, nor have we been created to feed Him, the verse, "*I have not created the jinn and humankind but to (know and) worship Me (exclusively). I demand of them no provision, nor do I demand that they should feed Me. Surely God—it is He Who is the All-Providing, Lord of all might, and the All-Forceful,*"[37] (51: 56–58) means that those in need of provision or provided with food cannot be deities and are not worthy of worship.

- **A brief, succinct speech is sometimes more detailed and clearer than an elaborate one. This is especially so when the speech is made to express different meanings, and composed of parts, and it is therefore difficult for the audience to understand the speech in its entirety and to comprehend the purpose for its utterance.**[38]

- **Guidance requires warning and promising, and refraining and encouraging together. These are the results of God's manifestations of majesty and grace.**[39]

- **The beauty of reference (referring or relating a part of speech to another) is based on the degree and beauty of the relationship between them. The degree and beauty of the relationship depend on the closeness or even sameness of the purposes in both parts referred or related to each other with a conjunction.**[40]

- **Just as the absence of relationship between speeches or parts of a speech makes referring or relating them to each other meaningless, so does an extremely apparent connection or relationship make their reference to each other unnecessary.**[41]

- **When the meaning of a word or speech is too apparent to utter it, such a word or speech is meant for another purpose required by the apparent meaning. Like this, when a judgment or conclusion in a speech is too apparent to state, another judgment is meant by the apparent one.**[42]

---

[37] *Suratu'dh-Dhariyat,* 51:56–58.
[38] *İşaratü'l-İ'caz,* "*Suratu'l-Baqara,* verse 5".
[39] *İşaratü'l-İ'caz,* "*Suratu'l-Baqara,* verse 6".
[40] *İşaratü'l-İ'caz,* "*Suratu'l-Baqara,* verse 6".
[41] *İşaratü'l-İ'caz,* "*Suratu'l-Baqara,* verse 14".
[42] *İşaratü'l-İ'caz,* "*Suratu'l-Baqara,* verse 8".

- **A high level of eloquence which throws simple minds and human free will into amazement and makes them unable to imitate it has purposes, one within the other, and indicates the goals that are connected with one another, houses several essential elements turned towards a single result, and contains many branches that bear different fruits.**[43]

The sub-purposes arising from the basic purpose support one another in order to fulfill vicinity rights, giving splendor and comprehensiveness to a speech. It is as if when one appears, the others also appear. The basic purpose distinguishes all the directions (right, left, front, back, etc.), and considers the relationships among them, placing all other purposes in the fortified castle of the speech. Thus, it is as if it employs many intellects to assist it, and each purpose in the assembly of purposes is a part to which all descriptions are turned.

A highly eloquent speech also considers, like an analogy starting from more than one premise that produces various results, several purposes that can be simultaneously both causes and effects in relation to each other. It is as if the speaker points to a family tree in the name of the permanence and multiplication of these purposes.

A third feature of a highly eloquent speech is that a single essential result it produces yields many other results and is based on different roots. Even though each root cannot be directly connected with this main, primarily intended result, at least it contributes to it. Despite the differences of the roots, the speech indicates the basic purpose embodied in the basic result, and ennobles it.

A speech also derives its power and vigor from its relationship with the underlying truth of universal existence, which is also called the life of the universe, universal life, or the universal conduct of affairs. If you look at the Speech of the All-Merciful, Who taught the Qur'an, you will see that this truth shines in all its verses.

A fourth point to be mentioned concerning a truly eloquent speech is that it has such a capacity and wording that there are in it seeds such that can grow into many shoots, and it gives rise to many conclusions, which contain many meanings and aspects. With this capacity, an eloquent speech reveals its power to produce numerous meanings and shows its

---

[43] *The Reasonings*, "The Second Part", pp. 94–96.

products. However, it concentrates all those shoots and aspects on the basic topic for which it is intended. It also keeps its merits and beauties in balance and sends each of its shoots to a different aim, appointing each of its aspects to a different duty.

For example, the Qur'an's narrative about Prophet Moses, upon him be peace , has numerous benefits. There is much more benefit here than the well-known kind of Arabian tree called *Tafariq Asa*, a tree which provides more and more benefit as it splits into parts. The Qur'an has taken it in its "Bright Hand" and employs it for many purposes. It uses each aspect of the narrative so wonderfully that those most advanced in eloquence cannot help but prostrate before its eloquence.

- **Fluency lies in avoiding conceitedness and pursuit of superiority through complexity and ambiguity, and therefore in not causing misconception or confusion, and in imitating the natural order, being clear and comprehensible, not diverting from the basic point in explanations and descriptions, and in the clarity of the purpose and the way that is followed to reach it. Affectations or feigned sentimentality, and the confusion of one's words with other words and feelings, damage fluency.**[44]

We should also avoid disordered detailing and rambling, and be careful that the arguments and meanings corroborate one another. Again, we should be a student of nature though the power of imagination, so that the Divine laws that operate in nature may be reflected in our work of art.

In addition, our concepts should correspond with the outer world. Supposing our conceptions are able to leave our minds and take on forms in the outer world, this world should be able to accept them and not deny their origin, saying, "These belong to me, or these resemble mine, or these are my own products."

We should advance to the purpose with determination, without deviating to the right or left, so that those who stand on the side will not be able to distract us from the purpose towards themselves. Rather, those who are on the sides should contribute to the main purpose from their own beauties and riches.

---

[44] *The Reasonings*, "The Second Part", pp. 96–97.

Furthermore, like the pivot around which speech turns and the purpose it follows, the common meeting points of the basic and secondary purposes should be clear.

- **The success and soundness of a speech lie in its ability to prove the main theme or thesis with all its elements, the foundations it is based on, and the means used to explain it.**[45]

To explain something more clearly, the material used to prove the basic point or main theme should not be corrupt, and the conclusion should be put explicitly and easily. The foundations upon which the conclusion is based should be so vigorous and powerful that they should be referred to as sources and sound arguments, and they must have the necessary equipment to remove doubts and answer any possible questions.

A speech is like a fruit-bearing tree. It has thorns or "bayonets" to protect against every attack. It gives the impression that it is a conclusion drawn after long discussions and an extract obtained after many, careful acts of reasoning. Furthermore, the speaker has so equipped the speech that it has the capacity to provide answers for any possible questions.

- **A speech is articulate to the extent that it is able to give the necessary aid to every fundamental part and every thought contained within it, and to clothe it in the most suitable style.**[46]

If the speech is in the form of a story, the speaker or writer should play the role of the hero. If you describe the thoughts and feelings of others on behalf of the hero, then you should embody the hero or let him be a guest in your heart or speak with your tongue. But if you dispose of your own property (if you take the role of the main character), then you should consider every element of the story according to its capacity and place, cutting and sewing the dress of style according to the stature of its capacity. This will enable every secondary purpose to appear in the dress of the style most suited to it.

In conclusion, the sufficiency of a speech lies in avoiding a style that is incompatible with the requirements of the purpose, or the occasion on which it is said, or the audience to whom it is addressed. Just as a speech displays the meaning through its purpose, arts, and the occasion on which it is said, the style also indicates the meaning, and the meaning, arts, and the occasion on which the speech is said, all contribute to the style.

---

[45] *The Reasonings*, "The Second Part", p. 97.
[46] *The Reasonings*, "The Second Part", pp. 97–98.

- Eloquence requires considering all of these points in a speech, and a speech derives its strength and beauty from them: Who says it? To whom is it said? On what occasion is it said? On what authority is it said? For what purpose is it said?[47]

- A speaker is not held accountable for all the meanings in a speech inferred by others from it. The speaker is responsible for the meanings construed by others only if he intended those meanings. Otherwise, the speaker is not called to account.[48]

- According to logic, analogies in the form of comparisons or parables do not offer certainty, and issues requiring conviction of belief must be based on logical proofs. Analogy is used in jurisprudence for potential solutions and for cases in which a fairly certain presumption is enough. However, there is one type of analogy which is stronger than logical proof and gives greater certainty than induction.[49]

For example, you point to the tip of a universal truth through a particular analogy based on concrete facts and base your conclusion on that truth. To teach that mighty truth and deal with particular incidents and realities in accordance with it, you show the general or universal law on which the truth is based in a certain, particular thing or event. For example, through the analogy that the sun is a single body that can be present in all shining objects at once because it emits light, we show this law of a truth: Light and things of light are not restricted. Distance, size, and quantity make no difference to such items, and they cannot be contained in space.

Another example: A tree's leaves and fruits are formed easily and perfectly at the same time and in the same center through a law of Divine Command. This shows the tip of a mighty truth and a universal law, and proves that truth and law, which is this: Like a tree, this vast universe is the result of that law and the manifestation of oneness. Therefore, it demonstrates the absolute existence and Unity of a Creator and Lord.

- A measure or means of comparison does not have to have actual existence, for its posited or supposed existence can serve as a measure, just like hypothetical lines in geometry.[50]

---

[47] *The Reasonings*, "The Second Part", p. 99; *The Words*, "The Twenty-fifth Word", p. 489.

[48] *The Reasonings*, "The First Part", p. 40.

[49] *The Words*, "The Thirty-second Word", p. 632.

[50] *The Words*, "The Thirteenth Word", pp. 554–555.

An absolute and all-encompassing entity has no limits or terms, and therefore cannot be shaped or formed; neither can it be determined in such a way that its essential nature can be comprehended. For example, an endless light undetermined by darkness cannot be known or perceived. But whenever a real or hypothetical bounding line of darkness is drawn, it becomes determined and known. In the same way, the Divine Attributes and Names (e.g., Knowledge, Power, Wisdom, and Compassion) cannot be determined, for they are all-encompassing and have no limits or like. Thus what they essentially are cannot be known or perceived. A hypothetical boundary is needed for them to become known.

This hypothetical boundary is our selfhood. The All-Wise Maker has entrusted each human being with selfhood, giving clues and samples to urge and enable him or her to recognize the truths about His Lordship's attributes and essential characteristics. Selfhood is the measure or means of comparison that makes Lordship's attributes and Divinity's characteristics known.

Human selfhood imagines within itself a fictitious lordship, power, and knowledge, and so posits a bounding line, hypothesizes a limit to the all-encompassing Divine Attributes, and says: "This is mine, and the rest is His." Selfhood thus makes a division. By means of the miniature measures it contains, selfhood slowly comes to understand the true nature of the Divine Attributes and Names.

For example, through this imagined lordship in its own sphere, selfhood can understand the Lordship of the Creator in the universe. By means of its own apparent ownership, it can understand the real Ownership of its Creator, saying: "As I am the owner of this house, the Creator is the Owner of this universe." Through its partial knowledge, selfhood comes to understand His Absolute Knowledge. Through its defective, acquired art, it can intuit the All-Majestic Maker's matchless, originative Art. It says: "I built and arranged this house, so there must be One Who made and arranged this universe."

Human ego or selfhood contains thousands of states, attributes, and perceptions that, to some extent, disclose and make knowable the Divine Attributes and essential Characteristics. Like a mirror, a measure, an instrument for discovering, or a letter which has no meaning in itself but serves the word's meaning, selfhood is a strand of consciousness from the thick rope of human existence, a fine thread from the celestial weave of humanity's essential nature, an "*alif (I)*" from the book of human identity and character.

- **An essential or intrinsic quality an individual has is common to the whole species, for qualities originating in the essence are shared by all individuals.**[51]

If a single spirit's permanence is established in the afterlife, this confirms the spirit's perpetuation after death. For the science of logic says that an essential or intrinsic quality an individual has is common to the whole species, for qualities originating in the essence are shared by all individuals. There are so many observations, incidents, signs and experiences indicating the permanence of the spirit that it is as certain as the existence of a continent that we have never visited. So there are numberless spirits which have left their corporeal bodies and continue to exist in the Intermediate Realm. They have a relationship with us; our prayers for them and acts of charity on their behalf reach them, and we receive their blessing in return.

- **The two parts of the affirmation of faith—I bear witness that there is no deity but God, and I bear witness that Muhammad is His servant and Messenger—attest to each other's truth. The first is the a priori argument for the second, and the second is the a posteriori argument for the first.**[52]

For Divinity demands Messengership to be known, and Messengership is possible by the Divine Being's appointment and instruction through Revelation.

- **In mentioning the things of the same or similar kind or quality in a speech, an arrangement from the less great or important to the greater or more important is preferred. This is called "the art of ascent" in eloquence. The art of descent is not standard.**[53]

- **Words or speeches are the molds or materialized forms of meanings, and grammar serves the expression of the meaning in the best way possible.**[54]

---

[51] *The Words*, "The Twenty-ninth Word", p. 537.
[52] *Gleams of Truth*, pp. 5, 30.
[53] *İşaratü'l-İ'caz*, "Basmala",
[54] *The Reasonings*, "The Second Part", p. 83; *The Gleams*, "The Twentieth Gleam", p. 216.

The Works of Bediüzzaman Said Nursi as References

Al-Mathnawi al-Nuri: Seedbed of the Light (2007), translated by Hüseyin Akarsu, The Light, New Jersey.

Barla Lahikası (Addendum of Barla) (2007), Şahdamar Yayınları, İstanbul.

Emirdağ Lahikası (Addendum of Emirdağ), vol. 1-2 (2007), Şahdamar Yayınları, İstanbul.

Gleams of Truth: Prescriptions for a Healthy Social Life (2010), translated by Hüseyin Akarsu, Tughra Books, New Jersey.

Hutbe-i Şamiye (The Damascus Sermon) (1996), Yeni Asya Neşriyat, İstanbul.

Hutuvat-ı Sitte (Sixs Steps) (2010), Şahdamar Yayınları, İstanbul.

İşaratü'l-İ'caz (Signs of the Qur'an's Miraculousness) (2007), Şahdamar Yayınları, İstanbul.

Kastamonu Lahikası (Addendum of Kastamonu) (2007), Şahdamar Yayınları, İstanbul.

Münazarat (Discussions) (1996), Envar Neşriyat, İstanbul.

Sünuhat, Tuluat, İşarat (2003), Envar Neşriyat, İstanbul.

The Gleams: Reflections on the Qur'anic Wisdom and Spirituality (2008), translated by Hüseyin Akarsu, Tughra Books, New Jersey.

The Letters: Epistles on Islamic Thought, Belief, and Life (2007), translated by Hüseyin Akarsu, The Light, New Jersey.

The Rays: Reflections on Islamic Belief, Thought, Worship, and Action (2010), translated by Hüseyin Akarsu, Tughra Books, New Jersey.

The Reasonings: A Key to Understanding the Qur'an and Its Eloquence (2008), translated by Hüseyin Akarsu, Tughra Books, New Jersey.

The Words: The Reconstruction of Islamic Belief and Thought (2013), translated by Hüseyin Akarsu, The Light, New Jersey.

Index

A

Aaron, 206
abdal, 387
ablution, 291, 442
Abraham, 223, 265, 435
Abu Bakr, 66, 127, 128, 130, 131, 227, 232, 488
Abu Hanifa, 350
Abu Jahl, 227
Abu Sufyan, 130
Adam, xi, 32, 100, 169, 175, 184, 337, 407
adhan, 62, 357
Afterlife, xii, 71
Ali, 36, 37, 66, 126, 127, 128, 129, 130, 131, 233, 264
All-Holy, 87, 222, 388, 403, 411
alms, 125, 188, 196, 197, 310, 327
America, 211
American, 54, 105, 211, 311
Angel, 79, 137, 387
Anti-Christ, 237
Arabia, 208
Arabic, 190, 191, 239, 345, 475, 502
Ascension, 86, 90, 104, 222, 228, 243, 361, 389, 390, 427
Asfiya, 40
atheism, 18, 52
Azrail, 79, 136, 137

B

backbiting, 242, 307, 345, 346, 376, 465
Barla, 276, 353
Basra, 238
Baydawi, 192, 512
beauty, 12, 17, 26, 71, 72, 84, 105, 106, 107, 122, 123, 134, 151, 156, 162, 167, 170, 172, 177, 182, 183, 212, 224, 250, 257, 263, 264, 272, 342, 354, 389, 398, 412, 414, 428, 440, 446, 450, 468, 507, 508, 514, 515, 516, 518, 522
Bediüzzaman, vii, viii, ix, xi, 10, 104, 125, 258, 282, 308, 323, 338, 422, 445, 460
belief, 18, 22, 30, 37, 39, 40, 41, 42, 43, 44, 46, 48, 49, 50, 51, 52, 56, 57, 58, 59, 60, 61, 62, 63, 64, 65, 67, 78, 101, 106, 107, 110, 111, 112, 125, 139, 142, 143, 150, 154, 163, 168, 175, 189, 190, 196, 205, 210, 211, 214, 215, 223, 237, 240, 252, 258, 260, 261, 262, 269, 270, 274, 275, 278, 279, 280, 281, 283, 286, 287, 291, 292, 293, 294, 296, 311, 316, 323, 324, 325, 329, 330, 331, 332, 334, 337, 338, 339, 343,

E

electricity, 90, 154, 166, 243, 244, 388, 389, 504

engineering, 23, 83, 102, 232, 401, 511

England, 211

enjoyment, 35, 43, 60, 107, 150, 249, 250, 254, 278, 279, 288, 303, 323

Enoch, 158

Essence, 84, 88, 106, 123, 156, 164, 172, 205, 338, 401, 409, 411

eternal, 4, 11, 16, 42, 45, 52, 53, 54, 58, 66, 68, 76, 85, 112, 113, 117, 124, 125, 126, 145, 146, 147, 148, 149, 150, 151, 152, 157, 163, 164, 168, 170, 171, 172, 175, 178, 181, 183, 184, 195, 203, 204, 205, 216, 222, 226, 240, 249, 252, 253, 263, 265, 266, 267, 270, 271, 278, 279, 280, 288, 289, 290, 294, 296, 297, 301, 303, 310, 311, 312, 313, 314, 316, 320, 322, 323, 324, 325, 329, 330, 332, 333, 335, 337, 340, 342, 352, 356, 397, 410, 414, 419, 423, 424, 425, 428, 438, 457, 461, 466, 473, 477, 484, 485, 487, 489

Europe, 181, 436, 440, 453, 459, 493

European, 211, 440, 441, 497

evil-commanding soul, 58, 138, 143, 252, 253, 279, 293, 316, 326, 330, 341, 367, 368, 373, 402, 424, 425, 468, 478, 481

examination, 36, 43, 51, 154

F

faith, viii, ix, xi, 9, 20, 22, 24, 25, 29, 30, 38, 39, 40, 41, 46, 61, 130, 135, 143, 161, 167, 177, 187, 208, 221, 223, 259, 275, 293, 328, 340, 343, 358, 363, 380, 381, 435, 443, 461, 464, 479, 480, 485, 486, 513, 524

falsehood, 9, 20, 30, 65, 143, 194, 213, 354, 455, 456, 472

family life, 342

fatalism, 117

Fatima, 126

Fiqh, ix

First World War, 454

forgiveness, 7, 37, 56, 57, 64, 111, 117, 139, 143, 282, 287, 290, 297, 301, 307, 317, 331, 353, 381, 416, 437, 465, 482

France, 211

freedom, ix, 12, 83, 86, 104, 205, 391, 446, 454, 489

G

Gabriel, 87, 136, 228, 387

generosity, 186, 252, 308, 315, 347

geometry, 401, 522

Ghazzali, 277, 350, 363, 382

glorification, 14, 76, 242, 257, 271, 273, 302, 355, 366, 368, 426, 427, 428, 429

God's Names, 240, 256, 311, 357, 362, 371, 426

Gog and Magog, 193

good morals, 174, 205, 305

Gospels, 191, 215, 235

gravity, 94, 104, 165, 244, 261, 262, 389, 452, 504, 508

H

hadith, 50, 66, 89, 112, 113, 114, 173, 194, 229, 270, 322, 327, 333, 336, 338, 456, 468, 490